Reflexive
Methodology

Reflexive Methodology

New Vistas for
Qualitative Research
Second Edition

Mats Alvesson and Kaj Sköldberg

Los Angeles | London | New Delhi
Singapore | Washington DC

© Mats Alvesson and Kaj Sköldberg 2009

First edition published 2000
This second edition published 2009
Reprinted 2010

SAGE Publications Ltd
1 Oliver's Yard
55 City Road
London EC1Y 1SP

SAGE Publications Inc.
2455 Teller Road
Thousand Oaks, California 91320

SAGE Publications India Pvt Ltd
B 1/I 1 Mohan Cooperative Industrial Area
Mathura Road
New Delhi 110 044

SAGE Publications Asia-Pacific Pte Ltd
33 Pekin Street #02-01
Far East Square
Singapore 048763

Library of Congress Control Number: 2008942798

British Library Cataloguing in Publication data

A catalogue record for this book is available from the British Library

ISBN 978-1-84860-111-6
ISBN 978-1-84860-112-3 (pbk)

Typeset by C&M Digitals (P) Ltd, Chennai, India
Printed by the MPG Books Group
Printed on paper from sustainable resources

CONTENTS

FOREWORD

In this second, revised edition of *Reflexive Methodology*, the text has been updated with the latest developments in the different areas treated. A chapter on the philosophy of science, including discussions of positivism, social constructionism, and critical realism, has been added as a background to the following chapters dealing with the four levels of reflection. The previous final chapter has been expanded into two, which further elaborate the discussion of the reflexive method and its four levels, and also contain concrete, practical examples of reflexive research processes.

Lund and Stockholm, February 2009

Mats Alvesson and Kaj Sköldberg

1

INTRODUCTION: THE INTELLECTUALIZATION
OF METHOD

Traditionally research has been conceived as the creation of true, objective knowledge, following a scientific method. From what appears or is presented as data, facts, the unequivocal imprints of 'reality', it is possible to acquire a reasonably adequate basis for empirically grounded conclusions and, as a next step, for generalizations and theory-building. So the matter has long been conceived, and no doubt many empirically oriented researchers in the social sciences still conceive it so, irrespective of whether they are examining 'objective reality' (social facts) or exploring people's subjective or intersubjective experiential worlds (meanings).

This view has been subjected to a good deal of criticism, however, much of which appeared towards the end of the 1960s and was directed against 'positivism'. But there has since been further criticism applying also to diverse variants of the qualitative method, sometimes automatically seen as 'anti-' or at least as 'non-positivist'. For the moment we will mention only such critique as stresses the ambiguous, unstable and context-dependent character of language, the dependence of both observations and data on interpretation and theory (interpretation-free, theory-neutral facts do not, in principle, exist), and the political-ideological character of the social sciences. One line of argument here starts from the notion that knowledge cannot be separated from the knower (Steedman, 1991: 53). Data and facts, as we will demonstrate, are the constructions or results of interpretation: we have to do something with our sensory impressions if these are to be comprehensible and meaningful. Alongside this general critique of the objectivist scientific view and the heavy focus on empirical data, more specific criticism is raised against various methodological conceptions and methods. The methodological conceptions and methods of the social sciences have been exposed to such a barrage of objections that one might have expected empiricists to lose their self-confidence and think of turning to some other branch of study instead.[1] But in fact the big risk seems to be that practising researchers stick in the same old rut, either repressing the criticism altogether or remaining more or less unaware of it. Many of the critics, on the other hand, tend to go to the opposite extreme and cut out empirical reality altogether – although exactly how they do this depends on their particular scientific orientation.

In the social sciences – to which we largely limit ourselves in this book – there is a clear division between the great mainstream of empirically oriented research, and various currents that are critical of 'empiricism' on diverse philosophical or theoretical grounds. To some extent this division overlaps with the dichotomy between scholars who adopt a robust and objectivist ontological approach and those with a consciousness- and experience-oriented, interpretive view of ontology and epistemology (Burrell and Morgan, 1979). But there are certain differences, since some representatives of this second approach are drawn towards the empiricist line – for example, some phenom-enologists and other advocates of rigorous qualitative method, assume that the very stringency of the method guarantees good research results. The critics of empiricism – ranging from historians of science, sociologists of knowledge, psychologists of science and linguistic scholars, to ideological critics and philosophers – claim that culture, language, selective perception, subjective forms of cognition, social conventions, politics, ideology, power and narration all, in a complicated way, permeate scientific activity. These elements leave their mark on the relation between empirical reality and/or attempts to force segments of reality into the research texts, so that the relation between 'reality' and 'text' (the research results) is at best uncertain and at worst arbitrary or even non-existent. To find support for this thesis we need only consider that, despite the wealth of different theories that exist in most fields in the social sciences, empirical results are generally found to 'agree' – at least in part – with the researcher's own premises, and that most researchers seem disinclined to change their point of view simply because a researcher with another theoretical base has presented empirical 'data' which contradict their own point of view.

A variety of ideas about how social reality is constructed – not only how it is rep-resented – by the researcher will be investigated in this book. We believe, with the 'anti-empiricists', that empirical social science is very much less certain and more problematic than common sense or conventional methodological textbooks would have us think. The great array of books on the 'qualitative method' does not differ decisively from the quantitative literature on this score. Nor as a rule are the former 'qualitative enough', in the sense of being sufficiently open to the ambiguity of empir-ical material and the complexity of interpretations. The focus on procedures and tech-niques implies an imitation of the quantitative methodology textbooks, and draws attention away from fundamental problems associated with such things as the role of language, interpretation and selectivity in research work, thus underrating the need for reflection. On the other hand, there are also certain risks involved in too strong an emphasis on this need. By problematizing research, we may come to overrate its dif-ficulties, which leads in the long run to a defeatist reaction, and perhaps even to ask-ing ourselves whether empirical social science has any reasonable function at all.

But we do not give up so easily, despite our ambition to take account of doubts about the ability of empirical material (data) to provide crucial input into research. We are not convinced that the opposite pole to methodological textbook wisdom – where it is claimed in a spirit of postmodernism or poststructuralism, for instance, that empirical reality can be ignored altogether – is in any way preferable. Nor is the phobia of empirical matters that characterizes much hermeneutic and critical theory to be recommended. It is our experience that the study of a confusing and contradic-tory, but often surprising and inspiring, empirical material has much to offer. It is precisely this combination of inspiration from the philosophy of science and empirical interests that provides this book with its *raison d'être* and, we believe, makes it unique. Most of the literature in the relevant field – broadly defined as ideas about how to conduct good social science research – is either empirically oriented or gives unequivocal priority to theoretical and philosophical considerations, which tends to make empirical research look odd, irrelevant, naïve or even, feeble minded. We try instead to manoeuvre between these two conventional – and safe – positions, which appear to us rather as a kind of methodological Scylla and Charybdis.

In our dealings with empiricism – broadly defined here as all research in which 'pure data' or uninterpreted 'facts' are the solid bedrock of research – we try to take account of the objections which have been raised by hermeneuticians, critical theorists, poststructuralists, linguistic philosophers, discourse analysts, feminists, constructivists, reflectivists and other trouble-makers who render life difficult for the supporters of either quantitative or mainstream qualitative methods. Against these trouble-makers – who explicitly or implicitly leave their readers despairing and irresolute vis-á-vis empirical research – we stubbornly claim that it is pragmatically fruitful to assume the existence of a reality beyond the researcher's egocentricity and the ethnocentricity of the research community (paradigms, consciousness, text, rhetorical manoeuvring), and that we as researchers should be able to say something insightful about this reality. This claim is consistent with a belief that social reality is not external to the consciousness and language of people – members of a society as well as researchers (who, of course, also are members of a society).

Before proceeding with our distinct approach to methodology, we relate it to and ground it in a broadly accepted thesis in philosophy of science: that how we interpret phenomena is always perspectival and that so-called facts are always theory-laden.

Ways of explanation and understanding

In explanatory models, it is usual to distinguish between *induction* and *deduction*.[2] An inductive approach proceeds from a number of single cases and assumes that a connection that has been observed in all these is also generally valid. This approach thus involves a risky leap from a collection of single facts to a general truth. Consider, for example 'there have never been any rocks on the bottom so far when I have dived into the water; therefore there are probably not any this time either …'. The weakness is, it appears, that the underlying structure or situation is not included in the picture, but only a mechanical, external connection. The method, as it were, distills a general rule from a set of observations; what comes out then becomes merely a concentrate of what is already included in the observations themselves.

A deductive approach, on the contrary, proceeds from a general rule and asserts that this rule explains a single case. This approach is less risky – at the price of seeming to presuppose what is to be explained: that the general rule always holds true, hence also in the current case. Moreover, it does not really appear to *explain* anything, but rather avoids explanation through authoritarian statements, rather as a parent under stress might answer an inquisitive child: 'Why do butterflies have wings?' 'Because all butterflies have wings, dear.' Thus, in deduction, too, we see a lack of underlying patterns and tendencies, which makes the model flat, bordering on the empty.

These two models are usually regarded as exclusive alternatives, but it would be difficult to force all research into them, if they are not to serve as a Procrustean bed. There are in fact other possibilities, and we will now present one of them.

Abduction is probably the method used in real practice in many case-study based research processes. In abduction, an (often surprising) single case is interpreted from a hypothetic overarching pattern, which, if it were true, explains the case in question. The interpretation should then be strengthened by new observations (new cases). The method has some characteristics of both induction and deduction, but it is very important to keep in mind that abduction neither formally (see note 5) nor informally is any simple 'mix' of these nor can it be reduced to these; it adds new, specific elements. During the process, the empirical area of application is successively developed, and the theory (the proposed over-arching pattern) is also adjusted and refined. In its focus on underlying patterns, abduction also differs advantageously from the two other, shallower models of explanation. The difference is, in other words, that it includes *understanding* as well.

Abduction is the method used in medical diagnosing and in diagnosing errors in technical systems; the interpretation of poetry is another field. It has had increasing impact in many areas of linguistics and the social sciences. Abduction is close to hermeneutics (Eco, 1990, cf. Chapter 4 in this book).

Induction has its point of departure in empirical data and deduction in theory. Abduction starts from an empirical basis, just like induction, but does not reject theoretical preconceptions and is in that respect closer to deduction. The analysis of the empirical fact(s) may very well be combined with, or preceded by, studies of previous theory in the literature; not as a mechanical application on single cases but as a source of inspiration for the discovery of patterns that bring understanding. The research process, therefore, alternates between (previous) theory and empirical facts whereby both are successively reinterpreted in the light of each other. In comparison, induction and deduction appear more one-sided and unrealistic, if we take into consideration how research is actually carried out; in other words, those who follow them too strictly risk putting a straitjacket on their research. Theory is poetry over facts, it has been said (Erslev, 1961). Maybe, but then as much a poetry *in and through* facts. Even though 'facts' are the surface of friction necessary to generate theory, theory is not a simple summary or description of 'empirical facts' as in natural history. The theory must also transcend 'facts' in order to achieve scope. 'Facts' thus serve to *occasion* the theory, while continually playing the role of critical tuning instrument and fount of new ideas for the theory.

Glaser and Strauss's induction from theory-free facts (Chapter 3 below) can be regarded as a counter picture to Popper's long dominating and one-sided thesis of *deduction from fact-free theory* (e.g. Popper, 1963).[3] In the latter case, it is a question of a kind of scientific virginal birth which should be as rare or miraculous for the practical researcher as its obstetric counterpart. Since Popper's influence has been so strong, Glaser and Strauss's thesis can perhaps be viewed as a polemically understandable one-sidedness. We argue, though, that there is a way beyond this polarization between induction and deduction.

Here it is fitting to quote what Alfred North Whitehead, influential philosopher and co-author (with Bertrand Russell) of *Principia Mathematica*, says about induction, and, implicitly, about abduction:

> This collapse of the method of rigid empiricism ... occurs whenever we seek the larger generalities. In natural science this rigid method is the Baconian method of induction, a method which, if consistently pursued, would have left science where it found it. What Bacon omitted was the play of a free imagination, controlled by the requirements of coherence and logic. The true method of discovery is like the flight of an aeroplane. It starts from the ground of particular observation; it makes a flight in the thin air of imaginative generalization; and it again lands for renewed observation rendered acute by rational interpretation.
>
> ... [T]his construction must have its origin in the generalization of particular factors discerned in particular topics of human interest ... In this way the prime requisite, that anyhow there shall be some important application, is secured. The success of the imaginative experiment is always to be tested by the applicability of its results beyond the restricted locus from which it originated. In default of such extended application, a generalization ... remains merely an alternative expression of notions [already] applicable ... (Whitehead, 1929: 4ff.)

Also, a theoretician of science like Bunge never tires of pointing out that it is not possible to generate theory by just condensing empirical data (see, for instance, Bunge [1967]; cf. also Toulmin [1953]).

Let us for the sake of simplicity illustrate with the traditional example of positivism – swans and their colours. Deduction would start by postulating that if a bird is a swan, it is white, and then draw the conclusion that if we meet an individual swan, it is white. Induction first meets one white swan, then another, then yet another ... and finally draws the conclusion that all swans are white. Abduction would at first observe a swan with a certain colour, and then show how, for example, the bird's genetic structure might generate a certain colouring. This underlying pattern then explains the individual case.

Neither induction nor abduction are logically necessary – i.e., they allow mistakes – yet we could not do without them, any more than without deduction, which is logically necessary at the price of empirical emptiness (it does not say more than its premises). Through induction, we draw, for instance, as children the conclusion that objects a, b, and so on fall to the ground if they are dropped, and therefore probably also all other objects. Abduction can, as was indicated above be illustrated by diagnostics and also with the interpretation of poetry. In the former case, we observe a symptom and from this draw the conclusion of an underlying pattern – i.e., a disease. In the interpretation of poetry, we see a certain pattern as an indication of a hidden but underlying pattern in the text. Since abduction is not logically necessary, it must be controlled against more cases. The physician must, for instance, compare with more symptoms (or patients); the interpreter of lyrics with more expressions, verses (or poems). A research process may rather be compared with a *series* of flights such as was described in the Whitehead quotation rather than with a single one (or even better with one long air trip with several intermediate landings). In other words, what is needed is a repeated process of alternating between (empirically-laden) theory and (theory-laden) empirical 'facts'.[4] This means a hermeneutic process during which the researcher, as it were, eats into the empirical matter with the help of theoretical pre-conceptions, and also keeps developing and elaborating the theory.[5]

The idea of theory application in contrast to induction has also been used as a learning strategy in artificial intelligence: expert systems with causal models ('deep models'), as a complement to previous heuristic rules-of-thumb models ('surface models'), which cannot explain the hidden patterns and tendencies behind processes (Hart, 1986; Steels and Van de Velde, 1986). In general, abduction remains a useful, topical method for learning systems in artificial intelligence (van der Lubbe, 1993), especially in situations with uncertainty and complexity (e.g. Esposito et al., 2007).

*

Abduction as an explanatory model also has connections to a perspectival approach. We are referring to Hanson's familiar and very important (1958) conclusion that *facts are always theory-laden*, a thesis for which he argued so convincingly that, despite other differences, there has long been almost complete consensus about it in the later philosophy of science (Hesse, 1980; Newton-Smith, 1990). The post-Kuhnian philosophy of science has gone even further along these lines, problematizing the very distinction between facts and theory, and thereby the very term 'theory-ladenness of facts' (see, for instance, Suppe, 2000). This does not, however, change our point in this section, but rather strengthens it. It was also for this reason that we put the word 'facts' within quotation marks above.

Hanson arrived at his conclusion among other things by interesting himself in what is meant by 'seeing'. There is evidence that we never see single sense-data, but always *interpreted* data, data that are placed in a certain frame of reference. Hanson used puzzle pictures as examples – ambiguous pictures that can be interpreted in two different ways, although their data are identical. Exactly the same set of lines can, for instance, be interpreted both as a bird and as an antelope, but not both simultaneously. (The idea goes back to the later Wittgenstein [1953].) Thus, we always lay a perspective into what we say, and not only that, but seeing is inseparable from the perspective, *it is perspectival*.

In the same way, a physician does not just 'see' a collection of black and white dots on an X-ray picture, but, for example, a certain shadow on the lungs, indicating a certain illness syndrome. The layman is literally 'blind' to this. A chess player does not 'see' a number of pieces that are then put together as a picture of the game, but views the whole board as a complex field of forces. Data are thus always contextually inserted in a semantic frame, which gives them their sense to begin with. This reasoning can be extended to research processes. Hanson rejected both induction and deduction as models for such processes. Induction is unsatisfactory since new knowledge does not constitute simple summaries, or condensations, of data, but an *explanation* of data. Deduction also gives a faulty picture of the research process, since it presupposes that scientific discoveries happen through airy speculation, which remains to be tested through empirical analysis. Instead, Hanson holds that through the work with the empirical material at a certain point a pattern emerges, and, as suggested by the title of the book – *Patterns of Discovery: An Inquiry into the*

Foundations of Science – this very pattern finding is at the heart of science. Hanson (1958) calls this process of pattern finding 'retroduction', which corresponds to what we have called 'abduction'; the latter term is the one most commonly used.

Qualitative and quantitative method

Having thus anchored our overall approach in this book to the overall principle of abduction and declared our scepticism towards induction as well as deduction, we proceed by indicating more specifically our view on methodology.

We deal in this book primarily with qualitative methods, but, as indicated, we do so in a somewhat unorthodox way. How 'qualitative method' should be defined is by no means self-evident. The consideration of open, equivocal empirical material, and the focus on such material, is a central criterion, although of course some qualitative methods do stress the importance of categorizations. The distinction between standardization and non-standardization as the dividing-line between quantitative and qualitative methods thus becomes a little blurred, which does not prevent it from being useful. Another important distinguishing feature of qualitative methods is that they start from the perspective and actions of the subjects studied, while quantitative studies typically proceed from the researcher's ideas about the dimensions and categories which should constitute the central focus (Bryman, 1989). Denzin and Lincoln (2005) strongly emphasize the researcher's presence and interpretive work in qualitative research:

> Qualitative research is a situated activity that locates the observer in the world. It consists of a set of interpretive, material practices that make the world visible. These practices transform the world. They turn the world into a series of representations, including field notes, interviews, conversations, photographs, recordings, and memos to the self. At this level, qualitative research involves an interpretive, naturalistic approach to the world. This means that qualitative researchers study things in their natural settings, attempting to make sense of, or interpret, phenomena in terms of the meanings people bring to them. (Denzin and Lincoln, 2005: 3)

This characterization of qualitative studies is valid for the majority of such research. Some language- and practice-oriented qualitative researchers are not, however, interested in the meanings or viewpoints of subjects (Silverman, 2006). Qualitative research then 'becomes not so much a question of deciding what a text or a textual extract might mean to a thinking subject as a matter of analysing the origins, nature and structure of the discursive themes by means of which the text has been produced' (Prior, 1997: 66).

We do not explicitly argue in favour of qualitative methods or against quantitative ones, even though it will be obvious that we are highly sceptical about the universal adoption of the latter in the social sciences, at least in their most narrowly codified forms. There is no reason to make a particular point of justifying the existence of qualitative methods, which are now well established in most social science disciplines, and even predominant in some (cf. Denzin and Lincoln, 2005; Silverman, 2006).

Consequently we will not engage in any further discussion of the advantages or disadvantages of quantitative and qualitative methods – a subject on which a good deal of often unproductive debate has already been held (Deetz, 1996). However, this debate does appear to be dying down, partly because the arguments have run dry and partly because polarization no longer seems to be as popular as it used to be in the discussions about method (see, for example, Bryman, 1989; Martin, 1990a). A common view is that the choice between quantitative and qualitative methods cannot be made in the abstract, but must be related to the particular research problem and research object. Sometimes – although in our view not nearly as often as seems to be the case today – a purely quantitative method may be appropriate, sometimes a purely qualitative one, and sometimes a combination of the two (Bourdieu and Wacquant, 1992).[6] Even in the case of mainly qualitative research it may sometimes be sensible to include certain simple quantifications. Although statistics on social phenomena often contain ambiguities, and conceal the social norms on which classifications are based (Prior, 1997), they may nonetheless sometimes have a certain value as background material in qualitative research.

In our view it is not methods but ontology and epistemology which are the determinants of good social science. These aspects are often handled better in qualitative research – which allows for ambiguity as regards interpretive possibilities, and lets the researcher's construction of what is explored become more visible – but there are also examples of the use of the quantitative methods in which figures, techniques and claims to objectivity are not allowed to gain the upper hand, but are subordinated to a well thought out overall research view (among them Bourdieu, 1984; Silverman, 1985). If we can avoid the trap of regarding quantitative results as robust and unequivocal reflections of a reality 'out there', there is no reason to be rabidly 'anti-quantitative'.

Reflective/reflexive research

Rather than arguing in favour of qualitative methods, the intention of this book is to contribute to what we call 'reflective or reflexive empirical research'. (For the time being we will use both these concepts synonymously. Researchers sometimes use them in a similar way. Later we will distinguish between them, viewing reflexive as a particular, specified version of reflective research, involving reflection on several levels or directed at several themes.) What does this mean? According to Bourdieu and Wacquant (1992) there are different varieties of reflexivity. These include ethnomethodological ethnography as text, social scientific studies of the (natural) sciences, postmodern sociology, critical phenomenology and the writings of authors such as Gouldner and Giddens (double hermeneutics). Bourdieu's own variety – where the researcher is seen as being inserted into a social field, with specific relationships of competition and power conditions generating a particular 'habitus', that is, a pattern of action dispositions, among the participants – also belongs here. Other discussions of reflexivity concentrate on the sociology of knowledge (e.g. Ashmore, 1989; Lynch, 2000; Woolgar, 1988) or the politics of doing and publishing research (Alvesson et al., 2008)

Thus in the literature there are different uses of reflexivity or reflection which typically draw attention to the complex relationship between processes of knowledge production and the various contexts of such processes, as well as the involvement of the knowledge producer. This involves operating on at least two levels in research work and paying much attention to how one thinks about thinking (Maranhão, 1991).

Calás and Smircich (1992b: 240) speak of 'a reflexivity that constantly assesses the relationship between "knowledge" and "the ways of doing knowledge"'. Briefly, for us this concept – which we will be exploring below – means that serious attention is paid to the way different kinds of linguistic, social, political and theoretical elements are woven together in the process of knowledge development, during which empirical material is constructed, interpreted and written. Empirical research in a reflective mode starts from a sceptical approach to what appear at a superficial glance as unproblematic replicas of the way reality functions, while at the same time maintaining the belief that the study of suitable (well thought out) excerpts from this reality can provide an important basis for a generation of knowledge that opens up rather than closes, and furnishes opportunities for understanding rather than establishes 'truths'.

Reflective research, as we define it, has two basic characteristics: careful interpretation and reflection.[7] The first implies that all references – trivial and non-trivial – to empirical data are the _results of interpretation._ Thus the idea that measurements, observations, the statements of interview subjects, and the study of secondary data such as statistics or archival data have an _unequivocal_ or unproblematic relationship to anything outside the empirical material is rejected on principle. Consideration of the fundamental importance of interpretation means that an assumption of a simple mirroring thesis of the relationship between 'reality' or 'empirical facts' and research results (text) has to be rejected. Interpretation comes to the forefront of the research work. This calls for the utmost awareness of the theoretical assumptions, the importance of language and pre-understanding, all of which constitute major determinants of the interpretation. The second element, reflection, turns attention 'inwards' towards the person of the researcher, the relevant research community, society as a whole, intellectual and cultural traditions, and the central importance, as well as the problematic nature, of language and narrative (the form of presentation) in the research context. Systematic reflection on several different levels can endow the interpretation with a quality that makes empirical research of value. Reflection can, in the context of empirical research, be defined as the _interpretation of interpretation_ and the launching of a critical self-exploration of one's own interpretations of empirical material (including its construction). Reflection can mean that we consistently consider various basic dimensions behind and in the work of interpretation, by means of which this can be qualified. In the course of this book we will indicate some reflective levels and principles, which we hold can be integrated in and stimulate empirical research.

Thus in reflective empirical research the centre of gravity is shifted from the handling of empirical material towards, as far as possible, a consideration of the perceptual, cognitive, theoretical, linguistic, (inter)textual, political and cultural circumstances that form the backdrop to – as well as impregnate – the interpretations. These circumstances make the interpretations possible, but to a varying degree they also mean that research becomes in part a naïve and unconscious undertaking. For example, it is difficult, if not by definition impossible, for the researchers to clarify the taken-for-granted assumptions and blind spots in their own social culture, research community and language. The main thrust of our approach is thus to try to stimulate critical reflection and awareness, in the first instance as regards qualitative research.[8] Empirical material – interpretations referring to 'reality' – remains important,

9

but we must proceed with care and reflection, pondering a good deal more upon what the empirical material means, and why we make just these particular interpretations, before forming any opinions of 'reality' as such. The research process constitutes a (re)construction of the social reality in which researchers both interact with the agents researched and, actively interpreting, continually create images for themselves and for others: images which selectively highlight certain claims as to how conditions and processes – experiences, situations, relations – can be understood, thus suppressing alternative interpretations. The aim of this book is to indicate some important themes in the data construction (interpretation) and text production (authorship) of research work, to conceptualize these in such a way as to stimulate awareness, and to provide ideas about care and reflection in planning, interpreting and writing during the research process.

This is, of course, an ambitious goal. Before the reader starts attributing fantasies of omnipotence to us, we should perhaps add that this book naturally does not start from scratch. In fundamental ways it is an inventory and critical review of the state of knowledge in the philosophy of (social) science, with particular relevance to social research and in particular to the qualitative method. There is much for us to build on. However, we will try to go beyond a simple inventory and general discussion. We also wish to present critiques of various positions, seeking to achieve integrations and to develop applications, and above all to suggest new ways of doing social research, through the development of a sufficiently flexible and mobile frame of reference for handling reflective elements.

Much philosophically oriented discussion remains uncoupled from empirical work. Many researchers probably feel like Melia (1997: 29), who states that '[t]he link between what a researcher does and the philosophical position set out to justify the method is often problematic'. We agree that this all too frequently is the case, which of course is highly unsatisfactory. Referring to philosophical ideas without really using them is pointless, bewildering and means a waste of the time and energy both for the researcher and for his or her unfortunate readers. Interplay between philosophical ideas and empirical work marks high-quality social research. While philosophical sophistication is certainly not the principal task of social science, social research without philosophically informed reflection easily grows so unreflective that the label 'research' becomes questionable. To avoid methodology being perceived as peripheral to research practice as a result of being 'intellectualized' is certainly a challenge. Against a perception that 'as the methods debates have become more philosophical, or at least epistemological, they have become less useful for the doing of research' (Melia, 1997: 35), we hope to contribute to a productive debate. Usefulness would then lead to research that avoids some of the pitfalls as well as being more reflective and creative due to a better interaction between philosophical-theoretical ideas and empirical-practical sources of inspiration.

Four elements in reflective research

Chapters 3–6 address four currents of methodology and philosophy of science, which we regard as important sources of inspiration: empirically oriented currents (in particular, grounded theory); hermeneutics; critical theory; and postmodernism. These four orientations indicate the reflective areas in which the social science researcher should be engaged – regardless of the specific methods he or she prefers. At this point we will content ourselves with a brief description of the chief contributions that have emerged from the different orientations, and give some indication of what we will discuss below.

1 *Systematics and techniques in research procedures.* Qualitative research should follow some well reasoned logic in interacting with the empirical material, and use rigorous techniques for processing the data. This is what most books on the qualitative method are about. We take up grounded theory (Glaser and Strauss, 1967) as a typical example of this methodological view. We will also briefly present ethnomethodology and inductive ethnography.
2 *Clarification of the primacy of interpretation.* Research can be seen as a fundamentally interpretive activity, which in contrast to – or at least to a greater degree than – other activity, is aware of this very fact. The recognition that all research work includes and is driven by an interpreter – who in the social sciences, moreover, often interacts with and contemplates other interpreters (the people studied) – here provides the key to a qualified methodological view. Thus method cannot be disengaged from theory and other elements of pre-understanding, since assumptions and notions in some sense determine interpretations and representations of the object of study. Hermeneutics is thus an important form of reflection.
3 *Awareness of the political-ideological character of research.* Social science is a social phenomenon embedded in a political and ethical context. What is explored, and how it is explored, can hardly avoid either supporting (reproducing) or challenging existing social conditions. Different social interests are favoured or disfavoured depending on the questions that are asked (and not asked), and on how reality is represented and interpreted. Thus the interpretations and the theoretical assumptions on which these are based are not neutral but are part of, and help to construct, political and ideological conditions. These dimensions are highlighted by critical theorists, among others.
4 *Reflection in relation to the problem of representation and authority.* It has been pointed out in recent hermeneutics that in many decisive ways the text is decoupled from the author. Postmodernism (poststructuralism) goes one step further and decouples the text from any external reality as well. The text lives its own life, as it were, and lacks any reference to anything outside itself. Texts only affect one another, and the consequence of this multiplicity of chaotic mutual influences is that the texts become fragmented or split. In this way both the author's (or in our case the researcher's) claim to authority, and the texts' claim to reproduce (not to mention 'mirror') some extrinsic reality, are equally undermined: the researching subject and the researched object are both called into question.

The reader may perhaps regard as incommensurable the different theoretical positions linked to the four themes introduced here. And so they are, at least in some cases.

However, it is possible to envisage research strategies which reinterpret important ideas from one or more of these positions, and put them into new contexts. Admittedly there are considerable differences between our four orientations, but the point here is not to integrate typical research from, for example, grounded theory and postmodernism, but to try to abstract principles and ideas from the four intellectual orientations, with a view to endowing qualitative research with a more reflexive character, while also stressing the importance of empirical material. The latter is often under-emphasized in the other three orientations, but is central to grounded theory and ethnomethodology, where certain ideas of research procedures may be useful. We are thus interested in interpreting certain insights gleaned from the different positions, which can be of general value to social science research, rather than proceeding from orthodox stances as regards these schools of thought.

These four areas for reflection (where the element of reflection is under-emphasized in the first one, namely grounded theory) provide, in the order given here, a certain logic. The interest in (unstandardized) empirical material that represents the core in (several variants of) the qualitative method, such as grounded theory, constitutes a kind of bottom line for research work. However, this bottom line is considerably less stable than is generally assumed. The focus on 'data collecting and processing' in most qualitative methodological theories is unreflective and should be impugned. Instead, a fundamental hermeneutic element permeates the research process from beginning to end. Interpretation rather than the representation of reality on the basis of collected data then becomes the central element. Even more strongly: there is no such thing as unmediated data or facts; these are always the results of interpretation. Yet the interpretation does not take place in a neutral, apolitical, ideology-free space. Nor is an autonomous, value-free researcher responsible for it. Various paradigms, perspectives and concepts, as well as research and other political interests, all bring out certain types of interpretation possibilities, at the same time as they suppress others, often under the guise of what is neutral, rational, right and correct. Interpretation as a political-ideological expression then represents an important complement to the hermeneutic brand of interpretation. An element of suspicion has thereby been introduced. To this is added the insight that even ideologically and politically aware researchers risk being steered by their own text production, where influences from prevailing, free-floating discourses can gain the upper hand and play their own fragmented game with the intentionally referential, supposedly politically aware, text. Any ambition to determine 'how things are' or 'how best to interpret a phenomenon' in this situation may then be regarded as illusory and doomed to failure. This idea inspires a problematization of the researcher's claim to authority.

On the basis of these preliminary considerations, and others which will be elaborated later on in the book, we thus claim that good qualitative research – and other research as well – should build upon a general awareness and a systematic, explicit treatment of the above-mentioned positions, and the problems, as well as the possibilities, which they indicate. How this can be tackled is the theme of the rest of the book. We will arrive, in Chapters 8 and 9, at a proposal for a reflexive methodology, built around a multi-layered, flexible structure of interpretation and reflection in which the systematic interplay of reflective areas is central.

Layout of the book

After this Introduction, we will in Chapter 2 give an overview of some important traditions that provide reference points for discussions in the philosophy of science and methodology: (neo-)positivism, social constructionism and critical realism. These offer a good ground for acknowledging the variety and tension in social research. They illuminate that social studies exist in contested terrain, encouraging a high level of thoughtfulness. We view knowledge of these traditions as important, but do not consider these broad streams to be sufficiently distinct to aid specific research work. Chapters 3–6 address the four main levels in a reflexive methodology which we will be discussing. First we consider a typical qualitative method with a rather strict empirical orientation, namely grounded theory. We see certain positive elements in it, but suggest that it gives too rational a picture of the research process and expresses a naïve view of empirical research. Chapters 4–6 deal with elements which, if they are taken seriously and applied to empirical research projects, can overcome the weaknesses in the empirically oriented methods, making it possible to go beyond these towards more sophisticated research processes: interpretation, political-ideological aspects, and the relative autonomy of the text.

In Chapter 7 we present some further important and topical influences that are highly relevant to a reoriented qualitative method, albeit in the nature of a comple- ment to the above-mentioned levels in the work of reflection rather than constituting fundamental elements of it. To these belong discourse analysis (the close empirical study of linguistic actions and expressions), feminism (gender research) and genealogical power theory (Foucault). These lines of argument carry further some of the insights from Chapter 6 and even to a certain extent from Chapters 4 and 5, but also go beyond what is treated in these chapters.

The thrust of the concluding chapters, 8 and 9, is to confront the four main levels with one another – that is, the handling of empirical material, interpretation, politics/ideology and representation/authority – with a view to creating a new and broader but also developable scope for qualitative methods. We indicate different ways of structuring our thinking on methodological issues, and point out some types of reflexive research in which the areas of reflection are given different weights depending on the research question and the knowledge interest. We also offer some concrete proposals on possible ways of coping with the complexity of the research process, and we discuss suitable levels of ambition in connection with the reflexive element.

The text presupposes some general cognizance of academic social science and a certain familiarity with qualitative method and the theory of science. Apart from this, it should be possible to read the book without any specific previous knowledge.

We have not explained terms which can be regarded as belonging to general knowledge; for those who are stuck for any particular word, an ordinary encyclopaedia should be able to help. However, parts of the book may be rather demanding, due to its research orientation and depending on the reader's degree of previous acquaintance with the field. But it is simply a matter of persevering! Without hard work there is nothing, except possibly methodological junk food, satisfying for the moment but leading to malnutrition in the end …

13

Notes

1. By 'empiricists' we mean those working in the field of science who place great faith in the capability of empirical research to reflect reality directly, and in the vital role of 'data' in science. Research is regarded primarily as a question of collecting, processing and analysing data, be it quantitative or qualitative. Theory and data are regarded as indisputably separate, and the value of the former is established by being tested against or emerging from the latter.

2. Within logic these are known as types of inference within the philosophy of science and also as types of explanation. This is true also of induction, which we take up below (see McMullin, 1982; Ruben, 1990).

3. In which one starts from a 'conjecture'. Like Glasser and Strauss, Popper to a certain extent slides between a more radical and a more attenuated version of his thesis. The radical thesis, however, predominates in both cases.

4. Cf. here also Yin (1984) about the replication of case studies.

5. We can also formally compare abduction, deduction and induction (Charniak and McDermott, 1985). This only fills the function of summary and schematic memory support; the formalization thus has no value in itself:

   Deduction (modus ponens variant) (1) If a, then b. (2) a. (3) Hence b.
   In the formalization of induction that follows, $P(x)$ means 'x has the property P'.
   Induction: (1) $P(a)$. $P(b)$ ... (2) Hence: for all x, $P(x)$.
   Abduction: (1) b. (2) If a, then b. (3) Hence a. In this last case, b is the (surprising) fact to be explained and a is the pattern that, were it true, explains the fact.

6. One view is that the problem should first be determined, and then the method. As a counterweight to technique-driven research – in which the questionnaire or the semi-structured interview, for example, are regarded as the solution to all problems – this is reasonable. But it is important to note that research problems cannot be determined independent of epistemological and theoretical starting-points. What constitutes an interesting and manageable research problem depends on the researcher's fundamental stance on methodological questions in the broad sense. More reasonable than the one-sided relationship of dominance between method (and theoretical considerations on methodological questions) on the one hand, and problems on the other, is a mutual relationship of influence between the two.

7. It could be argued that all research – indeed human life in general – is characterized by interpretation and reflection. In most books on method, including on qualitative method, these aspects are not salient. Interpretation is normally treated as a limited element, taking place after data have been gathered and categorized. Reflection is seldom mentioned and is normally constrained to technical matters and in relation to conclusions.

8. However, much if not all of what we have to say is also relevant to quantitative research. Actually a good deal of the criticism we make touches to an even greater extent on the quantitative methods, such as the adoption of a naïve view of language. Nor are the borderlines between the two orientations always clear-cut. However, in this book we do not address the question of what is specific to the quantitative method, but refer instead to the literature in the field of qualitative method and address themes of particular relevance to that field. In a way, a distinction that is more interesting than that between quantitative and qualitative research is one that distinguishes between reflective research and research in which the knowledge subject can avoid all critical examination, since it 'has been established as methodological reason' (Kittang, 1977: 33).

2

(POST-)POSITIVISM, SOCIAL CONSTRUCTIONISM, CRITICAL REALISM: THREE REFERENCE POINTS IN THE PHILOSOPHY OF SCIENCE

In this chapter we will discuss three overarching philosophies of science: positivism and post-positivism, social constructionism, and finally, critical realism. We take up the three orientations as a conceptual, terminologic, and thematic general background to the qualitative methodologies that follow. All three cut across the quantitative/ qualitative dividing-line. Although the main thrust of positivism is quantitative, there have been cases of qualitative positivism, for instance in historiography. Conversely, social constructionism is mainly qualitative, but quantitative social constructionist studies do exist. Finally, critical realism bridges quantitative and qualitative studies – there is no tendency for critical realists to favour either of these type of studies.

During the twentieth century, *positivism* became, and remained for a long time, the dominating philosophy of science. Theory and data, induction and deduction, law-like statements, verification and falsification, were key words. In the second half of the century, positivism came under increasing attack from internal sources – the post-positivists – as well as external opponents; and in the last third of the century, philosophical positivism rapidly deflated. Positivism has some similarities to the data-oriented methods discussed in Chapter 3, especially grounded theory; what is perhaps less well known is that it has also been alluded to by Foucault, and has some paradoxical traits in common with postmodernism; important ideas in post-positivism have been influential to postmodernist thought (see Chapter 6).

Social constructionism has increasingly emerged as an important perspective within social science and has even become predominant in some areas. Generally it can be said that for social constructionism, in contrast to positivism, reality is precisely *socially constructed*. (What this means in more detail, we will return to.) The important thing for research therefore becomes to explore how these social constructions happen. This approach is not particularly theory-oriented; rather the focus is on the 'disclosure' of how social phenomena are socially constructed. As we shall see, social constructionism is very rich and multi-faceted, so what has been said thus far is only a first indication of direction. Social constructionism has quite often been associated with postmodernism, and this may be true at a more superficial plane, although their roots and basic tenets are different; social constructionism has also made an inroad into grounded theory, and has been linked to hermeneutics and critical theory (sometimes called 'critical hermeneutics') as well. Feminism often emphasizes gender as a social construction.

According to *critical realism*, both positivism and social constructionism are too superficial, unrealistic and anthropocentric. For social constructionism, all knowledge is linked to our social constructions and should not rise – at least not too high – above these. For positivism, all knowledge comes to us as single sense-data, and theories are just human-made linkages between these single data. Critical realism, in contrast, asserts that there is a world independent of human beings, and also that there are deep structures in this world that can be represented by scientific theories; the latter therefore become central for this orientation. Critical realism has been presented as a possible successor to social constructionism, but whether this will transpire remains to be seen. In its emphasis on underlying patterns, critical realism shares some tangential points with hermeneutics and critical theory; in its searching for some kind of scientific laws, and in its view of the commonality of social science and natural science research, it shares ground with positivism.

Rooted in other traditions, social constructionism and critical realism constitute two important alternatives to positivist and post-positivist conceptions of science. In particular social constructionism but also critical realism presently draw great and increasing attention. They are often used as contrasts and as points of departure for debate and criticism.

In what follows, we present the orientations in chronological order. Initially launched in the nineteenth century, positivism was first out; social constructionism was introduced in the late 1960s; and critical realism in the 1970s. We shall give the most space to social constructionism since this is by far the most utilized orientation of the three in social science.

Positivism and beyond

The concept of 'positivism' has been central in the philosophy-of-science debate since the beginning of the nineteenth century, when Comte (1844) introduced the term, and through the twentieth century when logical positivism (later called logical empiricism) was topical. The sense of the positivism concept has often varied depending on who was doing the describing. The term 'positivism' has often been used in a derogatory sense, serving as a general invective. There is, though, a conceptual core. More concise and inclusive is perhaps Nietzsche's (1901/1967: 267) description of the approach as the doctrine that 'halts at phenomena: "there are only *facts*"'. To which Nietzsche promptly retorts: 'No, facts is precisely what there is not, only interpretations'. A little more elaborately, Feyerabend (1981: 16) describes positivism as 'any interpretation of science (and of theoretical knowledge in general), which applies an assumption equivalent to' the statement by the well-known positivist Hempel, 'Science is ultimately intended to systematize data of our experience.'

Etymologically, the word positivism comes from the Latin *positum*,[1] the supine form of *pono*, to put, set, place or lay. Thus, something is put, set, placed or laid; this something is given facts or data, and the one they lie in front of is the researcher.

Data are consequently something that *exists, is (already) there,* and the task of the researcher thus becomes to gather and systematize them. The underlying harvest metaphor is palpable. The researcher, as it were, collects the crops of the earth which are already there, and then prepares them as a tasty dish. Various positivist approaches have put a different emphasis on these two processes, the gathering and the systematizing, and have also described them in different ways. For positivist historians in the nineteenth century, data collection was more important than systematization, a systematization that was never allowed to lead as far as to theory, since this would mean the abandonment of facts in favour of speculation. In contrast, for Comte and also for the logical positivists in the twentieth century, theory, the systematization of data, was central.

Current social science positivists focusing on statistical analysis are found somewhere in between these positions: theory, seen as a summing of data, is accepted, but the theoretical propositions are both less encompassing and less systematized than the logical positivists' prescriptions of universally valid, formalized, axiomatic systems (prescriptions that the positivists' later inheritors in the philosophy of science have sharply criticized, see Suppe, 2000).

Data or facts should, according to positivism, be observable, and here is the link to empiricism (Harré, 1989). For modern positivism, what is observable also includes what is measurable or possible to register through some kind of instrument (Braithwaite, 1953: 8n). One approach within positivism, operationalism, even went so far as to reduce facts to measurable phenomena. A critical point against identifying observability with measurability is of course that this is all right when we talk about telescopes or microscopes; but even for these, a lot of interpretation beyond normal seeing is required. For other instruments, for instance a survey, the element of observation appears more distant or problematic. The logical positivists made a sharp distinction between theoretical language and observation language (reflecting the dichotomy between theory and empirical facts). The former was supposed to be translatable to the latter through so-called correspondence rules. As we shall see, this distinction was put in doubt by critics of positivism, who pointed out that all facts are theory-laden. If we talk about the results of measurements, this already presupposes both theories about the instruments that measure and theoretical preconceptions of what we measure (otherwise we would not know what to measure). For surveys, for instance, statistical theory lies at their basis, and the variables that are part of the measurements presuppose various social-scientific theories. The correspondence rules were also criticized for being a 'heterogeneous confusion of meaning relationships, experimental design, measurement, and causal relationships, some of which are not properly part of theories', while on the other hand more vague or diluted interpretations were criticized for being logically inconsistent (Suppe, 2000: 103).

Critics of positivism

In the post-war era, the positivist approach, and particularly logical empiricism, long dominated the scientific-philosophical discussion in the Anglo-American sphere. From the end of the 1960s, however, positivism was the target of strong and growing criticism, in particular from the Marxist left. The criticism did not diminish but rather increased in strength after the Marxist wave had ebbed away in the political disillusion of the 1970s. Structuralism, hermeneutics and phenomenology became the new banners under which many social scientists and humanists gathered. For the proponents of change, not least important was the access to something of a fifth column in the very camp of the enemy: Kuhn's ideas of paradigms and paradigmatic revolutions – ideas that had emerged from within a positivist environment. Kuhn's contributions, however, have somewhat unfairly come to obscure other important authors in the post-positivist tradition. Names like Feyerabend (1975), Hanson (1958) and Toulmin (1953, 1961) deserve to be mentioned in this context. Kuhn, Feyerabend, Hanson and Toulmin have been given the umbrella term 'historical relativists' (Suppe, 1977), since they held that scientific knowledge is historically and socially conditioned, and so is not absolutely true but relative in character.

The 'heart' of logical empiricism stopped beating on the 26 March 1969 at the opening day of a symposium in Illinois, when one of its foremost standard-bearers, Carl Hempel, openly admitted that he no longer accepted the basic theses of this approach (Suppe, 2000). (This does not of course prevent several of these theses from surviving *post mortem* in the social sciences.) Kuhn himself, even though his ideas are very topical in social science, has become more or less superseded by later developments in the philosophy of science: post-Kuhnian critics of positivism have turned away from historic relativism and, for good or bad, instead tried to form more general, timeless principles for theoretical knowledge (Preston, 2004).

If there is any common feature to be found in the just mentioned various alternatives to positivism, it is the following. The purpose of scientific activity no longer stands out as a statistical putting together of surface phenomena in an observed reality. Rather the important thing becomes to conceive this reality as an expression for, or a sign of, deeper-lying processes. For Hanson and Toulmin in the post-positivist school, the latter took the shape of law-like 'patterns' lying behind and explaining the manifestations of observed reality. The structuralists sought to trace structures that made their imprints on the matter of reality. The hermeneuticians interpreted the meanings that form the backdrop to and bring understanding of our language and actions. The Marxists and other dialecticians focused their interest on the hidden driving forces and mechanisms that in the form of in-built laws of movement, generated by contradictions, govern and develop the systems.

Thus, a transcending tendency is characteristic of the approaches critical of positivism: the observed reality is not all there is – and the researcher can reach behind it and reveal more fundamental layers, of which what we 'see' is a kind of projection or reflection. Such a way of looking at things was almost by definition excluded by the positivists, since (knowledge of) empirical reality was all that existed for them, and everything else was subjective constructions. Even scientific theories were conceived of as complex statements (systems of axioms) about generally observed relationships between surface phenomena. The parentheses around the words 'knowledge of' indicate the existence of differences in nuances between positivists in their attitudes to so-called theoretical entitities, i.e. what we have called underlying patterns or deep structures. On the one hand, there is the far-reaching opinion that these do not *exist*; on the other hand there is the opinion that we cannot *know* whether they exist or not (McMullin, 1982: 19). In both cases the attitude leads to a resistance to the use of theoretical entities as part of the scientific process. One might argue that at least the former kind of positivists would accept the use of such entities as a heuristic aid to find their theories. The theoretical entities could thus serve as a kind of useful fiction for the construction of theories. As an extension of this line of reasoning we might ask what the difference is in practice between positivists and their critics here. It is difficult to see why a positivist should take the roundabout way via deep structures and underlying non-observable tendencies, when it is much simpler and less time-consuming just to summarize data, which is the goal anyhow. The critics on their side aim precisely at theories that are *not* compilations of data.

The positivists' reduction to that which is observable (or even stronger, measurable) in reality is, in the view of the critics, not very justified. If there are hidden patterns, underlying rule formations, which govern the observed parts of reality, and whose exploration can contribute to explaining these observed parts, then this seems to be a legitimate area for research. Rather than beginning with survey-based measurements of large amounts of empirical data, or with guesses as to what the connections are between such data – both positivist approaches – another way becomes more reasonable: to carry out intensive studies of a small number of cases in order to retrieve through analysis the underlying patterns that are arguably reflected in the surface structures. These lines of thought have been held by post-positivists (Hanson, 1958; Toulmin, 1953), structuralists (Chomsky, 1968; Lévi-Strauss, 1962/1967) and dialecticians (Marx, 1967).

Later orientations such as different forms of postmodernism and poststructuralism (see Chapter 6) to a certain extent hark back to positivism by rejecting the idea of deep structures or underlying patterns. There are only surfaces (which can perhaps 'fold' – the fold metaphor is common in postmodernism/poststructuralism). In, for example, the case of Foucault (1972), this looking in the rear-view mirror happens explicitly, since he refers to himself as a 'positivist'. Even Latour (1996) can be mentioned in this context. A counter-reaction against surface thinking and a contention that underlying structures exist are found in the topical 'critical realism', which we discuss later in this chapter.

To take up the thread of postmodernism again, things are not that simple in this line of thought. As we shall see in Chapter 6, many proponents of postmodernism deny or bracket the existence of anything real outside language, to which linguistic statements would refer: texts only refer to other texts, not anything 'out there' (at least not accessible for research), as the jargon goes. If there is no extra-linguistic reality, there are also no hidden patterns to which the statements might refer. At the same time the postmodernists focused on tracing hidden but decisive cracks in the seemingly solid texts they studied: the so-called 'deconstruction'. The focus on the hidden behind the immediately familiar, palpable, is thus obvious even here.

Post-Kuhnian theoreticians (e.g. Suppe, 2000) in the influential 'semantic conception of science' have gone rather far in rejecting the idea of theories as direct reflections of reality. They introduce a third or middle term: *models*, which for them are more central than either theory or empirical data, and even constitute a kind of 'autonomous agents' (Morgan and Morrison, 2000). According to these 'model theoreticians', as they have also been called (Chakravarty 2001), researchers never directly compare theory and empirical data, as the logical empiricists argued; they compare *on the one hand* theory with models and *on the other hand* models with empirical data. For this line of thought, theories are almost a kind of Platonic 'non-linguistic' entities soaring over models and empirical data (Suppe, 2000). That theories contain non-observables – references to entities that cannot be observed – becomes nearly self-evident from such a stance. (The view of theories as non-linguistic has been criticized, for instance, by Hendry and Psillos, 2004, and Chakravarty, 2001.)

Beside the semantic conception of science there is also another post-Kuhnian orientation worth mentioning, the 'evolutionary' conception, in which the formation of theories is seen as a kind of Darwinian natural selection – the false or less true theories are weeded out by a kind of natural selection process. Through its evolutionary aspect, this orientation retains the time perspective on the scientific generation of knowledge that characterized Kuhn and other historical relativists, but without the relativism, for example Kuhn's idea that later paradigms are hardly more true than those they replace. Evolution and natural selection are thought to favour (ever) truer theories.

Theory vs empirical 'facts': verification, falsification and beyond

The clash between verificationists and falsificationists (or Carnapians and Popperians) in the philosophy of science is well known. Equally well known are Kuhn's paradigms. Lakatos's research programmes and Feyerabend's methodological anarchism are also important ingredients in post-positivist thinking, as are Toulmin's ideas. Less well known outside the philosophy of science as an academic field, post-Kuhnian approaches deserve more attention from social scientists.

With Carnap (1962) at the forefront, the logical empiricists had asserted the necessity of 'verifying' theories and hypotheses with positive examples. As against this, Popper's (1934/1972) ideas had a delayed but very strong impact, inverting everything and stating that theories, on the contrary, can only be 'corroborated' by repeated attempts at falsification. With his criticism, Popper directed a fundamental blow against logical empiricism, and theoretically refuted its most central theses.

Later critics, however, have had at least as strong objections to Popper's ideas. Kuhn (1970) showed in his analyses of scientific history that even the falsifications Popper had advocated as alternatives to the verifications he rejected, never occur in real research processes. He distinguished between two types of research. On the one hand the so-called 'normal research', where everything is focused on solving 'puzzles' within the frame of a thought structure – a 'paradigm' dogmatically regarded as given and the truth of which is beyond questioning. On the other hand the so-called 'paradigm shifts', scientific revolutions when one thought structure substitutes another, not on the basis of falsification, but for quite other reasons, including the capacity to attract supporters, who in time will come to dominate the research community.[2] Imre Lakatos (1970) tried to reconcile falsificationism with Kuhn's ideas, using his concept of 'research programmes'. These are reminiscent of complicated systems of fortifications, the aim being to protect the 'hard core' of the theory by different kinds of 'immunization strategies'. Such strategies were just what Popper had criticized. According to Feyerabend (1975), even great scientists will sometimes act like a kind of skilful con man or Machiavellian politician, who are good at hoodwinking the general public and their peer researchers by manipulating and forging data in various ways, and using micro-political tactics. This, too, is of course contrary to Popper's ideas of falsification.

An even earlier critic of positivism than Kuhn, Feyerabend and Lakatos was Stephen Toulmin. Avoiding the sometimes irrational overtones of the other three 'historical relativists', Toulmin (1953) held that theories are entities that are *used*, rather than entities that are *tested*. According to Toulmin, theoretical propositions can be compared with descriptions of rules. For rules, we first delimit the general area – here called the *domain* – indicating the type of cases for which the rule is valid. We do not say that the rule must necessarily hold for all these cases. In this way we stake out the rule's *area of application*. At American universities, there can, for example, be a general prohibition to walk on the lawns (the domain) – but not for 'Fellows', who fall outside of the area of application. To deprive other people of their liberty is generally forbidden – but not if they have committed crimes that lead to prison, something which falls outside the area of application. To kill another person is generally prohibited – except in war, which falls outside the area of application. And so forth.

In theoretical propositions, which thus express a kind of rules according to which reality functions, we first delimit the general domain, that is the types of cases in which the rules are applicable, and then successively try to map out the area of application within the domain, or, in other words, the cases within the general type for which the rule really is valid, and the cases that are exceptions. (Toulmin gives many examples of how this is done in scientific practice.) Positivism, on the contrary, regarded (in its deductive-nomological model) theoretical propositions as simply statements of universal relations like the prime example 'all swans are white'. If the statement is valid, it is true, otherwise it is false. As we have seen, matters are not as simple as that. Toulmin shows in many ways how positivism has ended up beside the road of scientific practice by failing to distinguish between the domain and the area of application for theoretical propositions. In particular this has been the case with physics, even though the latter has been the ideal model for positivism. Instead of verification/falsification, a procedure that, as we have pointed out (Kuhn, Feyerabend) seldom occurs in scientific practice, this research strategy therefore involves something else: *the successive establishing of a theory's area of application within a certain domain*. Concerning a *rule*, nobody asks 'it is true or false', but '*when does it apply?*'

Is it possible to generalize beyond the empirical base? A generalization of qualitative case studies is often called into question or regarded as unfeasible, something which has been seen as a weakness compared to quantitative setups. However, this depends on the epistemologic point of view. It also depends on what is meant by generalization. If we only accept surface regularities, there is of course no reason why a pattern that has previously been established should hold true for more occasions. Only a statistical study that can establish the probability that the findings have not emerged by chance is then justified to make a generalization – with a stated probability. In a perspective that accepts non-observables in the form of patterns and tendencies, common to and underlying several surface phenomena, *successive expansions of the empirical area of application within a certain domain* are both possible and desirable, even in qualitative studies. (For concise arguments in favour of generalizing qualitative case studies on the basis of knowledge realism, see also Tsoukas, 1989, and Danermark et al., 2002, Chapter 5.)

Many difficulties in the social sciences appear to be caused by importing a positivist view of how science 'should' be practised, a view that in its turn has been based on an erroneous picture of how the natural sciences really work. This is true of the issue we are discussing here, as well as of the issues of theory legitimation *vs* theory generation and the structure of explanations. The battle will then be for or against this supposed natural-science picture of scientific practice, whereby a lot of 'anti' approaches will ensue. This polarization risks losing what is really common to various branches of science, despite different subject matters. It is to the credit of the philosophy of science that emerged after logical empirism – for instance in the shape of post-positivism (Hanson and Toulmin) – that it has increasingly focused on how real research processes happen, contrary to previous, more prescriptive approaches.

In other words, positivism, by prescribing a formal logical form for theoretical propositions (universal judgements) has simply, as Toulmin (1972 and 1974, passim) points out, followed its tradition to *identify the rational with the logical*. (Something which also manifests itself in other ways, for instance in the requirement of theories to be formalizable as axiomatized systems.) But everything that is rational does not need to be formally logical even though the reverse is the case. If the research process is ensnared in a formal logical straitjacket, there is a risk that the qualitative counter-currents which will necessarily follow as a reaction, in the most extreme case will take on irrational overtones.

Among post-Kuhnians, adherents of the 'semantic conception of science' have particularly strongly, as we have seen, maintained that theory is never compared directly with empirical data, but with models; and models with empirical reality. There is also a two-way traffic between, on the one hand theory and models and, on the other hand models and empirical data: theories can be adjusted if they do not fit the results of the model, or the model can be adjusted; models can also be revised if they do not correspond to empirical results, and new empirical results can be sought out for further checking if the current ones do not agree with the model (errors in instruments, registrations, etc. can occur).

This conception of science, however, is 'methodologically naturalistic', i.e. it presupposes natural science (and especially experimental physics) as the paragon for all science; the models should, for example, be mathematically formulated and the theory be expressible in terms of state (or phase) spaces (Suppe, 2000), whence the semantic conception of science seems less applicable to the qualitative method in social science. McKelvey (2003) gives examples of why organization theory could be reformed from the semantic conception, and this seems rather quantitative. However, it should be kept in mind that the problematic is not unambiguous or simple; there is indeed qualitative mathematics (set theory, abstract algebra and topology are examples). The *basic* ideas in the semantic conception of science should also be applicable in qualitative research. What first comes to mind is of course qualitative models, but other ideational artefacts should also be considered. Metaphors, analogies and narratives often seem to play a similar role in qualitative research as quantitative models in quantitative research, pointing out a way to appropriate the semantic conception of science *malgré lui* for qualitative purposes. Such artefacts, re-presentations of, on the one hand empirical 'reality', and, on the other hand, theory, should then be considered as entities in their own right, irreducible to and potentially more important to the research process than either of these two, yet playing a mediating role between them.

The semantic conception of science claims to be epistemologically neutral, that is to be compatible with both realism and non-realism. Thus, the individual researcher can adhere to one or the other, in line with personal preferences, without either of them being at variance with the semantic conception of science. In particular when it comes to realism, one advantage is said to be the avoidance of the problems relating to the language–reality linkage (the problematic of representation), since theories are said *not to be linguistic* (and language includes also mathematical language). The argument for scientific theories' 'non-linguistic' character is that a theory can be expressed in different languages, and therefore it must be something that, so to speak, lies behind language. The argument seems doubtful – were it true, fiction in literature, for instance, would not be linguistic either, since it can be translated (albeit not always perfectly). Moreover, the problematic of representation with language is not avoided, since theories must always be expressed in some language (Japanese or Mathematese or …) and the same goes for models, whose representations of reality, even if these are visual, must always be expressed in words (Chakravarty, 2001).

The semantic conception of truth seems, despite its asserted neutrality between a realist and a non-realist view, to have clear preferences for the former. Its compatibility with a non-realist view is open to question, since the very root of the conception is a correspondence between theory and reality, based on Tarski's correspondence theory for truth.

Social constructionism

Social constructionism has been associated with all the orientations that we take up in Chapters 3–6 below. Its roots are in phenomenology, but it has more recently been related to postmodernism. There are also attempts to launch a social constructionist grounded theory, and sometimes both critical theory and hermeneutics have been associated with social constructionism, which also shares tangential points with ethnomethodology and with Foucault. As social constructionism is thus a very broad and multi-faceted perspective and furthermore has often been contrasted to, compared to, and seen as an alternative to, on the one hand, positivism, and on the other hand, critical realism, we treat it together with these two in the present chapter. For social constructionism, reality – or at least selected parts thereof – is not something naturally given. The study of how reality is socially constructed therefore becomes crucial for social constructionists.

23

The basic thrust of social constructionism can be described in the following four steps (taken from Hacking, 1999: 6, 12; note that we have changed Hacking's numbering):

1   In the present state of affairs X is taken for granted; X appears to be inevitable.

Social constructionist texts regularly begin with something that is regarded as self-evident, a taken-for-granted truth. The very point of social constructionism is then to prick a hole in this self-evidence by going further and showing that:

2   X need not have existed, or need not be at all as it is. X, or X as it is at present, is not determined by the nature of things; it is not inevitable.

This gives the 'aha experience' which is the main point of social constructionist texts. Many – though far from all – social constructionist texts then take one or two steps further, first to:

3   X is quite bad as it is.

And then to:

4   We would be much better off if X were done away with, or at least radically transformed.

Since social constructionism is so multi-faceted, these overarching characteristics are important in order to see, as it were, the forest and not just the single trees of the approach. (As to steps 3 and 4 above, it should be added that social constructionists are generally less systematic and confrontational in their criticism of societal phenomena than, for example, critical theorists: see Chapter 5.) Some try to be neutral or are only mildly sceptical. We will now look in more detail into Berger and Luckmann's classic work, which has become something of a cult book within the movement. After this we will take up two more recent important authors: Gergen and Latour. This is followed by a presentation of the variety of social construction. Finally we will present a few critical reflections and points of discussion.

Berger and Luckmann: reality as a social construction

Central author duo and pioneers for social constructionism,[3] Peter Berger and Thomas Luckmann, in 1966 published their book *The Social Construction of Reality*. The main inspiration for Berger and Luckmann was phenomenological (see Chapter 3 below). It was mediated by the Austrian Alfred Schutz, who in the 1930s became strongly influenced by the father of phenomenology, Edmund Husserl. Schutz, fleeing from Nazism, emigrated to the USA, and in his philosophy applied phenomenology to the common-sense world of everyday life. Berger and Luckmann developed this thinking in the area of sociology.

They were also influenced by other authors who had anticipated or been active within the area of knowledge sociology, such as Marx, Nietzsche, Scheler and Mannheim. All of these, who from the present perspective could be regarded as a kind of 'forefathers' to social constructionism, called into question the existence of a purely rational, objective knowledge, arguing instead that knowledge arises from processes more related to ideology, interests, or power.

Yet other sources of inspiration for Berger and Luckmann included sociological 'mega classics' like Durkheim, Weber and Mead. Durkheim presented as his basic rule that it was necessary to view 'social facts as things'. Weber, on the other hand, held that the subjective meaning content in social actions was the central issue. In their social constructionism, Berger and Luckmann wanted to join together these two polarized standpoints between objective macro relationships and subjective micro relationships (a polarity that has been something of a leading theme in much social science). Their solution placed the emphasis on the individual level and the social facts; the institutions remained secondary.

Berger and Luckmann held that:

> common-sense 'knowledge' rather than 'ideas' must be the central focus for the sociology of knowledge. It is precisely this 'knowledge' that constitutes the fabric of meanings without which no society could exist. The sociology of knowledge, therefore, must concern itself with the social construction of reality. (1966: 27)

Through this, the at first sight unsolvable conflict between Durkheim's and Weber's sociological position might be solved

> The central question for sociological theory can then be put as follows: How is it possible that sub-jective meanings *become* objective facticities? ... How is it possible that human activity ... should produce a world of things ...? In other words, an adequate understanding of the 'reality sui generis' of society requires an inquiry into the manner in which this reality is constructed. (1966: 30)

The authors begin to solve this question by first 'attempt[ing] to clarify the foundations of knowledge in everyday life, to wit, the objectivations of subjective processes (and meanings) through which the *inter*subjective common-sense world is constructed' (1966: 34). The 'phenomenological analysis' they hereby use is termed 'descriptive' and 'empirical', not 'scientific' (1996: 34). All consciousness is intentional – i.e., it is always directed against some object. But these objects can present themselves to us in different spheres of reality, for instance in dreams or the waking state. We live in several different realities – among others in that of the dream – but the basic one is the usual everyday world. This is experienced as in various ways pre-structured, objectified. It also presents itself for us as an 'intersubjective world, a world [we] share with others' (1966: 37). We continually remove ourselves from the everyday world to other, more secondary realities, or 'finite provinces of meaning' in Berger and Luckmann's terminology (taken from Schutz). These exist in unlimited numbers but a few important examples can be mentioned – theoretical science, art, religion, and the previously mentioned state of dreaming.

We share the everyday world with others. These others are experienced most characteristically in face-to-face situations. We '*typify*', according to Berger and Luckmann (Part 1, Chapter 2), these others in various ways, for instance as English, Brazilian, man, woman, child, grown-up, professor, nurse, police officer, etc. Everyday life is also filled with 'objectivations' (Part 1, Chapter 3). In these, a certain meaning content is given a material expression, which then becames more permanent and transcends the immediate, concrete face-to-face relationship. Signs, symbols and language are examples of such objectivations. (We return to the objectivation concept below.) Language is of course especially important in the building-up of 'a social stock of knowledge' (1966: 56). A prominent role in this social stock of knowledge is played by the build-up of routines for acting in various situations, something which functions as a sort of 'recipe knowledge' for actions (1966: 56).

Human beings differ from other animals in their less developed instinctual behaviour and in their great flexibility. In order not to become chaotic, human acting must therefore be confined by some form of stability. This happens through a 'social order'. Human beings are social in their nature, and Berger and Luckmann argue (inspired by the father of social interactionism, Herbert Mead) that even the expe-rience of a 'self' is developed in meaningful interaction with others. The social order is thus a human product, or more specifically 'an ongoing human product'; it is not something inherent in the 'nature of things', nor does it express any 'natural law'. People alienate, or *externalize*, themselves by necessity in their actions, and the social order is an expression of this (1966: 69–70).

Central to the social order is the process through which institutions emerge – *institutionalization*. What, then, is an institution? Berger and Luckmann mean that the forming of habits and routines, 'habitualization', happens continually in human acting. All the time, we develop habits, through which a certain way of acting can be repeated in similar situations. Berger and Luckmann describe institutionalization as 'a reciprocal typification of habitualized actions. Put differently, any such typification is an institution' (1966: 72). In every institution, actions of a certain type are supposed to be carried out by a certain type of actor. For example, our legal system as an institution stipulates certain penalties for individuals above a certain age who are aware of the consequences of their actions and commit certain crimes. Academic institutions stipulate certain rules of admittance for certain types of actors (students) and conditions of employment for others (researchers, teachers, administrators). And so forth. Through institutionalization, we are subject to social control: for example, the incest prohibition forbids certain kinds of sexual action. But this social control is already preceded by the typification whereby we define certain kinds of sexual action as incest and not others. This typification will of course vary between different cultures and societies.

We create within our social relations all the time new habits and routines in our actions, as well as new categories in our observing of others and their actions. Or in Berger and Luckmann's terminology, we habitualize and typify; these habitualiza-tions and typifications – these habits, routines, and categorizations – spread between actors, and as they do this, institutions, that is fixed patterns of thought and action, emerge: institutionalization occurs, for instance in the shape of family, religion, legal systems, sports, school systems, health care, hunting, etc. These institutions, originally created by people, by and by begin to be perceived as something external, objective, and given, that is, there occurs also an *externalization* and an *objectivation* (1966: 78).[4] Berger and Luckmann here draw on Hegel's and Marx's concept of alienation, in which people are viewed as estranged from their own activity, their praxis, which has been separated from them and therefore falsely comes to be understood as something external to themselves.

Through the need for meaningful mutuality in the social interaction, and for a coherent life – a 'biography' – there arises another need for coherence and unity, for integration, not only within but also between the institutions. Still, this integration, as different forms of 'institutional logic', is created by people, and is not the expression of any functionality or effectivity in the institutions themselves. Such institutional logics are the legitimizations of institutions, and a particularly important means for legitimizations is language. Whole 'bodies of knowledge' develop in this way, for instance theoretical formations in science, but there are also pre-theoretical bodies of knowledge that integrate knowledge in various areas on a pre-theoretical basis. The knowledge that is in this way alienated – externalized – from individuals will then be carried back to them, be internalized:

> Knowledge, in this sense, is at the heart of the fundamental dialectic of society. It 'programmes' the channels in which externalization produces an objective world. It objectifies this world through language and the cognitive apparatus based on language, that is, it orders it into objects to be apprehended as reality. It is internalized again *as* objectively valid truth in the course of social-ization. Knowledge about society is thus a *realization* in the double sense of the word, in the sense of apprehending the objectivated social reality, and in the sense of ongoingly producing this reality. (1966: 83–84, note omitted)

This knowledge is then transmitted not only betwen the individuals in society at a certain time, but also over time between generations, which is how traditions arise.

More specifically, experiences and knowledge are stored as memory layers in and between individuals, or as Berger and Luckmann (1966: passim) say with a geolog-ical metaphor, inspired by Husserl, they are '*sedimented*'. Language, through its intersubjective transferring of meaning, is an important means for collective sedimentation. The transferring of institutional meaning is an important aspect of this. Knowledge of the sense and meaning of institutions is transferred by special typifications – for example teacher and pupil – and by special control apparatuses. Rituals and symbols of various kinds are used as carriers of institutional, sedimented knowledge, for example 'fetishes and military emblems' (1966: 88). The sediments of knowledge in a society are legitimized, but these legitimations can differ from time to time. For example, at one time prisons can be legitimized from their pun-ishment function, at another time from their reforming function. Under a certain epoch universities can be legitimized from their educational function, under another epoch from their economic role in society.

In their typifications, individuals create different *roles* for themselves and others. Institutions cannot exist without being realized by human enactments in roles. Conversely, roles represent institutions. Institutions are also represented by many other things, like linguistic symbols, physical artefacts, and so on. But only human enactment in roles make the institutions, so to speak, come to life. 'The institution, with its assemblage of "programmed" actions, is like the unwritten libretto of a drama' (1966: 92).[5] Roles are very important for the development of the individual's self, since they are internalized and together will form a whole self, a subject. The roles further illustrate and mediate the basic dialectics between the institutional and the individual level of society. 'By playing roles, the individual participates in a social world. By internalizing these roles, the same world becomes subjectively real for him [sic!]' (1966: 91).

The extent of institutionalization can vary between different societies and times. Some societies are more or less pervaded by institutions; in others the institutionalization takes place mostly around a core. The institutionalization can also be segmented, so that, for instance, a certain institution is reserved for certain people or groups and is closed to outsiders. Cults are of course the extreme case of this. Institutions can also vary in the degree that they are *'reified'*, that is, they are perceived as physical things. (Berger and Luckmann took their inspiration here from Marx and his concept of *'Verdinglichung'*, which would translate as something like 'thingification'.) The reification is described as an extreme case of objectivation, but it is not always easy to see the difference, for example when the authors describe overarching theoretical formations as reifications – which originators would see these as physical 'things', one wonders.

Legitimization constitutes another layer in the objectivation of meaning. It integrates disparate meanings to a connected whole. This takes place both at the level of the single individual's biography and at the level of institutions. Legitimization becomes necessary when meaning is to be mediated to new generations for which it is no longer self-evident. Explanations and justifications therefore become possible, and this is the process of legitimization. Legitimization is therefore both cognitive and normative. Four levels of legitimization can be discerned. The first and the most rudimentary level is built into language: our very vocabulary, the words we use, legitimize ('counter-terrorism' instead of 'oil war', 'subprime loans' instead of 'reckless loans', for instance). The second level consists of proverbs and sayings, maxims, legends, etc. The third level contains explicit theories. The fourth and most important level creates entire *symbolic universes*. Such a symbolic universe orders and integrates within its framework *'all* socially objectivated and subjectively real meanings' (1966: 114).

Thus, individuals create their reality, the institutions and their legitimizations, but this created reality in turn creates the individuals. This happens through socialization, the social influence through which individuals internalize social norms and knowledge. In the primary socialization, the child learns the basics of what is important in society, and in the secondary socialization, the process is fine-tuned for the grown-up. In the primary socialization, the child learns via 'significant others'. The identity is built up through role-taking – another term from social interactionism – we see one another with the eyes of significant others, reflect over this, and successively generalize the experiences.

In secondary socialization we appropriate 'sub-worlds', rather than 'base-worlds' as in the primary socialization (Berger and Luckmann, 1966: 158). The secondary socialization, for instance the school system, involves less of significant others, and is more formalized and abstract; the people included in this are often interchangeable (for instance teachers, as compared to parents). Yet, even here life partners, for instance, can take on the role as significant others, maintaining the person's subjective reality, a reality that is always fragile and threatened by experiences that do not seem to fit in. More peripheral others function as a sort of 'choir' around the central, significant others. Another important means to maintaining a person's subjective reality is conversation. Through conversation with others, and perhaps above all through what is *not* said in conversation but is implied, we continually confirm our picture of reality. The need to maintain a subjective reality of course also means that it can change. The change can be continuous in the secondary socialization, when the present is interpreted in terms of the past. The change can also be radical, even transforming, when instead the past is interpreted in terms of the present. Examples of such radical changes encompass religious conversion, political brainwashing and therapy.

Socialization can fail. One extreme case is stigmatized individuals: lepers, pedophiles, mentally ill people, etc., under various periods. Less conspicuous examples can occur because of discrepancies in the socialization. This discrepancy can take place between significant others, so that for instance father and mother or parents and nursemaid convey different messages. It can also take place between primary and secondary socialization, for instance between parents and teachers. If several discrepant worlds for socialization are accessible in a society, then this paves the way for individualism and relativism.

Berger and Luckmann see the human organism as a 'biological substratum', which sets limits on the individual's sociality – the need to feed, sexuality, death, etc. But the social world also sets limits on the individual's biology, in how we eat, how we have sex, when and how we die, etc. Socialization itself constitutes an ongoing invasion of the sociological world into the biological one, by regulating time and space, against the spontaneous tendencies or active resistance of the organism.

The authors conclude by saying that they view their contribution primarily as a re-definition of knowledge sociology. Beyond this, they hope that their book will eventually become an important complement to structural analyses in sociology. They do not want to deny the importance of these analyses, or maintain that social constructionism must always be a part of them; however, despite a certain ambivalence, they are not enthusiastic over macro sociological approaches like structuralism, functionalism and systems theories, which they see as always running the risk of reification. Berger and Luckmann maintain that the dialectic between society and the individual that Marx had already pointed out 'in fact and generally, does exist' (1966: 209), but that it is necessary to move on and develop this dialectic on the basis of sociological tradition. In this work, they have sought to integrate other classical theories such as Durkheim's macro sociology, Weber's focus on individuals and understanding, and Mead's interactionist social psychology. (It should be added that this integration is done with a pervading phenomenological colour.) Finally, Berger and Luckmann hold that sociology is a humanistic discipline that must be carried on in a dialogue with philosophy and historiography.

Berger and Luckmann's book is very well written and its theses are unfolded with verve and enthusiasm. Its often suggestive terminology – 'finite provinces of meaning', 'symbolic universes' and so on – contributes to its rhetorical power. It integrates elements from major social-scientific classics such as Marx, Durkheim, Weber and

Mead. This integration is not just an eclectic putting together, but gains its unity through the philosophic canvas it is painted on, more precisely the phenomenology that was introduced by Husserl and further developed by Schutz in the area of everyday life. The book includes a whole spectrum of topical approaches in social science at the end of the 1960s. It is also a micro sociological protest against various macro sociological trends dominating at the time it was written. It is an attempt to solve a basic problematic of social science: the contradiction between the micro and macro, the individual and society.

That said, several basic aspects of Berger and Luckmann's book are problematic and can be called into question. We will leave these critical comments until the end of the present section on social constructionism. For now, we turn to two newer social constructionist thinkers, stemming from different national cultures and academic disciplines – the American social psychologist Kenneth Gergen and the French sociologist of knowledge Bruno Latour.

Gergen: a persistent critic of positivism

Gergen (1978, 1996, 2004) strongly emphasizes the importance of language, and in this respect his thinking borders on that of the postmodernists. Influenced, among others, by philosophers like Gadamer, Kuhn and Rorty, Gergen has struggled for many years against the dominating positivist orientation of his discipline. According to Gergen, knowledge is never abstract, objective and absolute, but always concrete, situated and tied to human practice. There is no Truth, only local truths.

The important theories that have formed our everyday thought and defined the problems of social science have, as Gergen (1982) shows, contained very little data, the most obvious example being Freud's works. These important theories have instead offered persuasive conceptions and ideas about the central issues of life, often calling into question both prevailing assumptions and predominating values. They have often led to intense and long-lasting debates. This should not come as a surprise, since Kuhn has pointed to roughly similar conditions within the natural sciences. There are reasons why certain theories are accepted rather than others, but this is not just a question of facts. The extension and use of certain theories, and even the results of these, are better explained by popularity cycles, boredom, career needs, and social and economic relationships. It is important for a theory to challenge established conceptions and question assumptions in previous theories to appear interesting and (reasonably) surprising, which is central to becoming influential (Davis, 1971). Empirical support is less important.

Gergen (1978, 1982), like many others has pointed out the insufficiency of theoretical claims for representation and of the hypothetical-deductive model as a way to think about the choice of theory. The various assumptions that are made – about the primacy of objective facts, the requirement of verification, the goal to reach universal atemporal results, and the impartial spectator – hide the nature and values of theories (Gergen, 1978, 1982). 'Facts' mean either the end or a suppression of a conflictual negotiation process which includes different interests and participants in the research process. A 'scientific procedure' often suppresses the element of negotiation and prevents us from investigating its character. The testing of hypotheses becomes, to a certain extent, self-fulfilling over time since the theory shapes that towards which the attention is directed and people react interactively in testing situations. All results are historical artefacts, both because of the theory and because people, partly as a consequence of social-scientific reports, change over time. The question is only if we accept the conditions and practices that are required to create the scientific artefact. Every theory carries with itself the values of a research community which often lets its concepts and interpretations substitute for those that are lived by the research subjects.

Gergen seems to us to have fought for so long – four decades! – against positivism in psychology that he, in contrast to Latour for instance, risks becoming a bit negatively dependent on it – something of an inverted mirror image. With some justification, he has been criticized for relativism, rather angrily by Ratner (2005) – a proponent of the older type of psychology that Gergen (2004) compares with the dinosaurs on their way to extinction. (For a counter-reply to Ratner, see Zielke, 2005.)

Gergen strongly advocates qualitative methods, which he believes have often been marginalized in favour of quantitative methods. He emphasizes the importance of a reflexive dialogue to set in motion hardened taken-for-granted assumptions which have emerged through collective processes of knowledge. Contrary to modernism, but like postmodernism, Gergen also very much emphasizes the instability and fragility of the human self, which he thinks has become particularly accentuated in our time of ever faster technological development and its influence on the individual. For Gergen (1989), this is a question of the ways in which human beings present their own (and others') inner self and gain credibility and legitimacy: 'What we take to be the dimension of self ... are symbolic resources for making claims in a sea of competing world construction' (1989: 75). Within more recent social constructionism, Gergen provides a contrast and represents something of a counter pole to Latour, to whom we now turn.

Latour and ANT: the 'second wave' of social constructionism

Within the sociology of knowledge, social constructionism has been particularly influential. Here, Bruno Latour with his investigations of scientific knowledge is incomparably the most well known name. He has been responsible for what can be characterized as a second wave of social constructionism, in which also non-human actors such as technical artefacts and the like can play an active role in the construction. By using social constructionist lines of thought on natural-science activities, Latour has aroused fury in some quarters, especially among American scientists, and also strongly contributed to the so-called 'science war' between, on the one hand French social constructionists and postmodernists, and on the other hand American natural-science realists, for whom the laws of nature are absolute, objective truths. A good early example of this is Latour and Woolgar's famous and controversial (1979) study of how knowledge is constructed socially in a laboratory. There were some predecessors – already at the beginning of the 1930s, Ludwig Fleck (1934/1979), who was a physician himself, investigated how medical knowledge is constructed; but

Fleck's book was long forgotten and it is Latour who made the great breakthrough. Latour followed *Laboratory Life* up with a book on the *Pasteurization of France* (1988), in which he showed that the reception and success of Louis Pasteur's groundbreaking ideas about micro organisms were socially constructed.

Latour has launched a very successful methodological programme, 'the actor-network theory' (ANT), where the actors do not only need to be humans. This idea is inspired by Greimas's (1983) semiotic theory of 'actants', a kind of generalized actor who does not need to be a person but can be an artefact, etc. The idea of non-human actors can at first sight seem a bit fantastic, almost science fiction, but on a closer look it appears less bizarre. In the context of organizations, for example, most of us know that organizations, organizational subunits, groups, etc. take on something of a life of their own. The same is true of technical systems such as IT systems in organizations or plans and projects: they have a life of their own and are not mere passive products. Machines and devices of various kinds can also be actants. To take a simplified illustration: when we stop at a red traffic light, we are influenced by the device on the street corner, which is thus not only a passive receptor of impulses from human subjects in its initial construction but also in its turn influences human subjects. Actor-network theory is also sometimes called 'actant-network theory'. For example, in Latour's (1996) book *Aramis* the main actor is a futurist personal rapid transit system which is later axed, and the question becomes, 'Who killed Aramis?'

In his extensive account of ANT, Latour (2005) strongly argues for a micro socio-logical 'bottom-up' perspective where the single actors, events and processual aspects play a decisive role. He rejects both a macro sociology of the Durkheimian type (in which 'society' becomes a kind of metaphysical substance according to Latour) *and* postmodern deconstructionism. The latter is described as ruins built on ruins. Instead ANT aims at following the traces of associations between actants; associations that are always in the process of dissolving and re-emerging. Latour describes himself as a social constructionist, on the condition that the word 'social' should not be misunderstood as some sort of macro phenomenon which is already there, instead of being created at the micro level. Other authors related to ANT are Callon (1980, 1986), who seems to be the one who first published the idea, and Law (1994). As to method, ANT uses vari-ous ways to follow the actor through interviews and ethnographic observation; there is also work with 'inscriptions', that is texts and the like (for instance databases and graph-ical material). For current applications of ANT, see Czarniawska and Hernes (2005).

Compared to the perspectives of his first studies, such as *Laboratory Life*, Bruno Latour (2004a and b) has later developed in a (more) realist direction. He describes himself as being in a state of permanent change and transformation, and provoca-tively refers to himself as a realist and a positivist[6] – even though he puts partly dif-ferent meanings into this than the usual ones. Actants can be both human and non-human, and it would then seem strange to claim that the latter do not exist or can be 'reduced' to constructions. Moreover, reality is not neutral to operations on it, but resists, so its existence cannot be disregarded. However, reality is fluid, since the construction work continues all the time. Latour is extremely critical of post-modernism, seeing it as a sterile and destructive nihilism. But he is also critical of more theoretical ambitions, such as those of Bourdieu. Instead, it is crucial to keep to pure descriptions of how actants create their networks; not even explanations should enter the picture, since the research subjects know better than the researcher what goes on. The researcher must not get up on any high horse but must be humble and let the actants speak. Latour's approach is in this way reminiscent of the empirically oriented lines of thought which we take up in Chapter 3 – in particular ethnomethodology, for which he has sympathies.

Latour problematizes conventional interpretations and conceptions of both terms in 'social constructionism'. The 'social' does not mean that the constructions are *made* by, *consist* of, something social – whether that be insubstantial phantoms of the brain or manifestations of overarching societal power structures à la Bourdieu – but that the *construction process itself* is social, with several actants participating, co-constructing. However, the word construction is also problematic, at least as it has been conceived, and this has to do precisely with the participation of several, even non-human, actants. The constructor is not a god who blows his spirit into a material. The construction is real, no chimera, and what we have is, thus, a *realist constructionism*.

But this does not mean that there is a 'both-and' of construction and reality. Then we are just building further on a false opposition. Discourse and reality, 'words and worlds', are not dichotomic pairs but end points on a continuum consisting of practices carried out by (human and non-human) actants. Instead of getting stuck in this opposition, Latour holds, we should pose the question of whether the construction is *good or bad*, something which is usually at the centre of questions concerning constructions in general, for example architectonic ones. (We might of course wonder: 'Good or bad *in relation to what?*') In any case, Latour's basic slogan, for which all other considerations must give way, is: 'Follow the actants' (Latour, 1999). Latour plays with the idea of substituting 'composition' for '(social) construction'; but he inclines after all towards keeping the term construction since it is well established. Latour's reflection over, and problematization of, the concept and the term social constructionism thus result, after due deliberation, in his decision to keep it.

Generally, we find Latour's ideas exciting, for instance the view of artefacts as more active than is usually assumed. Yet, like some other more recent French thinkers, he seems to have a tendency to overdramatize his own lines of thought, in his case so that the artefacts are almost transformed into living entities and tend to assume a science-fiction character. A certain coquettishness with one's own position, a kind of hide-and-seek towards the reader, is another part of the style. Latour is also among the most antitheoretical of the social constructionists, which is based in his reductionist catchphrase about following the actants – everything else is to be rejected. As is the case with grounded theory, we wonder how it is possible to do research – or any mental activity – without theoretical preconceptions, and what the point is with pure descriptions. Books like *Aramis* can be fun to read – for a while. Then the amount of describing voices becomes a bit wearying.

The variation of social constructionism

Social constructionism has successively spread to most areas of social science and in many cases – where not everybody follows Latour or Gergen – has become more or less dominant. An alliance, or convergence, with the postmodern orientation and Zeitgeist has contributed to its success – even though the coupling between these two lines of thought is not unproblematic, as we have seen. We will not try to list encyclopedically all conceivable authors in the social constructionist domain, since they are legion. Ian Hacking has playfully exemplified the host of social constructionist texts in an alphabetic sample. Thus, there are texts about The Social Construction of:

- Authorship
- Brotherhood
- The child viewer of television
- Danger
- Emotions
- Facts
- Gender
- Homosexual culture
- Illness
- Knowledge
- Literacy
- The medicalized immigrant
- Nature
- Oral history
- Postmodernism
- Quarks
- Reality
- Social homicide
- Technological systems
- Urban schooling
- Vital statistics
- Youth homelessness
- Zulu nationalism

(Hacking, 1999: 1, references omitted)

Further examples can be entered ad lib for most letters of the alphabet. Hacking comments that he has not been able to find a title with 'The Social Construction of X', but that was before the era of Googling. We found 'The Social Construction of X-rated films' (Kurti, 1983). There is great variety not only in the empirical examples authors use but also in their theoretical approach. Sometimes all possible orientations that can have any point in common with social constructionism are included in the latter, such as deconstructionism, Foucauldianism, grounded theory, poststructuralism, discourse analysis, etc. (see, for instance, Burr, 2003). Most social scientists probably adhere to the idea that society and its institutions are not given, but in some (wide) sense socially created. In this way, most of us are social constructionists. We have, however, wanted to conceive social constructionism as a fairly delimited approach. Nonetheless, it is necessary to point out the considerable variation even within the rather diffuse core area(s) of social constructionism.

We can discern – with an increasing degree of radicality – social construction as a critical perspective, a sociological theory, a theory of knowledge and a theory of reality (Barlebo Wenneberg, 2001). This makes four degrees of radicality within social constructionism: a critical, a social, an epistemological and an ontological. The critical variant is the mildest, and means impugning the 'natural' in what has previously and commonly been regarded as self-evident and natural, and instead showing that this is socially constructed. Youth or race can serve as examples. It is obvious that conceptions of these vary a lot, and that they tend to create the phenomena in question. The social variant means arguing that society is in some sense produced and reproduced by shared meanings and conventions and thus socially constructed. The epistemologic variant means as the name indicates that knowledge is socially constructed. In the ontological variant, finally, reality itself is a social construction.

Barlebo Wenneberg now contends that these four degrees of social constructionism make a kind of inclined plane, where it is easy to slip or glide inconspicuously from the first, relatively innocuous, position, all the way to the most radical position, that reality, including natural reality, is nothing but a social construction. From a relatively trivial remark that certain phenomena do not occur naturally but are social creations, we are driven to reflect over how these constructions in their turn have emerged. We are then into some kind of social theory such as, for example, Berger and Luckmann elaborate in the later part of their book (1966). But to be consequent, a theory of society must also tackle the issue of knowledge in society and how it is created. Then we have taken the step to the third variant of social constructionism, the epistemological one, in which knowledge is maintained to be a social construction. But if that is the case, it is a small step to start considering whether or not the object of knowledge, reality itself, is a social construction. Then we have taken the step to the fourth, ontological position, in which reality is a social construction.

*

Social constructionism is, as we have said, complex and varied and the overall picture is fragmented. One could probably say that in today's use of social constructionism there is a shift of emphasis from the former to the latter poles within the three related but distinct areas, that is from a critical perspective to ontology, from cognition to language, and from constructions of social phenomena to construction as a central aspect of research projects and claims. This coincides with an increased interest in postmodernism during recent decades, even though this interest has dropped during the last decade.[7]

Critique of social constructionism

Social constructionist texts and studies have the great merit of often being both fun to read and interesting, as well as exciting in their contents. They challenge common sense and not infrequently surprise the reader. Their value of attraction is usually higher than the mostly boring, not to say tinder-dry statistical investigations on the quantitative side, to which they have often been presented as the major qualitative alternative; but they are also more alluring than, for instance, texts in grounded theory generally are. This has probably contributed to the success of this orientation. But such success has its price, and we now come to our concluding critical points.

The Social Construction of Reality (Beger and Luckmann,1966), to start with the basic book of the movement, has, as we noted above, considerable merits and is a pioneering work, but critical reflections are possible at several points. To begin with, the central second part of the term 'social construction' remains not only undefined but also unexplained. What is 'construction'? The authors never give any answer to this; the term is just abruptly introduced in the text, like many other suggestive terms within the book. Etymologically, the term comes from the Latin *con-struo*: to staple, pile or order together, build. 'Construction' is a metaphor associated with planned activities such as those related to the erection of a building. The result of the building or construction process is an artefact, and the result of the social construction analogously would be a kind of social artefact, a social 'building' – an institution. Here, though, the metaphor limps along, because social constructions, especially in the social constructionist sense, are not planned activities. According to Hacking (1999), the very point of social constructionism and that which has brought the approach such success is that it shows how various, seemingly 'natural', phenomena are not at all natural but social. This recurs time and again in Berger and Luckmann's book. But through the metaphor of 'construction' they actually take this one step further: the terminology suggests that various natural phenomena are in fact not just social but also intentionally planned, thus almost manipulatively created: they are, as it were, human *fabrications*, and the *disclosure* of these manipulatory or arbitrary fabrications becomes an important part of social constructionism's enticement.

It is also possible to question the very starting point of the book, which becomes something of an axiom for the authors, namely the primacy of the individual, the individual as the one where everything begins and ends. The basic problem for Berger and Luckmann was how it is possible that subjective meanings become objective facticities. From this point of departure, and using the construction metaphor, they go on to think that the study of society must focus on how individuals construct society. As we have seen, the metaphor is skewed. But also, the primacy of the individual is anything but a matter of course. The authors seem to experience it as self-evident, but it is not. How do we know, for example, that the individual is not secondary and that overarching structures are the primary constructors – or rather creators – of individuals in the first place? But can this possibly be so? Well, Fuchs (2001), among others, has presented an elaborate theory of how individuals and individuality are created – or as he says, 'constructed' – by networks. Networks are, in this theory, the place where everyting begins and ends. And there are other examples of approaches where individuals do not have primacy. For postmodernists and poststructuralists, individuals are created by texts or discourses; the text/discourse is thus primary. Individuals and cognitions are seen as the 'result' of language (which is also a main point for non-cognitivist constructionists like Gergen). For more recent (alethic) hermeneutics (see Chapter 4), the very situation of understanding is primary, and the individual is a result of this. As to the macro–micro problematic which has permeated so much of social science, many attempts have been made to solve it, both before and after Berger and Luckman. Among the most successful are Bourdieu's (1979) theory of practice and Giddens's (1984) theory of structuration. Both also introduce a third element – a processual aspect which mediates between the individual and society.

Even if we were to accept the basic axiom of Berger and Luckmann that society and its institutions are built out of individual meanings, it does not follow that social science must necessarily be limited to studying how society is constructed. To take the analogy with houses: we can research into many other things than how a house was built, for example, its architecture, the strength of the materials, the plumbing, ventilation, price of the house, the rent, how people behave in it, etc.

A problem in any form of critical discussion of social constructionism more generally is that the orientation includes so many different positions, in between which advocates often move rhetorically under the pressure of various critiques and counter arguments (Barlebo Wenneberg, 2001). This is a common immunity strategy against critics. In addition there seems to be quite a lot of 'genuine' confusion and indecisiveness (Fleetwood, 2005). Correspondingly, there are many different versions of what people mean by 'construction' as well as 'social'. This means that any critique of social constructionism risks not 'sticking' as a consequence of the ambiguity and slipperiness of the target, and the critique may only be relevant for minor parts of the intended goal. What follows should therefore be read with some caution, as we also have problems in 'fixing' our object for critique.

Social constructionists hold that since social reality is a social construction, the only thing worth investigating is how this construction is carried out. This has profound consequences in that it leads to anti-theoretical tendencies (descriptivism and a reduction to the individual level of analysis). But since knowledge is always theory-laden and we never 'observe' anything (including social constructions) without theories, this neglects the decisive role of our theories in research. Theories that tell us anything about social phenomena 'beyond' the construction of these, hardly become possible. Yet, reflection over our theories, and the ensuing development of them, in order to better understand what we study, are an integrating part of research.

For this reason it can even be argued that theory is the most important aspect of research. Social constructionists tend, unfortunately, as Bourdieu has pointed out about micro sociologists generally, to stop where the real fun begins, instead of posing questions such as: 'Why do people construct society in the way they do?' and 'How do these constructions function, as patterns of social reality, once they have been constructed'?[8]

While some constructionists 'neutrally', and at times amusedly, seek to point at construction processes, others often tend to adopt a more sceptical perspective, regarding the patterns studied as something basically bad or evil, which we should not study as given (other than how they are *constructed*), just change or abolish. '[M]ost people who use the social construction idea enthusiastically want to criticize, change, or destroy some X that they dislike in the established order of things' (Hacking, 1999: 7). The abolishment is rather easy, since the patterns do not truly exist but are, so to speak, only make-believe; that is they are constructions – hence the penchant for voluntarism.[9]

Social constructionists pursue, to a greater or lesser degree, a nominalist line of thought, according to which reality is amorphous, without qualities, and is only provided with arbitrary patterns by the researcher (see, for instance, Hacking, 1999).[10] This anti-realism, more or less adhered to, is self-destructive, implying as it does that social constructionism itself is just an arbitrary pattern, invented by researchers. If everything is a social construction, then social constructionism is too, and there is no reason to believe in it, rather than any other taken-for-granted assumption. (See, for instance, Willmott's [1994b] criticism of the waverings and paradoxes this gives rise to, in his comments on Shotter and Gergen, 1994.) The interesting thing, following social constructionism itself, would instead be to study how social constructionism has been socially constructed or how specific social constructionist studies construct others' constructions. For some reason, though, such studies are conspicuous by their absence.

For radical constructionists view the many more 'conventional' social constructionists as a target for critique, when these only focus on the social constructions of the society being investigated. That also the researchers in their knowledge could be seen as an example of social constructions in operation is hardly considered. Some critics here talk of 'trivial construction' (von Glasersfeld, 1991). Potter suggests, for example, that Berger and Luckmann have a view on their own knowledge contributions as free from the studied citizens' social constructions, remarking that 'even though the authors spend considerable time considering the assumptions of the experienced reality of, for example, a car mechanic, Berger and Luckmann themselves seem to be able to look around the corner without any difficulties' (1996: 13). Radical proponents of this direction are then also eager to indicate their own social constructioning. This increases consistency and awareness in the research approach but at the cost of reduced opportunities to say something of social phenomena 'as such', that is beyond the construction work of the researcher.

Social constructionists – in all their variants – strongly object to what is called the 'essentialism' of other approaches. By essentialism is meant the opinion that various phenomena have some kind of immutable core of properties, their 'essence' (in Latin *essentia*). As against this, social constructionists argue that everything is instead constructed. The question is, however, whether social constructionism itself does not adhere to such an essence, one that is marred by real existence and is not just constructed but is 'out there'. We are thinking of the *construction*. This is something which is said to be perpetually ongoing, and central to what happens; the mystical force behind the curtain, to allude to Hegel. Without a continually ongoing construction, there is no social constructionism. The construction has, in fact, obvious characteristics of a social constructionist 'essence', an inherent, unchangeable, constant property of our reality. The social constructionist criticism of essentialism thereby has a boomerang effect; its fundamental views become self-destroying here too. This essentialism has its roots in the phenomenology which is the ideational background to social constructionism. An important ingredient of phenomenology was the so-called 'intuition of essences' (*Wesensschau*) behind phenomena, and in a corresponding way, social constructionists try to intuit hidden constructions-essences behind social phenomena.

A possible counter-picture could be that the construction of a specific phenomenon happens sometimes, but that for a major part of our time we do not indulge in a construction of the world in terms of men and women, competence, leisure time or whatever else it may be. On the other hand, one might always argue that it is typical of essences precisely that they do not always arrive at expression, so in that sense, the counter-picture is not a counter-picture but rather a confirmation.[11]

The question is also if social phenomena, which are always dependent on mutual, subjective attributions of meaning, cannot have a real, objective existence. Must they, as (inter-)subjective phenomena be mere collective creations of our mental processes, chimera of our imagination ... social constructions? Even if we agree that all social phenomena inevitably depend on mental processes and are infused with meaning, it is still possible to regard them as objectively, really, existing. For example, Searle has shown how there can 'be an objective reality that is what it is only because we think it is what it is' (1998: 113), through the 'collective attribution of status functions'. By this is meant that we, through collective intentions, assign to physical entities various symbolic functions. Take for instance money. When we have agreed that a certain type of paper slip, or a certain pattern of signs on a computer screen, represents money, we can heap all kinds of complex monetary functions on top of this. And we can – and do – link money to many further status functions, such as corporations, markets, governments, etc. This is a never-ending game, with real pieces from social life.

Critical realism

Critical realism, originated in writings by the philosopher Roy Bhaskar and in part inspired by Marx's view of science, has the ambition to be a more theoretical but also more realistic substitute for positivism and social constructionism in offering principles and ideas for science. Critical realists consider positivism and social constructionism as too superficial and non-theoretical in their way of doing research; analysis of underlying mechanisms and structures behind phenomena is what it takes to create theories that are not just concentrates of data. This orientation also has a radical vein: what is important is not just to explain the world but also to change it.

Overview

Critical realism is more and more often suggested as a counterweight and alternative to social constructionist ideas, and its increasing popularity can, to a large extent, be seen as a reaction against the spread of social constructionist and (overlapping with these) postmodernist ideas. Critical realism provides a ground for a critique of social constructionism, at a time when positivism has lost its appeal for most scholars. Some see critical realism as an attractive alternative, at least to the more radical versions of social constructionism. Critical realism is sometimes used as a stick to beat what is taken to be the ambiguous, confused and imprecise mixture of standpoints characterizing social constructionism and postmodernist thinking (e.g. Fleetwood, 2005).

Although critical realism has received a certain international attention, it is still, primarily, a British tradition. The English philosopher Roy Bhaskar, who is considered its founding father, has been developing the approach since the 1970s. It is intended to provide a philosophical grounding for science as well as an alternative to positivist and interpretive/constructionist approaches. The original target of critical realism was positivism, but nowadays more radical versions of social constructionism have become the main target of criticism, at least within the social sciences.

Critical realists stress the generalizing task of scientific activity. However, their stand is not to be confused with that of positivism, with its interest in predictable patterns. Instead, critical realism seeks to identify those deeper lying mechanisms which are taken to generate empirical phenomena. Bhaskar describes this as a shift from epistemology to ontology, and within ontology, as a shift from events to mechanisms. He thus turns against what he understands as misleading and antropocentric views, which give priority to epistemology, that is, questions concerning what and how we are able to know. Bhaskar refers to this as the 'epistemic fallacy'; by which he means the tendency to couple ontology and epistemology and to confuse that which exists with the knowledge we have about it (what we believe). These things should be kept separate, according to Bhaskar. Now, of course, science is a product of the social – moulded by a range of social, ideological and political conditions – 'but the mechanisms that it identifies operate prior to and independently of their discovery' (Bhaskar, 1998: xii).

The notion of reality as consisting of three domains – the *empirical*, the *actual* and the *real* – is a central one within critical realism. The *empirical* domain includes that which we can observe – things that happen and exist according to our immediate experience. The *actual* domain is a broader one, and refers to that which transpires independent of the researcher or any other observer who might record it. Finally, the domain of the *real* includes those mechanisms that are productive of different events and other 'surface phenomena'. According to critical realism, the task of science is to explore the realm of the real and how it relates to the other two domains. The empirical domain is more narrow and can be seen as a site of expression of the other two domains. 'Scientific work is instead to investigate and identify relationships and non-relationships, respectively, between what we experience, what actually happens, and the underlying mechanisms that produce the events in the world' (Danermark et al., 2002: 21).

It is the interest in mechanisms of a 'deeper dimension', which distinguishes critical realism from other traditions. It shares interest positivism's in the objective world, patterns, generalization, and in finding causalities, but it also diverges from this tradition in claiming that the study of the observable is too superficial, as it disregards the unobservable mechanisms that produce the phenomena that positivists seek to measure and explain. It is not possible to reduce the world to observable objects and facts, critical realists argue. Moreover, they do not accept a distinction between theory and observation, nor the interest in finding all-encompassing laws. Instead critical realism takes an interest in complex networks of theoretical and observable elements characterizing efforts going beyond the surface of social phenomena. It shares with a great number of qualitative approaches an interest in synthesis and context, but it also strongly emphasizes the objective nature of reality, and it argues that a focus on social constructions is insufficient and misleading. Indeed, most aspects of interest transpire beyond individuals' conception and definition of situations.

Social structure entails things that lie behind individual consciousness and intention. In other words, causal mechanisms operate largely independent from the mind and action of individuals.

Critical realists emphasize strongly the reality as such, as distinct from our conceptions of it. They talk about an intransitive dimension – the object of scientific inquiry – and a transitive – that is our conceptions of that object. Many versions of social constructionism assume that such distinctions are artificial, and that societal phenomena are integrated with our conceptions of these, including those expressed by the research community, which contributes to the production of social reality. For critical realists, however, reality exists independent from researchers' ideas and descriptions of it.

The relevance of knowledge is dependent on the nature, power and mechanism of the objective reality. However, this is not to say that research, if it only has good intentions and methodology, is flawless or stands in an unproblematic relation to that which is researched.

> While it is evident that reality exists and is what it is, independently of our knowledge of it, it is also evident that the kind of knowledge that is produced depends on what problems we have and what questions we ask in relation to the world around us. (Danermark et al., 2002: 26)

Social constructions, while they are acknowledged to exist by critical realists, are framed in an objectivist manner, and are granted a rather limited role. Constructions are taken to be constructions of something, for example a discourse, a social practice, or physical reality, a reality that exists independent of what the constructions look like. The fact that it is socially defined and produced does not make a societal phenomenon any less real, critical realists argue. The way they see it, there *are* sellers, buyers, men, women, entrepreneurs, paid workers, carers, social outcasts, the unemployed, etc. Put differently, constructions are objective phenomena. A contrasting view, embraced by constructionists and many interpretive researchers, would be to approach constructions as volatile processes, which are then understood in terms of their subjective grounding. The focus is then placed, not on discourses or physical phenomena as such, but rather on the interpretation of these. Research is no exception here. According to this (constructionist) view, objects of knowledge are constructed by researchers through different procedures and tactics, not least discursive ones. To Bhaskar, however, the question is rather: What characteristics of societies make them possible as knowledge objects?

The real is central to critical realism. There is a strong conviction regarding the real and the possibility of identifying it. Something is real if it has a causal effect, that is, if it affects behaviour and makes a difference. Reality does not just consist of material objects. Ideas and discourses are also real and can have causal effects. Ideas about, for example, 'race', men and age can explain patterns in the labour market, and they are real in the sense that they exist and work as mechanisms with causal effects. It is possible to identify at least four different types of realities; material, ideational, artefactual and social. A given entity can consist of several of these realities. Artefactual reality, for example, refers to a synthesis of the physically, ideationally and socially real. The socially real 'refers to practices, states of affairs or entities for short, such as caring for children, becoming unemployed, the market mechanism, or social structures' (Fleetwood, 2005: 201). Social structure is used to capture configurations of causal mechanisms, rules, resources, powers, relations and practices. Causality refers to the nature of an object, which tells us what a certain object can or cannot do in terms of its effect. And a causal account 'does not deal with regularities between distinct objects and events (cause and effect), but with what an object is and the things it can do by virtue of its nature' (Danermark et al., 2002: 55). Objects have power connected to their structure; the mechanisms which produce effects are outcomes of this structure. But sometimes the effect of mechanisms does not show at the level of the empirical, that is, as an observable event.

Critical realism emphasizes the ideal and possibility of causal explanation. However, as noted earlier, the approach is still different from that of positivism, which seeks to establish predictable patterns and the exact relation between cause and effect. To critical realists relations are complex and causality can exist on different levels. They generate tendencies rather than inevitable, specific and measurable conditions. Critical realism examines the different mechanisms which have implications in terms of different effects and events, the forces and characteristics that mechanisms produce, and the intricate connections between different structural levels, that contribute to the complexity of causal forces, and that make possible the treatment of these as single, isolated factors. Causality should thus not be understood in terms of universal, predictable patterns, but rather as contextual and emergent, in changeable societies. According to critical realists, social reality is often slow in changing, but still emergent and varied as a consequence of the different processes that are part of producing it. As part of the project of accounting for typical patterns, while avoiding the misconception of statistical regularity and predictability, critical realists sometimes use the expression semi-regularity, which indicates 'the occasional, but less than universal, actualization of a mechanism or tendency, over [a] definite region of time-space' (Bhaskar and Lawson, 1998: 13).

The term mechanism is central within critical realism. A generative mechanism can be loosely defined as that which is capable of making things happen in the world. Mechanisms are taken to exist, even when they are not triggered (at work), or when their effect is impossible to trace, due to the effect of other mechanisms. Normally, mechanisms exist as part of complex compositions, whose outcome might vary or even fail to appear. Danermark et al. (2002) take the example of a match. It has the causal effect of being able to catch fire, if that mechanism is triggered, but for that to happen action has to be taken and in addition objects with other capacities must not intervene (e.g. by wetting the match). The same goes for social phenomena although it gets somewhat more complicated here, due to the dependency on human conceptions and actions (which of course, to some extent, goes for the match and its flaming capacity as well). To illustrate the point, Danermark et al. (2002) take the example of paid work. The structure of paid work is claimed to have the causal effect of forming the situation of people in our type of society, by making us reason and act in certain ways. It makes us want and apply for jobs, and to acquire a suitable education, and it also makes us go to work every working day. 'And each time acts in this way, the mechanism which reproduces the wage labour structure is triggered, which in turns generates new actions of the same kind, and so on' (2002: 56). At the same time there are other conditions that counteract the above mentioned mechanisms, for example the need to care for small children in the home, self-sufficiency, unsatisfactory work, or a football game on TV.

Supporters of critical realism view the research process as a constant digging in the ontological depth of reality. In other words, reality is taken to be layered and research approaches which linger at a surface level are therefore discarded, be it social constructionism, hermeneutics, or positivism, which all depart from what is empirically given.

> In terms of the explanatory programme, the stratified nature of reality introduces a necessary historicity (however short the time period involved) for instead of *horizontal* explanations relating one experience, observable or event to another, the fact that these themselves are conditional upon antecedents, requires *vertical* explanations in terms of the generative relationships *indispensable for their* realization ... (Archer, 1998: 196)

Critical realism distances itself from both methodological individualism (a focus on the actor level) and holism (a focus on the collective level), in emphasizing the social as relational and emergent. It is especially critical towards the former, arguing that 'actors' accounts are both corrigible and limited by the existence of unacknowledged conditions, unintendended consequences, tacit skills and unconscious motivations' (Bhaskar, 1998: xvi). Or, as Archer puts it 'we do not uncover real structures by interviewing people in-depth about them' (1998: 199).

According to critical realists the experiment has much to command it, in terms of its capacity to generate elementary knowledge. (This is similar to the 'semantic science approach' that was touched upon in the previous chapter.) Through experiments it is possible to isolate and identify mechanisms. However, given the fact that objects of study in social science can be considered open systems and, in addition, very complex, experiments are still not considered that relevant and useful in the study of social conditions. Bhaskar goes as far as to say that in open systems: 'positivism's instrumentalist-predictive-manipulative approach to phenomena is completely out of place' (1991: 141). Examples of more suitable alternatives are:

- Counterfactual thinking, through which one tries to imagine what could be – 'What would it be like if X did not exist?'
- Social experiments, for example anticipating reactions in breaking norms, an approach that is also favoured by ethnomethodologists (to be addressed in Chapter 3 below).
- The study of pathological or extreme cases.
- Comparative analysis of different cases (Danermark et al., 2002).

In general, however, critical realism does not engage with methodological matters much. It is a philosophy that cannot directly contribute to the disclosure of structures and mechanisms that produce and impact a certain, chosen, object of study. Still it is a philosophy for and not about science. It is generally prescriptive and it can support research by offering an overall frame of reference and by 'affecting the questions put to reality, and the manner in which this is done' (Bhaskar and Lawson, 1998: 7).

Critical realism does not deny the value of definitions of the social reality that is produced. Of course, social phenomena are acknowledged to be different from those studied in the natural sciences, but the active construction of social reality by individuals, and collectives thereof, is still downplayed. It is argued that the structures that guide the reproduction and transformation of social activities should be studied in their own right. In addition, a division between structure and agency is emphasized. These two aspects should be studied separately rather than together, as suggested by structuration and action theories. Structural impact, it is argued, mediates an objective influence and thus forms actions and provides actors with guidance. Structures are consequently taken to precede and determine actions, which in turn are seen as capable of gradually changing the former. Proponents of critical realism look at the sharp distinction between structure and human action as important to the analysis and enlargement of a space for action, which in turn is connected to the critical agenda of critical realism.

Although the centrality of such agendas can be discussed, it is often argued that critical realism encourages the transgression of existing social patterns by placing emphasis on the emergent theme. The approach can contribute to an ideology critique by going beyond common conceptions and by showing the workings of mechanisms, as well as the predefinition of our space for action, by structures. The indebtedness to Marxist thinking of critical realism is shown clearly in its central concepts (underlying mechanisms, the level of articulation of reality), even if critical realism does not necessarily imply Marxist theory (some critical realists firmly reject a connection to Marxism). According to Archer (1998: 203) critical realism 'has a "cutting edge" through identifying contextual constraints upon our freedoms and specifying strategic uses of our freedoms for social transformation'.

Critique

Below we will raise two areas within critical realism that we find particularly open to critique. The first is the strong claim by critical realism to grasp reality. It is always problematic to say something about causes which are not visible to us. The second area concerns central concepts which tend to be somewhat broad and diffuse, and do not really support the strong claims that critical realists are making. We will, however, on the whole refrain from going into the more philosophical critique that radical constructionists direct towards critical realists (e.g. Willmott, 2005), although inevitably we will touch upon it in discussing the other two themes.

Objectivism and exaggerated claims

In reading critical realism one is struck by the confidence with which its proponents use the concept of objective reality, as a point of departure and reference for the knowledge that is produced. It is argued that 'it is the nature of the object under study that determines what research methods are applicable, and also what knowledge claims one may have' (Danermark et al., 2002: 70). And a central task of researchers is to identify 'the necessary, constituent properties of the study object, since these characteristics define what actions the object can produce' (2002: 70). It is almost as if the object of study discloses itself and then tells the researcher how it is most appropriately studied. So by defining the objective reality one is informed about what method to use and what outcomes in terms of knowledge can be expected. And by the same token, the correct identification of the 'necessary constitutive properties' will assist the researcher in figuring out the events that can be anticipated.

An alternative – and by far more realistic – approach departs from the notion that we can never describe the object as such, because we are always framed by our paradigmatic and methodological assumptions, a certain vocabulary and political stances (as we will discuss in the next chapter, preunderstanding and interpretation are also always central in research activities). To assume that the object of study, if appropriately defined, will direct the analysis, is a naïve conception, and to see the researcher as having privileged access to the object, seems pretentious. Different researchers have different views regarding the 'necessary constitutive properties' and even if one had the good fortune to find researchers sharing the assumption about such properties, they would most likely come up with different ideas on the nature of such properties, and they would probably also disagree over the events that the objects can be seen as capable of producing. Uses of different perspectives would probably lead to different properties and different produced objects.

To clarify our critique let us consider some of the accounts offered by critical realists that they argue illustrate their approach. Take the following statement for example: 'Structures divide the population – although seldom completely so – in to those with a positional interest in retaining and those with an interest in changing their structural location' (Danermark et al., 2003: 146). 'Beyond the main resource distributions there are relations behind ownership and those without property, those in power and those without, powerholders and the powerless, those discriminating and those discriminated against (2003: 148). According to this view it is the 'structure' that divides the population into this and that category. One could, however, argue that it is the author who does so. Let us explain. Without necessarily denying or even problematizing the idea of positional interests – although the concept of interest is not without its problems – it should be noted that the division of people, into those seeking change and those trying pre-empt it, is questionable in relation to the notion of a domain of the real (or the structure that is assumed to exist in it). Of course groups can be more or less arbitrarily defined, but still a group is never internally homogeneous; there are always different or even conflicting interests within a given group, and, in addition, a certain individual ambivalence is surely to be expected. In effect, the division according to 'structure' hampers empirical diversity. Moreover, it could be argued that the notion of 'structure', as a grand divider in society, is in fact just another guise for the researcher, who, albeit often unconsciously, has a certain interest in dividing the population in this or that way. Thus, a more or less successful attempt to describe an observed empirical pattern is mistaken for a causal explanation of that same pattern.

Possibly this mistake also informs the second argument paraphrased above, regarding the distribution of resources. It is argued that behind the distribution of resources, there are relations of power (between those in possession and those lacking resources). These relations of power referred to are almost by definition about the distribution of resources, and consequently cannot be used to explain that very same distribution. Perhaps it is more accurate to depict the distribution of resources as being 'in front of' (rather than behind) the distribution. In other words, first there is a certain distribution of resources, and from this follows certain relations of power. But even so the division remains problematic. No doubt there are large economic differences in society; however, it is not clear how many people in today's Western societies (which are the main concern of the critical realists discussed here) can be considered as completely lacking property and power.

Our point is thus that, unlike the arguments of critical realists, it is not so easy to assert the existence of structures, mechanisms, the constitutive properties of objects of study, and so on.

Modest claims are not the trademark of critical realism. Bhaskar (1991) himself, for example, speaks of the necessity to reclaim reality which has been kidnapped by dangerous forces, led by skewed ideas. This reclamation should happen in two ways. Firstly, from 'philosophical ideologies which have usurped or denied it – reclamation in the sense of lost property'. Secondly, 'from the effects of those ideologies that have – like stagnant and muddy water – covered it up – reclamation in the sense of land reclamation' (Bhaskar, 1991: 144). Bhaskar finishes by stating that once reality has been reclaimed it should 'be used, nurtured and valued in an ecologically sustainable and humane way for human emancipation, happiness and flourishing' (1991: 144). It is not totally clear whether he is being ironic or not, but most likely that is not the case, because unlike, for example, social constructionists and postmodernists, critical realists are not known for their light-hearted and humorous forms of expression; to them the mission is much too important. Having said that it is interesting to note that the most loyal and orthodox critical realists, having observed the later Bhaskar becoming drawn towards spirituality, have half-jokingly suggested that he himself ought to get his membership to the critical realist club suspended.

The unproductive concepts of structure and mechanism

Structure and mechanism are two of the most central concepts within critical realism. In fact, the merits of the approach can, to a certain extent, be judged on the basis of how well these two concepts function within the research process. The notions of structure and mechanism are related. 'The objects have the power they have by virtue of their structure, and mechanisms exist and are what they are because of this structure' (Danermark et al., 2002: 55). Structure is thus the key to it all. The structure can mobilize force given the right input. So what is structure then?[12] Structure is a collection of internally related objects, such as teacher–student or employer–employee. With social structure, positions, practices and roles become associated. Social structure is that context in which actions and social interaction transpire.

At first glance this image is quite appealing. Through observations we can surely spot indications of relations, roles and positions, we can grasp some of their implications. Indeed, language invites us to. Have you established that there are such things as teachers and students and that they are related in language use? But how much does this tell us? With the concept of structure, critical realism aims to do more than merely describe certain regularities and relations (conventionally, the concept of structure refers to such regularities). In fact, in their critique of positivism critical realists reject the importance of evident regularities and relations, but the latter is actually what Danermark et al. refer to in establishing the factual existence. But let us rest this discussion and move on to consider those 'forces' that the structure produces. If we exchange the term structure with its definition, as phrased by Danermark et al. (an internally related object), then we can read that objects have forces as an outcome of internally related objects. Internally related objects can trigger forces.

Let us now consider this in less abstract terms, taking the teacher–student example from above. The teacher–student relation, that is the structure (internally related objects), should, according to the logic suggested by critical realists, be capable of activating forces and mechanisms. But the question is then, does this 'structure' trigger anything automatically, and if so, what would that be – ambitious students, a subordination to authority, or maybe daydreaming related to a lack of interest in what the teacher has to say, or perhaps attempts to disrupt the tediousness through pranks, absenteeism or unruly behaviour in class, which in turn might cause the teacher to accumulate sick-leave days? Maybe what goes on in school between teachers and students is far more precarious, varied and processual, than the images suggested by objects, forces and mechanisms. In other words, the idea of Danermark et al. (2003) that the mechanisms exist as they are as an effect of this structure does not sit well with the variety and complexity of student–teacher relations that are likely to exist in many contemporary schools.

On paper and in an objectivist analysis, there are teachers and students, but a closer look may reveal a very different image. On closer inspection we might find guards and troublemakers, part-time marketers with the objective of producing satisfied 'customers', and students that have adopted a customer perspective on education, or collaborators in a job creation scheme (with school as a tool for reducing/ hiding unemployment) – that is, things that have less to do with learning and more to do with keeping young people off the streets. Perhaps teaching and learning are less central aspects of what actually goes on in many schools. In cases of inadequate teachers and very competent students the labelling, as we know it, might even verge on being misleading.

Surely critical realists can account for such conditions, and they do, through emergent structures and mechanisms. But the general stance shows a strong tendency to arrange the world in objective and sturdy categories. And while these refer to internally related objects, on the level of language, a closer and more open-minded look of what seems to be going on typically reveals a much more ambiguous view of the world. In fact, this is often the point with qualitative research; to transcend seemingly objective definitions of the world, and to show their limited value in trying to explain what is going on.

The concept of mechanism also poses certain problems. The flaming capacity of matches is one thing, because this capacity is quite easy to relate to a mechanism. But what are the mechanisms that follow from structure, which determine the force of objects? Danermark et al. (2003) take the example of the organization and positions of paid work. It is argued that the structure of paid work has the causal power of forming the life conditions of people. If this structure is about the relation of employer–employed there are by definition certain elements in these that are highly unspecific and do not say much about specific conditions. The life situation of people is determined by factual conditions, such as legislation, attitudes, labour market conditions, specific relations between the different people involved, the work organization, the machines, the organizational culture, managers, regional conditions, and the social security system, etc.

Proponents of critical realism would probably not deny that this is the case, and most likely they would attribute causal forces and mechanisms to all of these things. But is it reasonable to assume that a mechanism which reproduces the structure of paid work is triggered every time someone goes to work or applies for a job? Conceptualized this way, the mechanism metaphor becomes somewhat futile, that is, of course, if we disregard its, no doubt unintentional, comical value. 'I woke up this morning, feeling wretched not wanting to go to work. After some breakfast, with the feeling of agony still haunting me, I decided to activate (or the structure did so) the mechanism and reproduce the structure of paid work (= to go to work)'. It is our impression that critical realism uses the mechanism term in a much too literal sense. It appears to see the match example as a fairly good description of what is going on in social life. This point is, in our view, debatable.

Although critical realism acknowledges that social science, unlike natural science, mostly deals with open systems, a quite substantial part of the critical realist framework appears to be inspired by the world of physics. And when it leaves the realm of natural science and enters that of the social, the vocabulary of forces and mechanism does not work quite as well. Described in these terms, social phenomena come across as mechanical and often they run the risk of being overly simplified. They do not work quite as well in trying to explain complex matters, such as social relations in school or the organization of paid work.

To make the point even clearer, compare a recent comment made in an interview by Lisa Randall, one of the major names in theoretical physics at present, that it is simpler and easier to understand the universe than to understand the gender relations in a university organization.

Then again it is not always clear what mechanisms are, for instance as distinguished from underlying patterns (the latter are said to be revealed by abduction, the former via 'retroduction', and it is rather unclear what the difference really is). Not infrequently the hidden mechanisms in practical applications (for instance Danermark et al., 2003) become rather trivial and something that many positivists or social constructionists could well work with. The difference with, for example, Marx's more through-going analysis becomes evident.

Finally, it is our view that critical realists make too grand claims. They are utterly convinced about their approach to (what they take to be) objective science. Now, of course, they are aware of the precarious nature of research (as inevitably problematic and arguable), however, little space is granted to such discussions, apart from occasional confessions that come across as highly peripheral to what they otherwise consider themselves to be doing. In many ways critical realism expresses a view of the self as a deep-digging project, which exposes reality and frees it from the filth and mess caused by positivists, postmodernists and their like. But as a noble reality saving project the approach runs the risk of becoming rigid and lacking in terms of reflexivity, presenting subjective and arbitrary representations as self-evident and robust findings.

Some of these things can probably be explained by the orientation's underdog position against more established competitors and the need to use rather heavy polemics and simplifications. As an alternative to various antitheoretical currents, critical realism all the same constitutes a stimulating and provocative counter-picture.

So far then, we have quite a lot of critical comments; however, there are also merits to the approach. One is its position as a clear alternative to positivist and constructionist approaches. As a result, options within research become clearer and proponents of other frameworks are forced to think through their own perspectives. For too long anti-positivism has constituted a sufficient argument for choosing a qualitative approach; however, with the emergence of critical realism social science is faced with yet another option. This framework also offers a relevant critique against research that refrains from leaving the surface level; approaches that never go outside or beyond the empirical, to analyse other aspects that affect this level. Critical realism thus challenges social constructionists and wants to stimulate researchers to rise above and beyond the empirical, to move on to more daring and theoretical analysis.

Brief comparison

Postivism, social constructionism, and critical realism thus diverge substantially. Still one could say that they are all interested in reality – real facts in the first case, the social reality in the second, and the objective 'big' world in the third: the *factual* world is put up against the social world, and against this, the real, deep reality stands.

Many current debates frame social constructionism and critical realism as two main alternatives in outlining the development of social science (Fleetwood, 2005; Willmott, 2005). Two objections can be made against this argument. First of all, social constructionism is a very broad field, and the range of different approaches that fall under this label includes quite diverse viewpoints. Second, the range and influence of critical realism are still quite limited outside of Great Britain. Ideas about real, objective structures are perhaps not entirely in line with the contemporary sceptical spirit of our time (unless, of course, this is about to change).

Some commentators emphasize the similarities when comparing the orientations. For example, positivism and critical realism both maintain that natural science and social science can use the same philosophy of science. Critical realism accepts a constructionist element in research. There are streaks of realism within positivism, even though these are not predominant (its mainstream ontology is a subjective idealism – to regard data as subjective sense data and theories as instrumentalist summaries of data). Somebody might argue that the opposite of realism is not constructionism but idealism, in which the ideational is emphasized. Constructionism focuses on some phenomenon or object that is being constructed (Crotty, 1998). However, the construction itself is not a material thing, and neither, then, is the phenomenon or object under construction; they are both (inter)subjectively ideational. Delanty (2005) thinks that the main line of division is not between social constructionism and critical realism but between more radical and moderate variants of the former. Only extreme constructionists, such as the early Latour, deny the existence of underlying structures. We can of course establish various basic lines of division and options as to structures, constructions, interpretations, and so on. Extreme *vs* moderate social constructionism is here definitively a ground for drawing a main line of division. Yet, an even more fruitful distinction is probably that between a main or classical variant of social constructionism (exemplified by standpoints like those of Berger and Luckmann) and critical realism. The emphasis on (inter)subjective construction processes and outcomes, where socially defined and negotiated realities are central, generates rather different studies and understandings than critical realism's toning down of these in favour of an exploration of objective deep structures and mechanisms.

Final words

In this chapter we have considered positivism and post-positivism; social constructionism, a perspective that has become a dominating one within several disciplines of social science; and critical realism, a framework that competes with and has named itself as the leading alternative to and successor of the other two. This last claim remains to be realized. It can be mentioned, for example, that the approach is not very well known in the USA. Social constructionism, on the other hand, is doubtless a broad framework and there are different varieties and connections, many of these having much in common with, for example, hermeneutics and postmodernism, as well as some more recent versions of grounded theory. We have also raised some doubts regarding the term social constructionism and its, over time, more and more opaque (over)use (see also Fleetwood, 2005). This does not stop social constructionist thinking from being central to the social sciences of today, and it is important to consider how one relates to this approach. Social researchers also have reasons to consider their relation to critical realism, and its reflections regarding the deep dimensions of knowledge and reality, as an incipient alternative to positivism and social constructionism.

*

So far in this first part of the book, we have focused the discussion on the concepts of surface structure, underlying patterns, perspectives, knowledge-sociological conditions, relativism and dialogue. This is no coincidence; these concepts also point to the main emphases in the central chapters (3–6) of the book. Note that it is a question of emphasis; elements of the concepts appear in all these chapters. Even though the borderlines are of course fluid, the following generally is the case. In Chapter 3 about empirical orientations, empirical data and surface structures are at the forefront. Chapter 4 on hermeneutics contains an exploration of underlying patterns as its main aspect. The critical theory in Chapter 5 investigates various perspectives from a knowledge-sociological point of view, focusing on power and ideology. Postmodernism in Chapter 6, finally, takes up the problematic of relativism. Critical theory and postmodernism also emphasize, albeit each in different ways, the importance of dialogue. Critical theory strives for a rational dialogue, and to resist disturbances connected with power, ideology and dogma. Postmodernism emphasizes instead seminal clashes of meaning and disharmonies as a goal; in a wider perspective, the drift of this whole orientation is dialogue between texts, single individuals being seen as mere arenas for such dialogues.

Notes

1. See Heidegger's (1961/1991) interpretation.
2. MacKenzie and House (1979) propose Popper's falsificationism with 'crucial experiments' as a 'paradigm' for social science in a Kuhnian spirit. This brave idea appears, to put it mildly, neck-breaking, given that Kuhn among other things showed with his paradigm theory precisely that Popper's falsification method and 'crucial experiments' do not hold water.
3. There is a certain linguistic confusion about the concept itself; the terminology varies – sometimes the words 'social constructionism' are used, sometimes 'social constructivism'. We have chosen the former expression since 'constructivism' associates to other orientations in, for example, mathematics and developmental psychology. In this, we join Kenneth Gergen (see below), who strongly advocates the use of 'constructionism'.
4. Berger and Luckmann here use the term 'objectivation ' in a somewhat different sense than before (see above), when it referred to material objects as carriers of meaning.
5. Here the authors are carried away by their verbal drive. A libretto is, of course, not the basis of a drama in general but of a musical performance – an opera, operetta, musical, etc.
6. In this context, it is interesting to note with Hacking (1999) the subterraenean connections between positivism and social constructionism. The main work of the central figure in logical positivism, Rudolf Carnap, has, for example, the title 'Der Logische Aufbau der Welt', which would translate as 'The Logical Construction of the World'. This book has traits in common with the somewhat later ideas of one of the inspirers of social constructionism – T.S. Kuhn. As Hacking writes: 'The roots of social constructionism are in the very logical positivism that so many present-day constructionists profess to detest' (1999: 42–43).
7. This tendency does not hold true for Latour's influential ANT approach, where language and the researcher are given a less dominating place and postmodernism is totally dismissed.
8. A social constructionist might reply that the constructions are never finished, but are a continuous ongoing process. This may be true, as it is true of house constructions (houses are repaired, altered, etc.), but, as in the latter case, there are zones of relative stability constituting patterns for research.

9. The constructions being social and rooted in collective contexts can, however, be difficult to change (Czarniawska, 2005).

10. If the researcher provides the world with patterns, then what is there to abolish, we might ask. The answer is that 'common' people also, not only researchers, provide the world with patterns, and that it is these patterns – illusory or damaging ideas and ideologies – that are to be abolished. At a more philosophical level, the problematic harks back to Hegel and Marx with their thinking about alienation. The social world, which had originally been created by human beings, progressively becomes alien to them, and towers over them as an external threatening phenomenon. For Marx, the solution was, as is well known, to revolutionize this inauthentic world.

11. According to Latour, however, construction goes on all the time, and it has, as we have seen, real constructors as well as results (even though the latter are changing all the time, just like a city landscape).

12. The structure concept can also refer to 'small' structures, as in a workgroup structure, personality structure or emotional structure, but here we limit ourselves to social structures.

3

DATA-ORIENTED METHODS: EMPIRICIST TECHNIQUES AND PROCEDURES

In this chapter we describe some methods which are used in relatively close proximity to the empirical material. It is not a question of a one-sided presentation of data, since the methods also acknowledge the importance of theory. At the same time, however, theory is linked more intimately to the empirical material in these approaches than in the other orientations which we will study. It is not permitted to move too far from (what are seen as) the basic data, so research results tend to remain at a low level of abstraction. We focus in particular on grounded theory, with its background in the more general school of symbolic interactionism, since this seems to us to be an unusually distinct example of an empirically oriented method. According to Denzin (1994: 508) grounded theory is the most widely used qualitative interpretive framework in the social sciences, particularly since the appearance of Strauss and Corbin's bestselling textbook, *Basics of Qualitative Research*, in 1990. The chapter also includes a discussion of ethnomethodology, and a brief presentation of inductive ethnography. A minor contrapuntal motif occurs in that we let Bourdieu's ideas appear in confrontation and contrast with these various currents.

Grounded theory

Roots

Glaser and Strauss's 'grounded theory' has dual roots, one in symbolic interactionism in the person of Strauss, and the other in the statistically oriented positivism that was part of Glaser's intellectual luggage. General surveys of symbolic interactionism, such as Plummer (1991), usually mention grounded theory as a particular orientation with this movement. Although we do not altogether agree with this description, we do regard symbolic interactionism as the most important source of inspiration for grounded theory.[1]

Symbolic interactionism
Symbolic interactionism represents a qualitative methodological movement which appeared in the USA at the beginning of the twentieth century (Hammersley, 1989). The name 'symbolic interactionism' was launched in 1938 by Herbert Blumer, a

sociologist in Chicago. But the general line of thought is older than that, having arisen as a social-psychological and sociological movement at the beginning of that century in the Department of Social Science and Anthropology at Chicago University. The famous names here are Mead and Cooley (Blumer was a pupil of Mead, and Strauss of Blumer). The three main sources of inspiration were, in order of importance: American pragmatism, according to which truth became a question of practical utility; German neo-Kantianism, which emphasized the deeper idiographic study of particular cases rather than the nomothetic study of mass data; and German historicism, which gave priority to qualitative research over quantitative studies.

Following its first heyday in the 1920s and 1930s, symbolic interactionism consolidated its position during the 1940s and 1950s, but suffered a decline in the 1960s and 1970s. The main reason for this decline was pressure from 'hard' methods such as statistical method and structural functionalism on the one hand, and competition from the 'soft' side in the form of ethnomethodology, with its phenomenological cast, on the other. In addition, the movement was attacked from the political left for being cautiously reformist within the frames of the prevailing system. An article in 1973 even declared that symbolic interactionism was dead (Mullins and Mullins, 1973). However, reports of its death were greatly exaggerated; latterly its ideas have enjoyed a renaissance (Stryker, 1987). This triumph, which has meant that its methods have become fairly widely embraced, was accompanied by a certain degree of radicalization and a receptiveness to other methods such as postmodernism and feminism. But the victory was also bought at the price of fragmentation and a general dilution of the original ideas (Fine, 1993). Glaser and Strauss's (1967) book has had much the same history as the movement itself from the 1960s, with an initial relative lack of interest giving way to an enthusiastic embrace.[2] For many qualitative researchers, qualitative method is almost equated with grounded theory. According to Turner (1988: 112), 'the qualitative researcher has no real alternative to pursuing something very close to grounded theory'. And in the 1990s, as mentioned, Strauss and Corbin's (1990) work has become a bestseller. As we shall see, however, the book has not avoided criticism for having betrayed the original spirit of the method. Thus here, too, a book's history has paralleled that of the parent movement.

The intellectual goods which grounded theory retained from symbolic interactionism include the following central features, which we will look at in greater detail in the following pages: pragmatism, idiographic research, qualitative method, exploration, sensitizing concepts, social action, cognitive symbols, empirical orientation, and successive induction from empirical material. This list, and our presentation of its contents below, are not intended to provide an exhaustive description of symbolic interactionism. We simply hope to give a (necessarily) all too brief account of the ideas which are relevant to an understanding of grounded theory. The concepts have not been transferred automatically to grounded theory, but have acquired a special tint and developed in a particular way within that theory. There is thus no question either of simple repetition or of a cognitive break with the parent movement: grounded theory cannot be equated with symbolic interactionism, any more than its background in that movement can be ignored.

- *Pragmatism.* Social utility, social control as an outcome of research, constitutes the criterion of truth. Pragmatism has been described as an antitheoretical philosophy, which implies sticking as closely as possible to practical, empirical reality.
- *Idiographic* research rather than nomothetic. Particular cases rather than cases *en masse* should be studied. Idiographic knowledge, which appears especially in the humanities, is geared to the intensive study of unique phenomena. Nomothetic knowledge, which is found particularly in the natural sciences, calls for an extensive study of large amounts of data in order to discover general laws.
- *Qualitative* methods rather than quantitative. The latter, if they are used at all, are preparatory and secondary. It can be noted that this represents a reversal of the prescriptions for quantitative methodology, where the qualitative phase (if there is one at all) is regarded as preparatory and of minor importance.
- *Exploration.* Given the emphasis on qualitative methods, the explorative function is of central importance in the social sciences, with much higher status than it enjoys in the natural sciences with their emphasis on operationalization for the purposes of testing. A flexible method of data collecting, whereby the principles of selection are successively revised in the course of the research process, for example, is a result of this. Exploration should be combined with inspection, in which the preliminary concepts that were discovered are successively revised and complemented, while at the same time the empirical items to which the respective concepts refer are 'turned and twisted'.
- *Sensitizing concepts.* Instead of trying to create increasingly exact techniques in order to specify concepts, social science researchers should seek to create sensitizing concepts that stimulate them to perceive new relations, perspectives and world-views. Unlike in physics, where spatial and temporal relations dominate, empathy (as in Mead's 'taking the role of the other') and judgement are important ingredients in the social sciences.
- *Social action.* A microprocess – and not, for instance, a function or structure – is the main focus here (compare the later concept of 'structuration' in Giddens, 1984). This is *interactive*, that is to say it represents a relation between actors. It is also *symbolic* – symbols are being conveyed between actors – and so interaction is not regarded as external behaviour in a spirit of behaviourism. Thus the *intersubjective* (rather than, for example, the behavioural, psychological, structural or functional) is central.
- *Cognitive symbols.* People create and continually re-create themselves in contact with others; indeed, this self *is* ultimately a process. The self is not a passive medium or arena between internal and external stimuli and behaviours, dependent and independent variables, but a highly productive phenomenon of its own, the engine of the entire social process. The self is also a world of meanings, not an external structure or a set of variables. Meanings are interpreted primarily as cognitive. One criticism which has been raised against Blumer and other symbolic interactionists, is precisely that they underestimate the emotional elements in the creation of meaning, and overestimate the cognitive.

- *Closeness to the empirical material and successive induction*. Researchers should start inductively from the symbolic interactions of everyday reality, and not distance themselves too far from them. However, induction here differs from that of the classical and Baconian school in that it does not start directly from the data but proceeds in two phases: first, the intensive study of a limited set of data in single empirical cases, at which stage empathy is of crucial importance; and secondly, comparison between several cases with a concomitant extension of the empirical base.

Statistical positivism

It is worth emphasizing once more that symbolic interactionism was not the only source of inspiration for grounded theory. Its influence stemmed mainly from one of the two founders, namely Strauss. Glaser, the other founder, had studied at Columbia University under Lazarsfeld, famous for his development of statistical analysis within the social sciences. Bourdieu, for example, always refers to Lazarsfeld as the central figure in modern social scientific positivism (see, for instance, Bourdieu and Wacquant, 1992). Glaser (2005) strongly polemicizes against what he sees as textbooks overemphasizing the importance of symbolic interactionism for grounded theory, and even says explicitly (Glaser, 1992) that he used the statistical analytical method as his model for the qualitative method in grounded theory. Thus a positivistic form or model for quantitative analysis was infused with a new qualitative content. More generally, grounded theory took from Lazarsfeld's research programme a rigorous approach, and – to borrow a term from Bunge (1967) – what could be called a 'dataistic' conception of research: data are the alpha and omega of the scientific process. There was no counterweight to this in symbolic interactionism. On the contrary, the inductive element in interactionism helped to reinforce this position.

With these preliminaries behind us, we can now turn to a systematic exposition of the theory itself.

Theory generation, induction, qualitative data

The very title of Glaser and Strauss's book – *The Discovery of Grounded Theory: Strategies for Qualitative Research* – indicated the main elements in their methodology. It focuses on the *discovery* of theory, on *grounded* theory, and on *qualitative* research. In their foreword the authors declare that one of the main purposes of the book is to bridge the gap between 'grand theory' and empirical research (cf. postmodernism's current criticism of the 'grand narratives') – a gap which Blumer had already commented upon and which one of the great sociologists, Robert Merton, had tried to bridge with the help of a quantative verification method. In contrast to this, Glaser and Strauss put their main emphasis on the *discovery* rather than the verification of theory (and on qualitative research). However, they do not mean to place generation in any sort of opposition to verification, but simply to point out that far too much effort has been directed towards the latter (in Lazarsfeld's tradition of statistical analysis).[3] The main objective of research is the generation of theory, while verification is there to serve generation (Glaser and Strauss, 1967: 28). In their foreword, the authors also indicate their sources and procedures. The source of theory generation is empirical data, and the method of extracting the theory from these consists mainly of comparative analyses of a particular kind. The authors profile themselves in contrast to earlier qualitative research (for example, that of the above-mentioned Chicago school), which in their view was insufficiently rigorous and systematic, as well as trapped in the rhetoric of verification, instead of emphasizing what it was really involved in, namely the generation of theory. Thus in their own book Glaser and Strauss aim to formulate a set of more stringent and coherent methodological rules or canons, in and for the generation of theory from empirical data.

The authors claim that 'theory' has become synonymous with the theories of the 'great men' – Marx, Weber, Durkheim, Mead, etc. – theories that subsequent, less brilliant minds would only have to confirm through short-sighted exercises in verification. Against this Glaser and Strauss launched the rather liberating thesis that *anyone* can create their own theory, so long as they start from reality. Thus, not only geniuses, 'theoretical capitalists', can be creative in social science research. Even ordinary mortals can generate creative input as scientific entrepreneurs; they do not have to act as a verifying proletariat serving intellectual big business. Each one is the architect of her own theory. Certainly the theory should be tested, but this leads only to its modification, not its destruction, since a theory can only be replaced by another theory (Glaser and Strauss, 1967: 28). Otherwise it survives by the pure force of inertia. Here the authors are following ideas originally published by Kuhn during the early 1960s (see Kuhn, 1970).[4] Further, testing aims to *determine the empirical area of application* for the theory (Glaser and Strauss, 1967: 24), a notion which had already been put forward by the philosopher of science, Toulmin (1953).[5] For this reason, it might be added, we could even refrain from talking about 'verification' and 'testing', and refer instead to the *application of the theory*, not asking whether the theory is true or false, but when it applies, and under what circumstances it works.

Since grounded theory is derived from data, it is developed inductively, and Glaser and Strauss argue strongly against a 'logical deductive' view, which seeks instead to start from theories divorced from reality; here Blau (1955), in particular, with his formalized exchange theories, is exposed to some heavy flak. (This methodological debate between induction and deduction is not new; it has deep historical roots as far back as Bacon and Descartes, and even Aristotle and Plato.) The arguments which Glaser and Strauss raise against deductivism are often apt – for example, that its theories easily acquire a speculative stamp and therefore lose contact with the empirical base, so that testing is often impracticable; or, if it is undertaken nevertheless, then the empirical data are pushed by force into the categories of the theory.

On the other hand, one sometimes wonders about the mote in the authors' own eyes. The empirical materials can easily be reduced to common-sense categories. Admittedly, the authors point out that the personal and theoretical experiences which the researcher may bring to the task can serve as material for the generation of categories. They also guard themselves in a note (Glaser and Strauss, 1967: 3, fn. 3) by saying: 'Of course, the researcher does not approach reality as a *tabula rasa*. He must have a perspective that will help him see relevant data and abstract significant categories from his scrutiny of the data'. This perspective is not infrequently transformed into a rather transparent fig leaf as a cover for presuppositionless induction. Glaser and Strauss write, for example:

> An effective strategy is, at first, literally to ignore the literature of theory and fact on the area under study, in order to assure that the emergence of categories will not be contaminated by concepts more suited to different areas. Similarities and convergences with the literature can be established after the analytic core of categories has emerged. (1967: 37) [6]

In contemporary scientific theory, in the wake of Hanson (1958) and other postpositivists, there is by and large an agreement that all facts are theory-laden. It is thus not a question of a thin 'perspective'; instead, we always insert a whole set of cognitive and theoretical frames of reference into our perception of reality – a point made by Hegel (1952) in his polemic, written in 1807, against the inductivists and empiricists of his own time, and emphasized later by hermeneuticians such as Heidegger (1962). 'Reality' is *always already* interpreted. Thus data never come in the shape of pure drops from an original virgin source; they are always merged with theory at the very moment of their genesis. Given this reservation, Glaser and Strauss's idea – albeit in modified form – can be taken as a practical tip worth considering: 'Do not read *too much* about the technical area, so that you can maintain your fresh gaze'. The history of science can provide supportive evidence for this idea. Researchers of more modest learning sometimes prove more creative than those who are too well read in a field.[7] The risk with too much book-learning is to become over-dependent on earlier authorities and tangled up in all the old problems, so that it becomes difficult to see new possibilities. Boldness in the process of interpretation can, according to this line of reasoning, be enhanced by not having read too much about previous achievements – provided, of course, that the researchers are also capable of liberating themselves from induction and the unreflecting acceptance of the actors' spontaneous categories. This does not mean that we should simply turn to deduction: induction and deduction are not the only alternatives. There are others, such as abduction, which in simple terms means the ability to see patterns, to reveal deep structures (Hanson, 1958).[8] A general look through the broad outlines of the theoretical and empirical research field, followed as quickly as possible by a leap into one's own empirical material, can therefore be *one* possible strategy. However, too weak an insight into the research field also has its drawbacks, such as the possible reinvention of the wheel.

Critical reading is naturally an antidote to becoming caught up in the conventional wisdom or naïve orthodoxy of a field. One problem here is the risk of a *reverse*, negative binding to the established problems. Yet, to open one's eyes to established research, including its weaknesses, is a good starting position for spotting new possibilities. Another fruitful line in relation to early theory and research is to try to achieve a certain breadth in comparison to it, for example by learning something about empirical studies in neighbouring fields and reading up on alternative theories. The latter need not concern the specific area of application, but could be more fundamental, indicating various more general lines of interpretation. To be *generally* well read is always valuable – better than having read too much in a specialized area, or not having read anything at all. Thus a researcher's reading should have a certain breadth, not only for the reasons referred to, but also because seeing links between distant phenomena is a common feature of creative research.[9]

In the debate, the difference between theory generation and verification has usually been paired with another fundamental distinction, that between qualitative and quantitative data. Qualitative data are supposed to be mainly devoted to a preliminary explorative phase resulting in tentative hypotheses, while quantitative data are appropriate to the important phase in the research process, namely the testing of hypotheses. This, according to Glaser and Strauss, is an error on several counts. First, as we have seen, they assign considerably more weight to theory generation. Secondly, the two distinctions do not coincide; they cut across each other. Qualitative and quantitative data can both be used for the purposes of generation *and* verification. When it comes to the importance and use of qualitative or quantitative data, the authors adopt a similar position to the one they assumed on the question of the importance of generation versus verification. They certainly have no wish to exclude the use of quantitative data, but they focus on qualitative data because these are more appropriate to the study of complex phenomena and processes; since qualitative results are often the 'end product of the research' within an empirical area, beyond which the researcher has little motivation to move on (to quantitative verification); and, finally, since they provide the best – most 'adequate' and 'efficient' – way of acquiring the desired information (Glaser and Strauss, 1967: 18). The first argument, which is an echo of earlier discussions among the symbolic interactionists, seems fairly well justified. The other two arguments, on the other hand, are not particularly strong. The second applies after all only to the final product, the grounded theory, and not to the route by which it is reached; the third remains to be proven.

It is worth noting that Glaser and Strauss, both as regards the importance of quantitative versus qualitative methods and theory generation versus theory verification, simply turn the traditional positivist thesis on its head. Positivism claims that qualitative methods are a complement of minor importance to quantitative methods, and that theory generation is a prelude of minor importance to theory verification. In grounded theory, conversely, qualitative methods and theory generation emerge as the most important ingredients; quantitative methods and theory verification are seen as complementary to them. As a result, the boring type of puzzle research described and endorsed by Kuhn (1970) is avoided. The disadvantage, of course, is that the researchers risk reinventing the wheel – the same theory – over and over again, perhaps just giving new names to old concepts.[10] (This is naturally an extra drawback in the social sciences, where this disease is already rampant quite independent of Glaser and Strauss's methodology; witness, for example, in organizational theory the plethora of new names that have been attached over the years to Burns and Stalker's (1961) mechanistic and organic management systems, and launched as new theories.)

The theory criterion: practical utility

Another legacy from the tradition of symbolic interactionism, and more specifically from the strong element of pragmatism in this tradition, is the emphasis on the theory's *practical utility*. Glaser and Strauss return to this time and again. Among the requirements they propose for a theory is that it should be 'usable in practical applications – prediction and explanation should be able to give the practitioner understanding and some control of situations' (1967: 3); it 'must enable the person who uses it to have enough control in everyday situations to make its application worth trying' (1967: 245). We recognize here the symbolic interactionists' emphasis on 'social control' – a manifestation of instrumental common sense. The risk of entertaining such a criterion is, of course, that it reduces research to being the hand-maiden of the practitioners. Another expression of the same thing appears when Glaser and Strauss (1967: 3) claim that '[t]he theory must also be readily under-standable to sociologists of any viewpoint, to students and to significant laymen'. Here the above-mentioned risk is reinforced, since it is required that even the language be reduced to the actor level. Nevertheless this is logical, since if the actors are to be able to use a theory, it obviously has to be formulated in a language which is comprehensible to them. The problem with such a viewpoint is that it becomes difficult to achieve high-level theories; the theory-building will be inhibited by the reduction to the actor level. But science is not only systematized common sense. A comparison comes spontaneously to mind with the intuitionist current of common sense in mathematics. Kronecker, the foremost representative of this current in the nineteenth century, spoke out against Cantor – the heretical formalist who wanted to extend the field of numbers – with the majestic declaration: 'natural numbers have been created by God, everything else is the work of men'. Even if Glaser and Strauss do not cite the Superior Being in their argument, one gets the impression that 'practice' plays a similar role in their theories. Many scientific theories in the social and the natural sciences have had no immediate importance in practice; this first arose a long time – sometimes a very long time – afterwards. The 'user's manual' type of knowledge therefore has little to recommend it.

But, apart from this, does knowledge not have an intrinsic value of its own? What, for instance, is the practical use of knowing when and how the universe came into being – the aim of cosmologic science? Nothing at all, in either the short or the long term. And yet human beings are so made that they desire knowledge about just such matters. And the same applies to other branches of science as well. The Glaser–Strauss approach seems to confuse something which, other things being equal, can some-times be an *advantage*, namely practical utility, with a *condition*, that is, that scientific theory *must* be of immediate use and easily comprehensible to the relevant laymen. Things are not improved by Glaser and Strauss (1967: 98) going so far as to say expressly that research should be useful to 'consultations'.

Data and sources of data

Thus, grounded theory proceeds from (what are viewed as) empirical data. What is meant by 'data' in this context? The term that recurs in Glaser and Strauss's book is 'incidents'. Unfortunately the authors provide no definition, nor even a modest semantic investigation, of what this concept implies, even though it provides the base on which the whole of grounded theory rests. Here the reader is left in the lurch. But if we turn to a later book on the same subject, Strauss's *Qualitative Analysis for Social Scientists* (1987), we are given a lead: the word 'event' is used there as synonymous with 'incident'. If, further, we recall the fundamental

Mead–Blumer paradigm of symbolic interactionism, which we briefly accounted for above, then it seems reasonable to equate an incident with a 'social interaction'. And this equation in fact often appears to be valid, as an examination of the examples in Strauss's book in particular will show.

The whole question, however, is far from unambiguous: sometimes there are data which cannot be interpreted as events, sometimes there are events which cannot be interpreted as incidents, and sometimes there are incidents which cannot be classified as social interactions. In no small number of cases, the word 'data' seems to mean whatever Glaser or Strauss arbitrarily choose it to mean. Generally speaking, then, data in grounded theory can be described in vague terms as something empirical, often some event, often in the form of an incident, often in the form of some social interaction. By failing to make a conceptual examination of the basic unit in their methodology, the authors risk building their grounded theory on sand, particularly since they also fail to take into account that all facts are theory-dependent – a sin of omission which, it has to be admitted, they share with many other methodologies, not only the 'traditional' positivistic but also other qualitative methods which border on a positivistic style of thought.

A first prerequisite for grounding a theory on data is, of course, that some data do exist. It is thus important to consider where data can be 'found' – that is, the *sources* of data. Data can sometimes be thin or inaccessible in those places where they are traditionally sought in the social sciences. As regards the sources of data, grounded theory does provide a whole range of unconventional tips, apart from the traditional sources such as participant observation, interviews, etc. Glaser and Strauss devote an entire chapter (Chapter VII: 'New sources for qualitative data') to the subject, discussing a rather neglected area in social science, namely library research. In this context they mention documentary sources such as 'letters, biographies, autobiographies, memoirs, speeches, novels' (diaries could be added here); they then note such apparently far-off phenomena as 'deeds, jokes, photographs and city plans' (Glaser and Strauss, 1967: 161). They note that various tactics in library research are reminiscent of those in fieldwork. These include: going to the right shelves for sources about events versus choosing the right locale for observation or the right interview person; studying symposium proceedings versus taking part in symposia; checking what people involved say about events afterwards, through documentary sources versus interviews (Glaser and Strauss, 1967: 163).

Other tactics for the productive extraction of data involve the following (Glaser and Strauss, 1967: 167):

- Searching for *data caches* (e.g. collections of letters, interviews, speeches, article series, journals), which can prove to be veritable gold mines;[11] the only risk is that the researcher may become *too* engrossed in these, to the point of possessiveness.
- Using fictional literature associated with the studied area as a source of ideas.[12]
- Scanning written material with more remote ties to the studied area, in order to discover fruitful theoretical interlinkages.
- Keeping an eye open to serendipitous findings, or even randomly browsing, which often leads to seminal ideas.

- Looking for literature representing comparative groups who deviate from or fall outside one's own grounded theory.
- 'Pinpointing' in the literature details in hypotheses which have stemmed from grounded theory.

Library research obviously has an even more important role when it comes to the more general formal theory. The great advantage of this method is of course accessibility, which can lead to major cost reductions compared with field research. Another benefit is the great breadth of the available comparative material, in terms of time, space and other properties. Library research naturally also has its deficiencies, in particular gaps in the source materials and the fact that this has always been filtered through someone other than the researcher (Glaser and Strauss, 1967: 176–183). Altogether the chapter on library research is one of the most stimulating in the book, since it points out sources of data other than those traditionally sought, and discusses their use in considerable detail. Elsewhere in the book, Glaser and Strauss (1967: 67, 252) also recommend another unconventional data source – the researcher's own experience, or 'anecdotal comparison'.

Coding: from data to categories

Grounded theory starts from data in order to create *categories*, a procedure referred to as *coding*. The categories in turn have *properties*. Glaser and Strauss (1967) never really explain what they mean by categories, but it appears to be roughly a question of what other scientists refer to as *concepts* (Glaser, 1992: 38). The properties are then simply properties or determinations of the concepts. In the coding data are assigned to a particular category; similarly, the category is construed from the data. Glaser and Strauss (1967) provide rather scant information about how this procedure is undertaken. Strauss's (1987) book on qualitative method, on the other hand, is all the more informative on this point and includes many concrete illustrations of category creation by coding, mainly from the author's seminars in grounded theory. It involves a highly intensive analysis – word for word, line by line, or at least paragraph by paragraph – of a body of empirical material. As has been noted, the closer the material is to the empirical data, the better; the ideal is field-notes from participant observation, but interviews will also do.

The categories should be taken from the actors, or at least should be easily comprehensible to them (that is, they *could have been* taken from the actors). Essentially they are of two kinds: those which are found direct in the material, since they are stated by the actors ('in vivo codes'), and those which the researchers themselves construct from the material (i.e. in vitro coding) (Strauss, 1987: 33). The category can be generated from a single incident, after which any number of further incidents can be coded under this category, contributing to its development. The researcher simply (but industriously):

- reads the text (field-notes, interviews or documentary material) word by word, line by line, or at least paragraph by paragraph

- asks continually under which category the data in the text can be placed, particularly everyday or common-sense categories, easily understandable to the actors
- makes notes of these categories and of what further data fall under them.

By 'minute examination' (Strauss, 1987)[13] of data and categories, that is, by shifting them around in our minds in all possible ways – always with concrete everyday practice in mind – we think out possible properties of the categories, which can enrich them. More specifically, Strauss (1987: 27; see also Strauss and Corbin, 1990) recommends the use of a special

> *coding paradigm* … to code data for relevance to whatever phenomena are referenced by a given category, for the following:
>
> Conditions
> Interaction among the actors
> Strategies and tactics
> Consequences

The first and fourth concepts refer to causality: 'conditions' simply refers to causes, and 'consequences' to effects. The other two are largely self-explanatory. 'Interaction among the actors' refers to such relations as are *not* directly connected with the use of the strategies and tactics.

The following example of participant observation and the beginning of its coding illustrates the procedure (Strauss, 1987: 59–61):

> The portion of the first field note reproduced below records some observations done on a cardiac recovery unit, where patients are brought immediately after cardiac surgery. They are intensively monitored and cared for on a one-to-one, nurse-to-patient basis. The nurses are abetted by occasional visits of house physicians and, less frequently, by visits of surgeons. During the first postsurgical hours, patients are likely to be unconscious or barely sentient. Each is hooked up to numerous pieces of equipment, vital for survival or for monitoring their bodies. In one fieldnote, a young but highly skilled nurse is described as working on, around, and with a barely sentient patient. The observer was focused on details of her work with the equipment in relation to her patient care, and so reports exclusively on that. These field observational data have been specially coded for this book in order to illustrate coding procedures as they occur during the first days of a research project …
>
> 'I watched nurse T. working today for about an hour with a patient who was only four hours post-op. In general the work was mixed. She changed the blood transfusion bag. She milked it down, and took out an air bubble. Later she changed it again; later, got the bottle part filled through mechanical motion. She milked the urine tube once. She took a temperature. She put a drug injection into the tube leading to the patient's neck. She added potassium solution to the nonautomated IV. But, all the while, she had in focus (though not necessarily glancing directly at) the TV which registered EKG and blood pressure readings. Once, she punched the computer button to get the fifteen-minute readout on cardiac functioning. And once she milked the infection-purifier tube leading from the patient's belly. And periodically she marked down both readings and some of what she had done. Once the patient stirred, as she was touching his arm: she said quite nicely then that she was about to give him an injection that would relax him. He indicated that he heard. Another time, she noticed him stirring and switched off the light above his head, saying to him, "That's better, isn't it?" At one point, she assessed that blood pressure was not dropping rapidly enough, and told the resident, suggesting they should do something.'

After the analyst had scanned the field note, he focused on the first five lines, pertaining only to the blood transfusion equipment and what the nurse did in relation to it. His analysis took him several minute. Then he wrote the following lines, elaborating his brief notes, underlining those words which especially but not exclusively struck his attention. The analysis begins with the first line: 'She changed the blood transfusion bag.' His explanatory comments in brackets briefly indicate what is happening analytically.

'She *changed* ...' This is a *task* [a category, drawn from common experience].

'*She* changed ...' She is doing the task by herself. This apparently does not require any immediate division of labour [a category drawn from technical literature]. However, there is a division of labour involved in supplying the blood, an issue I will put aside for later consideration [raising a general query about this category].

'... *blood transfusion bag.*' 'Blood transfusion' tells us that this piece of equipment, the bag and its holder, requires *supplies* [a category]. Again, a fascinating issue, about which I can ask questions in a moment.

Let's look now at the '*changed*', qua task. What are its properties, or what questions can I ask about its properties? It is visible to others [the dimension here being visible–invisible]. It seems like a simple task. So it probably does not take much skill. It's a task that follows another (replace one bag with another). It seems routine. It doesn't take long to do. Is it boring or just routine? It's not a strenuous task either. And it certainly doesn't seem challenging. How often must she do this in her day's work? That is, how often does it take for the blood to get trans- fused into the patient? Or, perhaps, how much time is allowed to elapse before new blood is actually transfused to the patient between each bag? Or does that depend on her assessment of the patient's condition? What would happen if they temporarily ran out of the bags of blood? [Implication of safety to the patient, which will be looked at later.] I would hypothesize that if there is no immediate danger, then replacing it would have low salience. But if there were potential danger for certain kinds of patients, then there would even be organizational mech- anisms for preventing even a temporary lack of blood bags. Well, I could go on with this focus on the task, but enough!

Back to the division-of-labour issue now. Since the patient is virtually nonsentient, the nurse gets no help from him when changing the blood bag. It is a nonworking relationship – she is working on or for but not together with him. This means also that he cannot interfere with her work. He can't complain either, to her or anyone else, that he doesn't like what she's done or how she's done it [implicit comparison]. I know that some patients object to getting blood transfers, especially nowa- days, when they might be anxious about contamination of the blood [explicit comparison, with condition and consequence specified; also touching explicitly again on the supplies issue].

As for that issue: To begin with, there must be supplies for the equipment or it *is* no equipment, of no use whatever. Let's call it *equipment supplies* [category]. But those are very different supplies than for other equipment I have seen around the hospital. Thinking comparatively about those will tell quickly about the special properties of this particular equipment supply, as well as raise ques- tions about those supplies in general. Well, there are machines that use plastic tubing, which when it gets old must be replaced. Blood is a natural supply, not artificial – but the sources of both are somewhere? Where? [I will think about sources later.] Plastic tubing and blood are also replaceable. Blood costs more. Automobiles need gas supplies, but you have to go to a station for it, while blood supplies are brought to the user. What about storage of blood? Where on the ward or in the hospital is it stored? How long is it safe to store? And so on.

We leave this coding report here, although in the book it continues for two more pages. As this quotation shows, coding is a very extensive operation; Glaser and Strauss (1967: 112) speak of 'hundreds of pages' for a single project. (Add to this 'thousands' of pages which, according to the authors, may constitute the data for a single field study based on participant observation ...) Nor is coding to be taken lightly in using grounded theory. The methodology can be modified on various counts, but coding and theoretical memos – to which we will return later – are techniques which '*must*' be used, if we are to be able to speak of grounded theory at all (Glaser and Strauss, 1967: 8; emphasis added). It is a question of continually comparing newly coded data in a category with data previously coded in the same category, in order to develop the category's properties. The coding continues until a *theoretical saturation* is achieved, which occurs 'when additional analysis no longer contributes to discovering anything new about a category' (Strauss, 1987: 21).

Similar procedures in analytical induction, a related qualitative technique within symbolic interactionism, have been criticized for inefficiency (Hammersley, 1989).[14] A corresponding criticism of grounded theory might seem justified in this case: hundreds of pages of manually written coding notes sound somewhat extensive as a research effort. On the other hand, the advocates of grounded theory would presumably claim that while other techniques might have greater *efficiency* – with a satisfactory balance between performance and input – they nonetheless suffer from a lack of *effectiveness*, since they miss the empirical goal; for example, quantitative methods are often too crude to capture sophisticated social realities. Moreover, as Glaser and Strauss explain, the use of these tedious procedures means that less creativity and inspiration are required of the individual researcher; fine theoretical results appear on their own, as it were, but with a good deal of *per*spiration instead.

Many questions come to mind about the content of the coding process described above. For example, '*She* changed ...'. Strauss discusses this in terms of the division of labour, and looks particularly at the autonomy–heteronomy dimension. This bears evidence of a peculiar blindness. For us – and presumably for many others – quite a different angle would have seemed more relevant in connection with the italicized word. Why '*she*' and not '*he*'? Well, because the nurse is a woman. But *why* is the nurse a woman? Why is it worth noting the gender, in this context? Well, among other things, it is a question of routine work (see the whole discussion of routine in Strauss's analysis) and, even more, of a *caring, serving* task. The choice of words in connection with emptying the blood bag reinforces this further: '*milked*', instead of 'emptied' or some other synonym. Implicitly the nurse is here likened to a milkmaid, a peasant serving-girl in a high-tech caring environment. Strauss raises no questions on this point either, in his discussion of the category 'tasks' or even the category 'division of labour'.

Yet it would have been the most obvious thing to ask about the relative number of women among the nurses and of men among the physicians and administrators, about their relative wages and so on. The enigmatically illogical comment on possible *contamination of the blood* (AIDS!) and *the nonsentient* (!) patient's inability to *complain* is an error in thinking which becomes more understandable in light of the fact that certain groups in history (Jews, women) have tended to be accused of spreading

DATA-ORIENTED METHODS

the plague. The nurse's subdued, semi-averted profile in the field study is thus by a well-known twist suddenly transformed into the figure of the *woman-witch*. All at once the risk is here revealed as one of failing to problematize the spontaneous mental frames, the researcher's or the actor's, and of reducing oneself to common-sense conceptions. Science is more than systematized common sense.

In another sense, too, the whole analysis seems in some way desexed: it is, so to speak, *dumb* and *shadowy*. (On representations as silhouettes, see Ingarden, 1976.) The actors appear to be not people of flesh and blood, but some kind of shadowy Platonic beings. Where, for example, are the emotions of both the people involved, emotions which must be even more palpable in a borderline situation of this kind? How does it affect the nurse to find herself in conditions which must after all remind her of her own death? She does not even appear to have changed her expression throughout the observation period – at least, there is no note to this effect. She could equally well have been some kind of robot in a white coat. (Here there is of course a link with the lack of gender role analysis: the woman as an anonymous 'serving spirit'.) Furthermore, how does this borderline situation affect the researcher? Has he (Strauss) no feelings? Can the proximity of death be the cause of this shadowy mood of the whole description? There is no lack of indications, particularly in more recent hermeneutic literature, that the *death motif* does indeed give rise to the most radical repression and neutralization of existence (Heidegger, 1962).

Interestingly enough, the *patient* in the story despite being *nonsentient*, is ascribed emotions, very significantly in the shape of the *fear of death* (AIDS!).[15] We have on the one hand a researcher and a nurse who are conscious but *lack* emotions, and on the other an unconscious patient who *possesses* strong emotions. There seems good reason to interpret this as a projection of emotions from the researcher on to the patient. That is to say, the emotions are removed from those who *can* have them, and are transposed by way of a logical somersault to the one who *cannot* have them. The latter, moreover, does not fear the most immediate risk – death from heart disease – but AIDS (which is not even mentioned by name, only implicitly evoked).

In fact the whole coding scheme in this case can be regarded as such a process of repression to external 'neutral' things and relationships. The opportunities for trivializing the analysis are even greater since it focuses to such a high degree on *technology* ('equipment supplies' and so on). Technological rationality is particularly prone to inducing a loss of meaning, by reducing everything to external causal relationships (Heidegger, 1977). As a result of Strauss's interpretation paradigm – which in reality implies a limitation to exter-nal causal connections, ends–means relations and interaction (the four points in the cod-ing paradigm quoted above; see p. 63), that is to the study of effective and final causality – this tendency is further reinforced. Indeed, we can go one step further, and ask ourselves whether this interpretation paradigm has not come about as a theoretical repression mechanism, just because of Strauss's long and intimate research confrontation with ter-minally ill people in high-tech environments. The comparison between gas/automobiles and blood/people is thought-provoking in this context. Finally, it is worth pointing out that the legacy from grounded theory's 'parent', symbolic interactionism, has probably also left its mark here; this movement has often been criticized for its one-sided cognitive approach to research and disregard for emotional aspects.

Thus, despite its intentions, the coding operation is not really able to represent reality in an unambiguous way through an objective, unequivocal, sure and rational procedure. On the contrary, it is a question here of researchers interpreting what they think they are seeing, in light of their own unreflected frames of reference. Grounded theory suffers from two problems: on the one hand, an unreflected view of data processing is advocated, which brings with it a bias from pre-scientific categories of common-sense thinking; on the other hand, too much energy is spent on detailed coding operations.

Theoretical sampling

Theoretical sampling, a central principle in grounded theory, is described by Strauss as:

> a means whereby the analyst decides *on analytic grounds* what data to collect next and where to find them. The basic question in theoretical sampling is: *What* groups or subgroups of populations, events, activities (to find varying dimensions, strategies, etc.) does one turn to *next* in data collection? And for *what* theoretical purpose? So, this process of data collection is *controlled* by the emerging theory. It involves, of course, much calculation and imagination on the part of the analyst. When done well, this analytic operation pays very high dividends because it moves the theory along quickly and efficiently. (1987: 38–39; quotation marks omitted)

In grounded theory *any groups at all* can in principle be compared, in contrast to the traditional comparative method in which groups that are too different from one another are excluded as 'incomparable' (Glaser and Strauss, 1967: 50). This appears to be one of the advantages of Glaser and Strauss's methodology, since obviously it is possible in principle to find similarities and differences between *everything* in the world, and therefore in principle everything is comparable. Whether or not a comparison is made must naturally depend on the purpose at hand, not on the distance between entities in some abstract conceptual space. Comparisons between very different entities – 'maximizing the differences' – should be potentially fruitful, if we are to believe the various theories of creativity which emphasize the importance of seeing unexpected similarities in things that are very dissimilar (cf. Koestler, 1964).

Theoretical sampling has two main steps. In the first the differences between the groups are *minimized*, and in the second they are *maximized*. The emerging theory controls the process throughout. The first step, the minimizing of differences, aims to find quickly the basic categories and their properties (see, for example, the hospital study above). It is quite possible to start with a single case, for example, in order to minimize the differences. How is such a choice made? The authors do not address this question in any depth, but implicitly it transpires that it depends on the problem or purpose of the study. This purpose is regarded as initially fairly broad and unspecified; during the research process it may alter direction entirely – and not only 'may'; such a development is presented as the normal course of events. The second step – the maximizing of differences between comparison groups – enables the researcher to investigate these category properties in their greatest possible range, and to begin weaving them together into a more substantial theory. The technique used in both the first and second steps is the *comparison* of data in order to generate

DATA-ORIENTED METHODS

and develop categories and their properties: one incident is continually being compared with incidents noted earlier in the same category, in the same or different groups, which is what gives the procedure its name, the 'constant comparison method'.

One disadvantage of this process is that real organic relations between the incidents are broken, in that the incidents are being assigned to categories. Events are detached from the context of relationships in which they occur, and are instead linked to the actors' or the researcher's common sense. This makes it difficult to apply the method to the study of organizational relations, for example.[16] It would be like trying to analyse music by studying how people talk about and perceive individual notes ('incidents'): in this way we would never be able to discover the essential element – the *melody*.

From categories to theory

The properties of the categories are important, since they represent the branches and ramifications of the categories, through which these are woven together to form a theory. But how, in practice, is a theory created from a number of categories? Three main tactics are used. The first and most indispensable is continually to write memos on the theoretical ideas which always arise in the course of the coding, and particularly on the connections between the category properties. As we have seen, coding and memo-writing are a 'must' in grounded theory. The memos may be discursive; they may also include graphic representations such as diagrams, matrices, tables, graphs, and other more informal pictures. Out of the memo-writing, the theory gradually emerges; an illustrative example is graphic representation through matrices, in which the properties of two categories are related to each other (Strauss, 1987: 147).

The second tactic is to find the *core category*, the central concept around which the others revolve. This gives us, so to speak, the key to the theory. The core category can be identified with the help of the following criteria (Strauss, 1987: 36):

1 'It must be *central*, that is, related to as many other categories and their properties as is possible, and more than any other candidates for the position of core category.'
2 It 'must appear frequently in the data'.
3 It must relate 'easily … and abundantly' to 'other categories'.
4 It must have *clear implications* for a formal theory.
5 It must develop the theory.
6 It must allow 'for building in … the *maximum variation* to the analysis'.

The third tactic is to draw diagrams, or what many social scientists would call 'models', of the way the categories are related to one another. In Strauss's illustrations this is simply done with boxes and arrows. Obviously more advanced models can be envisaged, but the important thing is to make a graphic sketch of how the grounded concepts (the categories) hang together (Strauss, 1987: Chapters 8–9). A good idea is to start with the core category, and then to investigate how the other categories relate to it.

In the discursively presented theory, the various properties then specify *how* the different categories are interlinked in the theory, and in this way we get a conceptually *dense* (i.e. highly ramified) theory – something which is claimed as one of the great advantages of the methodology. In the author's study of the care of the terminally ill, for example, 'social value' appeared as one category and 'care' as another. It turned out that low social value (a property of the first category) was associated with a lower standard of care (a property of the second category). Both categories also had many other properties, while the study itself generated further categories. In grounded theory the different categories in the study, and their properties, are tied together into a fine-meshed network, and it has been illustrated above how one such mesh can look. Anyone who has struggled to develop an abstract and possibly anaemic theory so as to account for a little more of a colourful case material, will naturally recognize the great advantage of acquiring this more or less gratis, or at least as a natural part of the research process. As a result of this weaving together of the category properties, the *integration* of the theory is achieved in quite a different way than in more abstract theory formations. (Yet, as we have seen, this quality of grounded theory corresponds to the *dis*integration of the empirical material.)

Density and integration have a high price, however. Such close proximity to the actor level may result in no more than reformulations (at best) of what is already known at this level, implicitly or explicitly. The risk is thus that grounded theory creates trivial knowledge. This is illustrated by a discussion of a mastectomy as an 'invisible handicap' (Strauss, 1987: 308), and by a research seminar in grounded theory, where Strauss (1987: 159) instructs one of the participants: 'You have a translation of what she [the interview subject] is saying'. The fact that breast operations result in an invisible handicap (prosthesis) is hardly a surprising piece of knowledge; that scientific activity should constitute translations of what interview subjects say, on the other hand, is more startling. If we return to Glaser and Strauss (1967), the problem is palpable there, too. The finding that 'low social value' is linked to 'a low level of care' – the authors' prime example – is, for instance, not very ground breaking.

Another example of 'theories' developed from empirical bases failing to 'take off' is to be found in Starrin et al. (1984), which reports a study of unemployed women based on grounded theory. After extensive empirical work and considerable time spent on interviews and the processing and analysis of data, it is concluded that the unemployed women were either concerned to find paid work or had given up any such ambition, and that their attitudes to alternative activities were either active or passive. The two dimensions were combined, from which it emerged that some of the active women were disposed to find a paid job and were looking for one ('ambivalents'), while others were active in life in other ways without being dedicated wage-earners ('decentrers'); some of those who were passive in relation to alternative activities intended and were prepared to find paid work ('clingers'); while others were just generally passive and had no particular desire to find a job ('resigners'). A similar 'theoretical' result could possibly have been generated by brainwork, with less effort than the producing, coding and analysing of 1500 pages of interview transcripts.

Even more striking examples can be cited from Glaser (1993). Here we learn, for instance, that milkmen cultivate their customers; that prisoners suffer from the lack of privacy; that single women walking in open places employ various strategies to avoid contact with unfamiliar men; and so on. There is an imminent risk of belabouring the obvious.

Substantive and formal grounded theory

There are two kinds of grounded theory, substantive and formal (Glaser and Strauss, 1967: 32–35). The difference between them is said to be that the substantive theory is 'developed for a substantive, or empirical, area', while the formal theory is 'developed for a formal, or conceptual, area'. As examples of the first kind 'patient care, race relations, professional education, delinquency, or research organizations' are cited, and as examples of the second 'stigma, deviant behavior, formal organization, social-ization, status congruency, authority and power, reward systems, or social mobility'. Glaser and Strauss (1967: 33) stress in particular that both types of theory are to be found among the middle-range theories, somewhere between 'minor working hypotheses' and 'the "all-inclusive" grand theories', which Merton, too, had recom-mended as a way of bridging the gap between these low-level and high-level theories. Glaser and Strauss (1967: 90–92) seem to be suggesting that it is possible to generate both substantive and formal theories direct from data, but that it is preferable to start with the substantive theory, and then generate the formal theory from it. It is also possible to generate the formal theory from *earlier* theory, provided that this is substantive or at least has been based on substantive theory at a previous stage. (It is even possible to generate formal theory direct from data, but this is more difficult, and there is a risk that the outcome may be an abstract model of the 'logical-deductive' kind, which neither fits the data nor is usable in practice.)

The difference between substantive and formal theory is not, however, altogether clear. Sometimes the authors speak of the distinction as though it were a case on the one hand of theories of social *entities*, and on the other of *properties/relations* (in the illustration referred to above, for example). It seems as though Glaser and Strauss believe that entities are empirical, but properties or relations are conceptual, which is in fact a semantic *quid pro quo*. Sometimes, instead, it is a question of 'distinguish-able levels of generality, which differ only in terms of degree' (Glaser and Strauss, 1967: 33). But, to begin with, different levels of generality are not the same things as a difference between the empirical and the conceptual, since different generalities can refer both to theory and to its empirical referents. Secondly, different levels of generality are not the same as the difference between entities and properties, since both entities and properties can be more, or less, general. ('Dog' is thus more general than 'cocker spaniel', and 'covered with hair' is more general than 'shaggy'.)

A certain semantic confusion thus obtains. One mistake which the authors make is to posit an absolute distinction – albeit with fluid boundaries – between two phenomena whose differences are in fact relative. The whole thing boils down to a matter of *a lower or higher level of generality*, and in reality there are not just two such levels, but an arbitrary number of them. Which levels are chosen will depend on the purpose of the particular investigation. Glaser and Strauss describe, for example, how, via a substantive theory of 'social loss' (i.e. loss to society) and the way the hospital staff treated dying patients depending on how they evaluated this social loss, they extended their study to a formal theory of 'social value', quite inde-pendent of care situations. It is evident from this that the authors' dichotomy between the substantive and the formal simply represents two possible degrees on a scale of generality. Looking downwards – towards a lower level of generality – we could, for example, restrict ourselves to the study of professional or family losses. Looking upwards – towards a higher level of generality – we might extend the study to a consideration of value creation in society in general. What this shows is that Glaser and Strauss arbitrarily select two fairly close points on a scale of generality, designating these as 'substantive' and 'formal' theory. The authors further claim that studies of intensive care wards or fire service committees are both examples of substantive theory building, since they refer to empirically delimited areas. But nothing prevents us from studying them both in their common character, for instance, as (public) organizations for crisis management – which only serves to show once again the artificiality of the substantive–formal distinction. The term 'formal', furthermore, is misleading in this context, since the theory in question, according to Glaser and Strauss, may be either formalized or non-formalized. And even the term 'substantive' is dubious, since theories at a higher level of generality do not lack empirical substance either, so long as they are not purely speculative.

However, the discussion of the substantive and the formal can be useful as a recommendation and a *signpost* for qualitative researchers. Having created a theory at a certain level of generality or abstraction, they should not stop there, but should lift their gaze higher and investigate the possibility of further generalization. Often this may be possible by studying properties rather than entities. Ultimately, researchers might also consider the possibility of *formalizing* the theory, so long as this is not an end in itself but can produce greater theoretical power (cf. Sköldberg,1992a, on this research tactic).

Conclusion

As was mentioned initially, grounded theory is a much used qualitative method in international social science research – maybe even *the* must used method. This last is our subjective opinion, but the breadth of application can be suggested by a sample of more recent research in the area. Grounded theory has been used in studies of mathematical problem solving (De Hoyos Guajardo, 2004); parents' regulation of children's between-meal snacking (Freeman et al., 2005); heterodox economics (Lee, 2005); opportunities of academically talented women in Iran (Alborzi and Khayyer, 2008); natural science education (Maloney, 2005); interdisciplinary teamwork (McCallin, 2004); the discovery of deterioration in health care patients (Andrews and Waterman, 2005); consumers' spatial experience (Rosenbaum, 2005); cooperative synergies in the crane industry (Ng, 2005); and guardians to middle-level mathematics students (Johnston, 2008).

With its emphasis on the local, the provisional, the pluralistic, in its opposition to the 'grand theories', but also in a certain superficiality, grounded theory has at one level, points in common with postmodernism (see Chapter 6 below). However, there are also (much more) obvious differences, such as a generally uncritical attitude and a strong resistance to 'intertextual' influences from earlier theories. The movement also overlaps with positivism in regarding empirical data as (relatively) theory-free. Both share the ideal of being able to separate theory from empirical data, and thus also to test the relation between the two – although grounded theory sees verification as secondary. Further, they share ideals of objectivity, generalizability, reproducibility and predictability (Strauss and Corbin, 1990: 27). Yet grounded theory differs from positivism in its emphasis on understanding the symbolic meaning embedded in social interactions, on theory generation rather than verification, and on qualitative rather than quantitative data.[17] But, all in all, there is reason to take note of the similarities between grounded theory and a positivistic scientific stance, particularly since many authors have chosen to propose grounded theory as an alternative to the positivistic mode, and have thus over-emphasized the differences between the two (see, for example, Ekerwald and Johansson, 1989).[18]

Similarities to hermeneutics can be discerned in the very close and 'dense' reading of the text, but the differences are more marked, particularly as regards perceptions of the empirical material, which, as we shall see, in hermeneutics is always a result of interpretation, not a starting-point for interpretation. Grounded theory has (stronger) similarities with phenomenology, in its focus on the actor's perspective (although grounded theory does not go as far here as some other schools, such as ethnomethodology), and in its view of the possibility of theory-independent data.

It can be instructive – in the spirit of the authors' own thesis on the maximization of differences – to compare Glaser and Strauss's book on grounded theory with another methodological work published at about the same time. Bourdieu et al. (1991) starts from the philosophy-of-science tradition developed in France by Bachelard, among others. The authors apply these metascientific conceptions to the field of social science. They hold that the greatest danger in social science research lies in a reduction to common-sense knowledge. All knowledge admittedly has to *start* from such knowledge, but should not *remain* at that level. Moreover, social science must not only gradually free itself from this 'prescientific' conceptual world derived from the actors' own lifeworlds, but also conduct a genuine struggle to free itself, and this can only be effected by making a radical epistemological *break* (Bachelard's famous *coupure*), with the entire original semantics and terminology. Social science must *create* its own *social concepts* formed in an entirely different purview than the notions and frames of reference of the everyday world: [19]

> Sociologists would be less prone to the temptations of empiricism if it were sufficient to remind them, in Poincaré's words, that 'facts do not speak'. It is perhaps the curse of the human sciences that they deal with a *speaking object*. When the sociologist counts on the facts to supply the problematic and the theoretical concepts that will enable him to construct and analyse the facts, there is always a danger that these will be supplied from the informants' mouths. It is not sufficient for the sociologist to listen to the subjects, faithfully recording their statements and their reasons, in order to account for their conduct and even for the reasons they offer; in doing so, he is liable to replace his own preconceptions with the preconceptions of those whom he studies, or with a spuriously scientific objective blend of the spontaneous sociology of the 'scientist' and the spontaneous sociology of his object. (Bourdieu et al., 1991: 37)

Bourdieu et al. direct their criticism mainly at a positivist methodology focusing on statistical analysis in the tradition of Lazarsfeld, but it could equally well be applied to Glaser and Strauss's grounded theory. The arguments against a short-sighted empirical approach seem valid, since such an approach can never reach down to the *deep structures* in the empirical material but finds itself shackled to surface structures (see Chomsky, 1965). The focus is on the empirically (easily) accessible. But as scientific theorists as different as Bunge (1967) and Whitehead (1929) have argued: *it is never possible to distil (theories of) deep structures from data.*

Grounded theory and the constructionism of Bourdieu et al. can be regarded less as mutually exclusive alternatives in a dichotomy and more as positions close to the end-points in a spectrum of possible methodologies whose underlying dimension consists of the *distance to that which is studied.* ('Close' means that they do not coincide with the end-points.) In these terms Glaser and Strauss's grounded theory lies relatively close to the actor level, to that which is studied, while Bourdieu's construction of a social object is separated from the empirical level by a veritable chasm, an epistemological ravine. Beyond Bourdieu's constructionism, which in our view marks the site for genuine and fruitful grand theories, then, lie empirically empty, barren theories which – in so far as they are real theories and not conceptual frames or 'approaches' like Parsons's system – are simply ticking over, for want of that surface friction which empirical data supply. Beyond Glaser and Strauss's grounded theory, on the other hand, 'research' consists of mere reformulations of what the actors themselves are saying, or of the researcher's own common-sense ponderings.[20]

Grounded theory and the construction of social objects are thus two research modes, both of which can produce valuable results, depending on what is wanted. We could even, somewhat heretically, *combine* them, at the same time revisiting Glaser and Strauss by adding a new fundamental principle or golden rule to their methodology: **Try to effect an epistemological break with the actor level in the formal grounded theory (at the latest).**[21] The formal theory would then account for the deep structure and the substantive theory for the surface structure, upon which this is based. Such a golden rule would counteract much of what we see as the fundamental weakness in Glaser and Strauss's position, while also helping to preserve its strengths: the possibility and the right of all researchers to create new theories, the emphasis on theory generation rather than verification, the offensive utilization of qualitative methods, and the exploitation of new types of data. These are properties which make Glaser and Strauss's methodology still appear capable of development. The legitimation of a certain type of research, and the development of several individual methodological elements, are thus its lasting contributions, through which grounded theory has played a historically significant role in the liberation of methodology from the over-reliance on certain established devices such as quantitative analysis and the testing of hypotheses. Having said that, there is a need to go still further. The approach has its weaknesses, above all as a whole but, as we have seen, also in its individual parts. Here special mention should be made of the one-sided focus on data and, related to this, the disregard of the data's dependence on theory and the over-confidence in a technical machinery – the coding. Although such elements are not absent from symbolic interactionism, the positivistic tradition from Lazarsfeld is more tangible here. In part at least, grounded theory is built on a statistics-processing model (Glaser, 1992), something which should after all be foreign to the qualitative method. These weaknesses make urgent the need to investigate what can be learnt on other fronts of qualitative research, and we will devote the rest of this book to an exploration of these.

All in all, then, a further development and reformulation of grounded theory seems called for, building on a looser coupling to data and a more reflective focus upon the empirical material, combined with a bolder approach to the research process both in its foundations and theoretically. (A first step in the direction of such a reconstruction of grounded theory has in fact already been taken by Haig, 1995.) Despite the criticism we have directed at grounded theory here, it does have a good deal to offer that is of value. As we have seen, there are elements in this methodology which are useful in both big and small ways. Without being tied by individual prescriptions (not even by the coding procedure, the special trademark of the theory), it is possible, as many researchers in practice have done, to build on the general inspiration that grounded theory provides.[22] (It is, of course, important that this generalized inspiration does not lead to a kind of legitimization of methodlessness.) Another path is also quite possible: without paying too much attention to the whole, researchers could make their own choices according to individual taste, appropriating individual tips and techniques from the rich material on offer – provided that these can be integrated into an overall *interpretive* awareness. The present book aims to contribute to such an awareness.

Schism

In the preceding pages we have described the main features of grounded theory and have offered a critical examination of its content, referring mainly to Glaser and Strauss's original pioneering book. During the 1990s the two authors went their separate ways, and a schism arose between the originators of grounded theory. The conflict revolved around Strauss and Corbin (1990). Glaser (1992) mounts a scathing and sometimes very bitter attack on this book, which in his view betrays the original ideals of grounded theory. (For a more positive appreciation of Strauss and Corbin's book, as well as a discussion about the differences between it and the original theory, and the historical reasons for these differences, see Annells, 1996.) He further claims that it makes inadequate recognition of his own contribution, both as an originator of the methodology and for elaborating it further in his own later book (Glaser, 1978). Glaser's critique particularly targets Strauss and Corbin's over-emphasis on:

- preconceptions instead of an unbiased open approach
- the generation of categories from intensive analyses of a single incident, rather than from the constant comparison of incidents
- verification instead of generation
- rules in the research process, instead of the free emergence of theory from data.

Glaser appears from his own description as something of an 'orthodox', and Strauss as what we might call 'revisionist': Glaser wants to retain the original purity of the methodology, while Strauss in some ways moves closer to other methodological orientations. The fault-line seems to coincide largely with the question of the analyst's preconceptions, to which Glaser wants to assign a minor, negative role, and Strauss a greater, more positive one (cf. Strauss and Corbin, 1994). It is interesting to note in this context that the location of the dividing-line coincides with our main criticism of grounded theory.

Yet the question is not altogether a simple one. Admittedly it is correct, as Glaser points out, that Strauss and Corbin (1990) introduce a whole series of categories and preconceptions, in particular an interpretation 'paradigm' of a very rationalistic kind, which seems to have particularly upset Glaser.[23] Such a set of preconceptions does not occur in Glaser (1992). On the other hand, he does introduce one which may weigh as heavily as all of Strauss and Corbin's added together. He claims that the research question should always be concerned with exploring the *actors'* problem, their main worry. He also maintains that there is always one such overriding worry. This means, of course, that the analysis would be steered in a very radical way right from the start. Neither Strauss and Corbin nor Glaser argue for their respective preconceptions, but merely introduce them rather abruptly. Grounded theory's striving for a totally unbiased approach thus means that preconceptions come in anyway, but by the back door and in an unreflecting way, either in the shape of rationalistic assumptions or as adaptations to the actors' circumstances. We do not mean that it is always wrong to do research according to rationalistic assumptions, or to explore the problems of the actors; however, it would be wrong to limit qualitative research to either one of these principles. Rationalism certainly does not reign supreme in social or scientific contexts. And as to the actors' problems, to begin with it is not even certain that any such all-pervading problem exists (Sköldberg, 1991a, 1994): different actors may have different problems, and problems can anyway almost always be defined in different ways. Secondly, as Bourdieu points out, it may well be worthwhile to take account of the actors' spontaneous categories, but the analysis should not *stop* there; it must go on, to avoid the risk of falling into a naïvety imbued by unconscious, ideological, and thus prescientific frames of reference (Bourdieu and Wacquant, 1992).

Epilogue

Later, other revisionists have appeared. Haig (1995) thinks that grounded theory instead of being inductive, rather can be described as abductive (on abduction, see Chapter 2 above), which would nullify much of the criticism against this orientation for a naïve empiricism, etc. Charmaz (2000) has tried to reform grounded theory in a more social constructionist direction, and wants to position the approach between positivism and postmodernism, even combine elements of these. She emphasizes more strongly the conceptions of the research subjects, 'the study of experience from the standpoint of those who live it' (2000: 522), highlights the interactive character of data and analysis, and holds that categories and concepts emanate from the researchers' interaction with the field. Glaser (2002) reacts against this and insists on the objective character of data and interpretations – a point of view bound to appear somewhat aged for most adherents of qualitative methods. Whether a constructionist turn of grounded theory is possible or whether it remains a mixture of incompatible basic perspectives remains to be seen. In the meantime, Glaser on his part continues taking the sometimes thankless position of orthodoxy's staunch defender, repeating his well-known dictum 'All is data' (Glaser, 2007).

Clarke (2005), an earlier pupil of Anselm Strauss, accepts Charmaz's challenge and goes even further in breaking away from the positivist heritage in grounded theory. In her 'situational analysis' she considers the postmodern critique of traditional social science and tries to 'pull' grounded theory around the postmodern turn. Clarke focuses on the research situation itself, which she believes has been neglected in grounded theory. In this way, reflexivity enters the picture. The research situation is 'mapped' in three basics ways, inspired by Strauss and with analogies to Latour's actor-network theory (which is explicitly mentioned): (1) 'situational maps' of single human and non-human elements in the situation; (2) more overriding 'social worlds/arenas maps' playing a role in the situation; and (3) 'positional maps' laying out various positions from which the situation can be interpreted/judged/analysed. Analysis of discourses becomes central in contrast to the focus in much traditional social science on action, and here Clarke has been inspired by discourse analysis (see Chapter 7 below).

Somewhat humbly, Clarke presents her theory as a 'supplement' to traditional grounded theory, but the question is whether her programme does not signal an entirely new 'grounded theory' (perhaps even an un-grounded theory), or at least an entirely new variant of it. With this current development we take leave of grounded theory and move on to the second major approach in the qualitative area – ethnomethodology.

Ethnomethodology

Roots: phenomenology

Ethnomethodology, which also builds on close attention to the empirical material, has its roots in phenomenology, a German philosophical movement that emerged at the beginning of the twentieth century. Phenomenology is critical of modern natural science for having distanced itself – it is claimed – too far from its basis in everyday life, in this way creating an abstract world of its own, without having sufficiently analysed the foundations of ordinary human experience upon which it rests. 'Zu den Sachen selbst' (to the things themselves), the battlecry of the phenomenological movement, signalled a return to the concrete sensuous everyday – lifeword[24] – which positivism, with its rational 'scientistic' analyses, had drained of all substance and colour, leaving behind mere abstract formal structures, castles in the air set free from their earthly moorings. However, the pre-rational experience to which the phenomenologists wished to return was not the same as that of the British empiricists. It was 'lived' experience, not passive sense impressions, but perceptions which were as a rule already furnished with interpretation in the shape of objectives, values, meaning and the like: an interpretation to which Husserl – the man who launched modern phenomenology – gave the name 'intentionality' (Spiegelberg, 1982).

Thus experience itself becomes the point of departure. At the same time this implies disregarding the question whether or not it has an objective counterpart. (There are, after all, fantasies, hallucinations, delusions and so on.) It is the *phenomenal* world around which interest should be centred. The real world is, so to speak, cut off ('bracketed', to use Husserl's term). This is labelled 'phenomenological reduction', which thus means that we abstract from real existing objects, confining ourselves instead to the world of ideas. In this way Husserl claimed to have found an alternative to the subject–object problematic. The 'intentional objects' of interest here are neither subjective nor objective, but instead have the status of a third alternative – the 'lived'. We might perhaps ask how these differ from purely subjective mental phenomena, but the argument becomes clearer if we recognize that it is not a question of psychological processes in themselves but of their *content*, irrespective of the individual 'thinker'.

The first reduction was the 'phenomenological', mentioned above. The next step, the second reduction, is the *eidetic*.[25] The goal here is to leave the individual phenomenon behind, and to reach the so-called 'essence'. By this term the phenomenologists seem to be referring to what are otherwise generally called 'universals' – for example, the concept of the table rather than the table itself (Merleau-Ponty, 1973: 78–79; Spiegelberg, 1982: 99–102). In order to ascend from the individual phenomenon to something more general, some form of thought process is needed. Husserl distances himself from the method which involves analytical abstraction or similar activities. Instead he introduces a new technique, 'the intuition of essences' (*Wesensschau*). What is meant by this somewhat mystical-sounding term? It seems to refer simply to a kind of 'comparative analysis' of the elements of our thought processes. As a result of the 'imaginary variation' of a certain phenomenon, we should be able to reach something common – an 'invariance' to a whole group of phenomena, and this common something, this invariance, is precisely the 'essence'. For example, we have a red spot before our eyes. In our minds we vary the red colour by imagining all possible shades and nuances, thus moving on to the overarching concept of 'red', which refers to the common element in all hues and types of that colour. This general red then becomes something that we 'mean' when we look at some concrete red spot. We *see*, as it were, the general *in* the individual, in the various single phenomena – the intuition of general 'essences' (Haglund, 1977: 56; Husserl, 1913: 106–109; Merleau-Ponty, 1973: 78–79; Schutz, 1967: 113–116). As we realize, it is important in phenomenology not to *distance* oneself too far from the sensuous-concrete, in taking the step towards the general; the general is, so to speak, always embedded in the concrete, not detached from it. Husserl warns us not to lose all contact with concrete experience in creating general concepts. We '*see*' the general in the individual. (On the scrutiny of essences as a way of discovering previously unreflected meaning, see Merleau-Ponty, 1973: 61.)

There is one more step, a further reduction after the phenomenological and the eidetic, namely *transcendental reduction*. By this is meant that we pass on from studying universals, invariances, general phenomena – that is, essences – to investigate *how these are constructed*. Through what mental a priori structures do things acquire their properties? These structures have been labelled by Husserl, following Kant, 'the transcendental ego'. The productive, energy-filled ego is ultimately the creator of its own world. Here Husserl in fact lands in radical solipsism – only the ego exists; even the existence of external reality is in reality only an a priori category of the

transcendental ego, one of its ways to project itself, one of the ingredients or properties in the world which the ego generates, builds up. This line of reasoning has had
important implications for later research in the same tradition, whereby interest
came to be directed at fundamentally identical meanings between individuals, since
the transcendental ego also constructs the other individuals, including *their* transcendental egos, which are therefore *the same* (Schutz, 1967: 126). Traces of this can be
found in Garfinkel, the father of ethnomethodology (Garfinkel, 1967).

From the beginning Husserl had placed 'experience' (*Erlebnis*) in a 'stream of experience' (*Erlebnisstrom*) – that is, the individual experience was interpreted as an
element in a *process* (Husserl, 1913: 358). This brings us close to the historical aspect
of experience, in which Husserl began increasingly to interest himself towards the
end of his life. It implies that every individual experience must be seen as embedded
in and bearing the imprint of a conceptual world, with historical dimensions going
backwards in time and with allusions to the future; a world which is continually
changing, shifting its 'horizons' in past and future time, a lifeworld or *Lebenswelt*, to
use Husserl's famous term (Gadamer, 1989a: 247–251; Spiegelberg, 1982: 144–147).

This lifeworld, the world we live in every day, embraces not only various objects
but also other *people*, other 'selves'. These selves differ from the mindless objects in
the special attitude or intentional stance we adopt in relation to them, and which
consist of empathy (Gadamer, 1989a: 250). The only things which we can 'feel our
way into' in this intuitive way, are other selves, other people. Unfortunately, however, the solipsism remains, since empathy is an a priori structure of the self, and so
it is this which constitutes other people as also being selves (Schutz, 1967: 126;
Spiegelberg, 1982: 140).

Ethnomethodological research

For an account of phenomenological research models, see Moustakas (1994).
Phenomenology has been applied in a number of social science contexts (see, for
example, Giorgi, 1985; Karlsson, 1993; Sandberg, 1994; Silverman, 1970). A relevant development, which we discuss in Chapter 2, is social constructionism
(Berger and Luckmann, 1966; Gergen, 1985). For an outstanding work, inspired
by phenomenology and social constructionism, the reader is referred to Zuboff's
(1988) study of information technology and working life. In the present chapter
we look at another important application, namely ethnomethodology (Cicourel,
1964; Garfinkel, 1967; see also Heritage, 1984, and for a more recent overview
Holstein and Gubrium, 1994). Ethnomethodology is a direct heir of phenomenology in the third generation, inspired by second-generation German immigrants
to the USA (Gurwitsch, 1964; Schutz, 1967). It focuses on exploring how the
lifeworld emerges as a result of microprocesses in the form of social interactions,
which generate the common-sense knowledge of the participants. Its critique of
traditional social science is intense. Social science is conceived as moralizing
towards the everyday world of the social actors: 'We, the social scientists, know
better'. It is thus being assumed that abstract categories are superior to the actors'
own knowledge. The ethnomethodologists hold that such is not the case. On the

contrary, they *study* precisely this everyday knowledge, how it emerges and is shaped. Our actions in the lifeworld or everyday world are steered by (unreflected, never questioned) underlying expectations, implicit rules, and it is the task of the ethnomethodologist to elicit these.

> On the commuter train between Holte and Copenhagen I was once witness to a little scene, which could have been directed by Garfinkel himself. A young man who was to get off a few stops later tried unsuccessfully to *give away a bus token*. 'I don't need it myself', he said, 'go on, you can have it.' He turned to one passenger after another, but nobody wanted his bus token. Nobody even wanted to look at him. At least fifteen people rejected his offer, not by saying 'No thank you', but by not moving a muscle. The young man was good-looking, respectable and sober. He would presumably have ceased his little enterprise at once if somebody had accepted his token, but nobody did. When he got as far as me, I avoided looking at him as carefully as if he'd approached me with his flies undone. When the train stopped at the next station and a couple of new passengers got on, we felt: 'Aha! they don't know they're going to be offered a bus token.' At Svanemöllen the young man got off. Still with the token in his possession. In the train the passengers – for a fraction of a second – sought eye contact with one another, and small tentative smiles were exchanged. (Asplund, 1987: 129–130; our translation)

We will leave the reader to think about the implicit rules which may have been governing this little scene from everyday life, to which we will return later. In the meantime we will continue with some central ideas in ethnomethodology. Central concepts include 'indexicality' and 'reflexivity'. *Indexicality* – a phenomenon which Husserl had addressed under another name – implies that a meaning-bearing unit (a word, a behaviour, a happening) may have more than one sense. It is, to borrow a more illustrative expression from modern hermeneutics, *polysemic*, having several significations. This is because the sense of all meaning-bearing units is always *context-dependent, situation-bound*. Conversely, the same meaning can be expressed in several ways. The relation between sign and expression is thus many-to-many rather than one-to-one. In the view of the ethnomethodologist, earlier social science, inspired by the exactness ideals of the natural sciences, has fallen into the trap of trying to press all language into a scientific mould, in which definitions and conclusions stand to attention, and language resembles a classical French landscaped park rather than a more natural and wild English garden. The language of the real everyday world is considerably more rich, ambiguous and vague than the language of the natural sciences, and research which seeks to reduce it to the standards of the latter in fact mutilates it beyond repair.

Another important attribute is *reflexivity*. There is no one-way street between the researcher and the object of study; rather, the two affect each other mutually and continually in the course of the research process. A positivistic conception of research, according to which the object is uninfluenced by the researcher and the researcher is unaffected by the object, is thus untenable. Both researcher and object are involved in a common context, and are thus context-dependent according to the argument in the previous paragraph.[26] Pollner (1991) argues strongly that the 'radical reflexivity' of the original ethnomethodology, which had a truly revolutionary potential, has unfortunately been compromised by later writers, adopting a more mainstream position.

DATA-ORIENTED METHODS

Other central concepts in ethnomethodology include the following:[27]

- *Membership* – the competence to master a certain natural language game.
- *Accountability* – the actors' method for recounting their actions reflectively in common-sense terms.
- *Local practices and social order* – the way in which the actors creatively reproduce social rule structures in their concrete reality.
- *Unique adequacy of the methods, and becoming the phenomenon.* The first implies that researchers become competent in the lifeworld they study. 'Becoming the phenomenon' is an extension and intensification of this. Castaneda, for instance, in his controversial books (first in Castaneda, 1963) himself becomes the apprentice of a Mexican Indian sorcerer and glides into the magic universe of the shaman. (Castaneda was an ethnomethodologist and had studied under Garfinkel.)
- *Scenic display.* This is a legacy from Goffman's (1959) microsociology, referring to the actors' creative, dramatic performance in practice of 'local practices, implicit rules and knowledge, and accountability'. It can be explored using audio-visual aids (videofilm, audiotapes) as well as the 'incongruity experiments' in which ethnomethodology excels and which mean in one way or the other disturbing the conditions of the actors' common-sense ideas.

Which brings us back to the scene with the bus token and the commuter train.

> The young man who tried to get rid of a bus token was performing an ethnomethodological experiment as simple as it was consummate. The norms, rules and underlying expectations that he breached were of the following kind:
>
>> You don't give presents to strange people, especially not to strangers on a suburban commuter train.
>>
>> You don't give presents which are virtually worthless, and which thereby acquire an uncertain and ambivalent value.
>>
>> You don't give presents which, if they were accepted and used, might suggest that the recipient is either desperately poor or extremely mean.
>>
>> A young man with no particular socially distinguishing features does not give presents to people who are clearly middle-aged high income earners.
>>
>> A young man of no particular socially distinguishing features might perhaps *ask* middle-aged high income earners for a bus token, but the reverse situation is unacceptable.
>>
>> Etcetera. But above all the young man disturbed an atmosphere of dense automatism ... To ride on a suburban commuter train from Holte to Copenhagen is to be invisible. Or it is to *make oneself* invisible. And this calls for a good deal of effort. The young man with the bus token made the passengers visible. 'There you are now!' Once he had left the train, the return to automatism and invisibility was confirmed by subtle momentary glances, and smiles wiped off almost as soon as they appeared. (Asplund, 1987: 134–135; our translation)

One might object that if this interpretation is valid, then every deviant – for example, an addict on public transport or in a public place – is an (unconscious) ethnomethodologist, since the person concerned is revealing implicit rules by breaking them. The ethnomethodologist might agree with this. The question then becomes what the point is. That our actions are governed to a great extent by conventions (implicit rules, underlying expectations) is hardly news, nor that breaches of these rules lead to irritation, since one of the reasons why they were established in the first place was to smooth the path of social intercourse. To study these things in descriptive terms, as ethnomethodologists do, appears strangely pointless. The natural response seems to be, 'So what?' Ethnomethodology stops just when it begins to get interesting. We are left wondering *what generates the conventions*. Adopting Bourdieu's terms, we could ask, for example, how the *habitus* which is made visible by the incongruity experiments ties up with the *social field* in which the actors are embedded (Bourdieu, 1979; Bourdieu and Wacquant, 1992). The aspect of dominance which is central to Bourdieu's thinking in this context, is very evident in the relation between the well-to-do travellers on the train, belonging to the dominating stratum in society, and the young man, the outsider of uncertain status. Yet from this interesting problem the ethnomethodologists are hermetically sealed off, because of their phenomenological restriction to, and inclusion in, the lifeworld of the actor level.

Ethnomethodology has been applied in the most varied fields, particularly in medicine, the law, conversation, offices and bureaucracies, educational organizations, religion, art and scientific work. Recent publications include studies of diverse and interesting subjects such as eating disorders and grandparent caregiving (Beach, 1996); Alcoholics Anonymous (Arminen, 1996, 1998); Speaker's Corner (McIllvenny, 1996); computer games, schooling and boys at risk (Baskin and Taylor, 2007); interruptions in conversations (Bilmes, 1997); psychotherapy (Kozart, 2002) and classical music rehearsals (Weeks, 1996).

Ethnomethodology does not keep any sort of 'official manual' with instructions for research procedures, but has developed different 'local research cultures' using a variety of methodological devices. Their aim is often to shake up the taken-for-grantedness of the lifeworld – for example by questioning in practice social conventions – and in this way to spotlight the background expectations, the implicit rules. The following are some examples:

- *Zatocoding*. The ethnomethodologist writes down thoughts, references, quotations and the like on cards, as they occur. When a hundred cards are ready, the researcher provides them with an index in the shape of 'descriptors', and goes on to gather items for the next hundred cards, and the next. When several hundred cards have been indexed, the researcher begins to 'converse' with the cards, for instance by comparing all cases under a certain descriptor or different descriptors with one another. Boring though this procedure may sound, it nevertheless seems, just as in certain group-dynamic methods, to succeed in loosening up reality (Mehan and Wood, 1975) through its reflexive influence on the researcher.
- *Inverted lenses* are used to turn the visual field upside down, thus restoring the original image received by the optic nerve, before the brain has turned it the 'right' way up. In this way the observer can see reality with literally fresh eyes. Experiments with artificial arms and legs produce the same result on the motoric plane.
- *Incongruity experiments*. The experimenter behaves in a deviant mode in relation to some rule or expectation in a social context, in order to reveal the implicit rule

structure by an estrangement effect. For example, the experimenter starts treating customers as shop assistants, or guests in a restaurant as waiters, demands that his friends clarify their most everyday statements, or introduces new rules into a familiar game.

- *Unique adequacy of methods*, whereby the ethnomethodologist achieves competence in the domain studied by becoming a member of it.
- *Displaying the phenomenon* (*scenic display*) by clarification or confrontation of the theory with raw data, particularly in a concrete audiovisual form.

Conversation analysis

Conversation analysis (Atkinson and Heritage, 1984; Boden and Zimmerman, 1991; Sacks, 1992; Sacks et al., 1974) deserves special mention. It has been described as a 'neo-ethnomethodological' technique, and even for some ethnomethodologists as *the* current ethnomethodological technique (Bourdieu and Wacquant, 1992). According to Holstein and Gubrium (1994: 226), referring to Heritage (1984), conversation analysis has three basic prerequisites:

1 There are recurring structural features in ordinary conversation, irrespective of the psychological characteristics of the participants.
2 Conversation is context-bound, such that it 'is both productive of and reflects the circumstances of its production'.
3 '[T]hese two properties characterize all interactions, so that no detail can be dismissed as out of order, accidental or irrelevant to the ongoing interaction'.

Conversations are analysed by breaking them up into segments (in analogy with linguistics). It is then found that certain types of segment or 'slots' appear, irrespective of the content of the conversation. Telephone conversations which have been studied are thus normally introduced by the person receiving the call lifting the receiver and answering; greetings also generally occur, regardless of the subject of the subsequent conversation (Mehan and Wood, 1975). The result of this analysis may not perhaps seem too sensational.

In a similar example (Heath and Luff, 1993) a doctor is to make a diagnosis for a hernia patient; the situation is investigated with the help of a complicated and very detailed coding of the conversation that takes place. The doctor feels the patient's foot, and the latter says 'Agh'. The doctor makes no sympathetic comment, but simply goes on making the diagnosis. The fact that the patient says 'Agh' in a social interaction (not only in a private situation), and that the doctor goes on with the examination, are both presented as research findings. The external reader cannot help wondering whether it might have been possible to make these not particularly revolutionary observations without the intricate coding apparatus, and without claiming to be doing 'research'.

A more interesting example is provided by Greatbatch and Clark's (2005) book about management gurus and why they are successful. Using an ethnomethodological approach to study the gurus' ideas, the authors conclude, by way of conversation analysis, that it is their live presentation and performance rather than the content of the message or their written texts that bring the gurus their success.

A critique

We will conclude this exposition with a few critical remarks on the approach. Ethnomethodology seems to us to presuppose a transparent, rational, common-sense process, whereby the actors' lifeworlds are constantly being re-created, somewhat like a kind of sophisticated ant heap; the difference is that the messages are not mediated with the help of pheromones, but by words and gestures. The world consists of a number of semantically equal transcendental egos, communicating with one another without conflict, emotion or interruption. With Levinas (1989) we would claim that the differences between the participants are in reality very much greater than this. Thus, not only provocative ethnomethodologists stand for friction and conflict. We spoke above of 'deviating behaviour'; but this is hardly restricted to a well-defined, marginalized class of 'deviants'. On the contrary, conventions, etiquette, implicit rules are much more shifting, uncertain and flexible than the ethnomethodologists would have it. In human relations conventions are continually touching, overlapping and being misunderstood. Feelings, and emotional conflicts, obviously play an important role, which is largely suppressed by ethnomethodologists (Douglas and Johnson, 1977). If the meaning of social discourses is context-dependent, we could also ask, like Giddens (1976), how matters stand as regards Garfinkel's own (1967) theory, for example. Is it not, also, ambiguous, vague, fluid, uncertain and context-dependent? And what, then, does it actually say? Finally, as we have seen, ethnomethodology never asks the central question: which are the supraindividual structures – such as Bourdieu's social fields – that shape the actors' behavioural dispositions?

By adopting a short-sighted and detail-ridden focus on the actor level, the analyst risks becoming entangled in trivialities, as conversation analysis, for example, attests. The rigour of this procedure, combined with its far from amazing results, invites comparison with Horace's mountain that gave birth to a mouse. It is perhaps no coincidence that conversation analysis has even been described as 'enriched positivism' (Lynch and Bogen, 1994, quoted in Holstein and Gubrium, 1994); similarly, Atkinson (1988) criticizes conversation analysis for its narrow 'behaviourist and empiricist' approach. He argues that much contemporary ethnomethodology, especially but not exclusively conversation analysis, is characterized by empiricist and inductivist tenets, thus suppressing the seeds of a more hermeneutic and dialectic stance that he claims to have discerned in the early works of Garfinkel (for these two currents in ethnomethodology, cf. also Mehan and Wood, 1975). Parallels with grounded theory can also be noted. It should be pointed out, however, that conversation analysis in this version is not all-prevailing. Some writers in the last two decades have incorporated various more institutional, contextual and macro-related aspects (Drew and Heritage, 1993; Silverman, 1985, 1987).

Conversely, Garfinkel (1988) has advocated a less structured and more locally focused ethnomethodological orientation than conversation analysis. This has even led Maynard and Clayman (1991) to describe the former as 'ethnomethodology proper':

> a positive respecification of how investigators might approach sociology's most awesome phenomenon – the objective, immortal reality of social facts ... Sociologists can rigorously explicate that phenomenon as an accomplishment of actors' concerted work in making social facts observable and accountable to one another in their everyday lives.
>   This is, in a nutshell, the heart of the ethnomethodological enterprise.

However, Atkinson (1988) has described this and two other more recent and influential ethnomethodologists' texts in critical terms as follows:

> There are, therefore, self-imposed limitations that are extremely radical in their consequences. In the emphasis on description of work 'from within' and the absence of any sociological preoccupations, the analyst seems bound merely to recapitulate the observed sequences of activities with little or no framework for selection, or for the representation of those activities in any other discourse ... The radical stress on observable detail risks becoming an unprincipled, descriptive recapitulation devoid of significance. The stance advocated by Garfinkel, Lynch and Livingstone is reminiscent of the French *nouveau roman* of authors such as Alain Robbe-Grillet: minute descriptive detail is assembled in a hyper-realist profusion, until the reader loses any sense of meaning.

It would probably be possible to undertake a more positive evaluation of ethnomethodology than the above, from a postmodernist perspective. The criticism of 'grand theories' in orthodox social science, the emphasis on microprocesses and local life all point in this direction, as does the attempt to interpret phenomena as a self-referring ('reflexive') text in a continual creative process of coming into being. (For a similar assessment, cf. Holstein and Gubrium, 1994.) On the other hand ethnomethodology, despite its process aspect, lacks the local history anchorage that characterizes some postmodernism, at least in the humanities. More importantly, in the social sciences it also represents a markedly empirical field of research, while postmodernism is in many ways marked by philosophizing around topics such as subject, language and the authority of the researcher. Yet, again, a well-known writer with an ethnomethodological background like Bruno Latour – see, for instance, his *Aramis* (Latour, 1996) – is a good example of a happy melding between postmodernism and ethnomethodology, perhaps indicating that social constructionism may become something of a bridge between the two approaches.

Inductive ethnography

Grounded theory and ethnomethodology are naturally not the only examples of data-oriented qualitative methods. There are other established methodological currents, less closely bound by a systematic procedure and encouraging a somewhat freer approach.

One such current is ethnography. Fetterman (1989: 11) has defined ethnography broadly as 'the art and science of describing a group or culture'. There is an emphasis on 'the study of people in naturally occuring settings or "fields" by means of methods which capture their social meanings and ordinary activities, involving the researcher participating directly in the setting' (Brewer, 2000: 10). It typically implies fieldwork 'involving a sizeable amount of onsite observation' (Prasad, 1997: 102). But, more precisely, the term is used in several rather different ways. It is commonly associated with the branch of anthropological research based on fairly long periods of submersion in a local community. The idea is to show how social action in one world can be understood from the perspective of another culture (Agar, 1986: 12). But also briefer periods of exposure to the empirical material are currently sometimes denoted as ethnography (Atkinson and Hammersley, 1994). Silverman (1985) goes far in this direction, describing ethnography as any research involving observations of events and actions in natural contexts, and which acknowledges the mutual dependence of theory and data. In this way he seeks to distance himself from the view that sees observation or participant observation as pure technique.

Yet, like many other authors we would like to reserve the term for an anthropologically oriented method based on close contact with the everyday life of the studied society or group over a fairly long period of time and addressing cultural issues such as shared meanings and symbols (Prasad, 1997; Wolcott, 1995). The crucial thing is 'to have been there' (Geertz, 1988). A year's submersion in the society to be studied is often suggested as the typical ethnographic procedure (Sanday, 1979). If the object of study is not an alien local community but some part of the researcher's own society (a village, an organization, a subculture), however, the time requirement is generally less, since the researcher will already have considerable knowledge of the general context in which the study object is located. Unlike grounded theory, ethnography does not represent a coherent and clearly prescribed methodology; rather, it indicates a general research orientation, which can then assume a variety of forms. Some ethnographers refer in positive terms to grounded theory and/or phenomenology, which suggests that there is a considerable overlap.

However, ethnographical studies generally imply the charting of quite extensive sections of local societies or groups. Cultural or conceptual phenomena such as ideas, ways of thinking, symbols or meanings are frequently emphasized. Sometimes more attention is paid to behavioural patterns and (other) material conditions.

It is possible to distinguish between different kinds of ethnographies in relation to the main themes we discuss in this book (Baszanger and Dodier, 1997). Inductive ethnography strongly emphasizes data – quantity, quality and so on – while interpretive ethnography, critical ethnography and postmodern ethnography put the emphasis on bold (or bolder) interpretations, on critical reflection and the problems of representation and narration. We will return to these in subsequent chapters. Here we concentrate on the inductive ethnography, which strongly focuses on method as the key to good research.

Ethnography assumes that the researcher should have an open mind vis-á-vis the object of study. Naturally some theory or frame of reference must direct the work, but the purpose of this is to give some direction and system to the task, rather than to get in the way of crucial observation and analysis. Research success also presupposes ample access to comprehensive and abundant data of different kinds, and competence at handling these. Furthermore, personal involvement, flexibility and the opportunity for close contact with the subject of interest are required:

> An open mind also allows the ethnographer to explore rich, untapped sources of data not mapped out in the research design. The ethnographic study allows multiple interpretations of reality and alternative interpretations of data throughout the study. The ethnographer is interested in understanding and describing a social and cultural scene from the emic, or insider's perspective. The ethnographer is both storyteller and scientist; the closer the reader of an ethnography comes to understanding the native's point of view, the better the story and the better the science. (Fetterman, 1989: 12)

On the methodological side, a broad set of techniques is often vigorously applied: observation in natural contexts, studies of artefacts (material expressing cultural and social conditions), and interviews of various kinds – for example, with key informants and/or about individual life histories. Other techniques, such as projective tests, polls or questionnaires, can also be used. The broad set of methods that characterizes ethnography has led some scholars, such as Fetterman (1989), to point out the possibilities of triangulation. The coupling of ethnography and triangulation is not a strict one, however, as other types of research too, apart from the ethnographical, build on the triangulation idea (e.g. Martin, 1990a). The idea of triangulation is that, with the help of different kinds of methods, it is possible to better determine a particular phenomenon. For instance, one can combine qualitative and quantitative methods. The intention is to home in on the phenomenon to be studied. Critics claim that in reality this rather becomes 'homing out' – that is, the results point in different directions (Potter and Wetherell, 1987). Different methods capture different kinds of aspects, making it difficult on the basis of their combination to reach a coherent result. Another view of the breadth of ethnographical methods sees this as an advantage, enabling a richer and more varied material to be acquired rather than a well-substantiated one.

Less codified than grounded theory, ethnography gives more scope to the researcher's person and allows for a more flexible stance in relation to the data. In most ethnographies the hermeneutic element is somewhat more prominent. However, proponents of inductive ethnography share with grounded theory the assumption that the data studied provide the key to the result, and that theory and interpretation are secondary, relative to the data. According to Fetterman (1989), for example, theory should be chosen on grounds of its appropriateness, its simplicity in use, and its explanatory power. The ideological basis of theories often blinds rather than guides researchers on their way through the tangled mass of data in the field: when the theory no longer guides the researcher, it is no longer useful; when data do not agree with the theory, it is time to look for a new theory (Fetterman, 1989: 18). However, as we have already noted, such a conviction that the researcher can freely choose a theory, and that the data can simply determine the usefulness of a theory, is naïve. Theory is not something simple and clearly defined which can be freely chosen; rather, it is paradigmatically determined. Without assumptions, concepts and theory, nothing at all emerges as meaningful, as 'data'. Suitability, explanatory power and the ability to guide the researcher cannot be determined atheoretically or aparadigmatically, by reference to data. Even if the ethnographers believe that a certain theory is guiding them or that it possesses explanatory power in relation to their data, this is no guarantee that the research is going well. Since data, particularly in ethnographical research, are almost always ambiguous and open to a variety of interpretations, several different theories may well appear suitable – and the theory which the researcher finds helpful and which has been verified may still not be the one which does most justice to the empirical material or promotes the most creative thinking and interesting insights.

The ethnographical method is demanding of both time and resources, and often involves a good deal of personal frustration. This is presumably why it is not often used in any of the social sciences except anthropology. In organizational theory, for example, the method is more talked about than used (Rosen, 1991), even though there are a growing number of ethnographies of organizations (Schwartzman, 1993). It is easier and more convenient to turn to regulated observations and, especially, interviews. Nonetheless, interest in ethnography seems to have been growing in recent years. It has considerable advantages as regards the wealth and depth of possible empirical materials. Particularly in light of all the problems and limitations associated with interviews – whose ability to reflect anything other than the norms for behaviour in interview situations has been questioned (Alvesson, 2003; Potter and Wetherell, 1987; Silverman, 2006) – the ethnographical method does seem to be underutilized.[28] (We will return to the problems associated with interviews in Chapters 6 and 7.)

However, as will have already appeared, inductive ethnography suffers too much from a fixation on data. In recent years anthropologists in particular have expressed doubt about the ability of the various ethnographies to capture 'object reality' with the help of reliable methods (Clifford and Marcus, 1986; Hammersley, 1990; and see also Chapter 6 below). Yet, ethnographical studies which take hermeneutics, politics and the problems of representation and arbitrariness more seriously do not suffer in the same way from data fixation or from the claim to be able to mirror reality. We will return to these questions in later chapters, particularly in Chapter 4, one section of which addresses Geertz's interpretive cultural analysis.

Summary

In this chapter we have discussed three qualitative methodologies, all of which work in close proximity with data; some would perhaps call them empiricist or even 'hyper-empiricist' (which is how Bourdieu and Wacquant, 1992, describe ethnomethodology). Grounded theory and ethnomethodology in particular represent the 'microsociological revolution' (Collins, 1985) as opposed to various previously dominating forms of functionalist social science on the supraindividual (or macro) level, and to the statistically oriented 'data-crunching' type of social research. Common to these three currents is that they profile themselves in opposition to the lofty – but unfortunately empirically empty or at least difficult-to-apply and unrealistic – 'grand theories' in the spirit of Parsons and others (cf. Mills, 1959). At the same time they emphasize the advantages of qualitative as against quantitative methods, but – particularly grounded theory and ethnomethodology – seek to imitate the technical approach, rigour and codification of quantitative methodology. The result of this focus on the micro level, the anti-theoreticism and the minute calibrating of the methodology, leads naturally to a data-oriented or, if one prefers it, (hyper)empiricist stance.

One of the historic gains of these movements is that they have so strongly emphasized the importance of qualitative methods in the face of the hegemony and putative superiority (often not even questioned) of quantitative, positivistic research. They polemicize with dash and flair against the emphasis on verification and authority, whereby theory merely becomes a question of scholastic application of time-honoured classics, instead of individual creativity without too many side glances at the venerable – but unfortunately often rather dusty – old masters. Down with puzzle-solving, normal research: to everyone the right to think for themselves!

On the other hand, the weaknesses in these currents are also considerable. (The following critique is somewhat less valid for inductive ethnography than for the other two.) The descriptive focus entails a considerable risk of ending up with a frog's perspective, while the restriction to the actors' own perspective can lead to a trivialization of the research results. These currents miss the main part of the interpretive problematic, so that the data appear as more or less unmediated and pure, and the research process is endowed with a naïve character of gathering and threshing empirical material according to some sort of agricultural metaphor.[29] The recognition that preunderstanding possesses a certain importance does not compensate for this decisive weakness. Moreover, the whole problematic of the sociology of knowledge is disregarded – the influence of political and ideological structures on scientific work. Last but not least, the authority of the researcher is never questioned, nor is the discourse's (relative) independence of both 'reality' and researching subject a matter of discussion: the ambiguities and traps built into the language and the text remain an unexplored minefield. To these extensive and perilous domains of research we now turn in our continuing journey through the methodological landscape.

Notes

1. This does not mean that Glaser and Strauss's contribution can be *equated* with symbolic interactionism. Glaser and Strauss supplement the parent movement with their own creative elements, and – as so often in similar cases – all is of course not even in the spirit of symbolic interactionism. But its influence has been undervalued in the reception of grounded theory and, one might add, also underrepresented in the authors' own texts. Annells (1996), while referring to symbolic interactionism as the 'traditional ... theoretical underpinnings' of grounded theory, also discusses its postpositivist philosophical context, and even some current postmodernist affiliations.
2. Glaser and Strauss's book was originally received somewhat coolly, but during the 1980s it met with more interest and appreciation (Ekerwald and Johansson, 1989).
3. Here Glaser and Strauss anticipate the strong emphasis on the context of discovery, rather than on the context of justification, of the later post-positivistic science theorists (Shapere and others). The same applies to the related view of research as *process*. See, for example, Suppe (1977).

4. In another sense Glaser and Strauss are Kuhn's exact opposite, since they call for a multiplicity of different theories, thus coming closer to the theoretical anarchism of Feyerabend (1975). Kuhn's 'normal research', on the other hand, implies that *one* theory at a time has or should have (the border between descriptive and normative is blurred in Kuhn's exposition) the monopoly in a whole branch of research at any particular moment; the exceptions are the 'scientific revolutions' which occur when one monopoly is replaced by another. Glaser and Strauss transfer the idea from the macro plane (the entire research area) to the micro plane (the individual research process).

5. However, the authors differ decisively from Toulmin in that they do not regard data or (consequently) their area of application and their domain as theory-dependent.

6. In a manner typical of their times, the authors almost always speak of the researcher as 'he'. Female researchers are conspicuous by their absence from the intellectual world of Glaser and Strauss and their contemporaries.

7. Two comparisons can illustrate this. Lorenz was the great name of his times in theoretical physics, yet he was surpassed by the outsider, Einstein, partly because Einstein had the-capacity to think more freely and was less bound by authorities. Lorenz had reached the equations on which Einstein based his general theory of relativity, but, unlike Einstein, he never managed, in the *interpretation* of them, to free himself from the established ether concept. The discoverers of the genetic code, Crick and Watson, both in their way outsiders, were publicly scorned by Loria, the great learned man in their field, who never came close to the discovery himself. Other factors, too, obviously played a part, but the phenomenon is not uncommon in the history of science. Bohr, for example, called himself a dilettante; Darwin was self-educated; Marx was, in terms of education, a philosopher, not an economist; Freud a physician, not a psychologist; Wittgenstein an engineer, not a philosopher.

8. Hanson uses the less common term 'retroduction' instead of 'abduction'.

9. It should perhaps be added that creativity is not the only criterion of good research.

10. Compare Hammersley's (1989: 176–177) criticism of Glaser and Strauss for being non-cumulative: every piece of research starts from scratch.

11. Marx (1967) successfully used the English factory inspectors' public reports as an empirical source material for his theory.

12. Here and in the following points a reader who has absorbed the fact that theory should be grounded in empirical data, begins to feel slightly confused. Glaser and Strauss, however, produce the following line of argument:

> *Generating a theory involves a process of research*. By contrast, the *source* of certain ideas, or even 'models', can come from sources other than the data. The biographies of scientists are replete with stories of occasional flashes of insight, of seminal ideas, garnered from sources outside the data. But the generation of theory from such insights must then be brought into relation to the data, or there is great danger that theory and empirical world will mismatch. (1967: 6)

Apart from the apparent contradiction in the quotation (generation of theory from data or not?), the essence of the argument is clear: data-external theory sources should be used only heuristically, and with great caution; the link with the empirical material is the alpha and omega, otherwise there may easily be a lack of fit between theory and the empirical material.

13. This methodological technique is taken from Blumer; see Hammersley (1989).

14. See the influential article by Manning (1982), where the author advocates the use of analytical induction in ethnography.

15. No other new diseases have been visible in the discussion on contaminated blood. Among older diseases, hepatitis B is a possibility, but this has not been anything like as dominating in the medical or public debate as AIDS.

16. For the exploration of such relations, on the other hand, the reader is referred to another methodology in symbolic interactionism, namely 'pattern models' (Williams, 1976).
17. This last point, however, is not decisive in the present context. There is no given relation between philosophy-of-science position and type of data. For example, a qualitative postivist school existed in French and German historiography in the nineteenth century.
18. Compare, for example, Guba and Lincoln (1994: 110), who see grounded theory as an example of a revised version of positivism.
19. The same idea can be found in Taylor (1985b: 118): 'interpretive social science requires that we master the agent's self-description in order to identify our *explananda* but it by no means requires that we couch our *explanantia* in the same language. On the contrary it generally demands that we go beyond it'. And later he states:

> The view that I am defending here, which I can call the interpretive view … has to be marked off from two other conceptions. One is the original enemy, the natural science model, which I have been arguing against all along. And the other is a false ally, the view that misconstrues interpretation as adopting the agent's point of view … the interpretive view, I want to argue, avoids the two equal and opposite mistakes: on the one hand, of ignoring self-descriptions altogether, and attempting to operate in some neutral 'scientific' language; on the other hand, of taking these descriptions with ultimate seriousness. (1985b: 123)

20. At least it lies beyond in so far as the authors take, for example, Weber's bureaucracy theory and Durkheim's suicide theory as examples of grounded theories. There is some latitude in Glaser and Strauss's view between greater and lesser distance from the data.
21. By 'formal theory' we simply mean theories which are generalized beyond the empirical base in a particular study.
22. See, for example, Jönsson and Lundin (1977), in an article on myth-waves; or the theory of planning cultures in Sköldberg (1992a, 2000a), which was generated in the field of tension between a grounded and a more constructionistic method; or Voyer et al. (1996) on systemic-level organizational anxiety.
23. This is a further development of the 'coding paradigm' in Strauss (1987), which we discussed above.
24. The famous *Lebenswelt* of the phenomenologists was very important both to Heidegger's hermeneutics and to Habermas's critical theory. Bengtsson (1989) wants to distinguish between the lifeworld and the everyday world, but admits that this is not usual among the phenomenologists themselves.
25. The terminological usage varies as regards these reductions. Regardless of the terminology, the most important conceptual difference is that between the levels or phases in the reduction, which are here referred to as the phenomenological, eidetic and transcendental.
26. The same view is in fact shared by an influential current within modern natural science, the Copenhagen school in particle physics (Bohr, Heisenberg). It is a corner-stone of this approach that the object of study in an experimental situation is always affected by the researcher.
27. Unless otherwise stated, in the paragraphs below regarding the central concepts, fields and methods, we follow Flynn's (1991) socio-semantic analysis.
28. Some solutions to this problem are discussed in Chapter 4, in the section on source criticism. Conversely, the ability of participant observation to reflect anything other than the norms for behaviour in participant observation situations can, of course, be questioned as well.
29. This view is in fact expressed quite explicitly by Glaser (1992: 24): 'all data of whatever kind is grist for the mill of constant comparison to develop categories and their properties'.

4

HERMENEUTICS: INTERPRETATION
AND INSIGHT

Hermeneutics has sometimes been seen as the thinking par preference of our time (Kristensson Uggla, 2002, 2004; Vattimo, 1997), a thinking where the plurality of interpretations and understanding may collide and bring inspiration (Ricoeur, 1974). As we have seen, this book is characterized by, among other things, its span between empirically oriented and interpretive lines of thought. The present chapter takes up its position between the discussion of more empiricist approaches (Chapter 3)[1] and the more theoretical criticism of ideologies (Chapter 5). The span of the chapter parallels that of the book as a whole, albeit with less distance between the extremes and with its particular thematics. This applies, more especially, to the two main approaches in the area, namely objectivist and alethic hermeneutics, which, as we shall see, have followed rather a polemical line vis-á-vis each other and have often adopted diametrically opposite standpoints. (For another division, see Delanty, 2005.)

Yet of course there are not only differences between the approaches to be treated in this chapter; they also have traits in common. Chief among these is their emphasis on the importance of *intuition*. Knowledge is not to be acquired in the usual, reasoning and rational ('discursive') way. There is instead something of a privileged royal road to true knowledge of the world. This is achieved, not by laborious pondering, but rather at a stroke, whereby patterns in complex wholes are illuminated by a kind of mental flashlight, giving an immediate and complete overview. Knowledge is then often experienced as self-evident. Intuition implies a kind of inner 'gazing', separate from the more formal and non-perceptual kind of knowledge. In what follows, we shall discuss two types of intuition.

The first is the traditional *Verstehen* philosophy, with its emphasis on the re-enactment (*Einfühlung*) of the meanings that the originators of texts and acts – authors and agents – associate with these. This occurs above all in what we have termed the objectivist hermeneutics. It results in the *understanding of underlying meaning*, not the *explanation of causal connections*.

The second is alethic hermeneutics, with its focus on truth as an act of disclosure, in which the polarity between subject and object – as well as that mentioned above between understanding and explanation – is dissolved in the radical light of a more original unity (Heidegger, 1962: 44; for a discussion of the application of Heideggerian ideas to social science, with a focus on organization theory, see Sköldberg, 1998).

Roots[2]

Hermeneutics has its roots in the Renaissance in two parallel and partly interacting currents of thought – the Protestant analysis of the Bible and the humanist study of the ancient classics. The interpretation of texts – exegesis – is thus the point of departure. From the very beginning a main theme in hermeneutics has been that *the meaning of a part can only be understood if it is related to the whole.* Thus, a biblical text can only be understood if it is related to the whole Bible. Conversely, the whole consists of parts, hence it can only be understood on the basis of these. We are therefore confronted with a circle, the so-called *hermeneutic circle*: the part can only be understood from the whole, and the whole only from the parts (see Figure 4.1).

Whole

Part

Figure 4.1   *The hermeneutic circle: original version*

Hermeneutics solves this apparently unsolvable contradiction by transforming the circle into a spiral (Radnitzky, 1970: 23); you begin, for example, in some part, try tentatively to relate it to the whole, upon which new light is shed, and from here you return to the part studied, and so on. In other words, you start at one point and then delve further and further into the matter by alternating between part and whole, which brings a progressively deeper understanding of both.

This is the circle of objectivist hermeneutics. As we shall see, alethic hermeneutics advocates another circle, one between preunderstanding and understanding. Ricoeur (1981) introduced a 'hermeneutic arc' between explanation and understanding, constituting an oscillation between scientistic and humanist methods in the social science process, the former mainly structuralist in kind and the latter mainly hermeneutic (in particular alethic). In this way an element of scientific *theory* is inserted over and above the humanist interpretation. The importance of Ricoeur's melding of humanist and scientistic methods has been particularly emphasized by Kristensson Uggla (2004). Otherwise, hermeneutics, with its tradition of understanding, stands rather aloof from explanation-oriented, scientific theorizing. Heidegger (1982), for instance, held that by questioning texts he was engaged in disclosure, not theorizing. Vattimo (1997) even wants to return to religion and theology. The common trait of the hermeneutic circles (and more than two are conceivable) is that they present a processual, dialectic solution, alternating between the poles in a contradiction which at first sight, and regarded statically, seems unsolvable. Or to put it another way, they solve research situations of the 'Catch 22' kind by successive acrobatic jumps between the horns of the dilemma.

What was regarded as 'part' and 'whole' became much extended as hermeneutics developed. The 'part' was initially a passage from the Bible or from a book by some classical Greek or Roman author. Later, the domain in which the hermeneutic method applied expanded to include written texts generally, and finally in the 'universal hermeneutics' of Schleiermacher even to the spoken word. Ultimately, through the historical German school of the nineteenth century (Ranke, Droysen), interpretation was also extended from *linguistic* expression to (historical) *acts* in general.

The 'whole' was also subjected to a series of successive generalizations. Interest increasingly turned away from the Bible or some work from classical antiquity towards the *author* behind the work: if it is necessary to place a text in its context, in order to understand it, then the context should naturally also include the author of the work. Yet authors cannot be seen in isolation, either; they need to be placed in their social context – which can be further broadened to their whole historical background. In the final analysis, the entire world history becomes the whole to which it is necessary to refer in order to understand a single part.

Thus, from seeking to understand single textual passages from the whole of the Bible (and vice versa), the domain of hermeneutics has been successively widened to include the understanding of acts whose ultimate context is the whole of world history.

The interpretation of understanding has also become increasingly linked to *empathy*: understanding calls for living (thinking, feeling) oneself into the situation of the acting (writing, speaking) person. With the help of imagination one tries to put oneself in the agent's (author's, speaker's) place, in order to understand the meaning of the act (the written or spoken word) more clearly. The idea is that in the last instance the mind of one individual – especially its more creative, non-rule-bound aspects – is not accessible to the reason of another individual, trying to analyse it from the outside; only intuition can fully assimilate the mental universe of another human being. In so far as this empathy is complemented by the interpreter's broader or at least different stock of knowledge, it is even possible – and this constitutes one of the main theses of hermeneutics – for interpreters to understand agents better than the agents understand themselves.

By making a sharp distinction between the 'moral' and the 'natural' spheres – in our terms, liberal arts and social science on the one hand and natural science on the other – the eighteenth-century German philosopher Immanuel Kant came to influence the development of this problematic. Kant also analysed the role of intuition and held that this to some extent actively constructs our 'real' world, forming the raw material of perceptions. Intuition of the subject's mental process was indentified as self-consciousness. Even earlier the Italian philosopher of history, Giambattista Vico, had promoted the thesis of a radical disparity between historical and natural processes. Vico held that only the world constructed by humans, including society, was genuinely possible to 'understand'. Natural events must remain forever outside the possibilities of man's ability to understand *from the inside*, since they are not human creations; they can, however, be an object of certainty in 'mathematical' form (Caponigri, 1963: 459, 1971: 27; Gadamer, 1989a: 19–23; Hughes, 1961: 198, 428).

Vico emphasized above all the creative power of human beings – their 'poetic mentality'. This note was also struck by German Romanticism in the early nineteenth century, which brought a reaction against the rationalism of the Enlightenment by invoking the creative potency of the human spirit, rather than reason. These lines of thought were strengthened during the same century even more by the German 'life philosophers', Schopenhauer and Nietzsche. Here, 'life' comes to the forefront as a mystical 'creative power under the aspect of will', which cannot be *explained*, but only *understood* by inner intuition. Life, not thinking, becomes the central issue for philosophers who gaze yearningly from their ivory towers filled with dusty spiderweb-thin abstraction, at the burgeoning, fertile landscape outside. In the same vein the new natural science is regarded as too abstract and remote from life (Caponigri, 1971: 11ff.; Gadamer, 1989a: 231ff.).

The concept of 'experience' (*Erlebnis*) began to be used in the 1870s, eventually gaining the position of (irreducible) basic element for a whole generation of continental philosophers: experience is fundamental, always already given, something with which every exploration of reality or mental processes must *start*. 'Experience' differs from the 'perceptions' of British empiricists in two ways. First, it does not constitute a passive reception of something outside the subject; instead it is active, creating and provided with intention and meaning. Secondly, experience is more 'global' than a single perception: it covers an overall subjective situation, not an isolated fragment thereof, and it is also connected with the whole life of the individual, making up an organic part of this (Gadamer, 1989a: 60–70).

Around the turn of the nineteenth century and well into the twentieth, all these lines of thought – Kantian intuition including self-consciousness, the separation between nature and culture, life philosophy, and hermeneutics – converged into three successively emerging approaches, all of which took a pronounced stance against positivism: objectivist hermeneutics, phenomenology and alethic hermeneutics.[3] All three are still topical and relevant.

Objectivist hermeneutics

The wave of neoidealism[4] in Germany at the end of the nineteenth century and the beginning of the twentieth produced a whole galaxy of still very well-known authors – Dilthey, Windelband, Rickert, Simmel, Weber – active in fields of study such as philosophy, history, jurisprudence and sociology (Hughes, 1961). Dilthey, the influential philosopher of history, who belonged to an earlier generation than the others but was active into the twentieth century, is perhaps best characterized as a 'life philosopher' in the sense given above; the others, who raised the slogan 'back to Kant', are often classified as 'neo-Kantians' (see Spiegelberg, 1982: 109).

All neoidealists turned against the positivism of their time, and its methods (Hughes, 1961).[5] Positivism was to be confined to natural science. In general, a sharp boundary was drawn between natural and cultural science. 'Understanding' became the shibboleth of the latter: through a 'congenially intuitive', empathetic re-enactment (*Einfühlung*) of a past experience, the researcher would achieve an understanding of individuals in times gone by and of the meaning with which they imbued their behaviour.

Natural science should explain with causes, cultural science (the liberal arts and social sciences) should understand meanings: a dichotomy which has remained strongly influential (see, for example, Hollis, 1994;[6] Radnitzky, 1970; Roth, 1991; von Wright, 1971; for sharp critiques, see, besides Heidegger below, from different points of departure Fuchs, 2001 and Ricoeur, 2006). Besides this, in particular Dilthey (Gadamer, 1989a: 233–234) and Weber (1967: 97) emphasize the comparative method as a means of gaining the 'truth of a wider generality' than by intuitive understanding alone. The ambition for these authors was to put cultural science on an equal footing with natural science, through the development of hermeneuticians. Yet by accepting in this way natural science as the opposite pole, part of its problematic is also retained, especially the subject–object relationship. According to the objectivist hermeneuticians, there was a sharp dividing-line between a studying subject and a studied object (something the alethic hermeneutians strongly contested, as we shall see). To put it another way, they held that there is a certain objectivity in research – at least in *relative* terms (see under 'Canon 3' in the section on Betti's hermeneutic canons below).

Alethic hermeneutics

The hermeneutics discussed in the previous section is in the last analysis based on a polarity between a subject and an object. To this is tied a notion of correspondence, that is, ideally there ought to be a correspondence between the conceptions of an interpreting subject – the researcher – and an interpretation of something objective, occurring outside the researcher. This correspondence is the ultimate thrust of objectivist hermeneutic understanding, which thus becomes a kind of counterpart to the 'explanation' of natural science. The hermeneutics we shall discuss in the present section breaks radically with the subject–object problematic as well as with the twin concepts of understanding/explanation. To begin with, in this variety of hermeneutics understanding is nothing exceptional, achieved as the culmination of a scientific effort. Rather, understanding is a basic way of existing for every human being, since we must continually keep orienting ourselves in our situation simply in order to stay alive. It is this basic understanding that it is necessary to begin to explore; the understanding/explanation of cultural and natural science are at most its secondary derivatives.

Fuchs and Wingens (1986), for instance, emphasize this Heideggerian theme strongly, linking it with the problematic of contemporary philosophy of science, by regarding Kuhn's paradigms as hermeneutic 'forms of life' within natural science. (For the similarities between hermeneutics and Kuhnianism, see also Bernstein, 1983, and Caputo, 1987.) Rather than the study of an objective reality by a researcher/subject, natural science then becomes a collection of ways to live their understanding for a community of researchers. Researchers – be they natural or cultural scientists – are always members of a particular, historically and culturally conditioned, ever-changing 'lifeworld', and their practices are always already laden with theory and temporality (Heelan, 1997).

This also dissolves the boundary between natural and cultural science, since understanding as a form of life becomes basic to them both, rather than some more superficial aspects such as a correspondence to reality in the former and empathy in the latter. In line with his radically pragmatic view of science, Rorty (1991), too, supports such a dissolution of boundaries. Taylor (1991), on the other hand, while agreeing with the pragmatic picture, wants to retain dualism, since he holds that, unlike natural science, cultural science is directed towards self-understanding. Rorty's view, however, is that not even self-understanding is exempt from context and theory dependence (see Guignon, 1991, for an account of the Rorty–Taylor debate). Some alethic hermeneuticians thus underline the similarity, and others the differences, between natural and cultural sciences. It is possible that the differences in opinion are exaggerated in the heat of the conflict; in any case, all participants seem to agree that the natural and cultural sciences are both irrevocably marked by interpretations all the way down to the level of data, and by preconceptions in the generation of theory (on this compare especially Heelan, 1997). Thus we get a second hermeneutic circle: that between preunderstanding and understanding (see Figure 4.2).

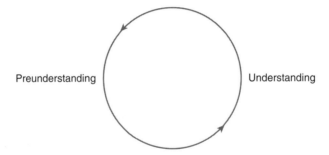

Figure 4.2   *The circle of alethic hermeneutics*

Alethic hermeneutics dissolves the polarity between subject and object into a more primordial, original situation of understanding, characterized instead by a disclosive structure. That is, the basic idea concerns the *revelation of something hidden*, rather than the correspondence between subjective thinking and objective reality. We shall explain this idea in greater detail later in the present chapter. Here a terminological observation can suffice. We have chosen to designate this hermeneutics *alethic*, with a neologism derived from the Greek *aletheia*, or uncoveredness – the revelation of something hidden (Heidegger, 1959: 102). This concept – alethic hermeneutics – embraces three sub-fields with different centres of gravity but without sharp borderlines between them: the existential hermeneutics presented by Heidegger in the book *Being and Time*, and by his pupil, Gadamer; the poetic hermeneutics in which the later Heidegger took an interest, which was developed in his wake by Ricoeur and others; and the hermeneutics of suspicion, represented in particular by Marx, Freud and Nietzsche.[7] All these transcend the subject–object problematic and all are in some sense preoccupied with the uncovering of something hidden. For the existential hermeneutics this hidden something constitutes an original structure of properties buried at the root of our existence, but for this very reason also forgotten. For the poetic hermeneutics, it forms an underlying pattern of metaphor or narrative. For the hermeneutics of suspicion, finally, it is something shameful – for instance in the form of economic interests, sexuality, or power – and therefore repressed.

Hermeneutical interpretation – a reconstruction

In this section, we shall present a reconstruction of the hermeneutic process, which combines the two seemingly conflicting mainstream approaches. For there are in fact overarching features belonging to both. Thus they are not quite as incompatible as might sometimes appear from their mutual polemics. Various standpoints adopted by adherents of the two schools tend to confirm this. For instance, Hirsch (1967), a proponent of the objectivist school, distinguishes between the author's original *meaning* with the text and the *significance* of the text (for us); the former is reconstructive, objectivist, the latter is currently relevant, alethic. Hirsch prefers a focus on the former but by no means excludes the latter. In a similar vein Skinner (1986d) holds that a focus on the intentions of the author is necessary for interpretation, but does not rule out further attributions of significance. According to Palmer (1969), an advocate of the alethic approach, the two hermeneutic approaches, which we have termed objectivist and alethic here, should be regarded as complementary rather than absolute opposites. Palmer prefers a focus on alethic hermeneutics but by no means rejects the objectivist approach, even though he seems to view the latter as more boring. It ought thus to be possible to combine the perspectives. This also applies to the relationship between the two hermeneutic circles 'part–whole' and 'preunderstanding–understanding', which we regard as complementary rather than opposed to each other.

Rules for interpretation are rejected by both the objectivist and the alethic school. Efforts to establish general rules have always faltered because the exceptions have proven to be more prominent, when it comes to their application to specific areas and cases. In the objectivist school, Hirsch (1967), referring to probability theory, has set up *ex ante* criteria for the validation of interpretations – albeit with the reservation that they hold true only for the original meaning of the text, as intended by the author, not its significance for the reader. For meaning is stable, in contrast to significance, which changes with, for example, the cultural or historical context. Thus, an interpretation of a text as regards the author's intended meaning is corroborated, according to Hirsch: (1) by checking it against other texts by the same author; (2) by checking it against other texts from the same culture or epoch, whereby the frequency of corroborating texts increases the validity of the interpretation at hand; and (3) by giving more weight to texts that are closer to the author in various property dimensions (in the extreme case the author's own texts) than to more remote texts (texts closer to the author can even overthrow very large sets of supporting instances from more remote texts). For decisions between interpretations where matters nevertheless hang in the balance, Hirsch recommends getting further information from the overarching generic level (to which genre does the text belong?), and from the micro level, where further (isolated) parts of the text in question can be subjected to renewed investigation in order to ascertain which interpretation would explain them best. In the event of a conflict between generic and micro level, the micro level is given precedence. Of course, cases can still occur in which the interpretations carry similar weight; then the interpreter should openly report and admit this fact. We shall return to Hirsch's proposal later, with certain essential modifications.

The alethic school, on the other hand, represented for example by Palmer (1969), rejects the distinction between meaning and significance, hence also criteria of the above type. Moreover, for existential hermeneutics the issue of validation is associated with a scientistic subject–object problematic, which this approach has left behind for a focus on how the actual situation of understanding works.[8] It is only natural that this focus should render the very process of understanding more important than its result. Or to put it even more strongly, the process becomes, as it were, its own result. Thirdly (the time-bound, for each individual specific) preunderstanding will always come into the picture – for instance, in the shape of problem direction or selection – before any set of criteria, and will leave its imprint on them: thus any such general objective set is impossible to establish. Alluding to Wittgenstein, we might say: try to draw a boundary line, and there is always the risk that somebody will trespass.

It is, however, possible to formulate a number of less stringent characteristics of the hermeneutic method, without thereby abandoning some form of systematization. For example, Madison (1988) advocates a view of the hermeneutic method as *casuistry*, in which judgement, practical (rather than theoretical) reason and argumentation become central elements. The argumentation leads not to some absolute truth in the sense of a correspondence between theory and reality, but to intersubjectivity – albeit provisory and 'discretional', never definitive or 'coercive'. Or, to quote Madison (1988: 71): 'Rationality has no other foundation than the uncertain communication among people whereby they succeed in working out mutual agreements'.

From this point of departure, Madison (1988: 29–30) tenders the following 'methodological principles'.

(a) *Coherence* – the interpretation should be logically consistent.
(b) *Comprehensiveness* – regard for the whole of the work.
(c) *Penetration* – the underlying, central problematic should be laid bare.[9]
(d) *Thoroughness* – all the questions raised by the text should be answered.
(e) *Appropriateness* – the questions should be raised by the text, not by the interpreter.
(f) *Contextuality* – the text should be set into its historical-cultural context.
(g) *Agreement (1)* – the interpretation should agree with what the author really says, without distortions.
(h) *Agreement (2)* – the interpretation should agree with established interpretations of the text.
(i) *Suggestiveness* – the interpretation should be 'fertile' and stimulate the imagination.
(j) *Potential* – the application of the interpretation can be further extended.

From an extra-hermeneutic perspective, it would be possible to impugn almost every item on this list (including, and in particular (a); we shall return to this below). Here we shall limit ourselves to some intra-hermeneutic observations. Points (b), (c) and (d) are actually the same principle, and concern the regard for the whole of the work. Point (e) appears to be in conflict with main alethic principles, since it would separate the interpreter from the situation of understanding and the text. Similarly point (g) appears to be in conflict with the basic ideas of alethic hermeneutics (to which Madison adheres). Madison also admits that it can sometimes be fruitful to let go of this principle. Point (h) seems excessively conservative, and is, moreover, opposed to (i) and (j). These last two can be fused into one, namely fertility in research; they are not specific to hermeneutics. Furthermore, we do not see any absolute or unsolvable contradiction between the Hirsch 'criteria' for an objective hermeneutics, which Madison fiercely criticizes, and Madison's own 'criteria' for an alethic hermeneutics – except just the basic stance, where we concur with Madison's (and earlier Toulmin's) ideas of a logic of argumentation rather than a logic of rational prescriptions.

In line with this, a hermeneutic interpretation can be said to alternate between certain aspects, each of which contains types of *arguments* for or against the interpretation. Central hermeneutic features are, on the one hand, the dialectics between interpretation as part and whole, and, on the other hand, the particular outlook of the interpreter (neither dominance nor prostration) as well as the special character of the matter interpreted. The aspects consist – in a somewhat different order – of the totality of the interpretation, what is interpreted, how one relates to the interpretation, and microprocesses within the interpretation. In what follows, we shall designate these four aspects – *pattern of interpretation, text, dialogue* and *sub-interpretation*. These aspects are of course not separated by watertight bulkheads; their mutual borderlines are to a certain extent blurred. The differences are relative, not absolute (in the same way as the traditional difference between theory and empirical data); thus the aspects indicate various emphases within the hermeneutic process rather than separate compartments of it.

Pattern of interpretation

This refers to the overarching set of interpretations of a certain text, that is, the coherent whole of partial interpretations. The pattern of interpretation corresponds loosely to the 'theory' of various extra-hermeneutic discourses. The pattern of interpretation should be internally consistent (cf. the internal control in Ödman, 1979, and the 'coherence' in Madison, 1988), since logical contradictions are strong counterarguments. The pattern of interpretation should also be externally consistent, in the sense that it either agrees with the other extant patterns of interpretation in the same area (Madison's 'agreement (2)'), or contains reasons for *not* agreeing with them. The pattern of interpretation should make individual details of the text understandable, while at the same time growing from them. The pattern of interpretation should also include 'facts' from the interpreted material, and above all should not be contradicted by them.[10] (Ödman's 'outer control', Madison's 'agreement (1)'). The pattern is elaborated in a dialogue with the text, starting from the interpreter's preconceptions, which will be transformed during the process. The pattern should yield a deeper understanding of the text, beyond what is immediately bestowed by reading (cf. Madison's 'penetration'). Since interpreters critically reflect upon their preconceptions, while also intending to let these be transformed, the pattern of interpretation is elevated above the common-sense level (in contrast to more empirically oriented methods such as those discussed in Chapter 3).

Text

What is interpreted is not 'facts' or 'data', but *text*. The text can be literal, consisting of written or spoken words. It can also be figurative, in that social acts are regarded as meaningful symbols, taking the text as model (see, for example Ricoeur, 1981). Facts emerge from the text via a process of interpretation. They are *results*, not points of departure. Thus, we see parts of the text *as* something, or more precisely as – in some sense – meaningful signs, whether we are reading a text written in letters of the alphabet or in social acts. These particulars are endowed with a deeper and richer meaning in light of the overarching pattern of interpretation. They in turn influence the pattern of interpretation, enriching and modifying it during the hermeneutic process. What are conceived as facts, as well as the selection of facts, are both affected by the whole research-sociological situation. The interpreter must become aware of this and be prepared to transform his or her frames of reference during the process: new 'facts' will thereby emerge and old ones disappear.

One important way in which this occurs is by placing the text itself in its *con*-text, its external socio-historical weave of connections (Phillips and Brown, 1993; Skinner, 1986b), corresponding to Madison's (1988: 30) principle of 'contextuality': 'An author's work must not be read out of context, i.e. without due regard to its historical and cultural context'. For example, in their hermeneutic study of letters from CEOs in the American oil industry to shareholders, Prasad and Mir (2002) insert the letters in their socio-political and historical context, and show how they can be interpreted and understood in this way.

This importance of contextualizing also holds true for 'authors' works' in the transferred sense of social actions. That is to say, just as we can relate single parts of a text to the text as a whole, we can also shift the perspective and regard the text itself as a part, seeing it in relation to its whole overarching context. The 'text' we are studying may be hooliganism at soccer matches, for example: single acts of violence are then parts, viewed in light of this text. But hooliganism should in turn be related to the prevalent socioeconomic conditions such as social segregation, poor cultural background, drinking habits, and so on. The context, however, is not absolute and immutable. On the contrary, originality in research can often be achieved by placing things in an entirely *new context*: see Rorty (1991) on the central role of such 'recontextualization'. Ideas for recontextualizations may come from familiarity or links with completely different fields of knowledge, and/or as a result of conscious 'forgetfulness' of earlier contextualizations.

Dialogue

In relation to the text, hermeneuticians neither take a *monologic* stance similar to that of positivism, nor do they proceed via a passive reception of the text as in grounded theory. Instead they use the procedure of asking questions to the text, and listening to it, in a dialogic form (Caputo, 1987). The questions originally emanate from preunderstandings, and will be developed or transformed during the process. A humble yet at the same time active attitude is thus recommended. The autonomy of the subject matter under interpretation must be respected, at the same time as we must 'enter' it. A dialectic between distance and familiarity provides the best attitude. Gustavsson and Bergström (2004) systematically used such a dialectic in their study of protests from neighbours against the building of a home for mentally disabled people. The authors' preunderstanding of protests and their knowledge of theories about this interacted with their encounters with the protests in this partic- ular case. In other words, we glide back and forth between the 'old' aspect imposed on the text in the shape of preunderstandings, and the new understanding. Eventually the borderline becomes less sharp than that to Alice's looking-glass world or in Wittgenstein's puzzle pictures, and the different aspects start to slide into each other. Questions directed at the whole also alternate with questions directed at the parts, and the two kinds can cross-fertilize each other. In this way the research problem will transform during the process, while at the same time the transformation will influence 'facts' as well as patterns of interpretation.

But there is also another facet to the dialogic approach. During the process of interpretation we enter into an imagined dialogue with the *reader* of our interpre- tation. That is, the process is not merely private, a simple relationship between an isolated researcher-subject and the object/facts studied, in which the Truth is estab- lished with logical necessity and by empirical 'testing' (verification/falsification): on this question, see Taylor (1991). What is important instead is to discuss arguments and counter-arguments and to reach the most plausible result, starting from current knowledge (always historically conditioned and provisory), in which theoretical, methodological and factual aspects interact. As Madison (1988) points out, instead of a *logic of validation*, we get a *logic of argumentation*.

It is also central to the dialogue that it is conducted within a specific *genre*. The genre – not, for example the word or the meaning – is the primary element in the communication in the sense of what comes first, according to Kent (1991), who develops Bakhtin's theory on this point. Genres are 'sets of reading expectations held by communities of readers and writers at specific historical moments, and these expectations obviously change over time' (Kent, 1991: 300). The genre is not a for- mal matter – there will never be a 'taxonomy' of genres – but a matter of commu- nication; the making of genres is an ongoing, open creation. Thus we should reflexively make ourselves aware of the genre and sub-genre in which we write, or which we confront when we try to transcend it. The different sciences develop and continually re-create their genres for presentation, and no one can adopt any posi- tion apart from these; the only way to transcend a genre is to master it. Good exam- ples of genres are found in scientific journals, which often accept papers on condition that they 'fit' into the genre the journal has created; as a result very good papers are often rejected because they do not fit into a genre. As was noted above, this is not some kind of irrational invention, but can be seen as a device for communicating to the readers. The genres play a similar role in judging theses at universities, or in evaluating applications for research project funding or applications for academic posts. The attitude to the genres ought neither to be that of a pseudo-radical, utopian revolt against their tyranny nor that of an unreflecting absorption into them, but rather that of a striving for development and transcendence based on critical reflection and distance. Finally, it should be pointed out that the genres do not constitute 'paradigms' in any of the senses Kuhn (1970) has given the term; in contrast to paradigms, genres are intimately linked to the actual *production of a text*. They could also be described as collectively accepted modes of presentation (cf. Skinner, 1986c).

Sub-interpretation

In the course of the process of interpretation we continually formulate sub-interpretations. When deciding between these, we work with certain background conceptions. Hirsch (1967: 179) has described these well, although he limits the area of application to the author's intended meaning with a text. As we saw above, however, his thinking hinges upon 'objective' criteria of validation, the existence of which in any case remains very dubious. If instead we are satisfied with more modest deliberations of plausibility in interpretations, starting from possible arguments *pro et contra*, and not from any claim to final truth, it is nevertheless possible to transfer this line of thought even to the meaning of the text irrespective of the author's intention ('significance', in Hirsch's words), as well as to the analysis of practices, that is of sets of social action, taking the text as a model.

Suppose, for instance, that we are trying to ascertain whether or not a person X in a country A has committed an act of sexual harassment, on a particular occasion. It is a case of word against word, and there is no further relevant information to be had about what happened on the occasion in question. Our interpretation has reached an impasse. There are then two ways of proceeding. The first is to investigate the previous biography of X – are there indications of sexual harassment in similar situations? Are there indications of *similar* actions (for example other types of abuse)? How frequent are such indications? The other way is to turn to some type or group of individuals to which X could be said in some way to belong. Is sexual harassment acceptable in some sense in X's national affiliation; gender in this nation; educational level and category; occupation … ? How frequent is sexual harassment in this type or group of individuals?

The more we narrow down the relevant group, the closer we come to X as a social person, and the higher is the interpretive value of our exploration. On the other hand, the greater the number of individuals who belong to the group, and the more they share a certain behaviour, the higher again is the interpretive value. Narrowing down takes precedence: for if we can establish a solid biographical background of previous episodes of sexual harassment on X's part, then the balance tips in the direction of a similar interpretation in the present case too, even if sexual harassment is very uncommon in X's particular culture. In both cases – the narrow and the wider class – the plausibility of the interpretation increases with the frequency of instances. As we mentioned, this is in the absence of further information, and as a probable, not a necessary or certain conclusion; in the case discussed, X *may* of course be innocent, but the information available indicates that the opposite assumption is more likely.

Thus we obtain the three following criteria for the assessment of plausibility in interpretations (Hirsch, 1967: 179):

1 A narrower class has more weight than a wider one.
2 The plausibility of the interpretation increases with the relative frequency of instances.
3 The plausibility of the interpretation increases with the number of members in the class (this, however, is subordinate to 1).

Caution: it is important to remember that the aim here is not a legal verdict. Legally, the guilt of the defendant must be established beyond all reasonable doubt, in order to minimize the risk of punishing innocent people. Here, instead, it is a question of reaching the most likely interpretation, given the existing information. If living persons are involved, great care should obviously be taken to anonymize the case.

We should also remember that what is meant by 'sexual' and by 'harassment' is time- and culture-bound just like anything else. Consequently, what is regarded as sexual harassment can vary according to the sociocultural context, and this applies to presumptive victims as well as to the researcher/interpreter. In addition, it is dependent upon the subjective experience of the victim. Harassment is a question of unwelcome, repeated, coarse advances of a sexual nature, and what is experienced as such can of course vary even within a given culture or epoch from a core of cases which are judged the same by practically all potential or real victims, to a grey zone beyond this, where assessments differ from one individual to another. Furthermore, there is also the possibility that individuals may change their opinions over time, or even that they may be chronically ambivalent. However, these are hardly the kinds of issues that have been discussed in the various well known cases of sexual harassment; rather these tend to be less subtle questions such as whether the alleged perpetrator really has said certain things or behaved physically in a certain way – utterances and behaviours which are regarded by consensus as sexual harassment under prevailing circumstances. Even so, we should remain aware of the possibility of cases that are hard to decide or are even undecidable, depending on the drift of meaning over time, between and within individuals and cultures.

The same method with the three criteria for validating the plausibility of interpretations can of course be applied not only to external events, but also to individuals' attitudes, intentions, motives, etc. *Why* did Y act in such and such a way in situation S? Y has not revealed his or her motives on the particular occasion, but are there earlier indications? A similar occasion? How similar? How many instances are there? How about people in Y's family, circle of friends, ethnic group; how about colleagues, fellow party members, academic peers . . .? How frequent is the proposed motive among these? We can also proceed to unconscious layers of motives, trying in our sub-interpretations to find patterns in the way of acting, related either to the single individuals or to their social affiliations, that agree with the single case, even though the ground is assuredly more unstable now. Earlier psychological and cultural studies are of course valuable here.

During the whole process, these sub-interpretations must be related to the overarching pattern of interpretation, transforming as well as being transformed by it and by the questions we put to the text. The pattern of interpretation will naturally change if the sub-interpretations change. New facts are created through the sub-interpretations, and old ones disappear; the same holds for new and old questions.

*

This entire process of emerging patterns of interpretation, textual analysis, dialogue and sub-interpretations should be permeated by the (workings on their own of the) two even more basic hermeneutic circles: that between whole and part, and that between preunderstanding and understanding.[11] As mentioned, these are characteristic of the two main hermeneutic currents, but they are different rather than contradictory, so that they may well be joined in the same research process. Hereby, the interpretation of the whole text is successively developed by the interpretations of its parts, and conversely the views of the parts are illuminated by the view of the whole. On the other hand, a similar alternation between preunderstanding and understanding is also taking place during the interpretive process. The understanding of a new text demands a preunderstanding; yet at the same time, preunderstanding – if it is to be developed – demands an understanding of the new text. Understanding must continually refer back to an earlier preunderstanding and preunderstanding must be fertilized by the new understanding. In sum, there emerges a hermeneutic 'basic circle' as shown in Figure 4.3.

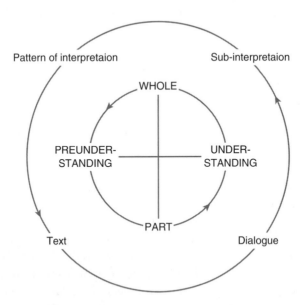

Figure 4.3   *The hermeneutic circle: basic version*

We have given in the foregoing some points to be considered with respect to interpretive plausibility. These provide supportive or critical arguments for or against an interpretation, arguments to which either the interpreter or external commentators/critics can refer during the process (the interpreter can, of course anticipate the critics). This obviously implies an openness to multiple interpretations. Even if, for example, the scales are tipped in favour of a certain interpretation, there is nothing to stop new arguments from appearing the very next day, radically altering the picture. A 'polyphonous' account of different interpretations, or at least of possibilities for interpretations, is, moreover, a form of honesty towards the reader; the researcher/interpreter does not adopt any false pose of ultimate authority vis-á-vis the circle of readers, but instead invites them into a dialogue about a number of alternatives, of which he or she prefers one (or several equivalent ones) on stated grounds. It should be emphasized once more that the above constitutes not a total or exhaustive set of a priori criteria, but a provisory systematization of certain extant arguments *pro et contra*. The list is thereby left open: further (types of) arguments can, and will certainly, emerge in the future, since all research engages in an ongoing process of re-creating its own methods (Feyerabend, 1987). What the considerations given here can do is, tentatively, to provide a basis for the future development of and inquiry into hermeneutics.

We shall now proceed to some of the more specific and developed variants of interpretation. A hermeneutic research process uses some of these under the general aspect of the 'basic circle' we have just presented. The variants can be combined fairly freely, for instance by alternating between them and letting them enrich one another.

Betti's hermeneutic canons

Betti (1967, 1980), the foremost modern exponent of the objectivist approach,[12] proposed four main criteria, or 'canons', which should guide hermeneutics. The first two refer to the object of the investigation, and the second two to its subject.

Canon 1. The hermeneutic autonomy of the object

That which is to be understood should be understood in terms of itself, of its own immanent standards and criteria, and more particularly of the original intentions behind it. This means, for instance, that a positivist study should be judged on positivist criteria and a grounded theory study on its own inherent criteria. Even if this is an appealing point of view, one could of course object that it leads to a lack of overarching criteria, and ultimately therefore to (a form of) relativism: every approach becomes a self-propelled unit, immune from critique and external impulses. As we shall see, however, canons 3 and 4 below establish a communication between researcher and researched, and consequently between their – potentially very different – research traditions.

Canon 2. The coherence of meaning (the principle of totality)

This is the principle of the harmonic whole. In each occurrence observed, a pervading wholeness of meaning is presupposed, which is reflected in each single part. Thus, canon 2 expresses the hermeneutic circle of part–whole, described above. What is whole and what is part is decided by the individual researchers, proceeding from their particular problematic. The part may, for example, be a word in a text, a clause, a sentence, a paragraph, or a section. The whole may be the text and in a wider sense the author behind the work, the historical background, and so on. The text constitutes the paradigm for the hermeneutic interpretation, providing the model even for the interpretation of *actions*, which in the interpretation can be read as a text, that is, a collection of meaning-laden signs, placed in their broader context.

Transferred to our field, social science, this means that hermeneutics has a double application. First, it is useful for the very extended sphere of research that consists in the interpretation of texts in the literal sense of the word: interviews, documents, notes from participant observation, as well as other researchers' theories, conceptualizations and so on – in short, the working field of *discourse*. Secondly, it can be used in the area of meaningful action, which has varying degrees of complexity, ranging from the actions of single individuals to group activities, and those of organizations, institutions, ethnic communities, nations and so on – in short, the working field of *practice*. These (complexes of) meaningful behaviour are studied *with the text as model*. Thus we read social action *as* text. And the relationship between the hermeneutic study of discourse and practice? The most complete picture will in all likelihood be provided if we combine these two ways of interpretation in a 'double hermeneutics' (Giddens, 1976), where practice stands for what is (more) immediate and discourse for what is mediated. Yet, whether it is a question of discourse or practice, we alternate between part and whole in the course of the interpretation.

Canon 3. The actuality of understanding

Understanding constitutes a creative, re-productive act, in which the researcher appropriates the meaning of the object, rather than mechanically mirroring it. The researchers carry around their own frames of reference, and inevitably make their interpretations in accordance with these. This is also the reason why interpretation always possesses only a *relative* autonomy, never an absolute one. Betti turned, for example, against the naïve conception of the older historical school, according to which historiography provides a direct parallel to the objectivity of natural science. There is, Betti maintained, in interpretation always an irreducible moment of reshaping, of subjective creativity with its point of departure in the researcher's already pre-existing frames of reference. The researcher is never a *tabula rasa*.

Hence, preunderstanding is important. On the other hand, according to Betti, *too* far-reaching an emphasis on preunderstanding and given frames of reference amounts to the disappearance of the object and its absorption by the subject, contrary to canon 1 above, which establishes the autonomy of the object. According to this canon, the proposal of the alethic hermeneuticians to substitute a preunderstanding–understanding circle for the hermeneutic part–whole circle cannot be accepted, for it transforms the dialogue between researcher and researched into a monologue – that of the subject itself. To this, the alethic hermeneuticians would probably reply that the difference between subject and object is an artificial distinction (polarization), and that real understanding is a more original phenomenon than either pole. In the view of these critics, understanding according to the subject–object problematic builds on all too theoretical and rational conceptions, rather than on practical or emotional ones. More on this below.

Canon 4. The hermeneutic correspondence of meaning (adequacy of meaning in understanding)

If the central role of preconception is thus rejected, and with it also the idea of an original fusion of subject and object, then the researcher has to establish a kind of 'resonance' with the object of the investigation, a 'congeniality' by which an invisible bond (of meaning) is forged between them. The interpreter submerges herself in the mental processes through which various forms of thought – even including those that have later been objectivized – originally came into being. In the literature on the subject, this re-enactment has been designated by other familiar terms, such as *Verstehen* and 'empathy'. By formulating ideal types and making comparative investigations, such congeniality can also be achieved at a supraindividual level, in relation to societal institutions and structures – social forms which possess a relative objectivity and autonomy.

Application: historiographic method (source criticism)

The Betti canons can be applied in many ways. One good example is provided by historiography, a competence of great, but unfortunately often neglected, usefulness in social science, particularly in case studies (Tsoukas, 1989). The main difference between historiography and social science case studies is that the latter are more linked to a theoretical interest. We cannot write about or research the now, since it has vanished in the stream of time as soon as we begin to reflect over it. The only thing we can write about is the past, since the future does not yet exist. But the past is no more, and what we have to deal with are just *traces* that we can interpret (Ricoeur, 2006). These traces are not 'facts' or 'data', but fragile, more or less uncertain, contradictory and 'polysemic'[13] bases for our process of interpretation, in which we can try to make provisory judgements of plausibility about happenings in the past. A common problem in the interpretation of qualitative material arises when there are contradictory statements, and when the statements appear uncertain for one reason or other, for instance because the interviewee is biased, because she is influenced by other people, because a long time has gone by since the reported event had occurred, and so on. The Japanese film *Rashomon* is a famous example of how radically different versions can be given of a course of events, so that in the end the uninitiated must call into question whether there is any underlying truth or meaning at all.[14] In order to solve such questions, historiography has elaborated a specific technique, which has been designated by various terms, and which we will refer to as *source criticism*: a hermeneutic (Betti, 1967; Ricoeur, 1988, 2006) but rigorous method, which sets up a number of criteria for the evaluation and interpretation of data.[15] Not only written text can be subjected to this; within historiography, the home of source criticism, an orientation towards oral history has emerged, something which also makes the method relevant for interviewing techniques (Thompson, 1978; Vansina, 1961).[16]

As Ödman (1979) points out, the borderline between 'historical hermeneutics' and the alethic hermeneutics which we will discuss later on is to some extent fluid. However, the source-critical aspect of historical hermeneutics can be largely assigned to the objectivist hermeneutics that we are discussing in the present main section. According to Helenius (1990: 188; our translation): 'The historiographic rules of source criticism are much the same as the interpretive rules of hermeneutics'. This is correct, to the extent that objectivist hermeneutics is what is referred to; as we shall see, the source criticism is intimately linked to the canons of objectivist hermeneutics.

What, then, does this method involve, more concretely? All source criticism is concerned with the question of *distortion of information*. Granted that the researcher observes reality not directly but through some kind of medium, there is a tripartite relationship reality–source–researcher. Obviously, much can happen on the route between reality and researcher. And it is this strategic highway that constitutes the area of interest for source criticism. First, however, a conceptual clarification: by 'source' we mean any entity that can provide the researcher with knowledge of a past event. The event has in some way or other left a trace and/or been reflected in the source – the medium – and the researchers acquaint themselves with this 'trace' or this reflection in order to gain answers to the questions about a time gone by.[17] What is a source, of course, also depends on the research problem. Anything that can be scrutinized by a researcher with the intention of finding information about the past becomes a source for this particular research. Or as Ricoeur expresses it (in the following quotation we change his term 'document' to 'source'):

> Nothing as such is a source even if every residue of the past is potentially a trace. For the historian, the source is not simply given, as the idea of a trace might suggest. It is sought for and found. ... For a historian, everything can become a source, including the debris coming from archeological excavations and other such vestiges but in a more striking way kinds of information as diverse and mercurial as price curves, parish registers, wills, databases of statistics, and so on. Having become a source in this way, everything can be interrogated by a historian with the idea of finding there some information of the past. (2006: 177–178)

The source critic is, at least to some degree, a knowledge realist, believing in the existence of an underlying reality, which is expressed, albeit in an incomplete, opaque way, in the sources.[18] This, incidentally, also holds for social constructionists, who speak about ongoing social constructions. Source critics would agree that their own interpretations are constructions. But source criticism is a hermeneutic way to achieve *better* interpretations (cf. Kristensson Uggla, 2004, on a '*striving* for truth'). 'Facts' are not just to be picked from the sources but must always be reconstructed by an often wearisome, precarious and, in the final result, always tentative process of interpretation. This reality does not itself need to be simple, unambiguous or non-contradictory; it may very well be complex, vague, or contradictory. This is important in our examples below, which generally stem from the first category above, both in order to simplify the presentation and to save space. Source critics of a time gone by sometimes thought they would reach the Truth with a capital T. A more modest and more recent attitude is, via the confrontation between interpretations recommended by Ricoeur (1974) for hermeneutics, to reach one (or more) interpretations that are *relatively* the best, given current knowledge. And all in a striving for knowledge (Kristensson Uggla, 2002, 2004).

It should also be kept in mind that source criticism is only a first and preliminary ingredient in historiography. A very broad investigation into the wider problematic of research is done by Ricoeur (2006), who divides the historiographic process into three 'phases': a documentary or documentary-testing phase, an explanation/understanding phase, and a presentation or writing phase. These phases are not separate in time, but necessarily overlap chronologically. No historian enters the archive without a project of explanation or understanding. 'And no one undertakes to explain a course of events without making use of some express literary form of a narrative, rhetorical, or imaginative character' (Ricoeur, 2006: 137). What we take up here is the first of these phases, the documentary test. As to the other two phases, Ricoeur strongly emphasizes both the importance of combining (traditional, scholarly) understanding with (a more scientistic) explanation, and that the narrative element in historiography does not mean that the latter can be reduced to literary fiction. To be sure, there are similarities, overlappings, between the two, but historiography differs from literary fiction in having its point of departure in a 'pact' between reader and author that the text concerns a real, albeit very hard to interpret, world, and its purpose is – even if merely provisorily, imperfectly and with narrative means – to try to reconstruct this world. The two phases of documentary testing and understanding/explanation are, furthermore, specific to historiography as compared to fiction literature.

Remnants and narrating sources

A preliminary classification of sources can now be made, from Betti's canon 1 on the judgement of the research object from the intentions behind it. From this we may draw a first distinction, namely between sources which offer unintended information, and those which provide intentional information (see, for instance, Le Goff, 1992). We will denominate these two types of source *remnants* and *narrating sources*. Thus, by 'remnant' is meant any source which cannot have been exposed to subjective distortion. In a narrating source, on the other hand, the information has passed through a subjective medium, and hence is always exposed to risks of distortion. A remnant is regarded (by the researcher) as a sign that something has happened. A narrating source says something about something that has happened. The remnant is regarded from its aspect of being the *effect* of an event; the narrating source from its aspect of *expressing* an event. In a source-critical evaluation, therefore, remnants are worth more (*ceteris paribus*, of course) than narrating sources.[19]

An illustration is provided by the problems surrounding the death of Raoul Wallenberg, the Swede famous for rescuing many Hungarian Jews from Nazism during the Second World War. In the last chaotic days of the war in 1945, Wallenberg was abducted by the Soviet military, after which he vanished without trace. Repeated enquiries and reminders from the Swedish government were without result until 1956, when Soviet authorities announced that he had died in 1947 in the Lubyanka prison. A death certificate signed by a certain Smoltsov, medical officer of the prison, was also produced, stating the cause of death as cardiac infarction. However, according to the testimony of several witnesses, Wallenberg had been seen in various camps after 1947, and the Swedish authorities therefore did not give strong credence to the Smoltsov certificate. The Swedish research team of Hans and Elsa Villius scrutinized the certificate source-critically in 1966, and came to the conclusion, mainly on linguistic grounds, that it was a true remnant. After the fall of the Soviet Union in the 1990s, Russian experts came to the same conclusion, based on an investigation of the handwriting, ink and type of paper.[20] The point is that neither of these two investigations said anything whatsoever about the content of the report – whether Wallenberg really died of a heart attack (which does not seem very likely, given that he was a young man) or was liquidated.[21] What the investigations do indicate is that Wallenberg really did die in 1947. Remnants are stronger evidence in terms of source criticism than narrating sources, and the certificate (even if its more specific content – the statement of a cardiac infarction – is mendacious) carries a heavier weight than later testimony.

From this it can easily be seen that the same source can be both a remnant and a narrating source, depending on the researcher's choice of aspect. The pyramids of Egypt, to take another example, are for most of us mute testimony to the building activities of the pharaohs, and hence remnants; for a pyramidologist, their construction expresses secret messages which have not yet been (entirely) decoded, and so in this perspective they are narrating sources. Or, to take an example closer to hand, (authentic) minutes constitute a remnant *of* a meeting, but also a narrating source *about* the same meeting. As a remnant they testify to the fact *that* a meeting has taken place; as a narrating source they tell us *how* it has taken place.

Authenticity

When the remnants have been sorted out from the narrating sources, the next source-critical evaluation consists in the control of *authenticity* – that is, whether or not the source *is* a source. We are still following Betti's first canon about the intention of the originator; now it is being applied to whether or not the individual concerned is sincere, in his or her purpose vis-á-vis the source. Forgeries are more common than we might think. An antedated document, for instance, is an inauthentic source as regards its given data. A more dramatic example is provided by 'Hitler's diaries', which were fabricated in East Germany and succeeded some years ago in duping even a world-class historian. The 'Piltdown Man' in palaeoanthropology, Burt's research on the psychology of twins (Broad and Wade, 1982), and the South Korean scientist who was recently disclosed to have falsified his results in stem cell research – all these are examples of very prominent researchers who have deceived or been deceived. The most fantastic example is surely the eighteenth-century scholar in Germany who kept finding more and more marvellous fossils; not even the small figures that began to appear engraved upon them made him suspect mischief – until one day he discovered a fossil bearing his own name. After this nasty prank by his colleagues he dedicated the rest of his life to buying back fossils that had been sold to various museums around the world. And if we turn to the really great names, it has been shown that according to the laws of probability neither Galileo's nor Mendel's experiments can have been conducted quite as they are presented. Maybe they were partly thought experiments, partly manipulated. The spectacular discovery of 'cold fusion' – a mega-event in the 1980s media – has largely been discredited since the results have not been possible to replicate by other researchers. As to the more thoroughly carried out but still controversial experiments with 'sonofusion' at the beginning of the twenty-first century, the final judgement is still open, since a replication of the experiment has proven varyingly successful and hard to interpret.

Bias

Thereafter, Betti's second canon, the one concerned with the coherence of meaning (the principle of totality) can be applied. Here, this takes the form of a *criticism of bias*, where bias refers to the interest (conscious or not) of the informant in skewing the information. Actually, these are not subtleties but only a more systematic application of the same judgement that every adult individual exerts when faced, for instance, with advertisements or the statements of politicians. We judge the potential bias of informants against their whole background situation. The stronger the bias suspected, the less value is attributed to information from that source. A single source which cannot be suspected of bias may possibly and with caution be used for the main outlines of a narrative. A single source, even if it is only suspected of bias, is considered worthless; and this evaluation is all the more easy to make if the bias is quite clear from the text. Note that this last refers to what the source intentionally says something about. A certain established bias – for instance, an ideological one – can, on the other hand, contain very valuable information from the perspective of *ideology research*: what message is being conveyed?

What is crucial to the criticism of bias is always to ask who is speaking, and with what purpose. Thus, one should not accept a single piece of information with a possible bias, but always try to complement it with information representing the opposite bias or with information from (relatively) neutral sources. From a source-critical point of view, one frequent practice in management literature is, for instance, quite condemnable: to uncritically accept managers' statements about their own companies, if there is even the slightest suspicion that the statements are made with the purpose of embellishing the image. Sources with a counter-bias or (relatively) neutral sources must complement this kind of information. Sources with a counter-bias might, for example, be people who work at the 'grassroots' level in offices or on the shopfloor. Another tactic is to look for 'black sheep' in the organization, as a counter-weight to the glossy pictures presented by the management. These counter-images are, of course, often as exaggerated as those of the management's, albeit in the opposite direction. They can, however, function as hints or clues that something here needs checking (for example, by recontacting the management). If, on the other hand, the black sheep agrees with certain elements in the positive picture provided by the management, then these elements deserve greater credibility. Relatively neutral sources can be sought, for example, in other lines of business which have some insight into the company at hand, but without being in a highly competitive or dependent relationship with it; or in groups within the company which stand somewhere between management and its opponents, and which are consequently not very interested in either whitewashing or blackening the image; or else in the community of external researchers.

Thus far we have spoken of the criticism of bias in terms of interest. However, as has transpired, even such things as ideological affiliation are usually subsumed under the criticism of bias. From this it is only a small step to go further and conceive of the criticism of bias as a more general evaluation of *perspectives* in a source. Then it is a matter of adding together different partial perspectives in order to gain a picture of the whole. What was said earlier about bias and counter-bias now appears as something of a special case, which concerns two opposite, partial perspectives, for and against. In other words, there might be a wider circle of partial perspectives which the researcher has to put together in order to reach a complete picture. The neutral source then corresponds to the informant, whose perspective better enables her or him to survey the whole. We may compare this with the much-quoted fable about the elephant and the five blind men. Each of these touched a different part of the animal – the trunk, the tail and so on – and drew entirely different conclusions about the nature of the animal, from their various partial perspectives. The story is often told with the purpose of 'proving' a relativist stance: reality is complex, elusive, and every interpretation is purely subjective. Yet this relativist moral of the story misses, or represses, one crucial thing: the role of the narrator. How does the story-teller know that the animal is an elephant? Like the narrator, the researcher should put together the partial perspectives that she encounters, in order to reach the conclusion that, metaphorically speaking, the animal is an elephant. Alternatively, the researcher can contact a sighted person, who from her perspective of seeing (better) will be able to survey the whole.

According to the influential French historian Le Goff (1992), the traditional source criticism is insufficient, since it does not involve influences on the source from overarching power structures. As just noted, though, this connection can be made by checking for bias. Overarching power structures and ideologies have been the favourite target of critical theory (see Chapter 5). In Chapter 8, we will consider the importance of alternating between different levels of interpretation: an interesting application of this could be provided precisely by critical theory and source criticism.

Distance and dependence

Canon 3, the actuality of understanding, has significance for two other aspects of source criticism, namely *distance* and *dependence*. In both cases, the researcher asserts her ability to interpret the event better than the informant. 'Distance' refers to the fact that the more remote the source is from the event in time and space, the less value it has. 'Dependence' refers to the number of hands the information has passed through from the source in question. It is well known that information becomes more distorted the greater the number of intermediaries. This is well illustrated by the game of Chinese whispers in which a story is whispered from one person to the next in a circle, until it returns totally unrecognizable to its starting-point. Thus, the greater the number of intermediaries on the way, the less valuable is the source. Two sources, of which one is the original and the other can be shown to be dependent on it, are consequently not worth more than one (the first). (Under canon 3, the generation of theory also enters the picture; the writing of history should not consist only of data-driven reporting, but should also create theory, taking its point of departure from the researcher's preconceptions and frames of reference.)

*

The above general principles entail a number of rules for source criticism, of which we give a sample below. *Caution*: in all cases the *ceteris paribus* reservation applies.

- A remnant is always worth more than a narrating source.
- A source the authenticity of which is in doubt, has no value.
- Since no source is entirely contemporary with the event (there is always a time gap, however small), never accept a single source for a concrete statement of fact; this takes at least two independent sources.
- A single source which does not suffer from effects of bias or dependence can possibly be accepted for the *main* structure of an account. (What the 'main structure' consists of then becomes a question for the conscience and 'clinical judgement' of the researcher.)
- If two sources, A and B, are mutually dependent, so that B takes the information from A, then their combined value is no higher than that of A alone.
- Primary sources have a higher value than secondary ones. (Alternatively, and more strongly: accept only primary sources.)
- A source that is more contemporary with the course of events in question has a higher value than one that is less contemporary.
- A source has less information value the more remote in time it is from the course of events it tells us about.
- The more reason there is to suspect a source of bias, the more reason there is to reject it. (Alternatively, and more strongly: reject all sources that can be even *suspected* of bias.)
- Two sources with a bias in the same direction are not worth more than one.

And so on. Minutes recording factual behaviours are thus worth more than interview information about the same behaviours; assessments of distant meetings are worth less than those of recent ones; secondary information is more important as clues for research than as evidence, etc.

The above rules, which for reasons of presentation and space have been set out somewhat crudely, should be used with practical reason and flexibility; they are not a methodological threshing-machine, through which data can be run. Furthermore, as has already been pointed out, they are valid only under the *ceteris paribus* condition. What was just said about minutes of meetings is, for instance only valid with respect to distance; that is, minutes are generally closer in time to the event(s) they report than are interviews, and are thus less exposed to distortions of memory than the latter, which may concern events months and years earlier. With respect to bias, on the other hand, both minutes and interviews can of course be exposed to distortion. In addition, it is necessary to check the extent to which the minutes are altered during the process of approval and thus are less contemporary with events than would appear at first sight. Also, both minutes and interviews can obviously be forged. Quantitatively, of course, minutes are often more meagre than interviews, although this can vary. Thus, when we relax the *ceteris paribis* condition, this method becomes ever more sophisticated and subtle. In sum, the rules for source criticism should be used rather like guidelines for style in writing – something to apply as an art and with *Fingerspitzgefühl*, rather than as a system of mechanical pulleys and levers for textual interpretation. Chapter 9 below provides a concrete, empirical example of the use of source criticism in research practice.

Empathy

The fourth canon, concerning the correspondence of meaning, implies that the researcher complements the source criticism (checking for authenticity, bias, distance and dependence) with *empathy*. By this is meant the intuitive understanding 'from within' of the object of investigation, whether the latter is a single individual or overarching social formations (in which case, as mentioned earlier, the researcher tries to re-enact the intentions behind their original creation). This means that empathy becomes more important the less value the sources at hand possess. Empathy also plays an important role by filling with inner meaning the merely external 'facts' generated by source criticism. Collingwood (1992) speaks of actions having an outside and an inside, that is, a behaviour and a meaning facet, and he maintains that the latter is accessible only through the 're-enactment of past experience', or empathy. Through empathy we fill and enrich with inner meaning the thin shells of outward behaviour which are the results of previous interpretation. Thus, the meaning for the acting subjects here becomes central.

Collingwood in fact goes even farther, claiming empathy as the necessary and sufficient method in all historiography. Thus any (degree of) the sources' correspondence with reality vanishes and is replaced only by their meaning. This anti-realist move has bearings to current discussions of historiography (Ricoeur, 2006). Here, the Holocaust appears as a touchstone and breaking point for the whole discussion of hermeneutic re-constructionism[22] and postmodern relativism: if there is no correspondence between language and reality, as held by the latter, how then can it be said that the Holocaust has taken place? A crucial debate is between on the one hand the meta-historian Hayden White, who holds that history writing does not really differ from fiction literature, and on the other hand Carlo Ginzburg, who holds that history writing is an 'evidential' science, since it builds on traces. White argues that the Holocaust falls outside normal historiography because of its terrible unicity, which makes it indescribable with the help of any narrative genres.[23]

Ginzburg, passionately defending a realist position, maintains that there is a very strong case for the Holocaust because of the amount of circumstantial evidence.

Source criticism: final words

Source-critical elements might be thought to deserve a wider spread in social science than they enjoy at present. They appear to be especially appropriate to case studies, since these have points in common with historiography. Further, interviewees' descriptions of certain factual circumstances are often accepted uncritically, even if they constitute the only source in the particular context. Yet we know that rationalizations and the like play many tricks with memory. It is, for instance, common to glorify one's own role in a process, depicting it as more central than it really was. An elementary source-critical checking of interview material would remove many mistakes on this score, which is all the more important since such material often provides the main bulk of the database in qualitative investigations. In general, all reporting in written form can be subjected to this hermeneutic technique. Even participant observation could easily be checked by source criticism, despite its efforts to effect the maximum reduction in both distance and dependence. But, as we remember from Chapter 3, it too uses written reports. Thus:

1 *Criticism of authenticity*. Is the observation genuine or fictitious? In natural science, where the results are easier to check, forgeries are not uncommon; even very prominent researchers have devoted themselves to such activities (Broad and Wade, 1982). There is no reason why things should be very different in the social sciences.
2 *Criticism of bias*. Which is the researcher's (possible) bias, and how can this have distorted her interpretations?
3 *Criticism of distance*. How long after the observation was made was it recorded, and in which situation?
4 *Criticism of dependence*. Can *other* stories, which the reporting person has listened to, possibly have influenced the structure or the content of the report (and the following analysis)? This is a phenomenon which could be termed *narrative contagion*: the classical problem of hagiography.

These four can then be complemented by empathy with the researcher as well as the other 'participants'.

Source criticism has long proved its value in historical research and, treated rightly, should not be underestimated. The problem is that previously it was often raised to the rank of a fetish among historians, and tended to replace theory; it then functioned as the legitimization of an empiricist, anti-theoretical stance (as in Germany and France during the nineteenth century). This, of course, runs the risk of reducing research to the compiling of facts, at best complemented by inductive low-level theory; we then end up in (a qualitative) positivism. Fortunately, there is a strong current among modern historians to adopt a more theoretical position. As Ricoeur (2006) has shown, source criticism can very well be combined with advanced models for understanding and explanation. It can also very well be used to complement a modern poetic hermeneutics of the kind we shall discuss later in this chapter. Interpretation in terms of narrative and plot, rather than the dry compilation of 'facts', renders the historiographic method more flexible and relativized than its outward image has sometimes suggested.[24]

Further, Collingwood (1992; for an introduction to his thinking, see Johnson, 1998), among others, has emphasized the importance of the researcher's alternating between the 'facts' resulting from the source criticism on the one hand and the theory that emerges as a pattern from these 'facts' on the other. It should be noted that in both cases, theory and empirical material, what we are dealing with are interpretations; the facts in question are thus by no means something immediately present, or given; they are the result of a process of interpretation. Hence, there are no pure facts, which is why the word was placed within quotation marks above. The researcher, according to Collingwood, 'interpolates' between these interpreted facts (which constitute *relative* fixed points or 'provisory nodes' of a kind), weaving in this way a sort of web over the whole. The researcher knows, for instance, that at a certain time entrepreneur A visited Mexico City and at a certain later time Houston, Texas; it then seems reasonable to assume that in some way or other A has moved between these places. The threads between the provisory nodes are in their turn woven together into a connected web, a theory. This global web, still according to Collingwood, must be 'coherent': a characteristic feature of all hermeneutic methodology (and a prime target for deconstructionist critics). But the process is not finished with the production of a theory, an overarching pattern of the whole. Even the 'facts', the relatively fixed points, are now reinterpreted in light of the theory … and so we are moving within the hermeneutic circle between part and whole.

It is instructive to compare this way of proceeding with grounded theory. First, facts are never immediately given; they are always already interpreted. But this means that the theory cannot be grounded in facts, since both theory and facts emerge from an interactive process of interpretation whose point of departure is the text. Second, Collingwood sharply rejects all methods that remove data from their context, since he holds that this leads to the creation of an artificial-abstract reality, and rips the historical patterns apart, thus making it impossible to discover them. (Or, as the saying goes: it is easy to make a fish soup out of an aquarium, but it is more difficult to make an aquarium out of a fish soup.)

In fact, Collingwood even takes a step further, and asserts that any interpretation of a past happening is subjective and historical, since it involves in a fundamental way the researcher's own time-bound frames of reference, values and so on. Consequently, there is no longer any Truth, with a capital 'T', in the sense of mirroring an objective reality in an absolute and purely rational subject, independent of time and space. With this historicity, this time-boundedness, we are touching upon the alethic hermeneutics which constitute the subject matter of the following sections.

Existential hermeneutics: back to basics

Being-in-the-world

The *existential* hermeneuticians who entered the stage from the 1930s onwards rejected the difference between subject and object, and oriented their interest towards what Heidegger (1962) called Being-in-the-world (*in-der-Welt-sein*).[25] We are irrevocably merged with our world, already before any conscious reflection, and the polarization between a thinking subject and an object is therefore a dubious secondary construction. Consequently, the concept of understanding in objectivist hermeneutics is called into question, since it builds on this polarity between an empathizing subject and a (human) object for empathy. Heidegger (1962: Division One, Chapter II, n.i; cf. Gadamer, 1989a: 254) coined the expression 'the hermeneutics of facticity'; that is, what is crucial is to 'understand' the factual-concrete. The really important concern is the ordinary world in which we live, before all abstractions, rationalizations and theoretical constructions. (Husserl, the father of phenomenology, later launched a similar concept: his famous 'lifeworld', an expression which for obvious reasons became more popular than Heidegger's not very catchy 'Being-in-the-world'. A better expression than either of these may be Gadamer's [1989a] simple 'belonging'.)

   Hence, what really matters is to study our place in the world. We are continually and without our own consent, thrown, as it were, into an existence in a world where we have to find our way. Husserl, the early philosophical guru of Heidegger, had maintained that the (transcendental) ego of man preceded everything – the world was a construction by the ego itself. For existential hermeneutics, this is an abstraction; instead we are 'always already' *in* the world. It should be emphasized, however, that the term 'existence' designates something concrete, individual. The existential hermeneuticians strongly dissociate themselves from any idea of supraindividual, law-like regularities, or any holistic approach. These constitute to them only further examples of misleading abstractions; instead only individual or at most interindividual relationships are valid, in principle. Therefore, what becomes central is neither single abstract egos, nor supraindividual wholes, but the study of individuals in concrete situations of life. In various ways, these thoughts have gained adherents in more applied research – for example: in Boss's (1988) daseinsanalysis, an existential psychoanalysis; the advocacy of an existential hermeneutic social science in Douglas and Johnson (1977); and Guillet de Monthoux's (1978) and Sotto's (1990) studies of organizations and corporations.

The structure of care

What Heidegger terms the structure of *care* plays a central role in the concrete life situations which are the focus of existential philosophy. As beings we are unique, in that we are faced, as it were, with a circular time horizon. We make plans for the future, on the basis of resources which follow us out of the past, and we make decisions in the present, with a view to the future as well as to this past. Future, present and past are thereby continuously reflected in one another in a circular flow of care. This has various consequences. We are placed in the world as the element of *possibility* in *reality*. We have built-in possibilities, thus freedom, and it is just this circumstance that brings difficulties. If individuals are free, then they are also free to *choose*; they have responsibility. On what criteria is this choice to be founded? The problem is that even these criteria are ultimately of our own making – we are those who provide the world with values. In spite of this, it is our responsibility to choose. Hence, we are 'condemned to freedom', as Sartre (1973) says. For Sartre, this freedom lies in a voluntarist (political) praxis; for Heidegger it lies in the reconquest of an original but forgotten unity and oneness (Fell, 1979: 418).

What matters under these conditions is to 'resolutely' take our responsibility, stand up to our fate and make decisions in a kind of heroically defiant attitude. The worst thing we can do is simply surrender ourselves to the circumstances and deny our possibilities of free choice – however circumscribed or baseless these may be; this constitutes an 'inauthentic' mode of action in contrast to the 'authentic' one, whereby we realize our own degrees of freedom as autonomous individuals. Incidentally, not to choose is also a choice – an inauthentic one. We 'fall' into an everyday world of trivial concerns. 'The cry of conscience' – an amplification of 'the voice of conscience' – calls us back to the authentic life. The cry of conscience, since this is not a low-keyed voice, but an abruptly striking *cry* to our innermost essence, a calling out for us, hitting with the force of a blow: *What are you really doing? Are you throwing away your own life?* (Heidegger, 1962).

Such situations have often been rendered in art, films and literature. Visually, this existential anxiety is portrayed in an unsurpassed way in Edvard Munch's famous painting, *The Scream*.[26] What am I truly doing? What is my life? Am I throwing away myself, my innermost possibilities, on trivialities? In the midst of career and family life, such questions can strike the individual in moments of icy, or, as Heidegger says, 'uncanny'[27] clear-sightedness, which changes her whole course of life. Through the 'anxiety' which ensues when we regard the everyday world in which we live, in its authenticity and wholeness, and thereby its meaninglessness, its emptiness, we are transposed into a mood which makes it possible to take non-trivial decisions, thus taking responsibility for and retrieving ourselves as individuals (Heidegger, 1962: 74; cf. Sartre, 1973: passim). This means a realistic view of ourselves and our possibilities – neither underestimating nor overestimating them. Everyday life, on the other hand, involves both, since it is submerged in trivialities and hence reduces our degrees of freedom; and also because it disregards death, which of course makes every existence *'finite'* (Heidegger, 1962: 278).

Let us elucidate and concretize this last point with an illustration from social science. Death is something of a taboo subject in organizational research (Sievers, 1990). The repression of thoughts about death might well lead to the trivialization and narrowing of organizational life: as Becker (1973) has pointed out, modern institutions can be seen as structures of escape from the knowledge of death. Morgan (1986) follows up this idea in a discussion relating to one of his eight metaphors for organizations – that of the psychic prison. Conversely, one of the present authors personally witnessed a case in which the approaching death of one terminally ill member over several years, far from having a depressing effect on the organization's consciousness, in fact contributed to raising it to a higher, more genuine and warm level. This person's office became something of a cult place, and the general feeling was one of relaxation and openness. Through the long-drawn-out proximity to death, the Being of life was revealed, transforming the organization in subtle ways – but finitude in organizations also means retirement and even the end of time-limited projects, as well as the possible threat of lay-offs. The effects of all these on organizations and their members deserve attention. Do they, for example, lead to escapism and trivialization or to a genuine consciousness? And if so, in what forms?

Understanding

From Husserl, and phenomenology, the existential hermeneuticians took over three ideas in particular. First, knowledge ought to be of an intuitive kind. Characteristically, Heidegger (1962) sees the concept of truth as undergoing one long Fall ever since Plato: from the 'disclosure' of a knowledge which is always already there, albeit at present concealed, to a principle of correspondence between proposition and reality. Truth means the liberation from illusions, and this liberation does not necessarily have to be expressed in a proposition which is then compared to a reality; such a comparison is only a derived and secondary aspect.[28] Thus, truth constitutes an insight, an intuition. Yet this intuition differs in important aspects from that of Husserl. The Husserlian variant of intuition was the so-called *Wesensschau* (literally 'gazing essences'), in which we use 'imaginary variation' – roughly speaking, a kind of thought-play at the very boundaries of a phenomenon, to explore its basic structure. By focusing on the phenomenon itself and thus regarding it in isolation from other phenomena, this variant of intuition obviously erases both history and spatial context. Instead, according to Heidegger, what is important is to see things in their context (*Umsicht*), and hermeneutically to see through (*Durchsicht*) the distortions resulting from the historical process. Traditional intuition wrested what was intuited (that is, gazed upon) all too far out of its spatio-temporal context. (However, other existential philosophers, such as Merleau-Ponty [1973: 104–107], have sided with Husserl here.) The web of connections, the historical context, is thus all-important. Ruin (1994) argues that historicity is a key concept, joining the various phases of Heidegger's thinking, together with what Heidegger himself referred to as the link between them, namely the question of the meaning of Being.

The second idea imported from Husserl was the conception of an original, 'lived' state, an *experience*, as the fountainhead of all knowledge. As was noted above, Husserl had extended this into a 'lifeworld' (*Lebenswelt*). The existential hermeneuticians regard us as 'always already' inserted in the world (*in-der-Welt-sein*) (Heidegger, 1962: ¶ 12, 13). We are, as it were, locked up in a spatio-temporal field. The world, however, is a world of what is meant, or intended. The individual constitutes a node in a net of meanings, and this net is her world. This *intentionality* provides the third important idea imported from Husserl. The time and space mentioned above are not physical, but *intentional* (Fell, 1979: 51). But as we have seen, we are always set in a context, and this context is also of a *practical* nature. Essentially, our understanding is not theoretical but aims at mastering a practical situation, thereby realizing the possibilities of our existence. Heidegger is not alone in having made this insight. It was also fundamental for the other of the two most influential philosophers of the twentieth century, (the later) Wittgenstein. As Taylor points out:

> A number of philosophical currents in the past two centuries have tried to get out of the cul-de-sac of monologic consciousness. Prominent in this century are the works of Martin Heidegger, Maurice Merleau-Ponty, Ludwig Wittgenstein. What all these have in common is that they see the agent, not primarily as the locus of representations, but as engaged in practices, as a being who acts in and on a world. (1991: 308)

For example, understanding comprises both emotional moods and so-called 'silent knowledge' (Polanyi, 1967). Intentionality thus becomes a pre-rational *preunder-standing*: it is no longer a question of a subject which passively, rationally and theoretically gazes at an object, but of an act of knowledge whereby subject and object are created in the first place. Thus, the very act of understanding is primary; subject and object are secondary (and misleading) categories.

What matters, therefore, is for individuals to *understand* the world in which they live. For this reason, hermeneutics becomes something which permeates the whole of existence. Every understanding, of the simplest everyday things, is at the same time a contribution to better *self*-understanding.[29]

The fusion of horizons

The same applies to the understanding of *others*. For there are other worlds to venture into, other individuals' meaning-fields to seek out. Every world is a 'horizon' of meanings, which signifies that it is determined by its outlook at any given occasion (here and now), the ultimate limit for the view, and the area in between. The word 'horizon' is also meant to refer to something flexible, something that changes or can change from one time to another (Gadamer, 1989a: 245–247, 302–307; the concept derives from Husserl). An individual can put herself into another individual's horizon, first moving into the other's meaning-field, using what we have previously termed 'empathy'. This, however, is not enough. For existential hermeneutics, prior to anything else ('always already') every individual is enmeshed in her meaning-field, intentional in time and space. In other words, she is never free from preconceptions inherited from the past, preconceived meanings. Nobody proceeds from a *tabula rasa* and this includes the one seeking to understand. This is Heidegger's *new version of the hermeneutic circle*: to understand presupposes preunderstanding, but at the same time preunderstanding is an obstacle to understanding. To prevent this from developing into a vicious circle, the existential hermeneuticians advocate a constant alternation between merging into another world and linking back into our own reference system. By means of this movement back and forth, we can successively come to an understanding of the unfamiliar reference system, something which also leads to the gradual revising and/or enriching of our own: there is a 'fusion of horizons' (Gadamer, 1989a: 306–307).[30]

Furthermore, it should be emphasized that all understanding from the very beginning is 'always already' coloured by *emotional moods*; there is thus no *purely* cognitive or rational understanding (Heidegger, 1962: Division One).

The original existential hermeneutics (the early Heidegger in *Being and Time*) focused attention on the elementary situations of understanding, which emerged as the basic phenomena. Later, interest was to a certain extent shifted to *texts*, in the later Heidegger,[31] in Gadamer, and, as we shall see below, even more in Ricoeur. They conceived language as the medium through which the lifeworld discloses itself, in sharp polemic against an instrumental view of language: words and the meaning of words are not something we construct, they are mediators of a living tradition. The important thing no longer consists, as in earlier hermeneutics, in the more or less psychological re-enactment of the intentions the author is supposed to have had, intentions which in any case must remain inscrutable. Now, instead, we enter the world of the *text*, with our own world in our luggage, so to speak, in order to 'fuse horizons' between the familiar and unfamiliar.[32]

Through the mediation of traditions, *historicity*, too, as we have already mentioned, becomes central. Every interpretation is historical, relative, in the sense that it always presupposes historically transmitted preconceptions, and also in the second sense that in order to be relevant, it is applied in the present time by the interpreter. Added to which, the interpreter projects it on a future, in the form of plans, expectations, and so on. Every interpretation thus contains the three aspects of time – past, present and future – as indissoluble moments. The mediation of these occurs precisely through language. Heidegger and his successors, however, avoid the two pitfalls of relativism and objectivism, since our *pre*understanding certainly renders all knowledge perspectival, but just in its character as pre*understanding* provides the condition of (some form of) reality, albeit by necessity always limited by a perspective (Wachterhauser, 1986). We always belong to a world, and only by theoretically/abstractly decoupling our mental activity from this world do we generate the relativism–objectivism polarity. Ruin (1994), too, characterizes Heidegger's thinking as neither relativism nor objectivism: interpretation is always historically conditioned, but this does not mean that truth is relative (to a particular epoch or culture); on the contrary, different facets of reality are revealed during different epochs or cultures (cf. Dreyfus, 1991, on the hermeneutic, pluralist realism of Heidegger).

Bohman (1991) attacks the problematic of relativism–objectivism in two other ways. On the one hand, he criticizes the notion of perspectives, background conceptions, and so on, as involving merely negative, *limiting* conditions; a notion that leads to relativism, as we cannot transcend our own perspective. Instead perspectives and the like should be regarded in a positive way, as enabling conditions; as such they are always open and can give rise to what we shall term in Chapter 9 a provisory rational knowledge. The tempering of this knowledge occurs through an intersubjective exchange, in which *shared* enabling conditions are mediated. On the other hand, Bohman asserts that we also have the possibility of transcending our perspectives by consciously reflecting upon them – a basic theme in the present book too. This undermines the relativist position. Yet, objectivism is no cure. For open perspectives always and inevitably render knowledge indeterminate, among other things precisely because we can always transcend to new knowledge. Thus we end up between relativism and objectivism, in a knowledge which is wavering, evasive yet at the same time at least temporarily valid.

Knocking at the text

Through language we reach the hermeneutic experience, the basic relation of understanding which the original hermeneutics explored. This can only be achieved by undertaking a *dialogue* with the text, which we approach neither as its master, nor by passively surrendering ourselves to it, but on an equal footing. First, what matters is to learn to *listen* to the text (and, for example, not to break it apart as in grounded theory). Second, it is important to learn to ask questions, something which Collingwood (1992) emphasized half a century ago: we cannot just sit passively and wait for the material to pose questions, but must actively take the initiative, go out and pose the questions ourselves. This can be done in a completely free and open way, somewhat like the Socratic technique of questioning. In existential hermeneutics, this method has been carried far; for instance, the interpreter uses the technique of asking questions line by line, sometimes even posing the *same* question again and again – like the cautious tapping at an object until it gives off a revealing sound, or knocking at a door until it finally opens. We ask the questions, examine the answer carefully, twisting and turning it, noting its shortcomings – and then put the same question again at the new level of knowledge that has emerged, from the positive contributions of the answer as well as from its shortcomings.

Sensitivity, the keen ear, is of the essence: to listen carefully to the text, as it were putting your ear close to it, in order to hear the answer as it emerges. The process is repeated time and again, whereby we ask the same question over and over, listening constantly to the text, until it no longer answers, or speaks to us so unclearly and faintly that the answer can no longer be heard. The idea is not to reach any final answer; instead the journey is its own reward. At the end of the voyage, the question itself has been dissolved and a *new question* has begun to manifest itself, so that the process can start all over again. The experiences gained in the course of the journey(s) are the prize, not some final Shangri-La of knowledge at the end of the road. A recent example is the new French – qualitative – sociology, where an interest in the symbolic, imaginary, goes hand in hand with the tactic of close listening which we described above; for only by this means is it possible to discern the play of the underlying symbolic forms, which are marginalized behind what at first sight appears to be the main message (Lalli, 1989). More on this in the section on poetics below.

The hidden basic question of the text

The dialogical technique is pushed to its farthest limits when used to inquire into *what basic, unspoken question lies beneath, and therefore generates*, a particular text. This corresponds to Madison's hermeneutic principle of 'penetration':

> A good interpretation should be 'penetrating' in that it brings out a guiding and underlying intention in the work, in this way making an author's various works or statements intelligible by seeing them as attempts to resolve a central problematic. (The need for this rule is especially apparent in the case of [texts of which] we possess only fragments.) (1988: 29)

In other words, our research problem now becomes: to what unspoken question is the text an answer? To a certain extent this means, as Heidegger used to put it, doing violence to the text, since it implies that we say something that the text neither says nor can say. We are now at the very limits of what can be described as dialogue and attentive listening, and at the edge of something that at worst can be described as arbitrariness or wilfulness, but at best succeeds in bringing forth the underlying yet hidden problematic of the text.

This can of course be justified by the existence in every text of much that is only tacitly understood; and this unsaid message – not what is openly stated – is actually the most important part of that which is communicated. The central purport stays, as it were, between the lines. However, the procedure can also be justified more on considerations of principle. For it has to do with the historicity of the interpretation. As interpreters we are always part of a historical-cultural tradition which has grown over a long time. We can never step out of this tradition (the fallacy of modernism), but simply to accept it uncritically would be to surrender to common sense or at least historical-cultural relativism (the fallacy of historicism). The solution to this dilemma of historicity lies, according to Heidegger, in a critical dialogue with the tradition concerned, successively laying bare its hidden roots. The true historical roots are, however, always evasive, and the point is therefore to discover them *such as they are reflected for the time and purposes of the interpreter: in 'another beginning'* (Ruin, 1994).[33]

There is of course a risk with this method – that we presuppose *a* basic question behind the text, when there may instead be several. All hermeneutics proceeds from the notion of a coherence of meaning, and if this does not exist, the method falters. We do not say that there is never an overriding coherence of meaning; but always to presuppose its existence seems to us too optimistic, or rather rationalistic, an assumption. Moreover, it is an assumption that can lead to serious fallacies, something which we have encountered in our own empirical research. (Sköldberg, 1991a, describes a research process which started from the notion of meaning coherence; eventually, though, the analysis of empirical material forced a radical break with this.)

Poetic hermeneutics

Hermeneutics has often been closely related to literary science, and this is the case both for the objectivist and the alethic branch. As was mentioned above, hermeneutics originally emerged from the study of written texts. Schleiermacher, who reshaped hermeneutics in the nineteenth century, had literary texts as his area of application. For (the later) Heidegger, literary language in the form of poetry (Hölderlin!) grew ever more important.[34] Gadamer (1989a) considered language to be central to hermeneutic preunderstanding; to him the essence of language – and thus also of understanding, thinking – at its deepest level was metaphorical-poetic, not logic-formal.[35] The rhetorical figures were not superficial decorations but shaped the thought in its very origin.

Ricoeur (1978a, 1978b, 1984, 1985, 1988) has devoted several major investigations to the hermeneutic problematic of metaphor and narrative. Ricoeur (1984: xi) is of the opinion that metaphor and narrative are intimately linked in an encompassing 'poetical sphere'.[36] The boundaries between them within this sphere are to some extent fluid. The integration between different aspects that the metaphor brings about corresponds to the 'plot' of the narrative, which joins its diverse elements. Both metaphor and plot constitute an act of 'productive fantasy', a 'semantic innovation', which through a 'schematic process' generates a new unity of the whole within the realm of language. The metaphorical expressions 'speak *of* the world, even though they may not do so in a descriptive fashion', but at a deeper level. The same applies, according to Ricoeur (1984: 78–82), to literary texts as such, including narrative ones, since the plot is not a copy of reality, but is transempirical (we cannot 'see' a plot, for it is always interpolated). This line of reasoning is also extended to non-fictitious texts.

It can be noted that Ricoeur thereby returns to the original hermeneutics, as *textual interpretation*, taking a roundabout way over empathy and existential situational analysis. This is quite deliberate. Ricoeur, to be sure, professes himself an adherent of existential hermeneutics, but has set up the goal of treading the way back, from the deep drilling of the earlier Heidegger and Gadamer, up to the surface of their true point of departure: the problematic of the human sciences.[37] The text in both the literal and the figurative sense hereby becomes central – in the latter case as a *model* for the interpretation of social action. In this way, the interpretation of symbols and semantics is 'grafted' (Phillips and Brown, 1993; Ricoeur, 1981) onto hermeneutics.

What was said earlier about Gadamer can now be further elaborated in the present context: we should keep in mind that unlike the ways of the older scholars of poetics, the literary science methods using a narrative and metaphorical analysis are *not* concerned with narrative structures and rhetorical figures as language ornaments, superficial linguistic decorations, but as the very heart of the texts, constituting basic *thought styles* (Sköldberg, 2002b; White, 1985a, 1985b). Thus, logic constitutes an epiphenomenon to poetics, rather than the other way round. The interest in narrative, what is told, the diachronic, has emerged as a humanistically inspired reaction against supposedly 'scientific', structuralist ideas about the primacy of the synchronic, timeless, in the shape of atemporal structures. The narrative is hence more fundamental than abstract models. The interest in metaphors, or rhetorical figures in the wider sense, has originated as a humanistically inspired reaction against an all too far-reaching rationalism, which regards language as something second to logical content; instead language permeates thinking in its very essence. Narrative and metaphorical analysis comprise two important branches of the application of poetics in social science, but they do not of course constitute exclusive alternatives; others are conceivable, but here we shall touch only upon those which have had the most impact.

Metaphors

An important aspect of the hermeneutic interest in poetics has thus pertained to metaphors. There are, as Ricoeur (1978b) points out, many ways of analysing this rhetorical figure. To conceive of metaphor as something which elucidates *similarity in difference* (Gadamer, 1989a) is one way. Ricoeur discusses this, following Hester (1967). Metaphor indicates some kind of correspondence between two different phenomena. For instance, 'My love, a rose' suggests similarities between the object of the tender flame and the botanic phenomenon (White, 1985a). Corresponding properties may be sweetness, beauty, fragrance, and so on. At the same time, of course, the two differ as much as flora and fauna. In this way, metaphor elicits a possible identity between very different phenomena. The better the metaphor, the more striking and surprising the correspondence.

The imaginary

The metaphor has often been conceived as something purely verbal. As a counter-weight, Hester (1967) points out the sensuous-intuitive, 'imagey' element, and maintains that this comes before the verbal formulation. Thus, we first *see* our beloved *as* a rose, and only afterwards put the similarity into words. Language, therefore, is primarily 'imagey', and not merely verbal. There is always a poetic 'aura' of images around the words, and for our metaphor we select some of these. Which image we choose depends on the angle of view, the perspective, and is thus subjectively conditioned. The possibilities for choice are naturally not unlimited; there are 'objective' degrees of freedom which depend on the properties of the two phenomena compared; if the boundaries are crossed, this results in what is known as a bad metaphor.

Such importance of the picture or image is also strongly underlined by the afore-mentioned French 'sociology of the imaginary' (Fourastié and Joron, 1993), which is devoted to a hermeneutics of everyday life (Grassi, 2005). 'Indeed, everyone's social experience is an unending work of metaphorical, imaginary production' (Lalli, 1989: 111; see also Tacussel, 1993). As does Ricoeur, this approach empha-sizes the polysemic in the metaphor, but it goes further than most hermeneuticians in its focus on the contradictory and open qualities of the interpretation: 'The "sociality" of the individual thus oscillates in contradictory symptoms and represen-tations, intertwined in individual life histories and producers of a multi-masked face: the social identity' (Lalli, 1989: 114). The influence from postmodernism is palpable here, and this approach also aims at describing a postmodern social life, more imaginary than rational, yet at the same time also more paradoxical, frag-mented, and marked by colliding image (Maffesoli, 1993a, 1993b) than is common in, or typical of, hermeneutics. On the other hand, Maffesoli (1993b) claims that the collision between the images generates an 'ethos', a 'cultural climate', which creates a certain coherence in and colours a particular social milieu; thus, the harmony, typ-ical of hermeneutics, is still there, albeit diluted. At least in part, this sociology of the imaginary lies on the borders of what can be called metaphorical, since the images no longer tend to stand for *something else*, but to constitute the basic, chaotic 'matrix' itself, which 'drives social life' (Maffesoli, 1993a). This, too, precludes a total overlap with postmodernism, for which there is only surface, nothing 'under-lying'. On the other hand, the idea of an underlying unity is characteristic of hermeneutics – the unified meaning that is to be extracted.

Root metaphors

An important application of the metaphor concept is the analysis of so-called root metaphors, that is, metaphors that underlie whole discourses. These also provide an illustration of the foundational analysis of different branches of science which Heidegger (1982) advocates as an element in a more basic phenomenology and hermeneutics. This is an instance of the central role the study of preunderstanding plays in existential hermeneutics. Root metaphors, like narrative structures, are an important form of preunderstanding, and by this token also a natural field for interpretive studies. Such a study has been made by Brown (1976, 1977), who proceeds from an apparently paradoxical 'cognitive aesthetics', that is, an aesthetic view of societal phenomena, which is – as the first part of the expression suggests – not only concerned with *l'art pour l'art*, but also intends to bring knowledge. This is combined with a 'symbolic realism', according to which:

> Adequate social theory must be both objective and subjectively meaningful; it must yield understanding of a person's consciousness and agency as well as explanations of social forces beyond their immediate control. (Brown, 1977: 27)

> Causal, lawlike explanation is itself an interpretative procedure, and interpretation itself can be a rigorous way of knowing. (1977: 33)

> The concept of aesthetic perception or the aesthetic point of view allows us to step outside the dreary debate between the 'objectivity' of measurement and causal explanation and the 'subjectivity' of understanding. Aesthetic perception is neither pure reflection nor ordinary awareness. Instead it combines the detachment of the former with the intuitive immediacy of the latter, though each is heightened and focused. (1977: 49)

The final quotation indicates that an aesthetic perception yokes a form of consciousness based on immediate, unreflected sensory experience to a more structured thought, resulting in a kind of fusion, where intuition enters in an indissoluble union with more reflecting categories. What we have, then, is something between the relatively empty, rational-formal thought and the substantial but relatively formless pure perception.

Brown identifies five root metaphors in sociology: organism, mechanism, language, drama and game. The difference between organic and mechanical is classic and goes back to the seventeenth century, when the new natural sciences broke with Aristotelian thought, in which the organism metaphor was central. Language, according to Brown, is a root metaphor not just for such approaches as symbolic interactionism and ethnomethodology, but also for French structuralism and others. Drama is often used unreflectingly as a metaphor for social phenomena, but has also been used deliberately by Goffman, for instance. Game as a root metaphor for sociology has two faces: von Neumann and Morgenstern's mathematical theory of games and Wittgenstein's language games. Brown's poetic analysis has many other interesting elements apart from the root metaphor discussion, but we shall not go into those here.

In the 1980s and 1990s, metaphors have aroused interest as a focus for understanding organization analysis and as an inspiration to new theoretical ideas. It has even been argued that we create our concept of 'organization' by seeing it *as* something, that is, by using a metaphor, and that the metaphor used is of decisive importance to our understanding of the subject matter as well as to thinking and theorizing in general. Morgan's (1980, 1986) work has been central in this respect (for a discussion, see Tsoukas,1991, 1993). Morgan speaks of metaphors used to conceptualize the totality, or at least all the elements of an organization which relate to a particular school or theory. (Metaphors can also be used to elucidate other more limited phenomena, as for instance when we speak of 'higher' and 'lower' positions in the hierarchy, or of 'sending' and 'receiving' as elements of communication. The latter harks back to a view of communication as 'dispatch by pneumatic tube'.) Morgan's (1980: 607) basic idea is that 'schools of thought in social science, those communities of theorists subscribing to relatively coherent perspectives, are based upon the acceptance and use of different kinds of metaphor as a foundation for inquiry'.

According to Morgan, the following metaphors have lead to or are suitable for organization analysis: machine, organism, population ecology, cybernetic system, loosely coupled system, political system, theatre, culture, text, language game, enacted sense-making, accomplishment, psychic prison, instruments of domination, schism and catastrophe. (Some of the sections of text dealing with these metaphors contain hardly any examples of studies in organization theory which have been influenced by the metaphor in question.) Other suggestions for metaphors which encapsulate existing lines of development and works on organization theory have been made by Berg (1982) and Mangham and Overington (1987), among others. Czarniawska-Joerges (1994) holds that 'superperson' is the dominating metaphor for organizations, which are described as though they act, make decisions, have needs, and so on.

Narrative

For the interpretation of intentionality in newer hermeneutics, time is central to the understanding of being – and not just any time, but precisely meaningful time, the time of man in the world (Ruin, 1994). According to alethic hermeneuticians, this concrete, meaningful time has tended to be repressed by Western thinking, either by a denial of it (in the form of timeless scientific models or timeless philosophical concepts, which would supposedly constitute the true reality behind occurrences in time), or else by deforming and draining it in various ways, leaving it thin and bloodless. The time aspect is thus central to alethic hermeneutics, yet – again – this applies not to any time (especially not to the disenchanted, meaning-bereft time of natural science), only to the always already meaningful and structured time, the action time of man in the world.[38] Transferred to social science, the inevitability of meaningful time would have interesting consequences. For it would mean that from a hermeneutic perspective, any operating with abstract models in the form of timeless generators 'behind' different societal phenomena creates an inauthentic knowledge. The examples are legion in social science, and include various structuralist and systems theory models as well as rational choice theories, in which time is either reduced to a non-entity or hollowed out into an empty shell devoid of meaning.

Thus far, we have presented the negative side of the critique. What, then, would a positive, constructive counter-proposition look like, one with a relevance for social science? We need to restore to knowledge a lost awareness of time. It may be asked whether this must be done by basing social science on another human science to which it has often been counterposed, since the latter is the science of time *par excellence*. We are thinking of historiography. Such a way out would of course be perfectly possible, as a hermeneutic social science. For example, Pettigrew (1985) has launched a research approach along these lines of thought, to be used for strategic studies of firms. But this resort is not necessary. As Ricoeur (1981) points out, the human sciences as a whole – including historiography and the literary and social sciences – have a common source just in the meaningfully temporal nature of their subject matter. This is the *narrative* aspect which has often been neglected, but which runs throughout all of them. One solution is therefore provided by narrative time (Ricoeur, 1988).[39] The meaningful time to be illuminated, thus, is the *time of narrative*. For this, as Ricoeur points out, analytical tools are available at the two principal levels of single actions (see, for example, Greimas, 1983) and the weaving together of actions into a plot (Frye, 1973; Propp, 1968).

Thus, the focus on the narrative – besides, as we must remember, constituting the other aspect of hermeneutics' basic interest in poetry – also has to do with the fact that every narrative moves through the fundamental medium of time. Ricoeur (1981: 278–279) maintains that the crucial aspect of narrative 'does not simply consist in adding episodes to one another; it also constructs meaningful totalities out of scattered events'. This implies that the narrative in general can be determined in terms of a combination of two dimensions, one chronological and one non-chronological, of which the latter provides the sense to the former, as *meaningful* time: a sequence of episodes and a significant configuration of these episodes which to a superficial view may seem separate. Knowledge without meaning-laden time becomes abstract and one-sided. Madison (1988: 99–100) has the following comment: 'Experience is meaningful, precisely because it can be *recounted*, and it can be recounted precisely because it has a temporal structure'. In arguing for a narrative paradigm for communication research, Fisher (1985: 34) maintains in a similar way: 'there is no genre, including technical communication, that is not an episode in the story of life (a part of the "conversation")'. Poststructuralists (such as Derrida, a former pupil of Ricoeur's) have been strongly influenced by the discussion of time in alethic hermeneutics, but have inserted it in their own problematic.[40]

*

Metaphor and narrative, constituting two aspects of poetics and expressing a productive, integrative, linguistic fantasy are also linked together in other ways. First, metaphor should be put into a context, a narrative, since all discourse is in some way or another narrative. Metaphor is seen against the backdrop of the narrative text of which it is a part; conversely, the narrative is influenced by metaphor: we have entered a part–whole hermeneutic circle. For example, Taylor's 'scientific management' can be seen as a tragic narrative in a triumphant genre (the victory of reason-rationalization over spontaneity by means of an obsessive regulation of work processes), and in this story the root metaphor of the organization as machine plays a central role (Sköldberg, 2002b). Secondly, there is a connection in terms of *'seeing as'*. Metaphor means seeing something as something else – the heart as a beggar, for instance (Shakespeare, *Timon of Athens*, Act 1, Scene 2) or society as a house with foundations and a superstructure (Marx). In the same way, narrative means that we see a series of isolated events as something else, namely a woven whole, a plot. This implies that aspect-seeing is a common basis for both metaphor and narrative, at the micro and macro level of discourse. Thirdly, metaphors and narrative support each other mutually (McCloskey, 1990). In economics, for instance, metaphors – in the guise of models – are the predominating form of poetics (as they are in physics: economics, after all has pretensions to be the physics of social sciences, or at least the nineteenth-century mechanics). Yet, when the metaphors (models) have to be explained, the economists turn to histories of economic processes, i.e. narratives. Conversely, in order to explain why economic stories happen as they do, economists turn to their metaphors (models). Thus, metaphors and narratives together form a self-supporting poetics of economic science, the basis of which rests on an allegory of self-interest.

The hermeneutics of suspicion[41]

The narrative perspective also provides an altered view of psychoanalysis, since – instead of models inspired by natural science – textual interpretation, oriented towards narrations and patterns of narrations, becomes central (cf. Fuerst, 2006). The topographical and dynamic categories of the Freudian conceptual apparatus have often been criticized for their sometimes naïve empiricist realism. The different 'entities' – the conscious, the preconscious, the unconscious; the ego, the id, the superego – which Freud distinguished in the psyche are actually, according to modern hermeneutics (Ricoeur, 1974), not entities at all, but *interpretations*. In this way Freud's unconscious becomes something that does not really exist, but is an *ascribed meaning*. This will apply in particular to the work of analysis itself, precisely as interpretation – something which hermeneutically provides the key to understanding the psychoanalytical approach.

There has been no lack of efforts to make of psychoanalysis an 'objective' science which would be subject to strict demands for evidence. Hermeneutically, this is completely fallacious and a total 'submission' to scientism and its image of the world (Ricoeur, 1974; cf. Lesche, 1986). Psychoanalysis can *never* be a discipline in the style of natural science. Its goals are quite different from those of a behaviourist psychology. These two areas of knowledge even operate with radically dissimilar material. A behaviourist psychology operates with observable behaviours. Psychoanalysis does not work with facts at all, but with the *life histories* of the analysands, kinds of texts that it is the task of the analyst to interpret meaningfully as coherent *stories* (see also Roth, 1991). In that the written discourse – the text – serves as a model of interpretation for the spoken discourse, the individual life histories are seen as symbols which can be endowed with a meaning only in the light of their context.[42] In contrast to the behavioural psychologist, the psychoanalyst does not aim at *adjusting* the patients to an often mendacious society, but seeks to give them self-insight through the understanding of their own biography, the story of themselves, as history. Such self-understanding may very well result in the very opposite of an adjustment to society. Thus, the subject becomes something which is constituted through discourse, interpretation, and which is not prior to these. The issue of the validity of interpretations should be solved by immanent demands on quality, complemented by stringent *argumentation* (modelled on jurisprudence), aimed at showing which of several possible conflicting interpretations is the most plausible (cf. Madison, 1988, on the hermeneutic method as a process of argumentation).

Psychoanalysis can be seen as belonging to the *hermeneutics of suspicion* which, apart from Freud, is also represented by Marx and Nietzsche. All three of these had probed behind what they conceived as an illusory self-consciousness to a deeper-lying, more unpleasant or 'shameful' one. In Freud the latter appeared as libido, in Marx as the economic interest, and in Nietzsche as the will to power. The concept of hermeneutics hereby undergoes a fundamental change. A characteristic of hermeneutics throughout its history has otherwise been the absence of such suspicion and instead a reverent attitude to the tradition mediated – a tradition which should be restored to its authentic meaning, and not stripped of its false deities by the interpreter tearing away the veil of illusion from the embarrassingly naked secret. The hermeneutics of suspicion can be regarded as lying on the borders of the thematic treated in the present chapter, which is why we do not treat it in greater detail. It overlaps on one side with Heidegger's disclosive view of truth and on the other with the criticism of ideologies by the Frankfurt school (see Chapter 5). It also has aspects in common with Foucault's texts (Chapter 7), which drew inspiration from Nietzsche's genealogical method – to search for the shameful, fragmented origin behind societal phenomena, whose origins have become mythologized, with the passing of time, as noble rationality and unambiguous clarity.

Ricoeur's idea of a hermeneutics of suspicion can also be widened to comprise a more general, distanced, sceptical and critical view of that which is to be interpreted. With the usual Ricoeurian bridge-building and reconciliating dialectics, this more general hermeneutics of suspicion should alternate with a closer, more Gadamerian way of interpreting. This of course also contributes to bridging the classical dichotomy between distanced explanation and close understanding (Ricoeur, 2006).

Geertz's hermeneutic ethnography

Geertz's (1973) method of studying cultures through 'thick description'[43] elicits several of the currents discussed in the previous sections; from our perspective, it can be seen as a set of elegant improvisations on some important themes within alethic hermeneutics. The concept of thick description is contrasted with a behaviourist 'thin description', which considers only the external behavioural aspect of action; thick description also includes the inner, meaningful aspect (Geertz, 1973: 7). It is important to pay attention to the rich layers of meaning and symbolism that characterize human action and social phenomena. A *culture* for Geertz is a coherent whole of a semiotic kind, the individual expressions or parts of which are constituted by symbols. Geertz, who is strongly influenced by Ricoeur, reads culture as a text:[44]

> As interworked systems of constructable signs (what, ignoring provincial usages, I would call symbols), culture is not a power, something to which social events, behaviors, institutions, or processes can be causally attributed; it is a context, something within which they can be intelligibly – that is, thickly, described. (Geertz, 1973: 14)

Furthermore, the whole is harmonious:

> Cultural systems must have a minimum degree of coherence, else we would not call them systems; and by observations, they normally have a great deal more. (1973: 17–18).

This is analogous, for instance, to the way in which a Beethoven quartet constitutes 'a coherent sequence of modelled sound' (1973: 11–12). How, then, is this wholeness, this coherence, obtained?

> [W]e begin with our own interpretations of what our informants are up to, or think they are up to, and then systematize those. (1973: 15).

Thick description is the first step in the interpretation of culture. The second, the creation of theory, is a pattern-finding process of 'generalizing within cases', in contrast to the procedure in positivism, which constitutes a deductive subsumption of a set of observations under a governing law. Geertz's inference is reminiscent of that in clinical studies: it 'begins with a set of (presumptive) indicators and attempts to place them within an intelligible frame' (1973: 26). Geertz (1973: 25–28) is of the opinion that the ideas for the theoretical interpretation must always be obtained from other, earlier, literature, and in that respect his position is of course diametrically opposed to that of Glaser and Strauss. Yet, if the two standpoints are viewed as relative rather than absolute, it seems unwarranted to exclude a priori any of these means of generating a theory – neither the (re)combination of previous ideas, nor the creative flashes of the researcher. In the former case, besides, there is always a higher or lower degree of originality, depending on the uniqueness of the new combination; conversely, in the latter case there is always dependence (ultimately on the alphabet), since without intellectual socialization we would not even be literate. In reality, then, it is more a question of different emphasis than of absolute differences.

Geertz demonstrates the applicability of the method with several examples, for instance from Indonesian culture (Bali). The very skill and the grasp of the whole in this type of analysis, however, may blind the reader to the problems associated with the basic harmony perspective underlying the analysis. This is a good example of what we referred to at the beginning of this chapter as canon 2, the coherence of meaning (the principle of totality). A criticism of this canon is that it presupposes what in fact remains to be shown in the individual case – namely that there really exists such a systematic coherence.[45] The assumption of global coherence is of course problematic: in a postmodern perspective, for instance, this is a decisive objection, since among other things postmodernism turns precisely against the conception of rationally homogeneous, overarching wholes.

In line with the narrative hermeneutics – and referring to Ricoeur (Geertz, 1973: 448n), Geertz (1973: 452) writes: 'The culture of a people is an ensemble of texts, themselves ensembles, which the anthropologist strains to read over the shoulders of those to whom they properly belong'. He also explicitly refers (Geertz, 1973: 449) to the three main hermeneuticians of suspicion whom we have already touched upon. One such text concerns the Balinese cockfight – a bloody spectacle performed by combatants armed with razor-sharp steel spurs, keen enough to cut the finger off an unwary onlooker, and surrounded by completely absorbed spectators, who in silent rapture imitate every movement of the feathered fighters. Geertz believes that we can certainly regard, and treat, a cultural phenomenon like cockfighting as, for instance, a rite or a pastime. Functionalist or psychological aspects can also be considered. However, the angle he chooses is a different one, whereby 'cultural forms can be treated as texts, as imaginative works built out of social materials' (1973: 449).[46]

What makes cockfighting interesting is the obsession with which it is embraced, and its extensive spread; well nigh every adult (male) Balinese engages in the 'sport' with great intensity, although it is officially forbidden in Indonesia, and although it seems to contradict the otherwise very restrained cultural world of the Balinese. The limitation to 'male' is important to remember; no women engage in cockfights. Cocks are actually seen as phallic symbols, and there is a flow of metaphors with these connotations between the cockfighting and other parts of social life.

After a detailed analysis of the intricate betting system, among other things, Geertz concludes that money plays a relatively small role. The strongest emotional charges do not occur where the money stakes are highest; rather they are associated with a similarity in status between the players, enmity between them, or a high status among them (Geertz, 1973: 441). At the same time, this provides a key to the interpretation of the riddle. The Balinese engage in cockfights neither for economic reasons nor for any other rational (or functional) reasons but, according to Geertz (1973: 443), as an 'art form' which like any other advanced art forms tells the participants and the spectators something about themselves and their society. Cockfighting is a status struggle, as displayed in a bloody and violent form which is usually subdued in the Balinese culture, in favour of the pleasantly understated, stylized choreography with which these actors conduct their social intercourse. Yet, historically the repressed brutality has, as Geertz points out, on occasion erupted onto the surface in the form of horrible massacres.

The cockfighting is a spectacle where nothing important actually happens (except to the cocks), but where the participants can, in a single white-hot moment, learn something about central but otherwise repressed themes in their culture, such as 'death, masculinity, rage, pride, loss, beneficence, chance' (Geertz, 1973: 443). It orders these existential themes 'into an encompassing structure [and] presents them in such a way as to throw into relief a particular view of their essential nature':

> [T]he cockfight renders ordinary, everyday experience comprehensible by presenting it in terms of acts and objects which have had their practical consequences removed and been reduced (or, if you prefer, raised) to the level of sheer appearances, where their meaning can be more powerfully articulated and more exactly perceived. (Geertz, 1973: 443)

Thus cockfights constitute a kind of 'aesthetic quanta' (1973: 445), displaying in a compressed form the life-and-death status relationships, which are otherwise masked in social life by a haze of elegant formalism, the ceremonial and etiquette. The cockfights tell us that violence is there, just beneath the surface, inseparably linked to the status system; and hereby they also describe what happens if the social control fails. *Lek* – the Balinese expression for the terror of losing one's social mask of courteousness – thus acquires a deeper and more ominous sense. If the surface veneer cracks, then destructiveness and violence threaten to break out like a lava stream, jeopardizing the actors and ultimately society itself.[47] The cockfights are ongoing stories, narratives in a highly dramatic form, speaking to the participants of their society's deepest secret.

Integration

Above, we have presented nine different hermeneutic themes, taking as our point of departure the hermeneutic 'basic circle' that we reconstructed at the beginning of the chapter:

1   Historiographic source criticism.
2   Empathy I (concerning the inside of actions).
3   Empathy II (interpolation between events).
4   Existential understanding of situations.
5   Poetics (metaphorical and/or narrative analysis).
6   Knocking at the text.
7   The fusion of horizons.
8   Reconstruction of the hidden basic question of the text.
9   The hermeneutics of suspicion.

The polemic between the objectivist and alethic schools has been intense. Yet, representatives of the two opposite orientations such as Hirsch (1967) and Palmer (1969) – while both emphasizing the greater importance of their own line of thought – seem to imply that the perspectives ought to be seen as complementary rather than mutually exclusive. This means that a hermeneutic process in practice should utilize both methods in order to be comprehensive. Let us pursue this idea a little further, observing that both objectivist and alethic hermeneutics contain various sub-orientations. By putting the two perspectives together we circle around the research problem, as it were, covering it from various angles. The same technique has been utilized, for instance, in modern poetry (Saint-John Perse), with the purpose of encircling elusive imaginary 'realities'. This is also in line with a Ricoeur-inspired view of hermeneutics, in which several different perspectives are confronted with one another in a *striving* for truth (Kristensson Uggla, 2002). The specific principle used here is in part inspired by Ricoeur (1984) and his different levels of 'mimesis' – creative re-construction. It differs somewhat in order from the foregoing presentation, when it comes to the positioning of poetics. We start with a focus on the author/originator (source criticism). Then we proceed via a focus on the actors of the text (empathy I and II, as well as existential understanding) to the text itself and its structure (poetics). After this, we concentrate upon the relationship of the text to the reader (knocking at the text, the fusion of horizons, the hidden basic question of the text, and the hermeneutics of suspicion). The hermeneutics of suspicion closes the circle, since it also directs the attention to the originator of the text. A new round of interpretation is then possible, enriched by the preceding results. See Figure 4.4 where the mimetic levels just mentioned provide the order of the sequence.

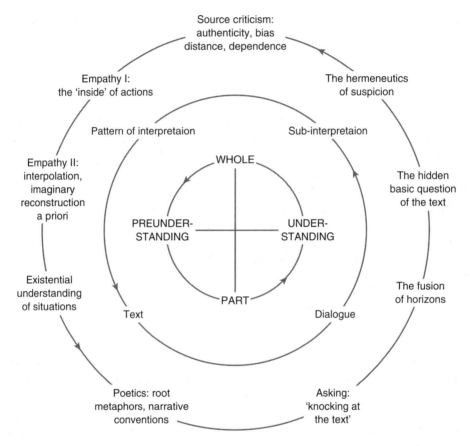

Figure 4.4 *The hermeneutic process*

As Bohman (1991) points out, there is a multitude of hermeneutic approaches, which cannot be reduced to a single one (Bohman mentions, for instance, the fusion of horizons), but are dependent on the academic discipline, research problem, theoretical context, and so on. In consequence, a particular hermeneutic process may use all nine themes, only one of them or some of them in combination. Elementary combinatorics tells us that this provides a hermeneutic typology with 512 different types in all to choose between. Combinations can build on themes which harmoniously support one another; or inversely they can build on competing themes, in which case the tension between them stimulates the interpretation. Figure 4.4 gives a total picture of the hermeneutic process as we have presented it in this chapter. The innermost circle is the most fundamental one, the inner core with an alternation between part–whole and preunderstanding–understanding. Next in importance comes the intermediate circle with an alternation between patterns of interpretation, text, dialogue and sub-interpretation. Finally, we have the outer circle, where the field is open for the choice of some theme or fruitful (new) combinations between two or more themes.

Critique

The newer, alethic branch of hermeneutics is often seen as the adequate answer to the criticism of foundational thinking, to which realist, objectivist and other similar conceptions of science have been exposed. No longer do we have the firm bedrock of data and theories, but instead everything is interpreted, and hermeneutics then becomes the natural way of proceeding (Shusterman, 1991). Yet, the question is whether alethic hermeneutics, too, may not be infiltrated by foundational thinking, albeit in a more subtle – but perhaps also more treacherous – form. If we start looking for such a foundation, it is not very difficult to find. Thus Gadamer, Heidegger's pupil, interpreter and successor, returns time and again to his notion that the absolute presupposition for hermeneutics is the possibility of a transparent understanding of the meaning of the whole, and that there *is* such a whole (Olsson, 1987). As to the two circles, 'part–whole' and 'preunderstanding–understanding', Gadamer (1989a: 293) seems – although he speaks of a 'decisive turning point' – to regard the latter circle as a development or completion of the former, in that the preunderstanding would refer to the whole of what is studied. An embryo of this development might be traced in that the earlier part–whole circle can be regarded from a subjective point of view, as 'the intuitive anticipating of the whole, and its subsequent articulation in the parts'. Thus, the preunderstanding of the researcher would refer to the whole, which would then be developed in greater detail in the shape of an understanding of the parts. Yet, we can critically note that the circles do not coincide: first, because understanding does not have to be a matter of the part but can equally well concern the whole; and secondly, because preunderstanding, too, can apply to the part as well as the whole. In any case, his reflection on these matters leads Gadamer to the conclusion that the process of interpretation must always proceed from a

'fore-conception of completeness'. But this, too, is obviously a formal condition of all understanding. It states that only what really constitutes a unity of meaning is intelligible. So when we read a text we always assume its completedness, and only when this assumption proves mistaken – i.e. the text is not intelligible – do we begin to suspect the text and try to discover how it can be remedied. (1989a: 293–294)

And Gadamer (1989a: 294) continues to maintain the utmost importance of 'an immanent unity of meaning', a 'unified meaning', which constitutes a cornerstone in his hermeneutics.

But is this not begging the question? Gadamer may be an extreme case, but the same line of thought recurs in other proponents of the alethic school. In his brilliant interpretation of Nietzsche, to be recommended as a pattern for every hermeneutic procedure, Heidegger postulates such a unified basis. He finds this in Nietzsche's incomplete *The Will to Power* (1901), concerning which he claims that the published – and in general fragmented, non-uniform, contradictory – works provide only its 'foreground'. The problem is only that parts of *The Will to Power* – it is unclear to what extent – are forgeries by Nietzsche's sister, his literary executor after his collapse and death. That is, in order to maintain the hermeneutic thesis of a systematic, overriding unity, Heidegger is forced to put the main emphasis on an unpublished work of doubtful provenance, and treat the published works as secondary material. The opposite would be the more normal way of proceeding.

And if we turn to Madison (1988: 29), one of the more recent advocates of an alethic hermeneutics, he includes, as we have seen above, 'comprehensiveness' and 'penetration' as two in a list of 10 methodological principles for hermeneutics. These two principles presuppose that the text is 'a "system", i.e. a unified whole', an emanation from a 'central problematic'.

The same attitude is found in the objectivist school – we merely need to think of Betti's second canon regarding the coherence of meaning (the totality principle). Skinner (1986a) admittedly criticizes a 'mythology of coherence' to be found among historians of political ideas, but does not abstain from advocating much the same mythology in another article (Skinner, 1986d). The question is whether the orientation towards a unitary meaning excludes the interpretation in terms of dissonance, ambiguity, and so on. Skinner (1986d) suggests that the interpreter should proceed from the supposition of rationality in the agents, which thus excludes possible contradictions from the very beginning. Hirsch, another proponent of the objectivist approach, has the following answer:

> By insisting that verbal meaning always exhibits a determinate structure of emphases, I do not, however, imply that a . . . text must be unambiguous . . . Ambiguity or, for that matter, vagueness, is not the same as indeterminateness. This is the crux of the issue. To say that verbal meaning is determinate is not to exclude complexities of meaning but only to insist that a text's meaning is what it is and not a hundred other things. Taken in this sense, a vague or ambiguous text is just as determinate as a logical proposition: it means what it means and nothing else. (1967: 230)

Thus, vagueness or ambiguity can permeate a text, and investigations in this mode are wholly legitimate for hermeneutics – we still have a meaning pervading the wholeness, namely a fuzzy one.[48] More difficult to combine with a hermeneutic attitude are breaking points and discontinuities in the interpretation itself. It becomes, for instance, difficult to assert that a text is sometimes vague and ambiguous and sometimes not, or that it is sometimes fragmented in a certain way and sometimes in another, if it is not possible to find something that ties the different interpretations together. Nor is it possible to assert the validity of several interpretations. For such a perspectivist stance will, according to Hirsch (1967), be guilty of one of two mistakes.

On the one hand, it only eclectically juxtaposes mutually incompatible emphases of meaning (perspectives). Yet, if the perspectives are incompatible, this means that it is necessary to make a choice; they cannot both be correct:

> It may be asserted as a general rule that whenever a reader confronts two interpretations which impose different emphases on similar meaning components, at least one of the interpretations must be wrong. They cannot be reconciled. (Hirsch, 1967: 230).

Against this, one might possibly argue for some kind of complementary principle, analogous to the wave–particle duality of quantum mechanics. On the other hand, it could then be objected that this irrationalistically makes a virtue of the necessity of contradiction, simply stating the fact instead of trying to solve or penetrate behind the problem of the contradiction (Lerner, 1991). Hirsch himself touches upon aspect-seeing, and adds the not particularly convincing comment (in the paragraph after the above quotation about ambiguity and vagueness):

> This is true even if one argues that a text could display shifting emphases like those magic squares which first seem to jut out and then to jut in. With texts of this character (if any exist), one need only say that the emphases shift and must not, therefore, be construed statically. Any static construction would simply be wrong. (Hirsch, 1967: 230)

But what if shifting emphases constitute an important category of perspectivism, and maybe not only that, but form the very nucleus of a perspectivist stance? Then it is not possible just to sweep the phenomenon under the carpet with a reference to the static–dynamic polarity, which is, on the contrary, an integrative part of the whole problematic. Hirsch describes the shift, the dynamic interpretation, as something marginal – the 'if any exist' in the quotation is revealing – besides the unambiguous, static interpretation. Deconstructively, on the other hand, it is possible to maintain that the oscillation between meanings in the interpretation is the more important facet, and then to take one step further and regard the text *itself* as vibrating with contradictory significances, independent of author as well as interpreter (cf. Bohman, 1991: Chapter 3, on the unavoidable indeterminacy of interpretations).

Problems connected with the presupposition of an unambiguous meaning permeate many social science issues. For instance, statements on 'leadership' on the part of a certain manager can be compared with statements issuing from the environment. If it is a question of specific behaviours on specific occasions, statements about these are easier to control and compare than if one is interested in somewhat broader patterns, such as style, properties, values, influence and so on, where matters are more complex. One possible outcome is that a set of statements about such phenomena will reveal a rather complicated picture with overlapping as well as contradictory information, not only between the manager in question and her or his environment but also within the utterances of various individuals. At least, the researcher should not proceed a priori from an assumption of harmony, but should take contradictions and variation seriously, and above all not try to force them into a uniform framework. (See, further, the discussion of discourse analysis in Chapter 7.)

Otherwise, the risk is high of ending up in a nostalgia for the decidable, simple and rational. A second possibility is simply that the researcher stipulates the criteria that are to be regarded as valid for the concept. This can of course be done, but the risk then is that the concept becomes ethnocentric; in certain cultures, for instance, concepts such as 'individual' do not even exist. Thus, in the final analysis we cannot close our eyes to the possibility of *undecidable* cases.[49] These can, by the way, also constitute 'specific behaviours on specific occasions'.

Hirsch's reasoning seems more convincing when he argues in the same text that perspectivism fails to relate the different interpretations to one another, but merely adds them together, as it were, without a structural meaning context. (See, however, Alvesson, 1996, for a comprehensive picture under the cloak of perspectivism, a picture in which the different interpretations are viewed as complementary.)

If, on the other hand, the emphases *can* be joined together, combined, then according to Hirsch (1967: 229) their *synthesis* is the right interpretation, not any single, partial perspective, since these – being partial – are simply false. The integration of the perspectives is itself the correct interpretation. The question then arises as to the nature of the relationship between the partial perspectives and their integration. According to the spirit of hermeneutics, this relationship should involve an alternation between the (subordinate) partial perspectives and (the dominating) synthesis. And so we are back in the hermeneutic circle.

Nevertheless, this whole narrow focusing on truth and correctness seems strangely misleading in the context, if we bear in mind that it is precisely a question of *interpretations*. Let us emphasize the skewness by analogy: nobody would maintain that a particular interpretation of a violin sonata by Mozart is *wrong* (unless possibly the performer plays out of tune). The same goes for a performance of Shakespeare's *King Lear*, or – coming closer to our methodology – an art critic's interpretation of a work of art, or a literary critic's interpretation of a literary work. On the other hand, it is possible to maintain that one interpretation is in certain aspects *better* than another. Which interpretation proves best will emerge during the course of the interpretive process (a process which incidentally also goes on within the interpreters themselves). In Madison's (1988) terminology, this is a logic of argumentation, not a logic of validation. Using this analogy, empirical 'facts' are presented as (one of many) arguments in favour of a certain interpretation in social science, not as one side in a theory–reality correspondence.

Actually, it is no coincidence that hermeneutics has taken the circle as its basic metaphor (the hermeneutic circles with which we are familiar by now). For at the very root of hermeneutics lies a circularity. And here the two hermeneutic circles coincide: the part–whole circle of objectivist hermeneutics and the preunderstanding–understanding circle of alethic hermeneutics. Hermeneutics presupposes as a general preunderstanding a basic, harmonious unity in the parts of the work, a unity which expresses itself in every single part: the postulate of the absolute foundation in the shape of uniform meaning. This hidden, basic precondition will then express itself in the interpretation, and in our analysis we reach via a circular route what we had presupposed … namely the harmonious, basic wholeness. In this way, the circle appears as the root metaphor beneath hermeneutics (thus, in this case it seems reasonable to speak of a uniform ground).[50] Also, the circle as symbol has tradition-ally always been seen as expressing qualities such as completeness, unity, harmony, wholeness (Cooper, 1978). This circle is then mediated in different ways by two sec-ond-order metaphors (part–whole and preunderstanding–understanding) by the objectivist and the alethic hermeneutics. Then it is, of course, also possible to ask, with Shklar (1986), what is in the *centre* of the circle: does this not become the researcher, the hermeneutician her or himself? And what, then, does this say about the latter's claims to authority . . .?

Like Hermes, the hermeneutician becomes the divine interpreter of the unearthly truth and harmony, hidden from ordinary mortals. The circle expresses divine per-fection and the interpreter is the prophet standing in the midst of the circle and bathing in the unearthly, glorious light.

This can seem like straining the criticism, but Fuchs (2001), among others, holds that hermeneutics, which as we have seen originally stems from religious interpre-tations of texts – exegesis – has never really freed itself from this root. The many prominent Christian hermeneuticians provide further substantiation. The most obvious example is undoubtedly Vattimo (1997), who explictly says that hermeneutics must retrieve its true meaning in regaining its basic connection with the Hebrew-Christian tradition, constitutive of the Western culture. It is no coinci-dence that not only Gadamer but also the contemporary and very topical hermeneutician Vattimo have been criticized for Western ethnocentrism (Ajagàn-Lester, 2004; Warnke, 1993).

So why not stop going round in circles and instead take the postmodern way out (Ihde, 1997)? This may sound reasonable, but requires some consideration. As we shall see in Chapter 6, this – a 'free play' of non-referential, intertextual signs – is not without objections either. If hermeneutics is well suited to the interpretation of texts possessing a basic harmony, then postmodernism is as well suited to dealing with contradictory wholes.

Both, however, are guilty of totalizing their perspective, one in the form of universal harmonizing, the other of universal fragmentation. More reasonable is instead to examine the situation at hand – harmonious or fragmented – and then choose the methodology suited to the conditions. Thus, one should be open to both interpretive possibilities, as well as to others of a more complex kind (Alvesson, 1993a; Sköldberg, 1994). Within hermeneutics (both approaches) and in postmod-ernism there is a rich flora of ideas and inspiration for the plucking – once we have managed to break the deadlock of *either* harmony *or* difference. An interesting alter-native, which combines aspects of both worlds, is provided by the French 'sociology of the imaginary' which we presented in an earlier section. This combines the hermeneutic interest in gaining access through interpretation to something under-lying, with postmodernism's higher acceptance of – not to say predilection for – contradictions and fragmentation, in the shape of a chaotic 'matrix' of colliding images, which are believed to lie behind the societal phenomena (Maffesoli, 1993b). Vattimo – who has also been characterized as a postmodernist – advocates a plural-ism of interpretive possibilities within a 'nihilistic vocation to hermeneutics', which, however, 'ends up in the arms of theology' (Vattimo, 1997: x) against the backdrop of a problematic synthesis of Heidegger and Nietzsche. From quite different points of departure, Caputo also strives for a deconstructive, more 'radical hermeneutics' beyond any fixation with harmony and freedom from contradiction:

> It is at this point that I want to insert a radical hermeneutic, a radically interpretive gesture, which consists not in finding meaning but in dealing with the breakdown of meaning, the shattering and foundering of meaning. It is not a hermeneutic which finally fixes meaning and truth once and for all but a hermeneutic fired by the dissemination and trembling of meaning and truth. It is a hermeneutic of the ébranler, possible only when the whole trembles. It is not a hermeneutic which gives comfort but a hermeneutic which is ready for the worst, which has been thrown out in the cold. (1987: 278–279)

Notes

1. Among which we include phenomenology (and its offshoots), which is otherwise often treated together with hermeneutics as a generally 'interpretive' approach; those two are also historically intertwined. Phenomenological roots appear particularly in the early Heidegger, which will become clear below.
2. The following account of the development of hermeneutics is based mainly on Gadamer (1989b).
3. Critical theory is sometimes also included under 'hermeneutics'. In this book, however, we have devoted a special chapter to it, on account of its radical character, which separates it from both objectivist and alethic hermeneutics.
4. The classical German idealism (without the neo- prefix) dominated German philosophy at the turn of the eighteenth century and the first half of the nineteenth, with Kant and Hegel its most prominent figures. After the death of Hegel, the idealist trend soon collapsed, to be succeeded mainly by various materialist approaches drawing their inspiration from natural science. The term 'neoidealism' refers to a return on a new basis to the idealist stance.
5. On positivism, see Chapter 2.
6. Hollis combines this dichotomy with another, namely that between holism and individualism, thus generating a two-by-two table, which he analyses in his book: systems; agents; games; actors.
7. The last of these has points of contact with the object of the next chapter, namely critical theory, and it is no coincidence that critical theory has sometimes been called critical hermeneutics (cf. note 3 above). The new direction that Heidegger gave to hermeneutics has often been termed 'ontological'. However, it is not so easy as has sometimes been thought to sort out the 'existential' from the 'ontological' in his work (see note 25 below). 'Alethic' is a broader term than either of these.
8. For a discussion of validation in interpretive research, see, for instance, Kvale (1989).
9. The choice of metaphor is rather interesting; we offer it to postmodern feminists as a clue to the deconstruction of hermeneutics.
10. Hirsch (1967) is of the opinion that counter-instances which overthrow patterns of interpretation do not emerge during the hermeneutic process, in contrast to the allegedly crucial, falsifying experiments of natural science. Our own research experience tends to contest this assertion: counter-instances have an annoying habit of emerging and demolishing exciting theories! Obviously, however, the counter-instances often provoke the revision or further elaboration of the pattern rather than causing it to be scrapped. As Kuhn (1970) and Feyerabend (1975) pointed out, this also applies to anomalies and the like in natural science.

11. Not infrequently the preunderstanding–understanding circle is seen as a further development of the whole–part circle (see, for example, Gadamer, 1989b). Preunderstanding is then regarded as the global meaning-context of a new and partial understanding of some special issue. This may well be true for the genesis of the alethic circle. Historical issues aside, though, the circles would seem to be more independent of each other. For a little reflection shows that we may equally well have partial preunderstanding(s) of an overriding, global experience.

12. See also Hirsch (1967), who has been inspired by Betti.

13. Having several meanings.

14. The same problematic is also dealt with by discourse analysis (see Chapter 7).

15. The term 'criticism of documents' (see, for example, Le Goff, 1992) seems too narrow for what we have termed 'source criticism'. Not only documents but also various kinds of non-documentary remnants from the past are used in historiographic research (more on this below).

16. It should be emphasized that in what follows we discuss *one* specific and basic historiographic method: source criticism and its complement, empathy. We do not go into the remaining spectrum of historiographic methods, such as the advances of the Annales school, or of mental history; for these we refer to articles and books which survey the subject (among them, Carrard, 1992; Tuchman, 1994).

17. A postmodernist, of course, would object that the trace is not a trace of any 'reality' but only of another trace, which is itself only a trace of another trace . . . and so on ad infinitum. As a rejoinder, the source criticist might, for instance, refer to Hegel's ironical comments on those who are awe-stricken by a 'bad infinity', or infinite regress. (The 'good infinity' constitutes the encompassing formula for the infinite series; in this case it might correspond to reality as an accumulation of traces made autonomous.)

18. This has made history writing a favourite target for postmodernists, who brand any form of realism an error, reflecting a fallacious subject–object problematic. This is combined with a (cultural) relativism, according to which any historian only writes according to her cultural bias. While agreeing that the cultural bias criticism certainly has some points, we must note that the postmodernists' totalizing of it into a 'nothing but' claim runs the risk of backfiring on themselves. For if everything is just an effect of the present culture, a social construction – then of course postmodernism is so too, and there is no basis for branding realism as false and postmodernism as the only true Gospel. In addition, long before postmodernism historians were aware of the effects of cultural bias on interpreters (historians themselves included).

19. This cannnot be countered by the argument that narrating sources (sometimes) contain more information than remnants. It would be like countering the claim that the Japanese make better cars than the Americans, by saying that the Americans make more (or bigger) cars.

20. According to the Swedish investigative TV programme, *Striptease*, 5 October 1994.

21. Former KGB employees have reported that cardiac infarction was a common euphemism for execution; it was used by henchmen who wanted to avoid possible retaliation in a later era with new relations of power.

22. This word was coined by the authors as an apt description of Ricoeur's position.

23. This may be contested, since Northrop Frye (1973), of whom White in his (1985a) theory makes extensive usage, thoroughly describes a genre that fits the Holocaust only all too well. A genre that may be termed 'demonic Tragedy' (Sköldberg, 2002b). White's argument of unicity can also be contested, for genocides have unfortunately occured more than once in the bloody history of humankind. There is also a risk in letting the very grisliness of the Holocaust make it a never repeatable event, since then we are less on our guard if something similar is on its way to happening.

24. Thus, the influential New History in France has in practice turned increasingly to the narrative and away from the quantitative mode. In this it negated its own original principles,

since it started out as the Annales school, whose programme included the strong rejection of a narrative tradition – the event-oriented historical positivism of the nineteenth century.

25. Of the two foremost proponents of existential hermeneutics, Heidegger and Sartre, Sartre accepted the designation 'existentialist', whereas Heidegger categorically rejected it; in this book we have used the term 'existential hermeneuticians' for both of them, which does not mean denying their large mutual differences. Ricoeur (1981) holds that Sartre and other existentialists have misunderstood Heidegger. The issue is not a simple one. Caputo (1987) has argued that Heidegger's problematic is closer to and has been much more inspired by the father of existentialism, Kierkegaard, than is often admitted by Heideggarians (including Heidegger himself). See also Caputo (1987) for extensive references on this subject.

26. An alternative interpretation is the psychological one which – in contrast to that of art criticism – has often sought to reduce Munch's art to symptoms of neurosis.

27. 'Unheimlich' is a characteristic and untranslatable etymological pun – we do not feel at home.

28. To take an example which Heidegger himself has used: when King Oedipus comes to know the truth about himself – that he has killed his father and committed incest with his mother – this is not a correspondence between a linguistic proposition and reality, but primarily a disclosure, a tearing away of illusion. Of course, had he wished to do so, Oedipus might have expressed this in words ('I have done A and B'), and conducted a positivist test to check whether the proposition corresponded to reality. Instead, as we know, he chose to put out his own eyes.

29. The focus on human practice and self-understanding as central to hermeneutics is also strongly emphasized by an Anglo-Saxon hermeneutician such as Taylor (1985a, 1985b, 1991), who for this reason (among others) terms himself a 'post-Heideggerian'.

30. For an application of Gadamer's ideas in culture research, see Agar (1986).

31. The later Heidegger did not use the word 'hermeneutics' about his ideas; according to Caputo (1987), however, they can be regarded as a radicalized hermeneutics (compared to Being and Time).

32. This line of thought can be carried further, and then ends up dangerously close to narcissism. A recurring theme in Ricoeur is that the main point of interpretation would be to better understand oneself. This disregards the interest in the unknown for its own sake. Interpretation certainly results in a widening of horizons, but this does not imply that a better self-understanding is necessarily the main point.

33. According to Caputo (1987), this signals a decisive difference between Gadamer's more cautious, conservative radicalism, with its 'fusion of horizons', and the later Heidegger's more radical hermeneutics.

34. For example, proceeding from his analysis of poems, Heidegger finds four primary entities between which everything in the world dwells, as if between some kind of poetical coordinates: earth, heaven, divinities and mortals (for a discussion of the relevance of this to social science, see Sköldberg, 1998). This can be regarded as his last effort to structure Being, and also as something quite basic to his later thought (on this, see White, 1978, who unfortunately repeats and paraphrases rather than explains Heidegger's evocative but enigmatic ideas on this point).

35. Here Gadamer (1989b) had different points of departure than Heidegger, whose later thinking he believed led in the wrong direction.

36. Signifying 'literary sphere'; 'poetics' means the study of literature, and should not be confused with 'poetry', which can constitute one of the objects of study for poetics.

37. As we saw earlier, the later Heidegger and Gadamer were already treading this path through their interest in textual interpretation.

38. Heidegger's thesis of the world as the screen on which Being reflects itself in the originary situation of understanding does not necessarily have to remain unchallenged. For a diametrically opposite – yet very non-Platonic – view, see Krishnamurti (1954), according to whom the understanding of Being, equivalent to freedom, is never possible in the 'net

of time', but only in the timeless now, with a radical dissolution of the preunderstanding which is always created by experienced time, that is, memory and expectations.

39. Prigogine and Stengers (1993) even extend narrative time from the human to the natural sciences, based on the concept of irreversibility and complexity theory.

40. Poststructuralists' view of temporality differs from hermeneuticians' in that it is conceived as a 'free play' rather than as an expression of human existence (e.g. Madison 1988: 99–100).

41. In this section we follow Ricoeur (1974).

42. Psychoanalysis as textual interpretation can also imply a focusing on the unconscious *language* as such: this is the case in Boothby's (1993) synthesis of Heidegger and Lacan in his view of psychoanalysis. Instead of narration, the linguistic metaphors become central here. An hallucination can, for instance, be seen as a pictorial illustration of an equivocal linguistic expression. Thus, a sun that in a wakeful dream at night is seen as 'rising' illustrates and concentrates in itself the many meanings of 'rising' which are burningly critical to the patient at the time. Boothby holds that this is compatible with the later Heidegger's orientation towards language. On the other hand, Boss's daseins-analysis, criticized by Boothby, renders psychoanalysis from the perspective of the early Heidegger. Boss interprets the sun hallucination mainly as an experience of Being.

43. The concept is borrowed from the Oxford philosopher Gilbert Ryle.

44. On culture as text, see also Phillips and Brown (1993).

45. For a more extensive discussion, see the final section of this chapter.

46. Apart from Ricouer's work already referred to, cf. also Palmer (1969: 24): 'The hermeneutic experience should be led by the text'.

47. As Geertz intimates, a similar interpretation could be made of the strange cleavage in Japanese culture between a courteous veneer and tendencies to naked violence – the famous sword and chrysanthemum.

48. Betti (1980: 79–80) is more sympathetic to such dissonance than is Gadamer, and he criticizes the latter's 'foreconception of perfection', according to which 'only that is understandable which forms a perfect unity of meaning'.

49. Interestingly enough, even the alethic school has difficulties with undecidability: Madison (1988: 115), for instance, wants to replace this concept – which he finds decon-structionist, negative, and testimony to the vanity of everything – with 'inexhaustibility'.

50. It is not without interest to note, in this context, that Heidegger repeats time and again, following the Greek philosopher Parmenides, as a property of his central notion of Being, precisely its *circular* (in the sense of closed in on itself, self-referring) shape.

5

CRITICAL THEORY: THE POLITICAL
AND IDEOLOGICAL DIMENSION

By 'critical theory' we mean the tradition in social science which includes the Frankfurt school and its associated orientations and writers.[1] The figures central to this tradition are those German (or German-born) social scientists associated directly or indirectly with the Frankfurt school, such as Habermas, Marcuse, Horkheimer, Adorno, Fromm, Apel and Offe. Other examples of scholars inspired by the Frankfurt school include Deetz (1992), Fay (1987), Forester (1993), Lasch (1978), Leiss (1978) and – although the link is slightly more tenuous – Sennett (1977, 1980, 1998) and Ziehe and Stubenrauch (1982). (See also Bernstein, 1985, and Thompson and Held, 1982, for a survey of prominent writers influenced to a varying extent by Habermas and critical theory.)

Critical theory is characterized by an interpretive approach combined with a pronounced interest in critically disputing actual social realities. It is sometimes referred to as critical hermeneutics. Its guiding principle is an emancipatory interest in knowledge. The aim of social science is to serve the emancipatory project, but without providing any given formulaic solution and without making critical interpretations from rigid frames of reference. The work of critical theory 'is open-ended and fallibilistic in ways quite distinct from the totalizing theoretical "systems" that have filled the intellectual graveyard of Western thought' (Morrow, 1994: 267). Critical theory consistently maintains a dialectical view of society, claiming that social phenomena must always be viewed in their historical contexts. Realized patterns must be understood in terms of negation, on the basis of their own opposite and of the possibility of social conditions of a qualitatively different kind.

Against the assumption that realized societal conditions are natural and inevitable – an assumption which underlies much empirically oriented research and even some hermeneutics – is posed the idea that societal conditions are historically created and heavily influenced by the asymmetries of power and special interests, and that they can be made the subject of radical change. The first-mentioned assumptions are regarded as plausible only to a very limited extent. The task of critical social science is to distinguish what is socially and psychologically invariant from what is, or can be made to be, socially changeable, and to concentrate upon the latter. The identification of regularities or causal connections should not therefore be one of the main goals of the social sciences.

Critical theory tends towards a fairly prominent theoretical or metatheoretical approach, and its level of abstraction often lies at some remove from the questions, concepts and interpretations that typify empirical research (in which we include work comprising its own empirical material, that is, research work involving first-hand experiences or the use of people's accounts about specific phenomena). One could even say that the insights of critical theory do not lend themselves easily to being used in empirical undertakings. The reader might thus question its relevance to a book such as this one, whose aim is to contribute to qualitative empirical research. As with hermeneutics, it is difficult to glean any clues about how to conduct meaningful empirical work from a reading of the central tenets of critical theory.[2]

As writers whose ambition is to provide good advice on methodology, we have thus voluntarily taken on a considerable challenge. We hope to link the metaunderstanding of critical theory to the more concrete field of empirical research, and to show how elements of the former can leave their mark on qualitative methods.

In this chapter we will describe critical theory and its development and note certain of its particular themes; we will also discuss the implications for critical methods and suggest some approaches to the conduct of meaningful social science, which maintains a critical and independent attitude towards existing social forms and counteracts their ossification. Critical theory provides guidelines and ideas about how the ideological-political dimension of social research can be made subject to reflection and awareness in empirical work and the production of texts.

On the critical theory of the Frankfurt school

Origins and early development

The Frankfurt school came into being at the end of the 1920s as a special independent institute of research, affiliated to the University of Frankfurt. Key names in the 1930s were Horkheimer, Adorno, Marcuse, Benjamin and Fromm. Knowledge stemming from sociology, psychoanalysis, philosophy, economics and aesthetics was combined here in a unique social science research environment. Traditional views on science were rejected, positivism was criticized, and attempts were made – without building alliances with any particular political parties or other institutions – to develop social theories that were philosophically informed and of practical political significance. Horkheimer and his colleagues confronted the neutral, objective researcher who follows specified methodological rules for acquiring knowledge about limited and testable causalities, with the independent, critical and socially and politically committed intellectual.

Instead of seeking to develop ideas about the universal, invariant regularities and fixed patterns in social relationships and processes, the members of the school perceived the task of social science as being to clarify the relationship between apparently given, empirical social conditions and the historical and social contexts from which they developed and within which they are re-created and – with time – changed. The idea is that social phenomena are best understood as changeable elements in a dialectical social development. The researcher contributes to this, or can do so at least in principle. Statements about society cannot be impartial. Rather, they tend to confirm or challenge existing social institutions and establish modes of thought. According to the Frankfurt school, social science should strive to develop an independent and critical stance vis-á-vis these institutions and modes of thought, and should call attention to contradictions in the way society functions. The inherent restrictions and irrationalities that inform modern capitalist society should be among the major subjects of research.

In the initial research programme, an outline was drawn up for a social theory based on both social philosophy and empirical research. The fundamental idea was to 'transcend the tension and abolish the opposition between the individual's purposefulness, spontaneity and rationality, and those work-process relationships on which society is built' (Horkheimer, 1976: 220).

Important sources of inspiration were Marx, Weber, Kant, Hegel and Freud. Obviously the school was also powerfully affected by the political climate then current in Germany and the development of authoritarian Stalinist communism in the Soviet Union. A number of studies on the authoritarian family and personality were initiated in the 1930s and 40s. The underlying idea was that economic and other 'objective' conditions – the crisis of capitalism, class conflict, and so on – provided a frame of reference for understanding, but that such explanations were insufficient. Any understanding of the obviously irrational ideas and patterns of behaviour characterizing Nazism and Stalinism that so many people were prepared to adopt called for work of considerable psychological depth. Some important results of this approach included the work by Adorno et al. (1950) on the authoritarian personality and Fromm's (1941) book, *Escape from Freedom*. In the former it was claimed, among other things, that authoritarian leanings – the tendency to categorize individuals according to various types of status, to glorify superiors, and to look down on those who are regarded as of lower rank (e.g. persons belonging to other 'races') – must be understood in light of an authoritarian upbringing, which in turn is associated with other general authoritarian tendencies in the workplace and in society in general. These are supported and re-created in their turn by authoritarian relations in the process of socialization. Fromm emphasized that people's desire to subordinate themselves in authoritarian relationships and ideologies was a mechanism for avoiding the anxiety that freedom and independence can engender.

Cultural pessimism and the critique of rationality

After Hitler's assumption of power, the original members of the Frankfurt school emigrated to the United States. Thenceforth the school could be described less as a specific intellectual milieu and more as a kind of common intellectual orientation. Under the less favourable working conditions that now prevailed, and owing to a certain pessimism about the progressive role that critically oriented knowledge could play, the original research programme was at least partially abandoned. This applied particularly to the ambition to conduct empirical studies, which after the first decade of the school's existence ceased to be a noticeable ingredient of critical theory.

The confrontation with the highly commercialized American culture left its impress on such classic works as Adorno and Horkheimer's *Dialectic of Enlightenment* (1979) and Marcuse's *One-Dimensional Man* (1964). Here the analysis focuses on the ability of the mass society, supported by the mass media and effective marketing, to achieve a standardization of needs, desires and wishes and to acquire control over responses. The far-reaching social control that typifies this sort of society, and which changes individuals into well-adapted and predictable consumers, dependent on society supplying them with an increasing volume of goods and services, is perceived by Horkheimer, Adorno and Marcuse as a threat to freedom of thought and independent opinions just as great – albeit not as barbaric – as the (more openly) totalitarian societies that had previously been the target of their fire. Adorno and Horkheimer are critical of the ideal of Enlightenment as such, based on the capacity of scientific and technological knowledge to control nature and on the development of a calculative, impersonal kind of reasoning. They claim that a privileging of this ideal leads to a form of rationality that pushes instrumental thinking so far as to produce its own opposite (irrationality), also turning the social into an object of rational, means-oriented action, permitting industrialized mass murder as in Auschwitz as well as the objectification and streamlining of human needs and desires. Thus the dominance of a technological rationality ultimately means that everything becomes subject to calculation and prediction; that man, nature and production are all transformed into objects of manipulation, vulnerable to unlimited control and readjustment.

> Marked differentiations such as those of A and B films, or of stories in magazines in different price ranges, depend not so much on subject matter as on classifying, organizing, and labelling consumers. Something is provided for all so that none may escape; the distinctions are emphasized and extended. The public is catered for with a hierarchical range of mass-produced products of varying quality, thus advancing the rule of complete quantification. Everybody must behave (as if spontaneously) in accordance with his previously determined and indexed level, and choose the category of mass product turned out for his type. (Adorno and Horkheimer, 1979: 123)

These works are imbued with cultural pessimism. According to Adorno and Horkheimer, social development and the ideals of Enlightenment are being wrecked by authoritarian and mindless social forms such as Nazism or Eastern bloc communism, or by the kind of rational control on which the triumphs of social technology in marketing, corporate leadership, education and the mass media are based. The latter turns the individual into an uncritical, passive object, well adapted to the logic of mass production and mass consumption which pervades all areas of society, from the aesthetic to the political. Politics becomes the arena of marketing and administration, rather than a setting for the continual formation of reflective political-ethical argumentations.

Critically constructive variants of critical theory

Although cultural pessimism pervades much of the thinking of the Frankfurt school, there are also variants which – alongside the basic critical tone – do contain clearly constructive and 'positive' elements. This does not mean, of course, that there is a simple critical–constructive dichotomy within critical theory (or in any other area). Critical studies aimed at emancipation from repressive institutions and ideologies can also make constructive contributions. Apart from Habermas (see next section), some of the work of Marcuse and Fromm also falls into this category of critical writings with a certain optimistic orientation.

In the works of Marcuse during and just after the student rebellion of 1968 there is renewed hope that social forces can be mobilized to question the dominant social logic, and that people can make themselves the architects rather than the victims of this logic (cf. Marcuse, 1969). After decades of largely unopposed capitalist social development, dramatic signs of dissatisfaction, questioning and fresh thinking emerged. Even though standardization, lack of imagination and a consumerist orientation still predominated, marginal groups were not subject to these pernicious influences to the same extent as before; they resisted and provided an important counterforce. Students and members of alternative movements could – the latter still can – be regarded as genuinely 'oppositional'. Compared to the working class and the trade unions they were less drawn into the logic of higher wages and the maximization of consumption. The main counter-forces of later decades are feminists and environmentalists. More recently, an anti-consumption movement represents a challenge to dominant logics and interests (Klein, 2000).

Habermas

A third, more optimistic variant of critical theory is propounded by Habermas. Habermas, Adorno's assistant during the 1950s, is usually described as setting the trend for the second generation of the Frankfurt school. Today he is the dominating figure in critical theory, and we will therefore devote more space to him than to others within this tradition.

Technocracy and the colonization of the lifeworld

In contrast to his predecessors' uncompromising – or, according to their opponents, 'indiscriminate' – criticism of modern society, Habermas holds a more balanced position. He shares with these others the view that a narrow, instrumental approach to rationality has become dominant. The optimization of means and the prioritization of effective goal-oriented action systems – institutions whose aim is to solve narrowly defined problems and to generate resources without regard to wider political or 'meaning' contexts – are what pervade the modern technological-capitalist society. Habermas claims that expertise and social engineering, supported by a narrow positivist view of science, have been handed the task of solving an increasing number of societal problems, while political and ethical debates and reflections are less prominent. People's ability to take up an independent political or ethical stance has been undermined. Technology, science and administration have increasingly taken over, and politics is becoming more and more a matter of administering the social apparatus. In this way, as Habermas sees it, science and technology have come to function as 'ideology'. Political conditions and decisions are thus concealed beneath a technocratic ideology, so that the problems formulated and the solutions suggested are those best suited to a narrow means–end logic (Habermas, 1971a).

A closely related element in Habermas's criticism touches upon what he calls the system's colonization of the lifeworld. By 'the system' is meant those aspects of society that have been detached from man's immediate cultural context, and which follow a more independent objectified logic. Here the crucial means of control are money and power (Habermas, 1984). The latter refers to a legal, formalized kind of power. (Other, more sophisticated but also more all-embracing views of power are now common. See, for example, Clegg, 1989, and the discussion in Chapter 7 below on Foucault.) The system dominates in the economy, administration and, up to a point, in politics. The lifeworld, a concept taken from phenomenology (see Chapter 4), stands for those contexts of meaning, that cultural horizon through which people seek to interpret and understand their situation and their environment. The lifeworld indicates the sphere of (always interpreted) concrete experiences, all that is close to human existence. Important media for control and coordination are values, norms and language.

By speaking of the system's colonization of the lifeworld, Habermas (1984) means that the system has expanded dramatically. Money, as a medium, regulates a growing section of existence. The system's continuing rationalization risks the impoverishment of our meaning context and of socialization. Existence is characterized by impersonal forces and influences bearing the seeds of fragmentation, as we are confronted by experts on everything from consumption to child-rearing and the orgasm – all of which has a destructive effect on socialization and the formation of personality (cf. Lasch, 1978, 1985). Habermas claims that the mass of psychological and social problems which burden the modern welfare affluent society can be regarded as a result of this.

While comprehensively criticizing these aspects of modern society, Habermas stresses that the possibility of a more progressive social development can also be discerned. On a number of points he supports Horkheimer and Adorno in their criticism of the less positive variants of the Enlightenment ideal, but also believes that these need not necessarily predominate. Habermas makes a particular point of the fact that the societies which have advanced furthest in social development have also passed the stage of authoritarian social relations, religious dogmas and other barriers that inhibit discussion and factual, rational argument. Political democracy, more education and information, and the kind of economic development that largely precludes any struggle for survival, have meant that a growing number of people possess what may be referred to as a modern consciousness. This in turn makes people more receptive to the opportunities provided by language and communication for testing established ideas and tackling or demolishing blockages associated with culturally established ideas and understandings. It is possible to question ideas and norms mediated by tradition and authoritarian institutions. Unlike the earlier Frankfurt school representatives, Habermas suggests that legitimation cannot (any longer) be reduced to an effect of the dominance of ideology. Instead there is an expectation of active legitimation through the use of argument (Delanty, 2005). Herein lies the potential for a broader 'rationalization' of our existence. This means that we need not simply let ourselves be steered by traditional ideas and values, but we can also scrutinize and question these, reaching out towards increasingly well-reasoned views. Habermas thus envisages social development proceeding along two dimensions – one technological-economic and the other political-ethical; he sees both as open to 'rationalization'.

The rationalization of the system and the tendency for thinking associated with economics, administration, law and social engineering to take over expanding areas of society, can in Habermas's view be counterbalanced by the rationalization of the lifeworld. This means that contexts of meaning, patterns of interpretation, the creation of norms, and social interaction from below are increasingly characterized by reflection and critical questioning. Key concepts for Habermas here are communicative action and competence (Habermas, 1984, 1990).

Habermas could be criticized for simply bringing together eclectically two incompatible approaches: that of the system and that of the lifeworld. His main line of defence (Habermas, 1986) against this criticism was to further define his concepts, thus displacing his opponents' objections rather than confronting them. The essence of the criticism remains largely unanswered. Another objection could be raised against the theory of 'the system', which in a social science perspective nowadays seems a little quaint, at least as Habermas uses it. It is hard to avoid the impression of a certain nostalgia in him for the clean, untainted rationality – a nostalgia expressed both in his system analysis and in his concept of communication, to which we will now turn.

Habermas's theory of communicative action

'Communication' in Habermas's terminology is something reciprocal. Thus not every transmission of messages or information is included. Communicative action contains the possibility of dialogue aiming to arrive at mutual understanding and agreement. Habermas starts from the opportunities offered by language. Here he is greatly influenced by Gadamer's hermeneutics, which stresses the possibility of achieving understanding in the meeting between individuals, through the merging of their initial – but flexible – horizons, ascending to a higher generality, which surmounts not only the individual's own particularity but also that of others (Gadamer, 1989a). Yet Habermas opposes Gadamer's consensus view of the connections of cultural tradition which enable this merging. Instead he posits a critical (deep) hermeneutics as opposed to a hermeneutics of reconciliation. His critical hermeneutics takes account of coercion and distortions within the tradition and in the interpretation. An element of explanation, as offered for example by Marxism or psychoanalysis, is necessary in order to tackle such distortions and to achieve the dialogue situations which according to Gadamer do exist, but which for Habermas are only a potential, a possibility to be realized (Habermas, 1971b). In his view all statements and meanings must in principle be suspected of bearing the imprints of ideologies, that is, of expressing power and implying socially determined restrictions for the understanding of the social world.

Habermas posits that under normal circumstances there is inherent in every statement the expectation and the claim to be comprehensible, credible (true), legitimate (in accordance with current value systems) and sincere. Without the theoretical possibility that these conditions are present, communication in the normal case would be meaningless. (There are exceptions such as humorous statements, literature and poetry, but these are not normally focused as objects of communicative action, and they will not be considered here.) There is no point in discussing anything unless it can be assumed that attempts at truth, sincerity, socially acceptable norms, and intelligibility dominate over lies, distortions, the expression of socially unacceptable norms, and incomprehensible statements. The use of language is based on the essential possibility that the former set of ingredients predominates. If elements of the second set are suspected, a participant would be inclined to terminate the conversation or at least to question any statements made in it.

That intelligible, true, legitimate and sincere statements will dominate a dialogue does not necessarily come about automatically, and it can of course happen that such elements are neglected altogether. There are nevertheless fundamental possibilities for testing speech acts critically, through dialogue, and for reaching consensus about what is regarded as intelligible, true, morally good and honest. Herein lies the basis of another broader and more basic view of rationality than the instrumental version that is normally predominant, and which corresponds to positivistic science, social engineering, and the reduction of politics to technology and administration.

The crucial point here is the possibility of undistorted communication, which is the basis for the 'highest' (or rather the broadest, most reflective) form of rationality – communicative rationality. Here it is not power, status, prestige, ideology, manipulation, the rule of experts, fear, insecurity, misunderstanding, or any other objectionable practices that constitute the grounds for the ideas and understandings which emerge. Rather, it is essentially one thing: the strength of the good, well-founded argument. In the context of communicative rationality, we no longer obey the priest because he has the monopoly on interpreting the word of God, or the duke because he has inherited a title and other privileges. Nor do we submit to the proposals of experts without first considering their validity, or blindly follow science and technology in order to reach political or ethical positions. We inquire into the authenticity of various imperatives and demand what can be recognized as reasonable arguments (or we rely on institutional arrangements which are perceived as based on rational grounds). Arguments claiming to be founded on rational connections can in principle be inquired into and discussed until consensus is achieved that a particular view is the right one (or at least acceptable), in the sense of being either true or appropriate in terms of certain well-considered needs and preferences.

This concept of communicative rationality carries with it connotations based ultimately on the central experience of the unconstrained, unifying, consensus-bringing force of argumentative speech, in which different participants overcome their merely subjective views and, owing to the mutuality of rationally motivated conviction, assure themselves of both the unity of the objective world and the intersubjectivity of their lifeworld (Habermas, 1984: 10).

Communicative rationality thus denotes a way of responding to (questioning, testing in conversation, and possibly accepting) the validity claims of various statements. A high level of communicative rationality thus signifies that perceptions are being based upon statements which are intelligible, that the statements reflect honesty and sincerity, that the statements are true or correct (given what we think we know) and that they accord with the prevailing norms. In language-based interactions, the fundamental assumption is that the author of a statement should be able to motivate it and fulfil the validity claims inherent in it, or alternatively be able to modify the viewpoint expressed. The crucial thing is that these four elements should be open to qualified scrutiny in a free dialogue. This means that there are fundamental and equal opportunities for terminating or exiting an ongoing interaction – for instance, a practical-instrumental problem-solving one – instead of accepting various statements, and engaging in the critical scrutiny of these may then lead to a common understanding. Also of vital importance is the individuals' competence in these respects, their reflective ability. Communicative action thus constitutes a potentially prominent aspect of social interaction in society, in societal institutions and in daily life. The ideal situation for conversation, which enables and is pervaded by communicative rationality, arises 'if and only if, for all possible participants, there is a symmetrical distribution of chances to choose and to apply speech-acts' (Habermas, cited by Thompson, 1982: 123).

Naturally this does not mean that the expressed views of everyone taking part in a discussion will carry equal weight. Depending on a number of factors – knowledge, experience, wisdom and (contingent thereupon) the weight of the arguments submitted – the opportunities for the various interlocutors to influence things will vary. The basis for a particular validity claim should, however, always be open to questioning. The status of a claim of knowledge, experience or another basis for authority must be communicatively grounded. In this way the scope, relevance and the reliability of statements made by experts can be ascertained, and reasonable weight can be ascribed to them. The clarification of legitimate asymmetries is therefore one element and aim (sub-goal) of good communication.

The opposite to undistorted communication is systematically distorted communication. Here various conditions will frustrate the achievement of a freely created consensus. Power relations, ideological dominance and so on infiltrate the communication process, making it difficult or impossible to question statements or to attain a high level of intelligibility, sincerity, correctness and legitimacy in the communication. Instead the dominating elements are asymmetrical social relations, mystification, insincerity, manipulation, rhetoric, distorted descriptions and disinformation. The important question to ask is: 'Are social norms which claim legitimacy genuinely accepted by those who follow and internalise them, or do they merely stabilise relations of power?' (Lukes, 1982: 137).[3] If the latter, then illegitimate asymmetrical power relations determine which views are developed and which are blocked. Alternatively, the social actors may be less prominent, and cultural blockages deeply engrained in society (taken-for-granted assumptions) are allowed to affect the discussion itself and its outcome.

Habermas distinguishes between the normatively and the communicatively achieved consensus, the former denoting a unity which results from an uncritical acceptance of common perceptions, either as a result of manipulations by an elite or because the cultural tradition transmits norms and taken-for-granted beliefs.[4] Instead, critical inquiry supports consensus achieved through communication. The very possibility and development of this ability to inquire critically, by way of dialogue, into statements are at the very heart of the 'rationalization' of the lifeworld. As this rationalization proceeds, the creation of meanings and values becomes less a question of uncritically accepting and reproducing traditional processes of socialization, and more that of mediating tradition while also inquiring into and changing it.

Habermas's argument takes place on a fairly abstract and theoretical level, and he does not take very much interest in the empirical or practical application of his ideas. In the latter context it is of course difficult to ascertain what is a normatively grounded and what is a communicatively grounded consensus, or to find examples of undistorted communication. Let us now look briefly at some of the criticisms that have been levelled at Habermas's position, before scrutinizing it more closely.

Critique of Habermas's theory of communication

Naturally, distortions in the process of communication are inevitable for a number of reasons. In this sense, communicative competence is no more capable of optimization than any other social attribute or ideal. This has been pointed out even by sympathetic critics. It is typically claimed that Habermas's views are intellectualized, and that the ambivalent and irrational character of fundamental social structures should be met by social action rather than endless argumentation and discussion (Bubner, 1982). It is also argued that rationally grounded consensus is often futile, since real preferences and conflicts of interest do not usually yield to the force of superior argument. Superior arguments are not practically possible, and in any case cannot make sufficient impact to resolve conflicting opinions and interests (see, for example, Giddens, 1982; Lukes, 1982). Brown (1994: 22) remarks that as Habermas's (communicative) concept of truth is separated from will, politics or compassion, it bears no necessary relation to practice. It could be said that Habermas's ideas ask too much of people's capacity for critical flexibility. Desires, norms and thinking are not as responsive to good arguments and to the twists and turns of conversation as one might assume. Even Habermas admits to this problem. He contends that instead of the ideal situation, genuine consensus, it may often be more rewarding and realistic to talk about compromises. Communicatively grounded compromises then differ from the pluralistic ideas about negotiated compromises unilaterally based on special interests and strengths. Habermas differentiates between legitimate and illegitimate compromises, depending on whether the fundamental principles for the creation of compromise are rationally grounded, that is, justified in communicative terms, or not (White, 1988). The problem of the will (capacity) to modify positions and convictions remains, but the idea of communicatively grounded compromises does reduce the problem of the 'realism' of his approach.

Another type of criticism emphasizes not only the practical inevitability but also the value of dissensus. A lack of consensus is healthy as it provides the possibility of perceiving and relating to the world in different ways and of avoiding blockages. This is the argument raised in particular by the postmodernists (for example, Lyotard, 1984; see also Chapter 6). Deetz (1992) agrees up to a point with Habermas's views on the importance and value of dialogue, but sees its value mainly in the opportunity it allows for revealing a multiplicity of meanings during the processes and for avoiding an unreflecting attitude towards oneself and the world. Thus in his view it is the generation of dissensus and conflict, as opposed to the achievement of consensus, that is the crucial ingredient.

Much of the criticism directed at Habermas seems to be related to his system-building ambitions, and concerns the limitations of the theory and a social or dialogue-based rationality. Habermas pushes his claims regarding the potential of language to achieve rationality a little too far. The theory can nevertheless serve as an ideal and a frame of reference, with whose help we may be able to understand the degree of communicative rationality in various social connections, thus indicating the crucial (albeit not exhaustive) dimensions of both emancipatory and repressive conditions. As Wellmer (1985: 62) points out, it is of less interest whether ideal communicative situations are historically feasible; the important point is how 'the deep structure of the grammar in our historical projects can be understood'. Another way of putting this is to say that 'the "regulative idea" of repression-free communication could serve as a thought-experiment through which we can question the legitimacy of certain institutions' (Ottmann, 1982: 96). But to regard Habermas's approach as a regulative ideal is problematic in empirically oriented contexts, since it is difficult to avoid gliding between this position and descriptions of actual conditions in relation to something both desirable and realizable. Critique must also be aware of the inevitable imperfections of human life and sensitively pay attention to 'surplus' distortions rather than indiscriminately raise its voice against everything that fails to comply with the ideal.

As we will be discussing in Chapter 7, the notion of undistorted communication may be called into question in a postmodernist perspective. In such a perspective, objections can also be raised against the whole idea of totalizing dialogue and communication as in the works of Gadamer and Habermas. Forget (1985: 143) criticizes the former for 'setting up a specific field as a universal absolute, the field of dialogue, of under-standing within dialogue, and of a specific interpretation of "communication" that exists only on the basis of exclusion'. Communication in a hermeneutic or critical(-hermeneutic) version implies the transmission of a message, a meaning, between inter-locutors. Following Derrida's 'Signature, event, context' (in Derrida, 1982), one might claim on the other hand that representations have a tendency to disengage themselves from the sender (the sender's intentions) and the receiver (the receiver's interpreta-tion), and to lead their own lives. They are also apt not to contain any unitary mean-ing for transmission, but rather to continually break down every distinct meaning and just as continually create new ones. This view involves the radical deconstruction (or 'detotalization', to adopt a term used by earlier critical theorists) of Habermas's con-cept of communication. (We will discuss Derrida further in Chapter 6.)

A possible, although partial response to this sort of criticism would be to reduce the ambitions of rationality and totalization characterizing Habermas's approach . An example of a more empirical and applied trend in Habermas-inspired research is provided in Forester (1989, 1993, 2003), where the notion of ideal situations of conversation and undistorted communication is played down. Instead Forester advocates the study of communicative action in terms of the production and reproduction of ideas, norms, trust and attention. By viewing human action and organizational structures in terms of communicative qualities, he develops what he refers to as 'a critical pragmatism'. This attempt shows how Habermas's theory of communication can be fruitfully linked to the issues of the social sciences, if we allow some unorthodoxy to seep into Habermas's rather abstract and philosophical theory.

Cognitive interest and epistemology

Habermas (1972) has compared various views of knowledge in terms of what he calls cognitive (knowledge-constitutive) interests. He differentiates between a technical, a historical-hermeneutic, and an emancipatory interest.

The technical cognitive interest concerns the development of knowledge used to create and nurture resources for man's survival, applicable to the production and distribution of food, clothing, the treatment of disease and so on. It presupposes that nature can be manipulated in a predictable way. The technical interest thus motivates research geared to the development of knowledge, and methods for maintaining control over objective or objectified processes. This calls for the isolation of objects and events and dividing them into dependent and independent variables, in order to ascertain regularities and causalities. The prediction and establishment of reliable procedures for the confirmation and falsification of hypotheses are of pivotal importance. It is the natural sciences and their applications – technology, medicine – that are the ultimate rationale for the technical knowledge interest.

The historical-hermeneutic knowledge interest is concerned with language, communication and culture. Radnitzky (1970) refers to this as 'a tradition-transmitting metainstitution'. The focus is interhuman understanding, both within the framework of certain cultures and between cultures, as well as between different historical eras. Actions, events, statements, gestures and texts are interpreted so that the distance between different individuals or traditions can be overcome. The primary interest thus concerns significations and meanings.

The third variety of knowledge interest is the emancipatory, which can be said to provide the inspiration for 'actions aiming at negation of pseudo-natural constraints' (Habermas, 1973: 176). This knowledge interest differs from the hermeneutic in that it attempts to identify sources of misunderstanding and ideological notions. Both structural and unconscious sources of social and psychological phenomena have to be investigated, which calls not only for insight but also for elements of what Habermas calls 'explanatory understanding'. Habermas cites Marx and Freud as examples of those working in the emancipatory mode. Psychoanalysis is regarded as the model for the emancipatory project. By way of self-reflection and the critical inquiry into ideas, perceptions, fantasies and so on, it is possible to counteract the psychological barriers that restrict man's potential. The intellectual insight thus acquired helps to combat repression. Marxism, as an idea, works in a similar manner on the social plane.[5]

The cognitive interest framework is a useful model for clarifying and sharpening the reason for doing research and for producing overviews of various research areas (e.g. Alvesson, Ashcraft and Thomas, 2008; Willmott, 2003). It is important to note that in certain respects there is a close relationship between the three varieties of cognitive interest. They are all necessary for an equitable individual and social existence. Knowledge about the laws of nature, about the technical solving of problems and the creation of resources – all these necessitate mutual understanding and a common linguistic tradition. The emancipatory interest is dependent upon empirical-analytical knowledge – not least in order to distinguish what is socially constructed from what is given by the laws of nature, thus enabling emancipation from stultifying dependence relations. Yet it is also, and above all in a high-tech society, concerned with critically scrutinizing the pervasive influence of techno-rational subsystems and the technical cognitive interest, as well as with counteracting the tendency of technocracy to supplant political and ethical positions as a governing principle in society.

The establishment of regularities and causal connections is thus reasonable in the domain of the natural sciences, but according to critical theory ought not to characterize the social sciences.[6] Such knowledge does not engender progressive development, but instead is apt to lock people into fixed and objectified categories. Apel (cited in Frisby, 1976: xxxiv) states that:

> social technology does not possess its ideal precondition in the model of the 'open society', but in a society which – on the basis of stable, quasi-archaic structures of domination – is split up into the informed and non-informed, manipulating and manipulated and subject and object of science and technology.

Apel also claims that social technologies (in business management, social work, teaching, psychology and so on) work best not when individuals articulate goals and norms on the basis of informed discussion and critique, but when they function almost as 'stupid' natural objects which can be studied in replicated experiments and manipulated for instrumental purposes under given conditions. Predictability and docility are not only prerequisites for social technologies; they are also a result of them (cf. Foucault, 1980, to be discussed in Chapter 8 below). In a socio-technologically advanced society, individuals develop a responsiveness to social control.

Critical theory therefore opposes the use in social contexts of experimental knowledge, or other types of regularity-seeking knowledge in imitation of the natural sciences. It warns us against social engineering and the expert-led handling of society's various inadequacies.

The advantage of the knowledge interest concept, according to Ottmann (1982: 82), is that it turns our attention to the fact that human interests 'are mediators between life and knowledge', something that 'leads us to suspect that a systematic foundation cannot be grounded exclusively either in life or in knowledge'.

Important elements in the discussion of the knowledge interest idea have revolved round the emancipatory ambition (see, for example, Fay, 1987; Ottmann, 1982). This is also what Habermas wants to stress, in opposition to the empiricists' and the social engineers' more limited conception of knowledge. Objections have been raised, among other things, against Habermas's intellectualist ideas about how emancipation is effected. It could be said that his conception of psychoanalysis as an emancipatory process by means of intellectual insight does over-emphasize the importance of the intellectual component and underestimate that which – at best – is the active ingredient, associated more with the expression and processing of emotions, empathetic reception and other non-cognitive elements. Objections to Habermas's conception of emancipation – and that of critical theorists in general – as an intellectual and rational project have come from several directions. Fay (1987) points to the difficulty of achieving a clear understanding of genuine needs and ideals, and the importance of non-cognitive conditions for emancipation such as external relationships, bodily (physical) factors, power conditions contingent upon the control of resources, and the inhibiting effect of tradition. On the other hand, one can hardly blame Habermas or critical theory for not encompassing the whole spectrum of possible factors contributing to emancipation; rather, critical social science should be assigned a reasonably limited role.[7] But we could also question the absence of any systematic or detailed consideration of political-economic realities in the transformation of theoretical ideas into emancipatory praxis. Is it reasonable to sever cognitive from non-cognitive aspects, in an analysis aiming at changing praxis, and to fairly strongly emphasize the former?

Another issue is concerned with the criteria for evaluating knowledge in terms of its contribution to emancipation. Identifiable outcomes in this respect – Have people managed to free themselves from constraints? Has suffering been abolished? – may not be a good criterion for assessing the value of knowledge, as the latter's relationships to social action and practical accomplishments are never simple or straightforward. An insightful study does not necessarily affect praxis in a distinct way. Hammersley (1992) points out that successful action may well be based on false assumptions, and that valid knowledge may be accompanied by unsuccessful action. He thinks that it is wrong to judge knowledge in terms of the pragmatic criterion of a contribution to emancipation.

A more general question is whether interest can constitute a foundation for knowledge development. The development of academic knowledge may be to some extent independent of the specific interests and purposes guiding its later use. This does not directly touch upon Habermas's ideas as they concern the knowledge-constitutive interests and not the uses of knowledge. The interest element in research is definitely worth considering, perhaps less as *the* foundation for the sciences than as a significant aspect in reviewing, evaluating and reflecting upon research.

Comparison between Habermas and early critical theory

Habermas has on occasion been called the 'last rationalist'. His whole project can be summarized as an attempt to investigate and support the possibilities of critical reason in a world where, paradoxically, the dominating perceptions of rationality can be regarded as the greatest threat to reason. He attempts at one and the same time to widen and to refine a view of reason as a critical, reflective and dialogue-stimulating faculty. Habermas's notion of rationality does not yield to the onslaught of positivistic, technocratic and bureaucratic notions of rationality. Nor does he succumb to the spirit of the times, as incarnated in the more extreme formulations of postmodernist ideas, where rationality and reason are regarded as beyond all rescue, and other ideals and means of evading relations of dominance are espoused (such as the body, pleasure, pluralism and nihilism – we will return to these in the next chapter).

Unlike other advocates of the intellectual tradition in which he is generally included, the Frankfurt school of critical theory, Habermas has abstained from functioning primarily as a 'fault-finding cultural critic' – to adopt the slightly malicious phrase that has sometimes been used about his predecessors (e.g. Adorno and Horkheimer, 1979). Instead he has constructed a systematic philosophy in which the theory of communicative action is the central theme. A crucial component of this philosophy is that evaluation and criticism are transferred or 'decentralized' to society's citizens, rather than being seen as the primary function of free and intellectual critics (Bubner, 1982). It is not in the first instance the task of Habermas's version of critical philosophy to reveal specific dominance relationships or ideologies. His major concern has been the grounding of critique and the indication of possibilities and obstacles to communication between individuals, pointing to the potential of dialogue to scrutinize existing dominance conditions so that well-founded positions can be achieved in ethical and political matters.

A similar conception of greater authority for the individual was also a leading idea in most of the earlier manifestations of critical theory. Even in that most culturally pessimistic of works, *Dialectic of Enlightenment*, in which 'the fully enlightened earth radiates disaster triumphant', Adorno and Horkheimer (1979: 3) discern a glimmer of hope that Enlightenment may yet be brought to some sort of critical self-awareness (Asplund, 1992: 57). But for Adorno and Horkheimer, as for Marcuse (1964), it is the trenchant comments on the technological and administrative control exerted by the social apparatus upon the thoughts, feelings and self-images of individuals in society, that typify the not (very) hopeful contribution of the intellectual social researcher to greater autonomy. It is possible to clarify one's own personal and social conditions and desires by brusquely identifying and grasping the obstacles standing in the way of this. By means of a sort of intellectual shock effect, the subject is shaken up so that the grip of the ego-administration is loosened. The style that characterizes much of this earlier work is thus very different from Habermas's. His dispassionate systematizations, his detailed discussion of earlier philosophers and social scientists, and his proclivity for long investigations, meticulous argumentation and innumerable subordinate clauses, have no equivalent in Horkheimer's and Adorno's polemical and sometimes fragmentary style.

Yet, as we have noted, there are many features common to the various advocates of critical theory. In surveying the tradition, most authors do not hesitate to group Habermas with the earlier Frankfurtians (see, for example, Bentz and Shapiro, 1998; Connerton, 1980; Held, 1980). The shared ingredients include an interest in emancipatory knowledge and the desire to promote a social science capable of stimulating autonomy, clarification, a sense of responsibility, and the democratic process. Critical theory perceives modern man as manipulated, objectified, passive and conformist in relation to the machinery of society and the dominant forms of rationality. Yet at the same time man is seen as partly or *potentially* autonomous, capable of self-reflection, and critical questioning.[8] The critique of positivism, technocracy and the ego-administration of private and public institutions which turn individuals into consumers and clients rather than active subjects, is also common ground for the various advocates of critical theory.

Critical theory and various political positions

Critical theory in relation to positions on the left and right

It might be thought that critical theory expresses a typical left-wing radical position, and that it would therefore only be of interest to those with such leanings. An opposition to certain attributes of established society and its development is part of the basic creed. Those who see contemporary society as in all vital respects the good society will find little of significance in critical theory.

As it is, most people would probably agree that the existence of cultural taken-for-granted assumptions, established ideologies, various kinds of power relationships and institutions, may at least sometimes obstruct or restrict people's thoughts and freedoms, and that a critical investigation might not be a bad thing. When institutionalized, even good ideas may turn into their opposite. Critical awareness can make it more likely that systems, goals, procedures, reforms, control and ideas are not taken for granted, but are reflected upon, and may thus work more 'positively'. Thus critical theory does not have to be based on a fundamentally negative view of society, but perhaps on a recognition that certain social phenomena warrant scrutiny based on an emancipatory cognitive interest; this project requires a *degree* of negativity. What is important in using critical theory is that problems are not treated as discrete phenomena which could be tackled with a bit of social engineering; rather they are viewed in light of the totality–subjectivity combination, that is, critical theory sees society in terms of culturally shared forms of consciousness and communication. Critical theory is an approach for those interested in identifying and exploring some of the absurdities of the contemporary time. These can be found in institutions, ideologies, interests and identitities that are central and often assumed to be good, self-evident and neutral.

Critical theory also lends itself well to the meticulous scrutiny of apparently progressive and emancipatory social changes and ideas. The Frankfurt school and associated groups harbour certain conservative and elitist features, although these are not particularly prominent in Habermas. They include the liberal education ideal, the opposition to mass culture and the conception of the autonomous individual – at bottom a classical bourgeois ideal, albeit one that is in clear opposition to many modern right-wing views. Market capitalism is hardly in full accord with bourgeois humanism – the latter's celebration of individuality, autonomy and a classical education conflicts with modern capitalism's commodification, commercialism and lifestyle pseudo-individualism. An example of a provocative attack made from within critical theory, and with a markedly conservative tone, is Lasch's (1978) critique of the lax modern habits of child-rearing. What undoubtedly identifies Lasch as a critical theorist is his ability to theorize on the modern ideology and practice in this particular field and to relate it to fundamental societal conditions associated with consumer capitalism, fragmentation, the influence of the professions, and the spread of psychological ideologies and techniques as a means of social control on business, on the market, and on socialization. His approach is thus much more than mere complaints about the breakdown of the family, permissive child-rearing and poor morals, when these are seen as phenomena that can be rectified by a tightening of moral attitudes.

It is thus possible for critical theory to work from other positions than that of an unambiguously leftist stance. Not only can the agents and ideologies of capitalism be the object of critical-theoretical investigation, but so can the public sector ('the social state'), trade union organizations and so on. Even social movements which in themselves accord with the ideals of critical theory by rejecting established ideas and values and seeking to reinforce the lifeworld, can still act repressively. The gender equality ideal, for instance, can be seen as a conformist force, through which a primarily money- and career-oriented middle-class ideology is disseminated by seemingly progressive interests with ready access to the mass media. The ideals may then acquire elements of dominance, with the result that existing money and career ideologies are further reinforced. (The thesis that 'women who do not work for a wage or do not seek a professional career, are repressed' may itself be repressive.)

Critical theory is grounded in a deep scepticism of technological-capitalist society; yet repressive institutions and ideologies that lock people into fixed and frozen positions and modes of thought can be critically scrutinized from conservative starting-points too. Sennett (1980) provides an example of this, when he describes how people trying to reject authorities often adopt these same authorities as a kind of negative model. In this way they are as blocked as they were before, constraining their freedom of thought and action through negative ties and rigid struggles with authority. Even revolutionary groups can fall into this trap. Resistance can thus entail the lack of freedom. People trying to avoid the constraints associated with hierarchy can easily create tyrannies of structurelessness, as witnessed in efforts to make organizations work in line with feminist ideals refuting hierarchy and bureaucracy (Ashcraft, 2001; Morgen, 1994). Critical research is wise to be open about suitable targets for critique and to not just focus on the usual suspects (capitalism, managerialism, consumerism, patriarchy, etc.).

A minimal version of critical research

On the basis of critical theory it would seem reasonable to conduct research from an emancipatory cognitive interest which critically interprets various empirical phenomena, with the purpose of stimulating self-reflection and overcoming the blockages of established institutions and modes of thought. However, a further implication of critical theory can also be envisaged: that the project is guided by some other cognitive interest than the emancipatory (hermeneutic, technical), but without having an 'anti-emancipatory' effect. This then becomes a sort of minimal variant of critical theory. One can envisage a project which, in the dialectic between reinforcing and questioning established institutions and ideologies, avoids the unequivocal adoption of either position. According to the conception of research as objective or neutral, all 'good' research would have to avoid both positions, but this view is naïve and antiquated in terms (at least) of the social sciences – something that not only the Frankfurt school and the poststructuralists but also Popper (1976), for instance, have claimed. In other words, it is a difficult task to avoid reinforcing the established social institutions and dominant interests, at least if one concerns oneself with socially important issues.

There is of course nothing wrong in itself with reinforcing existing values or institutions. Many of established society's fundamental values are shared by the advocates of critical theory (for example, the necessity to combat famine, personal violence, and abuse).[9] Nevertheless, one problem is that research often unconsciously purveys and reinforces existing patterns. Researchers are themselves prisoners of their own society and its taken-for-granted concepts, thus helping to reproduce the status quo.

A possible role for critical theory – as an example of a problem-identifying, questioning, research position – could be to *counteract* any such unconscious reinforcement of existing society's hold over thinking. Critical self-reflection thus has a limited emancipatory purpose, which is more about trying to prevent research from contributing to dominance and less about directly overcoming it. (Here there are strong parallels with poststructuralism: see Chapter 6.)

This is more difficult than one might imagine. If, for instance, we decide to study leadership, it can all too easily mean reproducing and reinforcing the 'leader' category's interests and positions, as well as contributing to the institutionalization of leadership as such. The ideas expressed in research about the nature of leadership not only reflect 'objective' conditions; they also constitute them. If 'strong' leadership receives a lot of attention in theory and research, then it acquires a certain importance in social practice. Both leaders and non-leaders come to believe that leadership is vital to operations, and will act accordingly. 'Leadership' becomes a regulative ideal for social relations in many contexts, strengthening and legitimizing asymmetrical social relations. The predominance of the leadership and management perspectives in business administration research may actually represent an adaptation to certain forms of institutionalized power, thus giving it an ideological alibi.

Let us take a completely different example: the study of the various consequences of 'unemployment'. Even such a study, which could be regarded as emancipatory, since it often points out the destructive psychological consequences of unemployment and speaks for a disadvantaged group, can mean that certain dominance relations are reproduced. If, for instance, on the basis of interviews with 'the unemployed' it is concluded that unemployment tends to be accompanied by psychological and psychosomatic problems, the research may in fact be helping to reproduce a particular attitude towards wage labour and unemployment that will reinforce existing work ideologies – which in many countries are still imbued with strong elements of the Protestant work ethic (Anthony, 1977) – and a dependence on the labour market. The consequences of being without a job may be contingent not only upon some 'law of nature' but also upon the social construction of 'unemployment', whereby part of the problem is just the production and reinforcement of the idea that people require jobs for the sake of their personal identity, self-esteem and ability to act. Even well-intentioned research can contribute to such construction.[10] It is thus important not to adopt too narrow or one-sided an approach to the problem, but instead to consider the social and historical contexts and to interpret the empirical material as socially constructed phenomena produced in part by dominant ideologies (together with material conditions, etc.). Research must not reproduce such ideologies uncritically and unreflectingly, nor take the legitimacy of the prevailing institutions for granted – but this is very hard to avoid.

Methodological implications

Critical theory and empirical research

As we have seen, critical theory is not primarily an empirically oriented approach. It could even be criticized for a lack of interest in empirical studies and for letting researchers down altogether in this respect (Bourdieu et al., 1991: 248). Critical theory offers more criticism of positivism and empiricism and less in the way of constructive methodological suggestions. Nonetheless it is possible, on the basis of critical theory, to develop practical guidelines for conducting reflexive empirical research.

Many empirical studies tend to allow little scope for critical theory or the emancipatory knowledge interest to work fully. This is because things that are simple to observe or to extract from interviews are not really what critical theory sees as an essential subject of research. Both totality and subjectivity – at least the deeper blockages in our consciousness which most urgently call for study – escape simple empirical methods. We can hardly go around asking people about their 'psychic prisons' or 'false consciousness', or about 'communicative distortions' and so on; nor do such things allow themselves to be readily observed.

Many of the views expressed in the rest of this chapter apply regardless of whether one accepts the fundamental idea of critical theory, namely that social science should be guided by an emancipatory cognitive interest, or whether one opts for a more limited adoption of the theory. The latter would mean accepting that reflexive research has to consider the ideological-political dimension that is characteristic of all social science, thus avoiding the uncritical reproduction of dominant ideas and institutions. However, the arguments below do acquire a rather different weight depending on whether the whole critical-emancipatory stance is adopted, or only the desire to avoid the uncritical reproduction or reinforcement of dominant ideas and interests.

The research question

The question that a research undertaking is to tackle should of course always be subject to careful consideration. If we take the political aspect of research seriously, then we have to pay equally serious attention to the special interests that any particular issue may or may not favour. As Forester (1983) pointed out, a decision to conduct research on a hospital, for instance, might help to reinforce ideas on the significance of medical and health care, while at the same time perhaps drawing attention away from preventive care. As we noted above, it is difficult for social science to avoid either cementing or impugning dominant patterns. What is researched and what is not researched involve political and research-political decisions with clear consequences.

Critical theory strongly supports the ideal of the independent critical researcher. Adorno (1976: 112) writes that 'the critical impulse is at one with the resistance to the rigid conformity of each dominant opinion'. One guideline for the independent researcher could be to pose various research questions that certain elite groups are reluctant to have answered, but which might be crucial from the perspective of some disadvantaged group. Another could be to ask questions that are an insult to common sense, the idea being to promote a kind of thinking which differs radically from established modes, in other words not simply adapting to the conventional views. An interesting example of this is provided by Burawoy (1979), who abstains from asking the all-pervading question, 'Why don't the workers work harder than they do?' and instead asks, 'Why do they work as hard as they do?' Another good example can be found in Asplund (1970). The author questions the assumption that the maximization of utility is both normal and rational – which means that deviations often have to be 'explained', since it is perceived as irrational not to try to maximize one's profits:

> Here one might conveniently ask oneself: Why the hell? Why can't it be assumed just as naturally that people don't try to maximize their profits? And if somebody does go in for maximizing his profit – surely this can be regarded as a phenomenon. (Asplund, 1970: 121)

A third example appears in Perrow (1978), who contends that research on 'human service organizations' (medical care, etc.) has been based upon the assumption that goals govern all such enterprises, and then proceeds to investigate how these goals may be better fulfilled. Perrow turns the problem around, maintaining that goals actually have very little relevance for such undertakings, which in reality are largely driven by external functions (employment, the regulations of deviants), and the interests of leaders and staff (harmony, job satisfaction, favourable conditions, and living up to norms about 'what it ought to look like'). The research question is therefore not 'How can we do more to achieve our goals?', but 'What actually drives these operations?' The uncritical acceptance of the first question reinforces the possibly inaccurate idea that the organization exists primarily for the sake of its clients and the official goals.

The ideal that the researcher poses the problem, in such a way that it goes against dominant patterns, may seem elitist and lacking in respect for society's institutions, including the political bodies. Should not researchers take seriously those things that politicians, business managers, trade unions and so on all deem to be important? Yes, but such issues should be subjected to critical scrutiny as much as taken for granted as guiding principles. The elites who are in a position to define major areas of research naturally do so from their own logic, and possibly from their own special interests. It is not certain, though, that they also represent wider or contradiction-free interests. And even if there were agreement between the views of an elite and those of a broader group – for instance between politicians and the population at large – those views still need not be taken for granted by the critical researcher. It is important that the legitimacy of the structures and processes which generate certain positions and opinions should be tested: for instance, to what extent are they the result of communicative debate, or can they be seen as an expression of systematically distorted communication (e.g. manipulation by the mass media)?

On purely practical grounds it can be difficult to undertake free research, since the critical approach is seldom supported by the funding bodies or by dominating groups within the research community at large. A restrictive factor, just as important as the 'objective' constraints, concerns the researchers' own self-discipline, their unreflecting attitudes, and conformism in relation to dominant positions in the research community. (In most disciplines the pressure to engage in 'normal puzzle-solving science' is very strong – see Kuhn, 1970.) The most important thing is that researchers should ask themselves the following kinds of question: Why do the funding agencies want this particular issue to be investigated? Is there (too) much fashion, opportunism or short-sighted thinking in this problem (or in the way it is formulated)? Does political correctness have too strong a grip on what is being expressed? Who will possibly gain and who will lose from an answer to this question (as formulated by the principal)? What is being taken for granted? At the very least reflexive research ought to consider and discuss the political aspects of a particular principal's interests, as linked to the given research topic.

Another issue concerns the critical researcher's relation to those being studied. One thing is to emphasize critical distance to generally defined elites and to broadly shared consensual views which may motivate the expression of alternative standpoints, another is how to relate to the specific individuals and groups that are studied. Here there are often difficult ethical problems which have been addressed by, for example, feminists in relationship to non-privileged groups, which the researcher should be careful not to address in an authoritative manner (Fine et al., 2000; Skeggs, 1997). Critical research of the Frankfurt and also Foucauldian type has not always shown that much ethical sensibility (Wray-Bliss, 2002). One problem is that in the critically distanced position there is an element of an elitist and arrogant attitude.

Now, the main problem characterizing critical research may not consist of any such external constraints and dependencies or ethical dilemmas, as these are quite visible and easy to reflect upon. Often more important is the researcher's tendency to conform to previously established patterns of thought about what is urgent and legitimate to research. The socialization process in the research community is tough. Moreover, researchers are members of society restricted by their cultural context. Cultural ethnocentrism is hard to avoid. Self-reflection and critical awareness seriously challenging ethnocentrism is not easy to achieve.

The role of empirical material

Even in critical projects that include empirical work personally conducted by the researcher rather than using the empirical work of others, the empirical material is still less central than in a study following textbooks on qualitative method. The focus shifts away from the empirical work itself and the data towards the interpretation and reasoned appraisal of the empirical material, which is further complemented by observations and interpretations of the surrounding societal context. (The researcher already possesses a thorough knowledge of this context from the 'ethnography of life', and just because it is impossible to place a formalized research procedure between oneself and this wealth of empirical material, there is no reason to ignore it. However, all this unsystematic empirical material must be subjected to particularly rigorous reflection about its significance and relevance.) Empirical material is not endowed with the same robust character here as in 'dataistic' qualitative research or objectivist hermeneutics.

There are three powerful reasons for not regarding empirical material as the whole truth, or as a decisive path to knowledge. One is that different phenomena should be elucidated in light of the totality–subjectivity combination, which means that only limited aspects of a phenomenon will lend themselves to being illuminated in a particular study. Interpretations of the phenomenon thus require much more than a body of well-defined empirical material which rarely addresses the social context as well as meaning/consciousness on an individual level.

A second reason concerns the social conditions, ideologies and communicative processes operating behind the backs of the subjects, in their subconscious, and which mean that the results of interviews and questionnaires are ambiguous. If the respondents in an in-depth interview maintain, for instance, that leadership is important in a workplace (in terms of work output or climate) what does this tell us? That leadership is *de facto* important? That it is important for these respondents (for their beliefs and actions)? That at a certain level they have adopted the ideology – recently propounded in prodigious amounts of popular leadership literature – that leadership is important? It may seem interesting enough that these people hold (or at least express) this view, but it may also be more important to understand what that view means, where it comes from and what consequences it may have. Perhaps it is just a 'semi-deep' notion which could easily change under different circumstances, or it is so deeply rooted that it has the effect of a quasi-natural law for the people concerned, that is they are highly responsive to the actions of their bosses. Perhaps there is even a natural law stating that most people are dependent upon leaders. (Historical variations suggest that this is not so, at least not in any specific sense.) Thus an empirical finding which states that a person (or *x* per cent of people) consider leadership (wage labour, high wages, independent work ...) to be important, or that there is a correlation between this and something else (satisfaction, cooperation, productivity ...) tells us very little. 'Facts' never stand alone in social contexts; on the contrary, the objects of social science express precisely that they are part of a social context.

A third reason for avoiding over-confidence in empirical data is that studies of what is deemed to presently *exist* fix our attention on the actual and draw it away from what *can be*. Empirical studies of unemployment, for instance, tend towards an exclusive consideration of the existing social organization with its rather rigid categorization of people according to their location inside or outside the labour market. If we stick strictly to the empirical material, we also stick to the bounds of thought and imagination which it imposes. Existing empirical patterns are treated as though they were more or less given, natural and neutral, not as episodes in a historical development. Trying to be 'strictly empirical' then means being non-dialectical. Forms of work organization, labour market arrangements and so on that break more than marginally with previous ones, are not permitted to inspire interpretations of the material. Such ideas are relegated to the extra-scientific sphere. But for critical theory the task of opening up lines of thinking bearing new potentialities in mind calls for the assessment of the dominating existing forms in imaginative ways. It is important to work with the recognition 'that all knowledge is "situated", will affect others and will help to open or shut down *different possible* futures' (Johnson, 2007: 96).

The importance of theoretical frames of reference

In critical theory the theoretical frame of reference possesses a special importance, not least in counterbalancing any tendency on the part of the researcher to get trapped by the empirical data – becoming swamped by observations, interview statements and other easily accessible material that seldom lends itself to direct or simple interpretation on the basis of an emancipatory cognitive interest. (Were this the case and interviewees were able to talk about communicative distortions, for instance, or about how they construct their own psychic or cultural prisons, then emancipatory research would be superfluous.) A well-developed theoretical frame of reference can also help us to make good interpretations, something which requires particular attention in critical theory as the idea is to go beyond surface meanings. It is necessary to consider not only what interview respondents (to stick to this type of empirical material) mean, and how we can understand their conception of the world and their way of imparting meaning to themselves and their situation, but also the totality of which they are a part and how, in combination with subconscious processes, this represents constraints and 'noise' in the way meaning is developed and existence is constructed (Morrow, 1994). In other words, several different theoretical considerations are needed in the research process. Kincheloe and McLaren express this as the researchers injecting 'critical social theory into the hermeneutical circle to facilitate an understanding of the hidden structures and tacit cultural dynamics that insidiously inscribe social meanings and values' (2000: 288).

Critical research demands at least three sorts of theory: a hermeneutic understanding of language and meaning, a social theory of society as a totality, and a theory of the unconscious (Deetz and Kersten, 1983). To this may be added an anthropological (alternatively a utopian-dialectical) theory or form of understanding, pointing at the relativity of cultural meanings, which helps prevent the researcher from getting stuck in the given empirical material and counteracts ethnocentrism.

These theories can almost be said to constitute metatheories, which on an overarching level guide the design of the research effort and the interpretations. They do not replace the need for specific theories associated with the area to be researched. Such specific theories do not necessarily have to accord with critical theory, which is able to refashion other theories so that they may on occasion be used in a critical approach. In fact, an important method in critical theory consists of the meticulous examination of existing theories and research that represent traditional (positivist, functionalist) thinking.

That critical theory researchers carry a substantial theoretical 'ballast' when it comes to interpreting empirical phenomena could be taken to mean that they do not see 'reality' as it 'is', but that they blindly read into it what critical theory suggests. One may find communicative distortions, ideological domination or the exercise of (illegitimate) power everywhere. As we have frequently pointed out, the interpretation of empirical material always springs from some mode of understanding and not directly from how 'reality' really 'is'. The (mis)understanding that 'objective reality' is revealed through the correct collection and systematization of 'data' implies a naïve empiricism, whereby unrecognized 'theory' built up from certain broadly based cultural common-sense notions informs interpretations. But perhaps there is reason to believe that critical theory is subject to even more 'blinders' than other methodological approaches? To a certain extent perhaps the heavy demands on the critical theorist to be well read and theoretically sophisticated can take so much time and energy that there is little time left for absorbing interesting impulses from empirical material. At the same time it is evident that the theory devotes more time and energy specifically to blinders (to use a not wholly adequate metaphor) than the orientations discussed earlier in this book. Because critical theory is interested in the processes that lead us to adopt particular ideas and take things for granted, it also enables an essentially more open attitude towards the material. Empirical material can thus contribute a great deal that is new compared to other approaches, if it is interpreted through a critical theory. It is nevertheless worth remembering that critical theory tends to under-utilize the potential of empirical material and may also be tempted to exaggerate the critical element. There is the risk of being caught in a negative binding to the targets of critique and that 'the usual suspects' are accused, assessed and condemned without open-minded inquiry.

Interpretations

Critical theory thus works interpretively, that is, its advocates are interested in the level of meaning and believe that social science is about providing various phenomena with content and meaning. Interpretations contain elements of both understanding and explanation (Morrow, 1994). As in ethnographic research and hermeneutics in Ricoeur's (2006) version, attention swings between closeness and distance. But critical research does make particular demands on distance, in order to relate the action level to the broader social, historical and economic context and in order to avoid being trapped by culturally shared meanings. What seems natural and self-evident should be problematized.

Some critical researchers distinguish between surface structure and deep structure (for example, Deetz and Kersten, 1983; Frost, 1987). Surface structure refers to the world in which individuals lead their conscious lives, where things are natural and existence is, or can be made to be, rational and comprehensible. Deep structure is here taken to refer to those unquestioned beliefs and values upon which the taken-for-granted surface structure rests. The aim is to be able to identify this deep structure, and in particular of course such beliefs and values as give rise to frozen social institutions and locked thought and action.

A good interpretation forces us to think – and rethink. Thus, in a sense, the interpretation must build upon the conceptions of people, but at the same time it must challenge and problematize them. Two principal foci are possible in this type of interpretation. One reveals the source of some particular distorted or repressive idea, while the other investigates the contents of the idea in question. The first takes account of *structures and processes* that lead to communicative noise or distort understanding and self-knowledge. Advertising provides examples when it promises an intimate connection between cigarette smoking and manliness, or between Pepsi-Cola and youth, popularity and charm (Leiss, 1983). Another example is the tendency for communication space (speech time) in social situations to be distributed asymmetrically in accordance with status hierarchies (Alvesson, 1996). Klein's (2000) study of the increased domination and infiltration of branding in a variety of domains is an excellent example of a revealing study. Here the point is not to show that the message or the particular practice is false. They may well be self-fulfilling 'truths': for instance, when men who smoke are exposed to the advertising message, they may experience themselves as more manly; or if managers consistently talk more than their subordinates in meetings, it may establish their central role, and the enormous investments in branding may lead people to fuse their sense of self with the brands they consume and identify with. Rather, the idea is to show how actors, well endowed with material and symbolic resources, are able to exert an influence which could be expected to give rise to biased and selective understandings. As critical theory in this version is concerned with the structure and the process rather than the possible espoused views of those reading the ads or of the manager's subordinates, it thus becomes a question of studying influencing processes rooted in domination. The other kind of interpretation takes into account the *content* of various conceptions and ideas. One may proceed, for instance, from people's ideas that management is important, or that the gratification of needs is a question of consumption. This content may itself be critically scrutinized in terms of plausibility.

Normally both types of interpretation are needed. Critical research thus considers both a certain mode of thought (or social institution) and its origins. Herein lies also a certain basis for examining the tenability of the interpretations. If any form of distortion can be shown, in terms of both the content and the origins of a particular conception or practice, then there is a strong case for a critical interpretation. If the message or conception seems plausible, or if there does not appear to have been any one-sided process influencing it, then no critical interpretation may be motivated. In the opposite case, if the conception can be shown to be problematic (false, misleading, blocked), and if it can be traced back to some one-sided influence (from tradition, dominant ideologies or groups with powerful resources), then there is good reason to make critical interpretations. In some critically inspired organizational studies, the illegitimate exercise of power by corporate leaders vis-á-vis their subordinates has been interpreted from both angles: in process terms, a dominant actor monopolizes communication and thus the definition of reality in a particular situation; in terms of content, messages are conveyed that give problematic representations of conditions and social relationship (Alvesson, 1996; Knights and Willmott, 1987).

Agreement with available empirical material is important, but critical research cannot be limited to making pronouncements solely on what is clearly corroborated by the empirical material. Empirical material which points unambiguously towards deep structures does not exist. However, as researchers we can and must make (self-)critical assessments of plausibilities.

Negations

An important principle, if interesting interpretations are to be produced, is to think in a dialectic way. It is in the state of tension between different realized ideas and practices on the one hand, and alternatives to these on the other, that it becomes possible to avoid getting caught by established ideas and institutions (Adorno and Horkheimer, 1979; Marcuse, 1964). By negating the existing order, it becomes possible to see it in a different and seminal way. Let us provide a couple of examples.

In contrast to contemporary consumption capitalism, where money provides the dominant medium and where so much activity, thought and need is focused on consumption as a source of gratification, status, self-esteem and identity, we can envisage a society without this consumption-maximizing logic, where a pronounced interest in possessing and consuming is seen as a problematic phenomenon. Instead of increases in wages and consumption being regarded as important natural forces, they can be seen as artificial (cultural). Instead of studying consumption as a way of gratifying needs, it could be researched in terms of illusions, broken promises and frustration. There are in fact numerous studies which interpret the whole modern consumption project – rising consumption and the possession of purchased goods and services as a means to happiness – in terms of failure (Hirsch, 1976; Kasser, 2002; Wachtel, 1983). As Fromm (1976) has said, we could see the whole of the twentieth century's economic development in the industrialized world as one gigantic experiment in hedonism, which has led to a clear conclusion: material well-being is not the key to human happiness.

Against the idea of (wo)man's profound dependence on wage labour in order to function well, we could posit the notion of (wo)man as a potentially active and imaginative being, who can act maturely and independently without being subordinated to an employer. If people in a specific society cannot manage this but are dependent for their well-being upon wage labour, that is, an administered existence, then this stands out as a phenomenon calling for investigation. How was this dependence on wage labour created? The wage-earning mentality and the social institutions which

169

support it – employers, trade unions, job centres and other bodies – can be seen as the expression of a peculiar societal construction in which the disciplining of human beings has in certain respects been pushed very far. (This is particularly obvious in light of the system's tendency to supplant human labour by technology, thus reducing the need for wage labour.) As the opposite of the employed wage labourer it is possible to launch the notion of a less constrained agent. The labour market conceived as a rational social institution can be compared with the idea of how formalized exchange relations and the market ideal (the system) have come to monopolize a particular conception of work as a life activity. This conception and the pseudo-naturalness of 'having a job' could then be seen as ideological effects. When researchers extend the labour market concept to include internal labour markets – the pricing and distribution of 'manpower' and its mobility within a particular administrative unit such as a company – this could be seen as reinforcing the system and the formal institutions and power groups that operate within it, at the expense of the lifeworld and an alternative conception of work.

By consistently seeking counter-images – not with a view to suggesting ideals but in order to provide meaningful contrasts – it is possible to make interpretations in which empirical phenomena are elucidated in the state of tension between the established order and the transcendental. It is important to stress that it is not a question of contrasting the existing order with some sort of utopia. Rather, it is about the way the empirical phenomena are conceptualized and interpreted in terms of the natural, neutral, unproblematic or the exotic, political, irrational, arbitrary. It is about making the familiar foreign (*Entfremdung*, estrangement), about problematizing the self-evident and pointing out that future realities need not be a reproduction of what exists today. A touch of imagination is required. Of course the risk of ending up with a utopia anyway is always there, but it should not be the goal. In our example of wage labour above, we were not trying to paint the system as inherently bad and to praise non-administrative forms of activity, but to encourage a more unbiased way of thinking about the meaning of wage labour.

Alvesson and Deetz (2000) suggest an overall framework for structuring the key components of critical research. This is divided into three major elements: *insight* (hermeneutic understanding in the critical tradition); *critique*; and *transformative re-definition*. The first element points at hidden or at least less obvious aspects and meanings of a chunk of social reality, the second shows the problematic nature of these meanings (and the material arrangements and social orders these indicate), the third undermines their seeming robustness by encouraging alternative ways of constructing this reality.

Critical research calls for at least the first two elements. The third may be included, but most critical work does not proceed beyond critique. Negations enter these elements both in the critique and in the suggestion for an alternative indicated in the transformative re-definition.

Critical ethnography and other forms of critical qualitative research

Apart from the general guidance that is concomitant upon the emancipatory cognitive interest, there is no definite or broadly agreed procedure for interacting with the empirical material proposed by advocates of critical theory. The literature of critical theory and qualitative method is sparse and seldom has anything very concrete to say about methodology in the sense of interacting with empirical material (see, for example, Kincheloe and MacLaren, 2000; Morrow, 1994). Without intending to cover all the possibilities, we would just like to indicate three versions of empirical research that appear reasonable in a critical-emancipatory perspective. We concentrate on ethnography as it relies on first-hand experiences and its combination of participant observation and interviews allows the researcher to go beyond relying solely on interview accounts. Critical research can certainly also lead to more structurally oriented studies (Morrow, 1994), but here the specific qualitative dimensions are less pronounced, so we do not treat such studies here.

Even if critical theory typically does not give priority to empirical studies one could consider a version of a more ambitious empirical bent – in the sense that extensive empirical material is of central importance. We could envisage studies more closely resembling conventional, inductive or interpretive ethnography. Researchers then work in a largely traditional manner, while also trying to consider themes and questions of interest in the domination versus emancipation context, and to interpret these in light of critical theory (or some other critical tradition).

Thomas (1993) cites the following points in connection with critically oriented research projects: ontology, choice of subject, method, analysis and the interpretation of data, discourse and reflection upon the whole research process. Thomas follows much the same model as that used by practitioners of inductive ethnography, but adds an element of a critical character. He suggests that critical ethnography accentuates the repressive, constraining aspects of culture, that it chooses its subject matter (focus) in terms of injustices, control and so on, that it is more inclined to scepticism with regard to data and informants, that it adopts a defamiliarizing mode in its interpretations (tries to avoid established ways of thinking and emphasizes whatever is non-natural, or strange, in the phenomenon under study), that it considers language in terms of power and reflects upon the research process itself, both as to how the researcher's involvement has affected the data and in terms of the broader relevance of the research, that is 'so what?'. Thomas contends that in such a form critical ethnography can counteract the focus on professional technique and authority that characterizes most empirical studies in the social sciences.[11]

A particularly important element in critical ethnography is the constant use of negation – trying to see things not as natural or rational but as exotic and arbitrary, as an expression of action and thinking within frozen, conformist patterns (Alvesson, 1993a; Alvesson and Deetz, 2000; Ehn and Löfgren, 1982; Marcus and Fischer, 1986).[12]

Since critical research demands a great deal of reflection, and since theory and empirical data cannot be simply and quickly integrated, the handling of an extensive body of empirical material becomes quite a complex matter. As has been shown, critical theory demands meticulous interpretation and theoretical reasoning in tackling the empirical material. One possibility is to select from a larger body of observations and other empirical indications such parts as appear important in light of the emancipatory cognitive interest. In practical terms this would mean that even if fieldwork is as extensive as in conventional ethnography, the compilation of empirical material and descriptions of the objects of study would be somewhat cut down, while more time could be devoted to the critical in-depth study of well-chosen themes.

One could envisage the result of a critical ethnography as being largely the same as an ordinary ethnography as regards the shaping of the text – with a focus on empirical descriptions but with interpretations of a more critical emancipatory character (see, for example, Jackall, 1988; Thomas, 1993). It can then be assumed that the critical theory element will become less distinct, making only a partial impact on the material. Such an approach can have the advantage of combining quite far-reaching consideration of the self-understanding of the subjects of the study on the one hand, with critical theory on the other. It remains closer to what can be represented empirically ('reality' as the members of a culture know it) in a reasonably simple way, and makes use of interpretations drawn from critical theory only when these appear most relevant and near at hand, that is to say without too much effort expended by the researcher in reducing the rift between the theoretical and empirical levels (Alvesson and Willmott, 1996: Chapter 7).

An alternative to the 'full-scale' ethnography is to go further in concentrating the empirical focus than suggested above. In the focused critical ethnography it is a question of making a fairly qualified interpretation of a more limited body of empirical material, on the basis of a relatively extensive basic knowledge about the object of study. Thus a possible research strategy could be to pick something out from within a broader empirical context which throws light on the undertaking or theme in question, and which is amenable to a critical interpretation (that is, touches upon aspects associated with the construction of reality, strongly asymmetrical relations of power, ideology, autonomy and communicative distortions), and to concentrate on that. The important point is that by way of interviews, observations and so on, the researcher has acquired a qualified understanding of the context in which the particular phenomenon occurs. This understanding, together with a theoretically sophisticated framework, will guide the choice of empirical focus. A limited empirical material is then the target of close readings and careful critical-interpretive readings. It seems that the empirical research projects most obviously bearing the critical theory stamp, at least within our own main field of organization theory, have concentrated upon the study of specific defined situations in which dominating actors have sought to define reality for their subordinates within an organization (see, for example, Alvesson, 1996; Forester, 2003). In the next section we will look at one example of this type of study.

A third variant of empirical studies, quite different from ethnography, is that the critical researcher works primarily on the theoretical level: using, synthesizing and interpreting existing studies, but adding some smaller empirical studies of her own, such as short ethnographies and interviews. The researcher's own empirical studies represent a small part of the research as a whole and are not subject to intensive analysis as in the variant mentioned above. This is a kind of mini-variant of empirical research, which can help to reduce the gap between critical theory and the field ('out there'). In this way the critical researcher can acquire more of an empirical 'feel', which will increase the accessibility and relevance of her undertaking. Readability and communicability can also be improved by using the researcher's own empirical material for the purposes of illustration (even though others' studies may also serve this purpose). The empirical work may also be used to complement a set of secondary sources. Examples of such an approach are Sennett's (1998) study of the corrosion of character in flexible capitalism and Klein's (2000) study of the increased dominance of branding.

An illustration: study of a workplace

Rosen (1985) studied an American advertising agency from a cultural perspective. The author was primarily interested in how dominance is exercised in dramatic forms, for example, how expressive situations are staged to reinforce dominant conceptions, and how this in turn helps to reproduce asymmetrical social relations in companies.

Over a ten-month period Rosen conducted participant observation in an advertising agency, Spiro and Associates, which had approximately 100 employees. He described and interpreted two specific and clearly defined situations, annual ceremonies in which all the staff joined in a spirit of festivity: an annual breakfast and a Christmas party (Rosen, 1985, 1988). Here we will discuss the first of these only.

Here Rosen (1985) sees the annual breakfast as an arena where the manipulation of symbols is very much in evidence. He provides detailed descriptions and interpretations of the context of the breakfast and what was said by the leading actors who spoke at it. He notes, for instance, that the breakfast takes place in one of Philadelphia's luxury hotels. Catering staff see to people's needs and food of the highest quality is served. The exclusive surroundings separate the advertising set from the others – their sense of belonging is underlined. According to Rosen, the luxurious setting also serves to indicate that 'access' to this sort of grandeur is possible for those who 'succeed', who get on in business life. Most employees normally have no access to such luxury, but on occasion it is theirs because they work at Spiro's. The situation implies that with more success at work comes more access to this world.

Rosen also dwells upon dress. Normally, different modes of dress will elicit differences in tasks and status. For those in higher positions, the norm system dictates very narrowly what is desirable – for example, strict, rather formal, expensive suits. Staff at lower levels generally have greater freedom. But at the breakfast everyone is subject to the same strict dress code. Here the requirement regarding a similar businesslike garb for all camouflages any differences. The idea of similarity and community is emphasized.

Rosen devotes a lot of space to the speeches delivered. He also describes in detail the tradition of making presentations to those employees who have completed a long period of working with the agency. On this occasion two people who had worked there for ten years received gifts. Others who had been there for more than five years were mentioned, whereupon they had to stand up to receive polite applause. Then came those with even longer periods in the company behind them. The last to be mentioned was a man who had been with Spiro's for 37 years; when he stood up he was greeted with very hearty applause. By the end, a quarter of the entire workforce had been on their feet. Rosen emphasizes the importance of calling attention to loyalty.

> The 'loyal' employee is likely to be more valuable to the employer than is the new, nonsocialized employee. The conditioned worker has internalized the rules of the form – control appearing as freedom – and through practice has probably increased skills, client relationships, and so on. (1985: 37)

The ritualized recognition of seniority, in the form of gifts and public affirmation, illustrates and strengthens the moral bond between employees and employer.

We will not dwell any further here on Rosen's interpretations. His work illustrates how apparently innocent and positive social activities can also be understood in terms of dominance: how specific elements of dominance can be symbolically created and recreated in social relationships. Rosen's chief method is a close reading, creating defamiliarization. He has extensive empirical work behind him, which provides him with fundamental insights into the broader organizational context of the focused situation. This in turn means that he can see through various statements in speeches, etc., which a less initiated listener might take at face value. He makes no attempt to present data in an aggregated form.

Rosen does not particularly concern himself with the participants' views regarding the breakfast. It may have been interesting to have had some light thrown on this, but one of the advantages of this type of participant observation is that the researcher is not dependent upon the ability of those present to perceive and transmit ideas about control and dominance – ideas that function albeit they are not altogether consciously registered, or are considered taboo, even though the subjects might be able to discuss them with some insight in an interview.

A weakness in this mode of representation is that there is sometimes a gap between empirical description and theoretical analysis, as the researcher's theoretical framework is used in a powerful way. The empirical material does not speak for itself in relation to critical interpretation, even though it is attended to in detail; instead argument, assumptions and deductions are given prominence.

Summary: critical theory as triple hermeneutics

Critical theory draws attention to the political dimension in research. Social science cannot maintain neutrality and objectivity in relation to social phenomena. What is focused on and thus the way it is represented and interpreted will tend to confirm or impugn existing conditions. Social science favours or disfavours different interests, whether the researcher wants this or not. Seldom, if ever, is it a matter of consistently confirming or disrupting established points of view and institutions, but instead is a mix of these qualities, sometimes at different levels. Challenging injustices in terms of unequal pay may, for example, reproduce the significance of money – the dominating medium and value in contemporary society.

In some cases the confirming and reproductive tendency is obvious. The interests and perspectives of elite groups are well represented in research. The perspectives and values of corporate management, for instance, pervade much of the research in the field of management and business administration. Various occupational groups are able to reinforce their strivings for professionalization – and thus their status and other privileges – if their areas of activity become the object of research intended to offer a scientific grounding for and legitimation of their work – for example, social workers and nurses. One field with obvious political links is gender research. It is hardly possible to disconnect the way the sexes are represented – or concealed – in research, from a gender-political and ideological context.

From the perspective of critical theory, such obvious connections between science and vested interests are not the most significant ones. Rather more important to note here is the way in which dominant institutions and ideologies are uncritically taken for granted and reproduced in research. As members of a society, researchers tend to take for granted phenomena in the particular society to which they belong, and thus to pass on its fundamental values unconsciously. In practice, reflection in research projects often focuses on very narrow sections of what is being researched. When researchers talk of their preunderstanding it is generally only a limited part of all the cultural and ideological imprints brought into a research project that is noticed.

Critical theory encourages much more, and more qualified, reflection than is characteristic of most mainstream social science. Research should promote critical reflection and emancipation from frozen social and ideational patterns. This applies not least to the researchers themselves. According to critical theory, the process of research must include self-reflection. The natural tendency to interpret existing social reality from a taken-for-granted cultural stance must be counteracted. It is a question of learning to maintain restraint in regarding social conditions and dominant modes of thought as natural, neutral and rational.

Critical research can be described as a kind of *triple hermeneutics*. Simple hermeneutics – in social contexts – concerns individuals' interpretations of themselves and their own subjective or intersubjective (cultural) reality, and the meaning they assign to this. Double hermeneutics is what interpretive social scientists are engaged in, when they attempt to understand and develop knowledge about this reality. Social science is thus a matter of interpreting interpretive beings. (In contrast to natural science, which certainly interprets, but interprets a non-interpreting reality. Nature itself is not, after all, involved in interpretation. But of course even here, data are constituted through interpretations.) The triple hermeneutics of critical theory includes the aforementioned double hermeneutics, and a third element as well. This encompasses the critical interpretation of unconscious processes, ideologies, power relations, and other expressions of dominance that entail the privileging of certain interests over others, within the forms of understanding which appear to be spontaneously generated. Critical interpretation involves a shift in focus, so that the balance between what appears self-evident, natural and unproblematic on the one hand, and what can be interpreted as the freezing of social life, irrational and changeable on the other, moves in favour of the second, thus enabling it to become the object of further scrutiny.

The critical-political dimension in research can be given more or less weight. We should hardly expect all social science to be primarily or exclusively guided by an emancipatory cognitive interest. Other knowledge interests also have their part to play. In reflexive research, this ideological-political dimension must be taken into account, but it need not be decisive for researchers' efforts. The minimum requirement, as we see it, is that researchers recognize that they are working in an ideological-political context in the broad sense of the term, where research – in so far as it is not regarded as trivial and is completely ignored – is embedded in the field of tension between the reproduction and/or reinforcement of the existing social order, and the challenging of that same order. In good research such a recognition should be discernible in the research context. Researchers should also avoid pandering to established thinking and dominating interests.

We have chosen critical theory as an exponent of political awareness in reflexive research. Criticism of this orientation can take several forms. The realism of the concept of undistorted communication can be questioned (even as an ideal type it remains somewhat too 'good'), and may be seen as a kind of telephone-wire metaphor in thinking about interference and success in the conditions for communication. The rationality concept is unreflecting in light of historical conditions, and seems to be more contingent on a particular cultural context – the reason-celebrating Western world – than Habermas acknowledges. The emancipation idea has a narrow intellectual focus, and pays too little attention to power relations and practical circumstances and constraints. Altogether, critical theory adopts too much of an 'intellectualizing' theoretical stance, which also makes it difficult to apply in empirical research. It is highly theoretical (implying a top-down theory) and easily prestructures empirical material, which tends to be perceived as fitting into the framework, assumptions, and vocabulary of critical theory. Critical research tends to 'leave unclear the methodological side of the interpretive process' (Denzin, 1994: 509). The idea that knowledge is always interest-driven also seems rather reductionistic. Is there no such thing as knowledge for its own sake? And of course a good deal of research is concerned with the researcher's own career ambitions rather than with any particular cognitive interest. In terms of reflexivity, critical theory tends to be one-sidedly focused on what are seen as the negative features of society and its institutions. In empirical studies it is important to be receptive also to the non-repressive, more 'positive' aspects of social institutions and to broaden the interpretive repertoire (Alvesson and Deetz, 2000). However, as will have become apparent from this chapter, we feel that critical theory has much to offer at the third level of interpretation, and that it provides a broad and powerful tradition in opposition to naïve notions about the neutral nature of research. We will now leave this level, and proceed to the fourth and last, focusing on language and the authority of the text.

Notes

1. Here we are following the accepted usage, although it is common for authors to deviate from it. Guba and Lincoln (1994: 190), for example, say that 'critical theory is (for us) a blanket term denoting a set of several alternative paradigms [to positivism] . . .'. Quite apart from the risk of confusion involved in breaking with the dominating usage of the term 'critical theory', it is not particularly helpful to lump together under the same label – as these authors do – a number of highly distinct schools, ranging from neo-Marxism and feminism to postmodernism and poststructualism.
2. Agger (1991) expresses a somewhat different view, claiming that, as with poststructuralism and postmodernism, the greatest strength of critical theory lies in its contribution to the methodological and empirical side. However, the methodological implications which he mentions are of a very general kind, such as the development of a post-positivist philosophy of science, and he makes hardly any reference to concrete empirical work. A more common view is that critical theory criticizes dominating ideas about methods without offering any alternatives.
3. Of course, the conditions for such an acceptance must be critically assessed.
4. The problem here is that it is difficult, if not impossible, to sort out problematic cultural ideas from a cultural tradition, which constitutes a necessary prerequisite for social life and speech acts.
5. It is important to note that it is a question of ideal types. That Marxism, then, in political contexts, is often exploited repressively rather than in a liberating mode is another thing. The contribution of psychoanalysis to emancipation can also be questioned. There are certainly anti-emancipatory elements, too, in both the practice and ideology of psychoanalysis. As we shall see later in this chapter, the movement may have helped to build a therapeutic culture which makes people exaggeratedly and self-centredly preoccupied with their mental inadequacy and dependent on therapeutic authorities (Lasch, 1978). Foucault (1978) has also stressed the ordering and forming nature of sexuality discourses. He notes that 'there has been a constant optimization and an increasing valorization of the discourse on sex' (Foucault, 1978: 23), leading not so much to a liberation as to a focusing and monitoring of certain aspects of the individual's inner life. However, both Marxism and psychoanalysis can, in principle, according to Habermas, work in an emancipatory way.
6. Critical theory claims that social phenomena are not primarily governed by regularities that go beyond historical and cultural variations. However, we should allow for the possibility that certain aspects of (wo)man's way of functioning, for example, are relatively constant, and are not simply 'mouldable' in relation to various societal conditions.
7. Some critical theorists, however, have emphasized the importance of drives and pleasures as a potential emancipatory force (Marcuse, 1955; see also Burrell, 1992).
8. Castoriadis (1992: 288) speaks of autonomy as 'the unlimited questioning of oneself about the law and its foundations ... It is the reflexive activity of a reason creating itself in an endless movement, both as individual and social reason'.
9. The extent to which these values are broadly shared is not, of course, beyond dispute. The media culture up to a point supports personal violence (action films) and physical abuse (the feminine ideal that encourages anorexia).

10. The possibility that there may be some 'natural law' type of relationship between (wage) unemployment and psychological problems within a particular cultural and social context cannot be excluded. Nor, in a short-term perspective, does it mitigate the problems to recognize the way different ideologies and social arrangements contribute to the constitution of them. In a wider context, however, it is important from a critical theory perspective not to give a narrow definition to the inquiry or to the interpretation and discussion of empirical results, but to take into consideration how a certain social context, in which a particular work ideology is central, helps to constitute the problems. Otherwise research may, in all humility, risk uncritically reproducing and reinforcing dominating ideologies about work and (wage) unemployment, thus adding to the problem it is seeking to solve.

11. A great deal of research is driven somewhat narrowly by the researcher's career interest, while its broader social meaning is slight or non-existent (Deetz, 1995). The kind of research environment that is closely geared to the number of publications in reviewed journals is particularly prone to see the combination of research and publication as a kind of game, in which publication becomes an end in itself. Another problem concerns studies oriented to practical applications, where an alleged 'use' rarely stands up to strict assessment in research terms, and where financial reward easily becomes the lodestar, rather than any open-minded interest in promoting the development of knowledge. In the case of such orientations, where the question 'so what?' is motivated on several grounds, critical theory can help to endow research with broader social relevance.

12. In Scheurmann (1984) a chieftain from a South Sea island gives his own anthropological and thought-provoking picture of contemporary Europe. He finds particularly interesting our habit of demanding money for everything – except for breathing. And that, he supposes, is only because we haven't thought of it yet …

6

POSTSTRUCTURALISM AND POSTMODERNISM: DESTABILIZING SUBJECT AND TEXT

The approach (or approaches) discussed in this chapter have their origin in the France of the 1960s, where the 'structuralist' field of ideas, represented by thinkers such as Lévi-Strauss, Lacan, Barthes and Foucault, began to dissolve and be superseded by a 'poststructuralist' (some, e.g. Habermas, would say neo-structuralist) approach. The most prominent figures in the latter line of thought were Michel Foucault and Jacques Derrida. Foucault himself, despite his own energetic protests, has often been designated as initially a structuralist. In his later writings, he falls somewhere between structuralism and poststructuralism. We shall present Foucault's ideas in Chapter 7. Poststructuralism brings with it crucial properties from structuralism, above all the linguistically inspired (Saussurian) thesis of language as a structural play with signs; yet it breaks with the conception of a dominating centre which would govern the structure, and with the conception that the synchronic, the timeless, would be more important than the diachronic, the narrative, that goes on in time. The text becomes a 'free play' with signs, without being anchored in either a producer of texts (subject) or an external world.

The roots of postmodernism can be traced back to a time after the Second World War, when a spirit of uncertainty, scepticism and pluralism began to spread in the Western world (Mirchandani, 2005). Its development thereafter has been described as 'a cultural movement which took off in the 1960s, broadened its scope and impact in the 1970s, became popular and fashionable in the 1980s and was routinized and academized in the 1990s' (Wilterdink, 2002).

The word postmodernism started to be used in the 1960s as an umbrella term for a group of American literary scholars, whence it slowly spread within their discipline and to other fields in the arts and humanities. To begin with, it was limited to rather narrow academic circles. Postmodernism also began to be used in the 1970s as a designation for a traditionally and locally inspired approach in architecture, in contrast to the ahistoric and super-rational functionalism. According to Jencks (1987), modern architecture died at a specific time and place, which can be determined as 15 July 1972, 13.32 p.m., when the ultramodernist Pruitt-Igoe housing complex in St Louis, Missouri, originally built in 1952, was blown up with dynamite, after having been long exposed to heavy vandalism by its residents, turning it into a slum. The complex was built according to all the purist principles of functionalism, with 'streets in the air', 'sun, space, and greenery', and according to a hospital metaphor which was supposed to infuse the inhabitants with cleanliness and health – but was not very well adjusted to their comfort. Despite the millions of dollars that went into the project to keep it alive and repair the damage, finally nothing but annihilation was left. A naïve rationalism had thus led to irrationalism. Postmodern architecture instead seeks rootlets to the small-scale, the local, and the historically emerged, whereas 'modern' architecture has devoted itself to cutting these off.

Thus, the approach started out as a high-cultural new trend within the arts, literary scholarship, architecture and philosophy (Wilterdink, 2002). Since the 1970s, especially under the influence of Lyotard's book, *The Postmodern Condition* (written in 1979), the term 'postmodernism' has become more and more common.[1] Here, the front line is drawn not merely against structuralism, but against a metaphysical inheritance of ideas, which is asserted to pervade all Western tradition from Plato onwards, and which has especially found expression in the eighteenth-century's Enlightenment movement – the birth of modernity: the notion that there are some rational, global solutions and explanations, some general principles which guarantee progress in the development of knowledge. According to postmodernism, however, these are not what they are asserted to be, but rather are kinds of myths or 'grand narratives', rhetorically coloured, dominant discourses that should be replaced by microhistories – local, always provisory and limited stories. Claiming to be no more than they are, these microhistories at the same time do not try to repress the power aspects, frictions, contradictions and cracks which unavoidably emerge in any discourse, either openly as in postmodernism or covertly as in metaphysics. Nietzsche, with his radical dissolution of dominant, rational discourses, was an important precursor to postmodernism (and poststructuralism). Heidegger and also Freud can be mentioned as inspirators (but hardly as forerunners).

Critical voices within the high-cultural field had already begun to be heard at that time, the 1980s, and in this area postmodernism had by then reached and passed its zenith. In the social sciences, the wave continued to grow during the first half of the 1990s, but from the middle of the decade it began to subside (Wilterdink, 2002). After the millennium shift, the relative decrease is particularly noticeable within sociology (Travers, 2006). Rather than a hot 'in' phenomenon with more or less revolutionary ambitions, postmodernism has become one part among others in the general social science repertoire (Crook, 2001).

This chapter takes up mainly those themes in what is marketed as poststructuralism (PS) and postmodernism (PM) that are relevant in terms of philosophy and methodology. On the other hand, we look only marginally at ideas about the postmodern society, etc. We begin by presenting a brief survey of some variants of PS and PM. This is followed by several sections devoted to some central figures and themes: Derrida and deconstruction, Lyotard's view of knowledge, ideas about the subject (the individual), and science and text production as narration and rhetoric. We then give an empirical illustration of research inspired by postmodernist ideas. Our critique comes later in the book, but in the penultimate section below we provide a more general critical evaluation. The chapter then closes with a discussion of some of the implications of PS and PM for empirical research.

Variants of poststructuralism and postmodernism

Poststructuralism and postmodernism are designations used in diverse ways. It is thus not possible to establish any definite relationship between the two.[2] Mumby and Putnam (1992: 467) see PS as one of many schools within PM, focusing on the discursive and linguistic patterns central to the production of subjectivity and identity. Derrida's idea of deconstruction is placed in the PS category by almost all those concerned, apart from some authors who simply 'omit' poststructuralism as a particular variant within the broad orientation which could be called 'PM/PS', and thus speak only of postmodernism. Foucault is generally ascribed to PS, but Margolis (1989), for instance, distinguished him sharply from Derrida and others, and regarded him instead as the 'typical example of a postmodernist'. His justification was that Foucault was not content with deconstruction – 'a reactive and parasiti-cal' attitude vis-á-vis texts – and introduced more 'holistic' attempts to rethink his-tory and dominating ideas with the help of alternative ways of understanding. (We will examine deconstruction in greater detail below.) This argument does not cut any ice with other scholars, who described Foucault as a poststructuralist on the grounds that he tried to rethink our conception of the subject and of the power and discipline which produce it. Foucault himself, like most of the other central figures in the schools concerned, distanced himself from labels altogether, and particularly disliked the designation 'postmodernism' (Foucault, 1983). Perhaps Rosenau (1992) best describes the difference between what most people have in mind referring to the two 'posts' when she writes:

> Post-modernists are more oriented toward cultural critique while the post-structuralists emphasize method and epistemological matters. For example, post-structuralists concentrate on deconstruction, language, discourse, meaning and symbols while post-modernists cast a broader net. (Rosenau, 1992: 3)

This is, however, more a matter of emphasis than substantive differences, so all efforts to divide up the intellectual world in PS and PM will be of limited value.

However, these somewhat philosophical themes constitute only part of all that has been launched in recent years under the rubrics of 'poststructuralism' and 'post-modernism'. In fact these terms – particularly postmodernism – have been used as catchwords for a multiplicity of different themes which in many cases have little to do with one another. In this connection we can mention various styles in architec-ture, art and literature (Foster, 1985), a certain conception of science and knowledge (Lyotard, 1984), a philosophical style, often with a powerful linguistic focus (Derrida, 1976, 1978a, 1978b), a certain cultural mentality, which either applies more generally (Daudi, 1990) or is restricted to the intellectual (Bauman, 1988), a certain social epoch which is regarded in modern Western countries as having begun some time after the end of the Second World War (Jameson, 1985), and which is characterized either by the computer revolution (Lyotard, 1984), or by the influence of the media and the 'imaginary' (simulations) (Baudrillard, 1983, 1985) or again by consumption having replaced production as the core element in the economy (Jameson, 1984). Other suggestions include de-differentiation – the breaking down of differences – within some appropriate societal sub-area such as scientific subdisciplines (Jameson, 1985), high and low culture (Lash, 1988), or the division of work in organizations (Clegg, 1990). Yet another view is that postmodernism can suitably be used to refer to the political changes in Eastern Europe and 'the death of communism' (Madison, 1991). The sprawling nature of the concept is also discussed by Alvesson (1995) and Wilterdink (2002).

Also as regards qualitative method in social science, various qualitative approaches have, without inhibitions, been sorted into the concept (Travers, 2006). Postmodernism, then, is a broad socio-cultural trend, and like its counterparts such as modernity, the Baroque period, the Renaissance and so on, it is not easily captured by ready-made definitions. (Even common social science concepts such as 'class', 'power' and 'culture' are notoriously resistant to definitions; the same goes, by the way, for some basic natural science concepts such as 'species' and 'mass'.) Possible alternatives to the terms of PM/PS might include 'deconstructionism', 'textuality', 'dialogic studies' or 'reflexivity', but as labels these are not unproblematic either.

There are differences also as regards political position. All variants seem to be possible. Sometimes poststructuralism is linked in people's minds with a leaning towards social criticism, but this does not necessarily hold. Many poststructuralist writers show no sign at all of a clear political commitment, which is one reason why they are sometimes described as conservative – 'Derrida is definitely conservative', according to Margolis (1989), for instance – or even reactionary (Newton, 1996). Since they leave the existing social 'reality' in peace, emphasizing that it is impossible to say anything definite about it, or to suggest social change in some direction, there may perhaps be something in this. Nonetheless, a tendency to stir things up, to problematize (dominating) forms of expression, can in itself be subversive. And since PM/PS is often combined with perspectives that are in some sense radical – feminism, for example – its ideas will naturally also tend in a similar direction.[3] We shall return to this later.

There are also considerable variations in views on the relation between critical theory and PM/PS. The great distance between Habermas in particular and postmodernism is often stressed. Habermas (1985) does not care for this group, and has criticized Foucault and others for neo-conservatism, while he himself has had to take the blame for the postmodernists' criticism of rationality (Lyotard, 1984; see below). But a number of writers emphasize common denominators – such as the criticism of modern conceptions of science; the general questioning attitude, for example of the Enlightenment tradition, including instrumental rationality; and the role of media and consumption. This especially concerns the more critical and subversive variants of PM/PS (Kincheloe and MacLaren, 2000). Many authors refer in favourable terms to, for example, both Foucault and critical theory (see, for example, Agger, 1991; Deetz, 1992; Sampson, 1989). In the present book we emphasize the differences more, but we also claim that both orientations offer important impulses towards a reflective social science, and that they can play complementary and balancing roles in a field that is thus charged with a constructive tension (Alvesson and Deetz, 2000).

After this discussion of the differences, perhaps a few words about what is 'typical' of much PM and PS as a philosophical and metascientific orientation would not be out of place. Particularly interesting here are the new ideas which have been introduced about language, meaning, the subject, the possibility and desirability of theoretical frames of reference, the importance of the imaginary, and the relation between the literary and the 'factual' in (social science) research styles and text production. Briefly, these ideas raise doubt about the ability of language and scholars to depict an external reality and to indicate the meaning (content) that language has traditionally been regarded as able to communicate. The problem of 'representation' thus moves centre stage. Language is considered to be ambivalent, evasive, metaphorical and constitutive, rather than unequivocal, literal and depictive. Since language is naturally of crucial importance in scholarship, this implies a problematization of traditional virtues such as objectivity, the mirroring of reality, clarity and rationality. As Brown puts it:

> [P]ostmodernism shifts the agenda of social theory and research from explanation and verification to a conversation of scholars/rhetors who seek to guide and persuade themselves and each other. Theoretical truth is not a fixed entity discovered according to a metatheoretical blueprint of linearity or hierarchy, but is invented within an on-going self-reflective community in which 'theorist', 'social scientist', 'target', and 'critic' become relatively interchangeable . . . (1990: 89)

Among other things, this means that the authority both of the researcher and of research is radically problematized. Can the researcher say anything about 'reality' which will be qualitatively superior to other people's statements about it? What about claims to 'truth', 'rationality', 'reason' and even the idea of a 'good interpretation'? Although PM and PS to some extent share with hermeneutics a deep scepticism of ideals such as rationality, universalisms and causal explanations, they do not embrace the idea of developing a best – or any – interpretation,[4] having a superior, revealing insight, or finding a singular holistic meaning. As Lincoln and Denzin (1994: 579) remark, 'if there is a center to poststructuralist thought it lies in the recurring attempt to strip a text, any text, of its external claim to authority'. (Poststructuralist writers themselves, of course, as a rule denounce any idea of a 'centre' to their 'thought'.)

Postmodernist and poststructuralist researchers draw attention to the problems surrounding the way theories are constructed, their assumptions, their rhetorical strategies and their claims to authority. Instead of an integrated theoretical frame of reference which guides an analysis towards unequivocal, logical results and interpretations, the idea is to strive for multiplicity, variation, the demonstration of inconsistencies and fragmentations, and the possibility of multiple interpretations.

Rosenau (1992) gives a good summary of the PM/PS project (albeit her final reference to subjectivity seems to be a lapse, as postmodernism goes):

> Post-modernists rearrange the whole social science enterprise. Those of a modern conviction seek to isolate elements, specify relationships, and formulate a synthesis; post-modernists do the opposite. They offer indeterminacy rather than determinism, diversity rather than unity, difference rather than synthesis, complexity rather than simplification ... social science becomes a more subjective and humble enterprise as truth gives way to tentativeness. (1992: 8)

That 'reality' can be represented in different ways is also a central theme, and the ideal that several voices should be heard is a cherished one. The very idea of truthful representation and interpretation is problematized, and it is claimed that social science cannot in fact reflect 'reality'; in many variants even reality is problematized and human experience is itself discursively constituted, that is, it 'exists' in, rather than outside, language. In more radical variations on these themes, 'reality' is presented as little more than a rhetorical stratagem, which is invoked and represented with a view to creating credibility and authority for a particular statement. Facts cannot be separated from fiction. According to Featherstone (1988), PM/PS abandons the normal social scientific ambition to adopt a rational approach, and to proceed from that to the presentation of reliable results, or interpretations which demonstrate the right or the best meaning of a phenomenon. Instead, postmodernists 'parasitically play off the ironies, incoherencies, inconsistencies and inter-textuality of sociological writings' (Featherstone, 1988: 205).

Let us now in more detail take up some authors and themes which have contributed to the establishment of this orientation, and deepen our understanding of what was adumbrated above. The discussion below naturally does not aim at a complete coverage of these actions but only at eliciting some important traits of their thinking. Various aspects, such as the Derrida–Foucault discussion and Derrida's criticism of Husserl, have been omitted. When it comes to the great inspiration for the approach, Nietzsche, our text has focused on the critical aspect of this many-faceted philosopher. The criticism can obscure the rich store of ideas to be found in this all too often misjudged thinker. (The accusations of anti-Semitism and proto-Fascism were refuted as early as 1950; see Kaufmann, 1974.) Nietzsche is above all the master of contrasting pictures, or counter-images, and to the extent that he has been criticized for lack of consistency, it is just this circumstance that is overlooked; one counter-picture does not need to be consistent with another. As Derrida (1989b) points out, there are several Nietzsches. Yet, behind picture and counter-picture there is something else again, which the Nietzsche critics have often overlooked but which inspired Derrida in his deconstruction.

Derrida and deconstruction

Several variants of postmodernism and poststructuralism constitute good examples of a thought style dominated by the rhetorical figure of irony (Lemert, 1992; Rorty, 1989; Sköldberg, 2002b, 2004). The irony is prominent in Derrida, perhaps the foremost proponent of this approach. Paradoxes, absurdities and jocular contradictions overflow here. In a discussion about Hegel, for instance, Derrida provokingly lets a parallel text run about the homosexual and criminal novel writer, Jean Genet. 'Anti-concepts' like *différance* are another example (more on this below). The famous thesis of 'intertextuality' shows how this ironic style of thought manifests itself at the level of processes, that is, how the texts are conceived as emerging over time. The single works are seen as similar to chaotic radio transmitters, decoupled from the illusory reality they intend to describe, and instead buzzing with the noise of the more or less intelligible fragments from the ethereal sea of collected world literature. The irony against a more 'objective', representational conception of the text could not be stronger.

Deconstruction

The ironic method used is 'deconstruction', which lays bare a hidden but decisive weakness in the text under study – a fracture in its seeming unity. Seeming, since the text at a certain point fails to draw the conclusions of its own premises. This sin of omission is shown to permeate the whole work. Aspects that have been repressed to the limit of non-existence are elicited through deconstruction to be central; thus the marginal is transformed into the principal.

Deconstruction thus means that an almost invisible crack in the façade of a work will prove to be a symptom of a flaw in the entire edifice; or, with a different metaphor, that there exists an apparently insignificant wound which is in reality bleeding through the entire body of the text.[5] So the *real* unity is not the systematic unity openly asserted in the text, but *another one*, now disclosed and previously repressed. Here we find a contradiction in PM/PS, since the programmatic dismantling of the work's unity gives rise to a new, second unity, which was previously hidden, repressed, subordinated.

In fact it leads to yet another unity, a third, for deconstruction does not rest content with this ironic topsy-turvy truth, but instead widens its application even beyond the work under study. It thereby creates in a further step a new problematic, which can then provide the basis for more general development. It is as if one were to point out that under the idyllic surface of the Walt Disney movie, *The Lady and the Tramp*, lies a latent violence which in fact dominates the scenic picture; and then widen this reasoning so that it is valid for more general forms of hostility underlying nice and gentle family movies as well as action movies, yet – and this is important – cannot be reduced to either idyll or violence but has a much wider bearing, for instance to other cinematic genres (comedies and so on) and even other forms of art (theatre, literature, opera, and so on).

Thus, in the first step of deconstruction we turn things upside down, and make the hitherto oppressed side the dominating one. However, we are not satisfied only with inverting the hierarchy between the two opposite sides, changing one from dominating to subordinate and vice versa. In the second step of deconstruction we undermine the difference between the two opposites as well as displace the whole opposition in favour of another notion (Krupnick, 1983). The two steps also explain the word 'de-construction'. The first step involves a destruction of the previously dominating picture, in favour of what was hidden, dominated. The second step involves a destruction of both these poles, but at the same time a displacement of them, and thus a construction of something new and wider, in which the two at most constitute special cases.

One example, and a basic one to postmodernism (Derrida, 1976, 1982): theories of meaning often proceed from the so-called 'conceptual triangle' term– sense–referent (Ogden and Richards, 1956), or, in another formulation, word– meaning –object (sign–signifier–signified). That is, as a concept a word specifies both a set of properties, which together constitute its meaning, and a number of real phenomena (referents) which possess these properties.

- *Unity 1: Between spoken word and reference.* Criticizing this, Derrida shows that in semiotic, linguistic, philosophical and other theories of meaning *the spoken word dominates over the written*, something which he terms 'phonocentrism'. This is because speech more immediately expresses its originator's intentions, including those that apply to an external referent. (For instance, a deceased person no longer speaks, yet his written words can live on, dissociated from him or her.) Phonocentrism leads into the wider and very well-known notion of *logocentrism*, which means that everything comes from and leads to *logos*, the divine word. Hence the tendency in modern Western thinking to relate everything to its logical-rational origin and/or rational goals and finalities.
- *Unity 2: Between written words.* Derrida's critique of Unity 1, and the alleged privilege of the spoken word, leads to the demonstration of the importance of the written word, with its detachment from its originator('s intended referents). Thus the initial hierarchy between the spoken and the written word is inverted. However, despite Derrida's intention to steer clear of wholeness and unity, in this way a new, second unity emerges – the unity of the written, self-contained text, something which a sceptical outsider might even be tempted to term 'graphocentric'.
- *Unity 3: Arche-writing.* Yet the process of deconstruction is not content simply to invert a hierarchy (in this case from the spoken to the written word). We must have a third stage, and this leads in turn to a further theory of so-called arche-writing, which is the precondition for both speech and writing, but in which the contrast between these two fades away to little more than a difference in degree. Even in speech there is a gap, a distance between that which is thought and that which is spoken, as well as between that which is spoken and that which is heard. Arche-writing is a 'free play' with non-referencing signs, which only address each other in an irresponsible frolic. So in a critical note, we may observe that arche-writing is a unity too, despite Derrida's programmatic intentions, to the contrary; albeit not a systematic unity of a semiotic or similar kind. In this closed room of self-referring signs, everything happens while at the same time nothing really happens at all: *plus ça change plus c'est la même chose.*

This self-referral in a closed room brings us to the 'intertextuality' which was touched upon above. The inconsistency is common to it as well, and hence our critique: Derrida pleads for a radical openness and the dismantling of all closed systems, while at the same time maintaining the thesis of 'texts', hermetically closed to the world, not referring to any external reality but only to themselves.

Différance and the metaphysics of presence

The free play of intertextuality can be referred to something which Derrida calls *différance*, and which has a double sense: it means both *difference* and *deferral*. Most things in the world can be regarded as a text, and a text consists, in accordance with the French structuralist tradition within linguistics (Saussure) which inspired Derrida, of a play with differences between signs. At the same time, the realization of the intentions of the author – his or her directions concerning referents – are, as it were, deferred indefinitely; they have only left a 'trace' in the work. Thus the text *makes itself autonomous*.

These differences and deferrals, in other words this *absence* in the form of so-called *différance*, is, in Derrida's opinion, much more important than the *presence* which he believes to have permeated the whole of Western (metaphysical) thinking. The critique of the metaphysics of presence is central to Derrida. According to this metaphysics, some underlying, more original or primordial – temporary or conceptually – principle is present in some more superficial, observable phenomenon. Thus what Derrida criticizes is a thinking in terms of manifestations: the idea that there is something 'behind' what we encounter, some hidden entity or power pulling the strings behind the curtain. But according to Derrida – and PM/PS in general – there *are* no hidden powers or entities, there are only surfaces. Examples of the metaphysics of presence are easily found, both in philosophy and in the social sciences. Philosophy furnishes such classical categories as: the presence of the essence in its phenomena; the manifestation of the substance in its accidents; the realization of the human being (as the goal of humanism); the transcendental ego of phenomenology, which generates its world; in existential hermeneutics, the understanding of Being which appears and discloses itself; the structures of structuralism with its central principles of generation, etc. Examples from social science might be the presence of the cause in its effects, the presence of the goal in the means, the presence of the deep structure in the surface structures, the intentions of the individual in her or his behaviour, the bases of power in the exercise of power, and so on.

Thus Derrida criticizes the whole of Western thinking for a metaphysics of presence. This is as abstract and simple a principle as it is basic, and it colours the whole of our mental world. Yet if we take Derrida's own ironic thinking into consideration, it seems to have difficulties in avoiding the same pitfalls. Thus, he writes that the absence (*différance*) has a 'presence' in the free play.[6] He seeks to guard himself in two ways. In the first place, *différance* is said not to be a concept. An unsophisticated reader would perhaps suspect this for being a sophism: if the word is not a concept, then what is it? And what is the difference (!) between a concept and a non-concept? That Derrida has written it?[7]

A second line of defence is that *différance* does not, in contrast to the metaphysical concept of presence, have any in-built goal or purpose (especially a final purpose for humankind), nor is it some kind of generative principle of origin. Both these points can be called into question. On the one hand, Derrida seems in fact to have a certain kind of human as a goal, namely what is usually called *homo ludens*, the playing human being, under (explicit) influence from Nietzsche's so-called 'overman'. Thus, this is the (human) *goal* for the play of differences and opposites that *différance* engages in: an individual who – like Derrida himself – plays with signs, happily liberated from every external responsibility for referents and similar boring matters. On the other hand, *différance* is most certainly a generative principle of origin; it is the source of the free play, and Derrida himself even says that it comes before the Heideggerian Being which otherwise is the original source of everything. It should be noted that this idea of nothingness or emptiness is by no means new, as we might be led to think, but has actually been around for millennia: in Buddhist philosophy (see, for example, Murti, 1980), which the postmodernists strangely enough ignore in their writings, it is completely central. Even 'free play' is, incidentally, anticipated in Indian philosophy, in the famous concept of *leela*, the divine dance of creation without goals and arising from pure joy. Thus, Asian philosophy is conspicuous by its absence – a sign of Western ethnocentrism as good as any criticized by PM, the uninitiated observer would think.

But we can take this one step further. In contrast to Indian philosophy, Derrida had an underlying, positive basis for the negativity, for the absence in free play. This basis is none other than *Nietzsche's will to power*. The free play is a Nietzschean play of *forces*, a self-referring 'economy' where different energies collide:

> Thus, *différance* is the name we might give to the 'active', moving discord of different forces, and of differences of forces, that Nietzsche sets up against the entire system of metaphysical grammar, wherever this system governs culture, philosophy, and science. (Derrida, 1982: 18)

However, with all due respect to this eminent thinker, it must be said that Nietzsche pursues the will to power as dogmatically as any of the thinkers he criticizes. The will to power is asserted, without an argument, as that to which everything ultimately can be reduced.[8] Thus it emerges that behind the difference, the absence, in Derrida's free play lies an ultimate presence: the Nietzschean will to power, dogmatically asserted. Despite his critique of the metaphysics of presence and the philosophy of fundaments, Derrida ends up in the same trap through his unreflected taking over of Nietzsche's equally unreflected will to power.

To sum up: all other thinkers are criticized for a metaphysics of presence, through which an ultimate ground is laid for these systems. As against this, Derrida poses free play, built on *différance*. But this means an *absence* in the form of differences in space and a deferral in time. According to Derrida, this differing, this absence, has a *presence* in the shape of free play. Thus Derrida is stuck in the same presence of metaphysics that he criticizes. This becomes even more evident in the fact that the differing can be assigned to a difference between various *forces* – Nietzsche's dogmatically conceived, reductionist thesis of the will to power, to which Derrida explicitly adheres. This will to power is thus the ultimate ground which – like Heidegger's Being, Kant's *Ding-an-sich*, Plato's Idea of the Good, Hegel's Absolute Idea, and so on – *manifests its presence* in the palpable.[9] Thus, although criticizing other authors for a metaphysics of presence, Derrida himself actually manages to end up in a *double* metaphysics of presence: first 'differance' is said to lie behind the present, and then the will to power is posited behind *différance*.

Freedom from references

Against the freedom from references in Derrida – the lack of external referents in the free play – we may counterpose another topical author, Kripke (1980), who takes the very opposite way in his critique of the conceptual triangle term–meaning–referent. Kripke objects to the primacy of *meaning* which has been pervading analytic philosophy from its cradle, with thinkers like Frege and Russell. Instead he maintains, with a heavy barrage of arguments, the *primacy of reference*. Words are, according to Kripke, not the 'definite descriptions' which Russell wanted to make of them, but '*rigid designations*', whose aim is to 'fix the reference'. This can be compared to giving a number to a runner before a race. The number does not describe the runner, but serves to identify him/her. On the contrary, descriptions can go wrong: 'Who is coming up there? Well, it is the winner of last year's New York Marathon'. Suppose that, unbeknown to the informant, the runner in question had been convicted of doping and been deprived of his win; then the description does not hold true. Another illustration: to describe, for instance, Derrida in a Russellian manner as 'the author of *De la Grammatologie*' would be misleading if closer examination showed that Derrida had used a ghost-writer for the book in question.

The conception of words as definite descriptions is related to a positivist, natural science way of thinking which puts definitions at the centre; a way of thinking which erroneously reduces the historical to the logical. This misses the point since, according to Kripke, designations by word do originate historically (in the case of Jacques Derrida more specifically when he was assigned his forename). Interestingly enough, Kripke's ideas (especially when used on classes) signal the possibility of a revival in modern philosophy of the concept of essence, as the rigid designation indicates something *essential* in the designed, the referent. Thus, postmodernism can be accused of 'senso-centrism': the (fluid) internal meaning devours everything, and nothing is left for the external reference. Instead, Kripke deploys a heavy battery of arguments to show that the reference in the semantic triangle in fact is *more* important than the meaning.

The play with signs and the market

It is probably no coincidence that postmodernism achieved its breakthrough precisely in the 1980s. One institution has emerged victoriously during this decade and left a deeper imprint on it than anything else. This institution is characterized precisely by differences and deferrals, more and more by a 'play with signs' and by a liberation from actors and the real underlying circumstances. We are thinking of the *market*, and more especially the *financial market*. (For an interpretation of the derivatives market – dealing with options and futures – in these terms, see Bay, 1998.) Particularly during the Roaring Eighties it was easy to conceive this as a free play in a vacuum, liberated from all references to mundane occurrences; a whirlwind of signs without regard to boring realities. The economic boom in the West during this decade, driven by Reaganomics, in combination with the internationalization automatization of the money markets, constituted its basis. The victory in the East of the market, with the fall of the command economy at the end of the decade, confirmed the trend (cf. Madison, 1991).

In such a social environment, postmodernism of course presents the perfect ideology. The light ironic playfulness against earth-bound troglodytes is the ideal attitude for a social world which has lost its anchor in reality. (Compare Baudrillard, 1983, on 'simulacra' – elusive images or chimeras which live their own ephemeral and capricious lives without being moored to any other reality than themselves.) This interpretation becomes ever more plausible if we specifically keep in mind that the counter-pole to the market – the command or plan economy – has been a favourite target for many postmodern critics. In line with this is also, for example, Min (2005), who criticizes the postmodernists' fixation on *différance* and believes, inspired among others by Hegel, that this fixation counteracts the necessary ethics and solidarity between people.

Sometimes, the hangover after the intellectuals' failure to gain response for their radical social ideas during the 1970s is given as an explanation for the broad breakthrough of postmodernism during the 1980s. Some of those who are counted among the foremost figures in postmodernism had early on been oriented towards Marxism (e.g. Baudrillard). In particular the disillusion over the failure of Marxism probably played a role (Wilterdink, 2002). Disillusion leads to a predilection for nihilism and relativism (Lash, 1988). Postmodernism can be conceived as a slightly transparent allegory for the preferred economic alternative, the market solution.[10] (Sometimes the transparency may be rather more than slight, as for instance in China where, according to the media, the postmodernists are criticized by the democratic opposition for a politically conservative attitude, supporting the bureaucratic ruling elite, since they regard it as a bulwark for the market economy.) Drawing similar conclusions, Wilterdink (2002) also emphasizes that neoliberalism and postmodernism are parallel currents with the same socioeconomic background. The beginning of the 1990s, with recessions and financial crashes in many Western countries, as well as the unexpectedly large difficulties preventing the market economy from functioning well in the East, may to some extent have shed new light on the ideological projection of the market – postmodernism.[11] These observations concern the reception of the approach and its possible deconstruction as 'markocentric' – alluding to a hidden model, the market, working as its invisible but generative centre. Naturally this does not gainsay, but on the contrary implies (since the centre is invisible), that single authors in the area can appear as anti-capitalist, socialist and so on (e.g. Clegg, 1990; Jameson, 1984; Touraine, 1992). Analogously, Derrida's critique of Heidegger for a metaphysics of presence does not contradict the latter's anti-metaphysical message.

The roots of the markocentric conception might incidentally be sought in two of the approach's paragons. That the economy of urges is so diligently referred to by PM/PS authors is hardly a coincidence – see, for instance, Derrida, cited in Spivak (1976: xlii):

> Following a schema that continually guides Freud's thinking, the movement of the trace is described as an effort of life to protect itself *by deferring* the dangerous investment, by constituting a reserve (*Vorrat*). And all the conceptual oppositions that furrow Freudian thought relate each concept to the other like movements of a detour, within the economy of differences. The one is only the other deferred, the one differing from the other.

Still less is it a coincidence that the great 'guru' of the approach, Nietzsche, had as the (never called into question, thus dogmatic) basic principle for his whole philosophy an *economy of free forces*, which he also designated as the 'will to power'. The anonymous market forces appear here, faintly disguised in German philosophic garb. The will to power as the 'eternal recurrence' is the central theme for Nietzsche, and the central problem in Heidegger's interpretation of Nietzsche (cf. Chapter 4). But what eternally recurs in the play of free market forces is of course nothing other than *profit*, generated by the market ever anew in its self-referring will to power 'beyond good and evil' which it inscribes in its shadowy agents. The delight over the word 'economy', emerging time and again among PM/PS authors, is indicative.

We might (deconstructively) ask what could lie *beyond* the economic metaphor for knowledge, either plan- or market-oriented. Our alternative is – as has been discussed above and will be further developed in Chapter 8 – dialogue, argumentation, the practical reason in an Aristotelian sense. Not in a *mediation* of knowledge/meaning between subjects but as the *creation* of knowledge in a discursive field. Both the actors and the dialogue between them have a degree of sovereignty, but this is a *relative* sovereignty, not an absolute; thus we end up neither in the problematic of the subject (absolutely sovereign actors) nor in PM (absolutely sovereign textuality), and so avoid two kinds of reductionism. This does not mean a rational, perfect, noise-free communication; noise, friction, misunderstanding, irritation and 'trouble' will always be there, and are indeed a precondition for the process. On the other hand, neither does it mean a 'paralogic' situation, where market competition trans-forms the actors into puppets. These possess an irreducible relative sovereignty, and it is in the interplay between the relative sovereignty of the actors and that of the dialogue that new knowledge is generated. Here we can, by the way, once again draw a comparison with Derrida (1989a), who in his critique of Gadamer's concept of dialogue points out that this is based on a fundamental axiom of 'good will' from the participants, and in connection with this says the following:

> It confers 'dignity' in the Kantian sense on the good will, to know that which in a moral being *lies beyond all market value, every negotiable price* ... So this axiom would stand beyond any kind of evaluation whatsoever and beyond all value, if a value implies a scale and a comparison. (Derrida, 1989a: 52; emphasis added)

Gadamer's concept of dialogue is certainly liable to criticism for an exaggerated harmonic view, as are incidentally also Habermas's ideas, which at this point are tangential to those of Gadamer; what is interesting here, however, is that Derrida criticizes the concept precisely for its lack of market adaptation. This confirms once more our picture of postmodernism as markocentric: a picture that is provided with further outlines by another of the movement's prominent figures, Lyotard.

The downfall of the grand narratives

Lyotard's (1984) discourse falls within a similar pattern of postmodernism and mar-ket: Lyotard objects to 'the grand narratives', kinds of myths or sagas that are told of and explain a vast number of occurrences, acquiring such power over minds that they come to function as absolute truths or dogma. Examples of this are system theories of different kinds, and Marxism; but even psychoanalysis, hermeneutics and other elaborated and coherent approaches are included in the same category. Like many postmodernists, Lyotard is concerned with the small, the local, the fragmented, historically emerged, contradictory and accidental, in contrast to the unified system buildings, the monoliths and the cathedrals of thought. (A forerunner here is the structuralist Lévi-Strauss (1967), with his recommendation of 'patchwork' (*bricolage*), an element which, even if it was subordinated in his writings, indicated future directions of thought – see Derrida, 1978a.) Lyotard especially emphasizes the importance of critically analysing the prevailing narratives, precisely in narrative terms. Even the seemingly 'truest' theories are stories, narrations, and a critical scrutiny of their narrative structure then becomes fundamental (see the parallel with Ricoeur in Chapter 4.)

Lyotard's critique can in fact be seen as an allegory for the critique of command and plan economies, in favour of the local, historically emerged, fragmented, temporary, apparently fragile but in reality powerful markets. The allegory is, to borrow de Man's (1983) term used in another context, 'half-conscious', since Lyotard explicitly rejects the thinking of plan economies but does not explicitly embrace the market solution in particular. However, he clearly says in the conclusion to his book, *The Postmodern Condition*, that there are no alternatives to capitalism; we can only work within it, and try to stretch its boundaries. In the shape of the so-called *temporary contract*, the market allegory finally becomes pretty transparent (the contract and contract law are, after all, the very cornerstone of the market):

> This orientation corresponds to the course that the evolution of social interaction is currently taking: the temporary contract is in practice supplanting permanent institutions in the professional, emotional, sexual, cultural, family, and international domains, as well as in political affairs. This evolution is of course ambiguous: the temporary contract is favored by the system due to its greater flexibility, lower cost, and the creative turmoil of its accompanying motivations – all of these factors contribute to increased operativity. In any case, there is no question here of proposing a 'pure' alternative to the system: we all now know, as the 1970s come to a close, that an attempt at an alternative of that kind would end up resembling the system it was meant to replace. We should be happy that the tendency toward the temporary contract is ambiguous: it is not totally subordinated to the goal of the system, yet the system tolerates it. (Lyotard, 1984: 66)

Lyotard also objects to another alternative, that of critical theory, and more especially in the form of Habermas's ideas. The thrust of the critique against the latter is that he has radically overvalued the importance of a communication free from disturbances and contradictions, and that he has given the wrong final goal – consensus – for the dialogue between actors. Lyotard too finds such a dialogue valuable, but he does not accept Habermas's harmonizing of it. Disturbances and contradictions will always be an element of every dialogue worth its name; and, what is more, the goal of the dialogue is not consensus (this is only an intermediary stage) but 'paralogy' – a fruitful dissensus which *undermines* the prevailing discourse. Consensus can either be based on the conception of emancipation, or else be a way to make the system function better. In the first case it is founded on a 'grand narrative', that is it claims to have found the Solution; in the other case it is instrumentally motivated, working through power interests. Both are objectionable. Besides, according to Lyotard it is impossible for the parties to a dialogue to unite in a Habermasian spirit around such overriding rules for the dialogue, since no overriding rules exist. Lyotard and Thébaud (1986) develop this line of reasoning into a notion of self-referring 'games' between different actors, with the will to power as a central ingredient. This may sound somewhat cynical as a prescription for (or a description of) dialogue, but, in their version, the will to power has a pluralist rather than a dominating character. Tension, dissensus and differences are irreducible elements of the game, which aims at creative development, not at a total victory over the opponent (since this means that the important aspect of tension would be lost). The Nietzschean influence is marked.

This same line of reasoning also holds for science, and here Lyotard refers with approval to the pluralism of Feyerabend (1975). Otherwise he maintains that in science such new theories as chaos and catastrophe theories, with their paradoxes and ambiguities, their interest in instabilities and undecidabilities, are superior to the classical, total and homogeneous systems *á la* Newton. The sciences are thus not completely *transparent* in their inner structure. Yet neither are they transparent vis-á-vis their object; Lyotard rejects a traditional thinking in terms of representation or mirroring, according to which truth in scientific discourses would be a mirroring in the subject of the object. Instead of correspondence, Lyotard holds what might be termed a *constructivist* thesis: that which is creative, or original in the theories, is the important thing in the scientific results. Similar ideas have been proposed by Deleuze (1983) in his discussion of Nietzsche, one of the foremost inspirations, not to say *the* foremost inspiration of postmodernism; and he too maintains the primacy of creation before representation, originality before the mimetic, action before reaction. But what, then, becomes of validity? Lyotard's answer is that every scientific 'language game' creates its *own* immanent rules of validation. Hence these cannot be imported from the outside, but are generated through the scientific discourse itself. At the same time, this of course means a criticism of the traditional positivist philosophy of science, according to which the overriding criteria for scientific activity can be established. It is therefore no coincidence that Lyotard concurs with authors critical of positivism such as Kuhn and Feyerabend, who have held similar opinions. Lyotard also considers the worth of knowledge from pragmatic, technologic criteria. Thus, it is not the truth content but the applicability that becomes decisive. A partly similar answer to the problem of validity is that this is decided by the *market value*, where knowledge is consequently conceived as goods sold on a market; see Berg (1989) for a discussion. This in turn further confirms the interpretation of postmodernism in terms of a half-conscious market metaphor, which we have just discussed.

The ideas of Lyotard may appear well turned. They have not, however, escaped critique. Rorty (1992) and Calhoun (1992), for example, argue that Lyotard, like postmodernists more generally, in a passion for pluralism against general rules and criteria for science, over-emphasizes the problem of relating different positions to each other.

> In most postmodernist accounts, the coming together of people from different traditions, or those abiding by different rules from within the same tradition, seems primarily an occasion for communication to break down, not for ... mutual learning and growth. (Calhoun, 1992: 266–267)

That the languages of different theories are not perfectly translatable and commensurable does not prevent a person from learning more than one language. Lyotard makes too much out of his insights about the problems of translations and diversity of criteria in science. Rorty argues that failures in finding a grand narrative that may serve as a universal translation manual do not need to obstruct the possibility of making peaceful social progress, within and outside science.

We can also ask what happens if we turn Lyotard's ideas against themselves. Does Lyotard himself not try to launch a general explanation of what is good and bad knowledge? And is it not, then, as totalizing as the scientific cathedral constructions he criticizes: a new 'grand narrative', but this time in a real super format, since it embraces all knowledge generally? He advocates a more relativist, wavering, ambivalent type of knowledge as a universal panacea for a humankind constipated in thought. But is it not the case that even this knowledge – that is, postmodernism itself – is relative and provisory (for a broad and systematic, Husserl-inspired critique of the lack of such self-referentiality in postmodernism see Detmer, 2003; cf. also Deetz, 1992)? Otherwise it becomes, to be sure, a 'grand narrative'. In other words: are not scepticism and undecidability merely a part of the cognitive process, and must they not be complemented by more synthesizing efforts? (Lyotard certainly talks about consensus besides dissensus, but this appears mostly as lip service; for him consensus, wholeness and harmony represent very marginalized values.) Thus, must not the palaces of the cities be raised, as well as the tents of the nomads? And besides, where are the *intermediate* constructions – the elegant lodgings of the merchants, the humbler abodes of the artisans, the miserable hovels of the poor, and the farmhouses with thatched roofs? Do they not all have their place – as well as parks, streets and squares – as part of the scientific landscape?

The question is, furthermore, why micro histories in themselves would in any sense be 'better' than overarching 'grand' narratives. Lyotard does not give any direct answer to this, but in all likelihood it is the devastating consequences of the totalitarian ideologies during the twentieth century that lie behind his standpoint. However, overarching grand narratives have always existed and will in all probability always exist. Instead of letting the neoconservatives, neoliberals, religious fundamentalists, etc. of our time monopolize these grand narratives, it might then be a good idea to try presenting alternative visions.

Criticism of the (humanistic) subject

Most writers who subscribe to PM or – even more – to PS, are not content with toppling traditional Western views on language and theoretical frames of reference; they also turn their attention to the idea of the individual. This word is in fact little used; what is interesting is the 'subject'. Both French structuralism and Heidegger had severely criticized the idea of the individual subject; PM/PS builds on and continues this critique, while at the same time developing it in new directions. These run counter to the tradition which, it is said, sees the conscious, autonomous, holistic and delimited individual as the bearer of meaning and as an active and 'acting' subject around which the social world revolves (see, for example, Collinson 2003, Deetz, 1992; Foucault, 1980; Hollway, 1984; Weedon, 1987; Willmott, 1994a). The poststructuralists regard the humanist idea of a single subjectivity, which at any given moment is fixed and complete, as a Western invention. The idea has been problematized even by writers who are not directly connected with this school. The anthropologist Geertz (1983: 59) sees it almost as an instance of Western ethnocentricity, to claim the individual as a coherent, unique, and, in terms of motivation and cognition, more or less integrated universe – a dynamic centre for consciousness, emotions, evaluations and actions which is external in relation to a specific social and natural background.

In opposition to the dominating notion of the individual, the poststructuralists want to demote the subject from its central position – decentre it, that is – shift the emphasis as regards what constructs perceptions, thoughts, emotions and actions to the linguistic and discursive context, which socially creates forms and expressions of subjectivity limited in time and space. By subjectivity is meant the individual's conscious and unconscious thoughts, emotions and perceptions, her self-insight and attitude to the surrounding world. Language is not an expression of subjectivity, but – it is claimed – constitutes subjectivity. The use of language triggers thoughts, ideas and emotions. From this it follows that subjectivity is something unstable, contradictory – a process rather than a structure. Thinking and actions 'depend on the circulation between subjectivities and discourses which are available' (Hollway, 1984: 252). How we speak and how others address us constitutes our subjectivity at any given moment, contingent upon the various discursive fields from which language emanates and in which we find ourselves. Depending on the way an individual is addressed – as a woman, an engineer, a New Yorker, a mother, a fashion junkie, a taxpayer or a skier – different forms of the subject (subjectivity) will be activated. These, in turn, may be interpellated (called upon) in a variety of ways due to the available discourses; different discourses will, for example, produce different meanings of motherhood. Various situations invoking a particular identity can in turn be represented in different ways: work may stand for heavy demands, stress, opportunity or challenge; gender may imply desirability, appreciation, a 'sex object' role or a gender trap; a particular relationship can be represented in terms of loyalty, demands, coercion, morals, sacrifice or free will. Thus, depending on the language, representation and discursive context, different forms of subjectivity are constituted. Weedon (1987: 34) writes that experiences have no innate essential meaning, but acquire their sense in language from discursive systems of meaning, which often contain contradictory versions of how social reality should be described.

Social structures and material conditions mean that discourses and language give expression to particular power relations, and lock people into various forms of subjectivity. Discourses do not therefore develop freely, nor do they operate in a random way. Certain discourses dominate – for instance, those which indicate perceptions and ideas about what is naturally male or female, or even the naturalness

POSTSTRUCTURALISM AND POSTMODERNISM

of talking about men and women as unitary and transcultural categories, the construction of sexuality, the meaning of consumption and material living standards. At the same time there are a number of discourses and languages that can take over from each other as pointers to subjectivity. Some writers within the approach we are discussing even want to get rid of the subject altogether. (For a review of the spectrum of positions within PM/PS, see Rosenau, 1992: Chapter 3.) But the majority share the idea of decentring the human subject, seeing it as an effect rather than the origin of social and discursive processes.

Feminists have been particularly prominent in adopting this idea. Butler (2004), Flax (1987), Fraser and Nicholson (1988) and Weedon (1987), for example, have pointed out the socially constructed and virtually arbitrary elements in every statement regarding what is male or female in terms of what is authentic and natural. At the same time they note the powerful inertia inherent in the dominant discourses which pervade and are embedded in material structures, laws, etc. We return to this in the next chapter.

This view of the individual turns a good deal of traditional social science on its head, with dramatic implications for the way in which everything – from cognition, motivation, identity creation, gender and values to social and cultural patterns – is understood. It ought perhaps to be pointed out that prior to PS/PM's appearance on the scene, much behavioural and social science had already landed a little outside the humanist idea of a conscious, knowing, integrated, rational subject. As (highly diversified) examples we could mention psychoanalysis, critical theory, behaviourism, role theory, social identity theory and – of course – structuralism. None of which means that PS/PM does not express new ideas with regard to the understanding of the subject.

One criticism of poststructuralism is that many of its proponents seem to over-emphasize the importance of the decentring of the subject, ascribing something approaching omnipotence to language and discourse. It could reasonably be claimed, however, that language is instead transformed into a supersubject. In many cases, a kind of linguistic reductionism seems to take over. (In this respect, PS only brings to an extreme the 'linguistic turn' of so much twentieth-century philosophy.) It seems likely that material life conditions may have an enduring influence, regardless of how exactly they are represented in language, and likewise that unconscious fantasies (which do not necessarily need to be understood in purely linguistic terms) may also play their role. Further, it seems reasonable to ascribe to the subject an ability to introduce its own 'touch' into the discourse, rather than simply viewing it as a kind of zombie or *tabula rasa* which can only awaken to a consciousness that is unequivocally determined by (whatever) discourse (some power allows to appear).[12]

Actually, it looks as if some (mostly second-hand or even vulgar) adherents of PM/PS are jumping to faulty conclusions: subjects are effects of discourses ... *and so of course* they must be volatile, constantly shifting, and so on. But the whole point of the critique of the subject is a *shifting of aspects*, the bringing in of a new problematic, not a discussion of the fickleness of the subject. Rather than seeing the subject as something pre-existing and definitive, PS conceptualizes it as an *outcome of a process of subjectivation*. Now, this outcome may of course be more or less stable, but this would depend on the stability of the discourses shaping the subject in question, and it is certainly not a foregone conclusion. If one holds that the so-called grand narratives are too strong, it is hard to escape the conclusion that this would have the effect of cementing the subject even further, given the dominance or even hegemony of the discourse. In this case it seems rather ill conceived to speak of the volatile, evanescent subject, since the said subject would be bolstered and stabilized by the overwhelmingly strong discourse that helped create it in the first place. On the other hand, if there are several contending smaller narratives, this would make the subject more volatile and so on, if one accepts the PM/PS idea that the subject is generated by the discourses, and not the other way round (and more especially if one accepts the idea that we live in an era in which the dominant grand narratives are, at least to some extent, breaking up). Yet it is hard not to grant some inertia, or even a good deal of it, to the subject, whether it is externally generated or not, if only for reasons of sedimentations. Thick layers of ideational 'matter' fill the bottom levels of the subject, and these are not so easily shed. It is a common experience that some people are more stable, inert and so on than others, and the PM/PS thesis of the volatile subject fails to account for this observation.

On the other hand PM has an important polemical point: it implies shaking up dominant modes of thought, rather than expressing a 'truer' view. By and large, the view of the individual championed by PS/PM can trigger the fruitful questioning of a certain over-confidence in uniformity and consistency in the way people function. We can certainly agree that greater sensitivity – rather than over-sensitivity – is desirable to contradictions, chance occurrences, variations and interactions between subjective, inner orientations developing over time and a discursive highlighting of subjectivity. The question then becomes central as to which subjectivities and identities are important and how these stabilize or vary with different social relationships and processes.

> There are a number of questions for study in this so to speak parallel processing, of identity at many sites. Which identities coalesce and under what circumstances? Which become defining or dominant and for how long? How does the play of unintended consequences affect the outcome in the coalescence of a salient identity in this space of the multiple construction and dispersed control of a person's or group's identities? (Marcus, 1992: 315–316)

Identity, by the way, may embrace almost everything: member of a family, employee, man, woman, TV viewer, elderly person, party supporter – all are examples of identities, related to different contexts. Identity may be defined as the individual's narrative about herself (cf. Ricoeur, 1992), about her self-definition – who am I? – her distinctiveness, and the continuity over time and across situations in which multiple identities (at least in post-traditional societies, identity is multiple rather than monolithic) are constituted.

Even if a general understanding of the subject is only slightly modified by poststructuralist insights, the consequences for concrete research could nonetheless be dramatic, regardless of the specific research orientation. Even if the subject behaves according to a psychology or a social logic that evinces a certain consistency (and more of it than PS/PM claims), it is quite reasonable to assume that in various linguistic contexts – which are the point of departure for empirical work – the subject is particularly sensitive to discursive variations, and here reveals significant divergencies. The significance of and sensitivity to discursive constitutionalizing are greater in 'discursively charged situations' such as conversations, than in many other contexts more socially and materially circumscribed. Consider, for example, interviews or polls, in which the subject is expected to respond to a particular communication; it is then an open question as to whether the discourses that confront the subject really lead to the expression of uniform and unambiguous insights, emotions, views, motives, plans and knowledge. Different ways of formulating questions or the different 'tracks' in which individuals land apparently by their own choice, can lead to a considerable variation in the current subjectivity – and in the empirical material that is being produced. (We return to this towards the end of the chapter, and to some extent in Chapter 7.)[13] In empirical research there are therefore good grounds for paying serious attention to the poststructuralist view of the subject.

The researcher as author

Many researchers of postmodernist inclination have also shown an interest in the importance of authorship. They maintain a shift in emphasis away from theory, data and interpretation, towards language and presentation as central elements in research. In particular, a number of anthropologists and other scholars in the culture field have claimed a central position in research work for authorship and the production of texts (Clifford, 1986; Geertz, 1988; Marcus and Cushman, 1982; Marcus and Fischer, 1986; Van Maanen, 1988, 1995). These writers differ a good deal from philosophers such as Derrida who emphasize the notoriously indeterminate character of language. The focus upon authorship means paying attention to the work on the research text in its entirety as a crucial element in, for instance, ethnographic studies. Thus the focus is not on deconstructions of delimited passages of text. Another difference is the interest in understanding cultures, that is, the 'reality' – even though this is seen as open in terms of how it may be represented – beyond the text. (What exactly is meant by this 'reality' is often left rather unclear as the emphasis is on the textual and fictional.) Thus the overall strategy as regards presentation is regarded as most important. An awareness of this and a certain experimentation with style are encouraged.

That anthropologists and other culture researchers in particular are interested in research as authorship, is probably connected with the character of ethnographic studies, especially those concerned with 'exotic' cultures. The wealth of empirical material, and the incredible number of choices the researcher must make, mean that the empirical reality can obviously never unequivocally determine the final text which reports 'the results of the research'. In the case of other more structured studies with more meagre (domesticated) empirical material, for instance standardized data, it may be easier to convince oneself and others that the conscientious representation of an empirical reality ('data' and the 'processing' thereof) can make a research text throw some (incomplete) light on this reality. However, all this really means is that the problem is concealed, not that it disappears. In anthropology it seems particularly pertinent to refer to the typical postmodernistic concern that research provides a totalizing description of a certain reality, in which the researcher speaks for the Other and blocks any alternative voices, since anthropology is historically closely associated with colonialism (these days mainly in the form of scientific imperialism and other forms of domination by Western ideas) and ethnocentricity. Furthermore, the subjectivity of the researcher is particularly prominent in ethnographic studies. Ethnographers can only pretend to a comparatively minor extent that an adherence to particular procedural methods guarantees scientific credibility, although they often try to. As we have argued in this book, not even procedure-steered qualitative (or quantitative) research ('mushroom-picking research') can avoid letting value-judgements, interpretations and a whole host of – often subconscious or non-reflected – choices as regards language, perspective, metaphors, focus, representation, and so on, pervade the whole research process. What is particularly obvious in the case of anthropologists and ethnographers is also important in the work of other kinds of researchers: authorship, style and text production are central to all research far beyond 'writing up the results' (cf. Alvesson, 2002; Richardson, 2000; Sköldberg, 2002b). Here, too, the author's voice implies silencing the voices of others.

Geertz (1988) writes that anthropologists have been obsessed with the idea that the crucial elements in ethnographic descriptions are connected with the 'mechanics of knowledge': how empathy and insight are achieved, how other people's thoughts and feelings can be verified and how the ontological status of the culture can be established. Against these fieldwork problems, he sets out what he calls the discursive problem. This questions a particular way of crafting a text – with the aid of vocabulary, rhetoric and a host of arguments, in combination with the researcher's 'signature' or writerly identity. After worrying for so long about the problem of fieldwork, it is now time for anthropology to take the problems of authorship seriously, Geertz argues. (See also Chapter 4 above, where we reviewed Geertz's view of culture as text.)

Questions of representation and presentation thus emerge as crucial methodological problems. The traditional view that the 'writing-down of results' is merely a limited part of the research process determined largely by theory, data collection, analysis and interpretation, is rejected. To underline the importance of writing and of the character of the text, the culture researchers who have focused on this aspect of research use various metaphors. Geertz's (1988) book has the subtitle *The Anthropologist as Author* and the anthology published by Clifford and Marcus (1986) is called *Writing Culture*. A book by Van Maanen (1988) is called *Tales of the Field*. The title is motivated by the story-like nature of field-notes and final reports, and the myriad decisions that a researcher has to make.

These authors' interests in the textual angle are shared to some extent by hermeneuticians such as Ricoeur. Compared with hermeneutic variants on the representation theme, which are concerned with the kinds of interpretations that are enabled or permitted by certain styles or certain root metaphors (Brown, 1977; Morgan, 1986; Sköldberg, 2000b; and see Chapter 4 above), the postmodernists emphasize what has been concealed as a result of the chosen form of representation, especially of dominant forms. It is noted, with critical irony, how a certain established style totalizes understanding, creating authority and legitimacy for a certain attempt at providing the truth or a good interpretation. Jeffcutt (1993) shows, for instance, how heroic, tragic, romantic and epic styles characterize organizational culture research, and points out their limitations. The hermeneutic ideal of indicating the right or most interesting meaning is rejected. (The line separating hermeneutics from postmodernism on this point is not necessarily a sharp one, especially not in the case of Ricoeur with his interest in narrative and polysemy.)

The fictive and political elements are emphasized instead, as crucial ingredients in the research process. A neutral, simple social reality that can be depicted or interpreted does not exist. Researchers must actively work with language and texts that have an ambiguous relation to significations and meanings – manifesting their local, contextual and arbitrary nature. Fictive elements – the more or less creative inventions of the author – cannot be avoided. What shape the fiction assumes is, in a certain sense, inevitably political. Innumerable choices are determined by values and interests. Representations are a question of what is selected or not selected for attention, and how what is observed is then presented. Here there is a definite link with critical theory, but postmodernist authors generally lean towards a more pluralistic view of society. This explains why ideas about 'the political' are more a question of the researcher's own (more or less arbitrary) choice in the face of a whole host of possibilities, and of the importance of language and the form of representation, than they are a question of the dominating social interests and ideologies underlying choices. Nonetheless, some postmodernist researchers stress the importance of paying attention to the *problem of representation* in two respects: on the one hand in the sense of the reproduction/construction of a particular reality (re-presentation), that is, how well this is captured and interpreted; and on the other, in the sense of what (and whose) interests and views (voices) the researcher is expressing (Linstead, 1993). The problem of representation therefore includes both an epistemological and an ethical-political dimension. This is well illustrated by the subtitle of Clifford and Marcus's (1986) anthology, *Writing Culture: The Poetics and Politics of Ethnography*. Despite their differences, critical theory and (certain varieties of) postmodernist ethnography tend to head in the same direction in terms of reformulating traditionally dominant (neo-)positivistic and inductive agendas for empirical research. The postmodernists emphasize more strongly that research constructs rather than depicts what is being researched. The fictive or literary elements in research are thus important (as they are in modern hermeneutics). Critical theory is far less anti-empirical or sceptical about the possibilities of saying something 'valid' or insightful about social reality. (Of course, there are strong variations within the two camps.)

Postmodernists and poststructuralists reject the traditional Western dichotomy in science which excludes certain expressive forms from the legitimate repertoire: rhetoric (by referring to well-defined, transparent linguistic forms), fiction (which is defined in a negative relation to facts) and subjectivity (which must be eliminated in order to achieve objectivity) (Clifford, 1986: 5). As these rejected elements are nonetheless both unavoidable and central constituents of social and humanist science, they must be made subject to reflection and expressed explicitly in the text, but without constituting the only feature to characterize an ethnography:

> [T]he maker (but why only one?) of ethnographic texts cannot avoid expressing tropes, figures and allegories that select or impose meaning as they translate it. In this view, more Nietzschean than realist or hermeneutic, all constructed truths are made possible by powerful 'lies' of exclusion and rhetoric. Even the best ethnographic texts – serious, true fictions – are systems, or economies, of truth. Power and history work through them, in ways their authors cannot fully control. (Clifford, 1986: 7)

Clifford indicates four conditions which prevent ethnographies (as other forms of social science) from depicting social phenomena:

1 It is always a matter of literary work, contingent upon linguistic tools that portray 'reality' in a particular way, *inter alia* through the metaphorical character of language and the local, contextual character of meanings.
2 Ethnographic writings cannot be objective as they are determined: *contextually* (they draw from and construct a certain social milieu); *rhetorically* (expressive conventions guide text production); *institutionally* (one writes within, and against, specific traditions, disciplines and audiences); *politically* (the authority to represent cultural realities is asymmetrically distributed); and *historically* (conventions and constraints change over time).
3 Cultures consist of multiple voices, but ethnographies can hardly present all of these, tending to concentrate on a few and often only one, either the author's own or somebody else's, presented on the author's conditions.
4 Cultures are perpetually changing, but it is difficult to avoid static descriptions ('"Cultures" do not stand still for their portraits', according to Clifford, 1986: 11).

In light of this, objectivity and pure data emerge as tantamount to mystification – or instances of naïvety. The distinction between fact and fiction thus becomes blurred. An understanding of scientific texts as historical constructions means that claims to 'truth' are perceived as rhetorical expressions, which can be constantly opened up to alternative interpretations. This in turn means that the reader becomes important. The text becomes less an expression of its own 'inherent' character than of the predispositions and creativity with which the reader approaches it (Brown, 1990). The text is open to different interpretations. In the perspective of postmodernist ideals, authorship is about increasing the opportunities for different readings. The reader becomes significant, not as a consumer of correct results – the right intended meaning from the text and its author(ity) – but in a more active and less predictable position, in which interesting readings may be divorced from the possible intentions of the author.

The key concepts and catchwords here include multiple voices, pluralism, multiple reality and ambiguity. The good research text should avoid closure, following a monolithic logic. Instead, inconsistencies, fragmentation, irony, self-reflection and pluralism must pervade the work – writing of the final text as well as the thinking and note-taking that precede it.

Empirical illustration

Postmodernist discussion of – or attempts at – empirical research are rather limited in character. There are a number of general arguments about how *not* to conduct, for instance, ethnographic research, but more concrete guidelines or examples of how it *should* be pursued are as yet few and far between. Most authors calling themselves postmodernists maintain a negative approach in this context: like the critical theorists, they are much more articulate and specific about what they are *against* than about what they are *for*.

Since text, language and representation are so central, many researchers see the empirical as synonymous with text, which is why they do not address any extra-textual reality – at least not directly. The deconstruction of texts, or of rather narrow social phenomena or incidents that appear in textual form or close to it (for instance, advertisements or public speeches) is a typical example of an application (see, for instance, Calás and Smircich, 1988, 1991; Linstead and Grafton-Small, 1990; Martin; 1990b).

In this section we will, however, offer a more 'ambitious' illustration: Taussig's (1987) study of colonial terror and shamanistic healing in Colombia, which provides an example of a postmodern, empirical ethnography.[14] The book is like a fragmented prism, whose every fragment glows with an intense yet impalpable and oscillating light, emanating the paradoxical, multiple and elusive 'meaning' of the object investigated. Taussig has been greatly influenced by Walter Benjamin among others, and at the beginning of his book he quotes the following passage from this author:

> Its method is essentially representation. Method as a digression. Representation as digression ... The absence of an uninterrupted purposeful structure is its primary characteristic. Tirelessly the process of thinking makes new beginnings, returning in a roundabout way to its original object. This continual pausing for breath is the mode most proper to the process of contemplation ... Just as mosaics preserve their majesty despite their fragmentation into capricious particles, so philosophical contemplation is not lacking in momentum. Both are made up of the distinct and the disparate; and nothing could bear more powerful testimony to the transcendent force of the sacred image and the truth itself. The value of the fragments of thought is all the greater the less direct their relationship to the underlying idea, and the brilliance of the representation depends as much on this value as the brilliance of the mosaic does on the quality of the glass paste. (Taussig, 1987: xvii–xviii.)

This quotation is central to Taussig's method. Description (representation) is what he regards as essential. This applies to texts such as letters, biographies and literary descriptions that are commented upon, as well as to oral testimonies, conversations and interlocutions in which Taussig himself participates. The description continuously creates the life it is commenting on: the commentary, the digression, are their own 'reality'. There is no uniform, underlying purpose or structure – something which explains the importance attached to interruptions. The particular is stronger and of greater importance than the general, which is only expressed in a vague, flickering and evanescent aura around the fragment. The interruptions are merely the other side of the fragmentation, which often acquires a dialectic, paradoxical appearance with essentially different or opposing pieces of the mosaic in juxtaposition to one another. The totality has been broken and there is nothing 'behind' the surface, behind the fragments: neither a particular aspect to which everything can be reduced as in the hermeneutics of suspicion, nor any form of harmonic meaning as in alethic hermeneutics. Certain general reflections are made in passing by Taussig, but these tend to be more or less submerged by the descriptions of particularities. This also ties in with his view that the descriptive representation is more important than the discursive.

In view of all this, Taussig finds a crucial technique in the *montage* – another idea borrowed from Benjamin. In fact it is not only a question of technique, for what is being investigated is itself regarded as a *montage*. The author participates in a seance during which he takes *yagé*, a hallucinogenic and purgative drug. Commenting on the seance, he criticizes the traditional view of rituals as creators of order (meaning) out of chaos. The *yagé* ritual is, rather, a *montage* of 'dialectical images' (as in surrealism), in sharp contrast to the established view which identifies the sacred with the ordered:

> The 'mystical insights' given by vision and tumbling fragments of memory pictures oscillating in a polyphonic discursive room full of leaping shadows and the sensory pandemonium are not insights granted to depths mysterious and other. Rather, they are made, not granted, in the ability of montage to provoke sudden and infinite connections between dissimilars in an endless or almost endless process of connection-making and connection-breaking.

> *Montage*: alterations, cracks, displacements, and swerves all evening long – the sudden interruptions, always interruptions to what at first appears the order of the ritual and then later on takes on little more than an excuse of order, and then dissolves in a battering of wave after wave of interruptedness into illusory order, mocked order, colonial order in the looking-glass. Interruptions for shitting, for vomiting, for a cloth to wipe one's face, for going to the kitchen to gather coals for burning copal incense, for getting roots of magical *chondur* from where nobody can remember where they were last put, for whispering a fear, for telling and retelling a joke (especially for that), for stopping the song in mid-flight to yell at the dogs to stop barking … and in the cracks and swerves, a universe opens out. (Taussig, 1987: 441)

In this context the shaman becomes merely 'a strategic zone of vacuity, a palette of imageric possibilities' (Taussig, 1987: 444). This is in radical contrast to the colonial view of the shaman as the 'wild man', half devil, half god: a version in which these imageric possibilities have ossified and become personalized in a particular figure. Expressed in dramaturgic terms, borrowed from Benjamin's discussion of Brecht's heroes, the shaman is to Taussig rather an 'empty stage' on which the contradictions of the drama may be played out. The shaman's 'place is to bide time and exude bawdy vitality and good sharp sense by striking out in a chaotic zigzag fashion between laughter and death, constructing and breaking down a dramatic space layered between these two poles' (Taussig, 1987: 444). This problematizes reality, transforming it into something wavering, uncertain. The *yagé* ritual combines in radical juxtaposition the fantastic with 'a heightened feeling of reality' (Taussig, 1987: 445). In the alternation between the fabulous and the intensified 'everyday', truth becomes an open experiment conducted by actors, rather than something concealed beneath the surface; it is the surface itself, in a state of continually interrupted and fragmented construction, that is the truth, and the actors create the surface by rendering their own representations while at the same time commenting upon this, thereby gliding between representation and representation-as-digression.

In an implicit critique of Eliade's (1974) study of shamanism, where an important symbolic element is held to be an *axis mundi* between heaven and earth – the central axis of the mythopoetic world picture – Taussig remarks that if we can speak at all about a world axis, then it

> stretches not from hell to heaven but oscillates back and forth between laughter and death in a montage of creation and destruction – figured for the shaman in the signs of sweet-smelling petals as against the smell of shit, flowers against frogs and lizards, birds as against snakes and alligators, clear-headedness as against nausea and drunkenness. (1987: 444)

Truth is therefore not abstract and other-worldly, but concrete, particular and sensuous – while at the same time being *open*, in an ongoing state of new creation by the actors, transcending the boundaries between the ordinary and the fabulous. In line with this, Taussig thinks that we should study representations – texts and oral accounts – irrespective of their possible references to any external reality, which in any case will remain problematic. The representation is (creates) its own reality, and there is no sharp limit or borderline between the fantastic and the real. This does not mean an advocacy of any 'magic realism', which Taussig regards as a literary upper-class phenomenon. It is more related to Bakhtin's dialectic and paradoxical, 'vulgar' poetics, where joking and seriousness, high and low, occur abruptly side by side.

Taussig's book has the merit that in its best sections it seems to re-create fragments of the swarming, elusive, chaotic life itself, with its union of beauty and cruelty, suffering and ecstasy, body and spirit. Yet the programmatic messiness, the concretion and the particularism do lead to an excess of impressionistic descriptions, and theory tends to be relegated to the Cinderella role; it becomes something which is done away with *en passant*, on the way to something more important – to fascinating new descriptions. Thereby the circle is in a way closed, and we are partly back to the empirically oriented approaches, albeit with new signatures and overtones. The interest among certain postmodernists in microsociological methods such as symbolic interactionism/ethnomethodology, and conversely the interest in the former among proponents of the latter methods, are no coincidence.

Critique of postmodernism and poststructuralism

In various contexts above we have levelled criticism at different versions of PM and PS, or at various themes within them. As a result of the great variations between different authors and between the views included within this approach, it is not altogether easy to provide an overall critique that applies to all or even the major part of PM and PS. The above-mentioned shift in meaning between more orthodox and extreme stances (for example, Derrida), and the less esoteric and more composite orientations (Weedon, Clifford and Marcus) certainly does not make things any better.

The former positions – often philosophical – are perhaps easy to criticize for lacking social interest and relevance, but more difficult to attack, being more consistent, whereas the reverse applies to the more eclectic variants. On some points, however, the target area seems to be reasonably large. Here we will primarily address what we consider relevant in the perspective of the empirically interested social scientist. Naturally such a perspective means that the level of philosophical sophistication is correspondingly set somewhat lower.

Lack of constructivity

An overriding comment is that postmodernism appears at the same time too sceptical and too dogmatic: too sceptical in that it shies away from more systematic theory; too dogmatic in that it moves within the hermetically sealed rooms of intertextuality. Both these features reveal a striking lack of dialectics: the first by counterposing criticism to systematic theory and excluding the latter; the second by counterposing intertext to external referent, again with the exclusion of the latter.

Postmodernism criticizes other orientations for totalization, closed systems. However, the very same approach constructs an extremely closed system through intertextuality – a 'free play' of meaningless signs, hermetically sealed off against referent and subject. (It was precisely such repetitious phenomena that Hegel [1967: 225] called 'boring', in his ironic remarks about authors who allow themselves to be impressed by what he called 'the bad infinity'.) Calhoun notes that:

> Ironically, in this way postmodernists are often the mirror image of the Enlightenment universalists they challenge, making of difference – especially Derrida's *difference* – an absolute as rigid as unitary identity or universalism is to their enemies. And if positive, unitary identity is a form of violence against difference, so absolutized difference is a form of violence against intersubjectivity or, more specifically, the human will to bridge the gap between people, traditions, cultures. (1992: 278)

Through its orientation towards a subversive undermining of established structures, postmodernism acquires a certain *parasitic* bias (Rorty, 1989), something which also appears in its numerous (ironic) comments and supplements, its focusing on the marginal and peripheral, rather than creating a knowledge of its own. It thus lacks an autonomous social scientific research area of its own. Other people's production of texts (for PS/PM, preferably problematic texts) is consequently a precondition of postmodernist work. Postmodernism's contribution, apart from general theoretical and philosophical expositions, is thus limited to comments and/or analyses which can only be understood within the specific (con)text at hand, that is, in relation to the text from which the analysis starts. Insights of broader interest can perhaps be created here, for instance if one delves into a typical or highly influential text, but it is hardly possible to accomplish a progression in knowledge development or produce anything of more general theoretical value. The new (quasi-)concepts created in the second phase of deconstruction represent attempts to achieve something of this sort, but they often falter just because PM is so afraid of theory, particularly during such tentative stages, or of saying anything positive of real relevance to groups other than the researchers-authors themselves. Castoriadis (1992: 16) notes a 'contemporary tendency of writers toward self-containment: writers write about writers for other writers'.

The lack of constructiveness is also connected with the fact that postmodernism 'seems to condemn everything, propose nothing', as if 'demolition is the only job that the postmodern mind seems to be good at' (Bauman, quoted by Billig and Simons, 1994: 6). Yet, knowledge advances not just through tearing down systems but also by building up new ones. The important thing is that the process does not *end*, either in system or critique. We must stay clear of both totalizations *and* hyperscepticism.[15] The dialectic between a transcendence of boundaries and synthesis drives the process of knowledge forwards. The transcending of boundaries leads to the breaking-up of old syntheses; yet the ground so broken becomes with time the object of a new synthesis at a higher level, and so on. (In line with this ideal, we have produced this book so that it involves a dialectic between transcendence and synthesis.)

Again, defenders of postmodernism's more developed forms have contended that it is slowly making its way from an epistemologic salvation movement to a more empirical, even though no longer so pretentious, orientation. It is possible to conceive interpretive empirical research as sensitive to variation, fragmentation and process. Postmodernism aims to capture these qualities (Alvesson, 2002).

From a partly other point of view, we can start reflecting over why postmodernism with its ideas of uncertainty and fragmentation has emerged in the later part of the twentieth century. Is it not the case that society itself has become ever more fragmented and uncertain, and does this not mean that we as social scientists should study this society? With such a leitmotif, social scientists have gradually

> deepened their research agenda beyond some of the admittedly sketchy and generalized themes of early postmodernism to rethink society's borders, industrialism, capitalism, and social relations: four key themes of modern social theory. New themes like time–space distantiation, risk society, consumer capitalism, and postmodern ethics give us an ability to continue to conceptualize the rapidly changing social world and to spawn new research here. (Mirchandani, 2005)

Even though the critique for destructivity has a good deal to say for it, postmodernism can also be interpreted and developed into more 'constructive' directions, with a good chance of catching more important currents – and sub-currents(!) – of the present time.

Linguistic and textual reductionism

Sometimes we also get a feeling that the commendable interest in language and text becomes exaggerated and results in a reductionist attitude. Certainly (literary) texts echo other texts, but that they would not therefore refer (ambiguously) to an external reality is too strained and over-dramatizing a thesis. Naturally it is a matter of a combination of the two. Social scientists often work just with texts – some theoretical, some comprising interviews with and documents from actors. Even if reverberations from previous literature on the subject can be demonstrated, it would be absurd to claim that these texts do not at all refer to an 'extratextual' social reality. The post-modern conception of text is in fact strikingly reminiscent of an idling engine in a driverless car.

It sometimes seems to be forgotten that in social science the text is a metaphor for a social phenomenon. (Arguably, the idea of a social science is to study the social.) The idea of the metaphor is that it generates insight by creating tension between the focal object (society, organization, man – or whatever is being studied) on the one hand, and a modifier of this object (text, discourse) on the other (see also Chapter 5 above). If the project is to be successfully completed, it is important that the researcher recognizes this tension and does not allow the metaphor to take command over what is to be understood. Thus society is not a text, but it is possible to understand certain aspects of it, if it is likened to a text (is seen as text-like). The tendency of postmodernist authors to emphasize the figurative, metaphorical nature of language ought to mean that they are quite clear on this point. Frequently, however, one gets the impression that the metaphor (the modifier) 'takes over' too much. What Derrida has said about literature and writing is transferred to the 'area of application' without any countering factor being introduced into the picture.[16] The focal object is thus not really allowed to influence the way the text is to be understood in the specific context. There is a risk of the metaphors creating too standardized a picture of rather dissimilar social phenomena. It almost seems as though insights from postmodernist literary theory and philosophy need only be translated to the area that is to be understood, and that no 'resistance' or addition of ideas or results of thinking and empirical studies within the area (no determination of the focal object) is necessary before the modifier is set to work. The logic that is claimed as characteristic of language makes its inexorable impact: people, organizations, or whatever is under investigation, are seen as adhering closely to the linguistic logic (Cooper, 1989; Shotter and Gergen, 1989). But differences between text and society (organization, (wo)man) must be taken into account (cf. Sangren, 1992; Thompson, 1993). Unless there is balance between the impacts of the two components of the metaphor, its value will be limited. Rather than being inspired by literature theory, social science becomes transformed into it.

In the postmodernist pervading fear of something 'outside' (subject, referent), it is not difficult to discern a longing to return to the mother's womb. Here, one may direct the same critique against postmodernism as it turns against other approaches: that of *marginalizing the external, that which in some ways 'lies beyond'*. In connection with Derrida's (1976) own discussions of Rousseau's sexual life, one might also ponder on masturbatory associations with the idea of a text that all the time only, as it were, touches itself. (The 'dissemination' metaphor is interesting here, as Derrida himself points out.) It can incidentally be noted that the problematic of intertextuality links to that of *rhetoric*, with a process of answers, and answers to answers as essential. Yet rhetoricians do not as a rule deny the existence of reality.

Later, Derrida has – which may come as a surprise for most postmodernists – actually denied that he meant what he said with his famous dictum 'there is nothing outside the text' (Derrida, cited in Caputo, 1997). By text he did not mean text

POSTSTRUCTURALISM AND POSTMODERNISM

(and by outside not outside, and by nothing not nothing), it appears. There has been discussion about this, and Caputo (1997), among others, has written that the literal interpretation in the form of text reductionism is almost ludicrous. 'Text' would instead mean everything – though then there is rather little point in saying that there is nothing outside the text; this follows so to speak by itself (and why, then, call it 'text', one wonders). The whole thing gives an impression of sliding, before criticism, between an extreme and a more ordinary position. It is not wholly uncommon that a thinker first makes a breakthrough and becomes famous on some extreme thesis, which through its very radicality is attractive. Confronted with critical comments that are hard to meet, the author makes a strategic retreat, diluting in various ways the thesis or theory, so that it becomes hard to attack – albeit at the price of triviality. This is a little reminiscent of Kuhn, who retreated before the choir of criticism, saying that everything is not at all a paradigm, and that paradigms are not paradigms, etc.

Also Foucault (cited in Spivak, 1976) has criticized Derrida for text reductionism, and in addition one that through a 'little pedagogy' exhorts its disciples to interpret *just about anything* in the holes of the text, in the undertext. Yet, almost all social scientists (and also humanists) who have joined the postmodern train have certainly interpreted Derrida in just the same way as his critics, namely as a text reductionist – and staunchly defended precisely this text reductionism. The difference is that the former adhere to and like a text reductionist point of view, whereas the latter reject it. On the other hand, what Caputo and the self-revising Derrida have said rather amounts to an announcement that postmodernism is not postmodern.

It is also possible to maintain that there is considerably more *structure* in intertextuality[17] than Derrida wants to admit. As, for instance, Frye (1973) and White (1985a, 1985b) have shown, there are *narrative deep structures*, which have a strong influence on the texts (see also Propp, 1968); for a social science application, see Sköldberg, (1994, 2002b). But deep structures presuppose a more systematic, theoretical textual level, transcending that of mere comments (or causeries). This leads into a more general reflection on the importance of theory. Research – to connect with our own activity – proceeds both through construction and destruction, system and critique. As we pointed out earlier, mere deconstruction becomes sterile, mere construction becomes dogmatic. Scientific activity cannot just limit itself to ironic comments – or grimaces – concerning existing systems. The risk with (many variants of) postmodern philosophizing is that it leads to an hostility to theory (as with Lyotard).

The perhaps exaggerated one-sided interest in language and text, and to an even greater extent the hostility towards theory, overlaps the fear of authority and totalization in research, which pervades PM and PS. In some orientations, especially in cultural research, there seems to be a keen anxiety lest a dominant voice should inform the text, as though this were a strong, clear and potentially dangerous pervasive social force. It is as if the researchers are envisaging an audience as eager to consume (social scientific) texts as they are unable to think for themselves. As Sangren (1992: 283) puts it, 'if "textual" authority were as efficacious as some literary critics imply, writers would be kings'. The text is thus ascribed an almost mystical power. Possibly the ghosts of the authors' fantasies of omnipotence and their self-centredness are haunting them. For those who work with words, the subtle nuances of language may be of greater importance than they are in a wider societal context: 'by making textual authority stand for cultural authority in general, the literary critic, as fabricator and deconstructor of that authority, places her/himself in a position of transcendent power – if not that of a king, at least that of a high priest' (Sangren, 1992: 283).

Another problem in much PM and PS is that the advocates of these movements often seriously contradict their own ideals and principles. According to Parker (1992), modernism is characterized by a belief in the possibility of communicating the results of investigations to other rational beings, whereas postmodernism sees this as a type of intellectual imperialism, ignoring 'the fundamental uncontrollability of meaning'. If we were to take this seriously, there would be no point in writing articles or books and sending them to scientific journals or publishers. All we would have left is the profession of poet or copywriter. In fact, however, it appears that few PM supporters take their own creed all that seriously, that they trust their reviewers and readers to be reasonably rational, and that they seek to control their own meanings. They send their work to journals for review, and seem to write according to 'modernistic' principles. This may, of course, be a matter of adaptation to constraints imposed by the mainstream academic community controlling publication and employment opportunities. Arguably, these constructions are 'real'. The theory, so cherished by poststructuralist writers in particular, that language is not transparent or expressive and cannot reflect a real world, is almost impossible to live up to in handling one's texts in the social sciences. Weedon (1987: 22) emphasizes the fact that language cannot reflect or express either the social or the 'natural' world's inner meanings, but also writes that '[w]e need to understand why women tolerate social relations which subordinate their interests to those of men and the mechanisms whereby women and men adopt particular discursive positions as representative of their interests' (1987: 12). One wonders what this statement is supposed to refer to. It seems to want to reflect 'actual' phenomena such as (a) women's tolerance, (b) their interests, (c) social gender positions, (d) mechanisms, and (e) discursive positions which represent the said interests. According to the poststructuralist creed, language can hardly make such reflections possible, at least not of the unequivocal kind that Weedon's statement implies. It could be added that even for a stubborn objectivist who does not doubt the reflective qualities of language, the entities that Weedon invokes are all too elusive to be captured by language, although a critical realist may easily find robust structures and mechanisms to explain how it fits together.

In our view, attention should not be focused on minor paradoxes and incongruities in research texts, as this can easily lead to pedantry and intolerance. But striking contradictions between different ontological positions – an extreme language-centred one, allowing only the deconstruction of texts, versus a hard-core realistic one, for instance – would justify some criticism.

Another example is the rejection by postmodernists of the author's authority in favour of the self-reproducing text. In practice – when it comes to one's own authority – the theory can be hard to follow. Derrida himself has, for example, threatened legal action to prevent the publication of an interview with him in the well-known French magazine, *Le Nouvel Observateur*, in an American anthology about Heidegger and Nazism. The publisher was forced to omit the interview, which had been included in an earlier edition of the book. The editor points out the curious fact that it is precisely Derrida who is willing to go to court in a copyright dispute – the same Derrida who in his philosophical seminars used to denounce all conceptions of copyright and the like as logocentrism, Western metaphysics, etc. The whole thing becomes even stranger if we bear in mind that it is a question of an interview, which involves two 'authors'; and that the publisher actually had been given permission by *Le Nouvel Observateur* to publish and translate the interview. See Wolin (1993: ix–xix). In fact, Derrida here goes much further, when his own interests are at stake, than many non-deconstructionist authors would be willing to go.

The Sokal affair

The discussion of postmodernism (and social construction) has found a focal point in the Sokal affair (often termed the 'Sokal hoax'). An American physicist, Alan Sokal, managed to get an article published in a postmodern journal, *Social Texts*, with the impressive title 'Transgressing the boundaries: towards a transformative hermeneutics of quantum gravity' (Sokal, 1996). After publication, Sokal disclosed that the whole article was full of nonsensical but serious-sounding jargon which anyone familiar with physics would have dismissed at a glance as a joke. In other words, the paper was a deliberate hoax, a parody intended to reveal the sloppy standards of postmodernism and social construction. Sokal has followed up this prank with a book (Sokal and Bricmont, 1998) which hit the intellectual Left Bank in Paris like a bomb. The outstanding physicist, Stephen Weinberg (1996), responded to Sokal's paper with an attack against relativism and social constructionism. These three critics have in common a realist and objectivist stance. Sokal, always a good polemicist, has invited anybody who thinks that reality is a social construction to jump out of the window in his office room on the twelfth floor. The critique is directed against much of the French intellectual establishment, such as Kristeva, Latour, Baudrillard, Lacan and Deleuze. It is notable, however, that the most prominent figures, Derrida and Foucault, escape the barrage with only minor bruises.

The Sokal affair is something of a watershed in contemporary academic life, reminiscent of the 'big' university feuds occurring over the centuries ever since medieval times and the fight between realists and idealists; but – as if to underscore the (post)modernity of the present discussion – much of it has been carried on via the Internet. On the one side the staunch realists and objectivists line up for the Truth as given by (natural) science, and on the other side the postmodernists and social constructionists draw their swords for the (inter)subjective humanities. The postmodernists have not addressed the accusations of sloppy thinking, the intimidation of their readers by using impressive sounding (but in reality meaningless) language from natural science, inconsistency, a fundamental lack of clarity, etc. Instead they have argued that the attacks are Francophobic, that the scientific realists have tried to exclude social constructionists from academic jobs, etc. As to the cultural differences, the American scientists do seem to have great difficulties in understanding the metaphoric use of language by the French intellectuals. This is evidenced, for instance, by Bricmont (1997) commenting on Latour's definition of postmodernity: 'one terms postmodern the feeling that the arrow of time is no longer straight, and no longer permits the clear organization of the past or the future'. Bricmont, speaking from the point of view of a physical scientist, apparently does not understand a single word of this, even though there is a thought behind it. On the other hand there is no denying the existence of too much excessive rhetoric and insubstantial phrase-mongering among the postmodernists. But then again, on the side of the realist critics, there is often a surprisingly crude, outdated positivist bias (which has long since been theoretically demolished by legions of philosophers of science).

The views of both parties appear somewhat extreme. On the one hand, the postmodernists maintain that reality is nothing but a social construction. As against this, there is of course always Sokal's 'window' argument. And it is rather painful to read Baudrillard's flood of verbosity on the atrocities in Bosnia (as is well known, he has argued that the Gulf War and similar happenings constitute simulacra, media events). On the other hand, the realists equally fiercely maintain that there is nothing (inter)subjective in reality, and that the natural laws are eternal, as is the final and objective Truth. As against this, the research of much history of science, philosophy of science *and* sociology of knowledge has definitively shown that there are substantial elements of subjectivity in natural science, too. In fact it would be strange were this not so: researchers are no robots, and this holds for natural scientists too. But there is also, for instance, the (dominant) Copenhagen interpretation of quantum mechanics, according to which subject and object are inextricably fused in the experimental situation: a mainstream view, which (for instance) the noted physicist, realist and philosopher of science, Mario Bunge (1967) spent much effort in combating: mainstream particle physics, according to Bunge, is not realist, which may come as something of a surprise to those who believe that everything outside PM/social constructionism is die-hard realism (one wonders also if they have never heard of that strong positivist but non-realist current, *instrumentalism*, see Chapter 2 above).

Leaving the polarized positions of the Sokal affair disputants, we believe that the question is not whether there is a reality, or if it is interpreted or not, but rather how much of reality is interpreted, and how. If the earth is hit by an asteroid tomorrow, wiping out all life on the planet, there will still have been a human history up to this fateful event, even if nobody will ever write about – interpret – this history. And if the Nazis had won the war, there would still have been a Holocaust, even if no one had been permitted to write about it, and all its traces had been wiped out. The interpretations would have differed, or rather been non-existent, but there would still have been a reality.

Final comment on the critique

From what has been said above, it appears that PM and PS – at least in their stronger versions – become somewhat difficult to take completely seriously in the context of qualitative empirical social science. They begin to resemble party manifestos or holy writs in a politically pragmatic and social world: people confess their faith on 'official' occasions, but their actual behaviour is often rather different. A rational style of presentation, efforts to accomplish a certain degree of control of meaning, attempts at establishing personal authority and a dominant voice that rejects others in order to try to change the power relations to the benefit of one's own career, an addiction to a realistic ontology and statements with a definite bearing on the world 'out there' – such sins are committed by many of those who confess their allegiance to PM or PS, just as by those claiming to have a 'modernist' stance. We could perhaps say that the pioneers preach PM but live – in their authorship – modernistically, at least part of the time. We could not really expect anything else. But this gives us an indication of the problems connected with many of these theses, once one goes beyond the programmatic statements and concerns oneself with social phenomena.

In spite of this PM and PS have important lessons from which qualitative methodology could benefit; much of interest can be gleaned from what we have been discussing. In the next section we briefly develop some of the points we consider to be valuable.

Implications for qualitative method

Most postmodernists do not talk about methodology. One could even say that postmodernism is anti-methodological. 'Anything goes' is one slogan in harmony with this orientation. What comes closer to method are introspective, anti-objectivist interpretation and deconstruction (Rosenau, 1992: 118). There are, however, some ideas suggested by postmodernistically inspired authors with empirical interests. They are not essentially different from what many other interpretive and critically oriented researchers have maintained. Interpreting material in different ways rather than relying on one clear-cut pattern is equally important to both. Ehn and Löfgren (1982) discuss some analytical methods for cultural research, and among other things emphasize *perspectivization* as a principle. This involves seeing familiar phenomena as strange, trying to differentiate one's understanding of empirical fragments (conversations, body motions, artefacts) from the primary impressions acquired from participant observation, trying to see different kinds of pattern, switching between levels of thought, and trying to think in similes (metaphors). Another principle is *contrasting* – attempting to understand phenomena in terms of what they do not mean. Here, however, it is necessary to be careful about simple dichotomies: pairs such as chaos–order, rationality–irrationality and man–woman can conceal important aspects. According to Ehn and Löfgren (1982: 112) '[I]n any specific culture there will not be just *one* chaos and *one* order, but several'. Ehn and Löfgren also advocate *dramatization*:

> Combine (in your mind) objects and incidents that seem to be incompatible. Turn social hierarchies upside down; let individuals switch roles, interests and language. Play and experiment with the empirical material as if it were a stage prop or a paper doll. Confront taboos, category divisions and sacred cows with everyday practice. Conduct thought experiments, perhaps putting down-and-outs in executive suites, Pentecostalists among hippies, a lady teacher among loggers. (1982: 113)

The authors point out that not only patterns and contexts must be taken seriously, but also contradictions and discrepancies. They warn against the risk of overemphasizing the former.

These suggestions bear a noticeable resemblance to Martin's (1990b) approach, although this text is intended to use a deconstructionist method. Ehn and Löfgren (1982) do not mention postmodernism or any of the authors usually included under this heading – many of whom, in fact, were not widely known at the time their book appeared. This suggests that, in terms of method, the differences between certain freer versions of interpretive research (of which Ehn and Löfgren's is a good example) and a more pragmatic version of deconstruction (as exemplified by Martin, 1990b, and others such as Mumby and Stohl, 1991), are not necessarily so great. (Often 'deconstruction' seems to be used in a rather loose sense, indicating a critical look at the claims of a text, not very different from, for instance, ideology critique.) Nevertheless, Ehn and Löfgren differ from mainstream PM in so far as they maintain that cultural meanings do exist and can be elicited interpretively; and, further, that it is possible and urgently necessary to create a coherent cultural analysis able to withstand the researcher's own test attempts and consequently to be both tenable and credible. The ontology is thus more 'stable' and the epistemology more 'rational' than PM and PS usually maintain.

The originality of PM and PS in relation to empirical research therefore does not lie primarily in ideas and suggestions about how to handle 'the data', even if the stricter versions of deconstruction do have their own distinctive character. Rather, the more specific contributions of PM/PS are associated with the three following points: first, their insistence on avoiding as far as possible the adoption of a definite viewpoint at the theoretical and interpretive level (many PM/PS authors would use other terms here – our usage is simply a matter of convenience), and to minimize the harm that can result from this; secondly, the insistence that research should be alert to the notorious ambiguities, differences and divergencies of things; and thirdly, the emphasis on the problem of authority – that all research is about the researcher ascribing to a particular phenomenon a certain definite, and thereby legitimized, meaning, which in turn upholds the authority of the researcher in relation to other voices (Alvesson, 2002). It should also be emphasized that the PM/PS literature provides only the vaguest indication of what ideals of multiple voices mean concretely in empirical studies (Kincheloe and MacLaren, 1994; Marcus, 1992). Starting from these vague suggestions of what constitutes good research, we will try here to develop ideas for a pragmatic postmodernist qualitative method. What follows represents a fairly free approach to making PM/PS useful in empirical work rather than a faithful application of core ideas within this orientation.

Pluralism

The *pluralistic ideal* entails several voices pervading the text. What 'several' means is difficult to say exactly. It depends on the research topic, the empirical material, theoretical points of departure, the form of the text (including any restrictions on length), and not least the researcher's (actual) and the reader's (expected) endurance. The text, naturally, should not be unduly long.

In light of our aim to make a contribution to empirical research, we start here at the empirical level and complement this later with the theoretical level. (We realize that the boundaries between empirical material and theory are very loose, so that the two 'levels' cannot be cleanly separated; empirical material is theory-impregnated and theory is not empty of observations and impressions.) In a research project and subsequent text the voices encountered in the site of research must come through in a sensitive and multifaceted way. Many researchers agree upon this, but as a rule the 'data' are 'processed' and interpreted giving priority to patterns and connections. This is, of course, very clearly so in quantitative studies but it is also a characteristic of most qualitative studies emphasizing procedures and rules. With the help of categorizations and aggregations the data are trimmed on the researcher's terms. In the process, the multiplicity in the voices is either toned down or disappears – all with the purpose of getting results. Admittedly, variations in the phenomenon (different experiences, meanings or values) are noted, but still in a stylized form, tamed by the researcher. The purpose of finding the regularities assumed to 'be found in the physical and social worlds' (Huberman and Miles, 1994: 431) calls for constraints in taking variation seriously and prevents the listening to and presentation of multiple voices.

Some authors see ethnography as the natural empirical approach in the postmodernist perspective. Linstead (1993: 98), for example, views it as a methodology that has the capacity to embrace manifold perspectives and situations; it can be regarded as the natural methodological and discursive response to epistemological and existential fragmentation. As we noted in Chapter 3 (and as Linstead also mentions), traditional ethnographies express a fundamentally empirical stance thus positioning themselves at a considerable distance from the ideals of postmodernism. It could also be argued that some versions of postmodernism entail a completely different focus from that of the ethnography, namely the deconstruction of limited segments of text. Perhaps we could say that PM indicates either of two extreme variants – the deconstructionist variant and the postmodern ethnography. In the former the researchers have a free rein in relation to the intended meaning of an author of a particular text, in the latter they restrain their own authority and are concerned that the voices associated with diverse forms of subjectivities should be heard. In principle there are no limits as regards methods – in the sense of techniques – which can be combined with PM or PS, except that they are not very compatible with strictly quantitative methods, which tend to over-emphasize unequivocality. Multiple perspectives can be emphasized in all qualitative material; in the close study of texts (passages of text) a much deeper analysis is required, while ethnographies yield multifaceted data as a result of assiduous empirical work. In what follows we look only at broader empirical ventures such as ethnographies and open or semi-structured interviews (usually with more than one or a few individuals), not at the deconstructivist variant.

As against the traditional research ideal of limiting the number of voices (categorizing and synthesizing), PM upholds the norm that these should be given ample space in the postmodernist text. In practice, this may mean that the researcher seeks variation in the empirical work (observations, interviews) as well as in a more ambitious interpretation of the empirical material. Different voices are allowed to speak. Even more crucial is to provide space for the appearance of multiple selves – as several vocal positions rather than a single autonomous and consistent core are assumed to characterize the individual. It is important to consider not only or mainly the dominant, but also and especially the marginal. Rather than searching for the atypical, the dichotomy of typical–atypical – the softer version of quantification that is sometimes applied to qualitative research – is avoided altogether. The ideal of pluralism may mean that the phenomenon is looked at from various angles. If leadership in a company is being studied, then perhaps older and younger people, men and women, ethnic groups, higher and lower management, non-management, management-celebrating positions ('management is important'), management-independent positions ('I am a professional') and management-rejecting stances ('I don't give a damn about the boss'), present and former managers and other employees – all these can have their say, that is, if such voices turn up in the material. (What turns up is, of course, partly a matter of what the researcher encourages to turn up through interventions such as asking questions or placing him or herself in a particular observation context.) Of course limits must be imposed, but the researcher must consider carefully what is being included and what is excluded. And why does he or she choose to exclude certain voices? Maybe some of these should be included? The problem of exclusion must be taken seriously by the PM-oriented researcher. It may be noted in passing that the problem is not a new one. As we noted in Chapter 4, it has been taken very seriously by source-critical scholars since the nineteenth century. The postmodernists give it a new turn, however.

It is not merely a question of listing various relevant categories. It is important to be sceptical about sociological fact-sheet categories. Different categories or identities, such as manager, woman or middle-aged, are not simply 'given'; they are also discursive constructions that produce effects.[18] Identities do not provide any basis for the expression of voices; rather, it is through the voices that identities are created. By interviewing someone *qua* woman, or asking someone to describe their relationship with their 'boss', we construct or fix a certain identity (such as 'woman' or 'subordinate'), and accordingly also an identity of dependence, independence or rejection in relation to the Other (man or manager). Identities or categories are themselves problematic: they fix and they exclude. All this must be carefully considered, and naïve linguistic clichés must be avoided, or rather consciously handled. For instance, we could get round the distinction between manager and subordinate by studying people as subordinate managers. Managers are generally subordinate to higher managers (Laurent, 1978). This could mean interviewing people in managerial positions in terms of their subordination, that is, in relation to their superiors. Alternatively, we could consider managers as dependent on their subordinates (for results, reputation, career), and study management in terms of how this dependence is handled. One could also avoid any reference to managers, whether subordinate or not, and ask more general questions, thus less strongly invoking and in the worst case even fixing the interviewee to a particular identity and, by implication, to a tendency to engage in a particular kind of story-telling. An interviewer could also explicitly vary the vocal positions through interpellating (calling upon) the interviewee in different and perhaps, at least in the context of management studies, non-conventional ways – for example as a parent, middle-aged, long-serving, religious. Whether the more open or the systematically varied approach is used, the variety of vocal positions and the accompanying, converging or diverging, stories that emerge should be sensitively presented/interpreted. What is important is to avoid becoming stuck on the 'manager' label and pinning the respondent's identity to it.

A well-grounded process of exclusion

It might seem as though we were suggesting an infinitely extensive empirical project. What is important is not to include all possible categories and voices that are at odds with established ones, but to reflect upon the process of exclusion and thus to avoid getting entangled in established categories and distinctions. We can then choose the carriers of various voices, some of which challenge dominant (linguistic) conventions. More important than attempting to include everything – or as much as possible – is to have a well-thought-out pluralism and a balanced multiplicity in the perspectives that the empirical landings offer.

The problem of exclusion naturally pervades all research and is also central in determining the research question. It is in itself politically and poetically charged, to use a typical PM slogan. This is emphasized in critical theory, but still more in PM, which maintains that even a politically well-thought-out (as against a 'neutral') research question entails a selective construction of the world, revealing as well as concealing. (It ought perhaps to be pointed out that PM/PS's concept of politics is partly neutralized in that it is applied primarily on the particular micro level, with a view to indicating the researcher's choice of representations of the reality to be expounded. The overall power structure and forms of ideological domination in society are thus not necessarily illuminated – according to parts of PM/PS there is nothing dominant (no essence) to reveal – and PM/PS can sometimes even draw attention away from these. The variations within PM/PS – not least in political terms – mean that on this point, as on so many others, we must be cautious in making generalizations.)

However, the exclusion problem is not simply a question of what groups and categories are being excluded, or of how the representation of these is made in processes of selection controlled by the researcher (who arrives at a particular picture of what is being studied). Even more important, perhaps, is how different voices which can be ascribed to individual subjects are handled or disregarded. According to PM, the individual does not speak with a single voice – or even a dominant one – but may represent different voices; for example, evaluations, thoughts, feelings, and how factual information is conveyed can be constituted in different ways. A single interview, for instance, can generate interpretations demonstrating that the subject is expressing multiplicity (multiple discursive constitutions). The ambiguity in the particular interview must be emphasized. Individuals, according to

PM and PS, are ambiguous, equivocal and inconsistent. (In Chapter 9, we will provide an illustration based on interview material.)

From the empirical point of view, we thus have a pluralism/exclusion problem in two dimensions: on the one hand, how *different* groups, categories and individuals can be represented or silenced in the research process and in the text; and, on the other, how different voices *within* these groups and individual subjects can be allowed space or be excluded. The important point here, as we have noted, is that silencing is partly effected through categorization (by locking subjects into identities), which is why a simple aggregate of groups provides no solution.

Cautious processes of interacting with empirical material

The way the researcher interprets, selects and narrates is of crucial importance to the very production of a plausible text. It is never a question of genuine pluralism, in the sense that a multiplicity of possible positions are really expressed on equal terms. The role of the researcher should not be limited to turning on the tape-recorder and then printing out the interviewees' stories. The labours – and satisfactions – of authorship cannot be avoided (Geertz, 1988: 140). According to Taussig (1987), the researcher nevertheless has roughly the same significance as other actors or voices. This seems to us to seriously undervalue the researcher-author's role. What can be attempted in PM/PS-*inspired* research is a *cautious* process of working with inclusions/exclusions in terms of representations and readings (a PM version of the interpretations) of the material. Again, as during and after the empirical work, theory and a frame of reference are naturally needed. And here, too, it is important to strive for some sort of pluralism, so that the multiplicity can be emphasized in a well-reasoned way. A good knowledge of different metaphors or theoretical perspectives, and the conscious use of this knowledge to guide the work of interpretation, are one possibility (Alvesson, 2002; Martin, 1992; Morgan, 1997; and cf. Chapter 4 above). Theory can be of particular importance when it comes to emphasizing voices that are usually silenced in the culture studied. If, for instance, women are particularly oppressed, no one may think of saying anything critical or problematizing about the situation, because the domination of women by men is regarded as 'natural' by men as well as women.[19] Theory can thus be used to 'detect' or support more 'research-driven' points about the marginalized – also in the absence of such alternative points of view being aired in, for example, interview statements.

Sometimes particular 'interests' or possible viewpoints representing them cannot be directly manifested in explicit voices. It is not possible to interview nature, for instance, on the effects of a certain production process or type of consumption (Shrivastava, 1994). Research can consider to advantage aspects beyond those that are tied to people's various selfish interests – for instance, questions connected with the well-being of animals and of the natural environment at large. (Views raised by animal rights activists and environmentalists may, of course, speak on behalf of animals and nature, but a study of hunting, a slaughterhouse or car drivers may not automatically include people with these orientations.) Even if postmodernist warnings against giving the researcher's elitism too much scope are sometimes justified, we do not hesitate to recommend that the researcher should examine critically which perspectives and voices are not being included, or which are too weak in a particular empirical material but could on good grounds be emphasized in light of the broader considerations that the position and schooling of the researcher should make possible.

Up to a point, the attitude towards ambivalence and the caution about ascribing a (dominant) meaning to phenomena held by PM/PS speak against the production of bold readings. These two principles – holding back any inclination to make a strong point and the researcher 'actively' reinforcing a weak voice or compensating for an absent viewpoint – need not necessarily conflict with one another. The dilemma may be handled *if* researchers allow their own bolder readings to be preceded or followed by alternative readings, and/or if they seek to represent the data in different ways so as to enable alternative readings. The important thing is that the descriptions should not be written in such a way that the researcher's main line of argument is presented as the only reasonable or unequivocably best one. In a PM/PS light, more researcher-driven initiatives should be a *complement* to what emerges in the texts (interview accounts and so on) produced in the empirical work, not an alternative set-up against the voices emerging in the empirical text material.

Avoiding totalizing theory

In a PM perspective, an element of scepticism and self-criticism with regard to *theoretical frames of reference* is fully justified. Most theories tend to engender unequivocality and define meanings. Instead we should seriously consider the possibility that 'the relationship between world and experience, text and reality, structure and action remains uncompromisingly problematic in a way that allows no given or traditional social theoretic solutions to impose order on what is not orderly' (Marcus, 1992: 323). Even if researchers avoid thinking in terms of systems and harmonies, emphasizing ambiguity, inconsistency, contradiction and fragmentation instead, they often do so from a frame of reference which gives priority to just this type of meaning (Alvesson, 1993a). Instead of assuming order, disorder is easily privileged. By using different theories or different metaphors for the research object, it becomes easier to emphasize and handle multiplicity. Totalizations are avoided if the researcher remains consistently aware of what his or her own interpretation conceals. By confronting a chosen interpretation with other interpretations, a play is initiated between a dominating and an alternative interpretation. Text and understanding are opened up. The point, for PM, is to avoid simple opposites, and so even the chosen alternative interpretation should be challenged in turn by yet another one. Derrida's ideas about 'conversion', that is, showing how a certain meaning is dependent upon a repressed opposite, and 'metaphorization' or demonstrating an overlap between two terms (Cooper, 1989; Linstead, 1993) exemplify how this can be done. A problem is that this appears best suited to fairly limited empirical materials – for example, texts. An alternative offering a wider application in terms of social phenomena consists of working with various root metaphors (see Chapter 4), and making parallel readings (Morgan, 1997). Another possibility is to look for metaphors for the chosen root metaphors, in order to initiate a 'play of metaphors' (Alvesson, 1993b). The metaphor initially chosen is then reframed with the help of another one. In the last two cases it is less a question of a detailed scrutiny of linguistic expression than of working with two or more comprehensive theoretical perspectives which allow for ambiguity.

A concrete way of working with parallel interpretations (multiple readings) could be to initiate a project by choosing two or three different perspectives that allow a productive combination of cooperation and competitiveness, collaboration and tension, and then to think out what questions these perspectives require. When the empirical study is completed, various distinct interpretations and analyses are made. The point is to avoid synthesizing at least too much or at too early a stage. Alternatively, some of the ideas and part of the material can be synthesized, while multiplicity, inconsistency and tension are also being stressed. The interpretations can then indicate both divergence and convergence, without prioritizing either. In the other alternative, the game of metaphors, the study is conducted more or less as usual, that is to say with a coherent frame of reference (root metaphor). The whole preliminary text, including the interpretations produced, is then subjected to a reinterpretation in which the chosen metaphor is elucidated with the help of a new one (Alvesson, 1993b). We can look at activities in companies in terms of 'strategies' (patterns in operations more or less contingent upon large and small decisions), for instance, but at the next stage look upon these strategies as *mantras* (Broms and Gahmberg, 1983). The text following the application of the second metaphor is written in such a way that new meanings and ambiguities are consistently empha-sized. (This could also be a way of breathing fresh life into the transition between the substantive and formal levels in grounded theory; see Chapter 3.) Cracks and openings are displayed and reinforced. We return to these ideas in Chapter 8.

Authorship and linguistic sensitivity

Another important point concerns the *style of research*. The suggestions mentioned have implications for this, which can hardly follow a monolithic logic any longer. Researchers cannot hide behind a bureaucratic methodological procedure and dom-inant conventions for writing, but must instead take responsibility for their texts and also make it obvious in the texts that they have done so. The presentation of different perspectives and aspects – due either to an attempt to introduce multiplic-ity into the research representations, or to the fact that an already interpreted and synthesized empirical material is exposed to different theoretical frames of reference – serves to open up the text. The reader's capacity for activity and reinterpretation is thus stimulated in a different way than when a text presents more unambiguous results, aiming to convince the reader that the author knows best and that the research results are true.

There are other ways of writing, too, that can make the downplaying of the researcher's authority easier and encourage a more active, creative reading of the text. Various authors have indicated alternative styles of writing, including confessional, impressionistic and ironic ones (Brown, 1977; Jeffcutt, 1993; Van Maanen, 1988). They differ from the more conventional realistic mode of presentation, and involve the reader in different modes of reading. Particular interest has been shown in the dialogic style, where the researcher and the informant share responsibility for the text. Here it becomes a question of 'negotiation' about how the described object should be represented (Marcus and Fischer, 1986). This diverges somewhat from the ideal of multiple voices, however, as the very idea of dialogue suggests that only two are involved, even though these two may be media for several expressed viewpoints. The researcher may also encourage a dialogue with the reader, by indicating pertinent problems and imperfections in the text. In this way it is possible to present the reader with interesting problems that the researcher has been unable to solve. The author is made visible and the reader is compelled to become involved. Appropriate parts of the researcher's subjectivity should emerge from the page. Avoiding jargon, rhetorical tricks, ritualistic references and other authority-promoting devices can also help to produce a more open text (Richardson, 2000). (On the tactics used by researchers to strengthen the authority of their texts, see Calás and Smircich, 1988, and Sangren, 1992.)

PM/PS's theory about the *subject's domination by context and language* – subjectivity as discursive construction – naturally has major implications for what can be expected from, for example, an interview. As will be seen in the next chapter, there is an increasing amount of empirical evidence suggesting how difficult it is to know what to make of interview statements (or, for that matter, of statements in general), and this evidence largely supports the more philosophical notions that have been launched by PM and PS. It is a big problem for those wanting to use empirical material to throw light on either social reality ('out there') or personal experience and meanings. How interviewees appear or represent reality in specific interview situations has less to do with how they, or reality, really are (or how they perceive a reality out there); rather, it is about the way they temporarily develop a form of subjectivity, and how they represent reality in relation to the local discursive context created by the interview. The important methodological implication of this is that it would be wise to avoid relying entirely on interviews (or, even more, on questionnaires, which, in view of the ambiguity and rich variety of language in the meanings ascribed by the respondents, are extremely unreliable). Participant observation is recommended as the method to produce empirical material on non-trivial phenomena, at least as a complement (that is, the ethnographic method). Yet even observations in the so-called 'natural context' are powerfully affected by the indeterminate nature of language. One problem here, of course, is the language of observation: from what is generally a large number of possible representations, which ones are chosen by the researcher? But it is important to note that observations of social conditions are often about linguistic actions (social interaction, after all, revolves around speech). These actions have the same ambiguous relationship to 'objective' conditions – broader chunks of social reality – and to people's way of imparting meaning to existence and to themselves, as interviews have. The point of ethnographies is that the data trancend the context of the interview (but, of course, come within a new context – that of participant observation). The availability of different perspectives increases, and the scope for more interesting interpretations is much greater.

Greater sensitivity to the meaning and character of language must also imbue the work of interpretation and writing. The belief that language can mirror a complex reality should be toned down considerably compared with what is usual today. Even if we do not fully accept the postmodernists' replacement of the mirror view of language (the non-problematical representational ability of language) by the idea that language is (only) constitutive, following a closed (referent-free) logic incapable of any form of representation, this problem of language as a representation of reality must nevertheless be taken into account. This might mean that language and language use become the object of study in their own right, rather than merely a medium for understanding what lies beyond language (see the following chapter on discourse analysis). It could also mean greater demands on micro-anchoring institutional-level concepts – coupling these more closely to actual processes (see, for example, Collins, 1981; Johansson, 1990; Knorr-Cetina, 1981; Sandelands and Drazin, 1989). As language provides an unstable foundation rather than a collection of stable building-blocks upon which to construct theories, the question is how high one should try to build – at least if one still maintains some idea about an empirical base and about theory's links (however tenuous) with 'reality'.

Research and the micropolitics of the text

One last, rather general, implication of PM and PS concerns the *political aspects of research*. Micropolitics has a different place on the agenda of this school (or schools), compared with critical theory, for instance. The research text is always, in some sense, about authority and consequently about power. As a result of a rather narrow focus on the 'politics of the text' and the encouragement for researchers to reflect upon their own claims to authority, there is a certain paradoxical risk of depoliticizing or trivializing the political, which becomes too researcher-centred. We have already mentioned the problems of narcissism and self-absorption.[20] However, this is not to deny the profound value of the insight that any statements we make, as researchers (or in any other context, for that matter) will always become the object of the *politics of representation*. How representations are made is always in some sense arbitrary, since there is no unambiguous relation between language and 'extra-linguistic' reality. One representation may block another possible one. Even descriptions and analyses that would appear good for some people – the emancipatory, for instance, or the apparently innocent (allegedly neutral) – are thus always potentially problematic. Even revelations are in some sense also obfuscatory. Once again we do not mean that this sort of perspective ought to be totalized, that is, regarded as an absolute central aspect of what research and text are all about. The consequence of this would be a complete inability to act, and a form of authorly narcissism. A recognition of the subtleties of language and the politics of the text has the direct implication for qualitative method that it emphasizes the importance of handling the problems of pluralism/exclusion with discernment. An open way of writing and the consideration of different theoretical frames of reference could offer one route towards the pragmatic and reflective handling of the problems of representation and writing.

Summary of pragmatic postmodern methodological principles

The ideals discussed above concerning multiple voices, well-reasoned exclusions, wary interpretations, caution vis-á-vis 'totalizing' theories and so on, need to be balanced by a scepticism against the ideal and possibility of 'adopting endlessly shifting, seemingly inexhaustible vantage points, none of which are "owned" by either the critic or the author of a text under examination' (Bordo, 1990: 42). Other modifying ideals include the value of taking empirical material seriously as an indication of some (ambiguous, often fragmented) social reality and maintaining a certain degree of analytical focus and depth. Based on this we have pointed to four central elements in pluralistic scientific research projects and texts, briefly summarized below.

- Pluralism in the potential of different identities or voices associated with different groups, individuals, positions or special interests which inform, and can be seen in, research work and research texts.
- Receptiveness to pluralism and variation in what individual participants in the research process convey (the possibility of multiple representations by one and the same individual participant).
- Alternative presentations of phenomena (for instance, the use of different sorts of descriptive language).
- Command of different theoretical perspectives (root metaphors), as well as a strong familiarity with the critique of and problems with these. This enables openness and different sorts of readings to surface in the research.[21]

It is hardly feasible in one and the same text to achieve a high degree of pluralism and a minimum of exclusion in all four of these dimensions. A possible research strategy would be to try to maximize one or two of the above inputs into the generation of pluralism, and to accept less consideration of pluralism in any of them that are not being maximized. What is crucial is the production of an open text, which stimulates active interpretation on the part of the reader; researchers should avoid 'closing' their texts by placing themselves too firmly between the reader and the voices researched.

Final word

Under the rubrics of postmodernism and poststructuralism – which are of course problematic representations of a large amount of research texts – a number of somewhat disparate ideas have been presented, which break radically with a realist point of view and also with orientations such as hermeneutics and critical theory. Not least, new ways of looking at language, theory and the authority of research have been emphasized. Some of these ideas – fragmentation, variation – are perhaps reflected in the design of this chapter.

We have rather brutally criticized some of the ideas in PM and PS on the basis of our own minimal belief in authority, and on grounds of the rather pragmatic stance which the context of qualitative empirical method implies. Let us now elicit a theme which we have only briefly touched upon above. A special problem concerns the relationship between the postmodern insights and what one can apply to one's own life.[22] As Sarup (1988) says, we (Westerners) live our lives as humanists: we perceive ourselves as active subjects, with goals, intentions and responsibilites, and as creators of meaning; but this is not necessarily how we theorize. There is certainly no reason to maximize the overlap between private and academic theories and beliefs – the point of research can even be to produce an epistemological break with the former (cf. Bourdieu et al., 1991). But too great a distance becomes problematic. Theories should be able to enrich our self-understanding and affect the way we act. If we were to fully accept, for example, PS's subject and language theories, start seeing ourselves as 'merely' linguistic appendices and abstain from all referential statements, the consequences for our existence would be absurd. We do not want to over-emphasize this point – a selective incorporation of insights from PM and PS is, as we have seen, quite possible and even desirable. Still, theories which are perhaps well suited to the desk or the armchair, but which can hardly be taken with complete seriousness in non-academic situations, risk becoming sterile and socially irrelevant.

An overarching comment on our part is that in their polemical enthusiasm PM and PS often aim too *high*. By adopting a stance that is pretty drastic and categorical, they make things difficult for themselves, even if they sometimes manage to market their ideas better this way (Alvesson, 1995a). This applies in particular to empirical research. PM and PS hardly encourage such activity, or even statements with any bearing on extra-textual conditions. However, as we have pointed out, our view of these orientations is not purely negative; we have found a great many interesting ideas and themes in both PM and PS, if taken with a large pinch of salt. Once again we would like to emphasize the many varied positions within the field, and to point out that we can take up only a few characteristic parts of the main lines.

This orientation (or rather the sum of the different variants) is important as a corrective to and a source of inspiration for more traditional views of research. The criticism against a naïve realism is considerably strengthened. The orientation also has advantages in its critique of the pseudo-rational, totalizing structures which are built into the social discourse, and which have petrified into giant, institutionalized mausoleums. (Even if we may ask whether these had not begun to crumble in the social sciences already before the arrival of PM on the scene.) The focus on the narrative, local, fragmented, and ambivalent has much going for it, as does the pointing out of the irreducible contradictions and instability in all human knowledge. If the idea of decoupling from the referents is not taken as something universally valid but more as an aspect worth careful consideration, it may communicate important insights. To the most valuable contributions also belongs an increased sensitivity to the importance of language, to what theoretical frames of reference and a monolithic style of research conceal, to how the subject (at least in part) is constituted by language, and to political aspects of research. PM and PS put the authority of research at the centre. They also encourage emancipation from and a more experimenting attitude in relation to established intellectual traditions.

Postmodernists are certainly right to question whether 'properties such as unity, identity, permanence, structure and essences, etc. are privileged over dissonance, disparity, plurality, transience and change' (Chia, 1995: 581). Rather than celebrating and privileging the second set of concepts, avoiding both forms of categorical thinking and being open to the selective use of each of them whenever it seems productive may be the most fruitful route to follow.

Notes

1. Architectural theory has contributed substantially to this (Jencks, 1987).
2. We report briefly here on the way the concepts are often used. In our own exposition we do not maintain any strict divisions between the two, even though in some situations one or the other may seem more appropriate.
3. Various writers distinguish between different forms of postmodernism in terms of politics. Rosenau (1992) talks about sceptical and affirmative postmodernists. The sceptics emphasize fragmentation, malaise, meaninglessness, absence of moral parameters and social chaos. The affirmatives, often less extreme, see some possibilities for positive social change. Foster (1985) makes a distinction between a postmodernism of reaction and of resistance, the former being happy with the status quo while the latter resists the contemporary (dis)order, without any (clear) political agenda. The latter category resembles the sceptics and their anti-subject, anti-humanist, anti-representation and anti-history position.
4. Some of the words used here are not normally used by postmodernists, or if they are used must be understood differently than in, for example, hermeneutics. While interpretation, for example, in conventional research is a matter of careful consideration of data in order to identify a pattern and point at a superior meaning or truth, if used in PM it is more a matter of accomplishing plural constructions and the multiplication of scenarios (Rosenau, 1992: 118). Basically, however, 'interpretation' is a concept within the general problematic and framework of hermeneutics – which is very far from 'deconstruction', its counterpart in PM (Hoy, 1996b).
5. Graff (1979) argues that postmodernism becomes tautological, since in every text it finds the same wounds that it presumes to exist there.
6. Derrida (1982) believes, to be sure, that *différance* does not constitute an absence, since this would either mean pure emptiness, or else would be directly linked to the concept of presence; he wants to eschew the absence–presence opposition in order to avoid the metaphysics of presence. *Différance*, then, would neither constitute something present, at hand, nor the absence of this (taken as non-existence, that is, emptiness, or else something which manifests itself in the present according to the classical metaphysics of presence – that of the essence in its appearances and so on). It is, however, difficult to see that *différance* could be anything else than just absence in either of the two senses Derrida gives this word. Deferral is the absence of something in time. Difference is the absence of similarity between two or more occurrences.
7. Besides, Derrida (1982: 21) tells us that *différance* actually *is* a concept.

8. Hayman (1980) maintains, influenced among others by Freud, that a highly developed capacity for introspection is the point of departure for and colours all the philosophy of Nietzsche. If this is correct, Nietzsche may through introspection have reached his idea of the will to power as fundamental to his being and then transferred this insight to his environment. (Hayman's biography should, however, be taken with some caution; its quality is uneven, since it tends too much to force a thesis – of Nietzsche's lifelong striving for madness – through refractory sources.)

9. The same thing is, by the way, true of a pre-postmodern author such as Foucault, whose genealogies in the wake of Nietzsche always aimed at showing that the historical origin of various cultural phenomena is not noble or rational, as represented in the conventional, received view, but an expression of the naked will to power in the different actors.

10. Berman writes about the Paris intelligentsia:

   It sounds as if, after the failure of their one great leap into actuality, back in May 1968, they resolved never to go out again, and dug themselves into a grand metaphysical tomb, thick and tight enough to furnish lasting comfort against the cruel hopes of spring. Their postmodern world makes a sensible retirement community, a fine place to stay cool. (1992: 46)

11. The fact that one of its leading proponents, Paul de Man, was revealed to have expressed Nazi sympathies during the Second World War, has contributed to undermining this orientation, especially in the USA.

12. Some PS authors address this issue. Weedon (1987), for example, mentions that the individual subject is not just a passive site for the play of discursive powers. She writes that 'the individual who has a memory and an already discursively constituted sense of identity may resist particular interpellations or produce new versions of meaning from the conflicts and contradictions existing between discourses' (Weedon, 1987: 106). This statement is not altogether representative of the entire text. Weedon elsewhere ascribes activity to discourses and portrays individuals as subordinate in relationship to these. The central theme is that 'subjectivity is an effect of discourse' (Weedon, 1987: 86).

13. One problem – among many others – is that research freezes a certain portrait of the individual. This is inherent in the way many kinds of scientific observations are conducted, where the researcher typically limits himself or herself to a specific context – for example, the laboratory or the psychoanalyst's couch (Rose, 1989).

14. Marcus (1994) refers to the study as 'post-postmodernist'. This term, however, designates what we mean by a more applied (later) postmodernism, in contrast to a more critical or negative (earlier) variant of PM.

15. A crucial aspect here is to insist that a sceptical attitude should be applied discriminately. Empirical claims, ideals and theories vary in terms of insights, pragmatic value, empirical support, and so on and should be evaluated accordingly. The problem with a non-discriminatory view is 'that you can say anything you want, but so can everyone else. Some of what is said will be interesting and fascinating, but some will also be ridiculous and absurd. Post-modernism provides no means to distinguish between the two' (Rosenau, 1992: 137).

16. And ideas of Foucault from his 'archaeological' period, in which he focused on discourses and even discursive structures ('epistemes'), are used to legitimize textual reductionism, whereby it is conveniently forgotten that Foucault, both before and (especially) after this period, by no means restricted himself to discourses but focused on *non*-discursive practices as well.

17. We find this term useful, if understood as less totalizing than normally understood in postmodernism, that is, with connections – however tenuous – to both subject and referent (signified).

18. The sensitivity to different (linguistic) identities emerged very clearly in an interview which one of us held with a woman in a company. The respondent answered questions about the workplace on the basis of her identity as an employee and lower-level manager, and spoke of the company in positive terms. To a question about the way she, as a woman, perceived her superiors, however, her answer was in quite a different key. She referred to them as 'male chauvinists'. Thus the activating of a gender identity produced an attitude to the organization that was radically different from what was otherwise expressed in the interview.

19. Representations, including 'the repression of women', are of course never unproblematic. This does not mean that they are unwarranted.

20. Postmodernism's critical impulse can also lead to depoliticization because its 'promiscuous critique' is aimed at everything, apparently without any underlying assessment of what urgently needs critical investigation in light of, for instance, emancipatory ideals or informed resistance, or, on the other hand, debureaucratization, personal responsibility, and individual initiative. As Billig and Simons (1994: 4) put it, 'critique is running rampant without political direction'. On the other hand, quite a few current social scientific writers embrace a (theoretically rather uneasy) alliance between postmodernism and left-oriented social constructionism, which points in the other direction. Not least many of the French opponents to Sokal and his realist colleagues belong to such an orientation.

21. All the points, but especially the third and fourth, overlap to some extent. The use of different metaphors affects both descriptions (preliminary interpretations/readings) and the more developed (hermeneutic) type of interpretation. But the emphasis can vary as regards pluralism, in that the researcher explores ambiguity and multiple meanings either in the preliminary interpretations or in the more concluding secondary work.

22. As Denzin (1997) remarks, the problems of representation (inability or difficulties in capturing social life) and legitimacy (the dismissal of traditional criteria for evaluating research) lead to the crisis of praxis (doubts about the capacity of social research to inform action).

7

LANGUAGE/GENDER/POWER: DISCOURSE ANALYSIS, FEMINISM AND GENEALOGY

In this chapter we discuss some orientations which we feel are of topical interest and too important to be excluded, but which we do not delve into in quite as much detail within the frames of our present project as the four previous ones. Whereas those embraced general themes which constitute the basis of reflective social science, the slightly more distinct orientations to be addressed below represent important complementary dimensions and angles of approach. Three dimensions, which most people would surely regard as fundamental, are *language*, *gender* and *power*: language is the medium in which we conduct our social lives and create our symbolical existence; gender is the fundamental dichotomous figure of thought characterizing our private as well as public lives; power entangles all of us in its constantly reinvented ruses and snares, which some scientists (such as Weber) even regard as the very texture of society, the fine-grained basic structure that holds it together.

Throughout the twentieth century, language has occupied a central position in philosophy, not least through the predominance – in separate thematic, cultural and geographical spheres – of Heidegger and Wittgenstein, and through French philosophy, which ever since the heyday of structuralism has found inspiration in linguistics through the work of Saussure. As was mentioned in the chapter on hermeneutics, interest in language has tended to move from limited linguistic units to larger textual units – discourses. The study of discourses is a topical theme in the social sciences, and we open this chapter with a section on discourse analysis. Discourse analysis deepens and varies the problematizations addressed in previous chapters as to how we handle language in empirical work, and contributes to questioning the assumptions underlying dataistic methods. In connection with qualitative methodology it is particularly relevant that discourse analysis demonstrates the problems of using interviews (the most common method in qualitative contexts), but also 'spontaneously' occurring accounts (documented in participant observation), in trying to find out 'how things are'.

Another main area has been, and still is, the study of *subgroups* within broader social formations. Class is such an area, although less central in recent years; nor is it connected to any great extent with qualitative method. Ethnicity is an emerging topic, but we cannot *yet* call it a strong theme in social science research.[1] On the other hand, gender now indisputably occupies a leading position in our research area, and will therefore be addressed below. A section addressing ethnicity and social class would also have been justified: the dominating thrust in contemporary research can be accused not only of male domination and inadequate reflection in terms of gender, but also of a predominance of white (Western) middle-class contributors and the overly powerful influence of their (our) culture. However, the point of this book is not to embrace all important topics, but to argue in favour of a reflective empirical social science, and to make concrete suggestions that could be relevant in this context. Feminism will have to represent the type of asymmetry that arises among social groups. Feminism – or, in a broader spectrum, gender research – is also particularly relevant to our argument here, since it has more to say about qualitative method than either class or ethnicity studies. Parts of feminism also consider these categories, emphasizing that one can't study gender abstracted from other social issues. And so the second section in this chapter deals with feminism. Feminism also has political-ideological dimensions, not least with themes concerning the destabilization of categories and mental sets which is characteristic of poststructural and, up to a point, also of critical theory. Feminism, moreover, here represents the lines of research which spotlight social groups, underprivileged both politically and in research terms.

Finally, the study of power is an evergreen, despite all the announcements of its demise, and it has even gained new ground, not least through the great interest in Foucault's writings which has swept through the research community. Foucault's thinking has a special methodological relevance, since he focused on the relation between power and knowledge. It is not primarily – or at least not only – power 'out there' that should be addressed in the present book, but power in a close connection with knowledge 'in here', in the research context. Foucault's notion of power is thus of great interest in the context of methodology – irrespective of the object of inquiry. We therefore devote the third section below to this type of power analysis. As we have seen, when Foucault elucidated the intimate link between knowledge and power, themes from phenomenology, hermeneutics, critical theory and poststructuralism also appeared in a radically different light.

The three chosen angles of approach appropriately complement our discussions in the previous chapters also in so far as they cut through one or more of these orientations. Several attributes of discourse analysis thus also appear in postmodernism. Feminism in its different versions has close points of contact with both critical theory and postmodernism. Foucault's writings border on the poststructural, as well as having a good deal in common with some versions of critical theory, and with the hermeneutics of suspicion in their Nietzschean variety. Language, gender and power are of course themselves closely related and, as we shall see, all three concepts overlap to some extent with one another in the separate presentations given below.

All approaches show some resemblance with social constructionism, in one sense or another. All avoid objectivistic assumptions and claims. (There are, however, versions of feminism that are more inclined to make claims about 'the truth' out there, like 'objective' discrimination, going beyond at least more radical forms of constructionism.) Discourse analysis looks at how reality is constructed in fine-tuned ways in language. Feminism studies the arbitrary construction of gender and gender differences disadvantaging females. Foucauldian power analysis shows how what is often understood as knowledge reflecting the world and/or providing us with valuable tools for handling it, means the imposing of order and other power effects, leading to the construction of specific institutions and norms which in a sense function as reality-producing.

Discourse analysis

Discourse is a widely and often vaguely used signifier in social science and language studies (Alvesson and Kärreman, 2000; Grant and Iedema, 2005). We don't have the intention here to cover all these uses, but will concentrate on discourse analysis, which focuses on the study of language in action, that is the detailed understanding of talk and text in a social setting.

Criticism of traditional views of language in research

As the previous chapters have indicated, it is rather naïve to think that social realities can be depicted in unequivocal terms. People's capacity for describing their interior realities or external conditions cannot be taken for granted, something which Wittgenstein (1953) pointed out half a century ago. It is pretty obvious that what people say in interviews, in writing, or in their everyday interactions, can differ from what they 'really' think, or that attitudes and behaviour may not always match each other very well. But the problem goes deeper than this. It can be questioned whether people actually have definite, unambivalent conceptions or values and atti-tudes which are (or can be) explicitly expressed at all. Let us imagine that we have skimmed off all the problems, such as dishonesty, self-deception, taboos, misunder-standings and interviewer effects, which to a greater or lesser extent leave their imprint on what people say (Van Maanen, 1979), thus creating for ourselves the 'ideal' situation for discussion, in which respondents as well as interviewer express themselves honestly, openly and clearly. But even under such 'optimal' conditions there is reason to doubt whether statements about the way people see reality, express experiences, or perceive themselves, for instance, actually reflect a particu-lar idea, belief or self-image in an unproblematic way. The problem is that, in order to be comprehensible and meaningful, utterances are necessarily context-dependent – not only in the obvious sense that people express themselves differently in public and private settings, to colleagues at work, to researchers, or in their personal diaries (social context), but also because what people say is contextually dependent at a more subtle level: as historians have also long pointed out (see Chapter 4), it may be affected by what has been said earlier in a conversation (by themselves or by some other person such as an interviewer), or by the way various utterances are organized (micro context). The way language is used does not so much reflect a person's inner, subjective world, as generate a version of this world that is in part a transient one. Neither accounts of subjectivity (feelings, attitudes, notions, values), nor ideas about the external world are consistent, partly as a consequence of there being no one-to-one relationship between language use and the phenomenon it is supposed to say something about.

All this implies a crucial critique of the so-called realistic view of language, which treats utterances as relatively unambiguous entry points to the understanding of actions, ideas or events. Two types of criticism can be raised here, one linguistic-philosophical and one stemming more from behavioural science studying accounts of people. The linguistic critique, formulated by Ricoeur and various poststructural-ists among others, emphasizes that language is by nature metaphorical, figurative and context-dependent, and not very successful at mirroring complex circumstances (see Chapter 6 above). Or, as Säljö (1990) puts it, language does not reflect reality but 'perspectivizes' it, that is, presents it in a special light. The critique from a behavioural science point of view concerns the assumption that people describing the same action or phenomenon will do so in similar ways, and that the same person describing the same attitude or idea in different contexts will always be consistent. But these are dubious assumptions; it is usually more reasonable, as the discourse analysts Potter and Wetherell (1987) point out, building on their research on people's accounts, to expect a low degree of consistency in both cases.

Let us illustrate this with an example from the advertising industry. Slater (1989: 122) has noted that: 'it is a cliché in the industry that agencies promise their clients total and infallible power over the consumer's behaviour while telling the public that it [the industry] has no power at all and merely reflects current trends or pro-vides information'. This can of course simply be regarded as a description of oppor-tunism; perhaps an adperson may 'really' hold one or other of these views, or a different one altogether. However, we could easily imagine that an advertising expert being interviewed in a research context – when there are no legitimation or pecuniary interests in expressing oneself in any particular way – could make state-ments expressing both these views, and perhaps even others, all during the same interview. Rather than trying to discover a 'true' or genuine belief of the impact of advertising, we could assume initially that there is no such clear-cut idea – or, if there is, that it is well concealed from human view. Better than speculating about the 'real' idea or belief would be to explore variations in people's statements on the issue. After all, utterances are what we can best relate to. Perhaps the average adver-tising expert has no consistent view of the effects of advertising, which is sometimes concealed by more opportune statements. Perhaps the experts' ideas on the subject are fragmented, not existing as an unequivocal or clearly defined part of their con-sciousness, but in a dynamic relation to a mass of other ideas, conceptions and asso-ciations. Every activation of the 'idea' or rather of these partially fragmented ideas also entails the introduction of many other such elements – which ones in particu-lar will vary, depending on the context in which the question has been raised (Alvesson and Köping, 1993). Perhaps the issue is better described as 'undecidable' than as a matter of a firm belief or attitude.

An important research orientation which has emerged in recent years, and which puts great emphasis on modes of expression, is discourse analysis (DA). Discourse analysis reveals a certain similarity with poststructuralism, in that people are assumed to be inconsistent and language is not seen as reflecting external or internal (mental) conditions. An emphasis on the 'undecidability' between language use and a reality 'out there' is also shared. Discourse analysis differs from poststructuralism (PS) mainly in that it is an empirical and systematic research endeavour, avoiding the sometimes rather wordy philosophizing that characterizes PS. Here we base our account and discussion of DA primarily on Potter and Wetherell (1987). Unlike many other writers we, following DA, include in 'discourse' all kinds of language use (speech acts) in oral and written social connections, that is, utterances and written documents. A discourse is a social text. The focus on discourse thus means a concern with 'talk and texts as parts of social practices' (Potter, 1996: 105).

Discourse analysis rejects a use of realist methods in social science which aim at mirroring extra-linguistic reality by finding patterns in empirical material. This applies to both quantitative and qualitative methods, in which the idea is to reduce dissimilarities and ambiguities by forcing people into a restricted variety of response or reaction alternatives (questionnaires, experiments), or by letting them speak or act more or less freely (open-ended interviews, field observations), and then developing categories which capture and reduce the variation. In this way, it is believed, we can discover interesting patterns in behaviour and/or ideas (meanings). The critique of quantitative endeavours is well known: in questionnaire studies the risk is that we only throw light on the way people put crosses on questionnaires (whereupon the slightest alteration in the wording of the questions or the alternative responses may give rise to new 'marking' behaviour), and that people in laboratory experiments are being asked to behave in artificial and simplified situations. Qualitative approaches are superior in the respects relevant here, but even these tend to over-emphasize the relation between utterances and underlying meanings or actual conditions. The discourse analyst feels that not enough serious attention is paid to the variations in what is said. All in all, the aggregating techniques used in behavioural and social science mean that consistency in utterances and accounts is over-emphasized, while inconsistencies are concealed. It is also felt that the existence of consistency – within a certain person's utterances or between the accounts offered by different individuals – cannot simply be taken as a guarantee of descriptive validity.

Potter and Wetherell (1987) claim that the failure of scholars to pay serious attention to variations in people's accounts, particularly in psychology, is a result of analytical strategies which have favoured the restriction, categorization and selective interpretation of utterances. *Restriction* means that the scientist 'locks' subjects by applying various techniques which force them into certain reaction patterns. This is the case in experiments, questionnaires and to some extent structured interviews. *Categorization* means that all accounts are referred to various broader categories, which are then treated as the primary empirical material. The fact that different evaluators may refer a particular utterance to the same category – a criterion of validity in content analysis – does not stop important distinctions and variations within a certain category from being missed. Similar evaluations can also arise because people share certain preconceived ideas of linguistic conventions (paradigms, school education), so that they may not necessarily be doing justice to the empirical material. *Selective interpretation* means that on the basis of the prestructured understanding – the theoretical framework and less conscious personal and cultural ideas and beliefs, including taken-for-granted assumptions and expectations – the scientist structures an account in such a way that a potential multiplicity of meanings is neglected in favour of what is regarded as a 'primary' meaning that the researcher believes expresses the core of what the respondent is communicating. (This critique can be directed at practically all qualitative research, in particular hermeneutics, and also at grounded theory, phenomenology and critical theory.)

Discourse-analytical research

Thus DA is interested in the discursive level only (which, as we have seen, refers to all forms of speech and writing), and emphasizes rather than seeks to reduce variations in language use. Consequently DA disregards, or at any rate tones down, the 'underlying reality' – including a socially constructed one – as the object of study (Potter and Wetherell, 1987).[2] There is no interest in the social constructions of institutions assumed to build up society according to authors like Berger and Luckmann. If on one occasion a person displays a certain attitude and on another a somewhat contradictory one, we cannot simply take this as reflecting what the person in question really thinks, nor can we regard one attitude as the real one and the other as somehow 'non-genuine'. Discourse analysis would claim that if we look at people's accounts in a sufficiently unbiased and detailed way, we will see that they almost always contain a good deal of variation. (Then, of course, this variation, or ambiguity, becomes the 'underlying reality' which thus, being excluded from the main entrance of DA, slips in through the back door.) The same event is described by different individuals in different ways, but – and this is the important point – the same individual also tends to describe the event in different ways. Potter and Wetherell demonstrate this in several convincing empirical examples. All this means that it is not really possible simply to say what is 'true' and what is 'not true'. This scepticism also includes doubt about the possibilities of making assessments about the beliefs and meanings that people 'really' hold. But it is possible to focus on utterances which reflect attitudes, and to ask oneself the following questions. On what occasions are the different attitudes expressed? How are the utterances constructed? In what contexts are they included and what functions do they fulfil? This is thus the task of discourse analysis.

Discourse analysis claims that through language people engage in constructing the social world. There are three aspects to this. First, people actively create accounts on a basis of previously existing linguistic resources. Secondly, they are continually and actively involved in selecting some of the infinite number of words and meaning constructions available, and in rejecting others. Thirdly, the chosen construction has its consequences: the mode of expression has an effect, it influences ideas, generates responses and so on. (Paradoxically, people, accounts, selections, influences, responses, etc. are apparently seen as real here.)

Discourse analysis starts from the following assumptions:

1 Language is used for a variety of functions and has a variety of consequences.
2 Language is both constructed and constructive.
3 The same phenomenon can be described in several different ways.

4 Consequently there will be considerable variations in the accounts of it.
5 There is no foolproof way yet of handling these variations or of distinguishing accounts which are 'literal' or 'accurate' from those which are rhetorical or incorrect, thus avoiding the problem of variation which faces researchers working with a more 'realistic' language model.
6 The constructive and flexible ways in which language is used should themselves be a central subject of study (Potter and Wetherell, 1987: 35).

Thus DA means studying conversations, interview statements and other linguistic expressions, without drawing any conclusions which are clearly 'beyond' the micro situations constituting the contexts in question. In other words, the conversations or the interviews themselves become the context of the accounts. Instead of treating interviews 'as a machinery for harvesting data from respondents, they can be viewed as an arena for interaction in its own right' (Potter, 1997: 149).

C.W. Mills (1940) presented similar ideas a good many years ago, when he noted the impossibility of capturing 'real' motives or 'real' attitudes with the help of language, and emphasized the strong social dependence of different accounts of motives. In different groups and at different periods in history the predominant linguistic expression of motives has varied enormously. Mills suggested focusing on 'the vocabulary of motives', that is, the way in which people account for and try to explain their motives.

Potter and Wetherell, amongst many others (such as Hammersley, 1992; Hollway, 1989; Silverman, 1985, 1994), warn the researcher against the risk of adopting the view of reality which the interview subject conveys as objective and real or even as a true expression of the subject's 'mental world'. Even apparently honest and reliable utterances must be understood on the basis of the specific context in which they are made and of the linguistic rules which imbue this context.[3] Honest and faithful accounts may very well contain contradictory or at least inconsistent utterances. (Among historians, this has been commonplace for centuries, even though they draw partly different conclusions; see Chapter 4.)

Potter and Wetherell (1987) provide several overall principles for conducting DA. One emphasizes the importance of approaching subjects' accounts in talk and writing '*in their own right* and not as a secondary route to things "beyond" the text like attitudes, events or cognitive processes' (Potter and Wetherell, 1987: 160). Another important principle is that it is not the size of a sample that is interesting, but the close study of nuances in possibly quite a small number of accounts. In conventional research the aim is to acquire a great mass of data demonstrating consistency, which can then be interpreted as meaning that the accounts may be able to reflect some kind of 'reality' beyond themselves. In DA consistency is also interesting, but only if the researcher wants to explore regularities and patterns in the use of language. Inconsistency and variation, as we have seen, are at least as interesting as consistency.

Discourse analysis is often interested in the accounts or documents which have arisen in the natural course of events, rather than in the interaction between participants and researchers. It may be a question of meetings, therapy or counselling sessions, news reports, scientific papers or whatever. If interviews are held, these differ from traditional ones, first, in that variations in the responses are as important as consistency;

secondly, in that techniques which allow variations in responses rather than reducing them play a prominent part; thirdly, in that the interviewees are regarded as active participants in a conversation, rather than as 'speaking questionnaires' (Potter and Wetherell, 1987: 165); and fourthly in that there is no intention to use the interviews in order to reveal what goes on inside people's minds or mirror external reality.

Interpretation does not, of course, focus on clear-cut patterns or 'gist'. Nuances, contradictions and areas of vagueness are also worth noting. The analyst should be interested in the way the accounts are organized, in details in the discourse, as well as in what is actually said or written, and not in vague notions about what may have been meant.

Potter and Wetherell are aware that their approach may seem esoteric, of academic interest only. But they claim a wide area of application for it. Language use is absolutely central to our lives. Social institutions and social relations are constructed and reproduced through communicative actions. Knowledge about them is important to many professions, and to the whole question of the influence to which people are exposed in a variety of contexts, as in political debates, for example.

Critique and evaluation of discourse analysis

We find the ideas of DA and associated streams such as conversation analysis and ethnomethodology exciting and worthy of serious attention. We agree that there are problems in regarding linguistic utterances as unequivocal mirrorings of external or internal realities. The capacity of language to represent (non-trivial) conditions and interior arrangements is limited. But we regard an exclusive focus on language use and speech acts as altogether too narrow an approach. If we constrain our research in this way, important (and admittedly difficult) questions are left unanswered. If all foci apart from the linguistic are excluded, there is a risk of the research becoming trivialized. Many crucial issues will then simply disappear. One disadvantage of DA, as of other linguistically focused endeavours, is that it empties people of psychological content in too radical a way. As Parker (1994: 244) points out, there is a tendency for 'a sustained refusal of appeals to individual mental mechanisms or intentions beyond or outside what can actually be read in a text'. Utterances are explained in DA by their effects, by what arises from them, and not by the intentions or cognitive processes lying behind what is said or written – a kind of functionalism that is problematic (Bowers, 1988). And, as we have seen, despite professions to what amounts to a textual reductionism, DA cannot avoid talking about these effects or functions as really existing 'out there'.

Our comments are concerned not so much with DA as a special field of research – which we find interesting and entirely legitimate, if narrow. Rather, we are looking at some of the implications which the approach can have for the kind of research which focuses more conventionally on ideas, actions and social patterns. What insights can discourse analysis contribute to qualitative methods with somewhat wider aspirations?

Discourse analysis – like other forms of critique of the realistic approach, such as poststructuralism and other linguistic-philosophical versions of 'anti-objectivism' – calls for more caution in drawing conclusions from accounts and speech acts about other social phenomena than these specific accounts and speech acts. On the other hand we see no strong, constructive reason for distancing ourselves altogether from the possibility of interpreting meanings in utterances – meanings which go beyond the utterances themselves and their microcontext. In the alternatives launched by Potter and Wetherell (1987) and other language-oriented behavioural and social researchers, there is a tendency to exaggerate and over-emphasize the importance of the inconsistency, variation and context-dependence of speech acts. As a counter-weight to a naïve realism, this is justified. But at the same time inconsistency and variation are naturally an expression of the yardstick used. A detailed study of utter-ances or word usage immediately reveals the overwhelming multiplicity of meanings. But the *relative* capacity of language in many cases to (equivocally) convey insights, experiences and factual information is also worth noting, as well as the *pragmatic* value of emphasizing its capacity to clarify phenomena. In contrast to the discourse analysts and the many modern linguistic philosophers and postmodernists who distance themselves altogether from the idea of representativity and instead stress the ambiguity of language and the wealth of variety in people's accounts, and also in contrast to the conventional representativity idea of the realists, we would like to emphasize the *partial* and *incomplete* ability of language to convey something beyond itself, and the *variation* in the relative consistency and value of different utterances as clues to phenomena other than their own language usage (Alvesson and Köping, 1993).[4]

There is also the need to distinguish between sense and reference. Ambiguity in sense does not necessarily imply ambiguity in reference, and vice versa. Secondly, an acceptance of ambiguity – in either of these meanings – does not equal an acceptance of non-realism. Thirdly, DA has a realist view of social constructions; these exist, can be talked about, etc.

This points to the need to remain reflective and sceptical, but not categorical, about the use of talk and language in our study. It is thus important to consider the extent to which various utterances can be appropriately treated simply as utterances, and how far they can be used as the starting-point for more extensive interpretations of other phenomena. Such other phenomena (than utterances) in turn contain two elements which should be kept apart: conceptions (values, ideas, motives, and so on) and 'objective' conditions. Thus we should consider interview statements, written documents and talk occurring spontaneously (written down in the case of participative observation), assuming that to a varying extent these can be interpreted on three levels:

1 The *discursive* level, at which language use and expressive mode do not stand for – or are not interpreted as – something else (for example, reflecting external conditions or the minds of the language users), but are themselves the object of study. What is then interesting, among other things, is the way different people in different contexts express themselves on the subject of their ideas, the motives of others, events and so on. In many situations this can in itself be an interesting phenomenon to study.
2 The *ideational* level, at which the researcher speaks of conceptions, values, beliefs, ideas, meanings and fantasies, on the basis of an interpretation of utter-ances during interviews and in natural situations.

3 The level of *action and social conditions*, where research aims to say something solid about relations, behaviours, events, social patterns and structures 'out there' which, without necessarily being ascribed an objective or robust character, nonetheless refer to something that cannot simply be regarded as language or as 'subjective conceptions' on the part of the studied individuals or collectives.

Research which pays serious attention to the ideas of discourse analysis, not simply limiting itself to the study of language use and speech acts, can thus systematically address these three levels, in the sense that the researcher consistently conducts explicit arguments about how the empirical material should be interpreted in relation to these levels, or at least tries to keep the levels in mind in the analysis and on occasion to refer more explicitly to them. To consider the problems and uncertainties in treating accounts as reflecting people's subjectivities as well as 'external social reality' would mean a healthy scepticism before using accounts in this way and a stronger appreciation of interesting research options in studying language in a social action context. Discourse analysis ideas could here be combined with and perhaps sharpen the source criticism of objective hermeneutics. Such research would consequently achieve fewer results (produce fewer interpretations) at the second and third levels – the two which normally predominate – and would instead make contributions spread over all three levels, although perhaps often with a certain emphasis on the first one. Despite the afore-mentioned drawbacks, DA focuses usefully on inconsistencies and variation at the level of utterances. Thus, taken beyond this level and applied to extra-discursive phenomena, the basic ideas of DA can contribute new, controversial and inspiring insights to qualitative research.

Feminism

Feminism means essentially that a women's or gender perspective is applied to a variety of social phenomena. These are often critically explored for the sake of promoting the interests of women, based on the assumption of gender being a dominating organizing principle in society, discriminating or in other ways disadvantaging females, in public and private spheres. Ridgeway and Correll for example, argue that sex categorization is 'deeply rooted in the socio-cognitive processes for organizing relations' and that 'both men and women have a deep cognitive interest in maintaining a clear-cut, reasonably stable framework of gender beliefs that clearly define (that is, differentiate between) "who" men and women "are"' (2000: 111). Such constructions privilege certain interests and freeze people into constraining relations and self-understandings. There are many brands of feminism (for a broad overview, see Calás and Smircich, 2006), which differ among themselves both politically and epistemologically. Liberal feminism strives for sex equality, but does not to any noticeable extent question other aspects of society apart from those which have a direct bearing on women's opportunities. Radical feminism distances itself from the male-dominated society in its entirety, and examines society critically with a view to promoting radical social change, in which an important element would be completely new gender relations. Several radical varieties have certain similarities with critical theory (see, for example, Benhabib and Cornell, 1987; Martin, 2003), although objections have been raised against critical theory – particularly in Habermas's later variant – for ignoring the gender dimension and treating issues in a biased way (Fraser, 1987; Meisenhelder, 1989). In terms of epistemology, all points of view are represented within feminism, from neo-positivism to postmodernism/poststructuralism.

This broad range naturally makes it difficult to do justice to feminism in a brief survey. The absence of any unified feminist approach, scientific or epistemological, also means that the different brands of feminism often tend towards different methodologies. We will limit ourselves here to pointing out the importance of the gender dimension and giving some indication as to how it can be considered even in research that is not primarily focused on gender conditions.

Before proceeding, we would like to point out that within gender studies there are also approaches focusing on men and masculinity and within these there are ideas on how to do research on men sensitively. For example, Schwalbe and Wolkomir (2003) address how to do interviews with men, considering the problems of dealing with men's response to culturally dominant forms of masculinity assumed to make men inclined to portray themselves as in control, autonomous, rational, etc. and thereby making interviews shallow and non-revealing as a way of accessing experiences, emotions, and so on. We don't go into this but just note this part of the overall field of gender studies, supplementing feminist work.

Allowing for considerable variations and conflicts within the movement as a whole, three central elements can be said to characterize mainstream feminism. First, gender represents an essential theme in the attempt to understand virtually all social relations, institutions and processes. Secondly, gender relations are seen as problematic since they are associated with conditions of dominance, inequality, stress and conflict. Thirdly, gender relations are regarded as socially constructed, which means that they are not given by nature, nor are they inevitable; rather, they are the result of socio-cultural and historical conditions, and can be radically altered by human action.

Feminists claim that research in general has been male-dominated, which has largely determined the questions addressed (or not addressed), and the way these have been answered. Even the way in which research is conducted and the criteria for what is 'scientific' reflect the often sexist values and ideas of men. Women as a category, their wishes, experiences and perspectives, have been disregarded. Traditional research contains more or less concealed expressions of sexism in its focus, its linguistic usage and its results. In this way the asymmetrical gender relations in society are legitimated and reproduced.

It is felt that feminism contributes to social science in the shape of a critique and re-evaluation of existing theories, most of which contain a gender bias and suffer from gender blindness. Another of feminism's contributions has been to indicate neglected areas such as sexual harassment in the workplace, or to show how elusive conditions can contribute to creating a variety of social structures. As an example, Harding (1987) cites the way in which changes in social practices as regards reproduction, sexuality and maternity have influenced the state, the economy and other public institutions. A third contribution of a more general theoretical kind concerns the development of new ways of 'theorizing' society. Acker describes a feminist paradigm, which she claims has not yet been developed, as follows.

> A new feminist paradigm would place women and their lives, and gender, in a central place in understanding social relations as a whole. Such a paradigm would not only pose new questions about women and gender but also help to create a more complex and adequate account of industrial, capitalist society. A feminist paradigm would also contain a methodology that produces knowledge for rather than of women in their many varieties and situations. (1989: 67)

Feminism also faces a dilemma when it comes to choosing between a focus on questions of immediate interest in a women's perspective, which may mean ignoring important conditions that indirectly determine gender relations, and bringing a gender perspective to bear on a broader set of social conditions, thus risking the perspective being regarded as indicating narrow aspects only of the phenomenon in question, or finding itself at a disadvantage vis-á-vis the more dominating perspectives.

Gender research has gradually been moving away from a view of gender as something simple and unequivocal (sex), as just one more variable to add to others, and towards a conception of gender as something rather complicated and difficult to pin down. Three fundamental approaches, to some extent corresponding to different phases in the development of this field of research, can be identified here (based on Harding, 1987; see also Oleson, 1994). As always in this type of overview, it is a question of simplification. (For alternative classifications, see, for example, Calás and Smircich, 2006.)

The gender-as-variable approach

The first approach concerns the gender variable. It is claimed that traditional (male-dominated) research disregards this, often generalizing between the sexes without taking account of possible differences. An understanding of gender, and in particular of women's (poor) conditions, thus requires that we differentiate between men and women and do not assume that research can treat them as the same, or that women's specific conditions can be disregarded. Thus any understanding of economic, social or psychological phenomena – ranging from the division of labour, class conditions, and wage-setting, to work motivation, recruitment and selection, leadership, and political and moral values – must start from the recognition that (among much else) possible differences between men and women in terms of situation, experiences, discrimination and so on must be taken into account. This is generally referred to as the 'gender-as-variable' approach. This approach, still common, is based primarily on a traditional scientific view which sets great store by 'objectivity' and 'neutrality'.

Many advocates of this perspective start from a fairly simple and unproblematic conception of gender. Few categories can be as easily ascertained as (biological) gender affiliation. But going on to examine the importance of gender, and what determines the special treatment of men and women, can be difficult.

This type of approach can be associated with quantitative or qualitative methods, although the former are probably more usual. With a few exceptions, the 'variable' approach corresponds to what Harding (1987) calls feminist empiricism. In all essentials, representatives of this perspective share the dominating epistemological and methodological views, but claim that the existence of social bias and negative attitudes to women, or simply ignorance about gender, leads to poor research. Their ambition is to improve the scientific quality of the research – objectivity, neutrality and exactness – by weeding out irrational (prejudiced) elements. This often means advocating a kind of gender-conscious neo-positivism. But even various ways of doing research distanced from the deductions, hypothesis-testing and copious measurements of other empiricist positions, can be linked to feminist empiricism. This could mean working on the basis of grounded theory, for example (Zuckerman, 1993), or of some other data-based method. Comparisons between groups of males and females are often central here.

Research from a feminist standpoint

The second approach emphasizes the importance of acquiring a broader and deeper picture of women's conditions and experiences. Here the ideal is to study various phenomena from the perspective of women or from a feminist point of view. First it has to be decided what one regards as women's interests and experiences (which may agree with or diverge from men's). Whereas feminist empiricism goes hand in hand with liberal feminism, the feminist standpoint research has more in common with radical and critical feminism. This standpoint research strongly emphasizes the political and practical relevance. It is not only a question of looking for the Truth in an abstract sense; even more important is to stimulate social change and emancipation.

In principle, there is an even larger area of application for this brand of feminism than there is for the gender-as-variable kind. Gender can theoretically be 'read' into anything. It is claimed (quite rightly) that science is traditionally conducted almost exclusively by men, and that the results to some extent bear the imprint of certain male-tinted assumptions, priorities, foci and even scientific ideas and methodologies. In particular, the dominating principles and rules of science are regarded as part of the general patriarchal domination. Positivism and the notion of the neutral and dispassionate scientist are seen as typically male inventions. In methodological terms, alternative approaches are preferred which can be seen as harmonizing more with the perspective of women, among other things allowing personal experiences and understandings to come to the fore (Acker et al., 1991). This means that it is important to give women a voice in research, and to describe and interpret social realities on the basis of their experience.

The feminist standpoint research is usually related to – and legitimated by – women's concrete experiences of discrimination and repression. Ferguson (1984) advocates a feminist attack on the bureaucracy, that is, on the more prevalent organizational forms and the kind of male-oriented rationality that characterize them, revealing itself in individualism, hierarchy, a lack of feeling, impersonality, the competitive mentality, etc. She calls for a critical understanding of the repressive character of modern organizations, based on 'the concrete and shared experiences' of women (Ferguson, 1984: 27).[5] Sometimes the position of females as outsiders to institutions created and ruled by a dominant group of men is thought to make certain deeper insights possible. Harding, for example, states that the personal experiences of women are a 'significant indicator of the "reality" against which hypotheses are tested' (1987: 7). Even though this perspective can be seen 'to be a product of its time' (Skeggs, 1997: 26), traces of it still play a role in some standpoint feminism.

One difficulty here is of course if there are 'genuine' experiences that simply are expressed in language or whether these experiences are constituted by discourse and follow rules for talk when being expressed. A DA advocate would be hesitant in treating statements as reality indicators, irrespective of the sex of the informant. Another problem is that the extent to which women's experiences are uniform is open to question. Women differ greatly among themselves, depending on ethnicity, nationality, class affiliation, age, profession, sexual orientation, and so on. There are also big variations as to individual background, lifestyle, life course and attitudes on political and ethical questions. When it comes to the micro level, we can see how historical change destabilizes women's positions, views and experiences. It has been suggested that claims to speak in the name of 'women' may in fact be no more than a manifestation of the ethnocentricity of white middle-class women. The risk is great that research which concentrates on 'the concrete and shared experiences' of women, will have a limited agenda.[6]

This applies in particular if – in the spirit of discourse analysis – we pay serious attention to the variations in accounts of experiences. However, it is possible to avoid the problem of over-generalization by focusing on historically and socially defined conditions, and to distinguish between different groups of women and their views, experiences and interests. Acker et al. (1991), for example, studied women at the end of their period of intensive mothering. But even these authors note in a postscript to the original version of their paper, which first appeared in 1982, that they had underestimated the variations associated with class and other differences.

Poststructural feminism

The third approach expresses a poststructuralist (postmodernist) position, and calls into question the gender categories which the other two approaches regard as given and unproblematic. The meaning of concepts such as men and women, male and female, is considered uncertain, unequivocal and shifting (Butler, 2004; Flax, 1987; Fraser and Nicholson, 1988; Weedon, 1987).

While empiricism and the women's perspective both try to discover stable grounds for a feminist science that at least in some respects will be better than traditional science, poststructuralism is sceptical towards the idea of any universal basis for reason, science, progress, or even the subject. Efforts by feminists to find the Truth – in the case of standpoint proponents, in the Genuine Female Point of View or in the authentic experiences of women – can be seen as yet another fault-finding grand narrative, blocking our understanding of multiplicity and equivocality, and silencing alternative voices.

Genders are seen as social and linguistic constructions, limited in time and space, that is, determined by existing ideas and conceptions about what 'man' and 'woman' mean, and by the social and discursive practices which create gender. Poststructuralist feminists emphasize the temporary and fragile nature of social constructions. Butler's (2004: 1) view of gender 'as a practice of improvisation within the scene of constraint' is here representative. Gender as labels and clues to identities and experiences is regarded as transient and contradictory. These feminists thus distance themselves from the emphasis given in the other two approaches to a particular women's perspective, based on the idea of women's unique and distinct experiences and interests. Instead of speaking of men and women as existing side by side, clearly separable as integrated and consistent subjects, it is emphasized that gender relations are the crucial point, and that these cannot be understood as unambiguous. 'The single most important advance in feminist theory is that the existence of gender relations has been problematized. Gender can no longer be treated as a simple, natural fact' (Flax, 1987: 627).

This brand of feminism thus shifts the interest from essential ideas of gender to an emphasis on diversity. There is a tendency to disregard the subject level as such. Gender is mainly a question of discourses on men and women – an approach which leads to an interest in destabilizing ideas and language usage, rather than saying anything definite or 'positive'.[7] Thus the critique which can be directed at poststructuralism (see Chapter 6) is also relevant here. Martin (1994: 631) criticizes the 'anti-essentialists' for hampering intellectual development in this field: 'In our determination to honor diversity among women, we told one another to restrict our ambitions, limit our sights, beat a retreat from certain topics, refrain from using a rather long list of categories or concepts, and eschew generalization'. However, not many scholars take the diversity view to this extreme. In reality, even feminist poststructuralists often avoid adopting a pronounced poststructural position of the type that completely disregards people of flesh and blood, and regards accounts of repression and injustice simply as linguistic expressions.

It is common for feminists tending towards poststructuralism to combine this philosophical position with some of the political commitments of the feminist standpoint. In discussing Weedon (1987) in Chapter 6 above, we drew attention to the contradictions and inconsistencies which such a mixed discourse can entail. Nevertheless, a consideration of the diversity and construction aspects emphasized by feminism, combined with an interest in an elusive and fluid 'real life' beyond purely textual-linguistic operations, is perhaps the most fruitful way forward for feminism and gender studies.

*

Thus, different combinations and/or syntheses of the three approaches do occur, not least in contemporary practical, qualitative empirical research. (As mentioned above, it is somewhat more difficult to envisage quantitative studies based on the feminist standpoint or – with even greater difficulty – the poststructural variants.) Elements of all three approaches can be taken into consideration, at least to some extent, if a researcher is empirically interested in a specific research area. It is possible to start from the 'variable' feminist approach, and study the gender-based division of labour, for example; then to go beyond this focus and look for instance at the social construction processes which lead to, and are reproduced by, this division of labour. In an analysis of conditions in the labour market and its organizations, for example, we could ask ourselves the following questions. How are the sexes distributed as regards tasks and social positions, that is, what does the horizontal and vertical gender-based division of work look like? How are privileges, etc. distributed? How do recruitment, selection and promotion operate in a gender perspective? Are there gender-specific experiences? What power and dominance conditions obtain? Do current power relations, priorities, ideologies, and so on, favour one of the sexes (normally men or particular men)? How are the sexes constituted by the organizational conditions, that is, how are men and women 'created' in organizations by language usage, interaction patterns and social practices? In what way can the organizations be described in a gender perspective? Can ideas, values, actions and practices be interpreted in terms of masculinity and femininity or as a multitude of various social constructions of masculinities and femininities? What ambiguities, variations, fragmentations, contradictions, openings, and so on can be invoked in different answers to these questions? That is to say, how can we break up all those uniform, seemingly robust, 'fact-finding' accounts which aim to give true answers? Of course it is not possible to go on mixing all kinds of questions endlessly, without some sort of limit; a coherent angle of approach and a frame of reference – at least at a meta level – for handling them are necessary. For examples of case studies that pay serious attention to the construction of gender, and at least touch on some of the themes mentioned here, see Hall (1993) and Leidner (1991).

Feminism and method

Is there any specific feminist method? As we have seen, there are big variations in method among women researchers (within as well as outside the field(s) of gender studies), of whom a not inconsiderable number tend primarily towards a traditional epistemological view. Yet it is often alleged that women's research is characterized by a qualitative approach, in which the subjectivity of both the researcher and the subjects studied is central – in the first case through empathy and commitment, and in the second through personal experience. This is sometimes assumed to be the kind of approach favoured by women in general, as they are less inclined than men to embrace the ideal of a split between the detached observing subject and the object being observed, but it is especially advocated in feminist research. A close and mutual relationship between researcher and subject is here seen as important: 'Unless a relationship of trust is developed, we can have no confidence that our research on women's lives and consciousness accurately represents what is significant to them in their everyday lives, and thus has validity in that sense' (Acker et al., 1991: 149). Procedures and formal methods are toned down. The research is characterized by an emancipatory knowledge interest, and is often oriented towards everyday life. There is a pronounced interest in ethics, solidarity and minimizing asymmetry in relation to the subjects of the study (Acker et al., 1991; Finch, 1984; Olesen, 1994). This approach has been criticized for its over-confidence in the existence of 'true' or 'genuine' experiences and in the possibility of capturing these (Hollway, 1989), and for the theoretical and practical problems entailed by the ideal of minimizing asymmetry in the relation between researcher and interview subject (Hammersley, 1992).

More generally, gender-related ideas about quantitative and qualitative data can also be noted, the former being regarded as 'hard' and 'masculine'. In an essay entitled 'Real men don't collect soft data', Gherardi and Turner (1987) reflect upon this in an ironical mode. They claim that the collection of hard data implies tough decisions, an impatience with 'nonsense', a hard core of material to build on and the expectation of concrete returns in hard currency on the projects concerned. Soft data, on the other hand, are for 'wets'.

Particularly in areas of typical female concern, such as assault, sexual abuse and power, which are difficult to define and extremely sensitive, women researchers have tried to reflect upon methods and develop them (Widerberg, 1992). A more general contribution to the methodological discussion from the feminist side appeared in Jagger (1989), where the central importance of emotion in all research is stressed. We will briefly review this author's very readable article.

Jagger attacks the traditional view which sees emotion in research as something clearly definable and incompatible with good science, something which can strike the less successful researcher like a disease. She regards the dividing-line between reason and emotion as artificial, and the notion of the unemotional, dispassionate scientist as a fiction. Research psychology supports Jagger: scientists are deeply committed to what they are doing, often showing little receptiveness to factual argument running against their paradigmatic convictions and vested interests (Bärmark, 1999). A study of the way scientists describe their own views and those of colleagues who champion positions opposite to their own, showed them claiming their own results to be based on empirical material and other rational grounds, whereas their competitors' results were said to be marred by irrational elements such as speculative ideas, social ties, personal investment in a particular orientation, and psychological attributes (Gilbert and Mulkay, referred to in Potter and Wetherell, 1987). This emotional attitude concerns not only theories and published results, but also elements in the research process. A study of anthropologists showed that they had strong feelings about their field-notes (Jackson, 1995; cf. Strauss, 1987).

Jagger argues against the view that emotion is a source of error or bias in research, and maintains that feelings do not simply express individual idiosyncrasies; rather, they are socially constructed at different levels. Emotions are dependent on the way people interpret situations, and are thus intimately connected with the cognitive level, with how people handle impressions and make judgements. Cultural expectations and norms are important here. Every feeling or emotion presupposes an evaluation of some aspect of the environment and, conversely, every evaluation of the judgement of a situation implies that those who share the evaluation can be assumed to react to it emotionally in similar ways. There is thus intersubjectivity in many emotional reactions. We only have to consider the central position occupied by values (expressed or unexpressed, conscious or unconscious) in all aspects of research – from the areas chosen for study to particular foci of attention and the words used in interviews, descriptions and analyses – to recognize that emotion is an important element throughout the research process. Emotions play their part not only in persons' thinking and in the attitudes they adopt on important research issues, but also in the specific observations they make.

> Just as observation directs, shapes, and partially defines emotion, so too emotion directs, shapes, and even partially defines observation. Observation is not simply a passive process of absorbing impressions or recording stimuli; instead, it is an activity of selection and interpretation. What is selected and how it is interpreted are influenced by emotional attitudes. On the level of the individual observation, this influence has always been apparent to common sense, which notes that we remark very different features of the world when we are happy, depressed, fearful, or confident. (Jagger, 1989: 29)

Emotions, as well as being important on the individual plane, are also social phenomena. Dominating norms and values naturally reflect the interest and cultural ideals of dominating groups, and this also applies to the way we perceive, interpret and react to feelings in various areas of life and in institutions such as science. The prevailing view of the 'scientific' as being dispassionate and unemotional, may be regarded as an expression of dominance conditions. Emotion is an inevitable and important part of the researcher's motivation and choice of orientation, and of the specific way in which the topic studied is handled. The research process should be explicitly guided by individual researchers' willingness to reflect upon and listen to their own feelings. At the same time, serious attention should be paid to the emotions of the subjects studied, regardless of what is being researched. None of this need imply 'emotional research', that is, research entirely under the sway of feelings. The point is that, irrespective of the research topic, this dimension is important. It is particularly important, still according to Jagger, to take illegitimate feelings into account, that is, feelings that are not fostered by elites and dominating norm systems.

It follows that self-reflection and the critical self-analysis of feelings are an important part of the research process, particularly in qualitative research. Naturally this is a question not of emotional catharsis, but of interpreting and processing one's feelings before and during the empirical and theoretical work. It does not mean that emotions should be given a more central position than observation, reason or action; but nor should they be second to any of these. In methodological terms this means that researchers should listen to their feelings and process them, for instance when performing interviews. What does the researcher feel in the face of the interview subject or the observed situation? What is the intuitive impression? Does the researcher hesitate to ask certain questions? What is the underlying tone in the descriptions given? To see research work as not only a perceptual and cognitive but also an emotional project can enhance its value.

These ideas are not specific to feminism. As we saw in Chapter 4, Heidegger strongly emphasized the inseparability of reason and emotion (for further discussion see Sköldberg, 1998). Much general critique of positivism has also emphasized the importance of the researcher's whole person. For example, Adorno (1974) wrote, in psychoanalytical mode and with a side-swipe at patriarchism, that even the highest objectification of the mind is nurtured by human urges and without these no insight will be produced; the kind of thinking that kills its father, the passion, must pay its price in the form of stupidity. Popper, while embracing a position very different from those of Jagger and Adorno, also acknowledged that 'without passion we can achieve nothing – certainly not in pure science. The phrase "passion for truth" is no mere metaphor' (Popper, 1976: 97). One could also envisage a researcher adopting Jagger's idea without paying any particular attention to the gender dimension. At the same time it is surely no coincidence that such strong opposition to the idea of the researcher as an emotional blank comes from the feminist camp. The ideal of the rational non-emotional, 'cool' researcher is a masculine one. And there are certainly several examples in women's studies of researchers considering and processing their own experiences and feelings as a systematic part of their method; one such is Widerberg (1992), in a study of sexual harassment.

Critical discussion of feminism

Feminism stresses the importance of a sensitivity to gender in research. Some texts suggest rather a narrow picture of gender relations, with men presented as repressors and women usually as victims or perhaps as members of an opposition movement. Certain issues, and the political thrust of some research, perhaps motivate such an angle, but there is a risk that the idea of male repression as the absolutely dominating element in gender relations leads to a rather blinkered view. For example, the claim in Harding (1987: 8) that the questions about women to which men want to find answers all too often stem from 'desires to pacify, control, exploit, or manipulate women', seems to be ascribing rather too evil a motivation to men in research contexts. Generally speaking, recent women's research is often less polemical and more open and self-reflective than earlier research (see, for example, Butler, 2004; Flax, 1987; Fraser and Nicholson, 1988; Gherardi, 1995; Skeggs, 1997). The influence of poststructuralism, and the multiplicity of rival approaches and critical debates within feminism have been important factors here. But also improvements in the situation of females over the decades in politics and on the labour market have played a role (Deutsch, 2007; McCall, 2005).

Some female researchers look with suspicion on men's participation in women's studies. They put a great emphasis on the ideals of closeness and empathy, and claim, on good grounds, that on some questions women find it easier to understand other women (Finch, 1984). While agreeing that shared gender sometimes is not only an advantage but almost a precondition in research, on many issues one may feel a sense of contact and mutual understanding with a person of the opposite biological sex, and also feel the opposite with someone who happens to have similar chromosomes and the same kind of anatomy as oneself. However, the other side of good research – the ability to distance oneself – is also important. The capacity to swing between empathy and understanding on the one hand, and a critical questioning, reflection, conceptualization and theoretical abstraction on the other, is the hallmark of good research (more than in literature or journalism, for example). In the research process, it is important to be able to look upon something as remarkable and exotic which could all too easily appear familiar and self-evident. It is not impossible that researchers of the opposite sex to the subject studied (and also of another ethnic affiliation or class background) may be able to contribute interesting aspects. At any rate we feel that ethnographies of 'masculine' leadership in business, for example, or military operations or big game hunting, written by (feminist) women, might be more interesting than those written by male business consultants, officers in the reserve or enthusiastic huntsmen (possibly weapons fetishists). Conversely, we would not rule out the possibility that male researchers – not necessarily pro-feminist – could generate interesting studies of women and of female settings. In fact we find the rather narrow emphasis on closeness, empathy and identification in some parts of women's research to be slightly worrying. Perhaps research conducted by men and women together would be best in order to optimize the closeness–distance relation – that is, if sex affiliation *per se* has any effects in terms of closeness/distance in connection with the study of a particular sex. Perhaps a more productive combination would be one person with a 'masculine' and one with a 'feminine' research orientation – which does not necessarily imply a male and a female person, as orientations do not stand in a one-to-one relation to people's biologies. (On ideas on masculinity and femininity, see, for example, Alvesson and Billing, 2009, and Marshall, 1993. Given that many women researchers have an objectivist-quantitative orientation, and that some men prefer interpretive approaches, the importance of gender should not be too strongly stressed. There is a risk that simply talking about men and women reproduces and creates gender stereotypes, as people almost always focus on and emphasize the differences. More important than the biological mix is, then, the combination of different gender-relevant experiences and attitudes.[8]

It is not our aim here to try to make any specific contribution to feminist scientific theory and method. However, our fundamental idea of presenting some dimensions that are central to qualitative research and that bring out its reflective element, is also relevant to feminism. In relation to mainstream feminism, the critique put forward by discourse analysts of the possibility of achieving genuine, deep, subjective experiences through various kinds of verbal accounts, seems particularly relevant. Without blindly claiming that experiences are solely constituted in discourse and textuality, serious attention should nonetheless be paid to the discrepancy between experience and linguistic expression. As we have already pointed out, we are a little sceptical of Potter and Wetherell's way of isolating the linguistic as an autonomous object of study, detached from subjective or 'objective' reality, but we do feel that wariness and caution are important before linking up accounts with 'real' experiences and factual conditions (Hollway, 1989). Thus, more consideration of gender discourses – including close studies of accounts of gender in field settings – are called for, before research can really begin to comment on phenomena 'beyond', or other than discursive acts, such as interview talk or everyday statements. (For an illustration of such a discursive focus, see Marshall and Wetherell, 1989.) The dynamic study of gender-construction processes – for example, how professions and behaviour are interpreted and/or described as 'male' or 'female' – also offers an appropriate line to follow (see Hall, 1993; Leidner, 1991).

More active attempts to introduce other metaphors besides patriarchy (society viewed as a system of gender repression) into interpretive work could also encourage a more reflective attitude. The problem is one from which all research suffers, namely that if we become hooked on a particular metaphor, it can get out of hand and 'take command of the world' (Asplund, 1989). It can often be advantageous to clarify gender-relevant phenomena from perspectives other than those triggered by concepts such as patriarchy, gender hierarchy or repression. For example, modern society can be viewed as one which breaks down rigid social boundaries, including those of gender. Organizations and other institutions can sometimes be described not only as gender-discriminating but also as equality-producing (Billing and Alvesson, 1994; Blomqvist, 1994). Much gender-based organizational research has adopted a narrow approach, staring blindly at the way women are disfavoured and completely ignoring or at least neglecting the possibility that a great deal of modern organizational practice – for example, the desire to exploit qualified personnel in a rational way – can favour women's professional lives. (The premises for such equality, which are not necessarily gender-neutral, should also be critically explored in a gender perspective – see Ferguson, 1984.)

Even more important, perhaps, is a willingness to consider other dimensions than gender. This does not simply mean increasing the number of variables, adding to 'men' and 'women' other sociological, institutionalized standard variables such as class, age or ethnicity, in order to pick out variations within the sexes, or focusing on issues where women are supposed to have a particular interest. In contrast to research focused solely on gender, we can consider an ideal in which the theory of gender and an interest in gender are part of the frame of reference and of the research topic, but in which researchers are also open to the idea that other non-institutionalized dimensions may prove to be at least as important. Under a broader approach, gender would not be given any preconceived priority over other aspects in a certain social context.

Discussion of gender in non-feminist research

Rather than criticize gender research, our aim here is to suggest ways in which other research can learn from it. The gender dimension is important in practically all of the social sciences, and it is important that even research not primarily or directly concerned with gender should develop a certain level of sensitivity to gender aspects. Ideally, gender researchers should broaden and vary their sphere of interest, and researchers in other fields pay more attention to gender dimensions than at present (Alvesson and Billing, 2009). This would help counteract what Acker (1989) has called the 'ghettoization of feminism'. At least a minimal insight into gender-sensitive categories and ways of thinking should be expected of all social science. An appropriate piece of advice, albeit a general one, is of course to read feminist (gender-research) writings, and to bear the subject of gender conditions constantly in mind. We cannot expect research which is not primarily concerned with the clarification of gender topics to achieve any great sophistication in its gender-related thinking, but it is possible to identify some intermediate forms between gender-blind (or gender-ignorant) research and feminist studies. The bottom line could be that non-feminist reflective research should not (unconsciously) operate as a conservative

247

force in gender relations, reproducing taken-for-granted ideas and gender-biased institutions.

We can envisage the following levels in considering the gender dimensions: avoiding the reproduction of asymmetrical gender relations and conserving traditional conceptions of gender; emphasizing gender conditions when they appear to be particularly relevant; and adopting gender metaphors as complementary perspectives.

To avoid reproducing the kind of gender thinking which entails conditions of social dominance, might be considered an obvious minimum requirement for all research. In a certain sense, however, it is an almost impossible task – even for intentionally feminist research, which seldom fully escapes blind spots and biases. However, the more serious forms of gender-blindness, such as stereotyping, should be eschewed. It may be a question of rejecting obviously gender-bound language, for instance the use of 'man' as an inclusive term for men and women, as in 'mankind' for the human race, or 'manpower' for human resources; or of assuming uncritically that general professional designations such as 'the manager' or 'the author' refer to a 'he'. It may be a matter of not generalizing from a male sample to people in general; or, if both sexes are included in a sample, of making a rough investigation to see whether any clear differences exist. If this proves to be the case, then the difference should at least be mentioned. Some thought should also be given to the nature of the research topic in gender terms: is it quite clear that it is 'fairly' gender-neutral, in the sense that it does not give a misleading picture of gender conditions, obscure asymmetrical relations of gender and/or represent a pronounced masculine logic?

What really matters is that researchers should stop now and again to think for a moment in gender terms. The advice to male gender researchers in Morgan (1981), namely that they should remind themselves from time to time that they are men, is probably useful even – or perhaps especially – for researchers who are uninterested in gender conditions. Considering the research for and the draft of a report as a masculine project may be a healthy exercise, encouraging reflections and revisions. If we had been still more practical by nature, or believed more in such devices, we might have made a kind of checklist of the traps that are easy to fall into. But we can mention one point worth thinking about: the number of women represented in reference lists and empirical material. If they are largely missing, then it is definitely time to stop and think. Perhaps the whole project expresses a fundamental gender bias? Perhaps the whole area or tradition is permeated by masculine attitudes? This is naturally not the same as suggesting that having a certain proportion of women among the references or subjects studied is a matter of urgent importance in itself, especially since it is not biology but the researcher's orientation that is of interest – not least in the context of gender studies. Such thinking in terms of representativeness and quotas seems to us too mechanical. We are suggesting inputs for reflection, rather than any definite formulae.

In a somewhat more ambitious vein, researchers could support the idea of gender-sensitive social science by developing a willingness to emphasize gender conditions, whenever the empirical material suggests that these are important, or of particular interest in the context. The empirical material itself does not, of course, generate any unequivocal picture in one direction or the other; it is the interpretive work which is decisive. But from the preparatory stages the researcher could be open to the idea of letting the empirical material be 'perspectivized' (angled) in gender terms, although some types of empirical material will better lend themselves than others to such an approach. For instance, there may be noticeable gender differences in the labour market, in educational situations and choices, or in consumption patterns. Given sufficient openness to the idea of registering such tendencies, the researcher can explore the occurrence and importance of these differences in greater detail. The point here is that researchers should have the interest and the ability to do 'justice' to the empirical material also from a gender angle. It is not only a question of trying to remain open-minded and unprejudiced (by championing and trying to live up to these virtues, researchers easily subordinate themselves to all forms of common sense and cultural ideas); a certain amount of work on gender theory and the learning of gender-sensitive categories is called for, in order to develop a degree of openness, if the empirical material is to be interpreted as relevant in gender terms. An atheoretical reliance on intuition – often guided by common sense and personal 'theories' – will often not do.

A third and more ambitious way of allowing for feminist ideas without directly defining the project mainly as gender research, is to include gender thinking as a complement to the other metaphors or perspectives adopted. The main interest is thus not in clarifying gender conditions or emphasizing the gender perspective as a key to the understanding of the object studied. But gender categories can often help to throw light on all kinds of things which are also – perhaps primarily – seen in terms of other categories. Ehn and Löfgren (1982), for example, see 'male' and 'female' as important cultural organizing principles, which can help us to understand different kinds of cultures. And here we can regard bureaucratic organizations (in the Weberian sense), or dominating leadership patterns – with the leader first in the pack, leading, planning, coordinating, controlling or communicating 'visions' to the others – as in some respects the bearers of 'masculine' principles (for good or ill) without reducing these manifestations to mere male inventions.

This means that researchers do not simply wait passively for the empirical material to 'produce' gender differences – for instance, men and women in the material obviously behaving in different (stereotypical) ways, or talking spontaneously about gender relations without being directly encouraged to do so. Instead the researchers actively mobilize gender perspectives in their interpretations. In this way they explore whether gender interpretations can produce anything interesting over and above what other perspectives are able to offer in specific instances, thus adding to their understanding of a phenomenon which may not be regarded primarily as having any particular gender interest.

This process can be illustrated by an ethnographic study of advertising agencies in which one of the present authors was involved (Alvesson, 1998; Alvesson and Köping, 1993). It was not originally intended that the study should focus on gender conditions. However, it turned out that the workplace division of labour followed a pronounced gender-based pattern. With few exceptions, the men in the studied agency occupied the top positions, while the women – who were younger and good-looking – were to be found in lower supportive roles. This simple, empirical observation led us to make a more detailed study of the division of labour by gender, and the theme of sexuality in general in advertising agencies. We did this by asking relevant questions and by going through interview reports and observation protocols, all the time bearing gender relations in mind. Thus some gender aspects emerged (we could be said to be following the second of the approaches just discussed). However, we then went further and introduced gender concepts into the theoretical frame of reference we were using to interpret other themes than the gender-specific distribution of tasks. The gender dimension was able to shed light on the theme of 'advertising work and identity' (which we were also focusing on, for other, non-gender-specific reasons), and we found it illuminating to describe the accounts of the character of advertising work (emotional, intuitive, non-rational) and the advertising agency's relations with its client companies (dependent, passive) in terms of femininity. In other words, gender theory was used as a complementary perspective in a workplace study which was not intended in the first instance as a gender-research project (see the third variant above).

Genealogical method: Foucault

For a couple of decades now, Foucault has been the leading name in research on power. As we mentioned at the beginning of this chapter, his work has a particular interest as regards reflection and methodology, since he focused on the intimate relationship between knowledge and power. Foucault (1972, 1973) originally advocated an 'archaeological method', in which the idea was to break with hermeneutic interpretation and with the positivist theory of correspondence or mirroring, and – disregarding the truth of statements as well as their (deeper) meaning – to map out the overarching rule systems in the thinking of whole epochs. The task he set himself was to track the ordered fields of knowledge, or 'epistemes', which are common to the discourses of a whole epoch, without undertaking any deep interpretations of the real meaning of the discourses or making a commitment as to their truth, in the sense of a correspondence to reality. Thereby, Foucault can be said to have started from a sort of radicalized phenomenology; as we saw in Chapter 3, Husserl had made a reduction from the aspect of truth, cancelling or bracketing it, and Foucault now continued with the aspect of meaning. This is no coincidence, since Foucault was a pupil of the much-reputed French phenomenologist, Merleau-Ponty.

The concept of 'discourse' was used by Foucault in a different sense than in discourse analysis. Foucault used discourse 'to analyse diverse configurations of assumptions, categories, logics, claims and modes of articulation' (Miller, 1997: 32). Discourse is thus seen more as a framework and a logic of reasoning that, through its penetration of social practice, systematically forms its objects, than as any use of language in a social context. The former can be referred to as (macro level) discourse and the latter as (micro level) discourse (Alvesson and Kärreman, 2000). Foucault's interest was more in how discourse constitutes objects and subjects than in the details of language use in social interaction.

The issue of power was continually present even in the early archaeological phase, but it was subordinated to discourse analysis and the interest in charting the forms of knowledge. Later, Foucault's interest in the problematic of power grew ever stronger, and he introduced a 'genealogy', in which the origins of discourses are studied, the clue being to treat the discourses as such, with their own distinctiveness and regularity, instead of some underlying ideas or conceptions underlying the discourses. At the very source of thinking the genealogist places randomness, discontinuity and power. That is, the discourses emerge not in a planned way, but aleatorily, as do their combinations; they disjoint over time and when they merge with each other they do so temporarily and partially rather than as continuing, homogeneous expressions of an initial thought; their origin is crassly materialistic, expressing diverse wills of power, not nobly governed by reason as claimed in the later rationalizations (Foucault, 1972).

In this genealogy of Foucault, the influence of Nietzsche looms very large, as is clear among other things from the fact that the latter originally created the genealogical method, including its designation. Foucault (1978, 1979) used the genealogical research programme in extensive studies of the development of the prison system and disciplinary surveillance, as well as in the history of sexuality. Archaeology and genealogy complement each other in that archaeology studies the forms of the discourses, and genealogy their (power-related) origins (Foucault, 1988). Archaeology provides the distance, the detached description of the discursive formations, and genealogy the engagement, the critically committed probing of the roots of societal practices (here, the ideas of Foucault approach those of critical theory). However, the complementarity is not equally balanced, for in the genealogical period of Foucault's thinking, genealogy dominates (similarly, genealogy had in fact already emerged on the Foucauldian scene during the archaeological period, but then as a subordinate element, dominated by the archaeological interest).

A second shift in the genealogical phase is related to the increased interest in power. Foucault then studied non-discursive as well as discursive practices, and the relationship between these. Previously, the discourses and (the archaeological) descriptions had been in focus; from the book *Discipline and Punish* onwards, phenomena like social institutions (Prison, Psychiatry, Family, Religion, Market, Sexuality, and so on) became ever more important. For instance, psychiatric knowledge is based on the separation, partitioning and control of (various groups of) mentally ill people. The power over these is a precondition for knowledge, enabling meticulous observations and classifications which would otherwise be impossible. At the same time, knowledge makes power possible: the exercise of power is not arbitrary, but the knowledge – the discourse of mental illness – is the basis of power, the functioning of the psychiatric institution.

Power and knowledge

Foucault's (1978, 1979, 1980, 1982) understanding of power breaks radically with more traditional approaches. He did not use conventional social science categories or concepts – such as individuals, structures, interests or ideologies – nor did he delimit or define power. For him power did not constitute some kind of abstract property that could be isolated and studied in itself. It lacks an essence and is not measurable; it exists only in relationships and when it is expressed in action. Thus, Foucault was not interested in who 'had' power over others, due to office, charisma, knowledge, or any other power base. Such an approach leads to the view of power as something unambiguous and centralized, a view which trivializes the phenomenon and causes us to disregard its multifaceted character. Power, according to Foucault, does not allow itself to be localized and fixed.

Hence institutions do not create power. Their role instead is to organize or, as it were, 'hang' already extant relationships of dominance on a more comprehensive instance: 'The Sovereign or the Law for the state, the Father for the family, Money, Gold or the Dollar for the market, God for religion, Gender for the sexual institution' (Deleuze, 1988, our translation). To comment on two of the quoted phenomena: sexuality exists before gender, and the sovereignty of royal power emerged in reality only as a device for the gathering together of micropowers. As regards the power of the king, Foucault showed, for instance, how the royal warrant of arrest (*lettre de cachet*) – a forerunner of today's voluntary admittance into psychiatric care – was the expression of a wish at the micro level to get rid of troublesome people in the family, in the workplace or in the neighbourhood, rather than of the power of the sovereign as an original, intrinsic attribute; instead the micro level uses this as a kind of 'public utility' for conflict resolution (Deleuze, 1988).

Power relationships can best be understood by examining the techniques and forms in which they are expressed. The exercise of power is the central issue; the practices, techniques and procedures which render power effective. It is in this context that we can speak of power in a fruitful way, according to Foucault:

> The isolation of 'meticulous rituals of power' is the conceptual basis for much of Foucault's later work. In *Discipline and Punish* and *The History of Sexuality* Foucault will identify specific sites in which rituals of power take place – the Panopticon of Bentham and the confession. He will use these to localize and specify how power works, what it does and how it does it. (Dreyfus and Rabinow, 1983: 110)

Thus, power is in principle everywhere. It is expressed in various micro contexts, and cannot be restricted to any particular unit or size, such as the nation-state, the management of corporations, capitalism, and the like. Institutions – schools, factories, hospitals – form fine-meshed nets of disciplinary influence. In a comment on *Discipline and Punish*, Geertz (cited in Hoy, 1986a: 143) writes that Foucault appeared to turn the conventional, progressive outline of history upside down, and painted the development as 'the rise of unfreedom'. The study of the 'micro physics' of power demands that we attribute effects of domination

> not to 'appropriation', but to dispositions, manoeuvres, tactics, techniques, functionings; that one should decipher a network of relations, constantly in tension, in activity, rather than a privilege that one might possess; that one should take as its model a perpetual battle rather than a contract regulating a transaction or the conquest of a territory. In short this power is exercised rather than possessed; it is not the 'privilege', acquired or preserved, of the dominant class, but the overall effect of its strategy positions – an effect that is manifested and sometimes extended by the position of those who are dominated. Furthermore, this power is not exercised simply as an obligation or a prohibition on those who 'do not have it'; it invests them, is transmitted by them and through

them; it exerts pressure upon them, just as they themselves, in their struggle against it, resist the grip it has on them. (Foucault, 1979: 26–27)

Foucault did not define power, nor did he formulate any clear theory of it, which is a natural consequence of his notion of power;

> instead he regards power as open arrangements of practices or open structures that are imposed in a multitude of forms and on a range of different social fields. In Foucault, there is no theory of power which delimits this analytic field; no theoretical order which sets the borders within which 'power' would 'be'. Power does not exist, but the practices in and through which power exists, these are potentially everywhere. (Beronius, 1986: 32; our translation)

Subjectivity itself, as a complex, contradictory, and shifting view of the self, is transformed or reproduced through social practices, which express power (Knights and Willmott, 1989: 541). While we conventionally believe that subjects – actors – are behind social practices (widespread ways of acting), Foucault took the opposite view. In his strategy for analysis, historically and culturally determined practices precede and form the subjects. The individual is an effect of power. As Delanty (2005) writes one finds in Foucault's writings 'a pervasive image of subjectivity being the product of a power game in which the rules are never revealed or understood by the participants' (2005: 111). Phenomena such as 'reason', 'madness', 'criminality' and 'sexuality' thus do not figure as natural objects which have an independent existence as part of the functioning of human beings. Instead they are regarded as non-natural objects which have been constituted in such a way that they are at the same time objects of particular forms of knowing and targets for historically specific reform and regulation projects (Beronius, 1991). Thus, madness is not merely something which exists in the heads of a certain group of people; rather it is through various techniques and procedures that madness during a certain epoch is panned out as a special object for knowledge and action (incarceration, treatment). There is a 'raw material' in the form of behaviours, gestures, biochemical processes and so on, but what is conceived as possession, immorality, the punishment of God, or mental illness is a consequence of practices for differentiation, classification and positioning at a material as well as a cognitive level.

Foucault's works are of great interest, not only to specialized power research, but also to all reflective social science, at least if it in any way concerns the subject. Different forms of knowledge are in the service of power, and they function in a disciplinary way, among other things by establishing normality and deviation. Established conceptions in science and other societal institutions of what is normal and reasonable thus contribute to regulating the self-consciousness and the actions of individuals. According to Foucault, knowledge cannot be extricated from power and made to mark neutral insights. Power and knowledge are parallel concepts, but of course not identical. Foucault, as Deetz (1992: 77) points out, had 'focused atten-tion on the power *in* rather than the power *of* knowledge'. The exercise of power and the application/development of knowledge have an intimate relationship with each other. Through classifying, codifying, calibrating, calculating normal curves for, and partitioning the phenomena, one handles and at the same time reaches knowledge of them. Knowledge and institutional control go closely together – in school, psychiatry, correctional treatment, sexual counselling, child-care, corporate management, and so on. Foucault's project aimed not at separating truth (science, knowledge) from ideology (roughly identified as prejudices, misconceptions), but at disclosing the mechanisms whereby the 'policy of truth' is constituted in a power–knowledge relationship. Knowledge is at the base of the exercise of power, while the exercise of power also produces knowledge. To put it another way, power becomes a crucial dimension in knowledge supported by institutional practices as well as institutional practices based on knowledge. Not only openly repressive knowledge but to a large extent even 'helping' and 'progressive' knowledge is linked to power and functions in a disciplinary way.

Hermeneutics occupies an important place in these disciplinary techniques; this applies also and even more strongly to the hermeneutics of suspicion which Freud represented, and through which individuals are supposed to be brought to an understanding of their true selves. Foucault held that these practices are interwoven with power, and that the hermeneutics is actually part of the problem. What matters is neither to interpret the everyday behaviour of individuals as in phenomenology, nor the hidden meaning behind these as in hermeneutics, but to focus on precisely such practices as the hermeneutic 'techniques' themselves. The human sciences, which include hermeneutics, play an important role in the disciplinary 'bio-power', in that they directly or indirectly regulate and thereby create the body of modern man. Bio-power can be described as 'a set of historical practices which produces the human objects systematized by structuralism and the human subjects explicated by hermeneutics' (Dreyfus and Rabinow, 1983: 103). Bio-power, the power over human life, which constitutes the paramount exercise of power in our present epoch, thus finds direct and palpable expression in institutional assemblages of regulations in the form of factories, hospitals, schools, universities, military barracks and prisons. For instance, discipline at the shop-floor level in factories is not introduced for purely economic reasons, but as a manifestation of the already existing strategies of bio-power. Here, we are transformed into objects within structures. But there are also methods for changing us into docile subjects. Thus, more subtle and indirect forms are provided by the confessional situation, where sexuality is at the centre. The whole modern therapy industry can be seen as an expression of this second, more manipulative aspect. The social welfarism in contemporary Western societies, with its continual interventions into the human life situation, can be assigned to the same group of indirect ruling, based on ideas of human science. In contrast to the older factory discipline, this is also the foundation of the softer methods of Organizational Behaviour, which build upon theories of motivation and other psychological theories for subjectivation in a desired direction – for instance, to a spectator rather than a participant status (Sotto, 1990).

Some methodological principles

It is not easy to develop specific methodological rules from the works of Foucault. Scheurich and MacKenzie (2005) refer to Foucault's general 'rules' for genealogy, as expressed in *Discipline and Punish*, as kinds of theses to explore and develop. One such rule is not to concentrate on the repressive effect of various systems of punishment, but to situate these in a relationship to 'positive' (productive) effects. Foucault's mode of working was unique and is best understood based on a thorough reading of his inspiring texts.

One can still note, however, that proceeding from his notion of power, Foucault formulated in *The History of Sexuality* (1978: 98–102) four 'rules' of method (not to be conceived as 'methodological imperatives', but as 'at most … cautionary prescriptions'). The rules are here exemplified with sexuality, but of course they can be used in other areas as well.

1 *The rule of immanence.* Power and knowledge are never separate but always fused: power/knowledge. Thus there is no 'pure' or 'innocent' knowledge. As we recall, power is also primarily local in nature. In the research process it is therefore appropriate to proceed from 'local centres of power-knowledge'. Such a centre is the confessional procedure, for instance the relationship between therapist and client in the therapeutic situation. Another is the body of the child, around whose sexuality an intense interest developed in the nineteenth century, so that it became surrounded by 'an entire watch-group of parents, nurses, servants, and doctors'.

2 *The rule of continual variations.* Relationships of power/knowledge are not static but in continual change. There are certain patterns of power/knowledge; however, these are not static but constitute 'matrices of transformation' which can be shifted in one direction or another with regard to the agents. Thus, for instance, the just mentioned interest in infantile sexuality gradually shaded over into the interest in adult sexuality with which we live today.

3 *The rule of double conditioning.* Local tactics and relationships must fit in with the overarching strategies; and conversely, the overarching strategies can only be specified in local tactics and relationships. Thus, Malthusian demographic policy as well as 'the medicalization of sex and the psychiatrization of its non-genital forms' took the family as an anchoring point, since it was local and relatively autonomous with respect to other power centres.

4 *The rule of the tactic polyvalence of discourses.* Discourses occur in the field of power, and for this reason they are never unambiguous, but complex, contradictory and unstable. One and the same discourse can, for example, be both an instrument of and an obstacle to power. Different forces in the field pull in different directions. It is therefore a question of examining where a certain discourse is situated, in the play between powers at the tactical and strategic level, rather than simply trying to establish that it is an expression or an effect of a certain global strategy.

The self and the ethics

At the end of his life, and during the completion of the later volumes of *The History of Sexuality*, Foucault began delving ever deeper into the history of classical antiquity.

He then came to realize that the formation of the subject (subjectivation) had started earlier and, in doing so also had not proceeded as he had previously envisaged it. More especially, it appeared that the ancient Greeks had undertaken an operation with power which, as it were, folded it into a self-reflection, a 'care of oneself' (Foucault, 1988), creating a self in much the same way as a sculpture. This provides something approaching a dimension of freedom beyond the two previously used (knowledge and power), and which – although freedom uses knowledge and power as the material from which to proceed – cannot be absorbed into them. In addition to the earlier basic questions, 'What do I know?' and 'What can I do?' there now emerges the question of self-identity, 'Who am I?' (Deleuze, 1988). This relationship to the self generates a subject, which is actually prior to the subjectivating process of the disciplinary techniques. We may therefore speak of a new – a third – ethical phase in Foucault's thinking, which was unfortunately interrupted by his untimely death in 1984, without having been fully developed. Thus, a third main dimension appears in Foucault's thinking, concomitant with and irreducible to knowledge and power, namely the self.

It should be noted that this view of the (active) formation of the subject differs radically from, and could be read as a critique of, the postmodern views of subjectivation which we discussed in the preceeding chapter. Such an active role of the self, reflecting on itself and thereby producing the subject, is of course excluded by postmodern ideas according to which the subject is generated by the discourse(s). True, even in the final phase of Foucault's thinking, the subject produced in the way indicated is coloured by forms of knowledge and power; yet the important thing is that it is *irreducible* to these. Thus the subject actually functions as a pocket of resistance to established forms of power/knowledge in the present age. But this subject is not the old, immutable individual; it is an ongoing process, a new, dynamic creation, waging a sort of (micro) guerilla war in favour of 'difference, variation, and metamorphosis' (Deleuze, 1988) as against the powers that be. It is especially worth observing that in this late Foucauldian version of subjectivation, the subject is *not* primarily a 'social construction', but a construction of the self reflecting on the self, albeit a construction that established forms of power/knowledge continually *try* to imprint with their crystallized patterns. The outcome of this struggle between subject and power/knowledge is always uncertain, never decided in advance, and never final.

*

Deleuze (1988) describes Foucault's social ontology in roughly the following way. Ultimately there is an amorphous mass of turbulent social raw energies in time and space. These are structured into free-floating strategies and power plays, which in their turn are sedimented into strata of the 'visible and sayable', that is discursive and non-discursive formations of practices, which are permeated by knowledge and power. The subject is created primarily by a folding-in of the social raw energy (especially under the aspect of time, in the form of memory) but will later be overdetermined by strategies and strata.

Critical views

There is a danger that a strongly Foucault-inspired power approach might become a kind of theoretical panacea. To see how apparently neutral or 'good' relationships and practices can be elucidated in terms of power is in principle very praiseworthy, but the risk is that the idea will command the empirical materials too strongly. This tendency can be traced back to Nietzsche's influence. We noted in Chapter 4 above that while criticizing the foundational philosophy, Nietzsche was himself engaged in operating with a reductionist foundation, namely the will to power, to which everything else ultimately recurs. This ready-made package is what Foucault takes over. It is difficult to think of any observation which could negate Foucault's view of power. Everything can be subordinated to Foucauldian terms, with the risk that such a perspective will find not only 'everything' but – as a consequence – also 'nothing'. Nor should the risk be underestimated that the presuppositions govern the result – that one finds what one is looking for, in this case local power/knowledge. The problem about a categorical linking of power and knowledge is that it ought to comprise Foucault's own project as well. Critics ask what power Foucault's own knowledge produces and how he regarded this (Dews, 1987; Walzer, 1986). Moreover, as we have seen, Foucault himself had at the time of his death entered a new phase of research so as not to be entirely swallowed up by the problematic of power.

Another problem concerns the limitations of the micro focus which Foucault advocates. The criticism against the idea that power has a centre or an essence is a cogent one, but this does not prevent some apparently crucial phenomena from escaping a Foucauldian perspective, for instance power relationships linked to economic relationships or the nation-state (Walzer, 1986). He objects to the importance of ideology, but as Clegg (1989) points out, it would be hard to understand the importance of leading neo-liberal politicians during the 1980s, not to mention communism and Nazism, if we disregard the ideological aspects. Walby (1992) is of the opinion that Foucault's concept of power becomes too scattered and that relationships between social classes, as well as fundamental aspects of gender relationships, are lost sight of. Newton (1998: 425) argues that Foucault neglected 'socially constructed stabilities in power relations'. A counter-argument is that Foucault was interested in the micro level and in specific forms of power, and that it was not his aim to investigate other kinds of phenomena. Another may be that he never aimed at being politically correct.

A third problem on which many critics have focused is the broad, pessimistic view of new forms of knowledge and technology. Everything tends to become a question of power and normalization. In any case, there are no guidelines for the identification of such occurrences as may possibly lie beyond these, or which constitute less 'negative' forms of power. Foucault's point of view involved an inability to distinguish positive features in technological, jurisdictional and medical advances, for instance (Dreyfus and Rabinow, 1986). Everything becomes 'problematic', and no clues are offered as to what is to be regarded as 'especially problematic'. Consequently, an analysis which is usually interpreted as political and critical risks transforming into its opposite, so that it lacks critical edge and becomes apolitical. Barring any form of normative stance from which the problematic sides emerge, this easily becomes a universal quality which can just as well be described as its counter-part. Something becomes 'problematic' (worth critically scrutinizing) only in the light of (the possible existence of) something 'unproblematic' or at least 'less problematic' (cf. Dews, 1987). On the other hand, this was a conscious choice by Foucault. With his orientation towards micro resistance, both theoretically and practically, against the current sites and strategies of power, he can be described as an eternal rebel or a Sisyphus figure in the spirit of Camus, rather than as a global revolutionary or, for instance, a critical theorist like those we discussed in Chapter 5. With his points of departure and his view of the nature of power and knowledge, this was of course also the only practical way out. Foucault himself maintained that he did not believe that everything he focused on was bad; on the other hand, most things were 'dangerous', and so it was important to observe and put up a resistance to the 'main danger' in every given epoch and situation; that is, what mattered was to choose the least dangerous of several dangerous alternatives. Consequently, Foucault characterized himself as a 'hyper- and pessimist activist' (Dreyfus and Rabinow, 1983).

Fourthly, Bourdieu and Wacquant (1992) criticize Foucault for focusing one-sidedly on the bodily, disciplinary bio-power and underestimating the more subtle 'symbolic violence' which permeates the various 'fields' of society. This critique may seem to miss the mark, since as we have just seen Foucault also included manipulative aspects of power. However, these constitute a roundabout route to the disciplining of the body, the bio-power, which is reached here in an indirect way. Foucault's conception of power is ironically described by Bourdieu and Wacquant as somewhat pubertal, reflecting the anxiety of the adolescent, faced with the disciplinary demands and institutionalizations of the grown-up world!

Naturally, the above points of criticism are hardly accepted by Foucault's advocates and, irrespective of how one sees their fairness, do not obscure the fact that Foucault remains a very important source of inspiration for social theory, and ought to have a strong impact on qualitative social research. One reason for this is his great original-ity, which among other things has found expression in his refusal to accept tradi-tional social science categories, which he had broken up and replaced by brand new ones. At the same time Foucault worked in the tradition of the great social science thinkers (Weber, critical theory and others) who trained the searchlights at the process of rationalization in modern society. Yet he provided this tradition with entirely new dimensions through his often very unexpected and creative conceptual formations and his displacements of the foci of investigation, linked at a more concrete level with detailed empirical studies, almost lifelike in their concreteness and vividness, inspired by the art of painting (Deleuze, 1988). Unfortunately, there do seem to be fewer detailed empirical studies strongly inspired by Foucault's work than discussions of it.

Some general implications for method

At first sight, Foucault's text may seem to belong to the fields of historiography or even the history of ideas. He himself rejected such labels – and rightly so, since he actually studied present-day society with a look in the rear mirror, that is, using the genealogic method. This means, of course, that Foucault's genealogy has much to offer all the social sciences. Moreover, in a social science which is inspired by, or uses, Foucault's genealogy, historicity is central. By searching for the often repressed, 'disgraceful' roots of the contemporary phenomena investigated, we obtain a new and different perspective on them. Our gaze is directed towards something other than that which is ordinarily regarded: look over there, it can also be seen in this way!

What is repressed is precisely that power is always intertwined with knowledge. Thus there is no 'innocent' or 'pure' knowledge. The general recognition of the power–knowledge relationship is of course crucial. It effectively destroys any notions of the eternally neutral, nobly rational or progressive nature of research. Even knowledge which claims to function in an emancipatory mode or to generate insights, can contribute to inscribing more or less limited forms of subjectivity via the ideals and conceptions of normality mediated. Various ideas of equality – including research and theory guided by this principle – shape and regulate our self-understanding by establishing norms for thinking, feeling and acting. Even 'progressive' poststructuralist ideas of process subjectivity, which seek to demolish fixed notions of the self (self-destruction as ideal) (see, for example, Deetz, 1992; Weedon, 1987), include a dimension of power in which the negative values that are given stability, consistency and 'essentiality' generate a new form for (desirable) subjectivity. A more fluid, playful, non-centred subject thus becomes the norm in light of which individuals are monitored and normalized – by themselves and others. That this is a flexible rather than a rigid procedure does not reduce the element of power in it.

The difficult way out of – or tactic for coping with – the power–knowledge linkage is to stimulate resistance, that is, efforts to wriggle out of various determinations and classifications. In the same vein as in the (other) poststructuralists, the surrendering of fixed categories becomes an important principle in the research process, which includes engendering scepticism even against apparently good ideas, such as taking a stance in the (determinate) interest of the underdog. (Foucault himself always took the part of the underdog, both in his writings and in political activism.)

Foucault's sources were mostly documentary. Yet, he also spoke with approval of the dialogic value of interviews and gave numerous interviews himself. How, then, should we use interview material in research? The following gives us a lead:

> [W]e must not imagine a world of discourse divided between accepted discourse and excluded discourse, or between the dominant discourse and the dominated one; but as a multiplicity of discursive elements that can come into play in various strategies. It is this distribution that we must reconstruct, with the things said and those concealed, the enunciations required and those forbidden, that it comprises; with the variants and different effects – according to who is speaking, his position of power, the institutional context in which he happens to be situated – that it implies; and with the shifts and reutilizations for contrary objectives that it also includes. (Foucault, 1978: 100)

That is to say, micropower is primary and we must study it in the specific interview statement without presupposing any overarching repressive mechanism. First and foremost: in what strategy or strategies does the discourse take part? Thus, what is said and *unsaid*, from the aspect of power? Here, as in postmodernism (and in this the procedure hence differs radically from that of hermeneutics), we disregard the originator of the statement as well as any underlying meaning, logic, or truth content in it (see Deleuze, 1988). The spokesperson only comes into the picture secondarily: who is speaking, what concrete position of power does this person have on this occasion, in what institutional context is she or he embedded, and under what displacements or possibly contradictory uses for different purposes? The general rule is to treat data, whatever their form, 'as expressions of culturally standardized discourses that are associated with particular social settings' (Miller, 1997: 34).

Deleuze (1988) strongly emphasizes the difference between the visible and the sayable, the non-discursive and the discursive, in Foucault's thinking. Perhaps the most relevant research practice, pertaining to the visible, would be detailed observation of specific arrangements and practices that show how power is expressed. If we adopt the ideas that power exists only in action, that a network of micropowers operates via different discursive practices in various contexts of human improvement in schools, social care, psychotherapy, consumer counselling, gender-equality projects, and so on, then observation studies become vital in the research process. Even limited situations can generate a host of interpretations. In Alvesson (1996), observations of a two-hour 'information meeting' led to a whole book with interpretations from a Foucauldian perspective (among others). A similar stance to that in the preceding paragraph on interviews should be taken here: that is, it is not a question of reaching the 'authentic' intention in the originator of the action, or the true meaning of the action, or some kind of logic of action, but of describing the strategies of which the action itself is part, disregarding the meaning or originator which only come into the picture in a secondary way. The basic overall rule is to treat all empirical material as expressions of culturally standardized discourses that are associated with particular social settings.

Final words

The three directions treated in this chapter connect to the themes that we addressed in earlier chapters. They also represent alternative entrances to, and themes for, a reflection on the broader level to which we try to contribute in this book.

Occasionally the directions are combined. There are discourse-analytic studies of gender (Marshall and Wetherell, 1989). Certain feminists are inspired by Foucault (Butler, 2004; Weedon, 1987). Despite the use of the common term 'discourse', Foucault and discourse analysis indicate very different kinds of studies. But there are also examples of approaches inspired by both orientations (Miller, 1997; Parker, 1991). Our rationale for addressing the three orientations is not, however, to contribute to their synthesis. Our purpose in grouping them in this chapter is instead that they are examples of highly significant contributions to reflective qualitative method, which add to and vary the insights communicated in previous chapters. We once again wish to underscore that these orientations are *examples* of great relevance to qualitative method in social science.

To a higher degree than the four main directions that form the pillars of this book, discourse analysis, feminism and Foucault's genealogy represent specific research programmes. (Feminism is, however, broader and more heterogeneous than the other two.) Their reflective capacities thereby become more directed and constrained.[9] They can offer a valuable input to hermeneutic, critical and postmodern reflection by problematizing what language expressions signify (the uncertainty of meaning) in social interaction, pointing at gender as a core dimension in political and ideological contexts, and showing how power is also present in seemingly good research (including that which aims to emancipate women) through the inseparability of knowledge/power. At the same time they give reflection a somewhat narrower focus and do not have the same general relevance as we think grounded theory, hermeneutics, critical theory and poststructuralism may have.[10] (This is no critique or ranking of importance. The last four directions' more general character may motivate critique for a lack of distinct contributions to social scientific knowledge about social phenomona.)

Our mode of structuring relevant knowledge within the intersection between philosophy of science and qualitative method is, of course, partly arbitrary. This is unavoidable, as thinkers and texts seldom lend themselves straightforwardly to categorization. It is possible to imagine other versions than those chosen here. Feminism may be seen as a political project, and we could have addressed it together with critical theory. Foucault could have been connected to postmodernism (if one emphasizes the philosophy of the subject and the anti-utopian attitude) or alternatively to critical theory (both are characterized by a resistance against ego-administration and processes of rationalization). Foucault, who himself mentioned his sympathy with the Frankfurt school, with which he became familiar very late (Foucault, 1983), and the early (gloomier) Frankfurt school could be combined, while Habermas's (more positive) communication theory could signify another position, and so on. Yet this would have meant forcing the approaches treated in this chapter into a context where they do not quite belong, which is why we have chosen the presentation here in order to elicit the complementary value of these currents.

Notes

1. For a survey and discussion of ethnic qualitative research, see Stanfield (1994).
2. The various schools differ somewhat on how they view the relationship between language use and an 'underlying reality'. Some concentrate on talk and utterances, and do not directly address the social context to which these belong. Others are interested in the social context, and view institutional conversations as culturally determined phenomena, as different conversation and communication cultures with different traditions and varied degrees of generality (Linell, 1990). Another dividing-line concerns whether the focus is on linguistic expression in the form of talk only or also in the form of (other kinds of) accounts. Conversation analysts often concentrate on institutionalized talk, which has a certain form and is somewhat repetitive and ritualized, such as discussions between professionals and laymen (Linell, 1990; Silverman, 1993). Discourse analysts are interested in linguistic expressions even in other forms – for example, in utterances not directly included in conversation and written texts (Potter and Wetherell, 1987). Thus interaction effects need not be central here. However, it has to be admitted that the difference between conversation and discourse analysis is not very strict.
3. Of course, an evaluation of 'honesty' is not a straightforward activity. Being viewed in this way may be seen as an outcome of the rhetorical acts of the person ascribed this moral virtue and trustworthiness. As Silverman (1993: 96) notes, 'maybe we feel people are at their most authentic when they are, in effect, reproducing a cultural script'.

4. Alert and ambitious interviewers often emphasize the ideal of establishing familiarity, dialogue and a relationship vis-á-vis research respondents, perhaps performing return interviews in order to further build on this and to be able to evaluate accounts for their consistency over time (see, for example, Collinson, 1992). Such ideals are important, but they only help to a limited extent to solve the problem, namely that accounts are characterized by the imperfections of language in their descriptions and transmissions of meaning, and that they tend to vary not only from one telling to another but even within a set of utterances produced on one particular occasion. What interviewers can attain at best – if they want to describe something beyond language use – is utterances that are 'more or less' consistent across different interviews and occasions. But if we pay serious attention to the ideas of discourse analysis, then we would probably expect return interviews first and foremost to yield abundant material for the study of variations in accounts. In Acker et al. (1991) a case is described involving four return interviews. The content of the interview accounts varied, something which the authors interpret as a development generated by the reflections which the dialogue-oriented interviews had encouraged. Other interpretations are of course possible – perhaps that the interviewees adopted the norms which the researcher represented, or developed their ability to present coherent stories (which does not need to mean more 'true', or, still less, clearer or better formulated stories). A further possibility is that the interviewee did not want to repeat herself but may have modified accounts in order to make them interesting. It is, of course, also possible to emphasize the randomness of how accounts may develop. The point here is that the variations in accounts often change over time, and that it is not a simple matter to interpret this. In very ambitious efforts to establish contact over time and perhaps complement interviews with other methods (informal interaction, observations) it is not, however, impossible that a certain 'stabilization' of the meanings expressed by research subjects can be found (see Skeggs, 1997, for an account of such a research project).

5. Ferguson (1984) can be said to represent a variant of the feminist standpoint in which the main interest focuses on the critical analysis of a patriarchal phenomenon, starting from an idea about a general women's point of view, while another variant is more empirical and experiential, starting from women's accounts of everyday life. (e.g. Acker et al., 1991).

6. Cf. Alvesson and Billing (2009). Not only do the variations among women themselves have a constraining effect on this research space; it is also reduced by the fact that a great many experiences and reactions are probably common to both men and women (within a particular social category).

7. The language focus is, however, typically less strict and narrow than in the case of discourse analysis.

8. An interesting question concerns the way feminists advocating a particular method as well as emphasizing the biological sex of the researcher look upon (biological) men who embrace in their method 'pro-feminine' ideals such as closeness, experience and anti-authoritative attitudes – as many male interpretive researchers do – compared to the (many) women researchers who use questionnaires and statistics and claim authority and rationality through references to their adherence to scientific methodology. Are the former or the latter to be preferred in gender research?

9. Many feminists would not accept this claim. It is, of course, possible to argue that gender is everywhere and that no social phenomenon can be understood without a consideration of this. Something similar may be said about, for example, language, power, class and culture (to invoke somewhat different aspects). The point here is to indicate a particular research strategy and roads to reflection, not to decide which phenomena are of greatest significance or are widely diffused.

10. At least, this may perhaps hold for Foucault, the power philosopher. However, there are many Foucaults, and the writer with the name Foucault may well be richer and more diverse (and more contradictory) than any of the approaches discussed in the previous chapters.

8

ON REFLEXIVE INTERPRETATION: THE PLAY OF INTERPRETIVE LEVELS

This chapter sets in motion the various themes we have touched upon, bringing them into play against each other. Our intention is thus to provide an overall frame of reference and some concrete ideas and suggestions, with a view to incorporating reflexive elements in – primarily – qualitative research.

We start with a short résumé of the main points raised in the earlier chapters and then look at some of the more typical responses to the critique of conventional empirical research – responses that pay serious attention to the constructed, political, gendered, linguistic nature of social research. We examine these responses critically, in particular tendencies to linguistic reductionism (totalization of the linguistic dimension). We then formulate a composite position which we call *reflexive interpretation*. Here we make a demand for reflection in research in conjunction with an interpretation at several levels: contact with the empirical material, awareness of the interpretive act, clarification of political-ideological contexts, and the handling of the question of representation and authority. In the next chapter we will indicate some methodological strategies that facilitate research in a spirit of reflexive interpretation, provide illustrations and discuss the criteria for good research. So as not to get stuck in a particular fixed position – which would counteract the reflective stance we are advocating – it is necessary to maintain a certain distance from the various positions discussed. Hence the importance of a little irony. Let us therefore describe the four trends with a touch of levity.

The four orientations in slightly ironical terms

Grounded theory is a doctrine for those with strong religious leanings, particularly of a Protestant persuasion. Success entails a process of purification, achieved by abandoning theoretical blinkers. Only then can diligent scholars see reality as it is, only then can they see the light. This blessed state is attained through hard, conscientious toil. Only the truly industrious – those who have collected an enormous amount of data and lifted them up into various category-containers, which in turn are stacked up to create a great cathedral-like structure, on top of which sits the theory (with a small 't') – can avoid the corruption and perils of free-thinking and hedonistic theoretical laxity, which allow the ungodly to think great, free and dangerous thoughts, abandoning the straight and narrow but rightful empirical path. Grounded theory is the path for petty bourgeois Protestants, where the accumulation of data leads to modest but certain returns in the form of a limited but secure stock of cultural capital. The grounded theorist is Luther's man.

Hermeneutics sees the light in a different way. The religious element in hermeneutics springs from its origins as a means for interpreting obscure passages in the Bible. The hermeneutician is well in touch with the powers above. God demands nothing; rather, a chosen few are granted divine inspiration. This comes from reading texts, either literally or metaphorically. Divine grace, manifest as a revelation of the text's underlying meaning, the sacred light, is achieved through an acceptance by the researcher of the circular process of the Catholic world order. The interpretation of the doctrine is one and undivided; pure Being has a Prophet, Hölderlin, and Heidegger is his infallible Vicar on earth. But reformists within the Church have started to talk about polysemy, that is ambiguity, and other such heretical inventions. The ancient Fathers of the Church must be groaning and turning in their graves: can this mean that the Only True Doctrine is being corrupted and that the Holy Trinity is transformed from unity in manifold into unbridled polytheism?

Critical theory also appreciates inspiration, but is anti-religious. Critical theorists thus differ radically from many Marxists, who have a more religious turn of mind, with a strong belief in the true doctrine and the good book (*Das Kapital*), and are interested in how the doctrinal teachings should be put into practice. Instead of missionary zeal, the critical scholar is driven by anxiety in the face of authority, and by paranoia. (In so far as salvation comes in at all, it is a question of being saved *from* religion.) The problem of authority leads to a sort of counter-dependence. Followers of critical theory distance themselves from and engage themselves in battle with existing institutions and authorities – which, for these theorists, exist to be opposed. Combat is a way of life. There is something pubescent about this approach (in parallel with a certain senescence). The paranoia is associated with the fear that Big Brother (capital, the technocrats, the market, the socialist state) is practising mind control. But the critical theorists will not subject themselves to control. Free thought is not only allowed, it is obligatory. Thought, to be worth the effort, must be bold and free. There is, however, a limit, which is set by pure, unrestricted rationality. 'Distortions' are not tolerated. Against any elements of friction the doctrine claims authority for itself, building an atheistic church based on horizontal as opposed to vertical communication as the means to the forgiveness of sins, and on the emancipation of the individual as a mark of favour.

Postmodernism is also characterized by the problem of authority. Here, however, the fear of being authoritarian oneself is as great as the fear of others being so; people seem to be impelled by the dread of suffering from delusions of omnipotence; power lies in the Word, and they have access to the Word themselves. The problem is that the beast cannot be controlled. To capture something in print is tantamount to black magic. Fearing its own innate strength, postmodernism becomes afraid of contact: getting in touch with reality (empirical material) – that is, with something beyond the bounds of the text – is risky, unpleasant and taboo. The fear of becoming (theoretically) tainted lies behind this. The purification idea is not altogether absent. But our own safe little sphere is secure. Here we can play at will, particularly with ourselves. This gives maximum satisfaction to the postmodernist. The postmodernist, like the critical theorist, is a freethinker, but in a pint-sized version. Here, thinking should be free but 'small'. Any more ambitous freethinking awakens the fear of the devil in postmodernists – the slumbering tyrant who uses his magical texts and his Grand Wicked Narratives to totalize existence for the man and woman in Academia as well as in the street.

Methodological strategies: resignation and linguistic reductionism

As we have seen, neither the research question, the cognitive interest, the vocabulary, the way of perceiving, representing, evaluating and weighting various elements that claim to say something about 'reality' (the empirical material), nor the theory and metatheory, the mode of depiction, the claims to authority, etc. can be taken for granted or treated in a simple manner. Rather they can – and must – all be problematized. Given the difficulty or even impossibility of describing or interpreting 'objective reality' (or people's intersubjective, socially constructed reality, or their interior psychological worlds), we could simply decide to stop doing empirical research and devote ourselves instead to theoretical problems, or we could tell people how empirical research should be conducted without doing any ourselves. This last strategy is not unusual. Thus, as we have already noted, there seem to be more scholars writing about postmodernist ethnography, or even about ethnography in general, than there are scholars actually engaged in this somewhat exacting art form (at least if by 'ethnography' we mean spending a long time on participant observation in a 'natural' environment). Resignation at the very idea of empirical research may thus be a possible methodological strategy (or anti-strategy). And there is certainly good cause to feel less self-confident about the possibility of providing good empirical answers to a whole lot of research questions to which the research community – and, even more, their sponsor organizations – currently expect answers to be provided.

We do not mean, however, that the ambition to do empirical research should be given up. On the contrary, this critique, and the insights it brings, can encourage greater freedom and, what is more, greater sophistication in attitudes towards empirical work, motivating a rather radical reorientation of ambitions and aims. Briefly, this implies less focus on what the empirical material can tell us about how things 'really are' and more about other virtues – creative ideas, for instance – that are not subject to the empirical norm which shackles us to the 'data'. Less concentration on the collection and processing of data and more on interpretation and reflection – in relation not only to the object of study but also to the researchers themselves and their political, ideological, metatheoretical and linguistic context – appears to be a reasonable and fruitful path for qualitative research to follow.

What can this entail in more concrete terms? Before offering our own ideas on this point, we will look at some attempts to provide methodological strategies which allow in particular for the criticisms raised in the postmodernist camp.

There are various responses to the wave of objections to conventional epistemology and method, which we have already presented and discussed. Geertz (1988) mentions four in the field of ethnography: textual positivism (a narrow focus on statements which are described in as much detail as possible, as in certain types of conversation analysis); shared authorship (in which the subject of an investigation talks in parallel with the researcher-author); 'confessionalism', in which the researcher and his or her reactions are central (cf. Van Maanen, 1988); and the idea that by means of self-examination the author can expel distortions or subjectivity so as to be able to relate freely to the reality studied. The last of these is a rather ambitious variant of what is traditionally advocated by inductive empiricists. In various contexts above we have touched upon all four types of response, but have not found any of them to be particularly successful. Textual positivism is all too narrow, and risks being unable to say anything of interest outside a narrow field of application. This applies also, albeit less emphatically, to discourse analysis. Shared authorship means either that the researcher has to collate various statements and do a substantial editing job on the material (statements made by the subject of the study), or that the researcher risks exposing the reader to long and often only moderately interesting reports. Moreover, such efforts are often limited to interview statements, easily grasped by readers. It is hard to imagine that any representative of the group studied would provide extensive documentation of detailed observations of situations and events. (This often demands hours of note-taking and transcription, and anyway presup-poses a training in participant observation.) Confessionalism has the advantage of replacing an objectivist style with 'the modest, unassuming style of one struggling to piece together something reasonably coherent out of displays of initial disorder, doubt and difficulty' (Van Maanen, 1988: 75). If taken too far, it easily slips into self-absorption and leaves limited room for other people's views – which are only interesting in so far as they affect the author. The idea that self-examination helps to get rid of theoretical and other ballasts, so that the empirical material receives maximum justice, is untenable. Without linguistic, cultural and theoretical ballast it is not possible for researchers to get their bearings, to make interpretations or to write anything that makes sense.

On the other hand, elements of all these variants can certainly be included as part of a reflexive methodology, but without dominating it. It is quite possible to imag-ine that part of a research effort could be associated with textual positivism or, per-haps more likely, with discourse or conversation analysis – which means that the researcher meticulously notes statements or conversations that are of particular interest, and interprets them in strict analytical terms. Recall our comment, when discussing discourse analysis in Chapter 7, that caution must be applied before going beyond the statement and using accounts as reflections of something else. The researcher can allow some particular representative (key informant) of the group being studied to express himself or herself in detail in the research text on a certain issue. It is also possible for researchers to describe specific, well-chosen situations or phases in their own explicit and conscious subjective perspective, thus being reflec-tive about how the researcher and research products interplay. (According to Van Maanen, 1988, confessional styles do not normally dominate ethnographic studies, but stand beside realistic accounts.) Self-examination and self-reflection are to some extent ingredients in all research. Thus, one or more of these working methods can be productively included in research, but without being allowed to dominate it. They may be helpful, without offering *the* solution to the problem of social science.

Another response is to focus on language and to discount the extra-linguistic, but to do so in a somewhat freer way than that favoured by the textual positivists and discourse analysts. We will consider this variant in a little more detail, since a rhetorical-linguistic focus is today a prominent alternative to conventional empirical research; it has some points of contact with postmodernism, with which it sometimes also overlaps (see Baker, 1990; Shotter and Gergen, 1989, 1994; Simons, 1989, Steier, 1991a). We will concentrate on a text by Gergen and Gergen (1991), which is a little more concrete as regards method than is customary in this field.

Gergen and Gergen (1991) argue that the fundamental character of language hinders empirical research which is aimed at establishing 'the truth', but also provides the possibility of saying something interesting along other dimensions. They perceive empirical research in a stricter sense as being both impossible and unnecessary, since it is based on the erroneous idea that language mirrors reality. Gergen and Gergen want researchers to direct their attention to the common language, which is not only an obstacle to objective knowledge on an empirical basis, but also constitutes a positive chance to escape from a locked position.

> The reflexive attempt is thus relational, emphasizing the expansion of the languages of understanding. The aim is to realize more fully the linguistic implications of preferred positions, and to invite the expression of alternative voices or perspectives into one's activities. (Gergen and Gergen, 1991: 79)

Research is a question of enriching the linguistic sphere. This may of course be interesting, but it means abstaining from – or even excluding the possibility of – saying anything about 'reality' as such, at least in terms of statements with some claim to truth. Reality exists, Gergen and Gergen and those of like mind presumably believe, but it cannot be accurately depicted with the help of language. Yet it is not necessary to totalize a non-realistic (non-representational) view of language to the extent that the Gergens – like many postmodernists and other linguistically interested social scientists – tend to do. The relative ability of language to tell us something about our individual and social reality – once certain linguistic conventions have become culturally established and are regarded as working 'tools' – can thus be taken seriously. Its ability to conceal and tie down certain phenomena, giving them an unduly robust and unequivocal character, must be continuously borne in mind. Language can be regarded as a blunt and equivocal instrument, which shapes and 'perspectivizes' rather than depicting or being totally dissociated from phenomena 'out there'.

Gergen and Gergen mean, for instance, that in the very definition of jealousy – built into the cultural code – as a 'negative emotional state generated by the attraction of a loved person to some other person', it is possible to conclude, a few steps later, that 'people who are low in self-esteem will be more highly prone to jealousy than those who are high in self-esteem' (Gergen and Gergen, 1991: 81). One objection here is that it is difficult to see how language as such makes this argument and this conclusion possible. Rather it is a question of advancing a certain argument, which admittedly requires the support of language; but emphasizing this point exclusively, or stressing the novelty value of a linguistic focus, is not convincing. Nor do our own empirical observations – to leave Gergen and Gergen's frame of reference for a moment – support this conclusion.

People who are said by others (and possibly by themselves) to be jealous, are not necessarily described as having low self-esteem. Whether the two concepts are often ascribed to one and the same person is, to return in part to Gergen and Gergen's frame of reference, an empirical question. It is also perfectly possible to claim the direct opposite, that jealousy often goes together with a high degree of self-esteem, as this inflates the ego sphere. The counter-argument that the ego is really weak, is a circular one, since it would mean that all types of self-esteem that are coupled with jealousy must by definition be described as weak. This of course demonstrates the problem of these authors' exclusively linguistic approach.[1] A possible research task – perhaps worth investigating beyond the scope offered by the desk and the dictionary – would be to relate statements regarding jealousy to statements about low or high self-esteem. People could be asked to think about themselves or some of their acquaintances in terms of degrees of 'jealousy' and levels of 'self-esteem'. It should then be possible to see whether 'jealousy' and 'low self-esteem' appear to be ascribed to the same person, and also to observe the variations in the statements, which are probably greater than Gergen and Gergen's language-focused line of reasoning would imply.[2]

Linguistic reductionism – restricting the field of research to the purely linguistic, completely cut off from references to 'real' actions, happenings, emotions, ideas, thoughts and so on – does seem pretty narrow and sterile. As a source of reflection, however, the approach undoubtedly has a certain role to fill. Respect for the distinctive character of language and its limited ability to reflect 'reality' is important. The ideas of Gergen and Gergen are also valuable for the critique of the tendency to naïvely equate correlations of statements with correlations of other phenomena 'out there'. Often the following of norms for language use leads respondents to questionnaires to produce responses which seem to show factual correlations. Seltzer and Bass (1990), for example, found that if subordinates tended to express positive sentiments concerning their managers in a questionnaire they were also inclined to say that their unit was effective. This was interpreted as supportive of the idea that a particular kind of leadership had a positive impact on performance. However, the outcome may equally well be seen as a result of the respondents complying with cultural rules for language use. If you express a very positive view of a manager, you are likely to say that the effectiveness of the unit is high (Alvesson and Deetz, 2000). One should perhaps add that estimations of the characteristics of a manager and the efficiency of a unit are normally quite uncertain, as indicated by the results showing that the large majority of managers were rated in very positive terms and that their units were described as very effective.

However, we would like to get beyond a focus on language and language use, consider broader aspects of qualitative research, and look at reflection on several levels, as a way of responding to the insights regarding the socially and textually constructed and constructing nature of research.

On reflection

Reflection means thinking about the conditions for what one is doing, investigating the way in which the theoretical, cultural and political context of individual and intellectual involvement affects interaction with whatever is being researched, often in ways that are difficult to become conscious of.[3] When we reflect, we try to ponder upon the premises for our thoughts, our observations and our use of language. Consequently, reflection is difficult. To Steier (1991a), the core of reflection (reflexivity) consists of an interest in the way we construct ourselves socially while also constructing objects ('out there') in our research. For without construction, and without a constructing and constructed self, there is no meaning:

> Nothing means anything on its own. Meaning comes not from seeing or even observation alone, for there is no 'alone' of this sort. Neither is meaning lying around in nature waiting to be scooped up by the senses; rather it is constructed. 'Constructed' in this context, means produced in acts of interpretations. (Steedman, 1991: 54)

The process of construction thus demands something to construct (out there, so long as we are not talking about pure objects of fantasy), a constructing subject (the researcher) and a social context that constructs the researcher (society, language, paradigms, the local research community). To put it simply: reflexivity, in the research context, means paying attention to these aspects without letting any one of them dominate. In other words, it is a question of avoiding empiricism, narcissism and different varieties of social and linguistic reductionism.

In the social sciences the 'object of study' can usefully be regarded as a social construction. After all, people construct their social reality. The point here is that this applies to the researcher as well. Von Glasersfeld (1991) speaks of trivial construction, when the researcher reserves social construction for the object of study, while implying that the researcher her or himself remains outside such constructing, and is able – in some sense objectively – to portray the social constructions. The objection that the researcher's constructing is ignored appears to apply to much mainstream qualitative research, including grounded theory, inductive ethnography and some versions of hermeneutics. The risk with a too far pushed social constructionism, as a reaction to the 'undersocialization' of neo-positivists and others, is of course an 'oversocialization' of research, where everything becomes reduced to social constructions (Danermark et al., 2002). Schools like critical realism can here function as productive counter-pictures to researchers focusing (only) on constructions of constructions.

In certain versions of postmodernism and poststructuralism (often taking a strict constructionist view) the emphasis is so firmly on one particular type of self-reflection that little energy is left over for anything else, such as empirical studies. It is often rhetorical or communicative aspects that attract attention, to the exclusion of everything else. Not only the critics but even several writers with a leaning towards PM/PS are concerned about the risks of self-reflective isolationism, self-absorption and impotent texts (Brown, 1994; Newton, 1996). Baker (1990: 235), for instance, is worried that excessive textual/rhetorical awareness could lead researchers into a house of mirrors, a self-sufficient meta-language which will isolate them from the rest of the world. To counter this tendency, according to Baker, it is necessary to widen our rhetorical and textual focus to include the researcher's recognition of her or himself as a rhetorician who is part of a social and political context. By writing ourselves into this and recognizing that we are engaged in persuasion within a social and consequently a political context, we can avoid narcissistic self-centredness.

In our view this suggested solution is too general and too closely linked to an emphasis on – and an overestimation of – what a textual/rhetorical angle of approach can capture. The whole idea of reflexivity, as we see it, is the very ability to break away from a frame of reference and to look at what it is *not* capable of saying. Simply to extend it, runs contrary to the whole idea of reflexivity.

In reflexive contexts there cannot be definite demands – at least not heavy ones – as regards theoretical consistency, in the sense that a particular ontological and epistemological position is strictly maintained throughout. The point of reflection is rather to break away from consistency and a narrow focus on a particular aspect, to question weaknesses inherent in the mode of thought one embraces (and is easily imprisoned within), to break up and change a particular language game rather than expanding it. This naturally applies even to postmodernism, whose supporters tend to claim that they have found the key to reflection, for example through emphasizing the fictional nature of research work and texts. In a certain sense we could claim that, like so many other reflection-oriented writers, Baker inadvertently illustrates the core of the problem with his adherence to a particular logic, rather than indicating new ways out.[4]

A major problem when it comes to the reflexivity of the postmodernists and (other) linguistically minded scholars such as Shotter and Gergen (1994), is that they limit the horizon too narrowly. The social element in attempts at emphasizing the dialogical dimension becomes a question of interpersonal interactions in the constructing of reality, while political, historical and social relationships are neglected (Newton, 1996; Willmott, 1994b). This can be compared, for instance, to Bourdieu (social fields) or critical theory (dominant ideologies or historical-cultural conditions), both of which in their particular way raise the question of how macrocontexts affect research work. To be a little unkind, we could thus say that the object of our criticism here represents a sort of 'reflective reductionism'. The reflective focus becomes too narrow. Certain aspects, in themselves vital, are overprivileged.

More reasonable is to demand some sort of consistency of the reflective researcher, at a metatheoretical level.[5] This level is more 'holistic' than the levels at which critical theory, poststructuralism, Foucault, gender theory, and so on, operate, since these deal with specific aspects of the conditions for the social sciences, the political and gendered nature of knowledge, the character of language, and so on. A reflexive metatheory, as we see it, is not merely a question of philosophical profundities or drawing attention to one single theme of reflection. Rather it is about initiating movement between different profundities of this kind and other more empirically based elements in research, which saves us from becoming locked into a particular philosophical position. Thus what we suggest here as a metatheory is no theory. It is more a framework for drawing attention to and mediating between various core dimensions of reflection, for initiating acts of reflection and maintaining movement between reflective themes. The framework gives multi-level reflective activities a certain structure and systematization. Reflection occurs when one mode of thought is confronted by another. Metatheory is about a comprehensive frame of reference for inspiring and structuring reflection. We call our suggestion for such a frame of reference 'reflexive interpretation'.

Reflexive interpretation

Breadth and variation in interpretation

In qualitative research we have identified four relatively distinct elements or levels which have been treated at length above (Chapters 3–6). As was noted in previous chapters, Giddens (1976) has suggested the concept of 'double hermeneutics' (the interpretation of interpreting subjects). According to this line of thinking the ideas embraced by critical theory could then be dubbed 'triple hermeneutics'. The next step should logically be called 'quadruple hermeneutics', a rather heavy term. A shorter alternative is *quadri-hermeneutics*. We will use this expression here, but with restraint.[6] The main point lies in the principle of reflection and interpretation rather than a definite number of levels; a movement instead of a static, four-tier structure. Nothing precludes the possibility that this movement may generate more (or less) than the four levels we have already touched upon. One can also use other intellectual sources than those we have emphasized. We have thus chosen the term *reflexive interpretation* as a way of indicating the open play of reflection across various levels of interpretation, exemplified in this book by the empirically based, the hermeneutic, the ideologically critical and the postmodernist. Just this variant can be called quadri-hermeneutics. Reflexive interpretation is therefore the main idea and quadri-hermeneutics an example of its application, in which the four levels are in focus.

Our use of the term 'reflexivity' has much in common with how other authors use it. We also view reflexivity as being about 'ways of seeing which act back on and reflect existing ways of seeing' (Clegg and Hardy, 1996: 4). It involves 'metatheoretical reflection that is a form of inquiry in its own right', but also 'an applied practice that, while drawing on general metatheoretical categories, is involved integrally … in the overall process through which research is produced' (Morrow, 1994: 228). We differ from other authors through the emphasis on a broader, multilevel area of reflection. In our terminology, research and methodologies strongly emphasizing one particular aspect are thus reflective in a specific way, but not reflexive.

The word 'reflexive' has a double meaning, also indicating that the *levels are reflected in one another*. A dominating level, for instance, can thus contain reflections of other levels. Two or more levels may be in a state of interaction, mutually affecting one another. (More on this in a later section.) We will denote this double nature by the term 'reflexive'. 'Reflective', on the other hand, we reserve for that aspect which consists of the focused reflections upon a specific method or level of interpretation. Most other authors seem to use the term reflexive in this sense.[7] We want to contrast the focused and somewhat specialized nature of reflection with the multidimensional and interactive nature of what we refer to as reflexivity. The breadth and variety in the reflexive work are emphasized. The term 'quadri-hermeneutics' is used exceptionally, only when we want to emphasize our example of reflexive interpretation.

'Interpretation' implies that there are no self-evident, simple or unambiguous rules or procedures, and that crucial ingredients are the researcher's judgement, intuition, and ability to 'see and point something out', as well as the consideration of a more or less explicit dialogue – with the research subject, with aspects of the researcher herself that are not entrenched behind a research position, and with the reader (cf. Maranhão, 1991).

In practice research glides, more or less consciously, between two or more of these levels: the handling of the empirical material, interpretation, critical interpretation and reflections upon language and authority. This applies to much good qualitative research, except for the most technical or 'recipe book' type, albeit often intuitively and unreflectively, in the sense that there is no explicit, advanced and multidimensional reflexivity. The different elements in reflexivity – to the extent that they can be isolated – often receive less attention than tasks such as the 'gathering and processing of data'. The point of reflexive interpretation is to bring out these aspects more clearly, both during the process of research and in the (final) textual product. There are thus greater demands on the researcher to address head-on the weighty problems of empirical research, such as the relation of language to reality and the position as regards the political context of the research. Reflexive interpretation is the opposite of empiricism and theoreticism (the use of a single, abstract framework offering a privileged understanding), and even what may be referred to as 'reflective reductionism': a one-sided emphasis on a specific aspect of research, for example, its gendered, discursive or rhetorical nature. Awareness of the problems can help reduce the difficulties and possible 'damage' which may be caused by claims that the research is presenting definite truths, authoritative interpretations, or superior insights about the constraints on freedom vis-à-vis the subjects studied. Reflexive interpretation also breaks with postmodernism, as this is usually formulated. The idea of reflexive interpretation is to allow room for elements other than the problematization of text–authority relations, and to avoid the latter dominating. A totalization or privileging of the rhetorical-textual dimension is rejected, not least because the empirical material does not get an adequate chance.

Let us investigate the four aspects or levels of interpretation (Table 8.1) that, after reviewing the current state of knowledge, we regard as central, and also the relations between them. Reflexivity arises when the different elements or levels are played off against each other. It is in these relations and in the interfaces that reflexivity occurs. This approach is based upon an assumption – and implies – that no element is totalized; that is, they are all taken with a degree of seriousness, but there is no suggestion that any one of them is the bearer of the Right or Most Important Insight. In this respect the approach differs from that of Gergen and Gergen (1991), for instance, which sees in language the solid basis for science, beyond which only quicksands lie, and from versions of feminism addressing the gendered nature of social phenomena as well as knowledge, but disregarding 'non-gendered' aspects.

We can start from the data-constructing level, where researchers make observations, talk to people, create pictures of empirical phenomena, make preliminary interpretations, and so on, and where the degree of interpretation is relatively low or somewhat unclear

Table 8.1   *Levels of interpretation*

Aspect/level	Focus
Interaction with empirical material	Accounts in interviews, observations of situations and other empirical materials
Interpretation	Underlying meanings
Critical interpretation	Ideology, power, social reproduction
Reflection on text production and language use	Own text, claims to authority, selectivity of the voices represented in the text

to the researchers themselves. We could speak of raw interpretations or of interpretations close to the empirical material or low-abstract interpretations.[8] This material is then subject to further interpretation of a more or less systematic kind, guided by ideas that can be related to academic theories (scientific paradigms) or to other frames of reference (cultural ideas or taken-for-granted assumptions, implicit personal theories, and so on). Ideally, the researcher allows the empirical material to inspire, develop and reshape theoretical ideas. It is thus not so much that objective data talk to the theory (data are after all constructions and dependent on perspective); rather that the theory allows the consideration of different meanings in empirical material. At the same time it must be emphasized that the researcher's *repertoire of interpretations* limits the possibilities of making certain interpretations. The repertoire of interpretations means that certain interpretations are given priority, that others are possible but are not so readily emphasized, while yet others never even appear possible. An economist who has learnt that self-interest lies behind everything is hardly likely to notice any empirical indications of altruism. The suggestion of any such thing either fails to be noted or is simply explained away. However, the possibility of reciprocity between the researcher (the theory) and what is being studied should be emphasized in the interpreter's construction of data. Unruly, ambivalent or unexpected empirical material (interview statements, incidents observed) can affect the interpretive repertoire. At the level close to the data, reflection is a question of reinforcing such reciprocity by influencing the interpretive repertoire.

The particular interpretive options open to the researcher are crucial in this context.[9] Four aspects appear to be of central importance: creativity in the sense of an ability to see various aspects; theoretical sophistication; theoretical breadth and variation; and an ability to reflect at the metatheoretical level. The first of these is to some extent a consequence of the other three, but over and above these are individual capacity, the research milieux, the researcher's network, etc., which all play an important part.

One condition for reflection in the interplay between empirical material and interpretations is thus the breadth and variation of the interpretive repertoire. If someone has dedicated almost all of her academic career to a particular theory, then her repertoire will be restricted. Prestructured understandings dominate seeing. The capacity for reflection, if not altogether eliminated, is at least reduced. Something which strongly overlaps with such a cognitive bias is the researcher's own emotions. (These two elements help to reinforce each other.) If one has worked a lot on a particular theory, one becomes, as a rule, emotionally attached to it. The empirical material will tend by and large to confirm the theory. Alternatively, recalcitrant data can always be dismissed by referring to the need for more research.[10] If, on the other hand, the researcher has at least some knowledge of two or more theories, and has a positive attitude towards these, then things will be different. Empirical material can then generate the consideration of some fairly disparate interpretations (or maybe several interpretations). Alternatively we could say that the construction of the data is undertaken with due thought, and that the 'data' – at least for a while – remain more open. (Ultimately, however, the researcher is compelled to exclude certain possibilities and to reduce the multiplicity of meanings.) The possibility of multiple interpretation enhances reflection (and vice versa). The formula for the latter, to put it somewhat mechanistically, then becomes: rich data (multiplicity of meanings) plus breadth and variation in the interpretive repertoire. This improves the chances for an 'empirically grounded imagination' (Norén, 1990).

On creativity and extensive reading

The trick, then, is to control theories (interpretive possibilities), without letting them control you. One remedy is to become familiar with alternative theories, which should not be too similar (such as several variants of psychoanalysis), plus a portion of metatheoretical reflection. The study of creative processes has shown that innovative thinking is often triggered by the fusion of seemingly disparate phenomena (Koestler, 1964). Hence it is important to be acquainted with material from several essentially different fields. This is *one* strategy for creativity. Another, which was discussed in Chapter 3, is to attempt mental blankness (*tabula rasa*) vis-á-vis preconceptions. However, together with an inductive approach this might lead to trivial research and common-sense reformulations in different words of the actors' own statements. What is important is to try to shut out common-sense preconceptions *as well*. Combined with an abductive approach, and with a less naïve attitude vis-á-vis the role of preconceptions,[11] the strategy may lead to interesting results. There is no radical conflict between these two strategies, the widely read and the 'blank' one. There is, for instance, nothing to stop someone from being widely read, while trying to shut out prestructured understandings within a narrow sector – the one focused on empirically.[12] It also ought to be possible to combine the two strategies for creativity by alternating between them (Gummesson, 1991). Further, the main emphasis may be placed on either of these. Such a shift of emphasis, however, must not be transformed into one-sidedness in either direction, which would risk ending up in well-read scholasticism or naïve ignorance. In practice the two strategies are likely to be linked with each other, since wide reading is difficult to combine with too myopic a reading, while shutting out a narrow sector of research presupposes some other forms of frames of reference – that is, if we are not to end up with purely mundane categories, and a consequent trivialization of the research results. An important point about the reading of theories of the type we touched upon in Chapters 5–7 is that they can contribute to a shutting out, precisely by providing powerful counter-views to more conventional thought and traditional theories, thus loosening the grip on these.

Shutting out can occur either before or during the research process – in the first case by trying not to read an undue amount within the narrowly focused field, and in the second by trying to forget it. An option in the second case is, of course, criticism of the received wisdom. However, there is some risk of being negatively fixated on this. Naturally, the best thing is to undertake many-pronged readings of existing research, which would include not only criticism but also attempts at finding new and fruitful facets. The problem is that all this is very difficult, and those who succeed in pulling it off elegantly may not need to engage in empirical studies in order to make an interesting contribution to knowledge. Another tactic could be to study opposi-tional, and preferably off-beat, unpopular, subversive or forgotten theories – a tactic favoured by Mandelbrot (1977), the father of fractal theory. It must be added that being widely read does not necessarily imply superficiality. On the contrary, a relatively systematic penetration of a few theoretical areas yields far more than easy pickings in a number of disparate fields. This is because every good theory is a systematic whole, and every application of such theories necessitates an understanding of their totality – that is, if the result is to be something more than shallow eclecticism.

As regards the literature of the section the researcher wishes to investigate, different approaches are called for, depending on the character of the literature itself, which can vary in the degree to which it either encourages or discourages creativity. If the liter-ature is characterized by a multiplicity of theoretical perspectives, or includes texts that are open (or can easily be made open) to different readings, then we can devote some time to our reading without risk. But if the literature is narrow and consists largely of statistical studies or other investigations of 'how it is', all from the perspec-tive of a highly unified dominant view, then – if we are concerned about creativity – we should be cautious about spending too much of our valuable time on reading it.

It should be added that the points raised above are connected with the creative aspect of research work. But research consists of a lot of other things, including relating any par-ticular contribution to other research and the presentation of the contribution in ques-tion. To avoid reinventing the wheel, the researcher should be acquainted with what others have done. The overall research process therefore demands reading within the focused area. Nor can background reading be avoided by adopting a shutting-out strategy – in fact particularly not then: if a researcher has used a shutting-out strategy in any of the above forms, then it is extremely important, *after* having developed an idea, to acquaint oneself with, and relate to, research within the relevant field.

Shutting out in the beginning should definitely not be used as a pretext for avoid-ing reading. Regardless of the risk of rediscovering the wheel, there is also an impor-tant ethical aspect here: how is an outsider to be able to distinguish between, on the one hand, researchers who have not read earlier authors and who present ideas, pos-sibly in slightly altered form, that are reminiscent of the earlier writers' work, and, on the other, researchers who have read the earlier authors but who do not mention their contributions and who simply put new labels on old ideas (introducing someone else's ideas as their own)? The principle is that the one who originally advanced an idea should be given due credit for it – which demands an extensive investigation of any potentially relevant literature. (Another principle is that the construction of new words for old concepts is not research.)

ON REFLEXIVE INTERPRETATION

On the role of metatheory

Metatheory, which to us means primarily critical theory and postmodernism (although one can imagine other variants), does not only encourage reflection; it also, in two ways, promotes creativity at the interface between the empirical material and its interpretation.[13] The first is by asking questions about what lies behind the initial, self-evident interpretations that the researcher sometimes automatically produces. Metatheories problematize the legitimacy of dominant interpretive patterns. Critical theory, for example, claims that it is very often the power of institutionalized structures and dominant ideologies that 'launches' the socially dominating theories cherished by the establishment, and that it is with these that the empirical material spontaneously 'agrees'. Foucault was similarly suspicious, albeit from a different angle. Secondly, metatheories provide alternative points of departure for thinking about what the empirical work produces. They may inspire the negation of what the data appear to be demonstrating, and/or they may highlight ambivalences and the potential for alternative representations. Thus the researcher's (and the reader's) thoughts are activated in such a way as to make attitudes to the empirical material (the idea that the data, or one's own interpretations of them, are correct) less self-evident or naïve. The traps of empiricism and preconceptions based on common sense are thus avoided; creativity is inspired. This is illustrated in Figure 8.1.

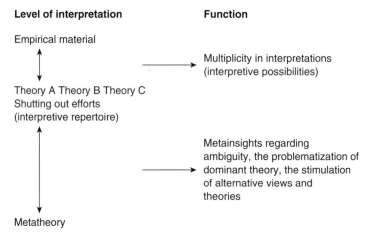

Figure 8.1 *Possible effects of an interaction between empirical material, interpretive repertoire and metatheory*

A consideration of several levels is thus of crucial importance. Reflection is promoted by the interaction between various levels, by the recognition that the different levels cannot be treated separately but must be continuously integrated. It is not just that the empirical material becomes meaningless and impenetrable without interpretation; it does not even exist without interpretation (data, as we have pointed out, are created through construction and interpretation). The interpretations require content in the form of empirical input or purely theoretical considerations. The character – in a sense, parasitical – of the metatheories (primarily postmodernism, but up to a point critical theory as well) requires someone's (someone else's) data or theory in order to have something to comment upon. It is at the interface of the various levels of interpretation that the inspiration to – and the possibility of – reflection are strongest. Herein lies also the potential for a problematization of metatheories. Obviously these cannot legitimize themselves – in the sense of being able to refer to some ultimate touchstone outside themselves. Narrow philosophy-of-science sophistication is not sufficient in relation to empirical research; rather, the value of metatheories depends on a proven ability to stimulate more reflective empirical research. Thus the metatheory does not directly determine how the empirical material is interpreted; instead, the material bears the imprint of the way the metatheory, via theories, can frame and guide the work of interpretation. The point is that while theories influence the interpretation of the empirical material, this material itself – filtered through the theoretical interpretations – provides the working material which the metatheories are indirectly plugged into.

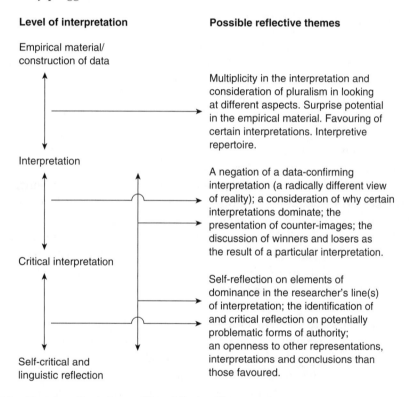

Level of interpretation

Empirical material/
construction of data

Interpretation

Critical interpretation

Self-critical and
linguistic reflection

Possible reflective themes

Multiplicity in the interpretation and consideration of pluralism in looking at different aspects. Surprise potential in the empirical material. Favouring of certain interpretations. Interpretive repertoire.

A negation of a data-confirming interpretation (a radically different view of reality); a consideration of why certain interpretations dominate; the presentation of counter-images; the discussion of winners and losers as the result of a particular interpretation.

Self-reflection on elements of dominance in the researcher's line(s) of interpretation; the identification of and critical reflection on potentially problematic forms of authority; an openness to other representations, interpretations and conclusions than those favoured.

Figure 8.2 *The interaction between different levels of interpretation*

It is thus not our intention to promote any particular level at the expense of any other. Rather, in a reflexive context all the levels should be seen as important, and should not be reduced to one another. This, together with the themes for reflection that are generated by the interaction of different interpretations, is illustrated in Figure 8.2. The vertical arrows to the left, indicating the interaction between various levels, should be self-explanatory. The long horizontal arrows refer to the outcomes of these interactions. The vertical arrow in the middle serves to illustrate one possible variant: working directly between the interpretive and self-critical/linguistic levels, thus largely bypassing the critical level. The short upper arrow means more emphasis on interpretation (with a sprinkling of critical thought), and the short lower arrow more emphasis on self-critical and linguistic reflection.

The whole point of the reflexive interpretation, in the specific version suggested here, is thus to define qualitative research as a matter of interpretation at four different levels and of reflections upon research work, by investigating, for instance, questions and themes that are highlighted and sharpened by interfaces and confrontations between levels. This means, as we have seen, that from handling the empirical material, the researcher moves distinctly through the metatheoretical field, making explicit reconnections to the empirical level.

Considering various directions and reversals

The movement can go in various directions, as – perhaps most obviously – when the provisionally interpreted material ('data') is subjected to interpretations of a hermeneutic kind, which in turn are subjected to critical scrutiny followed by rhetorical self-analysis and an attempt to tackle the problems of text and authority by opening up the text more clearly: drawing attention to the rhetorical nature of research texts, pointing out ambiguities in ways of dealing with the subject matter, indicating limitations and arbitrariness in what is being represented. But movement is also possible in the opposite direction. A relatively uninterpreted (data-bound, roughly interpreted) material can sharpen the reflection of a more philosophical, linguistic kind. For example, the empirical material may directly induce the (widely read) researcher to think in postmodernist terms, or at least indicate that the likelihood of a reasonably unproblematic representation is slim. Faced by ambiguous – varied, vague and incoherent – interview accounts, the researcher may feel, for instance, that descriptions of phenomena 'out there' are going to be difficult to make. Instead variations in accounts may be investigated, showing the fragility of a seemingly robust chunk of social reality. Or it may be that certain elements in the empirical material inspire deconstruction or some similar intensive treatment. The researcher may also encounter a rich material that he or she feels may be used in a varied way. Alvesson (1996) described an empirical case – an information meeting in a large company – which gave rise to multiple interpretations. Within the framework of a more extensive ethnographic study, the situation was documented and found to be of such interest that it was subjected to a separate exploration, which was published independent of the ethnography as a whole (except that knowledge of the background derived from this was used).

The empirical material may also stimulate the researcher to adopt rather different linguistic-philosophical positions. Certain phenomena lend themselves fairly easily to representation; in other cases the performative and constructive dimensions of language are more evident. Those who like to see theory and philosophy behaving in an orderly manner may think this sounds a bit too eclectic or even lacking in insight. Surely researchers should not swing from one position to another like this? We agree that the linguistic position of a text should not primarily resemble a weathercock. But it is possible to adopt a not altogether categorical or 'set' view of language. Tsoukas (1991), for instance, claims that a metaphorical linguistic position is appropriate for generating ideas and theories, but that this should be complemented by a more literal (mirroring) position in empirical studies and tests. It is a question here of 'deliberate inconsistency', albeit within the framework of a largely traditional view of the potential of language for transparency and reflective capacity. Departures from this view – which is characterized by the demand for conceptual precision and 'stringency' – are allowed only during the idea-generating phases.

Not infrequently texts appear to be unconsciously or unintentionally inconsistent on this point. Ironically enough, this perhaps applies mainly to researchers who themselves maintain a conscious and pronounced poststructuralist linguistic position. Poststructuralists with a social scientific interest, at any rate, sometimes find it difficult to avoid expressing themselves in a way suggesting that language can reflect external conditions. (We cited Weedon, 1987, in this context in Chapter 6.) A pronounced distancing from the 'mirroring' view of language – á la poststructuralists – easily leads to inconsistency. The theoretical position greatly limits the range of statements that are possible, and it becomes difficult to say anything about 'reality out there' – which it is all too tempting to do – without exceeding these limits. A less radically formulated view of the linguistic position, whereby the indeterminate, multiple and fluid nature of meanings is taken into account without being totalized (one-sidedly privileged), allows a certain discretion as to how language and the problem of representation can be treated more specifically in a study. Regardless of the researcher's basic philosophy, it can to some extent be constructive to consider the need for a problematizing (non-mirroring) conception of language in relation to the empirical material. Ethical considerations may come in here. Deconstruction, irony, rhetorical analysis, pointing out the notoriously indeterminate nature of statements – all this may be more appropriate in relation to texts which express the interests and ideologies of dominant actors, and may even appear tasteless in relation to socially disadvantaged groups or people who have been subject to abuse. No one, except perhaps a neo-Nazi, would – one might hope – regard the accounts of Auschwitz survivors as interesting texts for deconstruction.

In order to allow a certain latitude as regards attitudes to language, we could – as indicated above – adopt a position lying between a representative and a poststructuralism-influenced constructivist view, for instance seeing language as a 'perspectivist mirroring' or something along that line.

In other words, we mean that the consideration of the different interpretations and positions with respect to language, and the interaction between them, provides material for reflection and to counteract fixed positions, whether these be a matter of embracing seemingly definite and unambiguous empirical observations, a dominant line of interpretation, an authoritative critique, or a specific view of language and representation. The whole idea is to avoid getting stuck in a certain type of logic, be it empirical, hermeneutic, critical-theoretical or linguistic (gendered, classed, emphasizing the integral nature of power/knowledge, and so on), without making sure that space and energy remain for other positions. This sort of interaction between different kinds of epistemological reflective position does not of course guarantee advanced reflexivity – which is not primarily a question of the following procedures – but it does mean that the conditions for such reflection are improved.

Notes

1. In this connection, it is interesting to compare Bushman and Baumeister's (1998) experimental study on psychological factors behind violent behaviour. The author made a distinction between narcissism and having a high self-esteem. High self-esteem entails thinking well of oneself; narcissism involves passionately wanting to think well of oneself. Bushman and Baumeister found that while self-esteem is largely unrelated to violent behaviour, narcissism is highly related to violent behaviour.

2. The question is then what to do with the 'results', that is, the linguistic correlations or variations found. Reflexive research, as we see it, would consider both the possibility that the correlations/variations say something about the psychology of the subject of study ('beyond the purely linguistic'), and the possibility that it is a question of something else. An example of the latter could be that the statements are more about a cultural convention which is based upon the assumption that 'jealousy' and 'self-esteem' are linked in a particular way. (In a culture where 'jealousy' and 'low self-esteem' both have negative connotations, they might be connected in people's perceptions and/or statements.) Another possibility is that the statements are seen as the expression of attempts to produce particular effects: for example, 'I am jealous, but this depends on my low self-esteem', as constituting a creation of a particular self-image (which may partly justify certain actions, for instance control over one's spouse), or the evoking of a certain response, such as sympathy and support. It is such openness to multiple meanings that is important in reflexive research. It would also be reasonable here to investigate the statements in terms of gender and in relation to different types of social differentiation. There could be differences as regards the meaning of – and/or accounts of – jealousy, depending on class, society, ethnic group and so on – see Jagger's (1989) ideas concerning emotions, discussed in Chapter 7 above. One might ask oneself whether Gergen and Gergen's definition and their argument (above) may express a white American middle-class view of jealousy, rather than anything of a more general nature. Finally, there is also reason to note the expressions of power connected with the psychiatric and psychological normalizations to be found in the institutionalized discourses on jealousy – which are probably reflected in ('normal') people's statements about this phenomenon. (We could envisage statements such as 'People who are never jealous are out of touch with their emotions, and are not able to commit themselves', or 'Those who are very jealous are paranoid'. Too little or too much jealousy may be seen in terms of a failure to live up to the normalizations of psychology.) The indication of a multiplicity of different possible interpretations can produce rich and varied – and not only uncertain or unclear – 'results'.

3. In this section we will not distinguish between reflection and reflexivity, but see them as synonymous. In the next section, we will give reflexivity a specific meaning, which means that we use this term in a slightly different way than most other researchers.

4. All research is in some sense reflective. Often this element is limited and tied to a particular logic or theme, be it a formal method, gender relations, language or power that the researcher is trying to scrutinize. This can lead to situations of deadlock, which is contrary to the whole idea of reflexivity as we see it.

5. Note that throughout we are discussing consistency and variation here in connection with reflection. As to theoretical frames of reference and interpretations in connection with the empirical material, a certain coherence in terms of maintaining a theoretical line is necessary. To mix different kinds of argument, so-called 'mixed discourses' (Giorgi, cited in Sandberg, 1994), is hardly what we are advocating. Mixing is not the same thing as confrontation or carefully working with a multitude of discourses stimulating reflection. The latter presupposes that different themes have distinct identities and that the researcher is capable of changing levels and capable of variations in the thought mode.

6. The plausibility of subsuming postmodernism in an overall hermeneutic concept can be questioned. However, quadri-hermeneutics does not favour hermeneutics in any conventional sense. Nor are the aspects of postmodernism which we take into account the most radical, directly opposed to hermeneutics, but a more moderate variant in which an interest in multiple voices, fragmentation, restraint in the use of theoretical systems, or a reflective stance vis-á-vis the author's authority and the central meaning of the text, are not incompatible with interpretive empirical research.

7. Potter (1997: 146), like many authors, suggests that 'reflexivity encourages us to consider the way a text such as this is a version, selectively working up coherence and incoherence, telling historical stories, presenting and, indeed, constituting an objective, out-there reality'. For us, this somewhat narrow text focus is an example of reflection, but not reflexivity.

8. The ambition of the researchers is typically to restrain interpretations, to produce empirical material that is 'as close as possible' to the reality studied and that does not limit further interpretations.

9. As a rule, though, rich empirical material is less important than theoretical ideas, when it comes to the breadth and variation in the interpretations that can be made. In psychoanalysis, where the analyst has access to an abundance of information about the subject of the analysis after hundreds of hours of interaction, the empirical material is almost invariably perceived as suited to analysis in psychoanalytic terms. However, the character of the data is rather one-sided. What happens on the psychoanalyst's couch is quite different from the analysand's life in general. As a result of the particular way of working, the empirical material – despite its abundant character – is to some extent adapted to the theory. The most important point, though, is that the theory, which as a rule controls the rigorously socialized psychoanalyst, consistently makes it possible for everything to be interpreted according to the theoretical framework.

10. Alongside these individual factors, the social and political aspects of the research must also be observed. The individual researcher is part of a research community, and as such is often subject to conformist pressure. Cognitive and emotional fixations are often easier to understand in terms of collective as opposed to individual phenomena. The need for social identity and belonging, together with the threat of sanctions, make it difficult for anyone to break away on their own from the theories they are steeped in. A degree of conformism is often a precondition for a successful research career. The freethinkers who question the premises of a particular school are seldom appreciated. At the same time the differences in terms of openness and multiplicity in various research fields should be noted. In parts of the social sciences, no single paradigm predominates, something which can provide degrees of freedom and scope for the appreciation of new thinking.

11. Freeing oneself from preconceptions is, of course, a pious hope rather than an achievable goal. In the final analysis, a radical freeing (of the researcher) from preconceptions and cognitive conditioning entails the death of the ego (Krishnamurti, 1954), and even if Eastern philosophy sets great store by such a state, it seems a rather excessive demand to impose upon the qualitative researcher.

12. One problem here is that it is not altogether easy to decide upon the section that should be targeted for shutting-out efforts. To put it somewhat naïvely, perhaps a particular

object of study is seen as neutral in terms of gender, class or culture, while wider reading in the theories of gender, class or intercultural relations might have changed this attitude, motivating (further) attempts at reducing certain problematic preunderstandings in these dimensions, and instead cultivating a preunderstanding which would imply more openness and less prejudice in relation to them.

13. What constitutes – or rather, what functions as – a metatheory, is not something that can be established once and for all, as there is a relational element to consider. A metatheory is characterized by a significant distance from data, and functions primarily in relation to such theories as are used more directly in interpretation. In an empirical investigation of gender relations, for instance, some version of feminism would perhaps best be understood as a theory. But if something else is being studied which does not directly focus on the gender dimension, then gender theory can be used as a source of reflection upon the study: for example, is there a gender bias in the questions, the rea-soning, the focus, the language, or are certain problems being ignored? In gender research other theories are needed, more fundamental in the context, in order to promote reflection on the project in question (for instance, possible special interests associated with an emphasis on gender, the tendency to focus excessively on the gender dimension ['gender-reductionism'], ethnocentricity, problems of authority and language). A particular theory can only to a limited extent function as both a theory and a metatheory.

9

APPLICATIONS OF REFLEXIVE METHODOLOGY: STRATEGIES, CRITERIA, VARIETIES

In this chapter we will move further in terms of using our framework and ideas in research. We will indicate some methodological strategies that facilitate research in a spirit of reflexive interpretation. A rather long section provides two illustrations. In another section we discuss the criteria for good research. We then discuss the criteria for qualitative research, and in a following section will look at the importance of the way research is conceptualized, that is, which metaphor or metaphors are used for this activity. Some of the predominant metaphors used in qualitative research are noted; in particular, we consider some which avoid 'dataism'. Here we also touch upon ways of conceptualizing the role of the researcher. Our intention is to provide some suggestions on how to grasp the rather complex ideas and requirements associated with interpretation at several levels, which in our view is involved in a non-reductionist, high-reflective social science.

Methodological strategies in reflexive interpretation

In the previous section we gave in principle the same weight to various elements. In practice, however, it is rarely possible to conform to this model. One reason is that research work easily becomes unduly exacting. Another is that different researchers have different preferences, and that – depending on the problem and purpose of the research as well as what emerges during the process process – different projects point in different directions as regards the relative importance of the elements. We can conceive of different variants of reflexive interpretation, adapted according to where the emphasis lies. The point is that all four elements of interpretation should be present in the quadri-hermeneutic process – if we stick to this version of reflexivity – without any one of them predominating. A minus in one area or level of interpretations and reflection may be partly cancelled out by a plus in another. As before, we are describing envisaged ideal cases, rather than attempting to throw light on how research work is actually conducted.

In the empirically oriented study the primary consideration is to acquire good knowledge about a phenomenon through work with the production and cautious interpretation of empirical material. A *data-driven* study of this (reflexive) kind differs from data-centred approaches described in Chapter 3 above in that 'data' are regarded not as 'raw' but as a construction of the empirical conditions, imbued with consistent interpretive work. The attitude towards the empirical material thus becomes somewhat freer and demands are made for conscious interpretations. The demand for rigour in procedure is relaxed, and that for reflection in relationship to the interpreted nature of all empirical material is increased. Elements of political-ideological critique and self-reflection are also included, as well as the explicit handling of the problem of authority and representation.

In *insight-driven* research the emphasis is on the hermeneutic process. Insight into something implying a more profound meaning than that immediately given or conventionally understood, is the very lodestar in this research process. The work of interpretation is (more) central here, and the empirical material – texts in various forms – is the subject of attempts to assess meanings and develop revealing insights. The critical and postmodernist element acquire a weight similar to that in data-driven reflexive interpretation. In practice this may mean, for instance, that at the beginning and end of a study the researcher goes through all the levels, but during the main part of the process he or she keeps to the empirical and insightful interpretive levels.

Critical *emancipation-driven* research typically gives less weight to the empirical material in the form of constructed data. The wider context of which the relevant empirical material is a part cannot be mapped out in a concrete empirical study, which means that other elements than the researcher's own empirical material must be central here – for example, knowledge about society contingent upon societal membership, and reflective critical observations and impressions of social phenomena that one encounters or is actively participating in. As we have pointed out, emancipatory research demands much thought, and data-oriented work (interviews, observations) constitutes a relatively small part of the total story being produced. A combination of extensive empirical work and advanced critical interpretation would certainly be desirable, but time and resource factors tend to limit the former. Nevertheless, it is still important.

Postmodernist ethnographies contain more empirical material than emancipation-driven research, as there is a great interest in allowing, in a non-authoritarian manner, the voices of the subjects studied to be heard.[1] Alluding to the multiplicity of voices, we could speak of a *polyphony-driven* mode of research here. Interest in these multiple voices means that the degree of theoretical sophistication and the scope for the researcher's more advanced interpretations, are reduced – grand narratives and researcher authority suppress polyphony. But even a polyphonic study calls for a good deal of interpretive work, if the different voices are not to merge into a unison choir or a continuous uniform buzz. Critical theory stimulates reflection which encourages multiplicity; this in turn gives the marginalized quieter voices a greater chance of being heard, as well as enhancing the research project's political relevance over a broader field.

To some extent independently of the relative importance of the different elements in the research process, we could envisage different variants of the movement between the types of interpretation. One variant could be that once or twice, for example at the beginning and end of a project, the research could circle around outside and to some extent away from its 'core area', emphasizing interpretations and reflections other than those which principally characterize the project. Another could be that the researcher moves constantly between different elements, but devotes most of her or his time to the element(s) that dominate the project. Data-driven reflexive interpretation would thus include either infrequent, but important, ingredients of critical interpretation and linguistic reflection, or frequent but then more limited such ingredients. In the first case the research process is clearly divided into sequences, while in the second the mode of work is characterized by repeated moves between the various elements. The latter may call for more experience and ability; it requires the researcher to be able to switch easily between handling data and reflecting upon how this is done on the one hand, and alternative interpretive possibilities at different levels on the other.

Illustrations of a reflexive interpretation

We will now illustrate our ideas on reflexive interpretation on the basis of two concrete empirical examples. The first is based on very limited material, targeted for intensive interpretations. We use only one interview excerpt, but it is a rather detailed one, so that readers can evaluate our material for themselves. We will see how this text can be interpreted and reinterpreted, and how it is possible to reflect upon these interpretations. The second example is different, it summarizes a large scale research project addressing broad changes in a set of organizations. Here reflexive elements in the entire project are addressed on a more macro level.

Empirical example one: an advertising guru talks

In the following paragraphs the founder of an advertising agency talks about why he started the business, and what happened when he 'defected' from his former employer (N) in order to do so. We reproduce his own words (with only minimal editing) as he describes the sequence of events. The excerpt and parts of the following interpretation are taken from an ethnographic study of advertising and advertising agencies (Alvesson and Köping, 1993).

> There are many different reasons for starting a business of one's own. For a certain type of char-
> acter it is something you dream of. You want to see if the ideas, the thoughts and philosophies
> that you cherish within yourself can bear fruit. When is the right time to start? That may be diffi-
> cult to tell. This sort of situation may come up very early in your career. On the other hand you
> may lack the energy, the maturity or the opportunity to do anything about it. The reason I set up
> this agency was a feeling I had that I wanted to find out if I could cope on my own. The timing
> was incidental. The N business played into our hands by mismanaging their business so thoroughly.
> The more that came out about their affairs and the more fuss there was in the press, the more
> convinced I became that I wanted out. What was I to do? I enjoyed working with a lot of the
> people there. I also felt a certain responsibility for them, as I was still a departmental manager at
> N. Then I suddenly thought it would be much better to start my own business instead of just getting
> out (I knew I could make it on my own). So I spoke to two people, two key players who'd been

with me in the organization. I asked them whether they were interested in setting up a company. They were. (One was a copywriter, the other a project manager.) These two key actors then went round asking other people if they wanted to join us, and in the end seven more came in. Why not the rest as well? That's a good question, and it was a difficult decision to make. Should one take everybody, or only those one likes working with? I felt it was an enormous responsibility I was taking on. To employ ten people all at once is a great economic burden – somebody has to guarantee wages and costs. For this reason I felt I could only take the ones I really believed in. I think I was pretty tough, starting off with ten.

In this country there is something called 'breach of trust' and it is a legal offence. It is very important not to deceive one's employer when setting up a company like this. You might think I was doing so, as I had these ideas about starting my own business and I'd asked several colleagues to join me already. I hadn't asked any clients, though, and that's where to draw the line. I've been through all this before. I've defected before and been sued, but it's never come to anything. It is extremely difficult to get a conviction unless the defendant has actually embezzled money. I suppose you could talk about embezzling since the other party loses potential income, but in this business you never know from one day to the next whether a client is still with you!

A meeting was being planned for N in Amsterdam with Media Marketing and other part-owners in the business. It was to be what's known as a 'kick-off', and I felt this was the perfect moment to tender my resignation. I accosted my boss in the corridor just before the meeting and told him I was resigning: I was resigning and setting up my own agency; ten people would be going with me and I was leaving for home that night. Everyone was in Amsterdam and I could simply go home. They had no chance to start trying to persuade my allies to stay on and to force me out into the cold. You learn a few tricks over the years and I've been on the other end of it myself. It was quite deliberate on my part to grab the chance. If we hadn't gone to Amsterdam, I'd have done the same thing in Sweden of course. But events played into my hands and I had to act. It all sounds very ruthless, but that's how you have to play it in this game. You can't keep your hands absolutely clean every time. Even though I don't think, morally, that I'd all that much to be ashamed of. I think they'd a lot more to be ashamed of, letting the business run down as they had done. The company is not in Sweden any more. Things went downhill at tremendous speed. They tried to talk me into staying on, and I spent the night in Amsterdam. But they realized there was no point – I'd made my mind up. I'd also called Sweden to say that someone would be turning up at the agency to try to persuade you all to stay on. (Alvesson and Köping, 1993: 102–104)

Interpretations

This story has many facets. Interpreters of a discursive bent such as Potter and Wetherell (1987) could certainly fill innumerable pages with variously interesting comments and interpretations. Discourse analysis has inspired our interpretations, but we do not altogether privilege the discursive approach, contenting ourselves rather with two particularly interesting themes: motive and morality.

Primary interpretations

Before deciding what lines of approach can be adopted in interpreting the interview, various points must of course be considered. Some of these are of a technical nature – problems connected with misunderstandings, ambiguities, obscurities, undue influence on the part of the interviewer, and so on. In this case the two interviewers felt that the interview had been conducted satisfactorily. It was preceded by a few weeks of participant observation, which paved the way for a good understanding and ensured that contact (deep-level access) was easier to establish. Moreover, the interview subject was articulate and his speech well structured; his narrative needed little or no editing, either in producing a written document or on subsequent publication.

Nevertheless certain interpretations did precede the transcribing of the above material. Thus it is not a question of 'pure' data, categorized or interpreted only at a later stage. The fact that interpretation precedes data in all research is something we have been systematically maintaining throughout this book. One can talk about primary (or rough) interpretations, which are necessary if we are to avoid a mish-mash of unsorted sensory impressions. Primary interpretations are made before and during the interaction that such an interview entails: the researcher 'interprets' what and who can be asked, what has been said previously during the interview and what is being said now, what is interesting, and what it is possible to get an answer to. During the interview what is interesting and meaningful is also interpreted, what constitutes a comprehensible answer, whether the interview subject understands why the researcher wants his or her account, and so on. The tape also has to be interpreted so that the interview can be transcribed.[2]

The interview subject also makes interpretations. The interview is an expression of the interpretive work of the subject, both in relation to relevant aspects of life and in connection with the interview situation. What the subject says depends upon various ideas about the interviewer and the interview context at more or less unconscious levels. The acknowledgement that any empirical material is a construction, and consideration of the interpretive character of all observations, interview statements, questionnaire answers and the like are important elements in reflective research.

It may be difficult to separate preliminary interpretations from better-reasoned, secondary-level interpretations, in which the researcher does not construct but (further) interprets and explores 'data' in depth. Here we could speak of second-level hermeneutics. We are talking about interpretations of preliminary interpretations, such as the interpretation of the above excerpt. This kind of interpretation is generally explicit, conscious; the researcher typically realizes that other interpretations are possible. In the current case it is not too difficult to separate the levels of interpretation from one another. The preliminary interpretation has produced the above narrative. The next step is to take a closer look at it. In those (normal) cases in which it is necessary to edit the interview records – to render them meaningful or reduce them to a manageable length – or when complex actions or events are described, the two levels become increasingly intermixed.[3] An interpretation of what is happening during a meeting generally necessitates a more immediate interpretive effort than is needed to transcribe a taped interview. A merging of the two levels also occurs if the empirical material is very extensive and it becomes necessary to select from it before making a more meticulous interpretation. As we have noted, however, such complexities are not particularly relevant in our case, and we will therefore proceed to secondary interpretations.

Secondary interpretations

Important considerations in seeking to understand the above interview relate to the assessment of the nature of the statements made. Conventionally these are seen as mirroring (albeit incomplete and ambiguous) actual, that is historically correct, conditions (the conditions obtaining when the agency was founded) and/or the interview subject's (current) conceptions, ideas, values, motives. As the theme of the interview partly concerns the thoughts and motives of the subject at the time the agency was created, it is difficult to keep these two variants apart. However, we could claim that the 'factual' conditions include the subject's thoughts and motives at the time of the creation of the agency. The subject's perceptual universe thus refers to (present) perceptions of (earlier) 'factual' thoughts and motives.

There is thus a third possible focus, alongside the 'objective' and 'subjective' (perceptual) ones mentioned above, namely a discursive one (see Mills, 1940). It is interesting, in our view at least, to note how the founder expresses his motives. We do not therefore concern ourselves directly with the 'true' motives (for example, through empathy, like Collingwood in Chapter 4; hermeneutic theme 2), but with the use of words (hermeneutic themes 5–8). One argument in favour of this, as we have noted in Chapters 6 and 7, is also that statements that seem to spring from a uniform, holistic and rational subject should be treated with a certain caution. The manner in which people present themselves and their motives is greatly influenced by what is normative in terms of understandability and acceptability (Silverman, 1985, 2006). Social conventions therefore colour statements (Alvesson, 2003; Harré, 1989; Slugoski and Ginsburg, 1989). A second and more important reason for our focus is that a discussion of motives (the vocabulary of motives, as Mills called it) can say a great deal about what is typical of the whole sector or occupational group in question. (Of course, we cannot say too much on the basis of a single interview. But one interview, carefully interpreted, can give a great deal if it is combined with other qualified material. Here we will limit ourselves to an interpretation of the interview.) The way in which people show their understanding of the driving-forces and social conventions as regards modes of expression and legitimate motives, thus provides us with interesting insights into the values and ideals of advertising. It should be emphasized that we do not maintain that real or expressed motives always differ, or that they always agree. Even if we emphasize that the social context in which the motives are recounted – for example, the macrocontext of advertising and the microcontext of an interview with a researcher – naturally influences the choice of motive given, we do not therefore mean that 'actual' motives are system-atically corrected or distorted. We do not in fact delve into possible 'actual motives' at all. The method used is more that of a *horizontal fusion between researcher and text* (hermeneutic theme 7). In other words, with our preunderstanding (of advertising and the uncertainty of statements according to discourse analysis and also post-structuralism), we enter the process and alternate between distance and familiarity in relation to it.

At the beginning of the long quotation above, it is claimed that '[f]or a certain type of character it is something you dream of. You want to see if the ideas, the thoughts and philosophies that you cherish within yourself can bear fruit'. Here it is implied that there is a distinct and special type of person to which the founder implicitly belongs, which is special, which differs from others, and whose thoughts, emotions and philosophies are particularly worthy of being expressed and put to the test. The statement also implies that there is an inner urge in these individuals to start up on their own – the decisive factor behind launching one's own agency. The driving-force is therefore highly subjective, that is, linked to the person in question (and not to external influential factors such as economic conditions, God or the duty to support a wife and children). Alternative formulations of motive, such as the desire to earn money, to maximize self-determination and power, to give one's name to a company, to be able to handle difficult situations and so on, are not used. External restrictions and motivations do not stand out in the account. The situation in the parent company is reduced to a randomly determined 'right moment'. One might have expected the motives to be formulated so that external conditions could be described as an important background to the new start-up. But this was not the case, which was presumably no coincidence. It can also be noted that central to the founder's account was his setting up on his own. The other aspect, his 'defection', is only mentioned explicitly once in this whole long account. It is the inner impulse, the strong-willed actor, who is the subject of the description. To 'set up on your own' fits the image better than 'defecting', which is a rather more defensive measure.

Although the expression 'setting up on my own' appears frequently, the individual's right of ownership is not strongly emphasized. The founder's account does not refer to an ideology of small business, built on private ownership, independence and hard work. Rather than middle-class ideals, a kind of creator ideology is evoked. Commercial interest or some product idea are not mentioned, but rather the inner qualities of the founder (and his peers). The fundamental idea is to see if 'the ideas, the thoughts and philosophies that you cherish within yourself can bear fruit'. Rather than emphasizing a market or product orientation, a 'subjectivity orientation' is invoked as the grounds for setting up on one's own. The emotional dimension is stressed. For instance, the interview subject says 'The reason I set up this agency was a feeling I had that I wanted to find out if I could cope on my own'. This mode of expression is probably typical, precisely for the advertising industry. Such motives are socially acceptable and respectable. (More research would of course be needed before saying anything more definite.)

We would also briefly like to discuss the interview in terms of a story of morals – which might give a clue to moral talk in this industry. Here we would like to note that the hero in the story (the founder), albeit basically good, runs the risk of sounding morally slightly dubious. He talks about the clever tricks he uses to pre-empt countermoves on the part of his employer. Extenuating circumstances are emphasized: the protagonist has been on the receiving end of 'tricks' himself, and his employer 'had a lot more to be ashamed of'. Ethical problems, it is implied, are always cropping up in this line of business. The interview subject says that he subscribes to the norms of the business. He does not transgress these norms by contacting customers before setting up on his own. In the interview he states that he took on an 'enormous responsibility' and that it was 'pretty tough' starting off with ten people from his former workplace. (One might claim that the defection of the interview subject together with ten other – presumably skilled – workers was morally dubious, as in all probability it was a powerful contributing factor to the decline in the parent company. In the interview, however, this decline is mentioned as a reason why the subject's behaviour was morally correct.)

Altogether, this account leaves us with the impression of an industry where people are characterized by their strong inner, deeply subjective impulses (superordinate to purely instrumental considerations), and which, as regards moral issues and the rules of the game, is also somewhat jaded (Alvesson and Köping, 1993: Chapter 9). In the study there was a swing back and forth between the part (the interview) and the whole (the advertising industry). Another aspect was the alternation between preconception (about motivational inconsistencies within and between interview subjects) and conception (a deepening of the preconception in the form of variation analysis and inconsistency analysis).

Thus far we have a hermeneutic interpretation (theme 7), focusing on the vocabulary of ethics and motives. Now let us briefly bring in the two remaining levels. Elements of these – incidentally it is seldom possible to keep them clearly separate – may be traced in the above interpretation; but below we elaborate and delve further into them. We start with an interpretation inspired by postmodernism, although we could equally well have taken the critical-theoretical approach first.

Interpretations of authority and representation

The subject's account can be seen as a variation on the theme of the 'business-minded artist'. It seems important to people in advertising, particularly in leading positions, to uphold this identity. The interpretation can be given a psychological or a marketing-oriented slant. In the first case it is a question of strengthening one's professional identity by describing oneself in this manner. The identity is constituted by the action of narrating (Czarniawska-Joerges, 1994; Dunne, 1996; Giddens, 1991). In the marketing case it is a question of selling to those around one a certain orientation and a certain competence, which in the case of advertising is neither unambiguous nor clear, as we shall see. The interview could be seen as a bit of 'sales talk', in which the subject demonstrates his competence (Alvesson, 1994). He is a 'certain type of character', who wants to see if 'the ideas, thoughts and philosophies that you cherish within yourself can bear fruit'; he demonstrates the entrepreneurial spirit, smartness and some ruthlessness combined with a certain sense of responsibility. Perhaps he is saying that he is the right man for the industry, using the researchers as the medium for his message.

In order to reveal the pluralism in the subject's statements, we could point out the different sorts of identity invoked in the narrative. One such identity is that of the emotionally driven advertising person who wants to test himself and what he (less commonly, she) has within himself. Another identity is that of the instrumentally rational man, who effectively blocks his employer from taking counter-measures. We can thus discern here the voices of the romantic and of the cunning businessman. This multiplicity of voices in the quotation also includes a story about responsibility. The subject takes on the heavy responsibility of providing for ten people.

And there is another story about disloyalty and treachery vis-á-vis the former employer and former colleagues, whose future job security has been damaged due to the subject's defection. The point is that even if we take all these statements as an expression of the interviewee's subjectivity, as a temporary expression of how the individual is located in a net of subject positions produced by dominating discourses, it has to be said that this subjectivity is neither unambiguous nor consistent; rather, it means that several quite different discourses are constituting varied forms of subjectivity. These multiple voices in the text correspond well to post-structuralism's view of subjectivity, which can be compared with the subject's view that we humans have something 'inside ourselves' – alluding to the conventional Western view of the individual as a uniform subject, a view which is partly contradicted by the multiplicity of identities.

Another possibility would be to regard the statements as the reflection of a relatively coherent subjectivity – the expressions of ambition, values, motives and intentions seem to converge rather than indicate fragmentation. The researcher who decides not to respect in full the subject's claim to be believed, may be setting himself up as in some way *above* the subject. If statements are seen as the expression of cultural conventions, for instance the 'vocabulary of motives', then the subject's own wish that the descriptions be seen as genuine, as honest expressions of his or her own self-knowledge and ability to think and convey experiences, is being disregarded.

Against this it may be argued that the above interpretations do not give the researcher the kind of priority in interpretation attaching to other theories which consistently disregard the subject's self-understanding, and focus instead upon some superior theory (e.g. psychoanalysis or Marxism or something else). However, the interpretations advanced here do express a certain degree of authority on the part of the researcher vis-á-vis the interview subject. Discourses on motives and ethics are emphasized, while the individual's claim to be taken seriously is not fully accepted. (It is not wholly denied, but is met with some scepticism.) Certain ideas regarding subjectivity associated with discourse analysis and postmodernism endow the researcher with some advantage as regards being 'better' able to understand the sort of phenomena that the quotation expresses. The interpretation in question may thus be seen in terms of power, including the asymmetry of knowledge claims of researchers and 'natives'. The researcher presents him or herself as 'smarter' than the naïve object of the research. It should perhaps be added that, compared with most qualitative empirical material, the example just given (in which the statements lend themselves well to quotation in full, and have been so quoted in the published study of which they are a part) is relatively unproblematic in relation to the problem of representation and authority. One reason for this, we contend, is that the medium is words (which can relatively easily be put in a text) and not non-linguistic action (which is difficult to reproduce in the same way, since words and behaviour represent different kinds of media); another is that it consists of an account which requires only marginal editing before being reproduced; and a third is that the subject is allowed to speak at some length, both in the interview context and in the published text. Otherwise, in most qualitative studies, the researcher 'processes' the text far more extensively; the subject is steered during the interview, statements are edited (in order to be made comprehensible), the researcher has to interpret what the subject means and only selected parts of a previously edited interview are included (possibly in coded, that is, standardized, form). This is not meant as a criticism, since such modifications are often necessary in order to create a reasonably accessible and interesting text. In such cases there will be more problems to tackle in connection with authority and representation.

Critical interpretation

As previously indicated, critical interpretation may well challenge the perceptions and values of the individuals partaking in a given study. Here we can build on the idea mentioned above, that the interview subject expresses a market-oriented attitude in the story. It is presumably common that subjects express similar views of themselves. Interviews are about 'moral story-telling', as Silverman (1985) puts it. Interviewees often frame their accounts in a politically conscious manner, especially where members of social elites are concerned, but also other people with a stake in what is being treated. (As we have seen in Chapter 4, this is also fundamental to a historiographic source criticism of bias.) In interviews with senior managers, the picture that emerges of the subjects themselves and of their activities tends to have a positive charge: rationality, creativity, dependability, goal orientation, a willingness to change, a client and market orientation, a desire for the well-being of organization members – all these are claimed for the orientations of the interviewees personally, as well as for the companies and other organizations they represent. (There are, of course, exceptions: see, for example, Jackall, 1988; Watson, 1994.)

In a critical perspective we could ask a few questions about who exactly is allowed to speak when organizations are being studied, for instance. Corporate executives and other members of the elite are often greatly over-represented. In our present case, a top person has been interviewed. This may of course be sensible, but it is important to note it and to emphasize that the individual concerned has no better claim to the 'truth' than anyone else. The market orientation that can be discerned in the interview should not be seen as a 'natural' phenomenon, nor simply as a local one. It is not a 'given' that people should seize any opportunity to advertise their personal capabilities. But in a very commercialized society, where marketing relations are becoming increasingly important and where it is important to be good at 'managing impressions' and regulating images of oneself, one's profession and one's company, contemporary persons have internalized a market-oriented attitude (see, for example, Fromm, 1955; Klein, 2000; Lasch, 1978; Sennett, 1977). One has to be able to 'sell oneself' constantly. And particularly in the advertising industry, where it can be difficult for advertising executives and agencies to prove their competence, as the evaluation of performance is often arbitrary, it is important for practitioners to give the impression of being able to make some sort of unique and advanced contribution. The founder's narrative thus belongs to a particular cultural and economic ambience, and the statements must be understood in relation to this.

Several different contexts could be noted here. In a critical-theoretical perspective it is, for example, important to remember that the narrative is about advertising. Its critics claim, among other things, that advertising makes people materialistic, turning their attention to consumption as a route to happiness; that it glorifies youth, concentrates on outward appearance, encourages sexual stereotypes, makes people feel dissatisfied with themselves, vulgarizes language, encourages the waste of resources and adds to environmental degradation (Lasch, 1979; Leiss, 1983; Pollay, 1986). To thoroughly scrutinize the less obvious consequences of a particular societal institution – rather than accept it at face value and reproduce it in research as something natural and given – is an important ingredient in a critical interpretation. In the interview relatively 'low' ethical standards regarding 'internal' relationships in the business are signalled: smartness and tricks seem to be common. Our interviewee is, according to himself, morally far from clean, but the former employer is much worse and the interviewee has been the victim of tricks before. A certain correspondence between the morally dubious, 'smartness' nature of advertising products and the internal operations of the industry may thus be indicated. An ideology of entrepreneurialism seems to lurk here, legitimizing unethical behaviour.

Switching the position (back) to a postmodernist one could encourage a re-interpretation of these remarks as an expression of critical theory's inclination to impose a negative meaning to something, of 'lining up' the suspects and then convicting them with little doubt of CT's authority.

As discussed in Chapter 5, researchers should reflect upon the role of their work in relation to the reproduction or questioning of social institutions and ideologies. They must not hide behind the myth about the neutrality of research (nor about the superiority of emancipatory or deconstructionist ambitions) in relation to its subject matter. It is important to raise the perspective and not be too limited by observed behaviours or interview accounts, but to consider these instead in terms of the broader context.

These illustrations can suffice to show how critical interpretation and discussion – not necessarily narrowly directed at the reported empirical material, but still motivated by its presence – can be brought into the picture. After this, it might have been appropriate to return to the postmodernist level of interpretation and to comment upon the way critical theory stimulates reflection relative to the problem of representation and authority. We might also have returned to the empirical (preliminarily interpreting, data-constructing) and interpretive levels, modifying these according to what the postmodernist and critical interpretive levels have provided in terms of new insights. For reasons of space, however, we will not embark upon such routes here.

Empirical illustration two: changes in public sector organizations

Our second example, representing another extreme of how to use reflexive ideas, is a study of organizational changes in Swedish local and regional government. The investigation was set up as a series of case studies, chosen with respect to the phase of change (beginning, middle, or end) and type of change ('hard', i.e. structure or technology, or 'soft' changes, i.e. processes or people). This was based on pre-conceptions from the theory on the subject matter, discussions within the research project and its group of reference, and extensive literature studies. Three dimensions were assumed to be crucial to the study – problems, power and symbols. What problems lay behind the organizational changes and how were they solved? What power relations could be traced, and how did they change? What symbols characterized the organizational changes during their various phases?

The extensive empirical material stemmed from semi-structured interviews, written documents such as protocols, directives, information brochures and the like, and secondary literature from the relevant field. As Ricoeur (2006) has pointed out, it is important to distinguish between facts and events. The relation between these two is always and unavoidably problematic, since facts in contrast to events are constructed by the researcher. The event 'out there' is something we try to get a – however provisory and uncertain – grip on by constructing facts. (Event and fact thus have a different ontological status.) The process of interpretation begins with testimonies of different kinds, constituting the original material.

The testimonies are transcribed in different ways into documents, during which process some amount of information is always excluded or added. From a documentary-critical perspective, it is decisive to steer clear from both the naïvely credulous acceptance of whatever is in the documents and the extreme scepticism that rejects almost everything. What the informants uttered, and what could be obtained through secondary literature, was therefore not taken at face value but was regarded with a documentary-critical distance. The criticism of bias often proved most important. For example, managers often embellish their organizations' performance and culture, and this was so in the present cases too. Therefore it became necessary to take in complementary points of view. The criticism of bias was of course even more important for the information material received, which in many cases was more or less similar to advertising texts. The source value of the interviews was also often diminished because of the time that had passed since the organizational change had started. Dependence between sources was recognized both when interviewees used the same words for the same events and when linguistic expressions and fragments from organization and management literature came up (Peters and Waterman's management bestseller *In Search of Excellence* echoed for instance in several interviews).

Facts were constructed from an – as always – unreliable body of material by weighing the documents and their source values against one another in the light of the aspects mentioned, for the various 'events'. The empirical material was thus not something that was collected, but something that was constructed from facts through a documentary-critical process (hermeneutic theme 1 in Chapter 4 of this book). This of course means that facts are always provisory, until further notice; never final, 'hard' or even 'good', but fragile creations, yet those we can best achieve for the present moment, in the way just described.

For example, the following story was told. During a nationwide conference where representatives from other municipalities and organizations also took part, the manager of one local government had revealed in a speech that a certain change in his organization was going to be made shortly. 'And we were not told in advance. We heard of it only when he made his speech at the congress! We sat there as if struck by a lightning bolt!'

However, more than one single, possibly biased, source of information is generally needed for a source-critical re-construction of 'facts'. When this piece of information was checked with other informants, only a few of them could confirm the story while most either denied that the event had taken place or could not recall it. In another case study, employees from a different municipality told the same story in only slightly different words, with the event in the story taking place at the same occasion but with *their* top manager making the gaffe in question. Hence there was some basis for suspecting a dependence between the sources – and that what we had was a story that had travelled around, not necessarily based on any event at the conference mentioned. On the other hand, there could of course be a general culture in the municipalities of bringing up surprises in the form of organizational changes at conferences without telling staff in advance. However, as in the first case, only a very limited number of informants in the second case could recall the event. Informants from other municipalities than those directly concerned could not recall the event at all, or denied that it had taken place.

The conference in question had occurred rather recently, within the last two years, so the contemporaneity was acceptable, if not excellent. As to bias, the managers did not recall this incident, but they were naturally inclined to give a favourable picture of their own activities and their organization; on the other hand, some people lower down in the hierarchy might have grudges against their managers. As was mentioned, participants in the conference coming from other local governments and organizations could not recall the incident(s).

On the whole, then, weighing up the different aspects of source criticism against one another, it seemed more likely that the incident had not happened than that it actually had. Of course, there was a possibility that it had occurred in some weaker form than that which was told, but there was no evidence for that either, from any source. Could the manager(s) have said something innocuous that was interpreted differently by the employees in question? This is certainly possible, but the alleged incident concerned important pieces of organizational change, and it is not likely that revealing or not revealing this could be interpreted in extremely different ways.

If somebody had made a tape recording of the manager's speech, this would have been more palpable evidence for or against the event taking place, because of contemporaneity to the event and the absence of bias and dependence (provided, of course, that the tape was authentic, and that some individuals had not faked it for their own purposes); but no such tape recording (or stenographic recording) had been made.

In all, and always until further notice, the scales seemed to tilt slightly in favour of the event not having taken place. All this goes to show how tricky, fragile and beset with uncertainties the (source-critical) construction of 'facts' generally is. Facts are not something lying out there, waiting to be picked up; they are the result of a delicate, careful weighing of the values of information against one another on the different source-critical 'dimensions'. The empirical facts or data of a study are never the rock-solid ground envisaged by positivists and empiricists, but always a tenuous network. In this way, the aspects of source criticism can be used as *arguments* (not conclusive evidence) for or against a certain construction, always pending new information. The facts re-constructed are always provisory, pending further information.

So, barring new information, the (somewhat stronger) indications were that the event had not taken place, and for this reason it was not included in the presentation of the case. It would have been possible to go further (which the researcher did chose not to do), suspending the issue of truth (whether the event had taken place or not) and using the story in a Collingwoodian sense of what it *meant* (proceeding from hermeneutic theme 1, source criticism, to hermeneutic theme 2): it said something important about how these (minority of) employees from different local governments who told the story saw their managers – as people who were authoritarian in their leadership style and did not bother to inform their employees before starting an important change process, and in addition as insensitive and inconsiderate people who did not have any concern for the feelings of their subordinates. There was also, perhaps, a slight accusation of narcissism against the managers – that they liked posing in front of an audience and being admired for their initiatives but could not care less about their own employees.

This could have been extended into an interpretation of the story in a more existential way (hermeneutic theme 4), starting from the 'bolt of lighting' metaphor. Suddenly something crucial and totally expected is disclosed about an important person in our lives. We would not have dreamed of this, but now a gaping hole is torn in our (inauthentic) worldview; a naked truth of our existence is revealed, with a dire impact on our very lives. What do we do with this shattering experience: exit, voice or loyalty (leave, voice concern, or show loyalty) for instance (Hirschman, 1970), or are there other options? Perhaps the participants who did not recall or denied the story were really in a state of denial, suppressing the ugly truth, and the few who did recall it were the genuine people? What did they do with their insight?

The whole thing also spoke volumes about these employees' view of the organizational changes in general: the latter were something superficial, done in order to enhance the prestige of the management, but in reality hollow, and not anchored in the organization. This impression was substantiated by other statements, both by these particular interviewees and others. In fact, the telling of a story could be interpreted as giving an illustration of this attitude. The story then functions as an 'exemplar' (Gr. *paradeigma*, an illustrative, vivid example, often a story) in the second premise of an Aristotelian rhetorical enthymeme (Feldman and Sköldberg, 2002): good managers care about their employees, are considerate, not self-advertising and anchor their decisions among their subordinates. This manager behaved as told in the story. Hence this manager is a bad manager. The first premiss and the conclusion are implied, part of the subtext. (Note that this enthymemic logic is enticing but not binding: another version of the good manager may be one who takes initiatives, is charismatic and visionary, and does not wait for the inert bureaucracy of lower echelons before taking action.) Then we are already into hermeneutic theme 5, narrative and rhetorics.

Thus, all these further hermeneutic themes might also have been used, but the researcher chose source criticism (hermeneutic theme 1) as the main hermeneutic theme in this particular case, and also in the overall study. As a complement to source criticism, empathy (hermeneutic theme 2) was sometimes also used. The single 'facts' construed in this way were then put together, partly by being ordered chronologically, partly by interpolating between them, in a somewhat similar way to threading a pearl necklace (hermeneutic theme 3 in Chapter 4). The 'thread' was here constituted by the reasonable sequence of facts between already constructed facts. These were put together into a 'plot', a coherent story where motives, intentions, causes, context, etc. enter the picture (Ricoeur 1984; White, 1985a). Through this 'bottom-up' construction from never rock-solid and sometimes flimsy tracks of evidence, it mostly proved possible, in the way described, to gain reasonable interpretations of what had happened at the micro level.

More complex processes, on the contrary, proved harder to get a picture of with a preponderance of any interpretive version. This is also connected with pre-understanding. Already in the first case study it became necessary to go to what in this book has been described as the fourth level of reflection, postmodernistically inspirated reflection over patterns, authority and the nature of the researcher's text. This means a reflection over both preunderstanding and the various produced versions of the text, the latter in several consecutive versions which were rejected one after the other. The reflection finally took the form of a radical 're-framing' (rather than a mild, harmonious 'fusion of horizons' *à la* Gadamer). The preunderstanding that was part of the project's original 'baggage' was exposed to severe blows from the first case study onwards. In particular, this was so regarding the conception of a problem as a background to the organizational changes. It appeared that in the change process under study, and then in the later ones, decisions and actions were not taken against the backdrop of an experienced problem. Nor were problems always construed afterwards (March, 1981). The whole constellation of problems-solutions was largely absent from the organizational changes. Not infrequently, the changes were made because it was felt to be good to change, and because others did similar changes in the processes under study. The organizational changes had often been described enthusiastially and very positively in the media. These positive pictures were thus part of the preconceptions of the project. But at the interpretation of and the efforts to understand what happened, these preconceptions began to fall apart. Increasingly, the changes appeared hard to understand, enigmatic and confusing, which confirmed the impression of the first case. Also the actors themselves had difficulties in explaining them. For instance, they did not solve the problems they were claimed to solve. When the problems were scrutinized more closely, they even started to crack up, and it was doubtful whether there was any underlying problem. A question then naturally arose as to why the change had been implemented to begin with. Other phenomena included the displacement of problems (substituting an original problem for another problem); the dislocation of problems (the partial change of the original problem); and non-problems (the absence of problem as a background to change). In one local government, for instance, the bad economic situation was stated as an earlier major problem. Instead of solving this, the management had taken a series of steps that seemed decoupled from this problem (and moreover from one another). As a result, nobody talked anymore about the bad economy but everybody talked about the new 'package' of organizational changes – which in turn created new problems: a case of problem displacement.

The change symbolism was generally splintered. 'The no man's land' and 'the ship with torn sails' were typical overall symbols for the changes. 'A yellow, angular bird flying high' and 'a red elephant which despite its strength has difficulties drawing its load' were other overall symbols. The gawkiness of the bird and the difficulties of the elephant are significant. Associations to different perceptions gave similar results. The changes were on the one hand associated with fresh blue, green, and red colours, good forms such as circles, fine-tasting food or a refreshing astringency, and flower fragrance. On the other hand, there were comparisons with greyness, square- ness, tastelessness and stale tobacco smoke. An important element of the symbolism was *time*, referred to again and again. On the one hand, everything went too quickly; in this rashness there was no time to take a step back and reflect. On the other hand, things proceeded too slowly; there was a lack of dynamism in the changes. Actors from different levels in the organizations also experienced different time rythms, so that a 'struggle over time' emerged between those who wanted to hurry up and those who wanted to put the brake on.

Hence there was a general fragmentation in both problems and symbols. The pre- conception of an at least minimally homogeneous or cohesive picture in these aspects had thus been shattered. Instead the fragmentation had to be accepted and made the object of deeper consideration, still at the fourth level of reflection that focused on the documented texts *as texts*. What emerged was a kind of 'breach of style'. On the one hand, the changes were characterized by a strong trend towards cost efficiency and the centralization of information systems; on the other hand by the development of human recources and a decentralization (of the organizational structure). These two ambitions and orientations simply did not add up. Narratologically expressed, what was enacted was on the one hand a tragic drama with cutdowns and centralism, on the other hand a romantic comedy with the devel- opment of the individual coupled to a harmonious society of small-scale units. The incompatibility of these two narrative genres was expressed in a breach of styles that resulted in a dramaturgic satire: the more things changed, the more they remained the same, or as the French saying goes: *'plus ça change, plus c'est la même chose'*. And since the presupposed underlying problem complex for the organizational changes became more vague the more it was scrutinized, the narrative conventions and their breach of style emerged more and more as that which lay behind the discourse of the organizational changes and in the end the actions that followed on from this.

A postmodernist interpretation would open up the (radical) disconnection of representation from reality. In the change programme one can point at even more radical forms of texts being liberated from other texts. Reality in the form of the real, 'objective' nature of problems and conditions of municipalities fades away and becomes a matter of varied representations that live their own life within the 'real- ity' of change efforts. But also research efforts to capture the change programme becomes a form of hyperreality, where the talk and symbolism of those supposedly being knowledgable of the change projects seem disconnected from what was really intended, carried out and accomplished in the projects labelled as organizational change. The 'reality' that remains, after both the true nature of the situations and problems of municipalities as well as the efforts to accomplish progressive devel- opments fade away into a region of the un-knowable, surely hidden by a mess of incoherent and questionable truth claims by so called informants, is the varied and fragmented set of symbols, talk and other representations invented by people when asked by a researcher about what happened, why, how and what was the outcome. This kind of interpretation would then challange both dataistic (and realist) efforts to capture what really happeneded and hermeneutic lines of interpretation.

A minor element of the third level of reflection, inspired by critical theory, also figured in the study and can be emphasized even more. One point of critique concerned the very strong and prevalent ideology of decentralization, which was (and generally is) often conceived as a priori positive. This can be seen as an example of how an idea becomes fashionable and how most people uncritically follow the trend and the mass, conformistically reproducing a one-sided and naïve picture of the good. However, decentralization is often combined with a standardizing bureaucracy, to keep together the standardized sub-units (see, for instance, Mintzberg, 1983). The very 'charm' of the decentralization ideology is thereby undermined and transformed into its opposite. The study could have gone further with the ideology-critical level and deepened a discussion on how managerial ideologies and management gurus influenced the local government processes we studied. Rather than critical reflection and locally grounded decision-making, a seduction by the commercially successful pop-management industry – forming one of the most powerful ideology apparatuses of our time – led to mainstreamed mindsets and an adherence to recipes of sometimes quesionable relevance and value. As hinted at above, Peters and Waterman's bestselling *In Search of Excellence* was in vogue, and so were several other trendy management concepts and ideas of the era. A focus on how, concretely, these ideas seeped down into the organization, transforming it and in the process also transforming themselves, combining and recombining various ideational elements, would have been very interesting. It might have contributed further to an understanding of the fragmentation of the organizational discursive and non-discursive practices. Close-up studies of change projects sometimes reveal how various groups, depending on position, work situation and occupational background, make sense of the very purpose of a change initiative and the ways it is supposed to be implemented, very differently (Alvesson and Sveningsson, 2008). The critical eliciting of non-compatible managerial ideologies and trends behind the organizational changes could have contributed an emancipatory dimension to the study. Knowledge of this kind could have provided generally relevant input to more autonomous and reflective positioning efforts and inspiration to organizational actors to engage in communicative action, debating the validity of arguments about why, what and how things should or could be done in improving the public sector. Counter suggestions as to what really took place might also have been a part of the study (in fact a number of such suggestions were actually made).

Final comment on the two examples

We suggest that reflexive interpretation can be used in various ways in terms of the final production of a text. One possibility is that the contents of the above two sections are regarded as moments in the researcher's own thinking, which would lead to syntheses, or selections, of various interpretations and reflections for their ultimate presentation in a published text, albeit considerably shorter than the one

APPLICATIONS OF REFLEXIVE METHODOLOGY

above. (The two empirical illustrations above would in that case be more like the researcher's analytical work than finished research texts.) Another possibility is that the various levels of interpretation and reflection are given ample space and special sections in the text, roughly as has been done here. A finished research text would not then be altogether unlike the two presented above as regards the space allocated to, and the type of, reflexive interpretation. Something approximating the second variant, with a fairly lengthy reporting of reflexive work, may sometimes be preferred, in order to secure the importance of the reflection and – related to this – to increase commitment to work of this kind. We believe that intellectual work which directly affects the production of the text is more satisfactory, at least for researchers who enjoy writing. More care might be spent on the reflective work, if it is given more space in the final text. An obvious disadvantage is that this calls for a lot of text, forcing a concentration upon some well-chosen empirical material for interpretation. One possibility is to conduct extensive empirical work, for instance an ethnography, and then on the basis of some well-founded principle to select various parts for particular attention. The rest of the empirical material can then be used for a development of the researcher's own understanding, which ought to increase the quality of the interpretation of the focused material, and for complementary and balancing descriptions and analyses (Alvesson, 1996).

There are many factors which can affect the way the production of a text should be organized in relation to the ideal of reflexivity – the research task, the variant of reflexive interpretation chosen, the researcher's familiarity with the literature, the theoretical and institutional base, style, and so on – which mean there is little point in recommending any particular form as a universal standard. The ideals of reflexive-interpretive research may be combined with different forms and modes of presentation.

A note on the criteria for qualitative research

Some recent views

Throughout most of this book we have argued for a particular view of the way in which qualitative social research should be conducted. We will now discuss in a somewhat more comprehensive way some reasonable criteria for research, as a third alternative to prioritizing either data or theory.

The views advanced by poststructuralists, as well as critical theorists and a whole host of other non-positivist scholars, have gone beyond the truth criterion – theory confirmed by empirical evidence reflecting 'objective reality out there' – as the ultimate yardstick for science (Denzin and Lincoln, 1994). We have seen that many writers reject outright any notion that science can reliably mirror and explain 'reality'. In particular, the autonomy and ambiguity of language in relation to a non-linguistic reality are underlined. By emphasizing the researcher's active constructing of 'reality' – through perception, cognition and the handling of language as well as a social interaction with those being researched – a fundamental critique of traditional empirical epistemology emerges. The related notion of empirical material's dependence on theory strengthens the argument. To this we can add that because of the historical and changeable nature of social phenomena, what might be 'true' in one context may not be so in another. After all, published research also affects social conditions. As a rule this applies less to individual research projects or written works than aggregated research outcomes.

A consequence of all critique of conventional claims and the increasing distribution of views and ideals is that more and more people turn against the idea of general principles and criteria and suggest that 'the realization that social and educational inquiry is a practical and moral affair [means] that criteria must be thought of not as abstract standards but rather as socially constructed lists of characteristics' (Smith and Hodkinson, 2005: 922). Some researchers draw attention to the crafting of good texts as the central issue. Richardson (2000) suggests a combination of scientific and aesthetic criteria when assessing research. The latter aspects concern to what extent 'does the use of creative analytic practices open up the text, invite interpretive responses? Is the text artistically shaped, satisfying, complex, and not boring?' (2000: 937).

Von Glasersfeld (1991) rejects the traditional idea that knowledge should 'match' the world as it 'exists'; instead it is of central importance, as he sees it, that knowledge shows its value by its functionality. Knowledge must be judged by its ability to accomplish something. Similar ideas are expressed by Lyotard (1984), albeit from rather a different point of departure. The main criterion of good theory and research is a practical or *technological* value, that is, that it can guide action. It will be 'practitioners' who in the first instance will determine the value of knowledge on the basis of its ability to provide them with relevant insights and pointers. (In fact, in scientific contexts it is often the researcher's colleagues who account for this evaluation, but they will be keeping an eye on the theory's probable pragmatic value.)

We see this approach as a little problematic. It connects too easily with a technocratic approach, whereby knowledge is reduced to something in the service of various functionaries. There is seldom any very direct and specific link between more intellectual knowledge and practical usefulness in the same way as knowledge of a more pronounced pragmatic character is supposed to lead to immediate practical results.

It could also be said that the idea of ('real') pragmatic utility is based on some form of matching between the words used by the researcher and reality. The functionality of knowledge – 'can knowledge of psychological disorders lead to therapies for reducing anxiety?' for instance – can best be tested by studying the empirical results of attempts at using some particular knowledge.[4] Consequently the idea of functionality should not be separated too sharply from the idea of some kind of empirical testing, even though we certainly can – and ought to – differentiate between 'truth' and a technical-practical value.

Another criterion of good research has been suggested, namely that it should be 'pluralistic and democratic'. To be receptive to diversity is important; blockages and restrictions should be avoided, and in principle 'anyone' can offer a notion of how reality should be represented and/or interpreted. Since everyone is then contributing to the construction of social reality, they are also contributing to the creation of 'truth'. Social scientific knowledge cannot – as the positivists would wish – isolate knowledge objects from everything that is genuinely human. Peters and

Rotenbuhler (1989), referring to William James, maintain that our truths must be verified – made true. But this is not easy, since much of what we do has no effective impact, or does not 'function', which means that intentions, ideas and efforts to develop new practices do not fully materialize in social reality. The postmodernists' ideas about multiple voices come into the picture here, as does Gergen and Gergen's (1991) methodological suggestion about group conversations as a means of generating ideas and ways of talking about phenomena of which group members have both experience and knowledge (menopause, attempted suicide, unemployment, management and so on). As we also discussed above, they mean that the researcher and the subject should share the power in constructing meaning: '"Subjects" become "participants", and the number of interpretations (or theoretical possibilities) generated by the research is expanded rather than frozen' (Gergen and Gergen, 1991: 86).

The main criterion in constructivist research is somewhat vaguely expressed, but is thus liberal in its nature, and aims at emancipation:

> reality is not fixed or given; you partake in its creation and must ensure that reality does not rigidify. Hence, keep the options open and the alternatives fresh, and grant others the freedom you would want – while being considerate of them. (Ravn, 1991: 97)

This sounds alluring. On the other hand, we must ask whether the researcher's preconceptions are not to a certain extent 'fixed or given', providing a more or less rigidified version of (constructed) reality. And, with Bourdieu and Wacquant (1992), we may go further and ask what constructs the social constructor. This is the crux of social constructionism.

Deetz (1992) presents a somewhat different and more critical variety of the democratic ideal, by synthesizing ideas from critical theory and poststructuralism. Here there is a clearer idea about opening up (bringing about 'disclosure') towards socially dominant discourses. Instead of merely expressing the subjects' or participants' ideas and meanings, which provide diversity and dialogue, the researcher tries to indicate possible discourses which are never or weakly articulated among the subjects addressed. Deetz (1992: 341), referring to Foucault and to Weedon (1987), and to the ideal of process subjectivity, declares that 'the point of communication as a social act is to overcome one's fixed subjectivity, one's conceptions, one's strategies to be opened to the indeterminacy of people and the external environment'. This communication should apply to daily life but also to scientific texts. Good research therefore succeeds in breaking away from fixed forms of subjectivity.

The idea that, linguistically, good research makes new meanings and understandings possible, and thus also new action alternatives, gives us only rather a blunt criterion for good research. How do we know that the project has 'succeeded'? In particular, the disinclination to allow empirical material to provide a basis for assessing research makes the evaluation of theories and ideas more difficult. Even if data never have an unambiguous relationship with theory, the discussion of criteria becomes even more problematic if we deprive empirical material of any possibility of speaking for or against ideas. Moreover, an excessive focus on the linguistic and on the textualization of social and material conditions can easily lead to 'freedom projects' that consist of nothing more than armchair constructions which – if they were taken seriously and were to inspire concrete action – would frequently involve considerable practical problems in relation to material reality. The latter is generally much more inert or even intractable than linguistic constructions. The problem of criteria in the 'opening-up', 'direction-free' research is evident. The very definition of meaningful research makes it impossible to lay down any simple or unambiguous rules for evaluating the research in question.

Empirical material as argument

We agree with constructivists such as Gergen, von Glasersfeld and the poststructuralists that good research starts from the assumption that language follows a different logic from that of other phenomena (actions, social relations, ideas, etc.). The ideal that language should describe our objectively or socially constructed reality as exactly as possible, ought to be played down considerably. But that need not mean that the ideal of some sort of empirical tie or relationship should be completely abandoned. (Or that the link with the empirical material is formulated only in terms of 'functional fit', connected to a pragmatic or emancipatory value – presuming such things could be established.) One problem in this debate is that the various combatants seem to be advocating either a robust empirical ontology (or are said by their opponents to be doing so) – in recent years slightly modified with superficial references to the theory-impregnated nature of empirical material, which do not, however, seriously affect the approach – or to be abandoning all reference to empirical reality 'outside' language in favour of a one-sided linguistic focus. (Many of those who advocate a functional or pragmatic criterion as a yardstick of good research do so on the basis of a linguistic approach, among them Gergen and von Glasersfeld.) A strong feeling for the social reality under study can be insisted on as an important criterion for good research.[5] An ideal that theories and ideas should be well grounded in signs of empirical conditions and that it should be possible to use them in order to throw light upon these, does not mean championing the idea of language 'mirroring' reality. As we have already noted, it is possible to envisage a more ambiguous, uncertain and mediated relation between theory, researcher (research community), language and data than the naïve variants which positivists and inductivists appear to believe in, without ending up by adopting a linguistic or text-reductionist stance. In our view empirical material can inspire ideas and theories, endowing them with credibility, clarifying them and, in the case of theories, making them more stringent. Empirical material cannot unambiguously falsify or verify theories, but it can generate *arguments* for or against the championing of theoretical ideas and a particular way of understanding the world. Sometimes it can also be fruitful to allow interpretations of empirical material (interpretations of an already interpreted reality) to torpedo an idea or theory. Normally, though, the presence of the above-mentioned ambiguities (a relatively high degree of incommensurability between language and extra-linguistic empirical reality) means that such torpedoings are less likely. More commonly, the empirical work inspires modifications of theoretical ideas. The very nature of data, impregnated with theory and interpretation, naturally comes into the picture here, reducing the capacity to say clearly yes or no to a particular way of constituting and understanding a social phenomenon.

Thus, in our view, the criterion of confirmation through data should be played down relative to what books on method (qualitative and quantitative) normally suggest, and conceptions of the nature of empirical material should be changed as compared to traditional epistemology (cf. Guba and Lincoln, 1994; Kvale, 1989). Empirical material is still important. But it is a question of assigning it a considerably less clear-cut and robust character, of seeing it as an expression of negotiable, perspective-dependent interpretations, and as conveyed in an ambiguous language. *Empirical material should be seen as an argument in efforts to make a case for a particular way of understanding social reality, in the context of a never-ending debate.* The empirical material can have varying weight depending on the context and the degree to which it has been processed. This is different from ascribing to the empirical material the status of *referee in a dispute* between different (theoretical) stances. Data generated by questionnaires could then be treated as a relatively weak argument (even, and especially, as regards seemingly concrete 'facts' but in reality institutionalized social constructions such as salary, sex, age, etc.), while interpretations of empirical material generated by an extended period of participant observation can give greater weight to arguments about how to interpret social reality. Taking up the mirror metaphor again, we can say that empirical material resembles a picture in a hall lined with convex and concave mirrors (researchers, language, theories, reality), rather than the result of one single reflection of 'reality'. But data cannot *prove* anything.[6]

Criteria for empirical research

Silverman (1997: 25) suggests two criteria for evaluating any research, 'namely, have the researchers demonstrated successfully why we should believe them? And does the research problem tackled have theoretical and/or practical significance?' We agree that these criteria are important, but, as we have shown in this book, credibility is not a straightforward matter and the ideal of reflexivity indicates a need to take seriously other elements in addition to processing and rigorously analysing data. If the central importance of empiricist material as part of the search for truth is played down, then it should be possible to give other virtues more space. We can take off the empirical straitjacket which has restricted our freedom of thought or subordinated it to fixed procedures for depicting narrow segments of existing 'reality'. But this does not mean, as we have frequently noted here, that sloppiness is allowed or that 'anything goes'. On the contrary, a breaking up of all norm systems is the last thing we advocate, not even the norm that 'anything goes'. Other demands, different from the traditional ones – and to some extent more exacting – should be made. Good research, as we have sought to suggest in this book, should be characterized by the following features, to a reasonable extent at least:

- empirical 'arguments' and credibility
- an open attitude to the vital importance of the interpretive dimension to social phenomena

- critical reflection regarding the political and ideological contexts of, and issues in, research
- an awareness of the ambiguity of language and its limited capacity to convey knowledge of a purely empirical reality and awareness about the rhetorical nature of ways of dealing with this issue (the representation–authority problem)
- theory development based on the mentioned issues.

This leads to a reduced emphasis on and a somewhat freer view of the data-handling elements in qualitative research than we generally find in books on method. It is not as important to follow procedures in a detailed way. Just because other criteria have been brought to the fore, it does not follow that research becomes a capricious activity, making no demands. The criteria advanced above – that reality is ambiguous and that different vocabularies and methods of interpretation should be considered and explicitly accounted for – actually make higher demands on the researcher in terms of familiarity with a wide range of literature and viewpoints, as well as in terms of intellectual flexibility, receptiveness and creativity. It also stimulates coherence and thoughtfulness in the production of empirical material (see Skeggs, 1997, for a good example of highly reflexive and empirically ambitious research). The demand for the presentation of (the possibility of) different interpretations does not mean that the researcher has to regard all these as equally good or 'true'. Instead one interpretation can be emphasized, for example because it is perceived as matching the empirical material better than others, or because it seems more fertile or more likely to break new ground in terms of insights or theoretical ideas. If several interpretations are advanced, then the criterion must be that according to certain given yardsticks they are better than other interpretations and contribute more to knowledge. This position differs from what is typically advocated by postmodernists, who favour a pluralism of viewpoints as a value of its own and downplay criteria for evaluating interpretations.

Richness in points

In our view one important aspect of qualitative research concerns its *richness in points*. Research rich in points has some linkage to empirical conditions while also clearly going beyond what the empirical material (preliminary, first-order interpretations) is able to say. Its novelty value – developing insights, problematization of established ways of thinking – thus becomes important. It is a question of achieving an episte-mological break with everyday knowledge (see Bourdieu et al., 1991). An interpreta-tion rich in points appears reasonable in relation to the empirical material, but does not need strong support from it, in the sense of firm proof. The data can be said to *enable* and support interpretation, rather than unequivocally lead up to it. Empirical material can provide inspiration and arguments for interpretations. (Naturally it may also provide arguments for other interpretations than the preferred ones, and this must of course be carefully considered and addressed in reflexive research.) The empirical material may also render some particular interpretation impossible, or at least indicate that it is so implausible as to be pointless. Data can function generatively as a springboard for interpretations. More important still is to see the phenomenon under study *as* something (Asplund, 1970). The act of interpretation is therefore crucial. Here the empirical material (constructed data) comes into play, as does the repertoire of interpretations and reflective metatheory. Research rich in points is thus to be found in the field of tension between habile empirical contact, reported first-order interpretations (data), the imaginative and relatively free handling of these, and a well-judged combination of depth and breadth in the interpretive repertoire. In ambiguous empirical material, and not least in *rendering the material ambiguous in a thoughtful manner*, lie the conditions for richness in points.[7] Here, too, there is the possibility of a certain systematic approach in a creative and imaginative process. It is always easy to tell people (and oneself) that we should be imaginative, creative and free (in the sense of being unconstrained by established frameworks) in our relation to empirical material. But in the reflexive-interpretive research process there is the potential for facilitating these ideals. Using different starting-points and challenging earlier interpretations enables the supply of a seminal ambiguity to the material studied. As the alternative meanings and interpretations emerge, there are excellent opportunities for further creativity. Creativity, in our present context, can perhaps be regarded as one such step away from dominant and established angles of approach. Working with alternative theories engendered by a broader repertoire of interpretations, critical theory and postmodernism, stimulates just such a departure.

It is important to emphasize that an interpretive richness in empirical research – as opposed to more philosophically inclined studies – is to be found in the *tension situations* between empirical support and the freedom to express something creatively. The creative act implies going beyond the consensual views regarding the empirical material. Saying something creative and novel is thus not fully compatible with the ideal of maximizing intersubjectivity as the way of achieving 'objectivity'. If we limit ourselves to what everybody already agrees on, then it is difficult to say anything new or original, and there is a risk of repeating what everybody already knows (something which we criticized in Chapter 3). Research rich in points usually avoids definite statements about 'how things are' and emphasizes the importance of looking at things in some particular way, which allows a new understanding of the empirical situation concerned. Normally we have to envisage some sort of trade-off between empirical support and a richness in points, since these are inherently in opposition to one another. However, the richer the empirical material, the more likely it is to provide decent support for interpretations rich in points. (Good examples can be found in Jackall, 1988, and Kunda, 1992.) Otherwise we could envisage *either* that research achieves a great richness in points by means of strong empirical support – which would somewhat reduce the demand for creative, advanced interpretations – *or* that the empirical material provides some support for point-rich interpretations, but that these are achieved largely as a result of what is done in creative, inspired interaction with the empirical material. This may – together with other sources of inspirations – function generatively.

Original empirical material (original questions asked and/or creatively structured observations) can thus sometimes engender a richness in points, despite a lower level of sophisticated interpretive input. It is not easy to find any really good examples of such studies, as creative interpretations and interesting theoretical ideas typically go beyond what the empirical material unambiguously demonstrates. Mintzberg (1975), who studied the work of managers, could perhaps be counted as one such. Mintzberg made direct observations of a number of managers and noted that their typical working day consisted of a great number of very brief interactions with various other members of their companies. This diverged radically from earlier widely held notions about managerial work, which saw it as a more rational and systematic affair, consisting largely of planning, decision-making, control and so on. It is more common, however, for point-rich contributions to spring from significant creative interpretations of a more or less extensive body of empirical material, which by itself would not take us very far. (See, for instance, Freud, 1953; Foucault, 1979; Geertz, 1973; and Laing, 1960; cf. also Asplund, 1970.) It is interesting to note that the theories which are held to be important, for instance in organizational theory, are hardly popular because of their strong support in any empirical material, since the defects in this respect may be considerable, but still without affecting the popularity of the theory. Rather, these theories are popular because they appeal to the imagination, or because they are elegant or are perceived as breaking new ground (Astley, 1985; Weick, 1989).

Good research according to the criterion of interpretive richness thus enables a qualitatively new understanding of relevant fragments of social reality. This represents a break with earlier ideas, at least on certain points. Generative capacity, 'the capacity to challenge the guiding assumptions of the culture, to raise fundamental questions regarding contemporary social life, to foster reconsideration of that which is "taken for granted", and thereby to furnish new alternatives for social action' (Gergen, 1978: 1345), is thus important. The reader is encouraged to think and think again. Point-rich research stirs up problems. The suggestion at least of an 'aha!' response should be part of the normal reader's reaction. The idea is that rich and freely interpreted data should encourage imaginative richness, at the same time that the empirical material – as well as functioning as a generator – also sets limits on the imagination.

We do not want to advance this research ideal as the only right one, even from reflexive-interpretive starting-points. The latter can lead to research of different kinds; even a more down-to-earth, relatively concrete, data-oriented kind of research is acceptable, so long as the trap of empiricism is avoided and researchers consider carefully the constructed nature of data and are open to their ambiguities and ambivalences as well as the richness of alternative meanings. As we noted earlier, different sorts of research problems and aims must be allowed to influence the shaping of the research ideal – while at the same time problems and aims have to be determined reflexively. Richness in points can therefore sometimes be more prominent and sometimes less so, as a criterion of good qualitative research.

Reflexive interpretation and relativism

The problem of relativism, in the sense of a weak common norm system within the research community and the absence of criteria for evaluation, may also be avoided by strong intraparadigmatic demands combined with certain demands for interparadigmatic links in every research undertaking. The latter are related to our metacriteria for good – that is, highly reflective – research. (We are thus no longer talking about a richness in points as a possible criterion.) Since it is difficult to determine whether the criteria advanced in this book regarding a high level of reflection have been achieved in specific studies, the approach demands a certain capacity for dialogue in the research community, that is, even outside the delimited groups supporting particular schools. Interparadigmatic links are sometimes recommended as an ideal, in the form of a dialogue between various viewpoints. The problem of incommensurability prevents comparisons or the transferring of fixed criteria. However, some authors at least, for example Bernstein (1983), Morgan (1983) and Rorty (1992), contend that an incommensurability between paradigms does not exclude the possibility of reconciling some essentially different positions or of some attempt at least at mutual understanding (see Chapter 3). The argument against this view is that differences in language, political positionings and people's general inflexibility and intolerance prevent dialogue (Jackson and Willmott, 1987). The dominance relations and struggles for status in the research community do not facilitate responsiveness to good argument. Other obstacles to a healthy wide-ranging debate can be that 'debate is often influenced by contemporary fads and fashions (e.g. postmodernism?), and that academics are often schooled in fairly similar ways of thinking, with the consequence that the debate tends to narrow down rather than widen out' (Newton, 1996: 20). Theoretically there are thus possibilities, but in practice they often come up against difficulties.

The strong tendency for researchers to get stuck in a particular paradigm and to be captivated by their own language games is not an inevitable fact of nature; it can, at least to a certain degree, be reduced. Different disciplines at different times are characterized to varying degrees by tendencies towards dominance or pluralism. When the latter prevails it is not unusual for researchers to read up on various other fields and thus to acquire a certain understanding of perspectives other than their own. One way of strengthening such inclinations is to uphold metamethodological ideals which imply that the researcher's own position is not totalized, which is what we have advocated here. The pluralism thus encouraged *within* individual research projects would then correspond to an increased pluralism at the level of the research community.

The adoption of metaprinciples, such as quadri-hermeneutics, can generate a certain guarantee against specific epistemological positions which by definition detract from other positions. With a methodology for metainterpretations, and thereby for reflection in various domains (reflexivity), the researcher can at least be forced at certain spots to enter an interparadigmatic field. Such guarantees can counteract empiricism, hypercriticism and textual/linguistic reductionism, as well as an over-sensitivity to (the privileging of) gender, class or ethnicity issues. In this way it should be possible to increase a fundamental receptiveness to critical dialogue between positions.

Metatheories can function as 'pipelines' or liaisons, as it were, between paradigms, that is to say, the 'incommensurability' between these is not complete, as the metalevel makes it possible to construct a system of channels that maintains communication, even though the naïve dream of complete commensurability must remain a pious hope. This is yet another way in which the sterile dichotomy between relativism and objectivism can be overcome; we have discussed several others in this book.

Metaphors for research

Thus far in these two final chapters we have attempted to play elements from our exposition in the earlier chapters against each other, in particular the empirical, hermeneutic, critical-theoretical and postmodernist positions, and, based on these, to formulate a methodology guided by the philosophy of science. In this and the following sections we will supplement the theoretical exposition with slightly more detailed ideas about how to handle the ideals in concrete research work. It is a question of providing some cornerstones for everyday thinking about research and of how to avoid the problem of losing direction and impetus in a complex research process. We will thus depart somewhat from our main exposition and venture into the area of good advice.

What we have advocated in this book may also be formulated in terms of possible metaphors for research. As we have maintained – in particular, in Chapter 4 – a fruitful approach is to regard social phenomena in terms of the metaphors which we start from and which guide us in our thinking and writing. What are the metaphors for research in the kind of field we have been discussing, that is, qualitative social science?

A predominant image seems to represent research as *mushroom-picking*. (For readers in countries where mushrooms are bought in shops, the expression 'berry-picking' may be an alternative!) All the talk about the collection of data, the capture of data, the codification and classification of data, and so on, points to a metaphor of this kind. By carefully and painstakingly collecting and sorting through a sufficiently large amount of 'data', the raw materials are acquired to make a delicious dish that can be prepared according to the recipe book (cf. 'the processing of data'). As has become clear, we regard the mushroom-picking metaphor as unproductive, at least as the main metaphor for research. Empirical material – interview accounts, observations of social situations – should not be reified. The mushroom-picking metaphor might possibly facilitate some of the practical aspects, but it also expresses a naïve empirical view and stands in opposition to more reflective research ideals.

Talk of 'data collection' is unfortunately widespread in qualitative methodological contexts. We get the feeling that many people do not think of the concept as a metaphor. Even interpretive and critical scholars often use the expression (e.g. Rosen, 1991; Thomas, 1993; Van Maanen, 1995). Sometimes this may be justified for reasons of convenience – other expressions might mean more words and become unwieldy. And we should also remember that particular metaphorical expressions do not necessarily tell us all that much about what metaphors are used on a cognitive level. Certain sections of research may also be clarified or guided reasonably well with the help of this metaphor. Nevertheless, it remains too prevalent, even in research contexts where the demands on awareness and reflection are much higher than in the research we surveyed in Chapter 3.

One analogy, which like the mushroom-picking metaphor seeks to warn us about the pitfalls of traditional, dataistic methodology, invokes certain similarities between this and (early versions of) capitalism:

> In the world of science, as in the world of capitalism, it is a question of playing safe. Intellectual adventurousness is in some obscure way attractive, yet basically reprehensible, just like commercial freebooting. People imagine that life is so organized that all forms of saving – even of scientific data – will grow and yield compound interest. And they will grow on their own. The only thing we have to do is to invest sensibly and then to show great restraint. Stock-exchange quotations and significance testing may appear to resemble each other. So-called hard data are sometimes bewilderingly like hard currency. 'Data banks' ... (Asplund, 1970: 96; our translation)

Adorno's (1976) distaste at the idea of researchers as mere machines for registration, indicates a similar stance. So also does the widespread pejorative talk of 'data-dredging' with regard to research giving priority to the tedious, detailed processing of large amounts of data.

So much for metaphors with a negative charge, which reveal the traps into which the empirical research can fall. There are also examples of metaphors which seek to encourage in a more positive manner other, more 'interesting' views of the research process. Within grounded theory the stated aim is to 'discover' the theory. The problem is, of course, that a theory must – at least in part – be created, it is not just lying there waiting for the researcher-discoverer to find it, like an explorer discovering a hitherto unknown island (cf. Woolgar, 1983). Gadamer (1989a) talks about (hermeneutic) research as a 'fusion of horizons', while Czarniawska-Joerges (1992) uses the phrase 'insight gathering' instead of 'data collection'. Asplund (1970) suggests that the research process can be compared to a detective novel. It is about solving a mystery. Good research contains two central components: formulating the mystery and then solving it. In critical theory, defamiliarization and cultural criticism are possible metaphors for research (Ehn and Löfgren, 1982; Marcus and Fischer, 1986). (Defamiliarization, however, is also used more widely in cultural research.) Postmodernists have suggested some radically different metaphors for qualitative research (or at least certain varieties of it). Thus Clifford (1986: 6) talks about research as 'true fiction', while Brown (1990) refers to research activities as 'rhetorical constructions'. Research is authorship (Van Maanen, 1995). Certain other researchers cite metaphors that give more space to the social component in research, and in doing so they emphasize the importance of the interview subjects. Steier (1991b), for instance, sees social science research as 'co-construction', whereby the researcher in interaction with the research subject constructs the research object.

Following Morgan (1980, 1997), we could regard research as the development and application of metaphors for the object of study. Note that 'metaphor' here has acquired a double sense: the metaphor for research is thus both the development and the application of metaphors. Alvesson (1993b) contends that the theoretical frames of reference are often far more ambiguous than this, and that the explicit metaphors are affected in turn by second-order metaphors, which structure the first ones in various ways. The researcher's control over the metaphors that form the core of the frame of reference is therefore limited. It is suggested that 'research is better perceived as a struggle with the ambiguous and slippery interaction between metaphors at different levels, than as the development and application of a specific metaphor' (Alvesson, 1993b: 131). Here research is thus described as a rather refractory process, which includes different, perhaps contradictory, and partly unconscious ideas about what the researcher is dealing with. Denzin and Lincoln (2005) also emphasize the variety of elements in research work but use the metaphor 'bricolage' as indicating a more relaxed and playful process. The qualitative researcher is then viewed as a 'bricoleur' or 'maker of quilts', who is using the aesthetic and material tools of craftwork and making use of the various strategies, methods and empirical materials available.

Thus far we have looked at metaphors which illuminate the research process as a whole, or at least certain important parts of it. But there are also metaphors which throw light on some more delimited sections or dimensions of the process. 'Hard and soft data' represent a fairly typical case in point. Czubaroff (1989), following Toulmin, draws a parallel with jurisprudence and talks about the justification of research as a legal procedure. In Chapter 6 we saw how postmodernism and post-structuralism emphasize the literary qualities of science and the role of the researcher as author, as well as the poetic elements in texts. Yet perhaps the most important point to consider with regard to particular sections or dimensions of research concerns the metaphors that are used, more or less consciously, for language. Von Glasersfeld compares two such metaphors:

> Language does not transport pieces of one person's reality into another's – it merely prods and prompts the other to build up conceptual structures which, to this other, seem compatible with the words and actions the speaker or writer has used. (1991: 23)

Language as a means of conveying meaning is thus confronted here by language as inspiration or building blocks in the construction of concepts.

The point about the (root) metaphors discussed in this section is that, at best, they provide a holistic and suggestive picture of the phenomenon which facilitates thought and gives it an overall direction. The metaphor may provide guidance that counteracts the tendency to get caught in the struggle with empirical impressions, which easily leads the researcher to give priority to data management (codification, classification and so on) and thus to fall back on dataistic assumptions. By pointing out a few problematic metaphors – problematic in the sense of reinforcing empiricist assumptions – researchers acquire some guidelines which help them to avoid the particular trap in question. We will abstain from advocating any definite metaphors for research, but we do feel that the ironic metaphor of mushroom picking has some value as a counterweight to the ideas that dominate qualitative (and to an even greater extent quantitative) methodology. Otherwise, in accordance with our research ideal we would like to emphasize the value of having access to several different and complementary research metaphors. Exactly what ones are chosen will depend on what has personal significance for the individual researchers or what

APPLICATIONS OF REFLEXIVE METHODOLOGY

works generatively for them. The point is that having access to several different metaphors facilitates offering various comprehensive images of research, thus reducing the risk of latching on to a one-sided favourite conception. Having a favourite metaphor is both natural, desirable and inevitable, but the trick is to have a certain distance in relation to it, that is, an ability to look at one's favourite position from another angle. Metaphors should be chosen so as to stimulate reflection and movement between the levels of interpretation.

Let us sum up this section by considering possible views of (metaphors for) the individual researchers themselves, rather than for the research process. As mentioned, we regard it as unwise to see researchers as mushroom-pickers, at least with regard to the most essential components of their work. Another unfortunate view of researchers is represented by expressions such as 'calculators' or 'compulsive neurotics' – if we are to refer (inductively) to two metaphors which malicious colleagues have used to refer to mathematically minded social scientists and laboratory psychologists. (Laboratory experiments involve keeping everything under control; obsessive control is symptomatic of the compulsive neurotic.)

If we look back at the research identities presented in Chapters 4–7 in this book, for instance, we find that the researcher was seen as a mandarin (critical theory), an agitator (feminism) and an engine ticking over or a demolisher (poststructuralist). These are all useful counter-images. In a more positive spirit the researcher as field-worker, detective, cultural critic, partisan, free thinker, rhetorician and deconstructor of truths can all be cited.

The whole point of suggesting metaphors is not to stamp or stereotype individuals or positions, but to provide suggestive concepts that in practical ways can facilitate our own processes of reflection, and help us to resist the temptation to get stuck in a favourite position. A degree of (self-)irony is important here. With these examples we would like to encourage our readers to come up with some metaphors of their own, metaphors which work for them, seeing themselves *as* something.

Two kinds of emphasis in reflexive research

As a further element in our efforts to suggest how to more specifically work with reflexivity we return to the two major purposes with this, which can motivate somewhat different emphasis in reflexive methodology projects. One is to avoid or minimize naïve and problematic elements in research work, the other is to see new and interesting possibilities. In other words, the ideas are about how to increase 'reflexive rigour' and to work more creatively. The two are not unconnected. To avoid dividing up the population in pre-given categories like men and women, managers and co-workers, etc. (possible stupidities) is to open up far more interesting ways of interpreting gender and asymmetrical social relations.

Reflexive practices might usefully be differentiated between those that emphasize avoiding problematic or 'dangerous' things – intellectually, politically or ethically – and those that try to produce new insights. We refer to the former as D-reflexivity: D stands for deconstruction, defensive, destabilizing. We call the latter R-reflexivity:

R refers to reconstruction, re-presentation. There are of course no absolute distinctions between these two, the border is to some extent fluid.

D-reflexivity practices challenge orthodox understandings by pointing out the limitations of, and uncertainties behind, the manufactured unity and coherence of texts, as well as the way in which conformism, institutional domination and academic and business fashion may account for the production of particular knowledge. It engages with the problems, uncertainties and social contingencies of knowledge claims – whether empirical claims, concepts or theoretical propositions. By emphasizing how social science orders the world in a particular way, power/knowledge connections are illuminated and truth-creating effects are disarmed. These practices are conducted in attempts to counteract harm – to challenge efforts to stabilize the view of the world in a particular way, as well as to expose the unreflective reproduction of dominant vocabularies, rules or conventions in social research.

R-reflexivity is about developing and adding something; the person engaged in R-reflexivity is in the construction rather than the demolition industry. It means bringing in issues of alternative paradigms, root metaphors, perspectives, vocabularies, lines of interpretation, political values and representations; re-balancing and reframing voices in order to interrogate and vary data in a more fundamental way. Instances of alternative constructions and the reconstruction of fundamental elements of the research project are central to these reflexive practices. R-reflexive practices are employed to illuminate what is left out and marginalized: the (almost) missed opportunity, premature framing, the reproduction of received wisdom, a re-enforcement of power relations and unimaginative labelling. They provide alternative descriptions, interpretations, results, vocabularies, voices, and points of departure that could be taken into account, and show some of the differences that they would make. R-reflexivity aims to open up new avenues, paths and lines of interpretation to produce 'better' research ethically, politically, empirically and theoretically.

Of the perspectives addressed in depth above, postmodernism is of course mainly about D-reflexivity, as the aim of most versions of it is to undermine positive claims to results and contributions, while the others contribute more to R-reflexivity in that they encourage consideration of alternative views, even though critical theory and feminism also have a strong D-potential.[8] At the same time, the D and R division should not be exaggerated. When we talk about D- and R-reflexivity it is with reference to alternative contributions following on from reflexive projects, where the overall interplay between and confrontation of different points of view are central. D and R moments are always involved. A grounded-theory based reinterpretation of, for example, a Foucauldian or Frankfurterian interpretation can undermine this and create D-reflexivity effects.

We suggest that reflexive researchers might engage in practices that create a dialectic between D-reflexivity and R-reflexivity. This means moving between tearing down – pointing at the weaknesses in the text and disarming truth claims – and then developing something new or different, where the anxieties of offering positive knowledge do not hold the researcher back.

It is important that reflexivity is not just a ritual or a legitimation of the researcher's scholarship and general awareness of what s/he is up to. The researcher well versed in reflexivity can be tempted to take a 'holier than thou' position. (Our hope is that the reader of this book does not feel like this about its authors.) In the literature emphasizing its sophisticated reflexivity there is a tendency to demonstrate some such self-righteousness. But as we see it, a decisive criterion for successful reflexivity is whether it makes a productive difference in the delivery of research results. We believe some kind of tangible result should be demonstrated, such as thoughtful and creative research questions, ideas, concepts, challenges to conventional thinking, or suggestions for new research. Being productive does not necessarily mean being positive – negating or deconstructing ideas is also a productive outcome. Going through the intimate relation between the researcher and their knowledge in a reflexive loop should, we believe, lead to some novel (re)descriptions, (re)interpretations or (re)problematizations that add some quality to the text and the results it communicates. We thus believe that a vital purpose of reflexivity is to 'improve' empirical research and theorizing – producing fieldwork, texts or theoretical results that are 'better' in some distinctive way than they would be without reflexivity. The meaning of better is not self evident – it may be more creative, offering a broader set of ideas/interpretations, more ethically informed or sensitive, or it may not become ensnared by social conventions or fashions. Nonetheless, for us, reflexivity is not primarily an end in itself, but a means to make research better in some way (cf. Weick, 1999).

Some concrete suggestions

Finally, let us reduce the level of abstraction in our exposition even more, and provide some concrete suggestions about how the demands on reflexive research should be handled. Living up to ideals can be difficult. Part of the problem is that in qualitative research the researcher has to keep track of rather intractable material. Even if we play down the empirical work and reduce its extent compared to what seems to be common practice today, the problem remains that qualitative research often includes empirical material that is difficult to survey in its entirety. Since a simple sorting and categorizing of 'data' is not exactly encouraged in reflexively ambitious projects, the problem of achieving and maintaining an overview is in some sense greater in reflexive than in mushroom-picking research. In addition to the handling of the empirical material, the need to make continual interpretations at various theoretical and metatheoretical levels also requires a broad grasp of the material, familiarity with an extensive literature, a good memory, intellectual flexibility and cognitive capacity – as well as a cool head. A certain capacity to cope with cognitive dissonance is also needed. Being strongly religious about a favoured position gives limited space for reflexivity. As we have suggested above, various mixes of empirical work, meaningful interpretations, critical reflection and linguistic-textual self-reflection are possible – a specific strength in one area could motivate a reduction in demands in the other three. But it still has to be remembered that reflexive research in its quadri-hermeneutic variety, for instance, is more demanding than conventional qualitative (and to an even greater extent much quantitative) research.

One possibility, as we have noted above, is to divide a research project into different phases with respect to the reflective elements. We can thus talk about a *sequencing* of interpretations at deeper levels and reflection. By concentrating primarily upon empirical work and including certain definite spells during which one interprets one's own project in qualified reflective terms, it might be possible to reduce the difficulties. This could be arranged at the beginning of the project, in the middle of it, just before starting to compose a text, and/or during its final revision. Or, at a late stage in the work, a series of reflective notes or additional sections could be inserted, indicating alternative ways of reinterpreting and critically relating to the empirical material and interpretations presented. Naturally these should not look like dutiful postscripts or afterthoughts stuck on at the last minute. The idea of reflection is not only to reduce the naïvety of the research in relationship to the constructed nature of empirical material and themes such as power, politics or ideology, language, authority, gender, and so on, or to show how familiar the researcher is with the literature; the main point is to 'lift' a project, to generate more interesting, innovative and well-judged interpretations and qualified results.

We could also think of reflexive research as a research programme consisting of different sub-projects. The sequencing would then occur over time. Forms of reflection, in the more advanced sense, could then come in after the conventional empirical project is completed and has been reported on. Instead of immediately embarking upon a new empirical task, the researcher could reflect critically upon the previous project, not so much perhaps to find faults or weaknesses, although this is important for learning, but more to reinterpret earlier descriptions and ideas and to put them in a new context, thereby developing new knowledge. Reflexive interpretation, in the more ambitious way, would thus be taking place primarily at the programme level, with different components predominating in different sub-projects and research publications. One possible advantage of this is that it is perhaps easier to make reinterpretations of empirical material and earlier interpretations at metalevels when one has acquired a certain distance vis-á-vis the material. Another possibility is that researchers who collaborate with one another have – or develop – different specialities in reflective terms. This need not mean creating research teams consisting of (extreme) empiricists, hermeneuticians, critical theorists and poststructuralists. Such a collaboration would be difficult to organize in practice, and would anyway face problems in accomplishing a good interaction between the perspectives, if the initial points of contact and overlapping frames are too meagre. What we could envisage is rather that two or more researchers for instance, who have a basic approach in common – could as is necessary in research contexts – could individually delve more deeply into different areas, for example studying different complementary theories which would broaden their common repertoire of interpretations and ensure a certain reflective capacity. More generally, it is a question of acquiring a suitable combination of similarities and differences in the collaborative undertaking.

Finally, a warning about reflexive-interpretive research. The risk of failing in research is far from negligible. The same is true even if one starts from a more conventional methodological view, with a simplified and naïve idea of interpretation, language, political context and modes of presentation. Since even mushroom-picking PhD projects quite often fail to reach the minimum level for acceptability or achieve anything interesting or original, we can expect the successful completion of a reflective research project, with its higher demands, to be fraught with problems. On the other hand, the demands on reflexive researchers would surely have some salutary effects on motivation. The undiluted boredom of data-fixated research ('data-dredging') and the meagre scope for independent and creative thought can explain some of the failures, as people lose their inspiration and abandon a project. We believe even more strongly that the reflexive-interpretive approach can improve the outcome, in the shape of research which succeeds in saying something qualified and original. The risk that ambitious, multi-level reflection may lead to failure is naturally no reason to let social science (or other) research be exempt from the demands for hermeneutic, political and linguistic awareness, and for reflection developing such awareness and inspiring novel thinking. But it does mean that the individual researcher must carefully consider how these demands can be handled, what level of sophistication in terms of reflection can be managed, and how. Self-awareness, facilitated by sensitive listening to feedback on one's strengths and weaknesses as a researcher, is very important. As was mentioned in the discussion of various reflexive-interpretive methodological strategies, different mixes are possible as to interpretations at different levels, with different degrees of ambition and sophistication.

It is important to recognize, but not be overwhelmed by, the complexities of reflexive research. Conscious systematics for handling this problem are required. As in all qualitative research, it is not enough to rely upon the arguments of the recipe books; what is important is that the reflection is adapted to one's own personal abilities and conditions, and to the research task in hand. At the same time it must be pointed out that these personal competences are connected with what the researcher in question has read and studied. The research task is partly determined by reflection. Research questions informed by a consideration of a number of the themes covered in this book will, of course, differ heavily from the purpose of most conventional studies and the espoused interests of sponsoring organizations. To encourage rethinking on the part of the latter is a major intellectual but also pedagogical task.

Final comment: research as a provisionally rational project

In this book we have conducted a critical survey of a number of central currents in qualitative methodology and the philosophy of science. We have argued against prevalent methodological approaches and attempted to show the important lesson to be learned in the first instance from empirically oriented currents, hermeneutic, critical-theoretical, and postmodernist philosophies of science, but also from discourse analysis, feminism and genealogy. To put it polemically, we have argued that both 'recipe-book research' and 'theorizing in a vacuum' should be replaced by reflective activities, where the collecting, processing and analysis of qualitative data are regarded as a misleading description of what goes on, and as anyway being less central to research than the textbooks on qualitative method usually seem to suggest.

Using the term *reflexive interpretation*, we have sought to formulate a reasoned, comprehensive qualitative methodology (or metamethodology). We have not touched upon the technical level. This is mainly a question of the choice of focus, but also a reaction on our part against the obsession with techniques in traditional qualitative methodology. Nor do we consider that there is any need to add to what has already been said about methodological techniques. Recent years have witnessed a host of publications. The existing literature contains much about questions of access, about how to conduct interviews, about how to make notes during observations and so on – all of which is of value, provided the reader also possesses a metaunderstanding of the character of research work. But we claim that the decisive quality in qualitative research is not the way its different components are managed. Rather, what primarily determines its value is an awareness of the various interpretive dimensions at several different levels, and the ability to handle these reflexively. Good qualitative research is not a technical project; it is an intellectual one. In our view, reflection addressing a multitude of levels of domains, not the following of set procedures, characterizes the scientific in social science. Some may think that this leaves the criterion of demarcation vis-á-vis other well-reasoned activities (such as consultancy reports) too weak, and offers too loose a foundation for social research. We would not agree, maintaining instead that the special nature of social science is thus brought out quite strongly (without being exaggerated). The handling (constructing and further interpreting) of empirical material in a reflexive way, setting into motion reflections on several issues, at the same time as consistently admitting ambiguity, is what gives social science its distinctive hallmark. The framework presented in this book aims to provide a structure and direction, as well as to facilitate creativity and the transcendence of established ideas, while maintaining a flexibility on the level of research procedure and the interaction with empirical material.

Research according to the perspective (or rather metaperspective) presented here does not conform to any linear process or monolithic logic. It can be tempting to argue against, or heavily play down, the potential for rationality in (social science) research, as the postmodernists, the radical constructivists and others have done on a grand scale in recent years. We go along with them to the extent of agreeing that attempts to define empirical research as a supremely rational project are not particularly successful. On the other hand, we see no *constructive* reasons for taking up the opposite position. Instead we adopt the view of research as a provisionally rational project, in which the kernel of rationality is a question of reflection rather than procedure.

Provisionally rational, yes – but also provisionally rhetorical. For on closer scrutiny it becomes clear that the four interpretive levels that we have dealt with in this book, which we are proposing as major elements in a reflexive methodology, also correspond to the four main rhetorical figures, or 'master tropes', which in a wider perspective express four principal thought styles, and thus constitute a kind of 'poetic logic' (see White, 1985a; and, for a discussion in social science terms, Sköldberg, 2002b).

To the master trope of metonymy, which sees everything 'atomistically' as isolated from everything else, correspond the data-oriented approaches, and especially grounded theory, with their emphasis on isolated empirical data. Hermeneutics, the second level, expresses a stance where the meaning of symbols becomes central, thus manifesting the second master trope, metaphor, for which symbols and meaning of symbols are precisely the central concern. Critical theory deals with the influence of overriding systems, especially politics and ideology, on the lifeworld of people, thereby manifesting the third rhetorical figure, synecdoche, which expresses the relationship between whole and part. Postmodernism, as we have already mentioned, is permeated thoroughly by an ironical style of thought, and is therefore a very good example of the fourth and last master trope, or rhetorical figure, irony.

We shall not go into this deeper here, as we intend to do so elsewhere. It is just important to point out that not only are there rational reasons for choosing the four levels of reflexive interpretation which we have suggested for a qualitative method-ology, but there is also a poetic logic underlying this, shaping the subject matter by virtue of rhetorics and thought styles. In this sense, too, we see the position of the present book as a precarious balance between accepting the existence of some sort of reality 'out there', and accepting the rhetorical and narrative nature of our knowledge of this reality. There is an unstable and wavering relation between reality and rhetoric, but also a dynamism of re-construction, generated by this very instability, which we have tried to capture in this book.

Notes

1. We could envisage at least two variants of postmodernism in this context. As well as a polyphony-driven variant, which seeks to allow space for both the views of the subjects and for the multifaceted nature of empirical 'reality', a deconstruction-driven variant can also be mentioned, typically focusing on a narrow fragment of text. In our present con-text, which is about qualitative methods for empirical social research (and not literary theory), the former variant is of greater interest.
2. Conversation and discourse analysts try to minimize interpretations when transcribing recorded material. The reader sometimes has difficulty in understanding the transcript, which often gives a rather messy and incoherent impression, with incomplete sentences and so on.
3. To regard something as an event or an action is, of course, an interpretation.
4. The supporters of grounded theory emphasize both the agreement between theory and data, and the ability of theory to exercise control relative to action in the field in ques-tion. For some proponents of this direction, truth, as guaranteed by such traditional scientific virtues as 'theory-observation compatibility, generalizability, reproducibility, precision, rigor, and verification' (Strauss and Corbin, 1990: 27), and technical-functional value go hand in hand. On the other hand Glaser (1992: 67–69, 71–72) fiercely opposes this drift, referring to Glaser and Strauss (1967) as the original source of grounded the-ory, and pointing out that the basic idea of the whole book is the generation, not the ver-ification or testing, of theory.
5. Even if they do not always put it very clearly, most researchers with an interest in constructivism and the central importance of presentation (the text), subscribe to the crucial character of the empirical material. In certain cases criteria are used which are fairly similar to the conventional ones, albeit a little 'softer'. Guba and Lincoln (1994: 114) suggest trustworthiness, for instance, instead of internal validity, transferability instead of external validity, and confirmability replacing objectivity. Van Maanen (1995: 22)

declares that even if research acquires credibility in relation to social, historical and institutional forces, and even if textuality is pivotal in ethnographies, for instance, it is still necessary to maintain the traditional virtues such as 'presenting evidence, providing interpretations, elaborating analogies, invoking authorities, working through examples, marshalling the troops, and so on'. We agree that these criteria and elements of the work process are important in empirical research; but others can be even more important, as will be seen below. We wish to tone down the value of what can be clearly demonstrated empirically.

6. Apart from supporting various views on 'how it is' or (better) fruitful ways of describing and understanding 'reality', empirical material can also be used in other ways. It may be used, for example, to generate ideas, to illustrate or to encourage and guide critique and modification of theories, and to generate insightful descriptions through drawing attention to neglected dimensions.

7. A good idea in this respect might be not to deny the significance of an ordered observed world, but rather to take it as a powerful (and power-filled) product, and then to attempt to fracture these objectifications in order to reveal fuller potential and variety than are immediately apparent (Deetz, 1996).

8. This is not to deny that the sets of practices include some elements of both: destabilizing practices offer some sort of alternative understanding – even Foucauldian ideas on how knowledge produces rather than reveals truth says something about how subjects are created; in the case of multi-perspectivist practices, there is frequently a partial or minimalist deconstruction when one perspective is used to disturb another (Alvesson, 2002).

REFERENCES

Acker, J. (1989) Making gender visible. In R.A. Wallace (ed.), *Feminism and Sociological Theory*. Newbury Park, CA: Sage.

Acker, J., Barry, K. and Esseveld, J. (1991) Objectivity and truth: problems in doing feminist research. In M. Fonow and J. Cook. (eds), *Beyond Methodology: Feminist Scholarship as Lived Research*. Bloomington: Indiana University Press.

Adorno, T.W. (1974) *Minima Moralia*. London: NLB.

Adorno, T.W. (1976) On the logic of the social sciences. In T.W. Adorno, H. Albert, R. Dahrendorf, J. Habermas, H. Pilot and K.R. Popper, *The Positivist Dispute in German Sociology*. London: Heinemann. Paper first published in 1961.

Adorno, T.W. and Horkheimer, M. (1979) *Dialectic of Enlightenment*. London: Verso. First published in 1944.

Adorno, T.W., Frenkel-Brunswik, E., Levinson, D.J. et al. (1950) *The Authoritarian Personality*. New York: Harper & Row.

Agar, M.H. (1986) *Speaking of Ethnography*. Beverly Hills, CA: Sage.

Agger, B. (1991) Critical theory, poststructuralism, postmodernism: their sociological relevance. *Annual Review of Sociology*, 17: 105–131.

Alborzi, S. and Khayyer, M. with Johnston, T.L. (2008) Overcoming obstacles: opportunities of academically talented women in Iran. *The Grounded Theory Review*, 7(1): 11–41.

Alvesson, M. (1993a) *Cultural Perspectives on Organizations*. Cambridge: Cambridge University Press.

Alvesson, M. (1993b) The play of metaphors. In J. Hassard and M. Parker (eds), *Postmodernism and Organizations*. London: Sage.

Alvesson, M. (1994) Critical theory and consumer marketing. *Scandinavian Journal of Management*, 10: 291–313.

Alvesson, M. (1995) The meaning and meaninglessness of postmodernism. *Organization Studies*, 16(6): 1049–1077.

Alvesson, M. (1996) *Communication, Power and Organisation*. Berlin/New York: de Gruyter.

Alvesson, M. (1998) Gender relations and identity: masculinities and femininities at work in an advertising agency. *Human Relations*, 51(8): 969–1005.

Alvesson, M. (2002) *Postmodernism and Social Research*. Buckingham: Open University Press.

Alvesson, M. (2003) Beyond neo-positivism, romanticism and localism. A reflexive approach to interviews. *Academy of Management Review*, 28(1):13–33.

Alvesson, M. and Billing, Y.D. (2009) *Understanding Gender and Organization* (2nd edn). London: Sage.

Alvesson, M. and Deetz, S. (2000) *Doing Critical Management Research*. London: Sage.

Alvesson, M., Hardy, C. and Harley, B. (2008) Reflecting on reflexivity: reappraising reflexive practice in organisation and management theory. *Journal of Management Studies*, 43: 480–501.

Alvesson, M. and Kärreman, D. (2000) Taking the linguistic turn in organization research. *Journal of Applied Behavioural Science*, 36 (2): 134–56.

Alvesson, M. and Köping, A.-S. (1993) *Med känslan som ledstjärna. En studie av reklamarbetare och reklambyråer*. Lund: Studentlitteratur.

Alvesson, M. and Sveningsson, S. (2008) *Changing Organizational Culture*. London: Routledge.

Alvesson, M. and Willmott, H. (1996) *Making Sense of Management: A Critical Introduction*. London: Sage.

Andrews, T. and Waterman, H. (2005) Visualising deteriorating conditions. *The Grounded Theory Review*, 4(2): 63–93.

Annells, M.P. (1996) Grounded theory method: philosophical perspectives, paradigm of inquiry, and postmodernism. *Qualitative Health Research*, 6(3): 379–393.

Anthony, P.D. (1977) *The Ideology of Work*. London: Tavistock.

Archer, M. (1998) Introduction: realism in the social sciences. In M. Archer et al. (eds), *Critical Realism*. London: Routledge.

Arminen, I. (1996) On the moral and interactional relevancy of self-repairs for life stories of members of Alcoholics Anonymous. *Text*. 16: 449–480.

Arminen, I. (1998) *Therapeutic Interaction: A Study of Mutual Help in the Meetings of Alcoholics Anonymous*. Helsinki: Finnish Foundation for Alcohol Studies.

Ashcraft, K. (2001) Organized dissonance: feminist bureaucracy as hybrid form. *Academy of Management Journal*, 44(6): 1301–1322.

Ashmore, M. (1989) *The Reflexive Thesis: Wrighting Sociology of Scientific Knowledge*. Chicago, IL: University of Chicago Press.

Asplund, J. (1970) *Om undran inför samhället*. Lund: Argos.

Asplund, J. (1987) *Det sociala livets elementära former*. Göteborg: Korpen.

Asplund, J. (1989) *Rivaler och syndabockar*. Göteborg: Korpen.

Asplund, J. (1992) *Storstäderna och det forteanska livet*. Göteborg: Korpen.

Astley, W.G. (1985) Administrative science as socially constructed truth. *Administrative Science Quarterly*, 30: 497–513.

Atkinson, J.M. and Heritage, U. (eds) (1984) *Structures of Social Actions: Studies in Conversation Analysis*. Cambridge: Cambridge University Press.

Atkinson, P. (1988) Ethnomethodology: a critical review. *Annual Review of Sociology*, 14: 441–465.

Atkinson, P. and Hammersley, M. (1994) Ethnography and participant observation. In N. Denzin and Y. Lincoln (eds), *Handbook of Qualitative Research*. Thousand Oaks, CA: Sage.

Baker, S. (1990) Reflection, doubt, and the place of rhetoric in postmodern social theory. *Sociological Theory*, 8: 232–245.

Barlebo Wenneberg, S. (2001) Socialkonstruktivism. Positioner, problem och Perspektiv. [Social constructivism. Positions, problems, and perspectives.] Malmö: Liber.

Bärmark, J. (1984) Vetenskapens subjektiva sida. In J. Bärmark (ed.), *Forskning om forskning*. Stockholm: Natur och Kultur.

Baskin, C. and Taylor, R. (2007) Reciprocal Disconnectedness: computer games, schooling and boys at risk. *E-Learning*, 4(2): 150–160.

Baszanger, I. and Dodier, N. (1997) Ethnography: relating the part to the whole. In D. Silverman (ed.), *Qualitative Research*. London: Sage.

Baudrillard, J. (1983) *Simulations*. New York: Semiotext(e).

Baudrillard, J. (1985) The ecstacy of communication. In H. Foster (ed.), *Postmodern Culture*. London: Pluto Press. Paper first published in 1983.

Bay, T. (1998) AND … AND … AND. Reiterating financial derivation. Doctoral dissertation. Stockholm: Stockholm School of Business, Stockholm University.

Beach, W.A. (1996) *Conversations about Illness: Family Preoccupations with Bulimia*. Mahwah, NJ: Lawrence Erlbaum.

Becker, E. (1973) *The Denial of Death*. New York: Free Press.

Bengtsson, J. (1989) Fenomenologi: vardagsforskning, existensfilosofi, hermeneutik. In P. Månsson (ed.), *Moderna samhällsteorier. Traditioner, riktningar, teoretiker*. Stockholm: Prisma.

Benhabib, S. and Cornell, D. (eds) (1987) *Feminism as Critique*. Cambridge: Polity Press.

Bentz, V. and Shapiro, J. (1998) *Mindful Inquiry in Social Research*. Thousand Oaks, CA: Sage.

Berg, P.O. (1982) 11 metaphors and their theoretical implications. In P.O. Berg and P. Daudi (eds), *Traditions and Trends in Organization Theory. Part II*. Lund: Studentlitteratur.

Berg, P.O. (1989) Postmodern management? From facts to fiction in theory and practice. *Scandinavian Journal of Management*, 5: 201–217.

Berger, P.L. and Luckmann, T. (1966) *The Social Construction of Reality. A Treatise in the Sociology of Knowledge*. New York: Doubleday.

Berman, M. (1992) Why modernism still matters? In S. Lash and J. Friedman (eds) *Modernity & Identity*. Oxford: Blackwell.

Bernstein, R.J. (1983) *Beyond Objectivism and Relativism*. Oxford: Basil Blackwell.

Bernstein, R.J. (ed.) (1985) *Habermas and Modernity*. Cambridge, MA: MIT Press.

Beronius, M. (1986) *Den disciplinära maktens organisering*. Lund: Arkiv.

Beronius, M. (1991) *Genealogi och sociologi*. Stehag: Symposion.

Betti, E. (1967) *Allgemeine Auslegungslehre als Methodik der Geisteswissenschaften*. Tübingen: Mohr.

Betti, E. (1980) Hermeneutics as the general methodology of the Geisteswissenschaften. In J. Bleicher (ed.), *Contemporary Hermeneutics*. London: Routledge. Paper first published 1962.

Bhaskar, R. (1991) *Philosophy and the Idea of Freedom*. Oxford: Blackwell.

Bhaskar, R. (1998) General Introduction. In Archer, M. et al. (eds), *Critical Realism*. London: Routledge.

Bhaskar, R. and Lawson, T. (1998) Introduction: basic texts and developments. In M. Archer, et al. (eds), *Critical Realism*. London: Routledge.

Billig, M. and Simons, H. (1994) Introduction. In H. Simons and M. Billig (eds), *After Postmodernism. Reconstructing Ideology Critique*. London: Sage.

Billing, Y.D. and Alvesson, M. (1994) *Gender, Managers and Organizations*. Berlin/New York: de Gruyter.

Bilmes, J. (1997) Being interrupted. *Language in Society*, 26: 1–25.

Blau, P.M. (1955) *The Dynamics of Bureaucracy*. Chicago: University of Chicago Press.

Blomqvist, M. (1994) *Könshierarkier i gungning. Kvinnor i kunskapsföretag*. Studia Sociologica Upsaliensa 39. Uppsala: Acta Universitatis Upsaliensis.

Boden, D. and Zimmerman, D.H. (eds) (1991) *Talk and Social Structure*. Cambridge: Polity Press.

Bohman, J. (1991) *New Philosophy of Social Science. Problems of Indeterminacy*. Cambridge, UK: Polity Press.

Boothby, R. (1993) Heideggerian psychiatry. The Freudian unconscious in Medard Boss and Jacques Lacan. *Journal of Phenomenological Psychology*, 24(2): 144–160.

Bordo, S. (1990) Feminism, postmodernism and gender-scepticism. In L. Nicholson (ed.), *Feminism/Postmodernism*. New York: Routledge.

Boss, M. (1988) Recent considerations in daseinsanalysis. *The Humanist Psychologist*, 16(1): 58–74.

Bourdieu, P. (1984) *Distinction. A Social Critique of the Judgement of Taste*. Cambridge, MA: Harvard University Press.

Bourdieu, P. and Wacquant, L.J.D. (1992) *An Invitation to Reflexive Sociology*. Cambridge: Polity Press.

Bourdieu, P., Chamboredon, J.-C. and Passeron, J.-C. (1991) *The Craft of Sociology. Epistemological Preliminaries*. Berlin: de Gruyter. First published in 1968.

Bowers, J. (1988) Review essay on *Discourse and Social Psychology: Beyond Attitudes and Behaviour*. *British Journal of Social Psychology*, 27: 185–192.

Braithwaite, R.B. (1953) *Scientific Explanation. A Study on the Function of Theory, Probability and Law in Science*. Cambridge: Cambridge University Press.

Brewer, J. (2000) *Ethnography*. Buckingham: Open University Press.

Bricmont, J. (1997) 'Le relativisme alimente le courant irrationnel'. Interview with Jean Bricmont in *La Recherche*, May.

Broad, W. and Wade, N. (1982) *Betrayers of the Truth*. New York: Simon and Schuster.

Broms, H. and Gahmberg, H. (1983) Communication to self in organizations and cultures. *Administrative Science Quarterly*, 28: 482–495.

Brown, R.H. (1976) Social theory as metaphor. *Theory and Society*, 3: 169–197.

Brown, R.H. (1977) *A Poetic for Sociology*. Chicago, IL: University of Chicago Press.

Brown, R.H. (1990) Rhetoric, textuality, and the postmodern turn in sociological theory. *Sociological Theory*, 8: 188–197.

Brown, R.H. (1994) Reconstructing social theory after the postmodern critique. In H. Simons and M. Billig (eds), *After Postmodernism. Reconstructing Ideology Critique*. London: Sage.

Bryman, A. (1989) *Research Methods and Organization Studies*. London: Unwin-Hyman.

Bubner, R. (1982) Habermas' concept of critical theory. In J.B. Thompson and D. Held (eds), *Habermas: Critical Debates*. London: Macmillan.

Bunge, M. (1967) *Scientific Research* (2 vols). New York: Springer-Verlag.

Burns, T. and Stalker, G.M. (1961) *The Management of Innovation*. London: Tavistock.

Burr, V. (2003) *Social Constructionism* (2nd edn). London and New York: Routledge.

Burrell, G. (1992) The organisation of pleasure. In M. Alvesson and H. Willmott (eds), *Critical Management Studies*. London: Sage.

Burrell, G. and Morgan, G. (1979) *Sociological Paradigms and Organizational Analysis*. Aldershot: Gower.

Bushman, B.J. and Baumeister, R.F. (1998) Threatened egotism, narcissism, self-esteem, and direct and misplaced aggression: does self-love or self-hate lead to violence? *Journal of Personality and Social Psychology,* 75(1): 219–229.

Butler, J. (2004) *Undoing Gender*. London: Routledge.

Calás, M. and Smircich, L. (1988) Reading leadership as a form of cultural analysis. In J.G. Hunt et al. (eds), *Emerging Leadership Vistas*. Lexington, MA: Lexington Books.

Calás, M. and Smircich, L. (1991) Voicing seduction to silence leadership. *Organization Studies*, 12: 567–601.

Calás, M. and Smircich, L. (1992b) Rewriting gender into organizational theorizing: directions from feminist perspectives. In M. Reed and M. Hughes (eds), *Re-thinking Organization: New Directions in Organizational Theory and Analysis*. London: SAGE.

Calás, M. and Smircich, L. (2006) From the 'women's' point of view: feminist approaches to organization studies. In S. Clegg, C. Hardy, T. Lawrence and W. Nord (eds), *The SAGE Handbook of Organization Studies* (2nd edn). London: Sage.

Callon, M. (1980) Struggles and negotiations to define what is problematic and what is not: The sociology of translation. In K.D. Knorr and R. D. Whitley (eds), *The social process of scientific investigation*, 4: 197–219. Dordrecht: Reidel.

Callon, M. (1986) Some elements of a sociology of translation. In J. Law (ed.), *Power, Action and Belief: A New Sociology of Knowledge?* London: Routledge and Kegan Paul.

Calhoun, C. (1992) Culture, history, and the problem of specificity in social theory. In S. Seidman and D. Wagner (eds), *Postmodernism and Social Theory*. Cambridge, MA/ Oxford: Blackwell.

Caponigri, A.R. (1963) *A History of Western Philosophy, Vol III*. Notre Dame, IN: University of Notre Dame Press.

Caponigri, A.R. (1971) *A History of Western Philosophy, Vol. V*. Notre Dame, IN: University of Notre Dame Press.

Caputo, J.D. (1987) *Radical Hermeneutics. Repetition, Deconstruction, and the Hermeneutic Project*. Bloomington: Indiana University Press.

Caputo, J.D. (1997) *The Prayers and Tears of Jacques Derrida*. Bloomington: Indiana University Press.

Carnap, R. (1962) *Logical Foundations of Probability*. Chicago, IL: University of Chicago Press.

Carrard, P. (1992) *Poetics of the New History: French Historical Discourse from Braudel to Chartier*. Baltimore, MD: Johns Hopkins University Press.

Castaneda, C. (1963) *The Teachings of Don Juan: A Yaqui Way of Knowledge*. Berkeley: University of California Press.

Castoriadis, C. (1992) Power, politics, autonomy. In A. Honneth et al. (eds), *Cultural-Political Interventions in the Unfinished Project of Enlightenment*. Cambridge, MA: MIT Press.

Chakravarty, A. (2001) The semantic or model-theoretic view of theories and scientific realism. *Synthèse*, 127: 325–345.

Charmaz, K. (2000) Grounded theory: objectivist and constructivist methods. In N. Denzin and Y. Lincoln (eds) *Handbook of Qualitative Research* (2nd edn). Thousand Oaks: Sage.

Charniak, E. and McDermott, D. (1985) *Introduction to Artificial Intelligence*. Reading, MA: Addison-Wesley.

Chia, R. (1995) From modern to postmodern organizational analysis. *Organization Studies*, 16(4): 579–604.

Chomsky, N. (1965) *Syntactic Structures*. The Hague: Mouton.

Cicourel, A.V. (1964) *Method and Measurement in Sociology*. New York: Free Press.

Clarke, A.E. (2005) *Situational Analysis: Grounded Theory After the Postmodern Turn*. Thousand Oaks, CA: Sage.

Clegg, S. (1989) *Frameworks of Power*. London: Sage.

Clegg, S. (1990) *Modern Organization: Organization Studies in the Postmodern World*. London: Sage.

Clegg, S. and Hardy, C. (1996) Some dare call it power. In S. Clegg, C. Hardy and W. Nord (eds), *Handbook of Organization Studies*. London: Sage.

Clifford, J. (1986) Introduction: Partial truths. In J. Clifford and G.E. Marcus (eds), *Writing Culture: The Poetics and Politics of Ethnography*. Berkeley: University of California Press.

Clifford, J. and Marcus, G.E. (eds) (1986) *Writing Culture: The Poetics and Politics of Ethnography*. Berkeley: University of California Press.

Collingwood, R.G. (1992) *The Idea of History*. Oxford: Oxford University Press. First published in 1946.

Collins, R. (1981) Micro-translation as a theory-building strategy. In K. Knorr-Cetina and A. Cicourel (eds), *Advances in Social Theory and Methodology*. Boston: Routledge & Kegan Paul.

Collins, R. (1985) *Three Sociological Traditions*. New York: Oxford University Press.

Collinson, D. (1992) Researching recruitment: qualitative methods and sex discrimination. In R. Burgess (ed.), *Studies in Qualitative Methodology, Vol. 3*. Greenwich, CT: JAI Press.

Collinson, D. (2003) Identities and insecurities. *Organization*, 10 (3): 527–47.

Comte, A. (1844) *Discours sur l'Esprit positif*.

Connerton, P. (1980) *The Tragedy of Enlightenment*. Cambridge: Cambridge University Press.

Cooper, J.C. (1978) *An Illustrated Encyclopaedia of Traditional Symbols*. London: Thames and Hudson.

Cooper, R. (1989) Modernism, postmodernism and organizational analysis 3: the contribution of Jacques Derrida. *Organization Studies*, 10: 479–502.

Crook, S. (2001) Social theory and the postmodern. In G. Ritzer and B. Smart (eds), *Handbook of Social Theory*. Thousand Oaks, CA: Sage.

Crotty, M. (1998) *The Foundations of Social Research*. London: Sage.

Czarniawska, B. (2005) *En teori om organisering*. Lund: Studentlitteratur. B. Danermark, M. Ekström, L. Jakobsen and J.C. Karlsson (2002) *Explaining Society: Critical Realism in the Social Sciences*. London: Routledge.

Czarniawska, B. and Hernes, T. (eds) (2005) *Actor-Network Theory and Organizing*. Köpenhamn: Copenhagen Business School Press.

Czarniawska-Joerges, B. (1992) *Exploring Complex Organizations*. Newbury Park, CA: Sage.

Czarniawska-Joerges, B. (1994) Narratives of individual and organizational identities. In S. Deetz (ed.), *Communication Yearbook, Vol. 17*. Newbury Park, CA: Sage.

Czubaroff, J. (1989) The deliberative character of strategic scientific debates. In H. Simons (ed.), *Rhetoric in the Human Sciences*. London: Sage.

Danermark, B., Ekström, M., Jakobsen, L. and Karlsson, J. C. (2002) *Explaining Society: Critical Realism in the Social Sciences*. London: Routledge.

Danermark, B., Ekström, M., Jakobsen, L. and Karlsson, J.C. (2003) *Att förklara samhället* (2nd edn). Lund: Studentlitteratur.

Davis, M.S. (1971) That's interesting! Towards a phenomenology of sociology and a sociology of phenomenology. *Philosophy of the Social Sciences*, 1: 309–44.

Daudi, P. (1990) Con-versing in management's public place. *Scandinavian Journal of Management*, 6: 285–307.

De Hoyos Guajardo, M. (2004) Solutioning. *The Grounded Theory Review*, 4(1): 59–85.

De Man, P. (1983) *Blindness and Insight: Essays in the Rhetoric of Contemporary Criticism* (2nd edn). London: Methuen.

Deetz, S. (1992) *Democracy in an Age of Corporate Colonization: Developments in Communication and the Politics of Everyday Life*. Albany: State University of New York Press.

Deetz, S. (1995) The social production of knowledge and the commercial artifact. In L. Cummings and P. Frost (eds), *Publishing in the Organizational Sciences* (2nd edn). Homewood, IL: Irwin.

Deetz, S. (1996) Describing differences in approaches to organization science: rethinking Burrell and Morgan and their legacy. *Organization Science*, 7: 191–207.

Deetz, S. and Kersten, S. (1983) Critical models of interpretive research. In L. Putnam and M. Pacanowsky (eds), *Communication and Organizations*. Beverly Hills, CA: Sage.

Delanty, G. (2005) *Social Science* (2nd edn). Buckingham: Open University Press.

Deleuze, G. (1983) *Nietzsche and Philosophy*. London: Athlone.

Deleuze, G. (1988) *Foucault*. Minneapolis: University of Minnesota Press.

Denzin, N. (1994) The art and politics of interpretation. In N. Denzin and Y. Lincoln (eds), *Handbook of Qualitative Research*. Thousand Oaks, CA: Sage.

Denzin, N. (1997) *Interpretive Ethnography*. Thousand Oaks, CA: Sage.

Denzin, N. and Lincoln, Y. (1994) Introduction: entering the field of qualitative research. In N. Denzin and Y. Lincoln (eds), *Handbook of Qualitative Research*. Thousand Oaks, CA: Sage.

Denzin, N. and Lincoln, Y. (2005) Introduction: The discipline and practice of qualitative research. In N. Denzin and Y. Lincoln (eds), *Handbook of Qualitative Research* (2nd edn). Thousand Oaks, CA: Sage.

Derrida, J. (1976) *Of Grammatology*. Baltimore, MD: Johns Hopkins University Press. First published in 1967.

Derrida, J. (1978a) *Writing and Difference*. London: Routledge. First published in 1967.

Derrida, J. (1978b) *Speech and Phenomena*. Evanston, IL: Northwestern University Press. First published in 1967.

Derrida, J. (1982) *Margins of Philosophy*. Chicago: University of Chicago Press. First published in 1972.

Derrida, J. (1989a) Three questions to Hans-Georg Gadamer. In D.P. Michelfelder and R.E. Palmer (eds), *Dialogue and Deconstruction. The Gadamer–Derrida Encounter*. Albany: State University of New York Press.

Derrida, J. (1989b) Interpreting signatures (Nietzsche/Heidegger): two questions. In D.P. Michelfelder and R.E. Palmer (eds), *Dialogue and Deconstruction: The Gadamer–Derrida Encounter*. Albany: State University of New York Press.

Detmer, D. (2003) *Challenging Postmodernism: Philosophy and the Politics of Truth*. Amherst, NY: Humanity.

Deutsch, F.M. (2007) Undoing gender. *Gender and Society*, 21(1): 106–127.

Dews, P. (1987) *Logics of Disintegration*. London: New Left Review.

Douglas, J.D. and Johnson, J.M. (eds) (1977) *Existential Sociology*. Cambridge: Cambridge University Press.

Drew, P. and Heritage, J. (eds) (1993) *Talk at Work*. Cambridge: Cambridge University Press.

Dreyfus, H.L. (1991) Heidegger's hermeneutic realism. In D.R. Hiley, J.F. Bohman and R. Shusterman (eds), *The Interpretive Turn: Philosophy, Science, Culture*. New York: Cornell University Press. pp. 25–41.

Dreyfus, H. and Rabinow, P. (1983) *Michel Foucault: Beyond Structuralism and Hermeneutics* (2nd edn). Chicago: University of Chicago Press.

Dreyfus, H. and Rabinow, P. (1986) What is maturity? Habermas and Foucault on 'What is Enlightenment?' In D. Hoy (ed.), *Foucault: A Critical Reader*. Oxford: Basil Blackwell. Paper first published in 1982.

Dunne, J. (1996) Beyond sovereignty and deconstruction: the storied self. In R. Kearny (ed.), *Paul Ricoeur: The Hermeneutics of Action*. London: Sage.

Eco, Umberto (1990) *The Limits of Interpretation*. Bloomington: Indiana University Press.

Ehn, B. and Löfgren, O. (1982) *Kulturanalys*. Lund: Liber.

Ekerwald, H. and Johansson, S. (1989) Vetenskap som byråkrati eller som konst? *Sociologisk Forskning*, 2: 15–33.

Eliade, M. (1974) *Shamanism: Archaic Techniques of Ecstasy*. Princeton, NJ: Princeton University Press.

Erslev, K. (1961) *Historisk teknik: den historiske undersøgelsen fremstillet i sine grundlinier.* (2 uppl.). København: Gyldendal.

Esposito, F., Ferilli, S., Basile, T.M.A. and Di Mauro, N. (2007) Inference of abduction theories for handling incompleteness in first-order learning. *Knowledge and Information Systems*, 11(2): 217–242.

Fay, B. (1987) *Critical Social Science*. Cambridge: Polity Press.

Featherstone, M. (1988) In pursuit of the postmodern: an introduction. *Theory, Culture & Society*, 5: 195–215.

Feldman, M.S. and Sköldberg, K. (2002) Stories and the rhetorics of contrariety: the undertext of organizing (change). *Culture and Organization*, 8(4): 275–292.

Feldman, M.S., Sköldberg, K., Brown, R.N. and Horner, D. (2004) Making sense of stories: a rhetorical approach to narrative analysis. *Administration Research and Theory*, 14(2): 147–170.

Fell, J.P. (1979) *Heidegger and Sartre*. New York: Columbia University Press.

Ferguson, K. (1984) *The Feminist Case against Bureaucracy*. Philadelphia: Temple University Press.

Fetterman, D.M. (1989) *Ethnography. Step by Step*. Newbury Park, CA: Sage.

Feyerabend, P. (1981) Philosophical Papers (Vol 1). *Realism, Rationalism and Scientific Method*. Cambridge: Cambridge University Press.

Feyerabend, P.K. (1975) *Against Method: Outline of an Anarchistic Theory of Knowledge*. London: New Left Books.

Feyerabend, P.K. (1987) *Farewell to Reason*. London: Verso.

Finch, J. (1984) 'It is great to have someone to talk to': the ethics and politics of interviewing women. In C. Bell and H. Roberts (eds), *Social Researching*. London: Routledge.

Fine, G.A. (1993) The sad demise, mysterious disappearance, and glorious triumph of symbolic interactionism. *Annual Review of Sociology*, 19: 61–87.

Fine, M., Weis, L., Weseen, S. and Wong, L. (2000) For whom? Qualitative research, representations and social responsibilities. In N. Denzin and Y. Lincoln (eds), *Handbook of Qualitative Research* (2nd edn). Thousand Oaks, CA: Sage.

Flax, J. (1987) Postmodernism and gender relations in feminist theory. *Signs*, 12: 621–643.

Fleck, L. (1934/1979) *Genesis and Development of a Scientific Fact*. Chicago, IL: University of Chicago Press.

Fleetwood, S. (2005) Ontology in organization and management studies: a critical realist perspective. *Organization,* 12: 197–222.

Flynn, P.J. (1991) *The Ethnomethodological Movement: Sociosemantic Interpretations*. Berlin: de Gruyter.

Forester, J. (1983) Critical theory and organizational analysis. In G. Morgan (ed.), *Beyond Method*. Beverly Hills, CA: Sage.

Forester, J. (1989) *Planning in the Face of Power*. Berkeley: University of California Press.

Forester, J. (1992) Critical ethnography: on fieldwork in a Habermasian way. In M. Alvesson and H. Willmott (eds), *Critical Management Studies*. London: Sage.

Forester, J. (1993) *Critical Theory, Public Policy, and Planning Practice*. Albany: State University of New York Press.

Forester, J. (2003) Critical ethnography: on fieldwork in a Habermasian way. In M. Alvesson and H. Willmott (eds.) *Studying Management Critically*. London: Sage.

Forget, P. (1985) Argument(s). In D.P. Michelfelder and R.E. Felder (eds) *Dialogue and Deconstruction: The Gadamer–Derrida Encounter*. Albany, NY: State University of New York Press.

Foster, H. (ed.) (1985) *Postmodern Culture*. London: Pluto Press. First published in 1983.

Foucault, M. (1972) *The Archaeology of Knowledge*. New York: Harper and Row. First published in 1969. Includes *The Discourse on Language*, first published (as *L'Ordre du Discours*) in 1971.

Foucault, M. (1973) *The Order of Things: An Archaeology of the Human Sciences*. New York: Random House. First published in 1966.

Foucault, M. (1978) *The History of Sexuality. Vol. 1*. New York: Pantheon. First published in 1976.

Foucault, M. (1979) *Discipline and Punish: The Birth of the Prison*. New York: Vintage/Random House. First published in 1975.

Foucault, M. (1980) *Power/Knowledge*. New York: Pantheon.

Foucault, M. (1982) The subject and power. *Critical Inquiry*, 8: 777–795.

Foucault, M. (1983) Structuralism and post-structuralism: an interview with Michel Foucault, by G. Raulet. *Telos*, 55: 195–211.

Foucault, M. (1988) *The History of Sexuality. Vol. 3: The Care of the Self*. New York. Random House.

Fourastié, B. and Joron, P. (1993) The imaginary as a sociological perspective. *Current Sociology*, 41(2): 53–58.

Fraser, N. (1987) What's critical about critical theory? The case of Habermas and gender. In S. Benhabib and D. Cornell (eds), *Feminism as Critique*. Cambridge: Polity Press.

Fraser, N. and Nicholson, L. (1988) Social criticism without philosophy: an encounter between feminism and postmodernism. *Theory, Culture & Society*, 5(2–3): 373–394.

Freeman, R., Ekins, R. and Oliver, M. (2005) Doing best for children: an emerging grounded theory of parents' policing strategies to regulate between meal snacking. *The Grounded Theory Review*, 4(3): 59–80.

Freud, S. (1953) *The Interpretation of Dreams*. In J. Strachey (ed.), *Works. The Standard Edition of the Complete Psychological Works of Sigmund Freud, Vols 4 and 5*. London: Hogarth Press.

Frisby, D. (1976) Introduction. In T.W. Adorno, H. Albert, R. Dahrendorf, J. Habermas, H. Pilot and K.R. Popper, *The Positivist Dispute in German Sociology*. London: Heinemann.

Fromm, E. (1941) *Escape from Freedom*. New York: Holt, Rinehart and Winston.

Fromm, E. (1955) *The Sane Society*. London: Routledge & Kegan Paul.

Fromm, E. (1976) *To Have or to Be?* London: Abacus.

Frost, P.J. (1987) Power, politics, and influence. In F. Jablin (ed.), *Handbook of Organizational Communication*. Newbury Park, CA: Sage.

Frye, N. (1973) *The Anatomy of Criticism: Four Essays*. Princeton, NJ: Princeton University Press. First published in 1957.

Fuchs, S. (2001) *Against Essentialism: A Theory of Culture and Society*. Cambridge, MA: Harvard University Press.

Fuchs, S. and Wingens, M. (1986) Sinnverstehen als Lebensform. Über die Möglichkeit hermeneutischer Objektivität. *Geschichte und Gesellschaft*, 12(4): 477–501.

Fuerst, J. (2006) Hermeneutical practice and clinical psychiatry: the patient as narrative text. http://www.philosophy.ucf.edu/ah.html (11 January 2006).

Gadamer, H.-G. (1989a) *Truth and Method* (2nd revised edn). London: Sheed & Ward. First published in 1960.

Gadamer, H.-G. (1989b) *Destruktion* and Deconstruction. In D.P. Michelfelder and R.E. Palmer (eds), *Dialogue and Deconstruction. The Gadamer–Derrida Encounter*. Albany: State University of New York Press.

Garfinkel, H. (1967) *Studies in Ethnomethodology.* Engelwood Cliffs, NJ: Prentice Hall.

Garfinkel, H. (1988) Evidence for locally produced, naturally accountable phenomena of order, logic, reason, meaning, method, etc. in and as of the essential quiddity of immortal ordinary society (I of IV): an announcement of studies. *Sociological Theory,* 6: 103–109.

Geertz, C. (1973) *The Interpretation of Cultures.* New York: Basic Books.

Geertz, C. (1983) *Local Knowledge.* New York: Basic Books.

Geertz, C. (1988) *Work and Lives: The Anthropologist as Author.* Cambridge: Polity Press.

Gergen, K. (1978) Toward generative theory. *Journal of Personality and Social Psychology,* 31: 1344–1360.

Gergen, K. (1982) *Toward Transformation in Social Knowledge.* New York: Springer-Verlag.

Gergen, K. (1985) The social constructionist movement in modern psychology. *American Psychologist,* 40: 266–275.

Gergen, K. (1989) Warranting voice and the elaboration of the self. In J. Shotter and K. Gergen (eds), *Texts of Identity.* London: Sage.

Gergen, K. (1996) Social Psychology as Social Construction: The Emerging Vision. In C. McGarty and A. Haslam (eds), *The Message of Social Psychology: Perspectives on Mind in Society.* Oxford: Blackwell.

Gergen, K. (2004) 'Old-stream' psychology will disappear with the dinosaurs! *Forum: Qualitative Social Research.* 5(3). Art. 27, September. Online. www.qualitative-research.net/ fqs-texte/3-04/ 04-3-27-e.htm#zp. (20 September 2007).

Gergen, K. and Gergen, M. (1991) Towards reflexive methodologies. In F. Steier (ed.), *Research and Reflexivity.* London: Sage.

Gherardi, S. (1995) *Gender, Symbolism and Organizational Cultures.* London: Sage.

Gherardi, S. and Turner, B. (1987) Real men don't collect soft data. *Quaderno 13.* Dipartimento di Politica Sociale, Universitá di Trento.

Giddens, A. (1976) *New Rules of Sociological Method: A Positive Critique of Interpretative Sociologies.* London: Hutchinson.

Giddens, A. (1982) Labour and interaction. In J.B. Thompson and D. Held (eds), *Habermas: Critical Debates.* London: Macmillan.

Giddens, A. (1984) *The Constitution of Society: Outline of the Theory of Structuration.* Cambridge: Polity Press.

Giddens, A. (1991) *Modernity and Self-Identity.* Cambridge: Polity Press.

Giorgi, A. (1985) The phenomenological psychology of learning and the verbal learning tradition. In A. Giorgi (ed.), *Phenomenology and Psychological Research.* Pittsburgh: Duquesne University Press.

Glaser, B.G. (1978) *Theoretical Sensitivity: Advances in the Methodology of Grounded Theory.* Mill Valley, CA: Sociology Press.

Glaser, B.G. (1992) *Basics of Grounded Theory Research.* Mill Valley, CA: Sociology Press.

Glaser, B.G. (ed.) (1993) *Examples of Grounded Theory.* Mill Valley, CA: Sociology Press.

Glaser, B.G. (2005) The impact of symbolic interaction on grounded theory. *The Grounded Theory Review,* 4(1): 1–22.

Glaser, B.G. (2007) All is data. *The Grounded Theory Review,* 6(2): 1–22.

Glaser, B.G. and Strauss, A.L. (1967) *The Discovery of Grounded Theory: Strategies for Qualitative Research.* Chicago: Aldine.

Goffman, E. (1959) *The Presentation of Self in Everyday Life.* Garden City, NY: Doubleday.

Graff, G. (1979) *Literature against Itself.* Chicago: University of Chicago Press.

Grant, D. and Ledema, R. (2005) Discourse analysis and the study of organizations. *Text,* 25(1): 37–66.

Grassi, V. (2005) Introduction à la sociologie de l'imaginaire: une compréhension de la vie quotidienne. Ramonville: Érès.

Greatbatch, D. and Clark, T. (2005) *Management Speak: Why We Lisen to What Management Gurus Tell Us.* New York: Routledge.

Greimas, A.J. (1983) *Structural Semantics: An Attempt at a Method*. Lincoln: University of Nebraska Press.

Guba, E. and Lincoln, Y. (1994) Competing paradigms in qualitative research. In N.K. Denzin and Y.S. Lincoln (eds), *Handbook of Qualitative Research*. Thousand Oaks, CA: Sage.

Guignon, C.B. (1991) Pragmatism or hermeneutics? Epistemology after foundationalism. In D.R. Hiley, J.F. Bohman and R. Shusterman (eds), *The Interpretive Turn. Philosophy, Science, Culture*. New York: Cornell University Press.

Guillet de Monthoux, P. (1981) *Doktor Kant eller den oekonomiska rationaliseringen*. Göteborg: Korpen.

Gummesson, E. (1991) *Qualitative Methods in Management Research*. Newbury Park, CA: Sage.

Gurwitsch, A. (1964) *The Field of Consciousness*. Pittsburgh: Duquesne University Press.

Gustavsson, A. and Bergström, H. (2004) Pendlingen mellan olika tolkningsintressen. [Oscillating between different interpretive interests.] In S. Selander and P.-J. Ödman (eds), *Text & Existens. Hermeneutik möter samhällsvetenskap*. Göteborg: Daidalos. pp. 199–221.

Habermas, J. (1971a) *Toward a Rational Society*. London: Heinemann.

Habermas, J. (1971b) Der Universalitätsanspruch der Hermeneutik. In *Hermeneutik und Ideologiekritik*. Frankfurt: Suhrkamp.

Habermas, J. (1972) *Knowledge and Human Interest*. London: Heinemann.

Habermas, J. (1973) A postscript to *Knowledge and Human Interest*: Philosophy of the Social Sciences, 3: 157–189.

Habermas, J. (1984) *The Theory of Communicative Action. Vol. 1*. Boston: Beacon Press.

Habermas, J. (1985) Modernity – an incomplete project. In H. Foster (ed.), *Postmodern Culture*. London: Pluto Press. Paper first published in 1983.

Habermas, J. (1986) Entgegnungen. In A. Honneth and H. Joas (eds), *Kommunikatives Handeln. Beiträge zu Jürgen Habermas' 'Theorie des kommunikatives Handelns'*. Frankfurt am Main: Suhrkampf.

Habermas, J. (1990) *Kommunikativt handlande. Texter om språk, rationalitet och samhälle*. Göteborg: Diadalos.

Hacking, I. (1982) Language, truth and reason. In M. Hollis and S. Lukes (eds), *Rationality and Relativism*. Oxford: Basil Blackwell.

Hacking, I. (1999) *The Social Construction of What?* Cambridge, MA: Harvard University Press.

Harré, R. (1981) The Positivist-Empiricist Approach and Its Alternative. In I.P. Reason and J. Rowan (ed.), *Human Inquiry*. London: Wiley.

Haglund, D.A.R. (1977) Perception, time and the unity of mind. problems in Edmund Husserl's philosophy. Doctoral dissertation. Göteborg: Institute of Philosophy, Göteborg University.

Haig, B.D. (1995) Grounded theory as scientific method. *Philosophy of Education*. http://www.ed.uiuc.edu/EPS/PES-Yearbook/95_docs/haig.html (23 July 1998).

Hall, E. (1993) Smiling, deferring, and flirting: doing gender by giving 'good service'. *Work and Occupations*, 20: 452–471.

Hammersley, M. (1989) *The Dilemma of Qualitative Method: Herbert Blumer and the Chicago Tradition*. London: Routledge.

Hammersley, M. (1990) What is wrong with ethnography? The myth of theoretical description. *Sociology*, 24: 597–615.

Hammersley, M. (1992) On feminist methodology. *Sociology*, 26(2): 187–206.

Hanson, N.R. (1958) *Patterns of Discovery: An Inquiry into the Conceptual Foundations of Science*. Cambridge: Cambridge University Press.

Harding, S. (1987) Introduction: is there a feminist method? In S. Harding (ed.), *Feminism and Methodology*. Milton Keynes: Open University Press.

Harré, R. (1989) Language games and texts of identity. In J. Shotter and K. Gergen (eds), *Texts of Identity*. London: Sage.

Hart, P.E. (1986) Artificial intelligence in transition. In J.S. Kowalik (ed.), *Knowledge Based Problem Solving*. Englewood Cliffs, NJ: Prentice-Hall.

Heidegger, M. (1961/1991) *Nietzsche (Vol 1–4)*. San Francisco, CA: Harper Collins.

329

Hayman, R. (1980) *Nietzsche: A Critical Life*. Oxford: Oxford University Press.

Heath, C.C. and Luff, P. (1993) Explicating face-to-face interaction. In N. Gilbert (ed.), *Researching Social Life*. London: Sage.

Heelan, P.A. (1997) The scope of hermeneutics in natural science. *Studies in History and Philosophy of Science*, 29A(2): 273–298.

Hegel, G.W.F. (1952) *Phänomenologie des Geistes*. Hamburg: Felix Meiner. First published in 1807.

Hegel, G.W.F. (1967) *Wissenschaft der Logik. Erster Teil. Erster Band: Die objektive Logik*. Hamburg: Felix Meiner. First published in 1812.

Heidegger, M. (1959) *An Introduction to Metaphysics*. New Haven, CT: Yale University Press.

Heidegger, M. (1961/1991) *Nietzsche (Vol 1–4)*. San Francisco, CA: Harper Collins.

Heidegger, M. (1962) *Being and Time*. Oxford: Blackwell.

Heidegger, M. (1977) *Basic Writings*. New York: Harper & Row.

Heidegger, M. (1982) *The Basic Problems of Phenomenology*. Bloomington: Indiana University Press.

Held, D. (1980) *Introduction to Critical Theory*. London: Hutchinson.

Helenius, R. (1990) *Förstå och bättre veta*. Stockholm: Carlsson bokförlag.

Hendry, R.F. and Psillos, S. (2004) How to do things with theories. An interactive view of language and models in science. In K. Paprzycka and P. Przybysz (eds), *Idealization and Concretization*. Amsterdam: Rodopi.

Heritage, J. (1984) *Garfinkel and Ethnomethodology*. Cambridge: Polity Press.

Hesse, M. (1980) *Revolutions and Reconstructions in the Philosophy of Science*. Brighton: Harvester Press.

Hester, M.B. (1967) *The Meaning of Poetic Metaphor*. The Hague: Mouton.

Hirsch, E.D., Jr (1967) *Validity in Interpretation*. New Haven, CT: Yale University Press.

Hirsch, F. (1976) *The Social Limits to Growth*. Oxford: Oxford University Press.

Hirschman, A.O. (1970) *Exit, Voice, and Loyalty*. Cambridge, MA: Harvard University Press.

Hollis, M. (1994) *The Philosophy of Social Science*. Cambridge: Cambridge University Press.

Hollway, W. (1984) Gender difference and the production of subjectivity. In J. Henriques et al. *Changing the Subject*. London: Methuen.

Hollway, W. (1989) *Subjectivity and Method in Psychology*. London: Sage.

Holstein, J.A. and Gubrium, J.F. (1994) Phenomenology, ethnomethodology, and interpretive practice. In N. Denzin and Y. Lincoln (eds), *Handbook of Qualitative Research*. Thousand Oaks, CA: Sage.

Horkheimer, M. (1976) Traditional and critical theory. In P. Connerton (ed.), *Critical Sociology*. Harmondsworth: Penguin. Essay first published in 1937.

Hoy, D. (ed.) (1986a) *Foucault: A Critical Reader*. Oxford: Basil Blackwell.

Hoy, D.C. (1986b) Must we say what we mean? The grammatological critique of hermeneutics. In B.R. Wachterhauser (ed.), *Hermeneutics and Modern Philosophy*. New York: State University of New York Press.

Huberman, M. and Miles, M. (1994) Data management and analysis methods. In N. Denzin and Y. Lincoln (eds), *Handbook of Qualitative Research*. Thousand Oaks, CA: Sage.

Hughes, H.S. (1961) *Consciousness and Society: The Reorientation of European Social Thought 1890–1930*. New York: Random House.

Husserl, E. (1913) *Logische Untersuchungen, Vol. 2*. Halle: Max Niemeyer.

Ihde, D. (1997) *Expanding Hermeneutics*. http://ccmail.sunysb.edu/philosophy/Faculty/papers/Expherm.htm (13 February 1999).

Ingarden, R. (1976) *Det litterära konstverket*. Lund: Cavefors. First published in 1931.

Jackson, J. (1995) 'Déjà entendu': the liminal qualities of anthropological fieldnotes. In J. Van Maanen (ed.), *Representation in Ethnography*. Thousand Oaks, CA: Sage.

Jackson, N. and Willmott, H. (1987) Beyond epistemology and reflective conversation: towards human relations. *Human Relations*, 40: 361–380.

Jagger, A.M. (1989) Love and knowledge. *Inquiry*, 32: 51–176.

Jameson, F. (1984) Postmodernism, or the cultural logic of late capitalism. *New Left Review*, 146: 53–93.

Jameson, F. (1985) Postmodernism and consumer society. In H. Foster (ed.), *Postmodern Culture*. London: Pluto Press. Paper first published in 1983.

Jeffcutt, P. (1993) From interpretation to representation. In J. Hassard and M. Parker (eds), *Postmodernism and Organizations*. London: Sage.

Jencks, C. (1987) *The Language of Post-Modern Architecture*. London: Academy Editions. First published in 1977.

Johansson, O.L. (1990) *Organisationsbegrepp och begreppsmedvetenhet*. Göteborg: BAS.

Johnson, P. (1998) *R.G. Collingwood: An Introduction*. Notre Dame, Indiana: St Augustine's Press.

Johnson, R. (2007) Post-hegemony? I don't think so. *Theory, Culture & Society*, 24: 95–110.

Johnston, J.A. (2008) Pushing for privileged passage: a grounded theory of guardians to middle level mathematics students. *The Grounded Theory Review*, 7(1): 43–60.

Jönsson, S.A. and Lundin, R.A. (1977) Myths and wishful thinking as management tools. In P.C. Nystrom and W.H. Starbuck (eds), *Prescriptive Models of Organization*. New York: North-Holland.

Karlsson, G. (1993) *Psychological Qualitative Research from a Phenomenological Perspective*. Stockholm: Almqvist och Wiksell International.

Kasser, T. (2002) *The High Price of Materialism*. Cambridge, MA: MIT Press.

Kaufmann, W. (1974) *Nietzsche: Philosopher, Psychologist, Antichrist*. Princeton, NJ: Princeton University Press. First published in 1950.

Kent, T. (1991) Hermeneutics and genre: Bachtin and the problem of communicative interaction. In D.R. Hiley, J.F. Bohman, and R. Shusterman (eds), *The Interpretive Turn. Philosophy, Science, Culture*. New York: Cornell University Press.

Kincheloe, J. and McLaren, P. (1994) Rethinking critical theory and qualitative research. In N. Denzin and Y. Lincoln (eds), *Handbook of Qualitative Research*. Thousand Oaks, CA: Sage.

Kincheloe, J. and McLaren, P. (2000) Rethinking critical theory and qualitative research. In N. Denzin and Y. Lincoln (eds), *Handbook of Qualitative Research* (2nd edn). Thousand Oaks, CA: Sage.

Kittang, A. (1977) Hermeneutikk og litteraturvitskap. In H. Engdahl et al. (eds), *Hermeneutik*. Stockholm: Rabén & Sjögren.

Klein, N. (2000) *No Logo*. London: Flamingo.

Knights, D. and Willmott, H. (1987) Organizational culture as management strategy: a critique and illustration from the financial service industries. *International Studies of Management and Organization*, 17: 40–63.

Knights, D. and Willmott, H. (1989) Power and subjectivity at work. *Sociology*, 23: 535–558.

Knorr-Cetina, K. (1981) Introduction. The micro-sociological challenge of macro-sociology: towards a reconstruction of social theory and methodology. In K. Knorr-Cetina and A. Cicourel (eds), *Advances in Social Theory and Methodology*. Boston: Routledge & Kegan Paul.

Koestler, A. (1964) *The Act of Creation*. London: Hutchinson.

Kozart, M.F. (2002) Understanding efficacy in psychotherapy: an ethnomethodological perspective on the therapeutic alliance. *American Journal of Orthopsychiatry*, 72: 217–231.

Kripke, S. (1980) *Naming and Necessity*. Oxford: Blackwell.

Krishnamurti, J. (1954) *The First and Last Freedom*. London: Gollancz.

Kristensson Uggla, B. (2002) Slaget om verkligheten. Filosofi – omvärldsanalys – tolkning. [The battle of reality. Philosophy – context analysis – interpretation.] Stockholm/Stehag: Brutus Östlings bokförlag Symposion.

Kristensson Uggla, B. (2004) Tolkningens metamorfoser i hermeneutikens tidsålder. [The metamorphoses of interpretation in the age of hermeneutics.] In S. Selander and P.-J. Ödman (eds), *Text & Existens. Hermeneutik möter samhällsvetenskap*. Göteborg: Daidalos.

Krupnick, M. (1983) Introduction. In M. Krupnick (ed.), *Displacement. Derrida and After*. Bloomington: Indiana University Press.

Kuhn, T.S. (1970) *The Structure of Scientific Revolutions* (2nd edn). Chicago: University of Chicago Press. First edition published in 1962.

Kunda, G. (1992) *Engineering Culture: Control and Commitment in a High-Tech Corporation.* Philadelphia: Temple University Press.

Kurti, L. (1983) Dirty movies – dirty minds: the social construction of x-rated films. *Journal of Popular Culture*, 17(2): 187–192.

Kvale, S. (1989) To validate is to question. In S. Kvale (ed.), *Issues of Validity in Qualitative Research.* Lund: Studentlitteratur.

Laing, R.D. (1960) *The Divided Self.* London: Tavistock.

Lakatos, I. (1970) Falsification and the methodology of scientific research programmes. In I. Lakatos and A. Musgrave (eds), *Criticism and the Growth of Knowledge.* Cambridge: Cambridge University Press.

Lalli, P. (1989) The imaginative dimension of everyday life: towards a hermeneutic reading. *Current Sociology*, 37(1): 103–114.

Lasch, C. (1979) *The Culture of Narcissism.* New York: Norton.

Lasch, C. (1985) *The Minimal Self.* London: Picador.

Lash, S. (1988) Discourse or figure? Postmodernism as a 'regime of signification'. *Theory, Culture & Society*, 5: 311–336.

Latour, B. (1988) *The Pasteurization of France.* Cambridge, MA: Harvard University Press.

Latour, B. (1996) *Aramis – The Love of Technology.* Cambridge, MA: Harvard University Press.

Latour, B. (1999) For Bloor and beyond: a reply to David Bloor's anti-Latour. *Studies in History and Philosophy of Science*, 30(1): 113–29.

Latour, B. (2004a) A prologue in the form of a dialogue between a student and his (somewhat) Socratic professor. In C. Avgerou, C. Ciborra and F.F. Land (eds), *The Social Study of Information and Communication Study.* Oxford: Oxford University Press.

Latour, B. (2004b) Why has critique run out of steam? From matters of fact to matters of concern. *Critical Inquiry*, 30(2): 25–248.

Latour, B. (2005) *Reassembling the Social: An Introduction to Actor-Network-Theory.* Oxford: Oxford University Press.

Latour, B. and Woolgar, S. (1979) *Laboratory Life: The Social Construction of Scientific Facts.* Beverly Hills: Sage.

Law, J. (1994) *Organizing modernity.* Oxford: Blackwell.

Laurent, A. (1978) Managerial subordinacy. *Academy of Management Review*, 3: 220–230.

Lee, F.S. (2005) Grounded theory and heterodox economics. *The Grounded Theory Review*, 4(2): 95–116.

Le Goff, J. (1992) *History and Memory.* New York: Columbia University Press.

Leidner, R. (1991) Serving hamburgers and selling insurance: gender, work, and identity in interactive service jobs. *Gender & Society*, 5(2): 154–177.

Leiss, W. (1978) *The Limits to Satisfaction.* London: Marion Boyars.

Leiss, W. (1983) The icons of the marketplace. *Theory, Culture & Society*, 1(3): 10–21.

Lemert, C. (1992) General social theory, irony, postmodernism. In S. Seidman and D. Wagner (eds), *Postmodernism and Social Theory.* Oxford: Blackwell.

Lerner, E. (1991) *The Big Bang Never Happened.* New York: Random House.

Lesche, C. (1986) Die Notwendigkeit einer hermeneutischer Psychoanalyse. *Psyche*, 40(1): 49–68.

Levi-Strauss, C. (1962/1967) *The Savage Mind.* Chicago, IL: The University of Chicago Press.

Lévi-Strauss, C. (1967) *The Savage Mind.* Chicago: University of Chicago Press. First published in 1962.

Levinas, E. (1989) *Time and the Other.* Pittsburgh: Duquesne University Press. First published in 1947.

Lincoln, Y. and Denzin, N. (1994) The fifth moment. In N. Denzin and Y. Lincoln (eds), *Handbook of Qualitative Research.* Thousand Oaks, CA: Sage.

Linell, P. (1990) De institutionaliserade samtalens elementära former: om möten mellan professionella och lekmän. *Forskning om utbildning*, 4: 18–35.

Linstead, S. (1993) From postmodern anthropology to deconstructive ethnography. *Human Relations*, 46: 97–120.

Linstead, S. and Grafton-Small, R. (1990) Theory as artefact: artefact as theory. In P. Gagliardi (ed.), *Symbols and Artifacts: Views of the Corporate Landscape*. Berlin/New York: de Gruyter.

Lukes, S. (1982) Of gods and demons: Habermas and practical reason. In J.B. Thompson and D. Held (eds), *Habermas: Critical Debates*. London: Macmillan.

Lynch, M. (2000) Against reflexivity as an academic virtue and source of privileged knowledge. *Theory, Culture, & Society*, 17: 26–54.

Lynch, M. and Bogen, D. (1994) Harvey Sacks' primitive natural science. *Theory, Culture & Society*, 11: 65–104.

Lyotard, J.-F. (1984) *The Postmodern Condition: A Report on Knowledge*. Minneapolis: University of Minnesota Press.

Lyotard, J.-F. and Thébaud, J.-L. (1986) *Just Gaming*. Manchester: Manchester University Press.

MacKenzie, K.D. and House, R. (1979) A paradigm development in the social sciences: A proposed research strategy. In R. T. Mowday and R. M. Steers (eds), *Research in Organizations: Issues and Controversies*. Santa Monica, CA: Goodyear.

Madison, G.B. (1988) *The Hermeneutics of Postmodernity*. Bloomington: Indiana University Press.

Madison, G.B. (1991) The politics of postmodernity. *Critical Review*, 5(1): 53–79.

Maffesoli, M. (1993a) Introduction. *Current Sociology*, 41(2): 1–5.

Maffesoli, M. (1993b) The social ambiance. *Current Sociology*, 41(2): 7–15.

Maloney, K.M. (2005) Adventuring: A grounded theory discovered through the analysis of science teaching and learning. *The Grounded Theory Review*, 4(3): 29–58.

Mandelbrot, B. (1977) *The Fractal Geometry of Nature*. New York: Freeman.

Mangham, I. and Overington, M. (1987) *Organizations as Theatre*. Chichester: Wiley.

Manning, P.K. (1982) Analytic induction. In R. Smith and P.K. Manning (eds), *Qualitative Methods*. Cambridge, MA: Ballinger.

Maranhão, T. (1991) Reflection, dialogue, and the subject. In F. Steier (ed.), *Research and Reflexivity*. London: Sage.

Marcus, G. (1992) Past, present and emergent identities: requirements for ethnographies of the late twentieth-century modernity worldwide. In S. Lash and J. Friedman (eds), *Modernity and Identity*. Oxford: Blackwell.

Marcus, G. (1994) What comes (just) after 'post'?: The case of ethnography. In N. Denzin and Y. Lincoln (eds), *Handbook of Qualitative Research*. Thousand Oaks, CA: Sage.

Marcus, G. and Cushman, D. (1982) Ethnographies as texts. *Annual Review of Anthropology*, 11: 25–69.

Marcus, G. and Fischer, M. (1986) *Anthropology as Cultural Critique*. Chicago: University of Chicago Press.

Marcuse, H. (1955) *Eros and Civilization*. Boston: Beacon Press.

Marcuse, H. (1964) *One-Dimensional Man*. Boston: Beacon Press.

Marcuse, H. (1969) *An Essay on Liberation*. Boston: Beacon Press.

Margolis, S. (1989) Postscript on modernism and postmodernism. Both. *Theory, Culture & Society,* 6: 5–30.

Marshall, H. and Wetherell, M. (1989) Talking about career and gender identities. A discourse analysis perspective. In S. Skevington and D. Baker (eds), *The Social Identity of Women*. London: Sage.

Marshall, J. (1993) Organizational communication from a feminist perspective. In S. Deetz (ed.), *Communication Yearbook, Vol. 16*. Newbury Park, CA: Sage.

Martin, J. (1990a) Breaking up the mono-method monopolies of organizational analysis. In J. Hassard and D. Pym (eds), *The Theory and Philosophy of Organizations*. London: Routledge.

Martin, J. (1990b) Deconstructing organizational taboos: the suppression of gender conflicts in organizations. *Organization Science*, 1: 339–359.

Martin, J. (1992) *The Culture of Organizations. Three Perspectives*. New York: Oxford University Press.

Martin, J. (2003) Feminist theory and critical theory: Unexplored synergies. In M. Alvesson and H. Willmott (eds), *Studying Management Critically*. London: Sage.

Martin, J.R. (1994) Methodological essentialism, false difference, and other dangerous traps. *Sign*, 19: 630–657.

Marx, K. (1967) *Das Kapital, Vol. 1*. Berlin: Dietz. First published in 1867.

Maynard, D.W. and Clayman, S.E. (1991) The diversity of ethnomethodology. *Annual Review of Sociology*, 17: 385–418.

McCall, L. (2005) Gender, race, and the restructuring of work: organizational and institutional perspectives. In S. Akroyd, R. Batt, P. Thompson and P. S. Tolbert (eds), *The Oxford Handbook of Work and Organization*. Oxford: Oxford University Press.

McCallin, A. (2004) Pluralistic dialoguing: A theory of interdisciplinary teamworking. *The Grounded Theory Reveiw*, 4(1): 25–42.

McCloskey, D. (1990) *If You're So Smart: The Narrative of Economic Expertise*. Chicago: University of Chicago Press.

McIllvenny, P. (1996) Popular public discourse at Speakers' Corner: negotiating cultural identities in interaction. *Discourse & Society*, 7: 7–37.

McKelvey, B. (2003) From fields to science: can organization studies make the transition? In R. Westwood and S. Clegg (eds), *Point/Counterpoint: Central Debates in Organisation Theory*. Oxford, UK: Blackwell.

McMullin, E. (1982) A case for scientific realism. In J. Leplin (ed.), *Scientific Realism*. Berkeley: University of California Press.

Mehan, H. and Wood, H. (1975) *The Reality of Ethnomethodology*. New York: Wiley.

Meisenhelder, T. (1989) Habermas and feminism: the future of critical theory. In R.A. Wallace (ed.), *Feminism and Sociological Theory*. Newbury Park, CA: Sage.

Melia, K. (1997) Producing 'plausible stories': interviewing student nurses. In G. Miller and R. Dingwall (eds), *Context and Method in Qualitative Research*. London: Sage.

Merleau-Ponty, M. (1973) Phenomenology and the sciences of man. In M. Natanson (ed.), *Phenomenology and the Social Sciences*. Evanston, IL: Northwestern University Press.

Miller, G. (1997) Building bridges: the possibilities of analytic dialogue between ethnography, conversation analysis and Foucault. In D. Silverman (ed.), *Qualitative Research*. London: Sage.

Mills, C.W. (1940) Situated actions and vocabularies of motives. *American Sociological Review*, 5: 904–913.

Mills, C.W. (1959) *The Sociological Imagination*. Harmondsworth: Penguin.

Min, A.K. (2005) From difference to the solidarity of others: sublating postmodernism. *Philosophy & Social Criticism*, 31(7): 823–849.

Mintzberg, H. (1975) The manager's job: folklore and fact. *Harvard Business Review*, July–Aug.: 49–61.

Mintzberg, H. (1983) *Power In and Around Organizations*. Englewood Cliffs, NJ: Prentice-Hall.

Mirchandani, R. (2005) Postmodernism and Sociology: from the epistemological to the empirical. *Sociological Theory*, 23(1): 86–115.

Morgan, D. (1981) Men, masculinity and the process of sociological inquiry. In H. Roberts (ed.), *Doing Feminist Research*. London: Routledge & Kegan Paul.

Morgan, G. (1980) Paradigms, metaphors and puzzle solving in organization theory. *Administrative Science Quarterly*, 25: 605–622.

Morgan, G. (ed.) (1983) *Beyond Method*. Newbury Park, CA: Sage.

Morgan, G. (1986) *Images of Organization*. Newbury Park, CA: Sage.

Morgan, G. (1997) *Images of Organization* (2nd edn). London: Sage.

Morgan, M.S. and Morrison, M. (eds) (2000) *Models as Mediators: Perspectives on Natural and Social Science*. Cambridge: Cambridge University Press.

Morgen, S. (1994) Personalizing personnel decisions in feminist organizational theory and practice. *Human Relations*, 47(6): 665–84.

Morrow, R. (1994) *Critical Theory and Methodology*. Thousand Oaks, CA: Sage.

Mullins, N.C. and Mullins, C.J. (1973) Symbolic interactionism: the loyal opposition. In N.C. Mullins (ed.), *Theories and Theory Groups in Contemporary American Sociology*. New York: Harper & Row.

Mumby, D. and Putnam, L. (1992) The politics of emotion: a feminist reading of bounded rationality. *Academy of Management Review*, 17: 465–486.

Mumby, D. and Stohl, C. (1991) Power and discourse in organization studies: absence and the dialectic of control. *Discourse & Society*, 2: 313–332.

Murti, T.R.V. (1980) *The Central Philosophy of Buddhism. A Study of the Madhyamika System*. London: Unwin. First published in 1955.

Nietzsche, F. (1901/1967) *The Will to Power*. New York: Random House.

Newton, T. (1996) Postmodernism and action. *Organization*, 3(1): 7–29.

Newton, T. (1998) Theorizing subjectivity in organizations: the failure of Foucauldian studies. *Organization Studies*, 19(3): 415–447.

Newton-Smith, W.H. (1990) *The Rationality of Science*. London: Routledge. First published in 1981.

Ng, K.Y.N. (2005) Managing collaborative synergy in the crane industry. *The Grounded Theory Review*, 4(3): 81–103.

Norén, L. (1990) Om fallstudiens trovärdighet. FE-rapport, Department of Business Administration, Göteborg University.

Ödman, P.-J. (1979) *Tolkning förståelse vetande. Hermeneutik i teori och praktik.* [Interpretation, understanding, knowledge. Hermeneutics in theory and practice.] Stockholm: Almqvist & Wiksell.

Ogden, C.K. and Richards, I.A. (1956) *The Meaning of Meaning: A Study of the Influence of Language upon Thought and of the Science of Symbolism*. New York: Harcourt, Brace.

Oleson, V. (1994) Feminisms and models of qualitative research. In N. Denzin and Y. Lincoln (eds), *Handbook of Qualitative Research*. Thousand Oaks, CA: Sage.

Olsson, A. (1987) *Den okända texten*. Stockholm: Bonniers.

Ottmann, H. (1982) Cognitive interests and self-reflection. In J.B. Thompson and D. Held (eds), *Habermas. Critical Debates*. London: Macmillan.

Palmer, R.E. (1969) *Hermeneutics: Interpretation Theory in Schleiermacher, Dilthey, Heidegger, and Gadamer*. Evanston, IL: Northwestern University Press.

Parker, I. (1991) *Discourse Dynamics*. London: Routledge.

Parker, I. (1994) Reflexive research and the grounding of analysis: social psychology and the 'psy-complex'. *Journal of Community and Applied Social Psychology*, 4: 239–252.

Parker, M. (1993) Life after Jean-François. In J. Hassard and M. Parker (eds), *Postmodernism and Organizations*. London: Sage.

Perrow, C. (1978) Demystifying organizations. In R. Sarri and Y. Heskenfeld (eds), *The Management of Human Services*. New York: Columbia University Press.

Peters, J.D. and Rotenbuhler, E. (1989) The reality of construction. In H. Simons (ed.), *Rhetoric in the Human Sciences*. London: Sage.

Peters, T.J. and Waterman, R.H. (1982) *In Search of Excellence: Lessons From America's Best Run Companies*. New York: Harper & Row.

Pettigrew, A. (1985) *The Awakening Giant: Continuity and Change in Imperial Chemical Industries*. Oxford: Basil Blackwell.

Phillips, N. and Brown, J.L. (1993) Analyzing communication in and around organizations: a critical hermeneutic approach. *Academy of Management Journal*, 36(6): 1547–1576.

Plummer, K. (ed.) (1991) *Symbolic Interactionism, Vols 1–2. Classic and Contemporary Issues*. Aldershot: Edward Elgar.

Polanyi, M. (1967) *The Tacit Dimension*. London: Routledge & Kegan Paul.

Pollay, R.W. (1986) The distorted mirror: reflections on the unintended consequences of advertising. *Journal of Marketing*, 5 (April): 18–36.

335

Pollner, M. (1991) Left of ethnomethodology: the rise and decline of radical reflexivity. *American Sociological Review*, 56: 370–380.

Popper, K.R. (1934/1972) *The Logic of Scientific Discovery*. London: Hutchinson.

Popper, K.R. (1963) *Conjectures and Refutations: The Growth of Scientific Knowledge*. London: Routledge and Kegan Paul.

Popper, K.R. (1976) On the logic of the social sciences. In T.W. Adorno, H. Albert, R. Dahrendorf, J. Habermas, H. Pilot and K.R. Popper, *The Positivist Dispute in German Sociology*. London: Heinemann. First published in 1961.

Potter, J. (1996) *Representing Reality*. London: Sage.

Potter, J. (1997) Discourse analysis as a way of analysing naturally occurring talk. In D. Silverman (ed.), *Qualitative Research*. London: Sage.

Potter, J. and Wetherell, M. (1987) *Discourse and Social Psychology: Beyond Attitudes and Behaviour*. London: Sage.

Prasad, P. (1997) Systems of meaning: ethnography as a methodology for the study of information technologies. In A. Lee, J. Lieberau and J.I. DeGross (eds), *Information Systems and Qualitative Research*. London: Chapman & Hall.

Prasad, A. and Mir, R. (2002) Digging deep for meaning: A critical hermeneutic analysis of CEO letters to shareholders in the oil industry. *The Journal of Business Communication*, 39(1): 92–116.

Preston, J. (2004) Discussion: Bird, Kuhn and Positivism. *Studies in History and Philosophy*, 35: 327–335.

Prigogine, I. and Stengers, I. (1993) *Das Paradox der Zeit. Zeit, Chaos und Quanten*. Munich: Piper.

Prior, L. (1997) Following in Foucault's footsteps: text and context in qualitative research. In D. Silverman (ed.), *Qualitative Research*. London: Sage.

Propp, V. (1968) *Morphology of the Folk Tale* (2nd edn). Austin: University of Texas Press.

Radnitzky, G. (1970) *Contemporary Schools of Metascience, Vols I–II*. Göteborg: Akademiförlaget.

Ratner, C. (2005) Social constructionism as cultism (comments on: 'Old-stream' psychology will disappear with the dinosaurs! Kenneth Gergen in conversation with Peter Mattes and Ernst Schraube). *Forum: Qualitative Social Research*. 6(1), Art. 28 (January). Online. www.qualitative-research.net/ fqs-texte/1–05/05–1–28-e.htm (20 September 2007).

Ravn, I. (1991) What should guide reality construction? In F. Steier (ed.), *Research and Reflexivity*. London: Sage.

Richardson, L. (2000) Writing: a method of inquiry. In N. Denzin and Y. Lincoln (eds), *Handbook of Qualitative Research* (2nd edn). Thousand Oaks, CA: Sage.

Ricoeur, P. (1974) *The Conflict of Interpretations: Essays in Hermeneutics*. Evanston, IL: Northwest University Press.

Ricoeur, P. (1978a) Metaphor and the main problem of hermeneutics. In C.E. Reagan and D. Stewart (eds), *The Philosophy of Paul Ricoeur*. Boston: Beacon Press.

Ricoeur, P. (1978b) *The Rule of Metaphor: Multidisciplinary Studies of the Creation of Meaning in Language*. London: Routledge & Kegan Paul.

Ricoeur, P. (1981) *Hermeneutics and the Human Science*. Cambridge, MA: Cambridge University Press.

Ricoeur, P. (1984) *Time and Narrative, Vol. 1*. Chicago: University of Chicago Press.

Ricoeur, P. (1985) *Time and Narrative, Vol. 2*. Chicago: University of Chicago Press.

Ricoeur, P. (1988) *Time and Narrative, Vol. 3*. Chicago: University of Chicago Press.

Ricoeur, P. (1992) *Oneself as Another*. Chicago: University of Chicago Press.

Ricoeur, P. (2006) *Memory, History, Forgetting*. Chicago, University of Chicago Press.

Ridgeway, C. and Correll, S. (2000) Limiting inequality through interaction: the end(s) of gender. *Contemporary Sociology*, 29(1): 110–120.

Rorty, R. (1979) *Philosophy and the Mirror of Nature*. Princeton, NJ: Princeton University Press.

Rorty, R. (1989) *Contingency, Irony and Solidarity*. Cambridge: Cambridge University Press.

Rorty, R. (1991) Inquiry as recontextualization: an anti-dualist account of interpretation. In D.R. Hiley, J.F. Bohman and R. Shusterman (eds), *The Interpretive Turn. Philosophy, Science, Culture*. New York: Cornell University Press.

Rorty, R. (1992) Cosmopolitanism without emancipation: a response to Lyotard. In S. Lash and J. Friedman (eds), *Modernity and Identity*. Oxford: Basil Blackwell.

Rose, N. (1989) Individualizing psychology. In J. Shotter and K. Gergen (eds), *Texts of Identity*. London: Sage.

Rosen, M. (1985) Breakfast at Spiro's: dramaturgy and dominance. *Journal of Management*, 11(2): 31–48.

Rosen, M. (1988) You asked for it: Christmas at the bosses' expense. *Journal of Management Studies*, 25: 463–480.

Rosen, M. (1991) Coming to terms with the field: understanding and doing organizational ethnography. *Journal of Management Studies*, 28: 1–24.

Rosenau, P.M. (1992) *Post-modernism and the Social Sciences: Insights, Inroads, and Intrusions*. Princeton, NJ: Princeton University Press.

Rosenbaum, M. (2005) Beyond the physical realm: a proposed theory regarding a consumer's place experience: *The Grounded Theory Review*, 4(2): 23–61.

Roth, P.A. (1991) Interpretation as explanation. In D.R. Hiley, J.F. Bohman and R. Shusterman (eds), *The Interpretive Turn: Philosophy, Science, Culture*. New York: Cornell University Press.

Ruben, D.-H. (1990) *Explaining Explanation*. London: Routledge.

Ruin, H. (1994) *Enigmatic Origins: Tracing the Theme of Historicity through Heidegger's Works*. Stockholm: Almqvist & Wiksell International.

Sacks, H. (1992) *Lectures on Conversation, Volumes I and II*. Edited by G. Jefferson with Introduction by E.A. Schegloff. Oxford and Cambridge, MA: Blackwell.

Sacks, H., Schegloff, E.A. and Jefferson, G. (1974) A simplest systematics for the organisation of turn taking in conversation. *Language*, 50: 696–735.

Säljö, R. (1990) Språk och institution: Den institutionaliserade inlärningens metaforer. *Forskning om utbildning*, 4: 5–17.

Sampson, E. (1989) The deconstruction of the self. In J. Shotter and K. Gergen (eds), *Texts of Identity*. London: Sage.

Sanday, P.R. (1979) The ethnographic paradigm(s). *Administrative Science Quarterly*, 24: 527–538.

Sandberg, J. (1994) Human competence at work. An interpretative approach. Doctoral dissertation. Göteborg: BAS.

Sandelands, L. and Drazin, R. (1989) On the language of organization theory. *Organization Studies*, 10: 457–458.

Sangren, S. (1992) Rhetoric and the authority of ethnography. *Current Anthropology*, Supplement, 33: 277–296.

Sartre, J.-P. (1973) *Existentialism and Humanism*. London: Eyre Methuen.

Sarup, M. (1988) *An Introductory Guide to Post-structuralism and Post-modernism*. Hemel Hempstead: Harvester Wheatsheaf.

Scheurich, J. and McKenzie, K.B. (2005) Foucault's methodologies: archaeology and genealogy. In N. Denzin and Y. Lincoln (eds), *Handbook of Qualitative Research* (3rd edn). Thousand Oaks, CA: Sage.

Scheurmann, E. (ed.) (1984) *Papalagi. Tal av Söderhavshövdingen Tuiavii från Tiavea*. Göteborg: Korpen.

Schutz, A. (1967) *Collected Papers. 1. The Problem of Social Reality*. The Hague: Nijhoff.

Schwalbe, M. and Wolkomir, M. (2003) *Interviewing Men*. In J. Holstein and J. Gubrium (eds), *Inside Interviewing*. Thousand Oaks, CA: Sage.

Schwartzman, H. (1993) *Ethnography in Organizations*. Newbury Park, CA: Sage.

Searle, J.R. (1998) *Mind, Language, and Society: Philosophy in the Real World*. New York: Basic Books.

Seltzer, J. and Bass, B. (1990) Transformational leadership: beyond initiation and consideration. *Journal of Management*, 16: 693–703.

Sennett, R. (1977) *The Fall of Public Man*. New York: Vintage.

Sennett, R. (1980) *Authority*. New York: Vintage.

Sennett, R. (1998) *The Corrosion of Character*. New York: Norton.

Shklar, J.N. (1986) Squaring the hermeneutic circle. *Social Research*, 53(3): 449–473.

Shotter, J. and Gergen, K. (eds) (1989) *Texts of Identity*. London: Sage.

Shotter, J. and Gergen, K. (1994) Social construction: knowledge, self, others, and continuing the conversation. In S. Deetz (ed.), *Communication Yearbook, Vol. 17*. Newbury Park, CA: Sage.

Shrivastava, P. (1994) Ecocentric management for a risk society. *Academy of Management Review*, 20: 118–137.

Shusterman, R. (1991) Beneath interpretation. In D.R. Hiley, J.F. Bohman, and R. Shusterman (eds), *The Interpretive Turn: Philosophy, Science, Culture*. New York: Cornell University Press.

Sievers, B. (1990) The diabolization of death: some thoughts on the obsolescence of mortality in organization theory and practice. In J. Hassard and D. Pym (eds), *The Theory and Philosophy of Organizations: Critical Issues and New Perspectives*. London: Routledge.

Silverman, D. (1970) *The Theory of Organizations*. London: Heinemann.

Silverman, D. (1985) *Qualitative Methodology and Sociology*. Aldershot: Gower.

Silverman, D. (1987) *Communication and Medical Practice*. London: Sage.

Silverman, D. (1993) *Interpreting Qualitative Data*. London: Sage.

Silverman, D. (1994) On throwing away ladders: rewriting the theory of organisations. In J. Hassard and M. Parker (eds), *Toward a New Theory of Organizations*. London: Routledge.

Silverman, D. (1997) The logic of qualitative research. In G. Miller and R. Dingwall (eds), *Context and Method in Qualitative Research*. London: Sage.

Silverman, D. (2006) *Interpreting Qualitative Data* (3rd edn). London: Sage.

Simons, H. (ed.) (1989) *Rhetorics of the Human Sciences*. London: Sage.

Skeggs, B. (1997) *Formations of Class and Gender*. London: Sage.

Skinner, Q. (1986a) Meaning and understanding in the history of ideas. In J. Tully (ed.), *Meaning and Context: Quentin Skinner and his Critics*. Oxford: Polity Press.

Skinner, Q. (1986b) Motives, intentions and the interpretation of texts. In J. Tully (ed.), *Meaning and Context: Quentin Skinner and his Critics*. Oxford: Polity Press.

Skinner, Q. (1986c) 'Social meaning' and the explanation of social action. In J. Tully (ed.), *Meaning and Context: Quentin Skinner and his Critics*. Oxford: Polity Press.

Skinner, Q. (1986d) A reply to my critics. In J. Tully (ed.), *Meaning and Context: Quentin Skinner and his Critics*. Oxford: Polity Press.

Sköldberg, K. (1991) *Reformer på vridscen: Organisationsförändringar i kommun och landsting*. Lund: Studentlitteratur.

Sköldberg, K. (1992) The alchemy of planning cultures: towards a theory of strategic change. *Scandinavian Journal of Management*, 8: 39–71.

Sköldberg, K. (1994) Tales of change: public administration reform and narrative mode. *Organization Science*, 5(2): 219–238.

Sköldberg, K. (1998) Heidegger and organization: notes towards a new research program. *Scandinavian Journal of Management*, 14(1/2): 77–102.

Sköldberg, K. (2002a) *Tracks and Frames: The Economy of Symbolic Forms in Organizations*. London: Elsevier.

Sköldberg, K. (2002b) *The Poetic Logic of Administration: Styles and Changes of Style in the Art of Organizing*. London: Harwood/Routledge.

Sköldberg, K. (2004) Postmodernism as organizational *ricorso*: the 'final' trope of irony. In U. Johansson and J. Woodilla (eds), *Irony and Organization*. Stockholm: Liber Abstrakt.

Slater, D. (1989) Corridors of power. In J. Gubrium and D. Silverman (eds), *The Politics of Field Research*. London: Sage.

Slugoski, B. and Ginsburg, G.P. (1989) Ego identity and explanatory speech. In J. Shotter and K. Gergen (eds), *Texts of Identity*. London: Sage.

Smith, J. and Hodkinson, P. (2005) Relativism, criteria, and politics. In N. Denzin and Y. Lincoln (eds), *Handbook of Qualitative Research* (3rd edn). Thousand Oaks, CA: Sage.

Sokal, A.D. (1996) Transgressing the boundaries: toward a transformative hermeneutics of quantum gravity. *Social Text*, 46/47: 217–252.

Sokal, A.D. and Bricmont, J. (1998) *Intellectual Impostors: Postmodern Philosophers' Abuse of Science*. London: Profile. First published in 1997.

Sotto, R. (1990) *Man without Knowledge: Actors and Spectators in Organizations*. Doctoral dissertation. Department of Business Administration, Stockholm University.

Spiegelberg, H. (1982) *The Phenomenological Movement* (3rd edn). The Hague: Nijhoff.

Spivak, G.C. (1976) Translator's preface. In J. Derrida (ed.), *Of Grammatology*. Baltimore, MD: Johns Hopkins University Press. pp. ix–xxxvii.

Stanfield, J.H., II (1994) Ethnic modeling in qualitative research. In N.K. Denzin and Y.S. Lincoln (eds), *Handbook of Qualitative Research*. Thousand Oaks, CA: Sage.

Starrin, B., Larsson, G. and Willebrand, K. (1984) Upptäckande metodologi. *Sociologisk Forskning*, 3–4: 15–28.

Steedman, P. (1991) On the relations between seeing, interpreting and knowing. In F. Steier (ed.), *Research and Reflexivity*. London: Sage.

Steels, L. and Van de Velde, W. (1986) Learning in Second Generation Expert Systems. In J.S. Kowalik (ed.), *Knowledge Based Problem Solving*. Englewood Cliffs, NJ: Prentice-Hall.

Steier, F. (ed.) (1991a) *Research and Reflexivity*. London: Sage.

Steier, F. (1991b) Reflexivity and methodology: an ecological constructionism. In F. Steier (ed.), *Research and Reflexivity*. London: Sage.

Strauss, A. (1987) *Qualitative Analysis for Social Scientists*. Cambridge: Cambridge University Press.

Strauss, A. and Corbin, J. (1990) *Basics of Qualitative Research*. Newbury Park, CA: Sage.

Strauss, A. and Corbin, J. (1994) Grounded theory methodology: an overview. In N. Denzin and Y. Lincoln (eds), *Handbook of Qualitative Research*. Thousand Oaks, CA: Sage.

Stryker, S. (1987) The vitalization of symbolic interaction. *Social Psychology Quarterly*, 50: 83–94.

Suppe, F. (ed.) (1977) *The Structure of Scientific Theories* (2nd edn). Urbana: University of Illinois Press.

Suppe, F. (2000) Understanding scientific theories: an assessment of developments 1969–1998. *Philosophy of Science*, 67 (Proceedings): S102–S115.

Tacussel, P. (1993) Imaginary and social aesthetics: epistemological proximity. *Current Sociology*, 41(2): 33–42.

Taussig, M. (1987) *Shamanism, Colonialism, and the Wild Man: A Study in Terror and Healing*. Chicago: The University of Chicago Press.

Taylor, C. (1985a) *Human Agency and Language: Philosophical Papers 1*. Cambridge: Cambridge University Press.

Taylor, C. (1985b) *Philosophy and the Human Sciences: Philosophical Papers 2*. Cambridge: Cambridge University Press.

Taylor, C. (1991) The dialogic self. In D.R. Hiley, J.F. Bohman and R. Shusterman (eds), *The Interpretive Turn: Philosophy, Science, Culture*. New York: Cornell University Press.

Thomas, J. (1993) *Doing Critical Ethnography*. Newbury Park, CA: Sage.

Thompson, J.B. (1982) Universal pragmatics. In J.B. Thompson and D. Held (eds), *Habermas: Critical Debates*. London: Macmillan.

Thompson, J.B. and Held, D. (eds) (1982) *Habermas: Critical Debates*. London: Macmillan.

Thompson, P. (1978) *The Voice of the Past: Oral History*. Oxford: Oxford University Press.

Thompson, P. (1993) Post-modernism: fatal distraction. In J. Hassard and M. Parker (eds), *Postmodernism and Organizations*. London: Sage.

Toulmin, S. (1953) *The Philosophy of Science*. London: Hutchinson.

Toulmin, S. (1961) *Foresight and Understanding*. London: Hutchinson.

Toulmin, S. (1972) *Human Understanding: The Collective Use and Evolution of Concepts*. Princeton, NJ: Princeton University Press.

Toulmin, S. (1974) The structure of scientific theories. In F. Suppe (ed.), *The Structure of Scientific Theories*. Urbana, IL: University of Illinois Press.

Touraine, A. (1992) *Critique de la modernité*. Paris: Fayard.

Travers, M. (2006) Postmodernism and Qualitative Research. *Qualitative Research*, 6(2): 267–273.

Tsoukas, H. (1989) The validity of idiographic research explanations. *Academy of Management Review*, 14: 551–561.

Tsoukas, H. (1991) The missing link: a transformational view of metaphors in organizational science. *Academy of Management Review*, 16: 566–585.

Tsoukas, H. (1993) Analogical reasoning and knowledge generation in organisation theory. *Organization Studies*, 14: 323–346.

Tuchman, G. (1994) Historical social science: methodologies, methods, and meanings. In N. Denzin and Y. Lincoln (eds), *Handbook of Qualitative Research*. Thousand Oaks, CA: Sage.

Turner, B.A. (1988) Connoisseurship in the study of organizational cultures. In A. Bryman (ed.), *Doing Research in Organizations*. London: Routledge.

Van der Lubbe, J.C.A. (1993) Human-like reasoning under uncertainty in expert systems. In R.J. Jorna, B. van Heusden and R. Posner (eds), *Signs, Search and Communication. Semiotic Aspects of Artificial Intelligence*. Berlin, New York: de Gruyter. pp. 113–133.

Van Maanen, J. (1979) The fact of fiction in organizational ethnography. *Administrative Science Quarterly*, 24: 539–550.

Van Maanen, J. (1988) *Tales of the Field. On Writing Ethnography*. Chicago: University of Chicago Press.

Van Maanen, J. (ed.) (1995) *Representation in Ethnography*. Thousand Oaks, CA: Sage.

Vansina, J. (1961) *Oral Traditions: A Study in Historical Methodology*. London: Routledge.

Vattimo, G. (1997) *Beyond Interpretation: The Meaning of Hermeneutics for Philosophy*. Stanford, CA: Stanford University Press.

von Glasersfeld, E. (1991) Knowing without metaphysics: aspects of the radical constructivist position. In F. Steier (ed.), *Research and Reflexivity*. London: Sage.

von Wright, G.H. (1971) *Explanation and Understanding*. London: Routledge.

Voyer, J.J., Gould, J.M. and Ford. D.N. (1996) *Systemic Creation of Organizational Anxiety: An Empirical Study*. http://www.sol-ne.org/res/wp/org_anxiety.html (12 February 1999).

Wachtel, P. (1983) *The Poverty of Affluence. A Psychological Portrait of the American Way of Life*. New York: Free Press.

Wachterhauser, B.M. (1986) Introduction: history and language in understanding. In B.M. Wachterhauser (ed.), *Hermeneutics and Modern Philosophy*. New York: State University of New York Press.

Walby, S. (1992) Post-post-modernism? Theorizing social complexity. In M. Barrett and A. Phillips (eds), *Destabilizing Theory*. Cambridge: Polity Press.

Walzer, M. (1986) The politics of Michel Foucault. In D.C. Hoy (ed.), *Foucault. A Critical Reader*. Oxford: Blackwell.

Warnke, G. (1993) *Hans-Georg Gadamer: Hermeneutik, tradtiton och förnuft*. Göteborg: Daidolos.

Watson, T. (1994) *In Search of Management*. London: Routledge.

Weber, M. (1967) *The Theory of Social and Economic Organization*. New York: Free Press. First published in 1922.

Weedon, C. (1987) *Feminist Practice and Poststructuralist Theory*. Oxford: Basil Blackwell.

Weeks, P. (1996) A rehearsal of a Beethoven passage: an analysis of correction talk. *Research on Language and Social Interaction*, 29: 247–290.

Weick, K. (1999) Theory construction as disciplined reflexivity: Tradeoffs in the 90s. *Academy of Management Review*, 24: 797–806.

Weick, K.E. (1989) Theory construction as disciplined imagination. *Academy of Management Review*, 14: 516–531.

Weinberg, S. (1996) Sokal's Hoax. *New York Review of Books*, 8 August: 11–16.

Wellmer, A. (1985) Reason, utopia and the dialectic of enlightenment. In R.J. Bernstein (ed.), *Habermas and Modernity*. Cambridge, MA: MIT Press.

White, D.A. (1978) *Heidegger and the Language of Poetry*. Lincoln: University of Nebraska Press.

White, H. (1985a) *Metahistory: The Historical Imagination in Nineteenth-Century Europe*. Baltimore: The Johns Hopkins University Press. First published in 1974.

White, H. (1985b) *Tropics of Discourse. Essays in Cultural Criticism*. Baltimore: The Johns Hopkins University Press. First published in 1978.

White, S. (1988) *The Recent Work of Jürgen Habermas*. Cambridge: Cambridge University Press.

Whitehead, A.N. (1929) *Process and Reality: An Essay in Cosmology*. Cambridge: Cambridge University Press.

Widerberg, K. (1992) Hur mycket kvinna får jag vara som vetenskaps-man? *Kvinnovetenskaplig tidskrift*, 3: 58–63.

Williams, R. (1976) Symbolic interactionism: fusion of theory and research. In D.C. Thorns (ed.), *New Directions in Sociology*. London: David and Charles.

Willmott, H. (1994a) Bringing agency (back) into organizational analysis: responding to the crises of (post)modernity. In J. Hassard and M. Parker (eds), *Towards a New Theory of Organizations*. London: Routledge.

Willmott, H. (1994b) Social constructionism and communication studies: hearing the conversation but losing the dialogue. In S. Deetz (ed.), *Communication Yearbook, Vol. 17*. Newbury Park, CA: Sage.

Willmott, H. (2003) Organization theory as a critical science? Forms of analysis and 'organizational forms'. In H. Tsoukas and C. Knudsen (eds), *The Oxford Handbook of Organization Theory*. Oxford: Oxford University Press.

Willmott, H. (2005) Theorizing contemporary control: some post-structuralist responses to some critical realist questions. *Organization*, 12: 747–80.

Wilterdink, N.A. (2002) The sociogenesis of postmodernism. *European Journal of Sociology*, 43(2): 190–216.

Wittgenstein, L. (1953) *Philosophical Investigations*. London: Blackwell.

Wolcott, H. (1995) Making a study 'more ethnographic'. In J. Van Maanen (ed.), *Representation in Ethnography*. Thousand Oaks, CA: Sage.

Wolin, R. (1993) Preface to the MIT Press edition: note on a missing text. In R. Wolin (ed.), *The Heidegger Controversy. A Critical Reader*. Cambridge, MA: MIT Press.

Woolgar, S. (1983) Irony in the social studies of science. In K. Knorr-Cetina and M. Mulkay (eds), *Science Observed: Perspectives in the Social Study of Science*. London: Sage.

Woolgar, S. (ed.) (1988) *Knowledge and Reflexivity: New Frontiers in the Sociology of Knowledge*. London: Sage.

Wray-Bliss, E. (2002) Abstract ethics, embodied ethics: the strange marriage of Foucault and positivism in labour process theory. *Organization*, 9(1): 5–39.

Yin, K.K. (1984) *Case Study Research: Design and Methods*. Beverley Hills, CA: Sage.

Ziehe, T. and Stubenrauch, H. (1982) *Plädoyer für ein ungewöhnliches Lernen. Ideen zur Jugendsituation*. Reinbek: Rowohlt.

Zielke, B. (2005) The case for dialogue. (Reply to social constructionism as cultism, Carl Ratner.), *Forum: Qualitative Social Research*, 6/2, Art. 13 (May). Online. www.qualitative-research.net/fqs-texte/2–05/05–2–13-e.htm (20 September 2007).

Zuboff, S. (1988) *In the Age of the Smart Machine: The Future of Work and Power*. Oxford: Heinemann.

Zuckerman, I.G. (1993) Breaking out: the emergence of autonomous self-hood in women through psychotherapy and the women's movement. In B. Glaser (ed.), *Examples of Grounded Theory*: 219–251. Mill Valley, CA: Sociology Press.

INDEX

Please note that page references to footnotes will be followed by the letter 'n', while those in *italics* relate to diagrams.

causality 42, 63, 66
causeries 208
ceteris paribus reservation 109, 113, 114
Chakravarty, A. 20
Charmaz, K. 75
Chicago School 56
child-rearing practices, and critical theory 160
Christianity, and hermeneutics 139
Clark, T. 82
Clarke, A. E. 75–6
Clayman, S. E. 83
Clegg, S. 149, 257
Clifford, J. 200, 201, 310
cockfighting, example of hermeneutic ethnography 132–3
coding, in grounded theory 62–6, 73
cognitive aesthetics 126
cognitive interest 155–7
cognitive symbols 54, 55
coherence of meaning, in hermeneutics 105–6, 131
coherence of principle 98, 105–6
Collingwood, R. G. 114, 116, 122
Colombia, shamanistic healing in 202, 203
colonization of lifeworld 149–50
communication
    critique of Habermas's theory 153–5
    distorted/undistorted 152, 154, 155
    repression-free 154
communication space 168
communicative action theory, Habermas 150–3, 158, 261
communicative rationality 151, 152
comparisons 62, 67
comprehensiveness 98, 99
Comte, A. 16, 17
concepts 62
conceptual triangle term-meaning-referent 186, 188
confessionalism 266–7
consensus 153, 192–3
construction 36, 38, 41, 52n, 73, 269
contextuality 98, 100
continual variations, rule of 255
contrasting principle 212
conversation analysis 82–4, 261n
conversion 218
Cooley, C. H. 54
Copenhagen school 90n
Corbin, J. 53, 54, 74, 75
core category 68
Correll, S. J. 236
correspondence of meaning, hermeneutic 107
correspondence rules 17
correspondence theory 23
creativity 274–5, 306

critical ethnography/critical qualitative research 170–3
critical hermeneutics *see* critical theory
critical pragmatism 155
critical reading 58
critical realism 39–49, 269
    critique of
        objectivism and exaggerated claims 44–6
        unproductive concepts of structure and mechanism 46–9
    and positivism 40, 42, 43, 49–50
    quantitative and qualitative method 15
    and social constructionism 49, 50
critical research
    minimal version of 160–2
    qualitative method 170–3
critical theory 2, 16, 144–78, 264, 276
    cognitive interest and epistemology 155–7
    critically constructive variants of 147–8
    definitions 144
    and empirical research 162
        role of empirical material 164–6
    of Frankfurt school 145–8
    of Habermas 148–55
        early critical theory compared 157–9
    and hermeneutics 140n
    interpretations 167–9
    methodological implications 162–73
    negations 169–70, 171
    and postmodernism 182
    and political positions
        left and right 159–60
        minimal version of critical research 160–2
    research question 162–4
    and social constructionism 16
    strength of 177n
    theoretical frames of reference 166–7
    triple hermeneutics 175–6, 271
    workplace, study of 173–4
criticism of bias 111–12, 115, 292, 294
critique, in critical research 170
cults 28
cultural pessimism 146–7
cultural science 94, 95, 96
culture 127, 130–1
cybernetic system, as metaphor 127
Czarniawska-Joerges, B. 127, 310
Czubaroff, J. 311

Danermark, B. 42, 46, 47, 48
data 1, 2, 3, 6, 17, 87
    in grounded theory 58–9, 60–2
    hard and soft 242–3
    qualitative and quantitative 58–9

data *cont.*
    sources of 61
    systematization of 17, 98
data-driven research 283, 284
data-oriented methods *see* ethnography; ethnomethodology; grounded theory
de Man, P. 225n
de Saussure, F. 227
death, as taboo subject 118
deconstruction 19, 181, 185–6
    Derrida on 181, 184–91
deduction 3–4, 5, 6, 57
deep structures 19, 167, 168, 208
Deetz, S. 154, 170, 253, 302
defamiliarization 310
deferral 186
Delanty, G. 253
Deleuze, G. 193, 256, 259
density 68, 69
Denzin, N. 7, 53, 183, 226n, 311
dependence 112–14, 115
Derrida, J. 154, 179, 182, 209–10
    on deconstruction 181, 184–91
    on *différance* 185, 186–8, 224n
    on Husserl 184
    on metaphysics of presence 187, 188
    on text 207–8
Descartes, R. 57
descriptions 189, 202
detective novel metaphor, research process 310
Dialectic of Enlightenment (Adorno and Horkheimer) 147, 158
dialogue 31
    and communicative action 150, 151, 154
    hermeneutical interpretation 100–2
    with text 122
différance 185, 186–8, 190, 224n
Dilthey, W. 94, 95
Discipline and Punish (Foucault) 251, 252, 254
discourse analysis 227, 228, 229–36
    assumptions 232–3
    criticism of traditional views of language in research 229–32
    critique and evaluation 234–6
    and gender 240
    and poststructuralism 230–1
    principles for conducting 233
    research, discourse-analytical 232–4
    sense and reference 235
discourse/discourses 106, 195–6, 227, 250, 281n
    tactic polyvalence, rule of 255
The Discovery of Grounded Theory (Glaser and Strauss) 56

343

distance 112–14, 115
distortions
　of communication 152
　and critical theory 264
　eliminating 266
　of information 108
　of memory 114
distribution of resources 46
domains 21, 40
double conditioning, rule of 255
double hermeneutics 8, 106,
　175, 271
Douglas, J. D. 117
drama, as root metaphor 126
dramatization 212
D-reflexivity 312, 313
Durkheim, E. 25, 29, 90n

economic metaphor 191
ego, transcendental 77–8, 117
Ehn, B. 212, 213, 249
eidetic reduction 77
Einfühlung (empathetic
　re-enactment) 91, 94–5
Einstein, A. 88–9n
Eliade, M. 204
emancipation-driven research 284
emancipatory cognitive interest 155,
　156, 157, 160, 170
emotions 66, 120, 243–4
empathy 78, 93, 114–15
empirical material 2–3, 10, 12,
　231, 273
　see also data
　as argument 303–4
　cautious processes of interacting
　　with 217–18
　and critical theory 164–6
　and grounded theory 54, 55, 57,
　　62, 69
　limitations of 165
　and theory 281n
empirical orientation 54
empirical research/empiricism 1–2,
　3, 18
　and critical theory 162
　and empirical material 164–6,
　　217–18
　in reflective mode 9
emptiness 188
Enlightenment 94, 147, 149,
　180, 182
epistemes 250
epistemic fallacy 40
epistemology 8, 40, 155–7
Erlebnisstrom (stream of
　experience) 78
Escape from Freedom (Fromm) 146
essence 77
essentialism 38
ethnicity 227, 228
ethnography 265
　character of 198
　critical 170–3

ethnography *cont.*
　defined 84
　as empirical approach 214
　hermeneutic 130–3
　inductive 84–7
　and objections to conventional
　　epistemology 266
　postmodernist 284
　and social phenomena, failure to
　　depict 201
　subjectivity of researcher 199
ethnomethodology 54, 76–84
　conversation analysis 82
　critique of 82–4
　phenomenology 76–8
　research 78–81
events, and facts 294
evolution 20
exclusion problem 216–17
exegesis (interpretation of texts)
　92, 139
existential hermeneutics
　Being-in-the-world 117
　dialogue with text 122
　fusion of horizons 120–1,
　　288, 310
　hidden basic question of text
　　122–3
　structure of care 117–19
　subject-object relationship 98
　understanding 119–20
experience 78, 94
experiments 43, 81
explanatory understanding 155
exploration 54, 55
externalization 26, 27

facts 1, 3
　see also data
　and events 294
　reconstruction of 108
　and theory 4, 6, 17, 20–3, 30, 57
falsification 20, 51n
Fay, B. 157
Featherstone, M. 184
feminism 196, 228–9, 236–50
　see also gender
　critique of 245–7
　gender-as variable approach
　　238–9
　ghettoization of 247
　and method 242–5
　poststructural 240–2
　research 239–40
　and social constructionism 16
feminist empiricism 238
Ferguson, K. 239, 262n
Fetterman, D. M. 84, 86
Feyerabend, P. K. 16, 18, 20, 21,
　140n, 193
Fleck, L. 31–2
fold metaphor 19
Forester, J. 155, 163
forgeries 110, 114

Forget, P. 154
Foucault, M. 15, 23, 179, 181,
　225n, 302
　on Derrida 208
　on Frankfurt school 261
　genealogical method of 250–60
　and hermeneutics of suspicion
　　130, 254
　on knowledge and power 228,
　　229, 251–4
Frankfurt School of critical theory
　130, 145–8, 149, 158, 159,
　161, 261
　critically constructive variants of
　　critical theory 147–8
　cultural pessimism and critique of
　　rationality 146–7
　origins and early development
　　145–6
free play 179, 187, 188
freedom from references 188–9
Freud, S. 30, 129, 130, 155, 180
Fromm, E. 146, 148, 169
Frye, N. 141n, 208
Fuchs, S. 36, 95, 139
functionalism 179

Gadamer, H.-G. 30, 121, 123, 124,
　135, 136, 139, 297, 310
　and Habermas 150, 154, 191
Galileo 111
game, as root metaphor 126
Garfinkel, H. 78, 83
Geertz, C. 195, 199, 252, 266
　hermeneutic ethnography
　　of 130–3
gender 227–9
　see also feminism
　in non-feminist research 247–50
gender-as variable approach 238–9
gender-blindness 237, 248
genealogical method 250–60
　methodological principles 254–5
　self and ethics 255–6
generality, levels of 70–1
generalization 21
generative capacity 307
Genet, J. 184
genres 101–2, 114
Gergen, K. 30–1, 38, 51n, 267–8,
　270, 272, 280n, 302
Gergen, M. 267–8, 272, 280n, 302
Gheradi, S. 242
ghettoization of feminism 247
Giddens, A. 8, 36, 83, 271
Ginzburg, C. 114–15
Glaser, B. G. 4–5, 53, 54, 58, 88n
　on coding *see* coding
　conflict with Strauss and Corbin
　　74–5
　on data 60, 61
　on practical utility 59, 60
　on theory generation 56–7
global coherence 131

meetings, minutes of 114
Melia, K. 10
membership, concept 80
memo-writing 64, 68
Mendel, G. 111
Merleau-Ponty, M. 119, 250
Merton, R. 56, 70
metaphorization 218
metaphors 23, 124–7, 129
    bolt of lighting 296
    construction 36
    economic 191
    fold 19
    and gender thinking 249
    geological 27
    harvest 17
    mushroom-picking 309,
        310, 312
    for organizations 118
    for research 309–12
    root 126–7, 138, 218, 311
    second-order 139, 310
    text as 127, 207
metaphysics of presence 187, 188
metatheories 166, 271, 276–8,
    282n, 308–9
method
    intellectualization of 1–12
    qualitative and quantitative 7–8
methodological strategies 265–8
    linguistic reductionism 268
    resignation 265
micropower 259
microsociological revolution 87
Mills, C. W. 233, 288
Min, A. K. 190
Mintzberg, H. 307
Mir, R. 100
mixed discourses 281n
model theoreticians 19–20
models 19, 22, 68
modernism 31
montage 203
moral story-telling 289–90, 292
Morgan, D. 248
Morgan, G. 118, 127, 310
Morgenstern, O. 126
motives, vocabulary of 288, 291
Mumby, D. 181, 213
Munch, E. 118, 142n
mushroom-picking metaphor 309,
    310, 312

narrating sources 109–10
narrative 23, 124, 127–9, 132
natural science 22, 30
    and cultural science 94, 95, 96
    and social science 48
Nazism 146, 147, 257
negations 171
neoidealism 94, 140n
neo-Kantianism 54, 94
neoliberalism 190
networks 36

Newton, T. 257
Nietzsche, F. 16, 94, 130, 136,
    180, 184
    and Foucault 251
    and Heidegger 191
    introspection in work of 225n
    'overman' of 187
    'will to power' 136, 188, 191,
        256
nothingness 188

objectivation 26, 28, 51n
objective reality 1, 39, 265, 300
    and critical realism 41, 44
objectivism 44–6
objectivist hermeneutics 91, 92,
    94–5, 133, 136
observability 17, 18, 19
Ödman, P.-J. 99, 108
One-Dimensional Man
    (Marcuse) 147
ontology 8, 40
organism, as root metaphor
    126, 127
organization theory 22, 59
    metaphors 127
Ottman, H. 156
Overington, M. 127

paid work, example of mechanism
    42–3, 48
Palmer, R. E. 97, 98, 133
paradigms 18, 20, 51n, 62, 95, 102
Parker, I. 234
Parmenides 143n
Parsons, T. 87
participant observation 63–4
part-whole hermeneutic circle 116,
    135, 138, 139
    canons, hermeneutic 106
    interpretation 97
    metaphors and narrative 128
    and roots of hermeneutics
        92, 93
    sub-interpretation 104
passion 244
Pasteur, L. 32
Pasteurization of France (Latour) 32
patchwork 192
pattern models 89n
pattern of interpretation 99–100
Patterns of Discovery. An Inquiry into
    the Foundations of Science
    (Hanson) 7
penetration 98, 99, 100, 122
Perrow, C. 163
perspective 6, 57, 112
    'bottom-up' 32
perspectivization 212
Peters, T. 294, 299
Pettigrew, A. 128
phenomenological reduction 76–7
phenomenology 24, 25, 76–8
    and grounded theory 72

phenomenology *cont.*
    and hermeneutics 140n
    and lifeworld 149
        see also lifeworld
    and social constructionism 23
philosophical ideas 10
philosophy of science 6, 72, 260
phonocentrism 186
Plato 57
plausibility, in interpretations 103,
    104, 168
play with signs 179, 189
Plummer, K. 53
pluralism 193, 213–16, 308
PM *see* postmodernism
poetic hermeneutics 97, 115,
    123–30
    metaphors 124–7
    narrative 127–9
poetry 4, 5
political aspects of research 11, 176,
    221–2
    left and right, positions on
        159–60
    micropolitics of text 221–2
political system, as metaphor 127
Pollner, M. 79
polyphony-driven research 284
Popper, K. 4, 20, 21, 51n, 161, 244
population ecology, as
    metaphor 127
positivism 16–23, 48
    and critical realism 40, 42, 43,
        49–50
    critics 1, 15, 17–20, 94, 244
        Gergen as persistent
            critic 30–1
    example 5
    grounded theory contrasted
        15, 71–2
    logical 16, 17
    quantitative and qualitative
        method 15, 59
    and social constructionism 51n
    terminology 16–17
    textual 266, 267
    theory versus empirical 'facts'
        20–3
    verification and falsification 20
The Postmodern Condition (Lyotard)
    180, 192
postmodern turn 76
postmodernism 2, 23, 125, 264
    see also poststructuralism
    critique of 204–12
        lack of constructivity 205–6
        linguistic and textual
            reductionism 206–10
        empirical illustration 202–4
    and ethnomethodology 84
    exclusion problem 216–17
    and grounded theory 15, 71
    growth of 180
    and Habermas 182

postmodernism *cont.*
  and hermeneutics 139
  as markcentric 190, 191
  and positivism 15, 19
  and qualitative method 212–22
  and reflection 269, 270
  researcher, as author 198–201
  roots of 179
  sceptical and affirmative 224n
  totalizing theory, avoidance of
    218–19
  variants of 181–4, 318n
post-positivism 15, 18, 19, 20
poststructuralism 2
  see also postmodernism
  critique of 196, 204–12
  and discourse analysis 230–1
  exclusion problem 216–17
  feminism 240–2
  and positivism 19
  and reflection 269
  and structuralism 179
  on subjectivity 195
  and time aspect 128
  variants of 181–4
potential 98
Potter, J. 230, 231, 232, 233, 234,
  235, 246, 286
power
  and knowledge 228, 229, 250,
    251–4, 258–9
  micro-physics of 252
  relations of 46
  study of 228
practical utility 59–60
practice, theory of 36
pragmatic utility 301
pragmatism 54, 55, 155, 222, 235
Prasad, A. 100
preconceptions 274, 281n
presence, metaphysics of 187, 188
preunderstanding-understanding
  hermeneutic circle 121,
    138, 141n
  and alethic hermeneutics 96, 135
  interpretation 97, 98
  and roots of hermeneutics 92
  sub-interpretation 104
primacy of meaning 189
primary interpretations 286–7
properties, categories 62, 68–9
Protestantism 263, 264
  work ethic 161
PS *see* poststructuralism
Psillos, S. 20
psychic prison metaphor 118, 127
psychoanalysis 129–30, 143n, 157, 177n
public sector organizations, changes
  in 293–9
Putnam, L. 181
puzzle research 20, 59, 87

quadri-hermeneutics 271, 272, 281n
*Qualitative Analysis for Social
  Scientists* (Strauss) 60

qualitative method 2, 15, 31, 54, 55
  case studies 21
  critical research 170–3
  grounded theory 58–9
  and postmodernism 212–22
  and quantitative method
    7–8, 231
qualitative research
  criteria for 300–9
    empirical material as argument
      303–4
    empirical research 304–5
    reflexive interpretation and
      relativism 307–9
    richness in points 305–7
  and critical realism 47–8
  and semantic conception of
    science 22
quantitative method 15, 231
  and qualitative method 7–8, 231
questionnaires 231

radical feminism 236
Radnitzky, G. 155
Randall, L. 48
rationality/rationalism 75, 94,
  98, 176
  communicative 151, 152
  critique of 146–7
  and logic 22
rationalization 150, 153
Ratner, C. 31
reading
  critical 58
  extensive 274–5
  multiple readings 219
realism, and semantic conception of
  science 23
realist constructionism 33
reality
  see also critical realism
  artefactual 42
  domains of 40
  and empirical material 10
  interpretation of 58
  and language 267
  layers of 18
  objective *see* objective reality
  possibility in 117
  representation of 184
  as socially constructed 23, 24–30,
    37, 211
  and text 2
recontextualization 100
reductionism, linguistic and textual
  206–10
references
  freedom from 188–9
  theoretical frames of 166–7
reflection 9, 11, 12, 269–71
  see also self-reflection
  in critical research 171
reflective research
  characteristics 9
  elements in 11–12

reflective research *cont.*
  emphasis in 312–14
  or reflexive research 8–11
reflexive interpretation 271–8, 317
  breadth and variation in 271–4
  creativity and extensive reading
    274–5
  illustrations 285–300
    advertising agency founder
      285–93
    public sector organizations,
      changes in 293–9
  metatheory, role 276–8
  methodological strategies 283–5
  primary interpretations 286–7
  and relativism 307–9
  secondary interpretations 288–90
reflexivity 79, 176
re-framing 297
reifications 28
relations of power 46
relativism 18, 31, 307–9
remnants 109–10
repertoire of interpretations 273
representation 11, 23, 199
  politics of 221
  problem of 183, 200
  of reality 184
research
  as authorship 198
  dataistic conception of 56
  discourse-analytical 232–4
    see also discourse analysis
  empirical, criteria for 304–5
  feminist viewpoint 239–40
  language in, criticism of
    traditional views 229–32
  metaphors for 309–12
  normal versus paradigm shifts 20
  originality in 100
  political character of *see* political
    aspects of research
  as provisionally rational project
    316–18
  reflective *see* reflective research
  style of 219
research procedures 11
research programmes 20–1
researchers 6, 20
  and alethic hermeneutics 95–6
  authority of 183
  as authors 198–201
  and critical theory 163, 164
  emotions of 66
  independent, ideal of 163
  male 237, 245, 262n
  own experience 62
  and qualitative research 7
  and source criticism 112–13, 116
  and study object 45, 85
  subjectivity of 199
resignation 265
resistance 160
resources, distribution of 46
responsibility 117, 118, 290